Fodor's

OREGON

P9-CCQ-729

Welcome to Oregon

Rugged beauty, locavore cuisine, and indie spirit are just some of Oregon's charms. The Pacific Northwest darling is home to hip Portland, whose happening foodie and arts scenes are anchored by an eco-friendly lifestyle. Smaller cities draw you in, too: you can sample microbrews in Bend, see top-notch theater in Ashland, and explore maritime history in Astoria. Miles of bike paths, hikes up Mt. Hood, and rafting in the Columbia River Gorge thrill outdoors enthusiasts. For pure relaxation, taste award-winning Willamette Valley wines and walk windswept Pacific beaches.

TOP REASONS TO GO

★ **Portland:** Terrific food, eclectic music, boutique hotels, and culture galore.

★ **Seafood:** Fresh crab, sea scallops, razor clams, oysters, and salmon.

★ **Wine:** Perfect Pinot Noir, Pinot Gris, and more in the Willamette Valley and beyond.

★ **The Coast:** Scenic strands, tidal pools, whale sightings, headland walks.

★ **Mountains:** From majestic Mt. Hood to the mighty cliffs surrounding Crater Lake.

★ **Scenic Drives:** In the Cascade Range, along the Pacific, through evergreen forests.

Contents

Fodor's Features

Whale-Watching in
the Pacific Northwest 31
Wine Tasting in
the Willamette Valley 202

MAPS

Chapter 1

EXPERIENCE OREGON

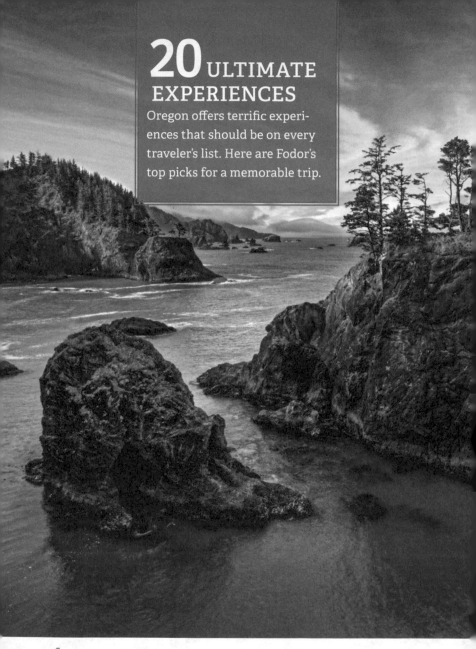

20 ULTIMATE EXPERIENCES

Oregon offers terrific experiences that should be on every traveler's list. Here are Fodor's top picks for a memorable trip.

1 | Explore the rugged Oregon Coast

Oregon's shoreline is truly unlike any other on the continent. The northern half draws visitors to Astoria, Cannon Beach, and the Tillamook Creamery. The southern stretches woo solitude seekers. *(Ch. 4)*

2 Keep Portland weird

A doughnut shop (Voodoo Doughnut), a sprawling temperate rain forest (Forest Park), and a bookstore (Powell's City of Books) are top attractions here. *(Ch. 3)*

3 Crater Lake's blue waters

Crater Lake reaches depths of nearly 2,000 feet and sunlight filters down 400 feet, making it one of the most striking sights in the West. *(Ch. 8)*

4 Drive Oregon's byways

For a wild road trip, check out Oregon's lesser-known scenic byways, which loop through river gorges, the sunny high desert, and off-the-grid territory far from the reaches of cell towers. *(Ch. 4, 6)*

5 Dip in natural hot springs

The volcanic forces that shape Oregon's landscapes come with steamy perks: dozens of soothing hot springs gurgling in all corners of the state, from rustic cabin resorts to lush national forests. *(Ch. 6)*

6 Time travel at the Painted Hills

Part of the John Day Fossil Beds National Monument, the distinctive stripes seen in the Painted Hills represent more than 30 million years of geological history. *(Ch. 10)*

7 Race a dune buggy

The Oregon Dunes National Recreation Area stretches for more than 40 miles between Florence and Coos Bay. A dune buggy is the quickest way to explore this expanse. *(Ch. 4)*

8 Wine tasting in the Willamette Valley

This swath of fertile, hilly countryside is home to more than 500 wineries and has earned a reputation as one of the finest producers of Pinot Noir in the world. *(Ch. 5)*

9 Get high (legally)

In 2014 the state was among the first to legalize cannabis for recreational use for anyone over 21 years old, and today it claims one of the highest densities of licensed vendors in the country. *(Ch. 3)*

10 Shakespeare in Ashland

One of the country's best regional performing arts organizations, Ashland's Tony Award–winning Oregon Shakespeare Festival puts on more than 700 shows every year. *(Ch. 9)*

11 Hike the Trail of Ten Falls

True to its name, the marquee 7.2-mile trail in Silver Falls State Park passes no fewer than 10 tumbling cascades, shrouded in a dense evergreen forest of Douglas firs and sword ferns. *(Ch. 5)*

12 Bohemian Eugene

This counterculture hub in the Willamette Valley has attracted freewheeling crowds since the 1960s, who've settled here and opened vegetarian restaurants, organic farms, and bike shops. *(Ch. 5)*

13 Portland Pride

The annual Pride Waterfront Festival and Parade (June) has become one of the West Coast's largest celebrations of queer identities and human rights. More than 60,000 people attend. *(Ch. 1, 3)*

14 Take a brewery tour of Bend

Bend has earned bragging rights for the most breweries per capita. Explore them by bus, electric bike, auto rickshaw, glorified golf cart, or horse-drawn carriage. *(Ch. 7)*

15 Ski or hike Mt. Hood

Snowcapped Mt. Hood is the only place in the Lower 48 where you can hit the slopes year-round. Or you can come to hike the trails that start near the Timberline Lodge Ski Area. *(Ch. 6)*

16 Hike or climb Smith Rock

The state park's sheer cliffs rise from the straw-colored high desert like a stone cathedral, while the mostly flat, and easily accessible, 2.5-mile river trail follows the course of the Crooked River. *(Ch. 7)*

17 Go whale-watching

You can spot resident whales year-round on the Oregon Coast, but prime whale-watching is early winter and spring. Start at the Oregon State Parks–operated Whale Watching Center in Depoe Bay. *(Ch. 4)*

18 Visit the "Alps of Oregon"

Ride the Wallowa Lake Tramway—the steepest tram in North America—up to the 8,150-foot summit of Mt. Howard and you might feel as if you've taken a gondola lift all the way to Switzerland. *(Ch. 10)*

19 Dive into Oregon Trail history

Retrace the riveting 2,000-mile journey that brought thousands to the Pacific Northwest at two world-class cultural centers and interactive museums in eastern Oregon. *(Ch. 10)*

20 Tour the Columbia River Gorge

The Columbia River Gorge's basalt cliffs rise from moss-covered forests along both sides of the West's grandest waterway, providing some spectacular vistas. *(Ch. 6)*

The Best Things to Do in Portland

SPEND SATURDAY AT THE MARKET

Start your Saturday with a tour of the convivial, tree-shaded Portland Farmers Market in the South Park Blocks by Portland State University, where you can listen to live music, score local snacks, and savor delicious breakfast fare.

GO BREWERY-HOPPING IN NORTH PORTLAND

There are several Portland neighborhoods where you can walk among three to five excellent craft breweries (the Pearl District and Central East Side leap to mind), but the North Mississippi Avenue area has some especially terrific beer venues and is pretty to walk through, too.

ATTEND A FESTIVAL AT TOM MCCALL WATERFRONT PARK

This sweep of green that fringes the Downtown section of the Willamette riverfront hosts fantastic festivals from spring through fall. The park and adjoining promenade are lovely for a stroll, jog, or bike ride.

BIKE THE BRIDGES AND RIVERFRONT

Rent bikes or use the city's bike-share program to venture out on two wheels up and down the riverfront promenades on both sides of the Willamette River, and also to pedal across some of the city's distinctive bridges, such as the historic Hawthorne Bridge and the Tilikum Crossing Bridge.

FEAST AT A FOOD CART POD
Portland is home to numerous bustling and reasonably priced food cart pods. Stop by for a progressive lunch or dinner by sampling dishes from two or three different vendors. The offerings are diverse, and there's also a great selection of craft beer and artisanal coffee.

WATCH THE SUNSET AT MT. TABOR PARK
This leafy and hilly East Side park set atop an extinct volcanic cinder cone is lovely for light hiking and heavy napping all day long, but it's especially dramatic at dusk, when you can picnic or laze on a blanket and watch the sun set over Downtown and the West Hills.

EXPLORE THE MILES OF AISLES AT POWELL'S
Set out on a book-buying adventure at the iconic Powell's City of Books, one of the largest and most famous bookstores in the world. You'll find an exhaustive selection of both new and used books.

Explore the gardens

HIKE THE HILLS TO PITTOCK MANSION
Just minutes from Downtown, hike through dense Douglas fir and cedar groves in one of the nation's largest urban forests, Forest Park.

STROLL THE JAPANESE AND CHINESE GARDENS
Two of the city's loveliest green spaces are devoted to the serene design aesthetics and native plantings of Japan and China.

WATCH A MOVIE AT A HISTORIC PUB THEATER
Portland abounds with handsomely restored vintage theaters, many of them from the early 20th century and located in hip, historic neighborhoods.

SMELL THE ROSES
Visit Washington Park's incredible International Rose Test Garden, then venture over to North Portland's Peninsula Park & Rose Garden for more floral exploring.

SPEND AN AFTERNOON AT THE MUSEUMS
The Portland Art Museum, the Oregon Historical Society Museum, and the OMSI are all excellent.

Roadside Attractions and Offbeat Museums in Oregon

PREHISTORIC GARDENS
Built in the 1950s by an amateur paleontologist, who traveled the world studying fossils in museums and archives, Prehistoric Gardens looks like a real-life Jurassic Park, except the 23 dinosaurs inhabiting this temperate rain forest are—thankfully—life-size sculptures.

SHANIKO GHOST TOWN
Oregon's many ghost towns captivate the imaginations of road-trippers and photographers with the mysteries of who might've called these frontier communities home. Shaniko in central Oregon is a picture-perfect example.

ENCHANTED FOREST
Take a literal walk down Storybook Lane in this old-school theme park to see scenes from popular fairy tales and nursery rhymes brought to life, including folk art–inspired statues of characters such as Little Red Riding Hood and the Seven Dwarfs.

THE FREAKYBUTTRUE PECULIARIUM
A truly peculiar roadside attraction found in Portland's Inner Southeast, the Freakybuttrue Peculiarium— that's a mashup of "freaky but true"—looks like a do-it-yourself Ripley's Believe It or Not! museum. It's the brainchild of several local artists, who fill the gallery and adjoining shop with a menagerie of macabre art and oddball kitsch.

OREGON STATE HOSPITAL MUSEUM OF MENTAL HEALTH
Visit a former insane asylum in Salem that served as the primary set for the legendary 1975 blockbuster *One Flew Over the Cuckoo's Nest*, starring Jack Nicholson. Volunteers operate the nonprofit museum which explores the somber history of psychiatry through artifacts such as straitjackets sewn by patients and now-regrettable treatment devices.

THE OREGON VORTEX AND HOUSE OF MYSTERY
In southern Oregon between Grants Pass and Medford, there's a place that seems to defy all the laws of physics—where a ball rolls uphill and a person's height appears to change as they move. Optical illusion or some strange paranormal activity? That question has made The Oregon Vortex and House of Mystery a popular diversion since the 1930s.

PAUL BUNYAN STATUE

Statues of this mythical logger are common roadside sights in the American West, though North Portland's 31-foot-tall Paul Bunyan smiles confidently as the king among them. The unmissable sculpture went up in 1959 to mark the 100th anniversary of Oregon's statehood. Neighbors have kept Bunyan in good shape over the years, with periodic renovations and fresh paint—that likely explains his perennially pearly concrete smile.

COLUMBIA RIVER MARITIME MUSEUM

See shipwreck artifacts, to-scale models, full-size vessels, military weapons, and more inside the Columbia River Maritime Museum, which sits about 10 miles from the mouth of the Columbia. Outside on the riverside dock, you can tour the lightship *Columbia*, which formerly plied the region's waters as a floating lighthouse.

EVERGREEN AVIATION & SPACE MUSEUM

A small town set amid rolling farm fields and vineyards may not seem the most obvious location for a museum of the caliber of the Evergreen Aviation & Space Museum, but that's one of the many surprises of this McMinnville-based institution. An awesome assortment of flying machines is on display—most notably Howard Hughes's iconic "flying boat," the *Spruce Goose*, which has a wingspan longer than a football field and its end zones.

PETER IREDALE SHIPWRECK

When the tide is low on the beach at Fort Stevens State Park, you can stroll up to the ghostly remains of the Peter Iredale, a four-masted steel ship that ran ashore here in 1906. It's the most accessible of the thousands of stranded vessels along the Coast.

Wineries That Define Oregon's Willamette Valley

KING ESTATE WINERY

King Estate immediately stands out from the smaller-scale outfits clustered along Territorial Highway, the main touring route in the quieter southern stretches of the valley, and it's easy to spend an entire day here touring the winery complex.

WILLAKENZIE ESTATE

A dynamic 420-acre estate—diverse in elevation, soil, and microclimates—inspires terroir-driven wines in this acclaimed winery.

CARLTON WINEMAKERS STUDIO

Taste wine from more than a dozen winemakers all under one roof at this one-of-the-kind collective, which functions as a kind of incubator for boutique and experimental labels.

ARGYLE WINERY

This stellar winery, in the North Willamette Valley, works with a variety of cool-climate grapes, though the founders built their names on elegant, aromatic, and remarkably ageable sparkling wines—relatively unique in the world of Oregon wine.

SAFFRON FIELDS VINEYARD

The contemporary art and architecture are as notable as Saffron Fields Vineyard's signature Pinot Noir. Inside, multimedia work from the owners' personal collection dominates. Outside, acclaimed Japanese landscape architect Hoichi Kurisu designed the gardens.

PENNER-ASH WINE CELLARS

Wine critics of the caliber of Robert Parker consider the women-led team at Penner-Ash Wine Cellars among the nation's top producers of Pinot Noir—considerable praise in a region where that's the top grape.

DOMAINE DROUHIN

Old World meets Oregon at this 225-acre estate in the Red Hills of Dundee. When the winery opened in 1987, it shone a bright spotlight on this still-burgeoning grape-growing region and firmly established Oregon as a world-class destination for Pinot Noir.

Chehalem Winery

CHEHALEM WINERY

The team at Chehalem Winery puts their values into actions, earning LIVE, Salmon-Safe, and B Corp certifications—a fancy way of demonstrating their commitment to the land and community. Their signature single-lot Pinot Noir and white varieties are worth a swirl, too. Make an appointment to tour the winery or visit the rustic tasting room in downtown Newberg.

THE EYRIE VINEYARDS

David and Diana Lett defied conventional wisdom when they founded The Eyrie Vineyards in 1965, helping to kick-start a Pinot Noir frenzy that's shaped the valley's vino reputation. Today, David's son, Jason Lett, oversees the McMinnville-based operation and continues to turn out top Pinot Noir, Pinot Gris, and several other varieties.

ABBEY CREEK WINERY

You might spot a DJ spinning hip-hop tracks in this laid-back tasting room, where you can pair small-batch Pinot Noir, Pinot Gris, and Gewürztraminer with imported Brazilian hot sauces. Owner Bertony Faustin personally oversees every aspect of his boutique operation, from the planting of estate vines to producing about 1,500 cases per year and pouring flights for guests.

WHAT'S WHERE

1 Portland. With its pedestrian-friendly neighborhoods and public transit, Portland is easy to explore. The city has become a magnet for fans of artisanal food, beer, wine, and spirits, and its parks and bike lanes make it a prime spot for outdoors enthusiasts.

2 The Oregon Coast. Oregon's 360-plus miles of rugged shoreline are every bit as scenic as the more crowded and famous California coast. Oregon Dunes National Recreation Area, the Oregon Coast Aquarium, Cannon Beach, and the Columbia River Maritime Museum are key highlights.

3 The Willamette Valley and Wine Country. Just beyond Portland city limits and extending south for 120 miles to Eugene, the Willamette Valley is synonymous with exceptional wine-making.

4 The Columbia River Gorge and Mt. Hood. Less than an hour east of Portland, the Columbia Gorge extends for about 160 miles along the Oregon-Washington border. Just 35 miles south of Hood River, iconic Mt. Hood is renowned for hiking and skiing.

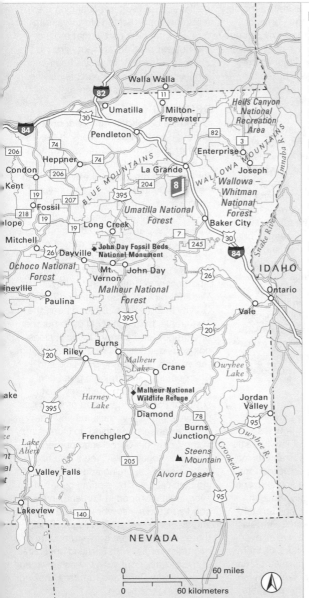

5 **Central Oregon.** The swath of Oregon east of the Cascade Range takes in a varied landscape, with Bend as the regional hub. Make time for the Old West–inspired town of Sisters and rock climbing and hiking in Smith Rock State Park.

6 **Crater Lake National Park.** The 21-square-mile sapphire-blue expanse is the nation's deepest lake and a scenic wonder. You can drive the loop road around the lake, hike, or take a guided boat tour.

7 **Southern Oregon.** Artsy Ashland and the gold rush town of Jacksonville have sophisticated restaurants, shops, and wineries. Nearby, Oregon Caves National Monument is a fascinating natural attraction, while Klamath Falls has some of the best birding and wildlife-viewing in the state.

8 **Eastern Oregon.** The vast and sparsely populated eastern reaches of the state promise plenty of memorable sights and recreational opportunities. The Wild West town of Pendleton, the picturesque mountain town of Joseph, and historic Baker City are among the top destinations here.

Oregon Today

POLITICS

Oregon has a reputation as a Democratic stronghold: nearly all of the state's major officeholders are Dems, and Portland ranks among the most progressive cities in America, though Oregon's origins as a whites-only state and the lingering presence of white supremacists belies the state's reputation as a liberal epicenter. In rural areas, especially the eastern two-thirds of Oregon and southern sections of the coast, you will encounter decidedly more conservative attitudes, with a mix of socially right and libertarian types, who retain a strong distrust of what they perceive as big-government regulation. On the other hand, the Republican Party seldom fields candidates for mayoral and city council elections in the state's largest city, which has half-jokingly been dubbed the "People's Republic of Portland" for its decidedly left-of-center vibe. And since the divisive 2016 presidential election, rallies and protests for a wide range of issues remain a mainstay in the city's streets. Due to the electoral dominance of the Portland metro area in statewide elections, Oregon voters passed a ballot measure in 2014 to legalize cannabis for recreational consumption (as opposed to medical use).

EATING

It's hard to think of another part of the country with a culinary scene that's both inventive and sustainable while still eschewing overly high prices and formality. Oregon chefs have been at the forefront of the locally sourced and seasonal dining movement, especially those in Portland, Eugene, Ashland, and stretches of the northern coast and Columbia Gorge. Farmers' markets thrive all over the state, and restaurants flock to them for local produce such as hazelnuts, marionberries, pears, and chanterelle mushrooms as well as for artisanal products ranging from aged goat cheese to spicy kimchi. Even in small towns like Joseph, Grants Pass, and Depoe Bay, you'll find stellar eateries with oft-changing menus featuring sophisticated Northwestern fare. But the best part is that most of the hottest chef-driven spots around the state offer meals that cost a fraction of what you'd pay for comparable cuisine in San Francisco or even Seattle.

DRINKING

Oregon is beyond merely beer obsessed, although craft ales are clearly at the forefront of the state's assiduous attention to beverages. Portland is well regarded for longtime breweries like Widmer that helped kick-start the local industry, but you're more likely to find serious fans hanging out at newer spots like Breakside Brewery and Ecliptic Brewing. There are many acclaimed beer makers outside the Portland area—consider Rogue in Newport, Pfriem in Hood River, Ale Apothecary in Bend, Yachats Brewing in Yachats, Ninkasi in Eugene, and Terminal Gravity in Enterprise. Beyond beer, the state ranks third in the nation in number of wineries, and plenty of *vino* aficionados consider Oregon Pinot Noirs among the world's best, with Pinot Gris and Chardonnay also earning a great deal of praise. The Willamette Valley, just south of Portland, has been producing top wines for a few decades now; new wineries are also popping up increasingly in the Columbia Gorge and southern Oregon's Rogue Valley. You'll also find coffeehouses sourcing and house-roasting high-caliber, single-origin beans, in every neighborhood in Portland, in every good-size town elsewhere in the state, and even in a few small villages. Finally, there's Oregon's fast-growing bounty of microdistilleries, with Portland once again at the forefront but with towns as varied as outdoorsy Bend and remote Brookings also joining the action.

ENVIRONMENTALISM

Oregon's embrace of eco-friendly practices permeates just about every aspect of the state. Sustainable design plays an increasing role in real-estate projects—even the Oregon Convention Center, the largest in the Pacific Northwest at nearly 1 million square feet, has attained the highest level of LEED-certified "green" construction. Portland has become a prime example in promoting high-density development and reining in suburban sprawl; the city maintains a strict urban growth boundary, which was instituted in the early 1970s as part of a then-novel statewide policy. The state is home to thousands of square miles of undeveloped wilderness—Oregon ranks behind only Alaska, Nevada, Utah, and Idaho in its percentage of public lands. As you travel around, it's easy to encounter examples of this eco-conscious ethic, especially in terms of the fast-growing number of hotels, farms, restaurants, coffee roasters, breweries, and wineries that adhere strictly to environmentally friendly practices.

THE OUTDOORS

Oregon offers plenty of activities for outdoors enthusiasts. Just 60 miles east of Portland, Mt. Hood (the state's highest mountain) is the only place in the Lower 48 where you can ski year-round (although trails are limited in summer). There are three different facilities on this mammoth, snowcapped mountain. Timberline Lodge Ski Area is the one that remains open year-round, and its runs pass beside the venerable 1930s Timberline Lodge. Nearby Mt. Hood Skibowl has less interesting terrain but the most night-skiing acreage in the country. Around the north side of the mountain, you'll find the most challenging and extensive terrain at Mt. Hood Meadows Ski Resort, which offers some 2,150 acres of winter snowboarding and ski fun. Of the many excellent places for white-water rafting in Oregon, the Rogue River offers some of the most thrilling rides. Several outfitters offer trips along this frothy, 215-mile river in the southwestern part of the state, from half-day adventures well suited to beginners to multiday trips that include camping or overnights in local lodges. The lush Silver Falls State Park, about 25 miles east of Salem, is so impressive that serious campaigns to admit it to the national park system have taken place recently. In the meantime, it's something of a secret treasure. The 8,700-acre swath of skyscraping old-growth Douglas firs climbs into the foothills of the Cascade Range, where rain and melting snow supply the torrent that roars through 14 different waterfalls, several of them more than 100 feet tall.

10 Distinctive Places to Stay in Oregon

In Oregon you can, of course, book a room in a luxurious hotel. But a wide range of one-of-a-kind places to stay reveal the state's personality, with funky tiny house villages in central neighborhoods, literary resorts along the beach, tree houses in the woods, and historic mountain lodges that have starred in horror films.

Bay Point Landing, Coos Bay. The words *luxury* and *RV* rarely appear in the same sentence, but they make sense together at this upscale campground resort, with vintage trailers and modernist cabins for rent. ⊕ *www.baypointlanding.com*

Caravan—The Tiny House Hotel, Portland. A complex of about a half dozen ingeniously designed and truly minuscule (80 to 160 square feet) houses, Caravan is situated along hip and artsy Northeast Alberta Street. Each of these bungalows on wheels has a kitchenette. ⊕ *tinyhousehotel.com*

Heceta Head Lighthouse, Florence. Occupying the same dramatic promontory as a working lighthouse, this Queen Anne–style bed-and-breakfast has views of the Pacific that inspire many a marriage proposal. ⊕ *www.hecetalighthouse.com*

McMenamins Kennedy School, Portland. The quirky McMenamins company has adapted dozens of buildings around Oregon as pubs, restaurants, and hotels— from a former asylum to this 1915 elementary school in Portland's funky Northeast neighborhood. ⊕ *www.mcmenamins.com*

Minam River Lodge, Eagle Cap Wilderness. There are only three ways to reach this remote wilderness lodge: via an 8.5-mile hike, a horseback ride, or charter plane; the private chef greets you with hearty meals prepared with ingredients from the on-site garden. ⊕ *www.minam-lodge.com*

Out 'n' About Treesort, Cave Junction. Live out your Swiss Family Robinson fantasy at this 36-acre forest resort in southern Oregon, where you climb ladders and swinging bridges to reach a collection of tree houses. ⊕ *www.treehouses.com*

Suttle Lodge, Sisters. Presiding over a peaceful lake in the Deschutes National Forest, this lodge and cabin resort pairs retro summer-camp vibes with some of central Oregon's finest craft cocktails in the lodge bar. ⊕ *www.thesuttlelodge.com*

Sylvia Beach Hotel, Newport. Perched on a cliff overlooking the sandy shores of Nye Beach, this circa 1912 hotel—named for the famous expat bookseller—has decorated each of its 21 rooms in honor of 21 different literary luminaries. ⊕ *www.sylviabeachhotel.com*

Timberline Lodge, Mt. Hood. This iconic 60-room lodge on the upper slopes of Oregon's highest peak, which famously starred in Stanley Kubrick's *The Shining*, is buried beneath many feet of snow for much of the year. Admire the 96-foot stone chimney in the lobby. ⊕ *www.timberlinelodge.com*

The Vintages Trailer Resort, Willamette Valley. Smack in wine country, this 14-acre property contains 35 resorted midcentury camping trailers, each stylishly upgraded with modern amenities and, of course, pour-over coffee. ⊕ *www.the-vintages.com*

Flavors of Oregon

Short of tropical fruit, there aren't too many types of food that don't grow somewhere in Oregon. Myriad fish and shellfish species dwell off the coast, while tree fruits line the windswept Columbia Gorge, and berries grow wild and on farms in the fertile Willamette Valley. A host of other fruits, vegetables, greens, and produce thrive in the temperate climate. Ranch lands, dairy farms, and acres of wheat and other crops round out an abundance that changes with the seasons.

NATURAL BOUNTY

Few states can match Oregon's agricultural diversity, which is good news for both chefs and food-crazy locals.

Nuts: There's a reason why hazelnuts—also known as filberts—are the official state nut. Oregon produces 99% of the country's hazelnuts, which add a toasty-sweet flavor to meat, salads, desserts, coffee drinks, and more.

Berries: Blueberries, blackberries, and strawberries thrive in the lush Willamette Valley. But the state is home to lesser-known berries highlighted in local preserves, baked goods, and sweet sauces. Subtly tart loganberries are a cross between blackberries and red raspberries. Marionberries have a slightly earthy flavor, and are sometimes dubbed "the Cabernet of blackberries."

Produce: Farmers' markets and restaurant menus are filled with locally grown staples like chanterelle mushrooms, rhubarb, kale, spinach, onions, lemon cucumbers, green beans, potatoes, peaches, cherries, apples, and pears.

Cheese: Open an Oregonian's refrigerator and you're likely to find a fat yellow brick (or a diminutive "baby loaf") of Tillamook cheddar from the century-old collective of coastal creameries. The state's broad swaths of grazing lands generate milk that fuels dozens of artisanal cheese producers. Some of the country's best blue cheese comes from the Rogue Creamery in southern Oregon.

SEAFOOD

With more than 360 miles of coastline, bays, tide flats, and estuaries, Oregon has a stunning variety of fish and shellfish off its shores. Restaurants and locals are attuned to the seasons, from the start of Dungeness season to the best months for oysters.

Salmon: Oregonians know king salmon as Chinook salmon, but make no mistake—the largest Pacific salmon reigns as the prize catch of the state's native cuisine. Silvery coho salmon also swim in the state's coastal rivers. Oregon salmon is phenomenal simply grilled or roasted. Perhaps the most traditional way to cook salmon is to smoke it, a regional practice that originated with Native American tribes.

Crab: Dungeness crab may be named for a town in Washington, but Oregon harvests more of these prized crustaceans than any other state. They are a delicacy simply boiled and served whole, but picked meat often appears in crab cakes or as a focal point in modern regional dishes.

Shellfish: Low tide on Oregon's beaches can yield thin razor clams or a variety of bay clams. Mussels also grow in clusters along rocky coastal stretches, while oysters are harvested in several spots. Mussels and clams are delicious steamed (perhaps in an Oregon wine or beer) or in a creamy chowder. Oysters are enjoyed raw on the half shell or lightly battered and fried.

Ocean fish: Pacific halibut, sole, rockfish, hake, lingcod, and the prized albacore tuna are all fished off the Oregon Coast. The Columbia River also offers up freshwater favorites like steelhead trout and Columbia River sturgeon.

PACIFIC NORTHWEST RESTAURANTS

Chefs across the country are in the throes of the farm-to-table movement, but in Oregon the close connection between chef and producer has long bypassed trend status. It's simply how things are done. Restaurants like **Clyde Common, Higgins,** and **Paley's Place** have been producing organic, locally sourced dishes since well before these approaches became national ideals.

Cuisine here tends to be modern and unfussy—a simple, slightly edgy celebration of what grows nearby. Dishes can have Asian, French, or other global influences, but the ingredients ground them solidly in the Northwest. But there is perhaps no more authentically Oregon preparation of meat or fish than cooking it with a crust of hazelnuts.

Portland is assuredly the epicenter of the state's restaurant scene, but wine-country tourism has helped spread noteworthy cuisine to the Willamette Valley, Hood River and the Columbia Gorge, Bend, the Rogue Valley, and the coastal wine region.

Since it was first inhabited, Oregon has looked to the ocean to feed its population. Nevertheless, eastern Oregon cattle ranches provide a ready supply of sustainably raised beef that chefs love to showcase. The recent nose-to-tail dining trend has generated interest in other meats, including rabbit, pork, goat, and lamb, sourced from Oregon farms.

WINE

Pinot Noir grapes have been the central force of Oregon wine-making since the industry took root in the 1960s. Frustrated by Pinot's poor performance in California, a few intrepid winemakers headed north to test out Oregon's cooler climate. The Willamette Valley's climate is similar to that of France's Burgundy region, where Pinot Noir grapes have reigned for centuries. The rich farmland on the valley floor isn't optimal for grape growing; most vineyards spread across the hillsides that ring the valley, taking advantage of higher elevation, thinner soil, and cool ocean breezes.

Oregon played a central role in America's rediscovery of this famously finicky grape. Today the state is the country's top producer of Pinot Noir. Oregon has 16 official wine-growing regions, though the vast majority of wineries are clustered in the Willamette Valley. Grapes also flourish in parts of southern Oregon and the Columbia Valley along the Washington border.

After Pinot Noir, **Pinot Gris** is the second-most-prevalent wine varietal in the state. The delicate and dry yet fruity white wine is something of an unsung hero, since its darker Pinot cousin earns so much acclaim. Chardonnay, Merlot, and Riesling round out the state's top wines. Oregon wines are generally highly affordable, and deliver a great value for the money, although top Pinot Noirs can cost a pretty penny.

Unencumbered by the wine-making traditions of France, or even California, Oregon vintners have taken the lead in growing organic grapes and producing wines using sustainable methods.

Portland with Kids

Many of Oregon's best kids-oriented attractions and activities are in greater Portland. Just getting around the Rose City—via streetcars and light-rail trains on city streets and kayaks, excursion cruises, and jet boats on the Willamette River—is fun. For listings of family-oriented concerts, performances by the Oregon Children's Theatre, and the like, check the free *Willamette Weekly* newspaper.

MUSEUMS AND ATTRACTIONS

On the east bank of the Willamette River, the **Oregon Museum of Science and Industry** (OMSI) is a leading interactive museum, with touch-friendly exhibits, an Omnimax theater, the state's biggest planetarium, and a 240-foot submarine moored just outside in the river. Along Portland's leafy Park Blocks, both the **Oregon History Museum** and the **Portland Art Museum** have exhibits and programming geared toward kids.

In Old Town, kids enjoy walking amid the ornate pagodas and dramatic foliage of the **Lan Su Chinese Garden.** This is a good spot for a weekend morning, followed by a visit to the **Portland Saturday Market,** where food stalls and musicians keep younger kids entertained, and the cool jewelry, toys, and gifts handcrafted by local artisans appeal to teens. Steps from the market is the **Oregon Maritime Museum,** set within a vintage stern-wheeler docked on the river. And just up Burnside Street from the market, **Powell's City of Books** contains enormous sections of kids' and young adults' literature.

PARKS

Portland is dotted with densely wooded parks—many of the larger ones have ball fields, playgrounds, and picnic areas. The most famous urban oasis in the city, **Forest Park** (along with adjoining **Washington Park**) offers a wealth of engaging activities. You can ride the MAX light rail right to the park's main hub of culture, a complex comprising the **Oregon Zoo, Portland Children's Museum,** and **World Forestry Discovery Center Museum.** Ride the narrow-gauge railroad from the zoo for 2 miles to reach the **International Rose Test Garden** and **Japanese Garden.** From here it's an easy downhill stroll to **Northwest 23rd and 21st Avenues'** pizza parlors, ice-cream shops, and bakeries.

OUTDOOR ADVENTURES

Tour boats ply the **Willamette River,** and a couple of marinas near OMSI rent **kayaks** and conduct **drag-boat races** out on the water. There are also several shops in town that rent **bikes** for use on the city's many miles of dedicated bike lanes and trails. There's outstanding **white-water rafting** just southeast of Portland, along the Clackamas River. On your way toward the Clackamas, check out **North Clackamas Aquatic Park** and **Oaks Amusement Park,** which have rides and wave pools galore.

Nearby **Mt. Hood** has camping, hiking, and biking all summer, and three of the most family-friendly ski resorts in the Northwest—**Timberline** is especially popular for younger and less experienced boarders and skiers. From summer through fall, the pick-your-own berry farms and pumpkin patches on **Sauvie Island** make for an engaging afternoon getaway—for an all-day outing, continue up U.S. 30 all the way to **Astoria,** at the mouth of the Columbia River, to visit the **Columbia River Maritime Museum** and **Fort Stevens State Park,** where kids love to scamper about the remains of an early-20th-century shipwreck.

What to Read and Watch Before You Go

BEEZUS AND RAMONA
The first book in children's book author Beverly Cleary's Portland-based Ramona Quimby series is one of her most beloved. This title and others in the series are set on Klickitat Street in the same Northeast Portland neighborhood (near the Hollywood District) that was also the geographical focal point of the earlier Henry Huggins books.

FUGITIVES AND REFUGEES
Fight Club novelist Chuck Palahniuk penned this endearingly strange and sometimes seedy memoir and travelogue as something of a love letter to the weirder aspects of his onetime hometown, Portland.

GEEK LOVE
Katherine Dunn's National Book Award finalist novel from 1989 was inspired by the author's Portland upbringing and follows an Oregon family's strange trials and tribulations as part of a traveling carnival.

THE GOONIES
The beloved Richard Donner–directed teen adventure comedy was filmed entirely on the northern Oregon Coast, including Cannon Beach and Astoria, which is home to the historic jail in the movie and now serves as the Oregon Film Museum.

THE LATHE OF HEAVEN
The late sci-fi novelist and Portlander Ursula K. Le Guin set this award-winning 1971 novel in a futuristic and dystopian version of Portland (in 2002). There have been two TV movies made from the book.

LEAVE NO TRACE
The critically acclaimed 2018 movie is based on the novel *My Abandonment* by Peter Rock—itself inspired by a true story—and follows the plight of a military veteran and his daughter who live off the grid in Portland's expansive Forest Park until being found and relocated to a Christmas tree farm in rural Oregon.

MY OWN PRIVATE IDAHO
Locally based LGBTQ indie director Gus Van Sant's 1991 drama, starring Keanu Reeves and River Phoenix, was filmed primarily in Portland, with many scenes at what is now the posh Sentinel hotel. It's perhaps the most celebrated of several movies that Van Sant set and shot in Portland, including *Drugstore Cowboy* and *Paranoid Park*.

PORTLANDIA
This hit satirical sketch TV series, starring Carrie Brownstein and Fred Armisen, ran on the IFC channel from 2011 through 2018. The show was filmed at a number of recognizable spots around town, including the Vera Katz Eastbank Esplanade (in the opening credits), Prasad restaurant, Olympia Provisions, Paxton Gate, Caravan–The Tiny House Hotel, and Land Gallery.

SOMETIMES A GREAT NOTION
Although renowned Oregon native son Ken Kesey is more famous for *One Flew Over the Cuckoo's Nest* (the movie was filmed mostly in Salem), this second novel—also a movie—with its rich depiction of the travails of an Oregon logging family, is even better and provides rich insight into the region's personality and history.

WILD
Cheryl Strayed's 2012 memoir about discovering herself while hiking the Pacific Crest Trail inspired the 2014 Reese Witherspoon film of the same name. And though the book and movie cover her time on the trail in California and Washington, too, most of the movie is filmed in Oregon, especially Portland, the Columbia Gorge, and Ashland.

WHALE-WATCHING
IN THE PACIFIC NORTHWEST

The thrill of seeing whales in the wild is, for many, one of the most enduring memories of a trip to the Pacific Northwest. In this part of the world, you'll generally spot two species—gray whales and killer "orca" whales.

About 20,000 grays migrate up the West Coast in spring and back down again in early winter (a smaller group of gray whales live off the Oregon coast all summer). From late spring through early autumn about 80 orcas inhabit Washington's Puget Sound and BC's Georgia Strait. Although far fewer in number, the orcas live in pods and travel in predictable patterns; therefore chances are high that you will see a pod on any given trip. Some operators claim sighting rates of 90 percent; others offer guaranteed sightings, meaning that you can repeat the tour free of charge until you spot a whale.

COMMON PACIFIC NORTHWEST SPECIES

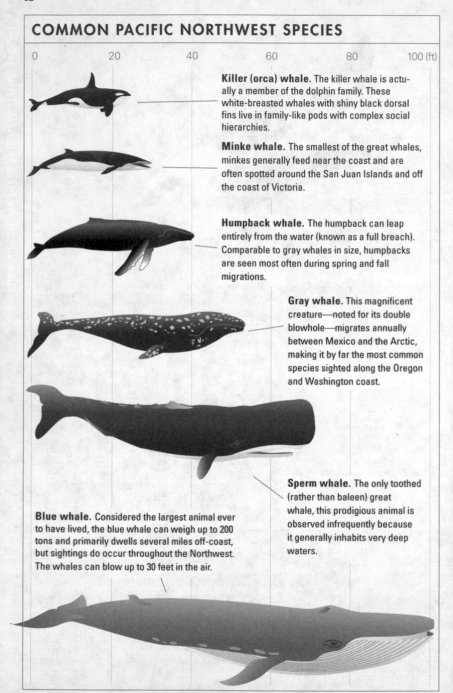

0   20   40   60   80   100 (ft)

Killer (orca) whale. The killer whale is actually a member of the dolphin family. These white-breasted whales with shiny black dorsal fins live in family-like pods with complex social hierarchies.

Minke whale. The smallest of the great whales, minkes generally feed near the coast and are often spotted around the San Juan Islands and off the coast of Victoria.

Humpback whale. The humpback can leap entirely from the water (known as a full breach). Comparable to gray whales in size, humpbacks are seen most often during spring and fall migrations.

Gray whale. This magnificent creature—noted for its double blowhole—migrates annually between Mexico and the Arctic, making it by far the most common species sighted along the Oregon and Washington coast.

Sperm whale. The only toothed (rather than baleen) great whale, this prodigious animal is observed infrequently because it generally inhabits very deep waters.

Blue whale. Considered the largest animal ever to have lived, the blue whale can weigh up to 200 tons and primarily dwells several miles off-coast, but sightings do occur throughout the Northwest. The whales can blow up to 30 feet in the air.

TAKING A TOUR

Spotting an orca in the Haro Strait between British Columbia and Washington

CHOOSING YOUR BOAT

The type of boat you choose does not affect how close you can get to the whales. For the safety of whales and humans, government regulations require boats to stay at least 100 meters (328 feet) from the pods, though closer encounters are possible if whales approach a boat when its engine is off.

Motor Launches. These cruisers carry from 30 to more than 80 passengers. They are comfortable, with washrooms, protection from the elements, and even snack-and-drink concessions. They can be either glass-enclosed or open-air.

Zodiacs. Open inflatable boats, Zodiacs carry about 12 passengers. They are smaller and more agile than cruisers and offer both an exciting ride bouncing over the waves and an eye-level view of the whales. Passengers are supplied with warm, waterproof survival suits. **Note: Zodiac tours are not recommended for people with back or neck problems, pregnant women, or small children.**

Most companies have naturalists on board as guides, as well as hydrophones that, if you get close enough, allow you to listen to the whales singing and vocalizing. Although the focus is on whales, you also have a good chance of spotting marine birds, Dall's porpoises, dolphins, seals, and sea lions, as well as other marine life. And, naturally, there's the scenery of forested islands, distant mountains, and craggy coastline.

MOTION SICKNESS

Seasickness isn't usually a problem in the sheltered waters of Puget Sound and the Georgia Strait, but seas can get choppy off the Washington and Oregon coasts. If you're not a good sailor, it's wise to wear a seasickness band or take anti-nausea medication. Ginger candy often works, too.

THE OREGON AND WASHINGTON COAST

A full breach in open waters is a thrilling sight

WHEN TO GO

Mid-December through mid-January is the best time for viewing the southbound migration, with April through mid-June the peak period for the northbound return (when whales swim closer to shore). Throughout summer, several hundred gray whales remain in Oregon waters, often feeding within close view of land. Mornings are often the best time for viewing, as it's more commonly overcast at this time, which means less glare and calmer seas. Try to watch for vapor or water expelled from whales' spouts on the horizon.

WHAT IT COSTS

Trips are generally 2 hours and prices for adults range from about $25 to $40.

RECOMMENDED OUTFITTERS

Depoe Bay, with its sheltered, deepwater harbor, is Oregon's whale-watching capital, and here you'll find several outfitters.

Dockside Charters (☎ 800/733–8915 ⊕ www.docksidedepoebay.com has an excellent reputation. Green-oriented **Eco Tours of Oregon** (☎ 888/868–7733, ⊕ www.ecotours-of-oregon.com) offers full day tours that depart from Portland hotels and include a stop along the coast at Siletz Bay, a 75-minute charter boat tour, lunch, and stops at state parks near Newport and Lincoln City.

Along the Washington coast, several of the fishing-charter companies in Westport offer seasonal whale-watching cruises, including **Ocean** Sportfishing **Charters** (☎ 800/562–0105, ⊕ www.oceansportfishing.com).

BEST VIEWING FROM SHORE

Washington: On Long Beach Peninsula, the North Head Lighthouse at the mouth of the Columbia River, makes an excellent perch for whale sightings. Westport, farther up the coast at the mouth of Grays Harbor, is another great spot.

Oregon Coast: You can spot gray whales all summer long and especially during the spring migration—excellent locales include Neahkanie Mountain Overlook near Manzanita, Cape Lookout State Park, the Whale Watching Center in Depoe Bay, Cape Perpetua Interpretive Center in Yachats, and Cape Blanco Lighthouse near Port Orford.

Chapter 2

TRAVEL SMART OREGON

2

Updated by
Jon Shadel

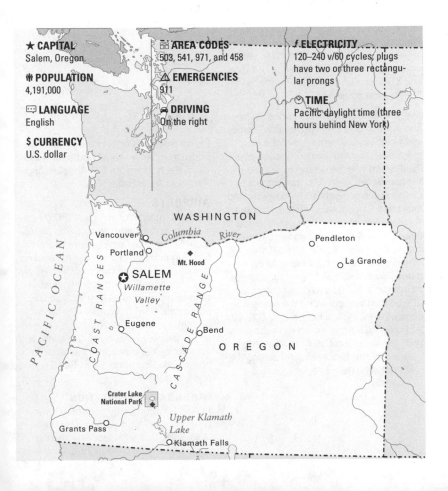

★ **CAPITAL**
Salem, Oregon

POPULATION
4,191,000

LANGUAGE
English

$ **CURRENCY**
U.S. dollar

AREA CODES
503, 541, 971, and 458

⚠ **EMERGENCIES**
911

🚗 **DRIVING**
On the right

ELECTRICITY
120–240 v/60 cycles; plugs have two or three rectangular prongs

TIME
Pacific daylight time (three hours behind New York)

WASHINGTON

PACIFIC OCEAN

Vancouver — *Columbia River*

Portland

Mt. Hood

★ SALEM
Willamette Valley

COAST RANGES

CASCADE RANGE

Eugene

Bend

Pendleton

La Grande

O R E G O N

Crater Lake
National Park

Upper Klamath Lake

Grants Pass

Klamath Falls

Getting Here

Except for Portland, you'll need a car to enjoy Oregon's cities, towns, coast, mountains, and wine country. Portland has outstanding public transportation options, such as a light rail (that goes to the airport), streetcar, buses, and taxis. This is not the case in most other towns in the state, so even if bus or train service exists between two points, you'll need a car to get around once you reach your destination.

Most visitors arriving by plane fly into Portland, home of the state's largest airport. There are smaller regional airports in Bend, Coos Bay, Eugene, Medford, and Pendleton. A smaller number of visitors arrive by Amtrak, which has major service connecting Portland, Salem, Eugene, and Klamath Falls with San Francisco, Seattle, and Spokane.

Major interstate highways connect Oregon with neighboring Washington, Idaho, and Northern California, making it easy to include the state as part of a regional Pacific Northwest road trip to Seattle, Vancouver, and environs. Interstate 5 is Oregon's major north–south freeway, and Interstate 84 cuts east–west across the northern part of the state from Portland through the Columbia Gorge and then southeast toward Boise, Idaho. Other major roads through the state, all of them offering plenty of beautiful scenery, include U.S. 101 up and down the coast, U.S. 97 north–south along the eastern edge of the Cascade Range, and U.S. 20 and U.S. 26, both of which run east–west from the coast through the Willamette Valley, over the Cascades, and across the state's vast eastern interior.

Travel Times from Portland to	By Car
Ashland/Medford	4½ hr
Astoria	2 hr
Bend	3 hr
Coos Bay	4 hr
Crater Lake National Park	4½–5 hr
Dundee	45 min
Eugene	2 hr, 5 min
Hood River	1 hr
Newport	2½ hr
Mt. Hood	1½ hr
Pendleton	3½ hr
Salem	1 hr

 Air

Flying times to Portland are about 5 hours from New York, 4 hours from Chicago, 2½ hours from Los Angeles, and 3¼ hours from Dallas.

AIRPORTS

Portland International Airport (PDX) is an efficient and modern airport with service to and from most major national and a growing number of international destinations. It's a relatively uncrowded facility, and both check-in and security lines tend to proceed quickly. It's also easily accessible from Downtown Portland, both by car and public transit. It serves as the primary gateway to the state, with connections to a handful of smaller airports, including Bend, Coos Bay, Eugene, and Medford.

GROUND TRANSPORTATION

PDX is 30 minutes by car from Downtown Portland, and is served by taxi ($38–$60), Lyft and Uber ride-sharing app service ($20–$40), light rail and bus

($2.50), and airport shuttle service ($14 one way, $24 round-trip). Consult the airport's website for a complete list of authorized shuttles and buses, rental car operators, app-based ride-share services, and more ground transportation.

Boat

CRUISES

From early April through early November, a few cruise lines offer excursions focused specifically on the Pacific Northwest, usually along the Columbia River, leaving from Portland. **Un-Cruise Adventures** offers seven-day excursions (some of them wine themed) along the Columbia and Snake rivers, calling at Richland (with access to Walla Walla), Clarkston–Hells Canyon, The Dalles, Hood River, Bonneville Dam, Portland, and Astoria.

American Cruise Lines runs seven-day excursions from February through April along the Columbia and Snake rivers, departing either from Portland or Clarkston (WA), on a Victorian-style stern-wheeler, the *Queen of the West*.

Bus

Greyhound buses travel to and within Oregon, providing frequent service to major cities, such as Portland, Eugene, and Medford. A modern alternative is BoltBus, which offers inexpensive daily fares on clean, Wi-Fi-enabled coaches between Eugene and Portland, and service farther north up to Seattle, Bellingham, and Vancouver, BC.

In Portland, TriMet operates one of the finest mass transit systems in the country with buses and streetcars connecting to MAX light rail stations, which provide faster service to the airport and suburban areas. Most buses stop every 15 minutes or so most of the day, every day. Service is less frequent outside rush hour. A single fare is $2.50, a daily pass is $5, and a monthly, unlimited pass is $100.

Car

Interstate 5 is the major north–south conduit for western Oregon (the most populous part of the state) and provides a straight shot at high speeds from California to Washington—provided there aren't traffic snarls due to slick conditions or summer road construction. Most of Oregon's largest cities, such as Portland, Salem, Eugene, Medford, and Ashland, are along Interstate 5. This makes driving between the major hubs the most practical way of exploring the state, as bus and train service is limited, and once outside Portland you'll need a car to get around.

For those who have the time, traveling U.S. 101 is an attraction in itself, as it hugs the Oregon Coast the entire length of the state with its incredibly scenic road. Make sure you want to commit to the coastal drive, which may be slow going in some parts, before getting on U.S. 101, because jumping back and forth to Interstate 5 adds a great deal of time to your trip.

The Cascade Range cuts through the middle of Oregon, which means that east–west journeys often wind through mountain passes, and can be either simply breathtaking (summer) or beautiful, slow, and treacherous (winter).

Interstate 84 is northern Oregon's major east–west artery—it enters the majestic Columbia River Gorge near Portland and continues east to Hood River, The Dalles, Pendleton, LaGrande, and Baker City. U.S. 26 provides access to Mt. Hood

Getting Here

from Portland and eventually connects with U.S. 97, leading to Bend.

CAR RENTALS

Unless you only visit Portland, you will need to rent a car for at least part of your trip.

Rates in Portland begin around $30 a day and $150 a week, not including Mult-nomah County's 17% tax on rental cars. Note that summer rates can be steep (easily as much as $65 per day or $300 per week for a compact); book as far in advance as possible, and if you find a good deal, grab it. All the major agencies are represented here.

In Oregon you must be 21 to rent a car. Non-U.S. citizens need a reservation voucher, passport, driver's license, and insurance for each driver.

GASOLINE

The first thing visitors notice in Oregon is that except in some very rural counties or late at night at some self-service pumps, it is illegal for customers to pump their own gas. Gas stations are plentiful in major metropolitan areas and along major highways such as Interstate 5. Major credit and debit cards are accepted, and stations often stay open late, except in rural areas, where you may drive long stretches without a refueling opportunity.

PARKING

Oregon communities offer plenty of on-street parking and pay lots. In certain urban areas, specifically Portland, there are sections of town where street parking is metered—Downtown parking meters take credit cards and parking spots can be hard to find, particularly during festivals and special events. Mass transit in Portland is a plentiful and efficient alternative.

ROAD CONDITIONS

Winter driving can present challenges; in coastal areas the mild, damp climate contributes to frequently wet roadways. Snowfall generally occurs only once or twice a year on the coast and in the valleys, but when snow does fall, traffic grinds to a halt and roadways become treacherous and stay that way until the snow melts.

Tire chains, studs, or snow tires are essential equipment for winter travel in mountain areas, which receive plenty of snow starting as early as October and running well into the middle of spring. If you're planning to drive into high elevations, be sure to check the weather forecast beforehand. Even the main-high-way mountain passes can close because of snow conditions. In winter, state and county highway departments operate snow-advisory telephone lines that give pass conditions. Review your route at ⊕ *www.tripcheck.com.*

RULES OF THE ROAD

Oregon drivers tend to be fairly polite and slower going, which can be a bit maddening for those in a hurry. Bicyclists are plentiful in Oregon cities and rural highways; drivers need to be especially alert to avert accidents, including when opening the car door after parking.

Car seats are compulsory for children under four years *and* 40 pounds; older children are required to sit in booster seats until they are eight years old *and* 80 pounds.

Oregon is a hands-free state. It is illegal to talk or text on a cell phone while operating a motor vehicle, and doing so will net you a hefty fine. Use a wireless headset device if you need to stay connected.

Taxi

Portland has several reliable taxi companies and is also well served by ride-share companies, such as Uber and Lyft. It can be expensive to get around town by cab, however, and you need to call for a taxi, as it's very difficult to hail them on the street. In Portland the flag-drop rate is $3.50 and then $2.90 per mile, and Uber and Lyft trips typically cost a fraction of the price. Make sure to ask whether the driver takes credit cards, whether there's a minimum fare, and whether there are charges for extra passengers. Other charges may include waiting times and airport minimums. Other larger communities in the state have at least one or two taxi companies, but you'll generally find that a couple of cab rides per day costs about the same as a daily car-rental rate.

🚆 Train

Amtrak has daily service to the Pacific Northwest from the Midwest and California. The Coast Starlight begins in Los Angeles; makes stops throughout California, western Oregon, and Washington; and terminates in Seattle. There are stops in both Portland and Eugene (as well as Salem, Albany, Chemult, and Klamath Falls); the 2½-hour trip between Portland and Eugene typically costs $22–$52.

Amtrak's Cascades begins in Vancouver, British Columbia; makes stops in Seattle, Tacoma, Portland, and Salem; and terminates in Eugene. The trip from Seattle to Portland takes roughly 3½ hours and costs $36–$65 for a coach seat; this is a pleasant alternative to the rather dull drive along Interstate 5. The Empire Builder begins in Chicago; makes stops in Milwaukee, WI; St. Paul, MN; Spokane, WA; and other cities before arriving in Portland. The journey from Spokane to Portland is 7 hours ($58–$127), with part of the route running through the Columbia River Gorge.

Essentials

🍴 Dining

Oregon has been a pioneer in the now ubiquitous farm-to-table movement. Pacific Northwest cuisine highlights regional seafood, locally raised meat, and organic produce. Farm stands are plentiful in the rural areas and are definitely worth a stop; almost all cities have at least a weekly farmers' market, and Portland has them daily most of the year.

All of Oregon's cities and prominent towns have some genuinely stellar dining options. Portland has become one of the top culinary destinations in the country, and Bend, Eugene, Ashland, Hood River, the Willamette Valley, and several towns along the coast—most notably Astoria, Cannon Beach, and Newport—have a few superb restaurants specializing in locavore-driven cuisine. Portland has also become quite famous for its wealth of food carts.

Oregon's wines are well regarded throughout the world, particularly those produced in the Willamette Valley and, increasingly, the Rogue Valley in southern Oregon and Columbia River Gorge. It's also one of the top states in the country for craft breweries, microdistilleries, and artisan coffee roasters. Portland again leads the way when it comes to beer, booze, and beans, but Bend, Hood River, and Astoria also have several nationally acclaimed producers, and you'll find notable brewpubs and coffeehouses throughout the state, even in small towns. The restaurants listed *in the chapters* are among the best in each price category. *For price categories, see individual chapters.*

MEALS AND MEALTIMES

Unless otherwise noted, the restaurants listed *in this guide* are open daily for lunch and dinner. Most people eat dinner between 6 and 9 pm, although in many rural areas—including some coastal towns—some restaurants close by 8 or 8:30, especially on weeknights.

RESERVATIONS AND DRESS

Regardless of the venue, it's a good idea to inquire whether reservations are needed on a weekend evening. We only mention them specifically when reservations are essential (there's no other way you'll ever get a table) or when they are not accepted. For popular restaurants, book as far ahead as you can (often a week is more than ample), and reconfirm as soon as you arrive. (Large parties should always call ahead to check the reservations policy.) Dress code policies are virtually unheard of in Oregon.

WINE, BEER, AND SPIRITS

Oregon's largest concentration of wineries is in the Willamette Valley between the northern Cascades and the coast, but you'll also find vibrant wine regions in the Rogue Valley and Columbia River Gorge. The Oregon Wine Board maintains a helpful website, with facts, history, and information on local wineries—Oregon has more than 700 wine-making operations, most of them open to the public.

Oregon has more than 250 microbreweries, with plenty of festivals and events celebrating its brews. The Oregon Brewers Guild also has links to breweries and information on events.

You must be 21 to buy alcohol in Oregon.

➕ Health and Safety

The greatest dangers in the Northwest are becoming lost or suffering an accident in the great outdoors. Don't hike alone, and make sure you bring enough water plus basic first-aid items. If you're not an experienced hiker, stick to tourist-friendly spots such as the well-marked trails in the national parks; if you have to drive 30 miles down a Forest Service Road to reach a trail, it's possible you might be the only one hiking on it.

When driving, take care to use only designated and maintained roads and check road conditions ahead of time when planning to pass through mountainous terrain from fall through spring—many roads over the Coast and Cascades ranges are closed in winter.

🛏 Lodging

The lodgings we list are the cream of the crop in each price category. We always list the facilities that are available, but we don't specify whether they cost extra; when pricing accommodations, always ask what's included and what costs extra. Properties are assigned price categories based on a standard double room in high season (excluding holidays), and excluding tax and service charges. Oregon room taxes range from 6% to 11.5%. *For price categories, see individual chapters.*

APARTMENT AND HOUSE RENTALS

An alternative to staying in a hotel is to spread out a bit and relax in a vacation rental. There are plenty of choices, particularly along the Oregon Coast, near Mt. Hood, and in central Oregon resort areas near Bend. Renting an apartment or a house is an especially attractive idea for long-term visitors or large groups and families.

BED-AND-BREAKFASTS

Oregon is renowned for its range of bed-and-breakfast options, which are found everywhere from busy urban areas to casual country farms and windswept coastal retreats. Many bed-and-breakfasts in Oregon provide full gourmet breakfasts, and some have kitchens that guests can use. Other popular amenities to ask about are fireplaces, jetted bathtubs, and outdoor hot tubs. An excellent resource is Airbnb, which is well represented throughout the state and is especially helpful if you're looking to stay in Portland's East Side, which has few hotels and commercial B&Bs.

CAMPING

Oregon has excellent state-run campgrounds. Half accept advance camping reservations, and the others are first come, first served. Campgrounds range from primitive tent sites to parks with yurts, cabins, and full hookups. Sites are located in and around Oregon's more spectacular natural sites, be it on the coast, the Cascade Range, or near the wine country. Privately operated campgrounds sometimes have extra amenities such as laundry rooms and swimming pools. For more information, contact the state or regional tourism department.

🎒 Packing

It's all about the layers here, as there's no other way to keep up with the weather, which can morph from cold and overcast to warm and sunny and back again in the course of a few hours, especially in spring and early fall. Summer days are warm and more consistent, but evenings can cool off substantially. August and September are the glorious, warm, clear months that remind Oregonians why they live here. Bring an umbrella or raincoat for unpredictable fall and winter weather. Hikers will want to bring rain gear and a hat with them, even if they're visiting in summer; insect repellent is also a good idea if you'll be hiking along mountain trails or beaches.

Essentials

🏃 Professional Sports

As the birthplace and world headquarters of Nike, running ranks among Oregon's most iconic competitive sports, especially in the city of Eugene, which, in 2021, will become the first city in the United States to ever host the World Athletics Championships. The Portland Trail Blazers, a National Basketball Association team, frequently sells out its home games at the Moda Center. Soccer is also a top spectator sport, with the Portland Timbers and Portland Thorns—competing in Major League Soccer and the National Women's Soccer League respectively—drawing rambunctious crowds to Providence Park.

💲 Taxes

Oregon has no sales tax—even in restaurants—making it a popular destination for shoppers, although many cities and counties levy a tax on lodging and services. Room taxes vary from about 6% to 11.5%.

📍 Visitor Information

FESTIVALS

Portland is the state's festivals hub, with many events taking place Downtown on the city's scenic Willamette riverfront, but you'll find plenty of engaging festivals elsewhere. Also keep in mind that Oregon is wild about farmers' markets—most towns in the state have one from spring through fall, and Portland has dozens. There's often live entertainment, arts and crafts, and prepared food at these bustling outdoor markets.

WHEN TO GO

There's no more scenic and enjoyable time to visit just about any part of Oregon than summer, which promises the driest, sunniest weather and mild temperatures, as well as lush, verdant terrain and the majority of the state's key festivals and gatherings—it's also the only time the road encircling Crater Lake is open. But summer can also mean crowds at popular destinations and, increasingly, threats of wildfire. The cooler but typically sunny days of late spring and early fall are a sweet spot for visiting more popular destinations such as the Oregon Coast, Columbia River Gorge, and Willamette Valley.

LOW SEASON

Spring and fall can be just as beautiful as summer, with blooming gardens and fall foliage, plus a calendar packed full of seasonal events such as flower festivals in April and May and harvest happenings in September and October. Weather, however, is hard to predict in early spring and late fall.

SHOULDER SEASON

During the winter months, from the coast to the Cascades (including Portland and the Willamette Valley), rain and gray skies are the norm and quite common in spring and fall. Winter is also the best time for whale- and storm-watching along the coast and bird-watching in southeastern Oregon.

HIGH SEASON

You should plan for occasionally intense (but dry) heat waves in the valleys, from Ashland clear north to Portland as well as east through the Columbia Gorge. Wildfires are a growing concern, mostly from July through September, when smoke and ash have the potential to cause unhealthy air quality. Even in summer, fog and rain can sometimes overpower the coast for a few days at a time.

On the Calender

JANUARY
Oregon Truffle Festival. Dinners and tastings elevate the Willamette Valley's signature fungus. ⊕ *oregontrufflefestival. org*

FEBRUARY
Newport Seafood and Wine Festival. Northwest vintners join fishers for this long-running local favorite. ⊕ *seafoodandwine.com*

Oregon Shakespeare Festival. Ashland's famed theater festival runs from March through October. ⊕ *www.osfashland.org*

Oregon WinterFest. Celebrate the region's winter sports with a mix of outdoors activities and indoor concerts in Bend. ⊕ *oregonwinterfest.com*

MARCH
Portland International Film Festival. The region's top film festival. ⊕ *www.nwfilm. org*

Wooden Shoe Tulip Fest. Every spring spectacular fields of brightly hued tulips spring to life. ⊕ *www.woodenshoe.com*

MAY
Portland Rose Festival. Arguably Oregon's most famous festival consists of numerous events and parties that culminate in a huge parade. ⊕ *www.rosefestival.org*

JUNE
Cannon Beach Sandcastle Contest. This one-day event features professional and amateur sand constructions. ⊕ *www. cannonbeach.org*

Portland Pride. One of the West Coast's largest Pride celebrations. ⊕ *www. pridenw.org*

World Naked Bike Ride. The wildly colorful event raises awareness for bike safety, body positivity, and a car-free lifestyle. ⊕ *www.pdxwnbr.org*

JULY
International Pinot Noir Celebration. Wine lovers flock to McMinnville, in the Willamette Valley, to sample fine regional vintages. ⊕ *ipnc.org*

Oregon Brewers Festival. Sample craft beer from the state's many craft operations. ⊕ *www.oregonbrewfest.com*

Waterfront Blues Festival. The largest blues showcase on the West Coast. ⊕ *www. waterfrontbluesfest.com*

AUGUST
Oregon State Fair. Old-school fair with vendors, competitions, races, and big-name entertainers. ⊕ *oregonstatefair.org*

Oregon Wine Experience. More than 100 Oregon wineries participate at this Jacksonville-based event. ⊕ *www.theoregonwineexperience.com*

SEPTEMBER
Feast Portland. Rapidly becoming one of the most talked-about culinary festivals in the country, with events and meals prepared by both local and national star chefs. ⊕ *www.feastportland.com*

Pendleton Round-Up. One of the country's most prestigious rodeos, drawing upwards of 60,000 participants and spectators. ⊕ *www.pendletonroundup.com*

OCTOBER
All Jane Comedy Festival. A multiday Portland festival showcases top women in comedy. ⊕ *www.alljanecomedy.org*

NOVEMBER
Portland Book Festival. Authors descend on Portland for this top literary festival. ⊕ *www.literary-arts.org*

DECEMBER
Holiday Ale Festival. Taste 50-plus beers and ciders brewed exclusively for the event. ⊕ *www.holidayale.com*

Great Itineraries

Best of Oregon Tour

With 10 days, you can get a taste of Oregon's largest city, eco-conscious Portland, while also getting a nice sense of the state's geographical diversity—the mountainous and sweeping coast, gorgeous Crater Lake, the rugged Cascade Mountains, and the eastern high-desert regions.

DAYS 1 AND 2: PORTLAND

Start by spending a couple of days in Portland, where you can tour the museums and attractions that make up **Washington Park,** as well as the **Lan Su Chinese Garden** in Old Town, and the excellent museums and cultural institutions along Downtown's leafy **Park Blocks.** This city of vibrant, distinctive neighborhoods offers plenty of great urban exploring, with Nob Hill, Hawthorne, Mississippi Avenue, and the Alberta Arts District among the best areas for shopping, café-hopping, and people-watching. If you have a little extra time, consider spending a couple of hours just south of the city in the **Willamette Valley Wine Country**—it's an easy jaunt from Portland.

DAYS 3 AND 4: OREGON COAST

(1½ hours by car from Portland to Cannon Beach)

Leave Portland early on Day 3 for the drive west about 100 miles on U.S. 30 to the small city of **Astoria,** which has several excellent spots for lunch and the **Columbia River Maritime Museum.** Pick the main scenic highway down the Oregon Coast, U.S. 101, and continue south, stopping at **Fort Stevens State Park** and the **Fort Clatsop National Memorial.** End the day in charming **Cannon Beach** (26 miles south of Astoria), which has a wealth of oceanfront hotels and inns, many with views of one of the region's seminal features, 235-foot-tall **Haystack Rock.** Be sure to check out the stunning beach scenery at nearby **Ecola State Park** and **Oswald West State Park.**

The following morning, continue south down U.S. 101. In **Tillamook** (famous for its cheese), take a detour onto the **Three Capes Loop,** a stunning 35-mile byway. Stop in small and scenic **Pacific City** (at the south end of the loop) for lunch. Once you're back on U.S. 101, continue south to **Newport,** spending some time at the excellent **Oregon Coast Aquarium** and Oregon State University's fascinating **Hatfield Marine Science Center.** Your final stop is the charming village of **Florence,** 160 miles (four to six hours) from Cannon Beach.

DAY 5: EUGENE

(2½ hours by car from Florence to Eugene with detour at Oregon Dunes)

Spend the morning driving 20 miles south of Florence along U.S. 101 to scamper about the sandy bluffs at **Oregon Dunes National Recreation Area** near Reedsport. Then backtrack to Florence for lunch in Old Town before taking Highway 126 east for 60 miles to the attractive college city of **Eugene,** staying at one of the charming inns or bed-and-breakfasts near the leafy campus of the University of Oregon. Take a walk to the summit of **Skinner Butte,** which affords fine views of the city, and plan to have dinner at one of the top-notch restaurants at the **5th Street Public Market.** Budget some additional time in Eugene the following morning to visit two excellent University of Oregon museums, the **Jordan Schnitzer Museum of Art** and the **Oregon Museum of Natural History.**

DAYS 6 AND 7: CRATER LAKE AND ASHLAND

(3 hours by car from Eugene to Crater Lake National Park or Prospect)

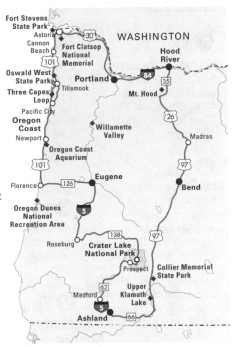

From Eugene, take Interstate 5 south for 75 miles to Roseburg, and then head east along Highway 138 (the Umpqua River Scenic Byway), which twists and turns over the Cascade Range for 85 miles to the northern entrance of **Crater Lake National Park.** Once inside the park, you can continue along Rim Drive for another half hour for excellent views of the lake. Overnight in the park or in nearby **Prospect.**

The following morning, take the lake boat tour to **Wizard Island** and hike through the surrounding forest. In the afternoon, head southwest on Highway 62 to Interstate 5, and then on to **Ashland,** 95 miles (about two hours) from Crater Lake. Plan to stay the night in one of Ashland's many superb bed-and-breakfasts. Have dinner and attend one of the **Oregon Shakespeare Festival** productions (March through October).

DAYS 8 AND 9: BEND
(3½ hours by car from Ashland)

Get an early start out of Ashland, driving east along scenic Highway 140, which skirts picturesque **Upper Klamath Lake,** and then north on U.S. 97, stopping if you have time at **Collier Memorial State Park,** to reach the outdoorsy resort town of **Bend.** Here you can spend two nights checking out the parks, mountain hikes, microbreweries, and restaurants of the state's largest city east of the Cascades. Be sure to visit the outstanding **High Desert Museum,** the **Old Mill District,** and **Mt. Bachelor Ski Area.**

DAY 10: HOOD RIVER
(3 hours by car from Bend)

From Bend, continue north up U.S. 97, and then northwest up U.S. 26 to **Mt. Hood,** 105 miles total. Have lunch at the historic **Timberline Lodge,** admiring the stunning views south down the Cascade Range. Pick up Highway 35 and drive around the east side of Mt. Hood and then north 40 miles up to the dapper town of **Hood River,** in the heart of the picturesque Columbia Gorge. Spend the night at one of the attractive inns, and try one of this town's stellar restaurants for dinner. From here it's just a 60-mile drive west along a scenic stretch of Interstate 84 to reach Portland.

Contacts

Air

AIRPORT INFORMATION
Portland International
Airport (PDX). ☎ *503/460–4234, 877/739–4636*
⊕ *www.flypdx.com.*

Bus

BUS INFORMATION
BoltBus. ☎ *877/265–8287*
⊕ *www.boltbus. com.* **Greyhound Lines.**
☎ *800/231–2222, 214/849–8100 outside U.S., 800/661–8747 in Canada* ⊕ *www.greyhound. com.* **TriMet Mass Transit.**
☎ *503/238–7433* ⊕ *www. trimet.org.*

Car

EMERGENCY SERVICES
AAA Oregon. ☎ *800/222–4357* ⊕ *www.oregon.aaa. com.* **Oregon State Police.**
☎ *503/378–3720* ⊕ *www. oregon.gov/OSP.*

🏛 Cruise

CONTACTS American Cruise Lines. ☎ *800/460–4518* ⊕ *www.american-cruiselines.com.* **UnCruise Adventures.** ☎ *888/862–8881* ⊕ *www.uncruise. com.*

Tours

CONTACTS EcoTours of Oregon. ☎ *503/245–1428*
⊕ *www.ecotours-of-oregon.com.* **Portland Spirit Cruises.** ⊕ *www.portland-spirit.com.* **TREO Bike Tours.**
☎ *541/676–5840* ⊕ *www. treobiketours.com.*

Train

TRAIN INFORMATION
Amtrak. ☎ *800/872–7245*
⊕ *www.amtrak.com.*

📍 Visitor Information

CONTACTS Oregon Brewers Guild. ⊕ *www.oregon-beer.org.* **Oregon Distillers Guild.** ⊕ *www.oregondistillerytrail.com.* **Oregon Parks and Recreation Department.** ☎ *800/452–5687 reservations, 800/551–6949 information* ⊕ *www.oregonstateparks. org.* **Oregon Wine Board.**
⊕ *www.oregonwine. org.* **Travel Oregon.**
☎ *800/547–7842* ⊕ *www. traveloregon.com.* **Travel Portland.** ☎ *503/427–1372, 888/503–3291* ⊕ *www. travelportland.com.*

Chapter 3

PORTLAND

Updated by
Andrew Collins

 Sights
★★★☆☆

 Restaurants
★★★★★

 Hotels
★★★★☆

 Shopping
★★★★☆

 Nightlife
★★★★★

WELCOME TO PORTLAND

TOP REASONS TO GO

★ **Play in the parks:** Head to Washington Park's Japanese Garden and International Rose Test Garden; stroll along the Willamette in Tom McCall Waterfront Park, or ramble amid the evergreens atop Mt. Tabor.

★ **View works of art:** Take part in the First Thursday Pearl District and Last Thursday Alberta Street art walks. Galleries stay open late, often with receptions and openings. And don't miss the superb Portland Art Museum.

★ **Embrace Portland's indie retail spirit:** Check out the many hip pockets of cool, maker-driven boutiques, especially in Nob Hill, the Pearl District, Hawthorne, and North Mississippi Avenue.

★ **Sample the liquid assets:** Visit a few of the dozens of superb local producers of craft spirits and beer, artisanal coffee and tea, and fine wine.

★ **Eat locally:** Plenty of visitors to Portland build their entire daily itineraries around eating; food trucks, cafés, and restaurants showcase the city's farm-to-table, locavore ethic.

1 Downtown. At the center of it all, Portland's Downtown boasts the Portland Art Museum, the Portland's Centers for the Arts, and the Portland Farmers' Market along with a slew of notable restaurants and the bulk of the city's hotels. Nearest to the Pearl District, Downtown's West End has become an increasingly stylish dining and retail area in recent years. Due west of Downtown lies enormous Washington Park, which contains many must-sees, including the Hoyt Arboretum, International Rose Test Garden, Japanese Garden, and Portland Children's Museum.

2 Old Town/Chinatown. Home to some great examples of Asian-inspired public art, the Lan Su Chinese Garden, and a fun if sometimes rowdy nightlife scene, this historic port district is also home to the famed Portland Saturday Market and the trendy Pine Street Market food hall.

3 Pearl District. Bordering Old Town to the west and Downtown to the north, this former warehouse district is now a posh warren of both historic and contemporary condos and commercial buildings housing upscale restaurants, bars, and retailers, including world-renowned Powell's City of Books.

4 Nob Hill. From offbeat to upscale, Nob Hill and adjacent Slabtown's shopping, restaurants, and bars draw a discerning crowd. Immediately west, Forest Park is the largest forested area within city limits in the nation. Trailheads are easily accessible from Nob Hill as well as from Washington Park, which lies just south.

5 Forest Park. Forest Park is the nation's largest urban forest. Trailheads are easily accessible from Nob Hill as well as Washington Park, to the south.

6 West Hills and Southwest. This expansive, green section of the city is home to Washington Park, which contains many must-sees, including the Hoyt Arboretum, International Rose Test Garden, Japanese Garden, and Portland Children's Museum.

7 North. The city's "fifth quadrant" sits on the peninsula formed by the confluence of the Willamette River and the Columbia River. Part working class, part creative class, it's home to the hip North Mississippi Avenue and North Williams Avenue dining and retail strips.

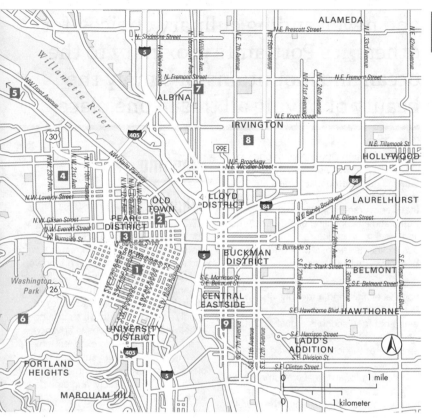

8 Northeast. Containing the Moda basketball arena, the Oregon Convention Center, the Alberta Arts District, and some of the city's least and most affluent neighborhoods, Portland's Northeast quadrant is also one of the city's most diverse neighborhoods.

9 Southeast. The several vibrant pockets of foodie-approved restaurants and independently owned shops—especially on Belmont, Hawthorne, and Division, and in the formerly industrial Central East Side—are highlights of this large quadrant that includes a number of attractive and historic residential areas. This neighborhood also has kid-popular draws like the Oregon Museum of Science and Industry (OMSI), Tilikum Crossing bridge, and Mount Tabor Park.

What distinguishes Portland, Oregon, from the rest of America's cityscapes? For some, it's the wealth of cultural offerings and never-ending culinary choices; for others, it's Portland's proximity to the ocean and mountains, or simply the beauty of having all this in one place.

Strolling through Downtown or one of Portland's many diverse and dynamic outlying neighborhoods, there's an unmistakable vibrancy to this city—one that's encouraged by clean air, infinite trees, and an appealing blend of historic and modern architecture. Portland's various nicknames—Rose City, Bridgetown, Beervana—tell its story.

Rich cultural offerings, endless recreational activities, and a friendly vibe make Portland universally alluring, but the white-hot food scene is arguably its top visitor attraction, especially its fervent embrace of the locavore movement. On a related note, the city maintains a strong appreciation for artisanal craftsmanship, which encompasses everything from coffee, beer, chocolate, and other edibles (recreational marijuana was legalized in Oregon in 2015) to furniture, jewelry, apparel, and household goods. These touchstones of modern urbanism have made Portland the kind of place that younger creative spirits, tech workers, and artists want to visit and live in.

Planning

When to Go

Portland's mild climate is best from June through September, when rain is a rarity and sunny days seem to go on forever. Hotels can fill up quickly during this period, and although a recent hotel building boom has greatly helped to increase supply and soften rates, it's still a good idea to book reservations in advance. Spring and fall are also excellent times to visit. The weather is still usually quite pleasant, prices for accommodations often drop considerably, and crowds are far fewer at popular attractions and restaurants. In winter, snow is uncommon in the city but abundant in the nearby mountains, which are hugely popular with skiers and snowboarders.

Average daytime summer highs are in the 70s, but heat waves usually two or three times per summer can lead to several consecutive days of temperatures topping out near or above 100 degrees; winter temperatures generally reach the 40s and low 50s during the day. Rainfall varies greatly from one locale to another. In the coastal mountains, for example, 160 inches of rain fall annually, creating temperate rain forests. Portland has an average of only 36 inches of rainfall a year—less than New York, Chicago, or Miami. In winter, however, even if it doesn't often rain hard, rainy or misty weather is common and can sometimes go on for days (especially in November and December). More than 75% of Portland's annual precipitation occurs from October through March.

Getting Here and Around

AIR TRAVEL

It takes about 5 hours to fly nonstop to Portland from New York, 4 hours from Chicago and Atlanta, and 2½ hours from Los Angeles. Flying to Seattle takes just under an hour, and flying to Vancouver takes just over an hour.

Portland International Airport (PDX) is an efficient, modern airport with service to most major national and a handful of international destinations. It's a relatively uncrowded facility, and both check-in and security lines tend to proceed quickly. It's also easily accessible from Downtown Portland, both by car and TriMet/MAX light rail.

AIRPORT
Portland International Airport

(*PDX*) This is the city's—and the region's—major airport. You'll find a pretty good selection of local restaurants and shops inside the terminal. ⊠ *7000 N.E. Airport Way, Portland* ☎ *877/739–4636, 503/460–4234* ⊕ *www.pdx.com.*

GROUND TRANSPORTATION

Taking the MAX, Portland's light rail train, to and from Portland International Airport is straightforward. The Red Line MAX stops right at the terminal, and the approximately 35- to 45-minute ride to Downtown costs $2.50. Trains run daily from early morning until around midnight—MAX won't be available to some very late-arriving passengers, but it generally runs early enough to catch even the first flights of the day out of Portland, which typically depart around 6 am. You purchase your ticket before boarding at one of the vending machines in the terminal and at every MAX stop, or by downloading the TriMet Hop Fastpass app and paying with your phone; tickets are also good on TriMet buses and the Portland Streetcar, and transfers within 2½ hours of the time of purchase are free. Uber and Lyft have dedicated pickup areas at the airport; the cost for either between the airport and Downtown averages around $25 to $35 (a taxi generally runs about $10 more).

CONTACTS TriMet/MAX. ☎ *503/238–7433* ⊕ *www.trimet.org.*

CAR TRAVEL

Although traffic has increased dramatically in recent years (Portland ranks as one of the worst cities in the country for traffic congestion), the city is a fairly easy city to navigate by car, and if you're planning to explore neighboring regions—such as the coast, Willamette wine country, and Columbia Gorge—it's best to do so by car, as public transportation options to these areas, especially the coast, is very limited. That said, parking Downtown can get expensive and a car isn't necessary for getting around the city itself. One practical strategy is going without a car during the days you plan to spend in the city center, and then renting a car just for those days when you're venturing outside the city or exploring some of the East Side neighborhoods, which have ample free parking. Most major rental agencies have Downtown offices, and renting Downtown can save you plenty of money, as you avoid paying the hefty taxes and surcharges that you must pay at the airport agencies.

Portland is easily reached via the West Coast's major interstate highway, Interstate 5, which connects Portland to Seattle (which is a three-hour drive north) and Eugene (a little over a two-hour drive south). Interstate 84 begins in Downtown Portland and runs east into the Columbia Gorge and eventually to Idaho. U.S. 26 is the main route to the Oregon Coast west from Downtown, and to Mt. Hood going east. The city's bypass freeways are Interstate 205, which links Interstate 5 and Interstate 84 before crossing the Columbia River north into Washington, and Interstate 405, which arcs around western Downtown. Most city-center streets are one way, and some Downtown streets—including 5th and 6th Avenues—are limited primarily to bus and MAX traffic (with just one lane for cars, and limited turns).

PARKING

Compared with many other major U.S. cities, Portland has a relatively abundant parking, even Downtown, both metered and in garages. The most affordable and accessible option is to park in one of several city-owned "Smart Park" lots. Rates start at $1.80 per hour (short-term parking, four hours or less), with a $16 daily maximum; weekends and evenings, the daily maximum is just $5. The best part about Smart Park is that about 400 participating merchants validate tickets, covering the first two hours of parking when you spend at least $25 in their establishments.

There are numerous privately owned lots around the city as well; fees for these vary and can be quite pricey, and Downtown hotels also charge significantly (as much as $40 to $55 nightly).

Downtown street parking is metered only, and enforcement is vigilant. You can use cash or a credit card to pay ($2 per hour) at machines located on each block (display your receipt on the inside of your curbside window) or by downloading the ParkingKitty app and paying with your phone. Metered spaces are mostly available for one to three hours, with a few longer-term spaces available on certain streets.

Outside the Downtown core, you'll find a mix of free and metered parking, with rates ranging from $1 to $2 depending on the neighborhood. In some free parking areas, time limits (usually an hour to three hours) are enforced. On the east side of the river, with the exception of the Central East Side (which has a number of metered blocks), free unmetered parking is the norm.

TRIMET/MAX TRAVEL

TriMet operates an extensive system of buses, streetcars, and light-rail trains. The North–South streetcar line runs from Nob Hill through the Pearl District, Downtown, and Portland State University campus to South Waterfront. The A and B Loop streetcar lines cross the Willamette River to the East Side via Broadway Bridge and the Tilikum Crossing Bridge.

MAX light rail links the city's eastern, southern, and western suburbs as well as North Portland with Downtown, Washington Park and the Oregon Zoo, the Lloyd Center district, and the Hollywood District and the airport. From Downtown, trains operate daily about 5 am–1 am, with a fare of $2.50 for up to 2½ hours of travel (transfers to other MAX trains, buses, and streetcars are free within this time period), and $5 for an unlimited all-day ticket, which is also good system-wide. A one-month pass costs $100. The ticket for riding without a fare is stiff.

You can pay your fare by purchasing a reloadable Hop Fastpass card at a number of grocery and convenience stores around town, downloading Hop Fastpass app and paying with your phone, or paying in cash on buses (exact change required) or at ticket vending machines at streetcar and MAX light rail stops. If you buy a physical ticket, hold onto it whether you're transferring or not; it also serves as proof that you have paid your fare. The most central bus routes operate every 10 to 15 minutes throughout the day. Bikes are allowed in designated areas of MAX trains, and there are bike racks on the front of all buses that everyone is free to use.

✉ *Ticket office at Pioneer Courthouse Sq., 701 S.W. 6th Ave., Downtown* ☎ *503/238–7433* ⊕ *www.trimet.org.*

Tours

BIKE TOURS

Portland is famously bike friendly, with miles of dedicated bike lanes and numerous rental shops. Also, a couple of great companies offer guided rides around the city, covering everything from eating and brewpub-hopping to checking out local parks and historic neighborhoods.

Cycle Portland Bike Tours and Rentals

BICYCLE TOURS | Trust your guide at this well-established outfitter to know Portland's popular and lesser-known spots. Tour themes include Essential Portland, Foodie Field Trip, and Brews Cruise, but you can also customize a tour. The well-stocked on-site bike shop serves beer on tap. ✉ *117 N.W. 2nd Ave., Old Town/Chinatown* ☎ *503/902–5035, 844/739–2453* ⊕ *www.portlandbicycletours.com* 🚲 *From $39.*

WALKING TOURS

Walk the Portland beat with guides who share their personal Portland knowledge, including history, food, brews, arts, and sights.

Portland Walking Tours

WALKING TOURS | A slew of tours are offered by this company, but it's the Beyond Bizarre tour that generates the most buzz. Ghost-hunter wannabes and paranormal junkies make this a popular tour that often sells out. There's also the Underground Portland tour, which highlights the city's sinister history, and a Chocolate Decadence excursion. ✉ *131 N.W. 2nd Ave., Old Town/Chinatown* ☎ *503/774–4522* ⊕ *www.portlandwalkingtours.com* 🚶 *From $19.*

Sights

One of the greatest things about Portland is that there's so much to explore, from both conventional attractions—museums, parks, and other amusements—to lively, pedestrian-friendly neighborhoods abundant with interesting, and usually independently owned, shops, restaurants, and bars. What makes discovering Portland's treasures even more enticing is that most of its attractions, transportation options, and events are relatively accessible and affordable.

The variety of Portland's parks is immense and includes one of the largest urban natural areas in the country (Forest Park). Other favorite Portland green spaces include Laurelhurst, Mt. Tabor, Powell Butte, and Washington parks.

Restaurants

Rising-star chefs and the foodies who adore them have been flocking to Portland for the better part of the past two decades. In this playground of sustainability and creativity, many of the city's hottest restaurants change menus weekly—sometimes even daily—depending upon the ingredients they have delivered to their door that morning from local farms. The combination of fertile soils, temperate weather, and nearby waters contributes to a year-round bountiful harvest (be it lettuces or hazelnuts, mushrooms or salmon) that is within any chef's reach.

And these chefs are not shy about putting new twists on old favorites. Restaurants like Le Pigeon, Beast, Ox, Ned Ludd, Tasty n Alder, and Bullard have all taken culinary risks by presenting imaginatively executed, often globally inspired fare while utilizing sustainable ingredients. There's a strong willingness in and around Portland for chefs to explore their creative boundaries. The city also excels when it comes to international dining, especially when it comes to Asian eateries, such as Pok Pok, Nodoguru, Aviary, Han Oak, and Langbaan. Other strengths include artisanal bakeries and pizzerias, coffeehouses, craft ice cream and doughnut shops, and vegan (or at least vegetarian) restaurants, and Portland also soars when it comes to gastropubs.

Many of Portland's longtime favorites and higher-end spots are concentrated in Downtown, the Pearl District, and Nob Hill. But many of the city's most exciting food scenes are on the East Side, along Alberta Street, Mississippi Avenue, Williams Avenue, Fremont Street, Burnside Street, 28th Avenue, Belmont Street, Hawthorne Boulevard, and Division Street, and sprinkled throughout the Central East Side or tucked away in many neighborhoods in between. Serious food enthusiasts will definitely want to make some trips to these vibrant, if out-of-the-way, neighborhoods. *Restaurant reviews have been shortened. For full information, visit Fodors.com.*

What it Costs in U.S. Dollars

$	$$	$$$	$$$$
AT DINNER			
under $16	$16–$22	$23–$30	over $30

Hotels

Portland has an unusually rich variety of distinctive, design-driven boutique hotels and historic properties, and though you'll find the usual mix of budget-oriented, midrange, and upscale chains here, if you'd rather avoid cookie-cutter brand-name properties, you're in the right place. The city has undergone a major hotel building boom since 2015, with most of these new and often chic and trendy boutique properties having opened Downtown, but the Central East Side, Lloyd District, Old Town, and Pearl District have also seen several notable new lodging additions. The influx of rooms has helped greatly to reduce hotel rates, which had become quite steep at one point—it's much easier to find good deals, even during the busy summer months. Portland has a few bed-and-breakfasts and an enormous supply of Airbnbs; the latter provide a great way to stay in some of the trendy East Side neighborhoods that lack hotels, such as Alberta, North Mississippi, Hawthorne, and Laurelhurst.

Downtown Portland is about a 20- to 25-minute drive from the airport. There are a number of chain properties near the airport, all offering much lower rates than comparable Downtown hotels. *Hotel reviews have been shortened. For full information visit Fodors.com.*

What it Costs in U.S. Dollars

$	$$	$$$	$$$$
HOTELS			
under $150	$150–$225	$226–$300	over $300

Nightlife

Given the city's unabashed passion for craft cocktails, beer, and local wines, it makes sense that Portland abounds with cool lounges and bars. Hard-core clubbing and dancing has a bit less of a following here than more casual barhopping, and Portlanders do like to combine noshing and sipping—you'll find an abundance of nightspots serving exceptional food (and often offering great happy-hour deals on victuals and drinks), and quite a few full-service restaurants with popular side bars and lounges. Nightlife and dining really overlap in the Rose City.

Portland has become something of a base for up-and-coming alternative-rock bands, which perform in clubs scattered throughout the city. Portland's top neighborhoods for barhopping are, not surprisingly, its favored dining districts, too—the West End, Pearl District, and Nob Hill on the west side of the Willamette River, within walking distance (or a streetcar ride) of Downtown hotels. On the East Side, head to the Alberta Arts District, North Mississippi Avenue, East Burnside Street in the 20s, the Central East Side, Belmont Street, Hawthorne Boulevard, Division Street, and Foster-Powell.

Performing Arts

Portland is quite the creative town. Every night top-ranked dance, theater, and musical performers take the stage somewhere in the city. Expect to find never-ending choices for things to do, from watching independent films, performance art, and plays to checking out some of the Northwest's (and the country's) hottest bands at one of the city's many nightclubs or concert venues. For a city of this size, there is truly an impressive—and accessible—scope of talent from visual artists, performance artists, and musicians. The arts are alive, with outdoor sculptural works strewn around the city, ongoing festivals, and premieres of traveling Broadway shows. One of the city's artistic strengths is its bounty of independent neighborhood theaters—many of these are historic, serve craft beer and light food, and show a mix of mainstream and independent films and film festivals.

Shopping

The shopping landscape in Portland has changed significantly in recent years, perhaps not quite as dramatically as the much-buzzed-about culinary scene, but in similar (pardon the pun) fashion. Specifically, those same hip and indie-spirited neighborhoods around the city that have become hot spots for food

and drink—areas like the Pearl District, Downtown West End, Alberta, North Mississippi, North Williams, Central East Side, Hawthorne, and Division—are also enjoying a steady influx of distinctive, well-curated boutiques specializing in edgy fashion and jewelry, handcrafted home accessories and household goods, and artisanal foods.

Activities

Portlanders avidly gravitate to the outdoors and they're well acclimated to the elements year-round. Once the sun starts to shine in spring and into summer, the city fills with hikers, joggers, and mountain bikers, who flock to Portland's hundreds of miles of parks, paths, and trails. The Willamette and Columbia rivers are popular for boating and water sports.

As for competitive sports, Portland is home to the Timbers, a major league soccer team with a devout local fan base, and NBA basketball's beloved Trail Blazers.

Visitor Information

"A&E, The Arts and Entertainment Guide," published each Friday in the *Oregonian* (⊕ *www.oregonlive.com*), contains listings of performers, productions, events, and club entertainment. *Willamette Week* (⊕ *wweek.com*), published free each Wednesday and widely available throughout the metropolitan area, contains similar, but hipper, listings. The *Portland Mercury* (⊕ *www.portlandmercury.com*), also free, is an even edgier entertainment publication distributed every other Wednesday. The glossy newsstand magazine *Portland Monthly* (⊕ *www.pdxmonthly.com*) covers Portland culture and lifestyle and provides great nightlife, entertainment, and dining coverage for the city.

CONTACTS Travel Portland Information Center. ⊠ *Director Park, 877 S.W.
Taylor St., Downtown* ☎ *503/427–1372,
888/503–3291* ⊕ *www.travelportland.
com.*

Downtown

Portland has one of the most attractive, inviting Downtown centers in the
United States. It's clean, compact, and
filled with fountains, plazas, and parks,
including a particularly pretty expanse
of greenery along the Willamette River.
Architecture fans find plenty to admire
in its mix of old and new. Whereas many
urban U.S. business districts clear out
at night and on weekends, Portland's
Downtown is decidedly mixed-use, with
plenty of residential and commercial
buildings, and an appealing mix of hotels,
shops, museums, restaurants, and bars,
especially in the hip West End district.
You can easily walk from one end of
Downtown to the other, and the city's
superb public transportation system—
which includes MAX light rail, buses, and
the streetcar—makes it easy to get here
from other parts of the city. A day pass is
recommended.

◉ Sights

Oregon Historical Society Museum

MUSEUM | Impressive eight-story-high
trompe l'oeil murals of Lewis and Clark
and the Oregon Trail invite history lovers
into this Downtown museum, which
goes beyond the dominant narratives of
white colonists and explorers to tell the
story of the state through myriad per-
spectives, from prehistoric times through
the racist era of "black-exclusion" laws
to the challenges of the present day.
The state-of-the-art permanent exhibit
Experience Oregon, which opened in
2019, comprises 7,000 square feet of
interactive galleries displaying a pair of
9,000-year-old sagebrush sandals, an

actual covered wagon, and hands-on
games. ⊠ *1200 S.W. Park Ave., Downtown* ☎ *503/222–1741* ⊕ *www.ohs.org*
⊠ *$10.*

Pioneer Courthouse Square

PLAZA | Often billed as the living room,
public heart, and commercial soul
of Downtown, Pioneer Square is not
entirely square, but rather an amphi-
theater-like brick piazza featuring five
food carts. Special seasonal, charitable,
and festival-oriented events often take
place in this premier people-watching
venue. Directly across the street is one
of Downtown Portland's most familiar
landmarks, the classically sedate **Pioneer
Courthouse**; built in 1869, it's the oldest
public building in the Pacific Northwest.
A couple of blocks east of the square,
you'll find **Pioneer Place Mall,** an upscale
retail center that spans four city blocks.
⊠ *701 S.W. 6th Ave., Downtown* ⊕ *www.
thesquarepdx.org.*

★ Portland Art Museum

MUSEUM | The treasures at the Pacific
Northwest's oldest arts facility span 35
centuries of Asian, European, and American art—it's an impressive collection for
a midsize city. A high point is the Center
for Native American Art, with regional
and contemporary art from more than
200 indigenous groups. The **Jubitz Center
for Modern and Contemporary Art** contains
six floors devoted entirely to modern art,
including a small but superb photography gallery, with the changing selection
chosen from more than 5,000 pieces in
the museum's permanent collection. The
film center presents the annual Portland
International Film Festival in March.
Also, take a moment to linger in the
peaceful outdoor sculpture garden. Kids
under 17 are admitted free. ⊠ *1219 S.W.
Park Ave., Downtown* ☎ *503/226–2811,
503/221–1156 film schedule* ⊕ *www.
portlandartmuseum.org* ⊠ *$20; free on
the first Thurs. of every month from 5–8
pm* ☉ *Closed Mon.*

★ Portland Farmers Market

MARKET | FAMILY | On Saturdays year-round, local farmers, bakers, chefs, and entertainers converge at the South Park Blocks near the PSU campus for Oregon's largest open-air farmers' market—it's one of the most impressive in the country. It's a great place to sample the regional bounty and to witness the local-food obsession that's revolutionized Portland's culinary scene. There's plenty of food you can eat on the spot, plus non-perishable local items (wine, hazelnuts, chocolates, vinegars) you can take home with you. There's a smaller Wednesday market, May through November, on a different section of the Park Blocks (between S.W. Salmon and S.W. Main). On Mondays, June through September, the market is held at Pioneer Courthouse Square, and at other times the Portland Farmers Market is held in different locations around town, including Nob Hill/Northwest, Kenton/North Portland, King/Alberta, and Lents/Southeast, and some 40 other farmers' markets take place throughout metro Portland—see the website for a list. ⊠ *South Park Blocks at S.W. Park Ave. and Montgomery St., Downtown* ☎ *503/241–0032* ⊕ *www.portlandfarmersmarket.org* ☽ *Closed Sun.–Fri.*

Tom McCall Waterfront Park

CITY PARK | FAMILY | Named for a former governor revered for his statewide land-use planning initiatives, this park stretches north along the Willamette River for about a mile from near the historic Hawthorne Bridge to Steel Bridge. Broad and grassy, Waterfront Park affords a fine ground-level view of Downtown Portland's bridges and skyline. Once an expressway, it's now the site for many annual celebrations, among them the Rose Festival, classical and blues concerts, Portland Pride, Cinco de Mayo, and the Oregon Brewers Festival. The arching jets of water at the **Salmon Street Fountain** change configuration every few hours, and are a favorite cooling-off spot during the dog days of summer. ■ **TIP→ Both the Hawthorne Bridge and Steel Bridge offer dedicated pedestrian lanes, allowing joggers, cyclists, and strollers to make a full loop along both banks of the river, via Vera Katz Eastside Esplanade.** ⊠ *S.W. Naito Pkwy. (Front Ave.), Downtown* ✛ *From Steel Bridge to south of Hawthorne Bridge* ⊕ *www.portlandoregon.gov/parks.*

★ West End

NEIGHBORHOOD | Sandwiched between the Pioneer Square area and the swanky Pearl District, this triangular patch of vintage buildings—interspersed with a handful of contemporary ones—has evolved since the early 2000s into one of the city's most eclectic hubs of fashion, nightlife, and dining. Boutique hotels like the Ace and Sentinel rank among the city's trendiest addresses. Along Harvey Milk Street, formerly the heart of Portland's LGBTQ scene, there's still a popular gay bar, but now you'll also find noteworthy restaurants and lounges like Clyde Common, Bamboo Sushi, and Multnomah Whiskey Library. Among the many independent shops, check out Cacao chocolate shop, Frances May clothier, and Union Way—an enclosed pedestrian mall with a handful of tiny storefronts. ⊠ *S.W. 13th to S.W. 9th Aves., between W. Burnside St. and S.W. Yamhill St., West End.*

 Restaurants

Bamboo Sushi

$$ | SUSHI | Claiming to be the world's first certified sustainable sushi restaurant, this Portland-based chainlet partners with nonprofits such as the Marine Stewardship Council and Monterey Bay Aquarium to ensure it sources its seafood from eco-conscious fishing operations. Bamboo has five locations throughout the metro area, including this stylish branch in Downtown's West End, where the counter seating fills for the weekday happy hour, served until 6 pm. **Known for:** creative, nontraditional signature rolls;

SKIDMORE
OLD TOWN
NATIONAL
HISTORIC
DISTRICT

Ankeny St.

S.W. Ash St.
S.W. Pine St.
S.W. Oak St.
S.W. Harvey Milk St.

S.W. 3rd Ave.
S.W. 2nd Ave.

MAX LIGHT RAIL

Morrison Bridge

S.W. 1st Ave.
S.W. Naito Pkwy. Front Ave.

Willamette River

Salmon Street
Fountain

Hawthorne Bridge

River Place
Marina

Sights ▼

1 Oregon Historical
  Society Museum......... **C6**
2 Pioneer Courthouse
  Square **E4**
3 Portland Art Museum ... **C6**
4 Portland Farmers
  Market **B8**
5 Tom McCall Waterfront
  Park **G6**
6 West End **D2**

Restaurants ▼

1 Bamboo Sushi............ **C2**
2 Bullard **D3**
3 Departure
  Restaurant + Lounge **E4**
4 Higgins................... **C6**
5 Il Solito................... **E3**
6 Imperial.................. **E3**
7 King Tide
  Fish & Shell............. **G9**
8 Maurice.................. **D1**
9 Mother's Bistro
  & Bar.................... **G2**
10 Tasty n Alder **C2**

Quick Bites ▼

1 Blue Star Donuts......... **C3**
2 Case Study Coffee
  Roasters **C4**
3 Good Coffee **D3**
4 Ruby Jewel
  Ice Cream................. **C2**
5 Stumptown Coffee
  Roasters **D2**

Hotels ▼

1 Ace Hotel **D2**
2 The Benson Hotel........ **E2**
3 Dossier Hotel............ **D4**
4 The Duniway **E5**
5 Embassy Suites
  Portland–Downtown ... **G2**
6 Heathman Hotel......... **D5**
7 Hi-Lo Hotel, Autograph
  Collection................ **G3**
8 Hotel deLuxe **A3**
9 Hotel Lucia **E3**
10 Hotel Rose............... **H5**
11 Hotel Zags **D7**
12 Kimpton Hotel Monaco
   Portland.................. **F3**
13 Kimpton Hotel Vintage
   Portland.................. **E3**
14 Kimpton RiverPlace
   Hotel..................... **G9**
15 Mark Spencer Hotel..... **C2**
16 McMenamins
   Crystal Hotel............. **C1**
17 The Nines................ **F4**
18 Porter Portland Hotel.... **F7**
19 Sentinel Hotel **C3**
20 The Woodlark **D3**

KEY

1 Sights
1 Restaurants
1 Quick Bites
1 Hotels
—○— Max Light Rail
– ← – Streetcar
.... Bus
🚲.... Bike only

Pioneer Courthouse Square is home to the iconic Mile Post Sign, which shows the distance to Portland's nine sister-cities as well as other international destinations.

choose-your-own sake flights; happy-hour nigiri set. $ *Average main: $18* ⊠ *404 S.W. 12th Ave., West End* ☎ *503/444–7455* ⊕ *www.bamboosushi.com.*

★ Bullard

$$$$ | **STEAKHOUSE** | In a city with the density of restaurants that Portland has, it takes a lot to stoke the level of buzz surrounding the opening of Bullard, a festive next-generation steak house in the lobby of the Woodlark Hotel. Drawing on his roots in Texas, *Top Chef* alum Doug Adams brings a Southwest-meets-Oregon flair ("Tex-Oregana," according to *The Oregonian*'s food critic) to signature dishes such as beef carpaccio and San Antonio chicken that lives up to the hype. **Known for:** mains large enough for two; house-smoked meats; pickleback shots. $ *Average main: $35* ⊠ *Woodlark Hotel, 813 S.W. Alder St., Downtown* ☎ *503/222–1670* ⊕ *www.bullardpdx.com.*

★ Departure Restaurant + Lounge

$$$ | **ASIAN** | This extravagant rooftop restaurant and lounge on the top floor of The Nines hotel seems fresh out of LA—a look and feel that is, indeed, a departure from Portland's usual no-fuss vibe. The retro-chic interior has an extravagant, space-age, airport-lounge feel, and the outdoor patio—furnished with low, white couches and bright-orange tables and chairs—offers panoramic views of the Downtown skyline. **Known for:** chef's tasting service with wine pairings; dedicated vegan menu; fantastic skyline views. $ *Average main: $25* ⊠ *The Nines hotel, 525 S.W. Morrison St., Downtown* ☎ *503/802–5370* ⊕ *www.departureportland.com* ⊗ *No lunch.*

Higgins

$$$ | **PACIFIC NORTHWEST** | One of Portland's original farm-to-table restaurants, this classic eatery, opened in 1994 by renowned namesake chef Greg Higgins, has built its menu—and its reputation—on its dedication to local, seasonal, organic ingredients. Higgins's dishes display the diverse bounty of the Pacific Northwest, incorporating ingredients like heirloom tomatoes, forest mushrooms, mountain huckleberries, Pacific oysters,

Oregon Dungeness crab, and locally raised pork. **Known for:** house-made charcuterie plate; tender duck confit; casual bistro menu in adjacent bar. $ *Average main: $30 ⊠ 1239 S.W. Broadway, Downtown ☎ 503/222–9070 ⊕ www.higginsportland.com ☾ No lunch weekends.*

Il Solito

$$$ | ITALIAN | The old-school sign outside and vintage photos at this handsome restaurant in Downtown's Hotel Vintage hint at the kitchen's deft handling of red-sauce Italian fare, including fried spaghetti Bolognese and bone-in chicken Parmesan. You'll find more than a few modern twists on this menu (or on the daily specials list) though, from crudo to chestnut ravioli with mushroom sugo along with an exceptional dessert of olive oil cake with mixed local berries and whipped mascarpone. **Known for:** skillfully prepared handmade pastas with interesting sauces; an extensive wine list favoring Italian and Northwest bottles; classic apps like garlic knots and fried hand-pulled mozzarella sticks. $ *Average main: $24 ⊠ Hotel Vintage Portland, 627 S.W. Washington St., Downtown ☎ 503/228–1515 ⊕ www.ilsolitoportland.com.*

★ Imperial

$$$ | PACIFIC NORTHWEST | Tall concrete pillars, exposed brick and ductwork, soft overhead lighting, and rustic wood tables and floors create a warehouse vibe at one of Portland's most defining restaurants, located inside the Hotel Lucia. Open for breakfast, lunch, and dinner, and serving up exemplary contemporary Pacific Northwest fare, menu highlights include Dungeness crab omelet, duck meatballs, grilled king salmon with corn puree and chanterelles, and meaty fare from the wood-fired rotisserie grill. **Known for:** Flat Top happy-hour burger; stellar cocktail program; wood-fired rotisserie-grill fare. $ *Average main: $25 ⊠ Hotel Lucia, 410 S.W. Broadway,*

Downtown ☎ 503/228–7221 ⊕ www.imperialpdx.com.

★ King Tide Fish & Shell

$$$ | SEAFOOD | One of only a handful of serious seafood restaurants in Portland, this casually upscale restaurant in the Kimpton RiverPlace Hotel overlooks the Willamette River and Tom McCall Waterfront Park, offering seating in a proper dining room as well as on a sweeping veranda (for the best views). Offering plenty of enticing starters (pickled deviled eggs with Dungeness crab, mussels with smoked-pork dashi, hamachi tostadas) as well as raw bar platters and a typically weighty whole fish catch of the day, the menu is well suited to sharing several dishes among friends. **Known for:** extensive late-night and happy hour menus; local king salmon with your choice of several sauces; a peaceful riverfront setting away from the bustle of Downtown. $ *Average main: $28 ⊠ Kimpton RiverPlace Hotel, 1510 S.W. Harbor Way, Downtown ☎ 503/295–6166 ⊕ www.kingtidefishandshell.com.*

★ Maurice

$$ | CAFÉ | Described by baker-owner Kristen Murray as a "modern pastry luncheonette," this dainty West End café has just a handful of wooden booth and counter seats and a minimalist-inspired white-on-white aesthetic. The menu features exquisite French–Scandinavian pastries, cakes, and sandwiches, as well as a full gamut of drinks, including wine, beer, cocktails, teas, and coffee. **Known for:** ever-changing, handwritten menu; assorted Swedish fika (snack) pastries; revelatory black-pepper cheesecake. $ *Average main: $20 ⊠ 921 S.W. Oak St., West End ☎ 503/224–9921 ⊕ www.mauricepdx.com ☾ Closed Mon. No dinner.*

Mother's Bistro & Bar

$$ | AMERICAN | FAMILY | Chef and cookbook author Lisa Schroeder dedicates her home-style, made-with-love approach to food to the comforting foods prepared by mothers everywhere. Clearly the theme resonates, as evidenced by the long waits on weekends, and even some weekday mornings for breakfast, which is arguably the best time of the day to sample Schroeder's hearty cooking; try the wild salmon hash with leeks or the French toast with a crunchy cornflake crust. **Known for:** down-home American comfort fare; fantastic breakfasts; drinks in the swanky Velvet Lounge bar. Ⓢ *Average main: $17* ✉ *121 S.W. 3rd Ave., Downtown* ☎ *503/464–1122* ⊕ *www. mothersbistro.com.*

Tasty n Alder

$$$ | **ECLECTIC** | Brunch draws even weekday crowds at this always-happening Downtown venture of celebrated Portland chef John Gorham, what you could label a "modern steak house," though the globe-trotting, tapas-focused menu evades easy categorization. For dinner, Tasty n Alder turns up the class, with a selection of steaks from family-run ranches, along with well-crafted original cocktails. **Known for:** brunch till 2 pm every day; "grown-ass" milk shakes (with alcohol, of course); Korean-style fried chicken. Ⓢ *Average main: $24* ✉ *580 S.W. 12th Ave., West End* ☎ *503/621– 9251* ⊕ *www.tastynalder.com.*

🍵 Coffee and Quick Bites

Blue Star Donuts

$ | **BAKERY** | **FAMILY** | If you have time for just one Portland doughnut shop, choose this light-filled spot on the street level of a glassy tower in the West End. Blue Star opens at 7 am and remains open until that day's fresh-baked stock sells out of popular flavors like blueberry-bourbon-basil, bacon-maple, and Valrhona chocolate crunch with a Boston-cream-style filling. **Known for:** brioche-based doughnuts; wildly inventive flavors; serving Stumptown Coffee. Ⓢ *Average main: $4* ✉ *1155 S.W. Morrison St., West End* ☎ *503/265–8410* ⊕ *www.bluestardonuts.com.*

Case Study Coffee Roasters

$ | **CAFÉ** | A first-rate independent café on a heavily trafficked Downtown corner by MAX and streetcar stops, Case Study serves small-batch, house-roasted coffee in a variety of formats, from Chemex to Aeropress to crowds of regulars. There is an additional Downtown location on S.W. 4th Avenue as well as coffeehouses in Hollywood and the Alberta Arts District. **Known for:** lattes made with scratch-made syrups; a pasty case stocked with goods from various local bakers; slow-drip cold brew. Ⓢ *Average main: $5* ✉ *802 S.W. 10th Ave., Downtown* ☎ *503/477–8221* ⊕ *www.casestudycoffee.com.*

★ Good Coffee

$ | **CAFÉ** | The Woodlark Hotel yielded its plant-filled lobby to the latest outpost from Portland roaster Good Coffee. The marble bar complements the sprawling seating area—a living room for an army of young freelancers, who set up shop at the communal table, on the blue banquet seats lining the street-facing windows, and the plush couches and armchairs. **Known for:** one of Portland's best cappuccinos; intriguing seasonal drink menu; tea lattes and matcha. Ⓢ *Average main: $5* ✉ *Woodlark Hotel, 813 S.W. Alder St., Downtown* ☎ *503/548–2559* ⊕ *www. goodwith.us* ⊗ *No dinner.*

Ruby Jewel Ice Cream

$ | **CAFÉ** | **FAMILY** | Portland's *other* critically acclaimed ice-cream shop (Salt & Straw tends to get far more attention), Ruby Jewel started in 2004 with ice-cream sandwiches in unusual flavors, such as lemon cookie with honey-lavender ice cream and cinnamon-chocolate cookie stuffed with espresso ice cream. Ruby Jewel's five cafés, including this central one in Downtown's West End, also dole out cones and dishes of ice cream with flavors like caramel with salted dark chocolate and chèvre with Pinot-grape swirl. **Known for:** ice-cream sandwiches locals line up for; root beer floats; relationships with regional farms and producers.

$ *Average main: $5 ⌧ 428 S.W. 12th Ave., West End* ☎ *971/271–8895* ⊕ *www.rubyjewel.com.*

Stumptown Coffee Roasters

$ | **CAFÉ** | A pioneer in Portland's artisanal coffee experience, Stumptown Coffee Roasters has expanded into a nationally revered brand. There are five local cafés, where hip baristas, well versed in all things coffee, whip up delicious espresso drinks. **Known for:** quintessential Portland roasts; sectionals and couches to lounge on in the Ace's lobby; pick-me-up before exploring the nearby Powell's City of Books. $ *Average main: $4 ⌧ Ace Hotel, 1026 S.W. Harvey Milk St., West End* ☎ *855/711–3385* ⊕ *www.stumptowncoffee.com* ⊗ *No dinner.*

 Hotels

Ace Hotel

$$ | **HOTEL** | The quintessential Portland hipster lodging, this flagship location of the buzzy Ace Hotels brand contains a Stumptown Coffee café as well as the very good Clyde Common restaurant and Pepe Le Moko bar, is a block from Powell's Books and the Pearl District, and is right in the heart of Downtown's ever-trendy West End neighborhood. **Pros:** prime West End location; unique design and artwork in each room; free city bicycles available for guests. **Cons:** offbeat decor and hipster vibe isn't for everybody; the cheapest rooms don't have private baths; on a sometimes noisy street. $ *Rooms from: $195 ⌧ 1022 S.W. Harvey Milk St., West End* ☎ *503/228–2277* ⊕ *www.acehotel.com* ⇌ *78 rooms* ⊙ *No meals.*

The Benson Hotel

$$$ | **HOTEL** | Portland's venerable grande dame may now be overshadowed by several other upscale properties in town in terms of luxury, but the Benson has hosted countless presidents and celebrities since it opened in 1913, and its guest rooms both capture the hotel's storied legacy while offering plenty of modern comforts, like fully stocked minibars, fluffy organic bathrooms and slippers, and super-plush modern beds. **Pros:** elegant public spaces; big discounts if you join free Coast Hotels rewards program; convenient location near West End, Old Town, and Pearl District. **Cons:** rooms and hallways are a bit dark; many bathrooms are quite small; pricey valet parking. $ *Rooms from: $240 ⌧ 309 S.W. Broadway, Downtown* ☎ *503/228–2000* ⊕ *www.bensonhotel.com* ⇌ *287 rooms* ⊙ *No meals.*

Dossier Hotel

$$ | **HOTEL** | This pale-stone, upscale hotel combines luxury with convenience, with Pioneer Square and the MAX just two blocks away, and West End and Pearl District dining within a 10-minute walk. **Pros:** close to Downtown dining and attractions; staff trained to help guests explore the city and nearby outdoors; excellent Mediterranean restaurant. **Cons:** pricey overnight parking; in a central but busy part of town; noise from nearby construction through 2023. $ *Rooms from: $220 ⌧ 750 S.W. Alder St., Downtown* ☎ *503/294–9000, 877/628–4408* ⊕ *www.dossierhotel.com* ⇌ *205 rooms* ⊙ *No meals.*

The Duniway

$$ | **HOTEL** | Adjacent to the city's venerable midcentury Portland Hilton, this newer (2002) Hilton-branded 20-story tower has been smartly redesigned and rebranded as the Duniway, complete with a scene-y restaurant and bar called Jackrabbit. **Pros:** a bold and captivating design theme; generally lower rates than comparable Downtown properties; decent gym and lap pool. **Cons:** convenient but busy Downtown location; bathrooms are a bit on the small side; very expensive overnight parking. $ *Rooms from: $215 ⌧ 545 S.W. Taylor St., Downtown* ☎ *503/553–7000* ⊕ *www.duniwayhotel.com* ⇌ *327 rooms* ⊙ *No meals.*

Embassy Suites Portland–Downtown
$$$$ | **HOTEL** | **FAMILY** | The grand lobby of the former Multnomah Hotel, built in 1912, offers an extravagant welcome to this all-suites hotel located close to both the riverfront and Old Town. **Pros:** close to West End and Pearl District shopping and dining; atmospheric old building; breakfast and evening drinks and snacks included. **Cons:** surrounding blocks can feel a bit seedy (though still quite safe) at night; expensive self- and valet parking; street noise can be a problem in some rooms. [$] *Rooms from: $305* ✉ *319 S.W. Pine St., Downtown* ☎ *503/279–9000* 🌐 *www.embassyportland.com* 🛏 *276 suites* 🍴 *Free breakfast.*

★ **Heathman Hotel**
$$$$ | **HOTEL** | The choice of countless celebs and dignitaries since it opened in 1927, this wonderfully atmospheric, art-filled hotel has undergone a stylish and contemporary redesign. **Pros:** stellar restaurant; central location adjoining Portland'5 Centers for the Arts, and a block from Portland Art Museum; outstanding art collection. **Cons:** some rooms are small; expensive parking; bar and restaurant can be crowded when there are performances next door. [$] *Rooms from: $309* ✉ *1001 S.W. Broadway, Downtown* ☎ *503/241–4100* 🌐 *www.heathmanhotel.com* 🛏 *150 rooms* 🍴 *No meals.*

★ **Hi-Lo Hotel, Autograph Collection**
$$$ | **HOTEL** | This dapper, old-meets-new boutique hotel—part of Marriott's indie-spirited Autograph Collection—occupies a masterfully converted 1910 Oregon Pioneer Building, a six-story structure with high ceilings, big windows, and the city's oldest restaurant, Huber's café, on the ground floor. **Pros:** close to Pearl District, West End, and Old Town; cool old building with midcentury modern vibe; very nice fitness center for a small hotel. **Cons:** street noise can be a problem; expensive valet parking; mid-rise building with not much of a view from lower floors. [$] *Rooms from: $259* ✉ *320 S.W. Harvey Milk St., Downtown* ☎ *971/222–2100* 🌐 *www.hi-lo-hotel.com* 🛏 *120 rooms* 🍴 *No meals.*

Hotel deLuxe
$$ | **HOTEL** | This retro-glam 1912 boutique hotel with its original chandeliers, gilded ceilings, black-and-white photography (arranged by movie themes), heavy drapes, and hip cocktail lounge evokes Hollywood's Golden Era, from the elegant rooms to the cozy 1950s-style Driftwood Room bar and swanky Gracie's restaurant. **Pros:** fun Old Hollywood vibe; close to Washington Park; nice touches like free bike rentals and evening champagne hour in the lobby. **Cons:** standard rooms are quite small; West End location is less central than other Downtown properties; expensive valet parking. [$] *Rooms from: $209* ✉ *729 S.W. 15th Ave., West End* ☎ *503/219–2094* 🌐 *www.hoteldeluxeportland.com* 🛏 *130 rooms* 🍴 *No meals.*

Hotel Lucia
$$ | **HOTEL** | Black-and-white celebrity photos from Pulitzer Prize–winner and native Oregonian David Hume Kennerly, comfy leather chairs, and stylish low-slung furniture adorn the rooms of this nine-story, 1909 European-style boutique hotel in the heart of Downtown. **Pros:** prime location near West End and Pearl District dining; artfully appointed rooms; two outstanding restaurants. **Cons:** limited shelf and storage space in the small bathrooms; expensive valet parking; busy Downtown location. [$] *Rooms from: $209* ✉ *400 S.W. Broadway, Downtown* ☎ *503/225–1717* 🌐 *www.hotellucia.com* 🛏 *160 rooms* 🍴 *No meals.*

Hotel Rose
$$ | **HOTEL** | This funky boutique property overlooking the Willamette River affords stellar views of the water, easy access to the waterfront park and the events that take place there (Rose Festival, Blues Festival, Gay Pride, and so on), and—as part of the Pineapple Hospitality chain—complimentary pineapple

cupcakes during the daily afternoon reception. **Pros:** central location on the riverfront; fitness center and free use of bikes; good restaurant (Bottle + Kitchen). **Cons:** rooms not facing the river have dull views; traffic noise is a problem for some rooms; rates can be steep when events take place on riverfront. [$] *Rooms from: $195* ✉ *50 S.W. Morrison St., Downtown* ☎ *503/221–0711, 877/237–6775* 🌐 *www.staypineapple.com/hotel-rose-portland-or* 🛏 *142 rooms* 🍴 *No meals.*

Hotel Zags

$$ | **HOTEL** | Decorated with local artwork, contemporary furnishings, and wood-and-marble accents, this boutique property (formerly known as Hotel Modera) is both upscale and accessible, and offers a location convenient to the Southwest Park Blocks and Portland State University. **Pros:** close to Portland State University and Saturday Farmers Market; inviting courtyard; great bar-restaurant. **Cons:** rooms on the small side; no on-site gym (but free passes to nearby 24-hour gym); a 10- to 15-minute walk from West End and Pearl District dining and nightlife. [$] *Rooms from: $215* ✉ *515 S.W. Clay St., Downtown* ☎ *503/484–1084* 🌐 *www.thehotelzags.com* 🛏 *174 rooms* 🍴 *No meals.*

★ Kimpton Hotel Monaco Portland

$$$ | **HOTEL** | This artsy Downtown Portland outpost of the Kimpton-operated Monaco boutique-hotel brand offers eclectic textiles and patterns, bright spaces and bold colors, interesting amenities like in-room yoga mats, extensive pet-welcoming items, and an evening social hour with local wines, spirits, and beers, and the overall sense that staying here is a lot of fun. **Pros:** vibrant, arty decor; convenient, central location; well-equipped fitness center and a full-service Aveda spa. **Cons:** design style may not suit all; pricey overnight parking; on a busy Downtown street. [$] *Rooms from: $230* ✉ *506 S.W. Washington St., Downtown* ☎ *503/222–0001, 888/207–2201* 🌐 *www.monaco-portland.com* 🛏 *221 rooms* 🍴 *No meals.*

Kimpton Hotel Vintage Portland

$$$ | **HOTEL** | This historic landmark hotel with a stylish two-story lobby takes its theme from Oregon vineyards, with rooms named after local wineries, complimentary wine served every evening, and an extensive collection of Oregon vintages served in the superb Bacchus wine bar and Il Solito restaurant. **Pros:** terrific on-site Italian restaurant and wine bar; several over-the-top spectacular suites; smart, contemporary room decor. **Cons:** pricey parking; some street noise on the lower levels on the Washington Street side; small gym. [$] *Rooms from: $239* ✉ *422 S.W. Broadway, Downtown* ☎ *503/228–1212, 800/263–2305* 🌐 *www.hotelvintage-portland.com* 🛏 *115 rooms* 🍴 *No meals.*

★ Kimpton RiverPlace Hotel

$$$ | **HOTEL** | With textured wall coverings, pillows made of Pendleton wool, and a color palette of slate blue, mustard yellow, and a variety of browns, this Kimpton-operated boutique hotel on the banks of the Willamette River captures the look and feel of the Pacific Northwest. **Pros:** stellar views and park-side riverfront location; outstanding seafood restaurant; several apartment-style suites with kitchens are great for families or extended stays. **Cons:** not many restaurants or shops within easy walking distance; some river views from rooms are blocked by trees; expensive parking. [$] *Rooms from: $249* ✉ *1510 S.W. Harbor Way, Downtown* ☎ *503/228–3233, 888/869–3108* 🌐 *www.riverplacehotel.com* 🛏 *84 rooms* 🍴 *No meals.*

Mark Spencer Hotel

$$$ | **HOTEL** | This family-owned hotel, with a prime location in the hip West End near Powell's Books and the Pearl District, is one of the better values in town, with most of its warmly decorated and spacious rooms containing well-equipped kitchenettes. **Pros:** steps from trendy West End and Pearl dining and shopping; afternoon tea and cookies and evening local wine tasting; most rooms have kitchenettes. **Cons:** some rooms are a bit dark; street noise can be a problem; no restaurant on-site. $ *Rooms from: $239* ✉ *409 S.W. 11th Ave., West End* ☎ *503/224–3293* ⊕ *www.markspencer. com* ⇌ *102 rooms* ⦿I *Free breakfast.*

McMenamins Crystal Hotel

$ | **HOTEL** | Travelers who appreciate good music and good beer—especially together—love this West End branch of the McMenamin brothers' unorthodox empire, which is home to three bars and a restaurant and is affiliated with the Crystal Ballroom concert venue a block away. **Pros:** priority access to tickets for Crystall Ballroom concerts; lots of bars and dining both on-site and on surrounding blocks; saltwater soaking pool in the cavelike basement. **Cons:** quirky vibe isn't for everyone; shared bath down the hall in most rooms; no TVs. $ *Rooms from: $125* ✉ *303 S.W. 12th Ave., West End* ☎ *503/972–2670, 855/205–3930* ⇌ *www. mcmenamins.com/crystalhotel* ⇌ *60 rooms* ⦿I *No meals.*

★ The Nines

$$$$ | **HOTEL** | On the top nine floors of a former landmark department store, this swanky Marriott Luxury Collection has the city's poshest accommodations, with luxe decor and two notable restaurants. **Pros:** stunning views; swanky vibe and cool design; outstanding Departure Restaurant on the rooftop. **Cons:** rooms facing the atrium can be noisy; expensive valet-only parking; on a very busy downtown block. $ *Rooms from: $359* ✉ *525 S.W. Morrison St., Downtown* ☎ *503/222–9996, 877/229–9995* ⊕ *www. thenines.com* ⇌ *331 rooms* ⦿I *No meals.*

Porter Portland Hotel

$$$ | **HOTEL** | This stylish, contemporary member of Hilton's hip Curio Collection brand is just a short walk from the waterfront, Keller Auditorium, and the PSU farmers' market, but you'll find plenty of reasons to stay on-property, from the roof-deck bar with sweeping mountain views to the well-equipped fitness center and inviting Portland Exchange coffee bar. **Pros:** close to South Waterfront and Portland State University; cool rooftop bar and other great dining options; nice gym with sauna, steam room, and lap pool. **Cons:** rooms have small closets; expensive parking; farther from Pearl and Old Town than most Downtown properties. $ *Rooms from: $285* ✉ *1355 S.W. 2nd Ave., Downtown* ☎ *503/306–4800* ⊕ *www.hilton.com* ⇌ *297 rooms* ⦿I *No meals.*

★ Sentinel Hotel

$$$ | **HOTEL** | The discerning common areas in this landmark, early-20th-century buildings capture Portland's maker aesthetic, with locally sourced textiles, furnishings, and goods. **Pros:** indie style meets luxury; well-equipped gym; spacious, well-designed rooms. **Cons:** pricey valet parking; uneven service in lobby bar; construction (through 2023) next door can get a little noisy. $ *Rooms from: $239* ✉ *614 S.W. 10th Ave., Downtown* ☎ *503/224–3400, 888/246–5631* ⊕ *www.sentinelhotel.com* ⇌ *100 rooms* ⦿I *No meals.*

★ The Woodlark

$$$ | **HOTEL** | The latest offering from the überhip Provenance Hotels brand connects a pair of stately early-1900s Downtown buildings that have been outfitted with well-curated local art, midcentury modern furnishings, and a slew of wellness amenities, from a first-rate fitness center to in-room streaming workout videos. **Pros:** exceptional dining and bars; artful, chic aesthetic; prime central location. **Cons:** some rooms are small; construction next door (through 2023) can get a little noisy; pricey valet parking. $ *Rooms from: $255* ✉ *813 S.W. Alder St., Downtown* ☎ *503/548–2559, 833/624–2188* ⊕ *www.woodlarkhotel. com* ⇌ *150 rooms* ⦿I *No meals.*

Nightlife

BARS AND LOUNGES

★ Abigail Hall

BARS/PUBS | Inspired by the legacy of Oregon suffragist Abigail Scott Duniway, the first woman registered to vote in Multnomah County, this elegant hotel lounge looks like a time capsule for a reason. A historian helped the design team re-create the early-1900s floral aesthetic of the historic Ladies Reception Hall, which originally inhabited this room. Behind the bar, the bartenders seem less tied to the history of the space, mixing up more than a dozen creative cocktails with quippy names. ✉ *Woodlark Hotel, 813 S.W. Alder St., Downtown* ☎ *503/548–2559* ⊕ *www.abigailhallpdx.com.*

Driftwood Room

BARS/PUBS | Once your eyes adjust to the romantically dim lighting, you'll find a curved bar, leather banquette seating, and polished-wood ceilings and walls in this Old Hollywood–themed bar in the Hotel deLuxe. The trendy cocktails are garnished with herbs culled from the hotel's garden. ✉ *Hotel deLuxe, 729 S.W. 15th Ave., Goose Hollow* ☎ *503/219–2094* ⊕ *www.hoteldeluxeportland.com.*

★ Headwaters at the Heathman

BARS/PUBS | At the elegant Heathman Hotel, you can enjoy Russian tea service in the eucalyptus-paneled Tea Court or beer, wine, and cocktails in the marble Headwaters lounge, a venerable old-world space that received a revamp in 2016 when local celeb chef Vitaly Paley took over. This is one of the city's most popular see-and-be-seen venues, especially before or after shows at nearby theaters and concert halls. ✉ *Heathman Hotel, 1001 S.W. Broadway, Downtown* ☎ *503/790–7752* ⊕ *www.headwaterspdx.com.*

Huber's

BARS/PUBS | The city's oldest restaurant (est. 1879) is notable for its old-fashioned feel and iconic Spanish coffee cocktail, which is set aflame at your table. The old bar in the back has great character. Huber's is on the ground floor of the historic Oregon Pioneer Building, which became the snazzy Hi-Lo Hotel in 2017. ✉ *Hi-Lo Hotel, 411 S.W. 3rd Ave., Downtown* ☎ *503/228–5686* ⊕ *www.hubers.com.*

Luc Lac Vietnamese Kitchen

BARS/PUBS | With a reputation as an after-work eating and drinking hangout among local Portland chefs and restaurant workers, this always-hopping Vietnamese joint offers well-executed cocktails, such as the Single Knight: Four Roses Single Barrel bourbon, pho syrup, Angostura orange bitters, and a Lapsang souchong tea ice cube. The kitchen turns out delicious eats until midnight on weekdays and 4 am on weekends. ✉ *835 S.W. 2nd Ave., Downtown* ☎ *503/222–0047* ⊕ *www.luclackitchen.com.*

★ Multnomah Whiskey Library

BARS/PUBS | Smartly dressed bartenders roll drink carts around the seductively clubby room—with beam ceilings, wood paneling, leather chairs, a wood-burning fireplace, and crystal chandeliers—pouring cocktails table-side. The emphasis, of course, is whiskey and bourbon—Multnomah has such an extensive collection in its "library" that staff need rolling ladders to access the bottles perched on the tall shelves lining the exposed-brick walls. ✉ *1124 S.W. Alder St., West End* ☎ *503/954–1381* ⊕ *www.mwlpdx.com.*

Raven & Rose

BARS/PUBS | Located in the ornate Victorian two-level Ladd Carriage House amid Downtown's office towers, this British Isles–inspired spot serves English-style pub fare and a worldly list of beers, wines, and cocktails in the Rookery Bar upstairs. Downstairs, you'll find a main dining room and a small lounge area. There's live music select evenings. ✉ *1331 S.W. Broadway, Downtown* ☎ *503/222–7673* ⊕ *www.ravenandrosepdx.com* ☾ *Closed Mon.*

Scandals
BARS/PUBS | This low-key bar is the lone remaining LGBTQ hangout in the West End, which used to be the city's gay nightlife district (most of the gay bars are now spread around the city, with a concentration in Old Town). There's a pool table, and light food service noon to closing. The plate-glass windows offer a view of Harvey Milk Street, and there's also popular sidewalk seating. ⊠ *1125 S.W. Harvey Milk St., West End* ☎ *503/227–5887* ⊕ *www.scandalspdx.com.*

LIVE MUSIC
McMenamins Crystal Ballroom
MUSIC CLUBS | With a 7,500-square-foot spring-loaded dance floor built on ball bearings to ramp up the energy, this historic former dance hall draws local, regional, and national acts every night but Monday. Past performers include Sleater-Kinney, Jefferson Airplane, Emmylou Harris, Tame Impala, and Angel Olsen. ⊠ *1332 W. Burnside St., West End* ☎ *503/225–0047* ⊕ *www.crystalballroompdx.com.*

 Performing Arts

PERFORMANCE VENUES
★ Arlene Schnitzer Concert Hall
ARTS CENTERS | The 2,776-seat Arlene Schnitzer Concert Hall, built in 1928 in an Italian rococo revival style, hosts rock concerts, choral groups, lectures, and concerts by the Oregon Symphony and others. "The Schnitz," as locals call it, is one of the venues that make up the Portland'5 Centers for the Arts umbrella organization. ⊠ *1037 S.W. Broadway, Downtown* ☎ *503/248-4335* ⊕ *www.portland5.com.*

★ Portland'5 Centers for the Arts
ARTS CENTERS | The city's top performing arts complex hosts opera, ballet, rock shows, symphony performances, lectures, and Broadway musicals in its five venues: the Arlene Schnitzer Concert Hall, the Keller Auditorium, and the three-in-one Antoinette Hatfield Hall, which comprises the Brunish, Newmark, and Winningstad theaters. The majority of the region's top performing companies call these venues home, including the Portland Opera, the Oregon Symphony, the Oregon Ballet Theatre, and the Portland Youth Philharmonic. ⊠ *Box office, 1111 S.W. Broadway, Downtown* ☎ *503/248-4335* ⊕ *www.portland5.com.*

CLASSICAL MUSIC
CHAMBER MUSIC
Chamber Music Northwest
MUSIC | Some of the most sought-after soloists, chamber musicians, and recording artists from the Portland area and abroad perform here during the five-week summer concert series; performances take place at a few different venues, primarily Reed College's Kaul Auditorium and the Lincoln Performance Hall at Portland State University. ⊠ *Box office, 2300 S.W. 1st Ave., Suite 103, Downtown* ☎ *503/294–6400* ⊕ *www.cmnw.org.*

OPERA
Portland Opera
OPERA | This well-respected opera company performs five or six productions a year, most of them Downtown at Keller Auditorium or the Newmark Theatre, but also occasionally across the river at the Hampton Opera Center. ⊠ *Downtown* ☎ *503/241–1802* ⊕ *www.portlandopera. org.*

ORCHESTRAS
★ Oregon Symphony
MUSIC | **FAMILY** | Established in 1896, the symphony is Portland's largest classical group—and one of the largest orchestras in the country. Its season officially starts in September and ends in May, with concerts held at Arlene Schnitzer Concert Hall, but throughout the summer the orchestra and its smaller ensembles can be seen at Waterfront Park and Washington Park for special outdoor summer performances. It also presents about 40 classical, pop, children's, and family concerts each year. ⊠ *Ticket Office, 909 S.W.*

Washington St., Downtown ☎ *503/228–1353* ⊕ *www.orsymphony.org.*

DANCE
Northwest Dance Project
DANCE | Founded in 2004, this first-rate contemporary-dance company performs several shows—typically including a world premiere or two—each season at different venues around town, including the Newmark Theatre and PSU's Lincoln Performance Hall. ⊠ *Downtown* ☎ *503/828–8285* ⊕ *www.nwdanceproject.org.*

Oregon Ballet Theatre
DANCE | This respected company produces several classical and contemporary works a year, including a much-loved holiday *Nutcracker.* Most performances are at Keller Auditorium and the Portland Center for the Arts' Newmark Theatre. ⊠ *Box office and studios, 0720 S.W. Bancroft St., Downtown* ☎ *503/222–5538, 888/922–5538* ⊕ *www.obt.org.*

FILM
Living Room Theaters
FILM | The boutique cinema, which has a lobby restaurant with a full bar, shows 3-D blockbuster, foreign, and independent films in, true to its name, living-room-like theaters furnished with spacious seats and movable couches and tables. You can dine and drink from your seat. ⊠ *341 S.W. 10th Ave., West End* ⊕ *pdx.livingroomtheaters.com.*

Northwest Film Center Whitsell Auditorium
FILM | Located adjacent to and operated by the Portland Art Museum, the Northwest Film Center's Whitsell Auditorium screens art films, documentaries, and independent features, and presents the three-week Portland International Film Festival every February. ⊠ *1219 S.W. Park Ave., Downtown* ☎ *503/221–1156* ⊕ *www.nwfilm.org.*

THEATER
Artists Repertory Theatre
THEATER | With a reputation for commissioning and staging new work by Pulitzer Prize–winning playwrights, this celebrated theater company performs seven to nine productions a year including regional premieres and classics. Starting with the 2019–20 season, the Artists Repertory is taking the show on the road—staging productions at other venues around the city, while they build new theaters on the site of its Downtown headquarters. Check the website for its "ART on Tour" showtimes and locations. ⊠ *Downtown* ☎ *503/241–1278* ⊕ *www.artistsrep.org.*

Oregon Children's Theatre
THEATER | FAMILY | This kid-centric company puts on four to five shows a year for school groups and families at Downtown's Newmark and Winningstad theaters. ⊠ *1111 S.W. Broadway, Downtown* ☎ *503/228–9571* ⊕ *www.octc.org.*

Shopping

CLOTHING
★ Frances May
CLOTHING | Commanding a prime corner shop in the fashion-forward West End, this grandmother-and-granddaughter-owned clothing retailer is one of the Pacific Northwest's most defining trendsetters—a favorite of stylish locals who come for that cool, understated look (casual to dressy) that Portlanders are known for. You'll find made-here labels like gender-neutral, organic line Olderbrother, as well as European faves like Acne and APC. Frances May also stocks jewelry, art books, and the city's own OLO Fragrances. ⊠ *1003 S.W. Washington St., West End* ☎ *503/227–3402* ⊕ *www.francesmay.com.*

Nike Portland
CLOTHING | It's safe to assume that Nike's flagship Portland store, just a short drive from the company's mammoth HQ campus in Beaverton, has the latest and greatest in swoosh-adorned products. The high-tech setting has athlete profiles, photos, and interactive displays. ⊠ *638*

S.W. 5th Ave., Downtown ☎ *503/221–6453* ⊕ *www.nike.com.*

North of West
SPECIALTY STORES | Embodying the growing consciousness about ethical fashion, this eclectic boutique opened in 2014 as a collaboration between several Portland designers, who shared a vision for opening a mission-driven store that elevated locavore goods and small-scale manufacturing. Today, you'll find the eponymous North of West line mingling with like-minded women's and kids' apparel, apothecary, and houseware brands. ⊠ *203 S.W. 9th Ave., West End* ☎ *503/208–3080* ⊕ *www.shopnorthofwest.com.*

★ Wildfang
CLOTHING | Founded by two former Nike employees, this queer-owned, women-centric retailer makes its values immediately clear, with its "Wild Feminist" T-shirt among its best-sellers. Wildfang's house collection of punkish, tomboy-inspired apparel shares this gallery-like shop with other minimally stylish brands that challenge gender conventions in the fashion world. ⊠ *404 S.W. 10th Ave., West End* ☎ *503/964–6746* ⊕ *www.wildfang.com.*

FOOD
Cacao
FOOD/CANDY | Chocolate fiends and sweet-tooths get their fix at this inviting storefront and café in the West End. Browse the huge selection of ultrafine, single-origin, artisanal chocolates from around the world, or order a cup of luscious house-made drinking chocolate. ⊠ *414 S.W. 13th Ave., West End* ☎ *503/241–0656* ⊕ *www.cacaodrinkchocolate.com.*

HOUSEHOLD GOODS AND FURNITURE
Boys Fort
HOUSEHOLD ITEMS/FURNITURE | If the name of this colorful West End emporium brings back memories of hanging out with friends in a rad basement rec room, you'll likely love this offbeat store curated by designers R. Rolfe and Jake France. They've stocked this high-ceilinged corner shop with a mix of artful items, including earthy-hued terra-cotta planters, model sailboats, and mounted wooden faux deer heads, plus old posters and games. ⊠ *1001 S.W. Morrison St., West End* ☎ *503/241–2855* ⊕ *www.boysfort.com.*

★ Canoe
GIFTS/SOUVENIRS | Form meets function at this design boutique with a niche selection of clean-lined, modern goods and gifts for every room in the home. You'll find curvy thick-glass bowls, modern lamps with sheer paper shades, polished-stone trays, Bigelow natural-bristle toothbrushes, and Chemex coffee kettles, with some goods produced locally and exclusively for Canoe, and others imported from Asia and northern Europe. ⊠ *1233 S.W. 10th Ave., Downtown* ☎ *503/889–8545* ⊕ *www.canoe.design.*

Tender Loving Empire
GIFTS/SOUVENIRS | The retail shop of the eponymous Portland record label founded by Jared and Brianne Mees carries not only music but also cool hand-printed cards, posters, and T-shirts, along with an artistic selection of handcrafted lifestyle goods, from pastel miniature vases and squiggle-shaped earrings to ceramic fox trinkets and illustrated prints. You'll find additional locations on Hawthorne, in Nob Hill, at Bridgeport Village, and in the airport. ⊠ *412 S.W. 10th Ave., West End* ☎ *503/548–2925* ⊕ *www.tenderlovingempire.com.*

 Activities

BIKING
BIKETOWN Portland
BICYCLING | Portland's bike-share program, in partnership with Nike, is affordable and easy to use. There are more than 125 stations throughout the city, and some

1,000 bikes, each with a small basket (helmets are not provided, however, so consider bringing your own). Just choose a plan (single rides start at 8 cents per minute), sign up (there's a one-time $5 fee), and you'll receive an account and PIN number that allows you to take out a bike. ⊠ *Portland* ☎ *866/512–2453* ⊕ *www.biketownpdx.com.*

SOCCER
Portland Timbers
SOCCER | Portland's major-league soccer team plays their 34-game season at the Downtown Providence Park from March through October. The city has many ardent soccer fans known as the Timbers Army. Sitting near this group means a raucous time with drumming, chanting, and cheers. The MAX stops right by the stadium. ⊠ *Providence Park, 1844 S.W. Morrison St., Downtown* ☎ *503/553–5555* ⊕ *www.portlandtimbers.com.*

Old Town/Chinatown

Old Town/Chinatown, officially known as the Skidmore Old Town National Historic District, is where Portland was born. The 20-square-block section—bounded by Oak Street to the south, Broadway to the west, and Hoyt Street to the north—includes buildings of varying ages and architectural designs. Before it was renovated, this was skid row. Vestiges of it remain in parts of Chinatown; older buildings are gradually being remodeled, and lately the immediate area has experienced a small surge in development, but the neighborhood can also feel a bit seedy in places. Portland doesn't have an LGBTQ district per se—the scene permeates just about every neighborhood of this extremely LGBTQ-welcoming city. But you'll find the highest concentration of Portland's gay nightspots in Old Town (and a few others close by in Downtown). MAX serves the area with stops at the Old Town/Chinatown and Skidmore Fountain stations.

Sights

Chinatown Gateway
PUBLIC ART | Located on West Burnside Street and Northwest 4th Avenue, this ornate arch is guarded by two bronze lions and decorated mythical creatures. It marks the entrance to Portland's once-thriving Chinatown. ⊠ *22 NW 4th Ave., Old Town/Chinatown.*

★ Lan Su Chinese Garden
GARDEN | In a twist on the Joni Mitchell song, the city of Portland and private donors took down a parking lot and unpaved paradise when they created this wonderland near the Pearl District and Old Town/Chinatown. It's the largest Suzhou-style garden outside China, with a large lake, bridged and covered walkways, koi- and water lily–filled ponds, rocks, bamboo, statues, waterfalls, and courtyards. A team of 60 artisans and designers from China literally left no stone unturned—500 tons of stone were brought here from Suzhou—in their efforts to give the windows, roof tiles, gateways (including a "moongate"), and other architectural aspects of the garden some specific meaning or purpose. Also on the premises are a gift shop and an enchanting two-story teahouse, operated by local Tao of Tea company, overlooking the lake and garden. ⊠ *239 N.W. Everett St., Old Town/Chinatown* ☎ *503/228–8131* ⊕ *www.lansugarden.org* ⌨ *$12.95.*

Oregon Maritime Museum
MUSEUM | **FAMILY** | Local model makers created most of this museum's models of ships that once plied the Columbia River. Contained within the stern-wheeler steamship *Portland*, this small museum provides an excellent overview of Oregon's maritime history with artifacts and memorabilia. The Children's Corner has nautical items that can be touched and operated. The *Portland* is the last steam-powered stern-wheel tugboat operating in the United States, and volunteer-guided tours include the pilot house

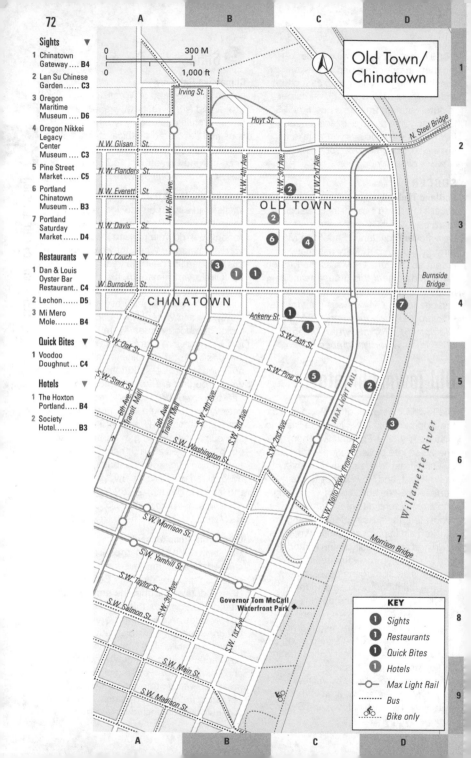

Old Town/Chinatown

Sights ▼
1 Chinatown Gateway **B4**
2 Lan Su Chinese Garden **C3**
3 Oregon Maritime Museum **D6**
4 Oregon Nikkei Legacy Center Museum **C3**
5 Pine Street Market **C5**
6 Portland Chinatown Museum **B3**
7 Portland Saturday Market **D4**

Restaurants ▼
1 Dan & Louis Oyster Bar Restaurant.. **C4**
2 Lechon **D5**
3 Mi Mero Mole......... **B4**

Quick Bites ▼
1 Voodoo Doughnut ... **C4**

Hotels ▼
1 The Hoxton Portland..... **B4**
2 Society Hotel......... **B3**

KEY
- ① Sights
- ① Restaurants
- ① Quick Bites
- ① Hotels
- ○— Max Light Rail
- .... Bus
- ○⚲.. Bike only

and engine room. ■**TIP→ Occasional four-hour cruises on the ship are also offered, about once a month, in summer; the cost is $88.** ✉ *Foot of S.W. Pine St., in Waterfront Park, Old Town/Chinatown* ☎ *503/224–7724* ⊕ *www.oregonmaritimemuseum.org* ✑ *$7* ⊗ *Closed Sun.–Tues. and Thurs.*

Oregon Nikkei Legacy Center Museum

MUSEUM | This Japanese American historical museum, just a short walk from the related historical plaza in Waterfront Park, pays homage to the dynamic Nikkei (Japanese emigrant) community that has thrived in Portland for generations. The museum occupies the stately 19th-century Merchant Hotel building, and the excellent rotating exhibits use art, photography, personal histories, and artifacts to touch on all aspects of the Japanese American experience in Portland and the Northwest, including the dark period during World War II of forced relocation to concentration camps situated throughout the U.S. West. ■**TIP→ You can also view an excellent interactive permanent history exhibit on the Nikkei Center's website.** ✉ *121 N.W. 2nd Ave., Old Town/Chinatown* ☎ *503/224–1458* ⊕ *www.oregon-nikkei.org* ✑ *$5* ⊗ *Closed Mon.*

★ Pine Street Market

MARKET | In a city where restaurants rank among the top sightseeing attractions, this bustling food hall in a handsome late-Victorian Old Town building offers visitors a one-stop opportunity to try food from some of Portland's most celebrated chefs. In one massive room, you'll find nine small restaurants with counter service and plenty of common seating. Highlights include one of the first U.S. branches of Tokyo's famed **Marukin Ramen,** juicy Southern-style burgers and throwback cocktails at **Bless Your Heart** (from John Gorham of Tasty n Sons fame), Spanish-inspired tapas and rotisserie chicken at **Pollo Bravo**, and a soft-serve ice-cream stand called **Wiz Bang Bar** operated by Salt & Straw. Bring your appetite, and brace yourself for long lines on weekends. ✉ *126 S.W. 2nd Ave., Old Town/Chinatown* ⊕ *www.pinestreetpdx.com* ✑ *Free.*

Portland Chinatown Museum

MUSEUM | Begun as a temporary exhibit on the city's Chinatown—more than 10% of Portland's population identified as Chinese American in the 1900s, making it the second-largest such community in the country—at the Oregon Historical Society Museum, this museum opened a 2,500-square-foot permanent space in late 2018 in the heart of Chinatown. Exhibits here document the community's continuously important contribution to the city, including the vibrant Chinese American–owned businesses that have prospered here since Portland's founding, as well as art, music, food, and important aspects of the community. The museum also presents rotating art and history exhibits as well as occasional concerts, lectures, and oral-history presentations. ✉ *127 N.W. 3rd Ave., Old Town/Chinatown* ☎ *503/224–0008* ⊕ *www.portland-chinatownmuseum.org* ✑ *$8* ⊗ *Closed Mon.–Wed.*

★ Portland Saturday Market

MARKET | **FAMILY** | On weekends from March to Christmas Eve, the west side of the Burnside Bridge and the Skidmore Fountain area hosts North America's largest ongoing open-air handicraft market, with some 400 vendors. If you're looking for jewelry, yard art, housewares, and decorative goods made from every material under the sun, check out the amazing collection of works by talented artisans on display here. The market also opens for holiday shopping during the week preceding Christmas Day, a period known as the Festival of the Last Minute. Entertainers and food booths add to the festive feel. ■**TIP→ Be careful not to mistake this market for the food-centric PSU Portland Farmers Market, which also takes place on Saturday, on the other side of Downtown.** ✉ *2 S.W. Naito Pkwy. at foot of S.W. Ankeny, in Waterfront Park,*

Lan Su Chinese Garden, in Old Town/Chinatown is the largest Suzhou-style garden outside of China.

Old Town/Chinatown ☎ 503/222–6072 🌐 www.portlandsaturdaymarket.com 🎫 Free 🕒 Closed Jan., Feb., and weekdays.

🍴 Restaurants

Dan & Louis Oyster Bar Restaurant
$$ | **SEAFOOD** | This Old Town landmark, located near the river and Voodoo Doughnuts, has oysters baked Rockefeller-style, stewed, and on the half shell, but the venerable 1907 restaurant offers plenty of other tasty local seafood, including steamed clams, Dungeness crab stew, and beer-battered cold-smoked salmon. The collection of steins, plates, and marine art fills beams, nooks, crannies, and nearly every inch of wall space. **Known for:** oyster stew; mix-and-match fried or sautéed combination dishes; endearingly old-fashioned ambience. *[$] Average main: $21 ✉ 208 S.W. Ankeny St., Old Town/Chinatown ☎ 503/227–5906 🌐 www.danandlouis.com.*

★ Lechon
$$$ | **SOUTH AMERICAN** | The menu of wood-fired, *carne*-intensive dishes at this bustling spot reads like a greatest hits of South American recipes, from Peruvian fried-chicken bites with fermented hot honey to brisket empanadas with ancho aioli to Argentinean-style 28-day dry-aged rib-eye steaks with cilantro butter. An added appeal is the location inside a handsome historic building just across the street from Tom McCall Waterfront Park, making it one of the closest dining options to the city's riverfront. **Known for:** plenty of seafood and vegetarian options; an emphasis on locally sourced and organic ingredients; great late-night tapas menu. *[$] Average main: $25 ✉ 113 S.W. Naito Pkwy., Old Town/Chinatown ☎ 503/219–9000 🌐 www.lechonpdx.com 🕒 No lunch weekends.*

Mi Mero Mole
$ | **MEXICAN** | Graffiti and murals decorate one concrete wall of this colorful Old Town eatery that serves some of the most flavorful Mexico City–style

street food in town. Regulars come for the tacos, burritos, quesadillas, and bowls filled with pork adobo, *albondigas* (meatballs) with a tomato-chipotle sauce, shrimp Veracruzana, roasted green chilis with a cream sauce, and about 10 other options, but there's also tasty ceviche and tamales with a daily changing selection of flavors. **Known for:** chilaquiles and breakfast burritos in the morning; extensive list of fine tequilas and mezcals, plus several handcrafted margaritas; the mole sampler with four types (pork mole verde, chicken, lamb, and butternut squash). [$] *Average main: $13* ✉ *32 N.W. 5th Ave., Old Town/Chinatown* ☎ *971/266–8575* 🌐 *www.mmmtacospdx.com.*

Coffee and Quick Bites

Voodoo Doughnut

$ | **BAKERY** | The long lines outside this Old Town 24/7 doughnut shop, marked by its distinctive pink-neon sign, attest to the fact that this irreverent bakery is almost as famous a Portland landmark as Powell's Books. The aforementioned sign depicts one of the shop's biggest sellers, a raspberry jelly–topped chocolate voodoo-doll doughnut, but all the creations here, some of them witty, some ribald, bring smiles to the faces of customers—even those who have waited 30 minutes in the rain. **Known for:** offbeat doughnut flavors; the bacon maple bar doughnut; long lines. [$] *Average main: $4* ✉ *22 S.W. 3rd Ave., Old Town/Chinatown* ☎ *503/241–4704* 🌐 *www.voodoodoughnut.com.*

Hotels

The Hoxton Portland

$$ | **HOTEL** | London's hipper-than-thou Hoxton brand opened this see-and-be-seen hotel in 2018 on the border between Old Town and Downtown. **Pros:** close to Pearl District and West End; stunningly designed bars and restaurant; rates include "healthy breakfast bag" (with fruit, juice, and house-made granola). **Cons:** many rooms are quite small; surrounding Old Town can be boisterous and loud; expensive valet parking. [$] *Rooms from: $189* ✉ *15 N.W. 4th Ave., Old Town/Chinatown* ☎ *503/770–0500* 🌐 *www.thehoxton.com* 🛏 *119 rooms* 🍴 *Free breakfast.*

★ **Society Hotel**

$ | **HOTEL** | This quirky, bargain-priced boutique hotel with simple, stylish, and affordable rooms and a gorgeous roof deck is just steps from Old Town nightlife and Lan Su Chinese Garden, and occupies an 1880s former boardinghouse for sailors. **Pros:** budget-friendly rates; gorgeous rooftop deck; airy lobby café with artisanal coffee and pastries. **Cons:** rooms are very small; nearby bars can get noisy at night; no on-site parking. [$] *Rooms from: $129* ✉ *203 N.W. 3rd Ave., Old Town/Chinatown* ☎ *503/445–0444* 🌐 *www.thesocietyhotel.com* 🛏 *39 rooms* 🍴 *No meals.*

Nightlife

BARS AND LOUNGES

Basement Bar

BARS/PUBS | Although officially part of the trendy Hoxton Hotel in Old Town, this speakeasy is located beneath the lobby and reached by an unmarked black door around the corner from the building's main entrance. Once inside this warmly lighted subterranean lair, you can curl up with a friend on a leather sofa, order a spendy but splendid cocktail, and munch on pork belly buns and crab rangoon dip. ✉ *2 N.W. 5th Ave., Old Town/Chinatown* ☎ *503/770–0400* 🌐 *www.thehoxton.com* 🕒 *Closed Sun.–Tues.*

★ **Ground Kontrol Classic Arcade**

BARS/PUBS | **FAMILY** | Revisit your teen years at this massive, old-school Old Town arcade filled with more than 100 classic arcade games and about 50 pinball machines, including vintage Atari,

One-of-a-kind items can be found at the Portland Saturday Market.

Super Nintendo, and Killer Queen. There are two full bars and a kitchen serving reliably good nachos, sandwiches, and ice cream sundaes—and now that you are no longer a teen, you can have as much as you like. Over 21 after 5 pm. ⊠ *115 N.W. 5th Ave., Old Town/China-town* ☎ *503/796–9364* ⊕ *www.ground-kontrol.com.*

★ Stag
BARS/PUBS | Drawing a diverse crowd of hipsters, tourists, and old-school clubbers, this Old Town hot spot cheekily bills itself a "gay gentlemen's lounge." Mounted antlers, leather chairs, and exposed-brick walls lend a rustic air, and male strippers dance on a small stage toward the back of the main room; a side bar contains a pool table. ⊠ *317 N.W. Broadway, Old Town/Chinatown* ☎ *971/407–3132* ⊕ *www.stagpdx.com.*

LIVE MUSIC
Roseland Theater
MUSIC | This spacious theater holds 1,410 people (standing-room only except for the 21+ balcony seating area), primarily stages rock, alternative, and blues shows, plus occasional comedians. Legends like Miles Davis and Prince have performed here, and more recent acts have included Hot Chip, Ingrid Michaelson, and Cat Power. ⊠ *10 N.W. 6th Ave., Old Town/Chinatown* ☎ *855/227–8499* ⊕ *www.roselandpdx.com.*

🛍 Shopping

CLOTHING
Compound Gallery
SHOES/LUGGAGE/LEATHER GOODS | One of a few spots in Old Town that special-ize in urban streetwear fashion, this expansive boutique carries Herschel backpacks, Japanese Kidrobot vinyl art toys, and clothing, footwear, and hats from trendy brands like Stüssy, UNDFTD, and Bape. The shop also collaborates on new products with local designers and artists. ⊠ *107 N.W. 5th Ave., Old Town/Chinatown* ☎ *503/796–2733* ⊕ *www.compoundgallery.com.*

HOUSEHOLD GOODS AND FURNITURE

★ Kiriko

CLOTHING | Shibori-style hand-dyed and intricately sewn textiles—both contemporary and vintage—form the basis for most of the products in this gorgeous Old Town shop that practically bursts at the seams with kimonos, boros, dresses, neckties, socks, dopp kits, wallets, and other items for the home and wardrobe. It's easy to lose yourself in this colorful space, where you'll also discover plates, bowls, tea sets, and pottery works. ✉ *325 Couch St., Old Town/Chinatown* ☎ *503/222–0335* ⊕ *www.kirikomade. com.*

Pendleton Home Store

CLOTHING | At this flagship lifestyle store—the headquarters are in the same building—of the world-famous textile and furniture purveyor, you can browse the company's new products before they're available online or in Pendleton's other shops around the country. The company's classic camp blankets—many of them with patterns inspired by Native American weavings and U.S. national parks—are a huge draw, but you'll also find pillows, pet beds, hats, backpacks, totes, sweaters, and other apparel. ✉ *210 N.W. Broadway, Old Town/Chinatown* ☎ *503/535–5444* ⊕ *www.pendleton-usa. com.*

SPECIALTY SHOPS

Serra Dispensary

SPECIALTY STORES | A beautifully designed cannabis shop in which carefully curated marijuana is displayed in blue ceramic dishes inside blond-wood cases, Serra stands out for its knowledgeable staff and decidedly artisanal aesthetic. They'll lend you a bronze magnifying glass if you want a closer inspection of the products, which also include cannabis-infused local chocolates, gummies, and other edibles. There's a similar branch in Southeast on Belmont Street. ✉ *220 S.W. 1st Ave.,* *Old Town/Chinatown* ☎ *971/279–5613* ⊕ *www.shopserra.com.*

Pearl District

Bordering Old Town to the west and Downtown and the West End to the north, the trendy Pearl District comprises a formerly rough-and-tumble warren of warehouses and railroad yards. Much of the Pearl is new construction, but dozens of the district's historic industrial buildings have been converted into handsome, loft-style housing and commercial concerns, too. You'll find some of the city's most buzzed-about restaurants, galleries, and shops in this neighborhood—the monthly First Thursday evening art walk is an especially fun time to visit. The Portland Streetcar line passes through here, with stops at ecologically themed Jamison Square and Tanner Springs parks.

Sights

Jamison Square Park

CITY PARK | FAMILY | This gently terraced park surrounded by tony lofts, shops, and restaurants contains a soothing fountain that mimics nature. Rising water gushes over a stack of basalt blocks, gradually fills the open plaza, and then subsides. Colorful 30-foot tiki totems by pop artist Kenny Scharf stand along the park's west edge. There are tables and chairs in the park, and wading in the fountain is encouraged. The streetcar stops right at the park. ✉ *N.W. 10th Ave. and Lovejoy St., Pearl District* ⊕ *www.explorethe-pearl.com* ⛫ *Free.*

★ Oregon Jewish Museum and Center for Holocaust Education

MUSEUM | FAMILY | This institution, which interprets the stories and lives of the state's vibrant Jewish community, also functions as an educational and inspirational resource that focuses on promoting tolerance and combating discrimination and persecution. The museum was established in 1999 and is the force behind Washington Park's poignant Oregon Holocaust Memorial, but it wasn't until 2017 that it moved into this beautiful new permanent home inside the 1916 DeSoto Building, on the leafy Park Blocks. The gallery on the upper floor contains permanent collections, including artifacts and artwork, and oral histories of the state's earliest Jewish residents as well as the profoundly moving historical exhibit on both the Holocaust and the valiant struggles of Jewish, Asian American, African American, Hispanic, LGBTQ, and other minority communities in the face of often strenuous intolerance in Oregon. ■ **TIP→ The ground floor features Lefty's, an excellent little lunch spot that has delicious sandwiches, salads, soups, rugelach, and other treats.** ✉ *724 N.W. Davis St., Old Town/Chinatown* ☎ *503/226–3600* 🌐 *www.ojmche.org* 🎟 *$8* 🕒 *Closed Mon.*

★ Powell's City of Books

STORE/MALL | A local legend, and rightfully so, Powell's is the largest independent bookstore in the world, with more than 1.5 million new and used books along with a good selection of locally made gifts and goodies. It's a top draw for any visitor, but serious book lovers can easily spend a few hours inside. The three-level store covers an entire city block on the edge of the Pearl District—maps are available at the info kiosks and rooms are color-coded according to book type. On the top floor, the Rare Book Room is a must-see, even if you're not planning to splurge for an 1829 volume of the Waverly Novels or an autobiography signed by Anwar Sadat; there are rare prints and mint-condition first editions in just about every genre. Be sure to look for the pillar bearing signatures of prominent sci-fi authors who have passed through the store that's protected by a jagged length of Plexiglas. Also check online for upcoming author readings, which take place three to five times a week and draw some of the world's top literary names. You'll find a branch of the popular Portland coffeehouse, World Cup, on the ground floor. There are also branches in Portland International Airport as well as a large outpost in the heart of the Hawthorne District, with its own coffeehouse, the Fresh Pot. ✉ *1005 W. Burnside St., Pearl District* ☎ *503/228–4651* 🌐 *www.powells.com.*

Tanner Springs Park

CITY PARK | Tanner Creek, which once flowed through the area, lends its name to this unusual urban wetland park that's surrounded by soaring modern condo towers. Today the creek flows underground, and this quiet, man-made oasis and spring with alder groves was built in the middle of the Pearl District as a reminder of what the area was once like. The Artwall was created using hundreds of upright railroad tracks and hand-painted fused glass. ✉ *N.W. 10th Ave. and N.W. Marshall St., Pearl District* 🌐 *www.explorethepearl.com/places/tanner-springs-park* 🎟 *Free.*

🍴 Restaurants

Andina

$$$ | PERUVIAN | This popular upscale Pearl District restaurant offers an inventive menu—a combination of traditional Peruvian and contemporary "Novoandina" cuisines—served in a large but nook-filled space that features live music most evenings. The extensive seafood offerings include several ceviches, grilled octopus, and a Peruvian-style paella that abounds with shellfish. **Known for:** Peruvian-style pisco sours; stylish yet casual lounge with great happy hour; ceviche with mixed fish and shellfish. [$] *Average main: $28* ✉ *1314 N.W. Glisan St., Pearl District* ☎ *503/228–9535* 🌐 *www.andinarestaurant.com.*

★ Deschutes Brewery Portland Public House

$$ | **AMERICAN** | The Portland branch of the Bend-based Deschutes Brewery typically has more than 25 beers on tap, including nationally acclaimed mainstays Mirror Pond Pale Ale, Inversion IPA, and Black Butte Porter, plus seasonal and experimental brews. On the food side, the kitchen has really upped its game in recent years, making this a worthy destination for elevated pub fare, such as Manila clams steamed in cider, porter-braised and smoked pork shoulder with grits, and plenty of sandwiches and salads. **Known for:** limited-release and seasonal beers; the IPA pretzel with cheese sauce and porter mustard; marionberry cobbler. [$] *Average main: $18* ✉ *210 N.W. 11th Ave., Pearl District* ☎ *503/296–4906* 🌐 *www.deschutes-brewery.com.*

Irving Street Kitchen

$$$ | **MODERN AMERICAN** | You might come to this hip Pearl District restaurant set inside a gorgeously transformed warehouse building just because you heard about the rich butterscotch pudding with roasted-banana caramel and peanut butter bonbons (it's available to go, sold in its own adorable canning jar); but chances are, once you see the exposed-brick-and-wood-beam walls, Edison bulb chandeliers, inviting central bar, and patio seats on a converted loading dock, you'll want to stay. And you'll be glad you did, as the well-executed Southern-influenced American dinner and brunch fare—including panfried soft-shell crab, organic fried chicken, and country ham with biscuits—is superb. **Known for:** wine by the glass on tap; terrific weekend brunch; decadent desserts. [$] *Average main: $27* ✉ *701 N.W. 13th Ave., Pearl District* ☎ *503/343–9440* 🌐 *www.irvingstreetkitchen.com* ⏲ *No lunch weekdays.*

★ Mediterranean Exploration Company

$$ | **MEDITERRANEAN** | Developed by cookbook author and celeb-chef John Gorham, this vegetarian-friendly tribute to Mediterranean cuisine occupies a handsome former warehouse on historic 13th Avenue in the Pearl. MEC (for short) is an energy-filled, open space with a mix of communal and individual tables (the food is served family-style)—it's surprisingly affordable considering the extraordinary quality and generous portions, particularly if you opt for the $50 tasting menu. **Known for:** chicken and lamb kebabs; Middle East–inspired cocktails; cardamom ice cream served with a pour-over of robust Turkish coffee. [$] *Average main: $22* ✉ *333 N.W. 13th Ave., Pearl District* ☎ *503/222–0906* 🌐 *www.mediterraneanexplorationcompany.com* ⏲ *No lunch.*

Oven and Shaker

$$ | **PIZZA** | A joint venture between James Beard Award–nominated chef Cathy Whims and renowned cocktail mixologist Ryan Magarian, this aptly named late-night spot specializes in creatively topped wood-fired pizzas and deftly crafted cocktails that rely heavily on local spirits and fresh juices. The salads and appetizers are also terrific, especially the radicchio version of a classic Caesar salad. **Known for:** great early-evening and late-night pizza deals; Tuscan brownie sundae with vanilla gelato, chocolate sauce; the Maple Pig pizza with apple butter, pork belly, smoked ham, maple mascarpone, and ricotta. [$] *Average main: $19* ✉ *1134 N.W. Everett St., Pearl District* ☎ *503/241–1600* 🌐 *www.ovenandshaker.com.*

Tanner Creek Tavern

$$ | **AMERICAN** | While both dining and drinking happen here, it's the airy, window-lined bar off the lobby of Pearl's surprisingly snazzy Hampton Inn that draws the biggest crowds, thanks to its lively buzz and—in warm weather—seating that spills out onto the sidewalk. Tuck into plates of familiar fare with creative twists, or for a more elegant repast, opt for a table in the intimate dining room

Coffee culture is strong in Portland—there are roughly 2,000 coffee shops in the city proper.

overlooking an exhibition kitchen. **Known for:** a fantastic happy hour with big portions of creative pub fare; flatbread pizzas with inventive seasonal toppings; deviled duck wings with balsamic-mustard glaze. [$] *Average main: $20* ✉ *Hampton Inn & Suites Portland-Pearl District, 875 N.W. Everett St., Pearl District* ☎ *971/865–2888* 🌐 *www.tannercreektavern.com.*

Von Ebert Brewing

$ | **AMERICAN** | Unquestionably, the tremendously varied and interesting beers—barrel-aged ales, small-batch seasonal sours, gluten-frees, German and Belgian styles—are the key draw of this cavernous brewpub, but the kitchen also turns out legit pub fare that makes this a great choice even for the hops-averse. Many of the best dishes have an Eastern European slant, such as the smoked trout salad and the bratwurst sandwich, but the pizzas are great as well. **Known for:** charcuterie and cheese platter; innovative seasonal beers; burgers and other hefty sandwiches. [$] *Average main: $12* ✉ *131 N.W. 13th Ave., Pearl District* ☎ *503/820–7721* 🌐 *www.vonebertbrewing.com.*

☕ Coffee and Quick Bites

★ Nuvrei

$ | **BAKERY** | You'll find some of the tastiest sweets—including heavenly pistachio-rose croissants and blueberry-blackberry scones—in town at this cozy patisserie and café a few blocks south of Jamison Square. Be sure to check out the ever-changing selection of fluffy macarons. **Known for:** house-made macarons; savory quiches and croissants; double-chocolate flourless cookies. [$] *Average main: $9* ✉ *404 N.W. 10th Ave., Pearl District* ☎ *503/972–1701* 🌐 *www.nuvrei.com* 🕘 *No dinner.*

Tea Bar

$ | **CAFÉ** | This minimalist space with white walls and blond-wood tables and chairs on the ground floor of one of the Pearl's tallest residential towers has giant windows looking out over Tanner Springs Park, which is also a lovely spot to sip one of the café's signature milk teas and tea lattes or savor a dish of lavender-matcha vegan ice cream. **Known for:** coconut-milk soft-serve ice cream; boba milk teas in taro, vanilla rose, and other notable flavors; ginger-lemon tea toddies with local raw honey. *[$] Average main: $7 ✉ 1055 N.W. Northrup St., Pearl District ☎ 503/227–0464 🌐 www.iloveyousomatcha.com.*

Hotels

★ Canopy by Hilton Portland

$$$ | HOTEL | This contemporary member of Hilton's hip Canopy boutique brand eagerly encourages guests to chill out and relax in the hotel's extensive—and gorgeous—industrial-chic lounges, one of which features complimentary evening beer and wine. **Pros:** quiet but central location near Pearl District; beautifully designed living room–inspired common spaces; rooftop gym with stunning views. **Cons:** a 10- to 15-minute walk from heart of Downtown; breakfast isn't complimentary; expensive valet parking. *[$] Rooms from: $259 ✉ 425 N.W. 9th Ave., Pearl District ☎ 971/351–0230 🌐 www.canopy3.hilton.com 🛏 153 rooms 🍴 No meals.*

Hampton Inn & Suites Portland-Pearl District

$$ | HOTEL | By far one of the most stylish and upscale properties in this midrange group of the ubiquitous Hilton chain, this contemporary hotel was built from the bones of a historic Pearl District building and it offers a number of great perks, including a lovely roof deck, a spacious lobby with local art and comfortable seating, a well-equipped fitness center and pool, and the excellent Tanner Creek Tavern restaurant and bar. **Pros:** lots of great dining and shopping nearby; quite chic for the brand; nice gym and pool. **Cons:** 10- to 15-minute walk from heart of Downtown; pricey valet parking; no room service from the excellent restaurant. *[$] Rooms from: $215 ✉ 354 N.W. 9th Ave., Pearl District ☎ 503/222–5200 🌐 www.hilton.com 🛏 243 rooms 🍴 Free breakfast.*

Residence Inn Portland Downtown/Pearl District

$$$$ | HOTEL | One of only a few lodgings in the Pearl District, this sleek, six-floor, all-suites hotel is set around a large courtyard with outdoor seating and a fire pit; it's within easy walking distance of the train station, several small parks, and many hip restaurants and retailers. **Pros:** many rooms can sleep six guests; proximity to Pearl District businesses; in-room kitchens. **Cons:** a little far from Downtown; pricey overnight parking; cookie-cutter room design. *[$] Rooms from: $304 ✉ 1150 N.W. 9th Ave., Pearl District ☎ 503/220–1339 🌐 www.marriott.com 🛏 224 suites 🍴 Free breakfast.*

Nightlife

BARS AND LOUNGES

★ Botanist Bar PDX

BARS/PUBS | This classy, food-forward basement lounge opened in 2019 to rave reviews for its use of high-quality artisanal spirits and fresh juice, shrubs, and spirits. The bar snacks here are substantive and delicious—whitefish ceviche, tuna poke nachos, Korean barbecue chicken. A popular boozy brunch is offered on Sunday. *✉ 1300 N.W. Lovejoy St., Pearl District ☎ 971/533–8064 🌐 www.botanistbarpdx.com.*

Pink Rabbit

BARS/PUBS | This elegant space with ambient pink lighting and suspended bubble lamps, named for a song by indie band The National, serves playfully named but seriously crafted cocktails like the sherry-and-gin-centric Sucker's Luck and the mezcal-driven Quiet Company. The Asian-influenced bar snacks are distinctively delicious—try taro tots with Thai ranch and chili sauce or the oxtail burger. The darkly seductive space makes an inviting milieu before or after a show at nearby Portland Center Stage. ✉ *232 N.W. 12th Ave., Pearl District* ⊕ *www. pinkrabbitpdx.com.*

Performing Arts

THEATER
★ Portland Center Stage
THEATER | Housed in a handsomely restored 1891 armory, Portland Center Stage puts on around 10 contemporary and classic works on two stages in the LEED-certified green building between September and June. These are first-rate productions with exceptional onstage and behind-the-scenes talents. ✉ *Gerding Theater at the Armory, 128 N.W. 11th Ave., Pearl District* ☎ *503/445–3700* ⊕ *www.pcs.org.*

💼 Shopping

CLOTHING
★ Keen Garage
SHOES/LUGGAGE/LEATHER GOODS | Known for its wildly popular and often playfully colorful hiking sandals, boots, and water shoes, this spacious showroom occupies a splendidly restored 1907 steamship factory that also houses this eco-concious company's headquarters. In addition to just about any kind of footwear you could need to tackle Pacific Northwest's great outdoors, you'll also find backpacks and messenger bags along with socks, pants, shirts, and other rugged outerwear. There's also a phone booth in the store from which you can call politicians in Washington to express support for a variety of environmental issues, from land and water conservation to clean air. ✉ *505 N.W. 13th Ave., Pearl District* ☎ *971/200–4040* ⊕ *www.keenfootwear. com.*

Lizard Lounge
CLOTHING | Shop until your caffeine levels drop at this expansive men's and women's fashion source in the Pearl District, where staff will pour you a complimentary cup of Stumptown coffee as you browse that particularly Portland mix of hip and hipster chic. Lizard Lounge carries everything from major midrange brands like Levi's and Ray Bans to higher-end clubbing labels, like G-Star, Nudie Jeans, and Naked & Famous. There's also a good selection of gifts and household items. ✉ *1323 N.W. Irving St., Pearl District* ☎ *503/416–7476* ⊕ *www. lizardloungepdx.com.*

Nau
CLOTHING | Specializing in men's and women's sustainable clothing, from rugged hoodies and urbane down jackets to dressier threads made with cotton, Tencel, and other breathable fabrics, Portland-based Nau ships all over the world, but you can try on products and ask questions at this sleek flagship retail store in the Pearl District. ✉ *304 N.W. 11th Ave., Pearl District* ☎ *503/224–9697* ⊕ *www.nau.com.*

GALLERIES
★ First Thursday
ART GALLERIES | This gallery walk the first Thursday of every month gives art appreciators a chance to check out new exhibits while enjoying music, wine, and light appetizers. Typically the galleries, which are largely located in the Pearl District, are open in the evening from 6 to 9, but hours vary. Beyond the galleries, you'll find a lively scene of street musicians, local art vendors, and food and craft beer stalls along N.W. 13th Avenue between roughly Hoyt and Kearney Streets, which is pedestrians-only during First Thursday. ✉ *Pearl District* ☎ *503/227–8519* ⊕ *www. explorethepearl.com.*

PDX Contemporary Art
ART GALLERIES | One of the Pearl District's longest-running and most respected art spaces, this large gallery features rotating exhibitions in a range of materials from an impressive roster of both local and national artists. The striking space, inside one of the neighborhood's oldest buildings, was designed by famous Portland architect Brad Cloepfil (famous

for the Seattle Art Museum, Museum of Arts and Design in New York City, and many others). ✉ *925 N.W. Flanders St., Pearl District* ☎ *503/222–0063* 🌐 *www.pdxcontemporaryart.com.*

HOUSEHOLD GOODS AND FURNITURE

★ Made Here PDX

GIFTS/SOUVENIRS | This spacious showroom across from Powell's carries an impressive and eclectic assortment of locally made culinary goods, housewares, fashion, jewelry, arts and crafts—even handcrafted skis and snowboards. The quality of everything here is consistently high—it's a perfect way to get a sense of Portland's vibrant "maker" culture, all under one roof. There's a second location on North Mississippi Avenue. ✉ *40 N.W. 10th Ave., Pearl District* ☎ *503/224–0122* 🌐 *www.madehereonline.com.*

Nob Hill and Vicinity

Fashionable since the 1880s and still filled with Victorian houses, Nob Hill is a mixed-use cornucopia of old Portland charm and new Portland retail and dining. With its cafés, restaurants, galleries, and boutiques, it's a great place to stroll, shop, and people-watch. At the southern end of 23rd, on the blocks nearest Burnside, you'll mostly encounter upscale chain shops, whereas more independent and generally less pricey retail proliferates farther north, which includes the more recently developed and up-and-coming Slabtown district.

👁 Sights

Bull Run Distilling

WINERY/DISTILLERY | A pioneer of Portland's burgeoning craft spirits scene, head distiller Lee Medoff opened this Slabtown distillery in a 7,000-square-foot warehouse in 2010, with a dream of creating an iconic single-malt Oregon whiskey. Today Bull Run operates two of the largest commercial stills in the state, turning out acclaimed whiskeys, vodkas, and aquavit. ✉ *2259 N.W. Quimby St., Slabtown* ☎ *503/224–3483* 🌐 *www.bullrundistillery.com* 🕒 *Closed Mon. and Tues.*

Slabtown

NEIGHBORHOOD | A formerly industrial slice of Northwest, this mini neighborhood epitomizes New Portland, with a walking-scale grid of stylish apartment buildings and repurposed warehouses filled with some of the city's most hyped restaurants. Come hungry, as the food scene is the star of Slabtown. Tasty highlights include cocktail lounges like Solo Club and Bar West, inventive tapas at Spanish eatery Ataula, craft beer at the bi-level Breakside Brewery, and handmade pasta at Grassa. While Slabtown loosely refers to the blocks stretching north from Lovejoy Street to the Willamette River, most of the action is sandwiched between Northrup and Thurman Streets. ✉ *Blocks stretching north of Lovejoy St., Slabtown.*

🍴 Restaurants

★ Ataula

$$$ | **TAPAS** | The son of a cook from Spain's Aragon region, renowned chef-owner José Chesa brings his passion for Spanish cuisine to this small restaurant on a side street just off N.W. 23rd Avenue. The food is served tapas-style, with everything meant to be shared, including the heaping paella platters. **Known for:** picturesque sidewalk seating; the dessert of toasted bread with olive oil, chocolate, and salt; outstanding wine list. [$] *Average main: $29* ✉ *1818 N.W. 23rd Pl., Slabtown* ☎ *503/894–8904* 🌐 *www.ataulapdx.com* 🕒 *Closed Mon. No lunch.*

Besaws

$$ | **AMERICAN** | Brunch is the signature meal at the longest-operating restaurant in Northwest Portland, which opened in

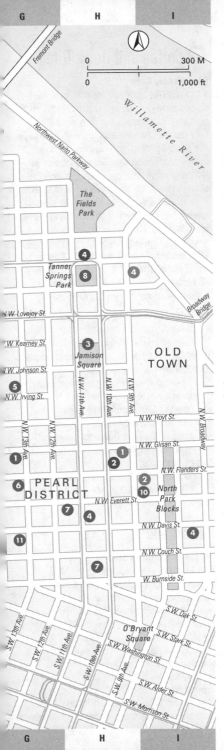

Sights ▼

1 Bull Run Distilling **B3**
2 Forest Park **A1**
3 Jamison Square
  Park **H5**
4 Oregon Jewish Museum
  and Center for
  Holocaust
  Education.................**I7**
5 Pittock Mansion **A7**
6 Portland Audubon
  Society....................**A7**
7 Powell's City of Books.. **H7**
8 Tanner Springs Park.... **H4**
9 Slabtown................. **B1**

Restaurants ▼

1 Andina **G6**
2 Ataula **B1**
3 Besaws **C2**
4 Deschutes Brewery
  Portland
  Public House **H7**
5 Irving Street Kitchen ... **G5**
6 Mediterranean
  Exploration Company... **G6**
7 Oven and Shaker **H7**
8 Paley's Place **C4**
9 St. Jack **B2**
10 Tanner Creek Tavern **I6**
11 Von Ebert Brewing...... **G7**

Quick Bites ▼

1 Commissary Cafe **E4**
2 Nuvrei.....................**H6**
3 Smith Teamaker..........**F2**
4 Tea Bar...................**H4**

Hotels ▼

1 Canopy by Hilton
  Portland.................**H6**
2 Hampton Inn & Suites
  Portland-Pearl District ...**I6**
3 Inn @ Northrup
  Station **D4**
4 Residence Inn
  Portland Downtown/
  Pearl District **H4**
5 Silver Cloud Inn–
  Portland..................**A1**

1903 as a beer parlor serving famished loggers and dockworkers. While the restaurant relocated from its original home in 2016 to the ground floor of a shiny-new Slabtown condo, Besaws's hefty helpings of American standards could still please the appetites of lumberjacks. **Known for:** hour-plus waits for weekend brunch; dedicated "day-drinking" cocktail menu; a group-friendly spot for special occasions. [$] *Average main: $20* ✉ *1545 N.W. 21st Ave., Slabtown* ☎ *503/228–2619* 🌐 *www.besaws.com.*

★ Paley's Place

$$$$ | FRENCH | Open since 1995 in an old Victorian house, this nationally acclaimed bistro helped put Portland's farm-forward restaurant scene on the map. Helmed by James Beard Award–winning chef-owner Vitaly Paley, who also operates Downtown's Imperial restaurant, Paley's serves Pacific Northwest meets French cuisine prepared with organic ingredients. **Known for:** iconic restaurant in a converted Victorian; glass case filled with an extensive cheese selection; porch and patio seating. [$] *Average main: $34* ✉ *1204 N.W. 21st Ave., Slabtown* ☎ *503/243–2403* 🌐 *www.paleysplace.net* 🕓 *No lunch.*

St. Jack

$$$ | FRENCH | This always-crowded Slabtown restaurant takes its inspiration from the *bouchons*, or rustic cafés, of Lyon, the culinary capital of France. The menu changes weekly, with recurring favorites including such shareable plates as pan-seared scallops drenched in a cognac, leek, and Gruyère sauce, with a bread-crumb crunch. **Known for:** superbly crafted house cocktails; mussels served with baguette; aged-cheese menu. [$] *Average main: $30* ✉ *1610 N.W. 23rd Ave., Slabtown* ☎ *503/360–1281* 🌐 *www.stjackpdx.com* 🕓 *No lunch.*

☕ Coffee and Quick Bites

Commissary Cafe

$ | CAFÉ | The concept for this cinema-inspired café comes from the history of the building it occupies—a former distribution hub for America's major film studios. Art deco lighting and design touches subtly reference the Golden Age of Hollywood, while the proprietor named her simple menu of sandwiches and salads in honor of stars from the silver screen. **Known for:** a popular spot for hanging with friends; light weekend brunch without any lines; fine espresso drinks prepared with locally roasted beans. [$] *Average main: $7* ✉ *915 N.W. 19th Ave., Suite A, Nob Hill* ☎ *503/593–5992* 🌐 *www.commissarycafe.com* 🕓 *No dinner.*

★ Smith Teamaker

$ | CAFÉ | At the center of Portland's locally steeped tea scene is Smith Teamaker's birthplace—a rustic tasting room opened in 2009 by the late entrepreneur Steven Smith, who the *New York Times* said "helped transform the nation's tea-drinking habits." Duck inside to learn about the tea's origin stories, sample different varieties at the tea bar, and leave with a few gift boxes. **Known for:** tea flights; tea lattes; chocolate and tea pairings. [$] *Average main: $5* ✉ *1626 N.W. Thurman St., Slabtown* ☎ *503/719–8752* 🌐 *www.smithtea.com.*

🛏 Hotels

★ Inn @ Northrup Station

$$$ | HOTEL | FAMILY | Near the Pearl District, bright colors, bold patterns, and retro designs characterize this Nob Hill hotel, which contains luxurious apartment-style suites with full kitchens or kitchenettes as well as patios (or balconies) adjoining most units, and a garden terrace for all guests to use. **Pros:** roomy suites have kitchens and feel like home; steps from Nob Hill shopping, dining, and the streetcar; free parking and streetcar tickets. **Cons:** the bold color scheme isn't for everyone; a 30-minute walk, or 15-minute streetcar ride, from Downtown; in demand, so it can be hard to get a reservation. $ *Rooms from: $239 ⊠ 2025 N.W. Northrup St., Nob Hill* 🕾 *503/224–0543, 800/224–1180* ⊕ *www. northrupstation.com* ⇨ *70 suites* �|◎| *Free breakfast.*

Silver Cloud Inn–Portland

$$ | HOTEL | The sole Portland branch of a small, Seattle-area, midpriced hotel chain is just a block from the lively upper end of N.W. 23rd Avenue and a great alternative to the bustle of Downtown. **Pros:** free parking; close to Nob Hill and Slabtown boutiques and dining as well as Forest Park hiking trails; easy access to bus and streetcar. **Cons:** gym but no pool; a bit of a distance from Downtown; front rooms face a busy street. $ *Rooms from: $189 ⊠ 2426 N.W. Vaughn St., Nob Hill* 🕾 *503/242–2400, 800/205–6939* ⊕ *www.silvercloud.com* ⇨ *81 rooms* |◎| *Free breakfast.*

Nightlife

BARS AND LOUNGES

Bantam Tavern

BARS/PUBS | Named for the miniature variety of fowl, this shot-glass-sized pub is refreshing for what it's not. In a city nearly obsessed with themed cocktail lounges, this 2018 addition to the 21st Avenue bar circuit has no discernible concept but plenty of character. In other words, it's a snug neighborhood hangout with a brief tap list of Pacific Northwest and German beers, classic and draft cocktails, and a concise selection of shareable entrées for late-night snacking. ⊠ *922 N.W. 21st Ave., Nob Hill* 🕾 *503/274–9032* ⊕ *www. bantamtavern.com.*

★ Pope House Bourbon Lounge

BARS/PUBS | Of the half-dozen hopping bars clustered around the intersection of 21st Avenue and Glisan Street, this whiskey lover's haven is the clear standout. Set in a Victorian home, with a covered porch and pocket-size patio, Pope House prides itself on its collection of more than 40 different Kentucky bourbon brands that pair well with the selection of Southern-accented small plates. ⊠ *2075 N.W. Glisan St., Nob Hill* 🕾 *503/222–1056* ⊕ *www.popehouselounge.com.*

★ Solo Club

BARS/PUBS | A Mediterranean air flows through this jewelry box of a bar, which specializes in highball cocktails and *amari*, Italian after-dinner digestifs. The bi-level Solo Club, with salt-block-adorned pillars and turquoise tiles, has a piazza-like patio that appeals to the parents of toy poodles, corgis, and other adorable dogs. ⊠ *2110 N.W. Raleigh St., Slabtown* 🕾 *971/254–9806* ⊕ *www.thesoloclub. com.*

BREWPUBS AND MICROBREWERIES

Breakside Brewery

BREWPUBS/BEER GARDENS | A large-scale mural of a rather serious-looking man marks the exterior of this craft brewery, where the atmosphere inside is far more convivial. Famous for its prolific range of beers and a face-sized soft pretzel, the industrial-styled brewpub spans two floors, with a sunny dining hall, a covered patio, and a mezzanine bar. Don't miss the rotating taps that showcase the brewmaster's experimental spirit. Breakside also has a second brewpub on Dekum Street in Inner Northeast Portland and a tasting room in the suburban community of Milwaukie. ⊠ *1570 N.W. 22nd Ave., Slabtown* 🕾 *503/444–7597* ⊕ *www. breakside.com.*

🎭 Performing Arts

THEATER

Northwest Children's Theater

THEATER | FAMILY | This long-running company presents four shows during its fall–spring season, geared to both the toddler and teen set. Performances are currently staged in the handsome Northwest

Neighborhood Cultural Center in Nob Hill. As of 2020, the company was looking for an eventual new permanent home, so check the website for updates. ⊠ *1819 N.W. Everett St., Nob Hill* ☎ *503/222–2190* ⊕ *www.nwcts.org.*

Shopping

GALLERIES
Twist

ART GALLERIES | This sprawling space in Nob Hill is well stocked with contemporary American ceramics, glass, furniture, sculpture, and handcrafted jewelry often with a whimsical touch. ⊠ *30 N.W. 23rd Pl., Nob Hill* ☎ *503/224–0334* ⊕ *www. twistonline.com.*

HOUSEHOLD GOODS AND FURNITURE
★ **Vía Raíz**

HOUSEHOLD ITEMS/FURNITURE | "Made in Mexico" is the manifesto at Vía Raíz. The Spanish name of this tiny, 220-square-foot boutique translates to "via roots," which sums up the shopkeeper's approach to elevating contemporary Mexican designers and artisans. Expect a rotating display of modern crafts, art, accessories, home goods, and coffee table books. ⊠ *2774 N.W. Thurman St., Slabtown* ☎ *503/303–3450* ⊕ *www. viaraiz.com.*

JEWELRY
★ **Betsy & lya**

JEWELRY/ACCESSORIES | Bright Santa Fe-esque colors and sleek geometric forms define the handmade earrings, bracelets, rings, cuffs, necklaces, and other stylish accessories at this beloved jewelry studio. On weekdays during production hours (between 10 am and 5 pm), complimentary artisan-led tours show you the magic happening in the production space, where you might glimpse anything from stone setting to metal soldering. ⊠ *1777 N.W. 24th Ave., Slabtown* ☎ *503/227–5482* ⊕ *www. betsyandiya.com.*

Activities

BIKE RENTALS
Fat Tire Farm

BICYCLING | For treks in Forest Park, rent mountain bikes at Fat Tire Farm, which is close to the park's Leif Erikson trailhead. The staff here really knows their stuff, from repair and maintenance help to advice on the best trails and routes. ⊠ *2714 N.W. Thurman St., Nob Hill* ☎ *503/222–3276* ⊕ *www.fattirefarm.com.*

Forest Park

One of the largest woodland city parks in the country, Forest Park stretches 8 miles along the hills overlooking the Willamette River west of Downtown. More than 80 miles of trails through forests of Douglas fir, hemlock, and cedar (including a few patches of old growth) offer numerous options for those looking to log some miles or spend some time outside.

◎ Sights

★ **Forest Park**

NATIONAL/STATE PARK | One of the nation's largest urban wildernesses (5,157 acres), this city-owned, car-free park has more than 50 species of birds and mammals and more than 80 miles of trails through forests of Douglas fir, hemlock, and cedar. Running the length of the park is the 30-mile Wildwood Trail, which extends into adjoining Washington Park (and is a handy point for accessing Forest Park), starting at the Vietnam Veterans Memorial in Hoyt Arboretum. You can access a number of spur trails from the Wildwood Trail, including the 11-mile Leif Erikson Drive, which picks up from the end of N.W. Thurman Street and is a popular route for jogging and mountain biking. ■**TIP→ You can find information and maps at the Forest Park Conservancy office, at 833 S.W. 11th Avenue, Suite 800, and on the website.** ⊠ *End of N.W.*

Thurman St., Forest Park ✛ Entrance at Leif Erikson Dr. ☎ 503/223–5449 ⊕ www. forestparkconservancy.org.

★ Pittock Mansion

HOUSE | Henry Pittock, the founder and publisher of the *Oregonian* newspaper, built this 22-room, castlelike mansion, which combines French Renaissance and Victorian styles. The opulent manor, built in 1914, is filled with art and antiques. The 46-acre grounds, northwest of Washington Park and 1,000 feet above the city, offer superb views of the skyline, rivers, and the Cascade Range, including Mt. Hood and Mt. St. Helens. The mansion is a half-mile uphill trek from the nearest bus stop. The mansion is also a highly popular destination among hikers using Forest Park's well-utilized Wildwood Trail. ⊠ *3229 N.W. Pittock Dr., Forest Park* ☎ *503/823–3623* ⊕ *www.pittockmansion. org* 🎟 *$12* ⊘ *Closed Jan.*

Portland Audubon Society

NATURE PRESERVE | The 150-acre sanctuary has a few miles of trails, including one known for ample woodpecker sightings, as well as access to the miles of trails in the adjoining Forest Park. There's also a hospital for injured and orphaned birds here, as well as a gift shop stocked with books and feeders. The society supplies free maps and sponsors a flock of bird-related activities, including guided bird-watching events. ⊠ *5151 N.W. Cornell Rd., Forest Park* ☎ *503/292–6855* ⊕ *www.audubonportland.org.*

West Hills and Southwest

Forming a natural western border of Downtown and Nob Hill, the West Hills extend as a high (up to around 1,000 feet in elevation) ridgeline from Southwest to Northwest Portland. Part of this lofty neighborhood is residential, containing some of the largest and finest homes

in the city, many of them with knockout views of the Downtown skyline and Mt. St. Helens and Mt. Hood in the distance. Technically, Downtown Portland is in the city's Southwest quadrant as are most of the attractions included in the West Hills section of town. But when locals mention Southwest, they're generally referring to the area south and southwest of Downtown, a mostly middle- to upper-middle-class residential district with a few commercial pockets.

◉ Sights

Council Crest Park

PARK—SPORTS-OUTDOORS | The highest point in Portland, at 1,073 feet, this 43-acre bluff-top patch of greenery is a superb spot to take in sunsets and sunrises. Along with nearly 180-degree views of the Portland metro area, a clear day also affords views of the surrounding peaks—Mt. Hood, Mt. St. Helens, Mt. Adams, Mt. Jefferson, and Mt. Rainier. A bronze fountain depicting a mother and child has been erected in the park twice; first in the 1950s and second in the 1990s. The peaceful piece was stolen in the 1980s, uncovered in a narcotics bust 10 years later, and then returned to the park. Trails connect Council Crest with Marquam Nature Park and Washington Park. ■**TIP→ It's quite busy on weekends, so visit on a weekday if possible.** ⊠ *1120 S.W. Council Crest Dr., West Hills* ⊕ *www.portlandoregon.gov/parks.*

Hoyt Arboretum

GARDEN | Some 12 miles of trails that connect with others in Washington Park and Forest Park wind through the 189-acre arboretum, which was established in 1928 and contains more than 2,000 species of plants and one of the nation's largest collections of coniferous trees. Pick up trail maps at the visitor center. Guided 90-minute tours ($3 suggested donation) are offered most Saturdays and Sundays at 11 am and 1 pm from April through October. Also here are

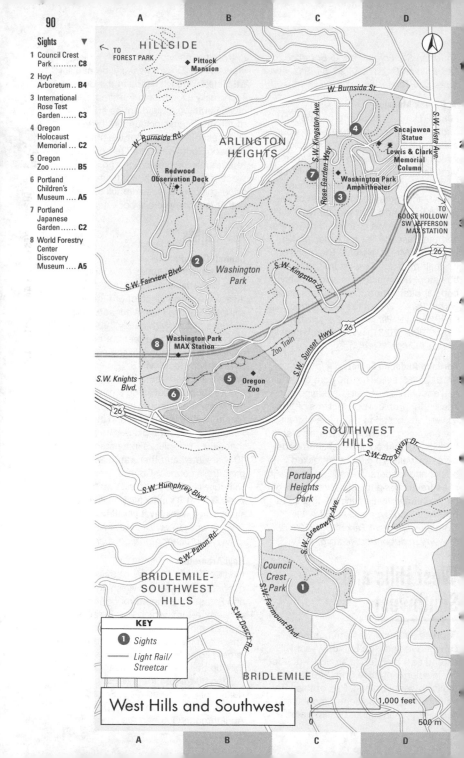

West Hills and Southwest

the Winter Garden and a memorial to veterans of the Vietnam War. The visitor center is a half mile from the Washington Park MAX station. ⊠ *4000 S.W. Fairview Blvd., Washington Park* ☎ *503/865–8733* ⊕ *www.hoytarboretum.org* ⊠ *Free.*

★ **International Rose Test Garden**

GARDEN | FAMILY | This glorious park within Washington Park comprises three terraced gardens, set on 4½ acres, where more than 10,000 bushes and some 550 varieties of roses grow. The flowers, many of them new varieties, are at their peak in June, July, September, and October. From the gardens you can take in views of the Downtown skyline and, on clear days, the slopes of Mt. Hood, 50 miles to the east. Summer concerts take place in the garden's amphitheater. It's a pretty but hilly 30- to 40-minute walk from Downtown, or you can get here via MAX light rail (either to Washington Park or Kings Hill/S.W. Salmon Street stations); then transfer to Bus No. 63 or Washington Park shuttle (May–October only). ⊠ *400 S.W. Kingston Ave., Washington Park* ☎ *503/227–7033* ⊕ *www. portlandoregon.gov/parks.*

Oregon Holocaust Memorial

MEMORIAL | This memorial to those who perished during the Holocaust bears the names of surviving families who live in Oregon and southwest Washington. A bronzed baby shoe, a doll, broken spectacles, and other strewn possessions await notice on the cobbled courtyard. Soil and ash from six Nazi concentration camps is interred beneath the black granite wall. The memorial is operated by the Oregon Jewish Museum and Center for Holocaust Education in Old Town, which hosts rotating history and art exhibits, films, concerts, and lectures. ⊠ *S.W. Washington Way and S.W. Wright Ave., Washington Park* ☎ *503/226–3600* ⊕ *www.ojmche.org.*

Oregon Zoo

ZOO | FAMILY | This animal park in the West Hills, famous for its Asian elephants, is undergoing a two-decades-long series of major improvements and expansions to make the zoo more sustainable and provide more stimulating spaces, education, and conservation opportunities, as well as improved guest amenities and event spaces. New in recent years are the Condors of the Columbia habitat, which includes a deep pool for condor bathing, a 30-foot aviary, and an elevated viewing area to see the condors in flight; and the Elephant Lands area, which features feeding stations, mud wallows, varied terrain, and deep pools to keep the elephants active, as well as one of the world's largest indoor elephant facilities. A state-of-the-art Zoo Education Center opened in 2017. Other major draws include the Africa Savanna with rhinos, hippos, zebras, and giraffes; Steller Cove, an aquatic exhibit home to Steller sea lions and a family of sea otters; and a troop of chimpanzees. More than a dozen summer concerts, featuring nationally known pop stars, take place at the zoo from mid-June through August. Take the MAX light rail to the Washington Park station. ⊠ *4001 S.W. Canyon Rd., Washington Park* ☎ *503/226–1561* ⊕ *www. oregonzoo.org* ⊠ *$17.95.*

Portland Children's Museum

MUSEUM | FAMILY | Colorful sights and sounds entertain kids of all ages where hands-on play is the order of the day. Visit nationally touring exhibits; catch a story time, a sing-along, or a puppet show in the theater; create sculptures in the clay studio; splash hands in the waterworks display; or make a creation from junk in the Maker Studio. The museum shares the same parking lot as the Oregon Zoo and can also be reached via the MAX light rail Washington Park stop. ⊠ *4015 S.W. Canyon Rd., Washington Park* ☎ *503/223–6500* ⊕ *www.portlandcm.org* ⊠ *$11.*

★ Portland Japanese Garden

GARDEN | One of the most authentic Japanese gardens outside Japan, this serene landscape unfolds over 12½ acres of Washington Park, just a short stroll up the hill from the International Rose Test Garden. Designed by a Japanese landscape master, there are five separate garden styles: Strolling Pond Garden, Tea Garden, Natural Garden, Sand and Stone Garden, and Flat Garden. The Tea House was built in Japan and reconstructed here. An ambitious expansion designed by renowned Japanese architect Kengo Kuma added a tea garden café, library, art gallery, and a new gift shop in 2017. The east side of the Pavilion has a majestic view of Portland and Mt. Hood. Take MAX light rail to Washington Park station, and transfer to Bus No. 63 or the Washington Park Shuttle (May–October only). ■ **TIP→ Knowledgeable volunteers guide daily public tours, which are free with admission; call ahead for times.** ⊠ *611 S.W. Kingston Ave., Washington Park* ☎ *503/223–1321* ⊕ *www.japanese-garden.com* ⊠ *$16.95.*

World Forestry Center Discovery Museum

MUSEUM | **FAMILY** | This handsomely designed, contemporary museum across from the Oregon Zoo contains interactive and multimedia exhibits about forest sustainability. A white-water raft ride, smoke-jumper training simulator, and Timberjack tree harvester all provide different perspectives on Pacific Northwest forests. On the second floor the forests of the world are explored in various travel settings. A canopy lift ride hoists visitors to the 50-foot ceiling to look at a Douglas fir. ⊠ *4033 S.W. Canyon Rd., Washington Park* ☎ *503/228–1367* ⊕ *www.worldforestry.org* ⊠ *$8* ☉ *Closed Tues.–Wed. early Sept.–late May.*

North

Somewhat dismissed historically as the city's "fifth quadrant," North Portland has come into its own in recent years, as the comparatively low cost of real estate has made it popular with young entrepreneurs, students, and other urban pioneers. North Mississippi and North Williams Avenues, which are about 10 short blocks apart, have become home to some of the hottest food, drink, and music venues in the city, and farther-out areas like Kenton and St. Johns are becoming increasingly popular.

Sights

★ Cathedral Park

NATIONAL/STATE PARK | Whether it's the view of the imposing and stunning Gothic St. John's Bridge, which rises some 400 feet above the Willamette River, or the historic significance of Lewis and Clark having camped here in 1806, this 23-acre park is divine. Though there's no church, the park gets its name from the picturesque arches supporting the bridge. It's rumored that the ghost of a young girl haunts the bridge, and that may be true, but if you're told that it was designed by the same man who envisioned the Golden Gate Bridge, that's just a popular misconception. Dog lovers, or those who aren't, should take note of the off-leash area. ⊠ *N. Edison St. and N. Pittsburg Ave., St. Johns* ⊕ *www.portlandoregon.gov/parks.*

★ North Mississippi Avenue

NEIGHBORHOOD | One of North Portland's strips of indie retailers, the liveliest section of North Mississippi Avenue stretches for several blocks and includes a mix of old storefronts and sleek new buildings that house cafés, brewpubs, collectives, shops, music venues, and an excellent food-cart pod, Mississippi Marketplace. Bioswale planter boxes, found-object fences, and café tables built from old doors are some of the innovations you'll see along this eclectic thoroughfare. At the southern end of the strip, stop by the ReBuilding Center, an outlet for recycled building supplies that has cob (clay-and-straw) trees and benches built into the facade. ⊠ *N. Mississippi Ave., North Mississippi Ave.* ⊕ *Between N. Fremont and N. Skidmore Sts.* ⊛ *www.mississippiave.com.*

North Williams Avenue

NEIGHBORHOOD | About a 10-minute walk east and running parallel to North Mississippi, the bike-friendly North Williams corridor is a much more recently developed area of almost entirely new, eco-friendly buildings and condos rife with trendy restaurants, nightspots, and boutiques. Highlights here include Eem, JinJu Patisserie, Vendetta, the People's Pig Barbecue, XLB, and Hopworks BikeBar, a branch of Hopworks Urban Brewery in Outer Southeast. ⊠ *N. Williams, from N. E. Monroe St. to N. E. Going St., North Williams Ave.* ⊕ *To get here on MAX light rail, get off at the Albina/Mississippi station* ⊛ *williamsdistrict.com.*

Paul Bunyan Statue

PUBLIC ART | Statues of this mythical logger are common roadside sights in the American West, though North Portland's 31-foot-tall Paul Bunyan smiles confidently as the king among them. The unmissable sculpture went up in 1959 to mark the 100th anniversary of Oregon's statehood. Neighbors have kept Bunyan in good shape over the years, with periodic renovations and fresh paint— that likely explains his perennially pearly concrete smile. ⊠ *Pacific Hwy. N and N. Denver Ave., Kenton.*

★ Sauvie Island

ISLAND | FAMILY | If it's a day to take advantage of gorgeous weather, then drive about a half hour northwest of Downtown, or 15 minutes north of St. Johns, to Sauvie Island. The largely agrarian 33-square-mile piece of paradise in the Columbia River has a wildlife refuge,

three beaches (including Collins Beach, which is clothing-optional), superb biking and hiking trails, and several farms offering seasonal "u-pick" bounty (and one, Bella Organic, offering an autumn pumpkin patch and corn maze). One excellent hike, and one of the few with free parking, is the Wapato Greenway, which is just 3 miles north of the bridge onto the island. The trail leads through a white oak savannah and around a pond, and you may see green horned owls, nuthatches, and deer. Part of the trail leads to a peaceful dock on the Multnomah Channel, where you can tie a boat or kayak. To get to the beaches, after crossing the Sauvie Island bridge, turn right; follow N.W. Sauvie Island Road to Reeder Road and follow signs. There's plenty of parking at the beaches, but a permit is required ($10 for a one-day permit, $30 annual, available at the general store at the base of the bridge). Keep in mind that visitors are banned from bringing alcohol onto the island from May to September. ⊠ *N.W. Sauvie Island Rd., Sauvie Island* ⊕ *Take U.S. 30 north from Portland to the Sauvie Island Bridge* ⊛ *www.sauvieisland.org.*

🍴 Restaurants

★ Eem

$$ | THAI | This impossibly delicious mash-up of Thai street food and Texas barbecue, a collaboration between the talents behind locally renowned restaurants Langbaan and Matt's BBQ, excels in both its playful approach and smoking-good execution. Potted plants and hanging basket lamps impart a subtle, relaxed beach bar vibe, perfect for enjoying tiki-esque cocktails with inspired names like Arranged Marriage and Act of God. **Known for:** colorful tropical drinks; chopped barbecue-fried rice with shishito peppers; rich curries with smoked brisket, lamb shoulder, and other barbecue staples. Ⓢ *Average main: $16* ⊠ *3808*

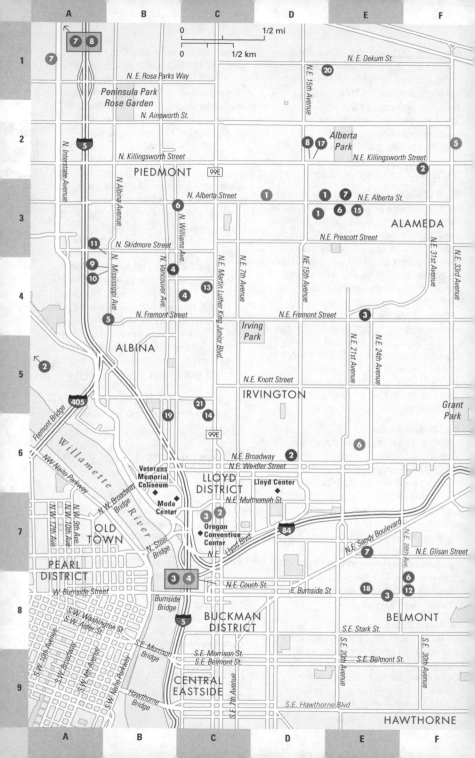

KEY

- 1 *Sights*
- 1 *Restaurants*
- 1 *Quick Bites*
- 1 *Hotels*

Sights ▼

1 Alberta Arts District **D3**
2 Cathedral Park **A5**
3 East Burnside and
  28th Avenue **E8**
4 The Grotto **I5**
5 North Mississippi
  Avenue.................. **B4**
6 North Williams
  Avenue.................. **B3**
7 Paul Bunyan Statue **A1**
8 Sauvie Island............ **A1**

Restaurants ▼

1 Aviary **D3**
2 Beast..................... **F2**
3 Dóttir **C8**
4 Eem...................... **C4**
5 Gado Gado............... **G6**
6 Güero.................... **F8**
7 Han Oak.................. **E7**
8 Hat Yai................... **D2**
9 Interurban **A4**
10 Lovely's Fifty Fifty **A4**
11 Matt's BBQ **A3**
12 Navarre **F8**
13 Ned Ludd **C4**
14 Ox Restaurant........... **C6**
15 Pine State Biscuits **E3**
16 Pizza Jerk............... **G3**
17 Podnah's Pit BBQ....... **D2**
18 Screen Door............. **E8**
19 Sweedeedee........... **B6**
20 Tamale Boy.............. **E1**
21 Toro Bravo............... **C5**

Quick Bites ▼

1 Bakeshop................ **H5**
2 Eb & Bean **D6**
3 Guilder **E4**
4 JinJu Patisserie......... **B4**
5 Pip's Original Doughnuts
  & Chai.................. **H4**
6 Proud Mary.............. **E3**
7 Salt & Straw
  Ice Cream............... **E3**

Hotels ▼

1 Caravan–The Tiny
  House Hotel **D3**
2 Hotel Eastlund............ **C7**
3 Hyatt Regency
  Portland.................. **C7**
4 KEX Portland **C8**
5 McMenamins
  Kennedy School **F2**
6 Portland's White House
  Bed and Breakfast....... **E6**
7 Viking Motel............. **A1**

North and Northeast

Food cart pods are found all over Portland like this one on Fifth Avenue in Downtown.

N. Williams Ave., North Williams Ave. ☎ *971/295–1645* 🌐 *www.eempdx.com.*

★ Interurban

$ | MODERN AMERICAN | A laid-back North Mississippi gastropub with an L-shaped indoor bar and a bi-level back patio with lush landscaping and a shaded pergola, Interurban is both a convivial drinkery and a fine spot for affordable, well-crafted American fare served from midafternoon until 2 am (hours start earlier on weekends, with brunch kicking off at 10 am). The kitchen creates consistently good and creative food, such as steak tartare and smoked-trout BLT sandwiches, and there's an extensive selection of cocktails and microbrews. **Known for:** terrific afternoon and late-night happy hour menu; salted-caramel French toast at brunch; pretty back patio. [$] *Average main: $15* ✉ *4057 N. Mississippi Ave., North Mississippi Ave.* ☎ *503/284–6669* 🌐 *www.interurbanpdx.com* 🕒 *No lunch weekdays.*

★ Lovely's Fifty-Fifty

$ | PIZZA | This unpretentious and airy neighborhood spot with wooden booths and whimsical fire-engine-red chairs is really two delicious dining options in one: the dining room serves inventively topped, crisp, wood-fired pizzas, and a small takeout counter dispenses homemade hard and soft-serve organic ice cream with flavors like hazelnut toffee and candied kumquat. Among the pizzas, you can't go wrong with the pie layered in shaved-and-roasted potatoes, sage, taleggio, and pancetta, and topped with an egg. **Known for:** innovative flavors of house-made ice cream; perfectly crispy wood-fired pizzas; beautiful seasonal salads with local greens. [$] *Average main: $15* ✉ *4039 N. Mississippi Ave., North Mississippi Ave.* ☎ *503/281–4060* 🌐 *www.lovelysfiftyfifty.com* 🕒 *Closed Mon. No lunch.*

Portland's Food Carts

Throughout Portland at any given mealtime, more than 500 food carts are dishing up steaming plates of everything from Korean bibimbap to brick-oven pizza to Texas-style barbecue to Oaxacan *tlayudas* (flatbread with toppings). The food-cart scene that's become a fixture in countless North American cities in recent years owes much of its popularity to Portland, which fervently embraced the movement in the 1990s.

Brightly colored and mostly stationary, the carts tend to cluster in former parking lots in pods ranging from 3 to nearly 60 establishments, oftentimes ringing a cluster of picnic tables or a covered awning. The city's rampant boom has led to the closure or relocation of some key cart pods, but others have opened, often farther from the city center, and you'll always find a handful of notable carts at any of the many farmers' markets around town. Arguably the most famous pod in the city, downtown's S.W. 9th and Alder cart community shut down in 2019 to make way for an impending Ritz-Carlton hotel development, but as of this writing, it's slated to reopen at some point along the North Park Blocks on the edge of the Pearl District and Old Town.

With plate prices averaging $7 to $10, carts provide a quick, inexpensive, and delicious alternative to traditional sit-down restaurants, and it's an easy way to sample Portland's extensive ethnic food offerings.

For up-to-date information on hours and locations, and the latest on openings, moves, and closures, check out the extensive local blog **Food Carts Portland** (⊕ *www.foodcartsportland. com*) and its corresponding apps.

Some Top Pods

Prost! Marketplace (4233 N. Mississippi Ave.): A snug encampment of about 15 pods that's adjacent to the excellent German-beer hall **Prost!** (where you'll also find restrooms), this fixture along North Mississippi contains some of the city's most vaunted carts, including the smoky Texas-style chopped brisket of **Matt's BBQ,** exceptional Mexico City–style street tacos from **Little Conejo,** and two-fisted smoked-meat sandwiches from **Pastrami Zombie.** There's also an expansive (and covered) wood-deck beer garden with taps from some of the best craft brewers in the Pacific Northwest.

Southeast, Portland Mercado (S.E. 73rd Ave. and Foster Rd.): A convivial collection of some 40 businesses, including food carts and crafts and gift vendors, the Mercado is devoted to Latin culture and heritage. Feast on *ropa vieja* (braised beef) and other Cuban delicacies at **Que Bolá?;** Venezuelan egg and sweet-pepper arepas at **La Arepa;** and Oaxacan mole blue-corn enchiladas at **Tierra del Sol.**

The Bite on Belmont (4255 S.E. Belmont): There are just 9 or 10 carts at this cozy but festive cart colony in Southeast, but the variety and quality is right up there with the best in the city, starting with **Viking Soul Food** and its delectable Norwegian meatballs and house-smoked-salmon wraps. There are also gooey-good casseroles with plenty of mix-in ingredients available (bacon, jalapeños) at **Herb's Mac & Cheese,** *bulgogi* cheesesteak sandwiches and Hawaiian plate lunches at **Namu,** and pints of local beer at **Hindsight Tap Cart.**

★ Matt's BBQ

$ | BARBECUE | Located in the Prost! Marketplace on North Mississippi, you'll often have to stand in line (it's worth it!) to experience the top food-cart *and* (Texas-style) barbecue joint in Portland. **Known for:** the hotmess sandwich (with brisket, sausage, jalapeños, and slaw); combo platters featuring brisket, ribs, sausage, pulled pork, and sides; outstanding craft-beer offerings elsewhere in this cart pod. $ *Average main: $10 ⊠ Prost! Marketplace, 4233 N. Mississippi Ave., North Mississippi Ave.* ☎ *503/504–0870* ⊕ *www.mattsbbqpdx. com.*

Sweedeedee

$ | MODERN AMERICAN | Although this modest white-brick storefront on a quiet street doesn't look like anything special from the outside, it produces some of the most memorable breakfast and lunch fare in North Portland, including savory bacon-lettuce-beet sandwiches on cornmeal molasses bread and sweet porridge with fruit and cardamom yogurt. This Southern-inspired eatery also offers up flaky-crust marionberry, salted-honey, and other delectable pies. **Known for:** seasonal fruit pies; hearty but fresh Southern breakfast fare; sandwiches on unusual house-baked breads. $ *Average main: $13 ⊠ 5202 N. Albina Ave., North Mississippi Ave.* ☎ *503/946–8087* ⊕ *www. sweedeedee.com* ⊗ *No dinner.*

☕ Coffee and Quick Bites

JinJu Patisserie

$ | CAFÉ | Dessert isn't the only offering at this modish East-meets-West patisserie, but these opulent treats—matcha-yuzu mousse tarts, fig-and–red wine chocolates, red velvet whoopie pies—are unquestionably JinJu's raison d'etre. For a more substantial breakfast or lunch experience, tuck into a five-grain Korean bulgogi bowl or a curried-chicken panini. **Known for:** exquisitely crafted pastries and cakes; artisanal chocolates; savory and sweet breakfast croissants. $ *Average main: $12 ⊠ 4063 N. Williams Ave., North Williams Ave.* ☎ *503/828–7728* ⊕ *www. jinjupatisserie.com* ⊗ *Closed Tues. and Wed. No dinner.*

Hotels

Viking Motel

$ | HOTEL | When this clean, family-run, midcentury motel opened in the late 1970s, it served the nearby shipyard; today, this eco-friendly property is one of Portland's best bargain lodgings, catering to savvy visitors who take the nearby MAX to Downtown Portland. **Pros:** low rates that include free parking and Wi-Fi; friendly owners who take great pride in the property's upkeep; just off Interstate 5 and a block from MAX light rail station. **Cons:** a 15-minute drive or 20-minute MAX ride from Downtown; very basic rooms; dated decor. $ *Rooms from: $95 ⊠ 6701 N. Interstate Ave., North* ☎ *503/285–4896, 800/308–5097* ⊕ *www. vikingmotelportland.com* ⌐ *26 rooms* ⌑ *No meals.*

Nightlife

BARS

The Box Social

BARS/PUBS | Aptly located in a boxy glass-and-steel contemporary building in the trendy North Williams Corridor, this low-key, self-proclaimed "drinking parlor" stands out in particular for its nicely balanced whiskey cocktails. Note the extensive use of house-made, sometimes barrel-aged, bitters, and the long list of premium whiskeys and small-batch bourbons. ⊠ *3971 N. Williams Ave., North Williams Ave.* ☎ *503/288–1111* ⊕ *www.bxsocial.com.*

BREWPUBS AND MICROBREWERIES

★ Ecliptic Brewing

BREWPUBS/BEER GARDENS | Fans of boldly flavored brews flock to this spacious, airy brewery and pub at the south end of the Mississippi strip, which also has a spacious patio that's abuzz with revelers on summer afternoons. Founder John Harris is as obsessed with astronomy as he is with beer, hence the cosmic names of beers, which include Quasar Pale Ale and Phobos Single Hop Red Ale. ■TIP➔ **Brewery tours are offered at noon three times a week.** ⊠ *825 N. Cook St., North Mississippi Ave.* ☎ *503/265–8002* ⊕ *www.eclipticbrewing.com.*

Ex Novo Brewing

BREWPUBS/BEER GARDENS | What began as a humble Portland homebrew operation in 2012 has blossomed into a highly esteemed craft-beer producer with brew-pubs in Oregon and New Mexico. You can quaff the company's hops-focused classics and distinctive seasonal one-off beers here at the original location, which also serves quite good bar fare, such as deviled eggs with pork belly burnt ends and pimento mac and cheese. ⊠ *2326 N. Flint Ave., North Williams Ave.* ☎ *503/894–8251* ⊕ *www.exnovobrew.com.*

Prost!

BREWPUBS/BEER GARDENS | At the northern end of the hip North Mississippi retail and restaurant strip, Prost! is an airy, amber-lit, contemporary bar special-izing in old-school German beers like Spaten Lager, Franziskaner Weissbier, and Erdinger Dunkel Weisse. Nosh on Bavarian pretzels and other Euro snacks or venture next door to one of the city's best food-cart pods, Prost! Marketplace. The owners also operate the excellent German pub Stammtisch, on N.E. 28th Avenue. ⊠ *4237 N. Mississippi Ave., North Mississippi Ave.* ☎ *503/954–2674* ⊕ *www.prostportland.com.*

LIVE MUSIC

★ **Mississippi Studios**

MUSIC CLUBS | An intimate and inclusive neighborhood music venue, with a seat-ed balcony and old Oriental rugs covering the standing-room-only floor, commu-nity-oriented Mississippi Studios offers high-quality live music performances every night of the week in a wide range of genres. Between sets, you can jump back and forth from the adjacent BarBar, a hip, comfortable bar serving delicious burgers and vegan fare and a covered back patio. ⊠ *3939 N. Mississippi Ave., North Mississippi Ave.* ☎ *503/288–3895* ⊕ *www.mississippistudios.com.*

Shopping

CLOTHING AND ACCESSORIES

Queen Bee Creations

SPECIALTY STORES | Since 1996, this stalwart along the rapidly developing North Williams strip has been creating fairly priced products to help you carry and organize your stuff in style. Many of these items—which include honeybee faux-leather messenger bags, canvas weekenders, and convertible tote-back-packs—are waterproof or water resistant, and everything is handcrafted in Portland. Wallets, eyeglass cases, notebooks, and other useful accessories are also available. ⊠ *3961 N. Williams Ave., North Williams Ave.* ☎ *503/232–1755* ⊕ *www. queenbee-creations.com.*

FOOD

★ **The Meadow**

FOOD/CANDY | Food writer Mark Bitterman (not to be confused with food writer Mark Bittman) knows a thing or two about salt—he's written popular books on the subject, and he's the owner of this tiny purveyor of gourmet finishing salts, some of them smoked or infused with unusual flavors, like cherry and plums, or saffron. At this flagship location (there's a second Meadow in Nob Hill, and others in Man-hattan and Tokyo) you can also purchase the additional magical touches you might need to create the perfect dinner party, from Oregon and European wines and vermouths, to fresh-cut flowers, aromatic cocktail bitters, and high-quality, single-or-igin chocolates. ⊠ *3731 N. Mississippi Ave., North Mississippi Ave.* ☎ *503/974–8349* ⊕ *www.themeadow.com.*

HOUSEHOLD GOODS AND FURNITURE

★ Beam & Anchor

HOUSEHOLD ITEMS/FURNITURE | Set on a busy street corner several blocks from the North Side's trendy North Mississippi strip, this once-dilapidated warehouse houses an upstairs workshop for makers of artisanal goods and an inspiring downstairs retail space where you'll find a carefully curated selection of lifestyle goods for every room in the home, many of them produced locally—some as local as upstairs. Among the hipster treasures, look for warm and soft camp blankets and Navajo rugs with vibrant prints, women's jewelry in a variety of simple-but-beautiful styles, Portland Apothecary bath salts and soaps, and quite a few larger pieces of distinctive furniture. ⊠ *2710 N. Interstate Ave., North Mississippi Ave.* ☎ *503/367–3230* ⊕ *www.beamandanchor.com.*

Mantel

CERAMICS/GLASSWARE | Set along North Kenton's bustling Denver Avenue strip, this splendid shop run by a former ceramics teacher carries pedestal vases, textured-glaze stoneware mugs, clay hanging planters, and other both artful and utilitarian household items designed mostly by local Portland artists. The aesthetic tends toward clean, simple lines and muted colors. You'll also discover glassware, jewelry, vegan soaps, and other items for the contemporary urban home. ⊠ *8202 N. Denver Ave., Kenton* ☎ *503/289–0558* ⊕ *www.mantelpdx.com.*

TOYS

Paxton Gate

TOYS | Here, science and biology mix with whimsy and imagination. You'll find everything from taxidermied scorpions and baby goats to ostrich eggs and ceramic chimes. It's a fascinating and strangely beguiling mix of goods, although not for the faint of heart. ⊠ *4204 N. Mississippi Ave., North Mississippi Ave.* ☎ *503/719–4508* ⊕ *www.paxtongate.com.*

Northeast

Still the epicenter of the city's relatively small—compared with other U.S. cities the size of Portland—African American community, Northeast has slowly gentrified over the last half century. In the Irvington, Laurelhurst, and Alameda neighborhoods, you'll find some of the largest, most historic homes in town. Northeast's outer reaches include one of the city's top neighborhoods for indie retail and dining, the Alberta Arts District, as well as inviting neighborhoods like Hollywood and Beaumont. This huge quadrant extends north to the Columbia River and way out east to the city border, and is home to some intriguing attractions like the Grotto and Rocky Butte.

Sights

★ Alberta Arts District

NEIGHBORHOOD | FAMILY | Arguably the first of Portland's several hipster-favored East Side neighborhoods to earn national attention, the Alberta Arts District (aka Alberta) has morphed from a downcast commercial strip into an offbeat row of hippie-driven counterculture and then more recently into a considerably more eclectic stretch of both indie arts spaces and downright sophisticated bistros and galleries. Favorite stops include Pine State Biscuits, Salt & Straw ice cream, the Bye and Bye bar, Tin Shed Garden Cafe, Aviary restaurant, Bollywood Theater restaurant, Urdaneta restaurant, Proud Mary coffeehouse, Ampersand art gallery and books, PedX shoes, and Grayling jewelry. Extending a little more than a mile, Northeast Alberta offers plenty of one-of-a-kind dining and shopping; you'll find virtually no national chains along here. The area is also home to some of the best people-watching in Portland, especially during the Last Thursday (of the month) art walks, held from 6 pm until 9 pm. The Alberta Street Fair in August showcases the neighborhood's offerings with arts-and-crafts displays and street performances. **■TIP→ Northeast Alberta is about a mile from the smaller but similarly intriguing North Mississippi and North Williams corridors; fans of indie dining and shopping could easily spend a full day strolling or biking among both areas.** ✉ *N.E. Alberta St., Alberta Arts District* ✥ *Between N.E. Martin Luther King Jr. Blvd. and N.E. 30th Ave.* 🌐 *www.albertamainst.org.*

East Burnside and 28th Avenue

NEIGHBORHOOD | A roughly T-shaped dining and retail district that's less defined but no less popular and impressive than some of the East Side's other culinary and shopping hot spots (like the Alberta Arts District and Southeast Division Street), this diverse neighborhood comprises a slew of mostly food-related ventures along East Burnside Street from about 22nd to 28th Avenues. Then, where Burnside meets 28th Avenue, you'll find several blocks of first-rate eateries as well as a handful of boutiques in either direction, heading north up to about Glisan Street and south down to about Stark Street. The historic Laurelhurst Theater anchors the intersection of 28th and Burnside, and top foodie haunts in these parts include Heart Coffee Roasters, Güero, Screen Door, Tusk, Navarre, Alma Chocolate, PaaDee and Langbaan, Laurelhurst Market, Crema Coffee + Bakery, Fifty Licks, Ken's Artisan Pizza, and several others. **■TIP→ The neighborhood isn't close to any light-rail stops, but you can get here easily from Downtown via Bus 20, and street parking is free and pretty easy to find.** ✉ *E. Burnside St. from 22nd to 28th Aves., and 28th Ave. from N.E. Glisan to S.E. Stark Sts., East Burnside/28th Ave.*

The Grotto

RELIGIOUS SITE | Owned by the Catholic Church, the National Sanctuary of Our Sorrowful Mother, as it's officially known, displays more than 100 statues and shrines in 62 acres of woods that adjoin Rocky Butte Natural Area. The grotto was carved into the base of a 110-foot cliff, and has a replica of Michelangelo's *Pietà*. The real treat is found after ascending the cliff face via elevator, as you enter a wonderland of gardens, sculptures, and shrines, and a glass-walled cathedral with an awe-inspiring view of the Columbia River and the Cascades. There's a dazzling Christmas Festival of Lights (late November and December, $12.50), with 500,000 lights and more than 160 holiday concerts in the 500-seat chapel, and an indoor petting zoo. Daily masses are held here, too. **■TIP→ Hours can vary seasonally, so call ahead if visiting late in the day.** ✉ *8840 N.E. Skidmore St., Northeast* ✥ *Main entrance: N.E. Sandy Blvd. at N.E. 85th Ave.* ☎ *503/254–7371* 🌐 *www.thegrotto.org* 🎟 *Plaza level free; upper level $8.*

🍴 Restaurants

Aviary

$$$ | **ASIAN FUSION** | Eschewing many culinary conventions, this visionary Alberta Street eatery serves up innovative dishes that sometimes push boundaries but consistently succeed in flavor and execution. The simple menu of small plates (order two to three per person) is influenced by Asian flavors and uses European cooking techniques, combining unusual ingredients that offer pleasing contrasts in flavor and texture, such as crispy pig ears over mildly sweet coconut rice, and hoisin-glazed beef brisket with a macaroni salad croquette and sour mango powder. **Known for:** vegetarian tasting menu option; knowledgeable, helpful service; artfully presented food. [$] *Average main: $27* ✉ *1733 N.E. Alberta St., Alberta Arts District* ☎ *503/287–2400* 🌐 *www.aviarypdx.com* 🕒 *Closed Sun. No lunch.*

Beast

$$$$ | PACIFIC NORTHWEST | This meat-centric exemplar of Portland's cutting-edge culinary scene is the domain of James Beard Award–winning chef-owner Naomi Pomeroy, who oversees a six-course prix-fixe dinner (and three-course brunch on Sunday) that changes weekly, depending on the meat at the market. Most dishes are prepared right before your eyes in the open kitchen: there might be an ahi crudo with smoked pine nuts and pickled ginger, or Wagyu coulotte with pink peppercorn–cognac sauce. **Known for:** communal seating overlooking open kitchen; some of the most creative meat-centric food in the city; sublime Sunday brunch. [$] *Average main: $118* ✉ *5425 N.E. 30th Ave., Woodlawn/Concordia* ☎ *503/841–6968* 🌐 *www.beastpdx.com* 🕒 *Closed Mon. No lunch except Sun. brunch.*

★ Dóttir

$$ | SCANDINAVIAN | Iceland bumps happily into the Pacific Northwest in this Nordic restaurant inside the hip KEX hotel, where roasted cabbage has never tasted so heavenly (it's flavored with whey caramel and apple vinegar)—follow this, perhaps, with the hearty (designed for two or more to share) plate of loin, belly, braised shoulder, and sausage of lamb with spiced lentils. The warmly lighted, atmospheric seating in the dining room–cum–lobby is at tables or the long, elliptical bar, a space that encourages lingering and socializing over one of "Grandma Helga's" chocolate-butterscotch doughnuts with black cardamom sugar and a glass of Campari. **Known for:** fantastic, often veggie- and seafood-centric starters; cool, living room-esque vibe; several house-brewed craft ales. [$] *Average main: $22* ✉ *KEX Portland, 100 N.E. Martin Luther King Blvd., Central East Side* ☎ *971/346–2992* 🌐 *www.kexhotels.com.*

★ Gado Gado

$$ | INDONESIAN | Bold colors play a central role in the look and culinary approach of this trendy restaurant, from the tropical-print wallpaper to the ornately ornamented tableware, and above all else in the consistently delicious Indonesian fare. Roti with coconut-cream corn, braised-beef *rendang* with kumquats, and Coca-Cola clams steamed with chilies and lemongrass reflect the kitchen's creative and sometimes surprising interpretation of a cuisine that's gotten very little play in Portland until recently. **Known for:** family-style ($55 per person) "rice table" featuring a wide selection of chef favorites; whole wok-fried Dungeness crabs; weekend brunch with mimosas. [$] *Average main: $17* ✉ *1801 N.E. Cesar E. Chavez Blvd., Hollywood/Rose City Park* ☎ *503/206–8778* 🌐 *www.gadogadopdx.com* 🕒 *Closed Tues. No lunch weekdays.*

Güero

$ | MEXICAN | This casual but inviting counter-service Mexican eatery decorated with leafy plants and green-and-white Talavera tiles specializes in hefty tortas stuffed generously with chicken pibil, braised beef, carnitas, and plenty of flavorful accoutrements like habanero slaw and pickled onions. If you'd rather go breadless, you can customize a "cart bowl" using most of the torta ingredients. **Known for:** excellent mezcal and tequila list; esquites (corn sautéed chili and garlic and topped with lime mayonesa and cotija cheese); several vegetarian and vegan choices. [$] *Average main: $12* ✉ *200 N.E. 28th Ave., East Burnside/28th Ave.* ☎ *503/887–9258* 🌐 *www.guerotortas.com.*

★ Han Oak

$$$ | KOREAN | Begun as a pop-up and still with somewhat limited hours, this clean and contemporary space lined with shelves of beautiful plates, glassware, and cookbooks produces some of the most exciting Korean fare on the West Coast. The carefully plated food is arranged as artful vignettes, and everything bursts with flavor, from hand-cut noodle soups to Korean fried chicken wings. **Known for:** fresh-fruit "slushy" cocktails; communal seating (that's expanded to outside in summer); pork-and-chive dumplings. $ *Average main: $26 ⊠ 511 N.E. 24th Ave., Kerns ☎ 971/255-0032 ⊕ www.hanoakpdx.com ⊗ Closed Tues.–Thurs. No lunch.*

★ Hat Yai

$ | **THAI** | Operated by the acclaimed chef behind Langbaan and Eem, this cozy and casual counter-service eatery takes its name from a small Thai city near the Malaysian border and its concept from that region's spicy and delicious fried chicken with sticky rice and rich Malayu-style curries with panfried roti bread. Other treats here uncommon to Thai restaurant culture in the States include fiery turmeric curry with mussels and heady lemongrass oxtail soup. **Known for:** the roti dessert with condensed milk; perfectly crunchy free-range fried chicken; good selection of Asian beers. $ *Average main: $14 ⊠ 1605 N.E. Killingsworth St., Woodlawn/Concordia ☎ 503/764–9701 ⊕ www.hatyaipdx.com.*

Navarre

$$$ | **SPANISH** | It's easy to miss this intimate storefront space whose kitchen produces stellar Spanish, French, and Italian food, but don't miss it. The menu changes daily and specials are written in red ink on the front window and always include some sensational seasonal dishes, from a simple summery radish-and-sweet-pea salad to foie gras on cumin toast. **Known for:** more than 50 wines by the glass; sourcing many ingredients from a local CSA; western Mediterranean cuisine, often with Basque influences. $ *Average main: $24 ⊠ 10 N.E. 28th Ave., East Burnside/28th Ave. ☎ 503/232–3555 ⊕ www.navarreportland.com ⊗ No lunch weekdays.*

★ Ned Ludd

$$$ | **PACIFIC NORTHWEST** | Named for the founder of the Luddites, the group that resisted the technological advances of the Industrial Revolution, this Northwest-inspired kitchen prepares its food the most low-tech way possible: in a wood-burning brick oven, over an open flame. Sourcing most of its ingredients locally (or carefully, if they come from afar), Ned Ludd's menu varies completely depending on the season and weather, and the from-the-earth theme continues through to the decor, which incorporates salvaged wood, dried flowers, and small succulent plants under glass domes. **Known for:** whole roasted trout with charred leeks; nice selection of craft ciders; a $60 per person family-style dinner option that features some of the kitchen's most interesting food. $ *Average main: $27 ⊠ 3925 N.E. Martin Luther King Blvd., North Williams Ave. ☎ 503/288–6900 ⊕ www.nedluddpdx. com ⊗ No lunch.*

★ Ox Restaurant

$$$$ | **ARGENTINE** | Specializing in "Argentine-inspired Portland food," Ox is all about prime cuts of meat—along with flavorful garden-fresh side dishes—prepared to perfection. In a dimly lit dining room with hardwood floors, exposed brick walls, and a bar against the front window, the flannel-shirt-and-white-apron-clad waitstaff serves beef, lamb, pork, and fish dishes cooked over flames in a large, hand-cranked grill. **Known for:** the asado Argentino platter (lots of amazing meaty grills); creative side dishes, a few of which could make a full meal; vanilla tres leches cake dessert. $ *Average main: $36 ⊠ 2225 N.E. Martin Luther King Blvd., Lloyd District/Convention Center ☎ 503/284–3366 ⊕ www. oxpdx.com ⊗ No lunch.*

Pine State Biscuits

$ | **SOUTHERN** | Loosen your belt a notch or two before venturing inside this down-home Southern restaurant that's especially beloved for its over-the-top breakfast biscuit fare. Pat yourself on the back, or belly, if you can polish off the Reggie Deluxe (a fluffy house-baked biscuit topped with fried chicken, bacon, cheese, an egg, and sage gravy), a masterful mélange of calorie-laden ingredients, or the gut-busting smoked-brisket-club biscuit sandwich, shrimp and grits, and andouille corn dog featuring locally made Otto's sausage. **Known for:** made-from-scratch seasonal fruit pies; arguably the best food stall at the Portland Farmers Market; the massive Reggie Deluxe sandwich. $ *Average main: $9* ⊠ *2204 N.E. Alberta St., Alberta Arts District* ☎ *503/477–6605* ⊕ *www.pinestatebiscuits.com* ☽ *No dinner.*

Pizza Jerk

$$ | PIZZA | The red-checked tablecloths, Tiffany-style lamps, and simple decor of this pizza joint might not inspire high expectations, but just wait until you taste the blistered-crust East Coast–style pies and slices. You can build your own pizza selecting from a long list of ingredients, or choose one of the signature favorites, like the white pie with ricotta and garlic, or the dan dan with sweet pork, chili paste, and mustard greens. **Known for:** thin-crust and cast-iron deep-crust pizzas; adult "slushies"; soft-serve ice cream. $ *Average main: $18* ⊠ *5028 N.E. 42nd Ave., Woodlawn/Concordia* ☎ *503/284–9333* ⊕ *www.pizzajerkpdx.com.*

Podnah's Pit BBQ

$$ | BARBECUE | Firing up the smoker at 5 every morning, the pit crew at Podnah's spends the day slow cooking some of the best Texas- and Carolina-style barbecue in the Northwest, including melt-in-your-mouth, oak-smoked brisket, ribs, pulled pork, chicken, whole trout, and lamb, all served up in a sassy vinegar-based sauce. Some sides, like the delicious green-chili mac and cheese, rotate on and off the menu, but the collard greens, barbecue baked beans, and the iceberg wedge, topped with blue cheese and a punchy Thousand Island dressing, are excellent mainstays. **Known for:** green-chili mac and cheese (when available); daily specials (fried catfish on

Friday, smoked lamb on Thursday); casual and lively vibe. $ *Average main: $18* ⊠ *1625 N.E. Killingsworth St., Woodlawn/Concordia* ☎ *503/281–3700* ⊕ *www.podnahspit.com.*

★ Screen Door

$$ | SOUTHERN | The line that forms outside this Southern-cooking restaurant during weekend brunch and dinner is as epic as the food itself, but you can more easily score a table if you come for weekday breakfast or lunch; a spacious second location opened in the Pearl District in early 2020. A large, packed dining room with canned pickles and peppers along the walls, this Portland hot spot does justice to authentic Southern cooking, especially when it comes to the crispy buttermilk-battered fried chicken with creamy mashed potatoes and collard greens cooked in bacon fat. **Known for:** fried chicken (with waffles at breakfast or brunch); seasonal side dishes, from praline bacon to spiced zucchini fritters; banoffee pie with shortbread-pecan crust. $ *Average main: $20* ⊠ *2337 E. Burnside St., East Burnside/28th Ave.* ☎ *503/542–0880* ⊕ *www.screendoorrestaurant.com.*

★ Tamale Boy

$ | MEXICAN | Though the cooks at this lively counter-service restaurant are adept at preparing tamales—both the Oaxacan style wrapped in banana leaves and the more conventional style wrapped in corn husks (try the version filled with roasted pasilla peppers, onions, corn kernels, and queso fresco)—the kitchen also turns out fabulous ceviche and *alambre de camarones* (adobo shrimp with bacon and Oaxacan cheese over flat corn tortillas). Be sure to check out the colorful murals that decorate the space and don't miss the chance to dine on the spacious side patio. **Known for:** El Diablo margarita with roasted-habanero-infused tequila and mango puree; table-side guacamole; hearty and filling tamales. $ *Average main: $11* ⊠ *1764 N.E. Dekum St.,*

Woodlawn/Concordia ☎ 503/206–8022 ⊕ www.tamaleboy.com.

Toro Bravo

$$ | TAPAS | The success of this wildly popular and impressively authentic Spanish tapas bar has spawned a popular cookbook and helped spur chef-owner John Gorham to create a restaurant empire in Portland. This bustling spot with closely spaced tables and a lively vibe turns out sublime, share-friendly dishes like fried Spanish anchovies with fennel and lemon, and Ibérico sausage and braised cuttlefish in ink. **Known for:** "chef's choice for the table" menu; molten chocolate cake and other rich desserts; extensive sherry list. $ *Average main: $21* ⊠ *120 N.E. Russell St., North Williams Ave.* ☎ *503/281–4464* ⊕ *www. torobravopdx.com* ⊘ *No lunch.*

☕ Coffee and Quick Bites

★ Eb & Bean

$ | CAFÉ | Choosing your flavor of silky, premium frozen yogurt at this hip dessert café is relatively easy, as there are only a few flavors offered at any given time, unique though they often are (honey-grapefruit and mango lassi, for example). It's the formidable list of toppings that may leave you overwhelmed, albeit happily so, highlights of which include coconut-pecan cookie, organic sour fruity bears, marionberry compote, cold-brew bourbon sauce, and nondairy peanut butter magic shell. **Known for:** inventive dairy-based and vegan flavors; seasonal fruit toppings (figs, blueberries, etc.); made-from-scratch waffle cones. $ *Average main: $5* ⊠ *1425 N.E. Broadway St., Lloyd District/Convention Center* ☎ *503/281–6081* ⊕ *www.ebandbean. com.*

Guilder

$ | CAFÉ | Clean lines, natural light, and angular, modern tables (some communal) define the Scandinavian aesthetic of this bi-level café in the mostly residential—and quite picturesque—Alameda neighborhood, close to Beaumont's commercial strip. Drop by to work or socialize over cappuccinos or "freelancer" cocktails (espresso and fernet), or dig into a bowl of porridge, a fried egg and avocado sandwich, or a salad of roasted beets with a dill-chive yogurt dressing. **Known for:** tartines and sandwiches; a well-chosen mix of espresso drinks and cocktails; spacious, airy dining rooms well suited to work or conversation. $ *Average main: $9* ⊠ *2393 N.E. Fremont St., Beaumont* ☎ *503/841–6042* ⊕ *www.guildercafe.com.*

★ Proud Mary

$ | AUSTRALIAN | Launched in 2009 in Melbourne, Australia, this third-wave coffeehouse that sources its beans sustainably from around the world opened a U.S. location on Alberta Street in 2017. In this light-filled postindustrial space, you can savor perfectly prepared espresso drinks alongside tasty breakfast and lunch fare, such as Singapore chili crab omelets and grilled croissant brioches with cured ham, blackened corn, and poached egg. **Known for:** avocado and other breakfast toasts; healthy, inventive salads; flat whites. $ *Average main: $12* ⊠ *2012 N.E. Alberta St., Alberta Arts District* ☎ *503/208–3475* ⊕ *www.proudmarycoffee.com* ⊘ *No dinner.*

★ Salt & Straw Ice Cream

$ | CAFÉ | FAMILY | This artisanal ice-cream shop began here with this still always-packed café in the Alberta Arts District and continues to wow the public with its wildly inventive classics as well as seasonal flavors (freckled-chocolate zucchini bread and green fennel and maple are a couple of recent examples). Locally produced Woodblock chocolate bars and house-made salted-caramel sauce are among the toppings, and the related Wiz Bang Bar in Old Town's Pine Street Market offers delicious soft serve. **Known for:** strawberry-honey-balsamic ice cream with black pepper; monthly rotating specialty flavors; flavor collaborations with local chefs and restaurants. $ *Average main: $5* ⊠ *2035 N.E. Alberta St., Alberta Arts District* ☎ *971/208–3867* ⊕ *www.saltandstraw.com.*

 ## Hotels

Caravan–The Tiny House Hotel

$$ | B&B/INN | This cluster of itty-bitty custom-built houses-on-wheels offers visitors the chance to experience Portland's unabashed offbeat side. **Pros:** a quirky, only-in-Portland experience; in the heart of Alberta's hip retail-dining district; all units have kitchenettes. **Cons:** these houses really are tiny; 15-minute drive or 35-minute bus ride from Downtown; often books up weeks in advance (especially weekends). $ *Rooms from: $155* ⊠ *5009 N.E. 11th Ave., Alberta Arts District* ☎ *503/288–5225* ⊕ *www.tinyhouse-hotel.com* ⊷ *5 cottages* ⦿ *No meals.*

Hotel Eastlund

$$ | HOTEL | This mid-20th-century Lloyd District/Convention Center property with a handy location on the MAX line offers quick access across the river to Downtown, and stylish rooms outfitted with California king beds, smart-technology gadgetry, and airy bathrooms with smoked-glass walk-in showers. **Pros:** next to Moda Center, convention center, and light rail stop; fashionable rooms with plenty of high-tech perks; see-and-be-seen restaurant with dazzling skyline views. **Cons:** surrounding neighborhood lacks charm and interesting dining options; area can be noisy during conventions or Moda Center events; rooms are a little compact. $ *Rooms from: $189* ⊠ *1021 N.E. Grand Ave., Lloyd District/Convention Center* ☎ *503/235–2100* ⊕ *www.hoteleastlund.com* ⊷ *168 rooms* ⦿ *No meals.*

Hyatt Regency Portland

$$$$ | HOTEL | Opened in 2020 and by far the city's largest hotel, the swanky 600-room Hyatt is steps from the Oregon Convention Center and Moda Center arena, and its wealth of dining options, appealing common spaces, a great 24-hour fitness center, and other top-notch amenities make it a favorite of business travelers. **Pros:** convenient location by convention center, Moda Center, and light rail; great Downtown skyline views from many rooms; excellent, well-equipped fitness center. **Cons:** pricey, especially during conventions; surrounding neighborhood lacks character; giant size can make it feel a bit impersonal. $ *Rooms from: $339* ⊠ *375 N.E. Holliday St., Lloyd District/Convention Center* ☎ *971/222–1234* ⊕ *www.hyatt.com* ⊷ *600 rooms* ⦿ *No meals.*

★ KEX Portland

$ | HOTEL | Opened in fall 2019, the first U.S. outpost of the hip, design-driven Reykjavík hotel–hostel has been developed expressly with the aim of encouraging travelers and locals to mix and mingle together, whether in the inviting lobby-restaurant or with friends in the cedar sauna. **Pros:** cool Icelandic design; hip bar and restaurant; reasonably priced. **Cons:** many rooms are bunk-style and share bathrooms; the very social vibe isn't for everyone; no on-site parking. $ *Rooms from: $140* ⊠ *100 N.E. Martin Luther King Blvd., Central East Side* ☎ *971/346–2992* ⊕ *www.kexportland.com* ⊷ *29 rooms* ⦿ *No meals.*

★ McMenamins Kennedy School

$ | HOTEL | FAMILY | In a renovated elementary school near Northeast Portland's trendy Alberta District, Oregon's famously creative McMenamin brothers hoteliers created a quirky and fantastical multiuse facility with guest rooms that feature original schoolhouse touches like chalkboards and cloakrooms and literature-inspired themes, a movie theater, a restaurant, a warm outdoor soaking pool, a brewery, and several small bars. **Pros:** funky and authentic Portland experience; room rates include movies and use of year-round soaking pool; free parking.

Cons: rooms have showers but no tubs; no TVs in rooms; 20-minute drive or 40-minute bus ride from Downtown. [$] *Rooms from: $145* ✉ *5736 N.E. 33rd Ave., Northeast* ☎ *503/249–3983, 888/249–3983* 🌐 *www.mcmenamins.com/kennedy-school* 🛏 *57 rooms* 🍴 *No meals.*

Portland's White House Bed and Breakfast
$$ | B&B/INN | Hardwood floors with Oriental rugs, chandeliers, antiques, and fountains create a warm and romantic mood at this lavish 1910 Greek Revival mansion in the historic Irvington District, where guests can gather in several common areas and stroll the landscaped gardens. **Pros:** over-the-top romantic; outstanding breakfasts included in the rates; a short drive or bus ride to several hip East Side restaurant and retail districts. **Cons:** in residential neighborhood 2 miles from Downtown; nearest commercial area is the rather bland Lloyd District; older house with some quirky details. [$] *Rooms from: $200* ✉ *1914 N.E. 22nd Ave., Northeast* ☎ *503/287–7131* 🌐 *www.portlandswhitehouse.com* 🛏 *8 suites* 🍴 *Free breakfast.*

Nightlife

BARS AND LOUNGES

The Bye and Bye
BARS/PUBS | An Alberta go-to specializing in creative drinks (sample the house favorite, the Bye and Bye, a refreshing concoction of peach vodka, peach bourbon, lemon, cranberry juice, and soda served in a Mason jar) and vegan fare, Bye and Bye has a big covered patio and a festive dining room. The owners also operate several other similarly trendy bars around town, including Century Bar, Dig a Pony, Sweet Hereafter, and Jackknife. ✉ *1011 N.E. Alberta St., Alberta Arts District* ☎ *503/281–0537* 🌐 *www.thebyeandbye.com.*

★ Expatriate
BARS/PUBS | Operated by Kyle Webster and his wife, celeb-chef partner Naomi Pomeroy of Beast (across the street), this intimate, candlelit spot has a devoted following for its balanced, boozy cocktails and addictively delicious Asian bar snacks, like Burmese curried noodles. Each of the eight nightly cocktails are meticulously crafted. ✉ *5424 N.E. 30th Ave., Woodlawn/Concordia* ☎ *503/805–3750* 🌐 *www.expatriatepdx.com.*

Hale Pele
BARS/PUBS | The riotously colorful lighting and kitschy retro-Polynesian decor of this island-inspired tiki bar creates the ideal setting for sipping tropical cocktails like the fruity Volcano Bowl (which serves two to three) or the potent Zombie Punch. The crab Rangoon dip and lumpia spring rolls are highlights among the small plates. ✉ *2733 N.E. Broadway, Lloyd District/Convention Center* ☎ *503/662–8454* 🌐 *www.halepele.com.*

Wonderly
BARS/PUBS | This dapper yet unpretentious neighborhood lounge anchored by a horseshoe-shaped bar is known for its generously poured "martini-and-a-half" and "Manhattan-and-a-half" cocktails, which are sure to calm your nerves after a long day. Folks also pile in for arguably the best bar food in Beaumont—the seared scallop with an egg, beet puree, and capers is a standout. ✉ *4727 N.E. Fremont St., Beaumont* ☎ *503/288–4520* 🌐 *www.wonderlypdx.com.*

BREWPUBS AND MICROBREWERIES

Culmination Brewing
BREWPUBS/BEER GARDENS | A bit cozier and neighborhood-y than many of Portland's brewpubs, Culmination is set inside a sustainably designed building with a dog-friendly patio in the Kerns neighborhood. It's a favorite of serious beer aficionados, always featuring at least 20 taps of often creative limited-release brews, including barrel-aged sours,

heady barleywines, and beers produced in collaboration with other craft labels around town. ✉ *2117 N.E. Oregon St., Kerns* ☎ *971/254–9114* ⊕ *www.culminationbrewing.com.*

 Performing Arts

PERFORMANCE VENUES
Moda Center
MUSIC | This 20,000-seat facility is home to the Portland Trail Blazers basketball team and the site of other sporting events and rock concerts. It's right on the MAX light rail line, just across from Downtown. ✉ *1 N. Center Ct., Lloyd District/Convention Center* ☎ *503/235–8771* ⊕ *www.rosequarter.com.*

FILM
★ Hollywood Theatre
FILM | A landmark movie theater that showed silent films when it opened in 1926, the not-for-profit Hollywood Theatre screens everything from obscure foreign art films to old American classics and second-run Hollywood hits, and hosts an annual Academy Awards viewing party. It also hosts a slew of film series and festivals, including the QDoc LGBTQ documentary film festival, the Grindhouse Film Festival, the Northwest Animation Festival, the Portland Latin American Film Festival, and POW, which showcases top women directors. ✉ *4122 N.E. Sandy Blvd., Hollywood/Rose City Park* ☎ *503/281–4215* ⊕ *www.hollywoodtheatre.org.*

 Shopping

CLOTHING AND ACCESSORIES
Cosube
CLOTHING | It might surprise you just how popular surfing is among Portlanders, but a visit to any of the major wave-producing beaches along the Oregon Coast— such as Oswald West State Park and Pacific City—will show you otherwise. This well-stocked shop inside one of Portland's most architecturally noteworthy new buildings carries everything you need for a day of cold-water surfing, plus stylish beach apparel, sunglasses, and skin lotions. You can also rent boards, wet suits, and gear, or take a lesson on how to shape your own board. Even if you're not looking for gear, stop by the shop's hip café, which serves Coava coffee, plus teas and light snacks. ✉ *111 N.E. Martin Luther King Blvd., Central East Side* ☎ *971/229–4206* ⊕ *www.cosube.com.*

pedX Shoe Shangri-La
SHOES/LUGGAGE/LEATHER GOODS | The fashion-savvy owners of this cool footwear emporium in a sleek contemporary showroom on Alberta opened in 2003 with a mission to bring urbane women's shoes and accessories to outer Northeast Portland. Here you'll find sturdy boots, sensible flats, and swanky pumps from brands like Camper, El Naturalista, Miz Mooz, and Vagabond, plus an extensive selection of jewelry, sunglasses, handbags, and other accents. ✉ *2005 N.E. Alberta St., Alberta Arts District* ☎ *503/460–0760* ⊕ *www.pedxshoes.com.*

FOOD
Alma Chocolate
FOOD/CANDY | What began as a modest table at Portland's farmers' market has grown into a nationally celebrated artisanal chocolate shop that takes great pride is sourcing just about every ingredient but the cacao locally, from the almonds and fruit in the fig-marzipan candies to the nuts and sea salt in the vegan hazelnut pralines. In the flagship shop on Northeast 28th, you can also munch on fresh-baked cookies and cakes, pick up jars of house-made caramel, and sip tea, espresso, and drinking chocolates. ✉ *140 N.E. 28th Ave., East Burnside/28th Ave.* ☎ *503/517–0262* ⊕ *www.almachocolate.com.*

Providore Fine Foods
FOOD/CANDY | This sleek gourmet market features the artisanal and local fare of several notable Portland purveyors,

including Little T Baker, Rubinette Produce, Arrosto (which turns out delicious Mediterranean-style rotisserie chicken), and Pastaworks, plus a lovely flower shop. It's a terrific source for picnic supplies, and there's table seating. ⊠ *2340 N.E. Sandy Blvd., Kerns* ☏ *503/232–1010* ⊕ *www.providorefinefoods.com.*

GALLERIES
Ampersand Gallery & Fine Books
ART GALLERIES | Part art gallery, part media store, this minimalist white-wall space on Alberta Street has monthly shows featuring edgy, contemporary art, and stocks a fascinating trove of photography and art books, vintage travel brochures, curious photography, pulp-fiction novels, and other printed materials of the sort you might find in a chest in a mysterious neighbor's attic. The owners also operate the cute Cord boutique next door, which stocks artfully designed household goods, from handcrafted soaps to aerodynamic coffeepots. ⊠ *2916 N.E. Alberta St., Alberta Arts District* ☏ *503/805–5458* ⊕ *www.ampersandgallerypdx.com.*

★ Last Thursdays on Alberta
ART GALLERIES | FAMILY | The Alberta Arts District hosts an arts walk on the last Thursday of each month. This quirky procession along 15 blocks of one of the city's favorite thoroughfares for browsing art galleries, distinctive boutiques, and hipster bars and restaurants features street performers and buskers, crafts makers, and food vendors. During the three summer events, from June through August, the street is closed to traffic from 6 to 9 pm, and many more arts and crafts vendors show their work. ⊠ *N.E. Alberta St. and N.E. 22nd Ave., Alberta Arts District.*

HOUSEHOLD GOODS AND FURNITURE
★ Crafty Wonderland
CRAFTS | Although the Alberta branch of this whimsically named arts and crafts gallery is smaller than the original Downtown location, it still showcases the handmade cards, books, apparel, jewelry, household goods, and toys of more than 60 carefully selected makers. Crafty Wonderland also hosts two huge annual markets, featuring works by about 250 artists, in May and December at the Oregon Convention Center. ⊠ *2022 N.E. Alberta St., Alberta Arts District* ☏ *503/281–4616* ⊕ *www.craftywonderland.com.*

JEWELRY
★ Grayling Jewelry
JEWELRY/ACCESSORIES | All of the locally made pieces at this friendly boutique have been carefully and exquisitely designed with sensitive skin in mind—every piece is nickel-free. The simply elegant lariat necklaces, chain-cuff earrings, and wrap rings are done mostly in silver and gold and displayed in a clean, unobtrusive storefront on Alberta Street. ⊠ *1609 N.E. Alberta St., Alberta Arts District* ☏ *503/548–4979* ⊕ *www.graylingjewelry.com.*

 Activities

BASKETBALL
Portland Trail Blazers
BASKETBALL | The NBA's Portland Trail Blazers play their 82-game season—with half the games at home—in the Moda Center, which can hold up to 20,000 spectators. The MAX train pulls up just a couple of blocks from the arena's front door. ⊠ *Moda Center, 1 N. Center Ct., Rose Quarter, Lloyd District/Convention Center* ☏ *503/797–9600* ⊕ *www.nba.com/blazers.*

Southeast

Vibrant pockets of foodie-minded eateries, craft cocktail bars, and funky indie boutiques make the closer-in sections of Southeast, especially the formerly industrial Central East Side, a must-visit. You'll also find the funky commercial sections of Hawthorne, Division, and Belmont west of the 30th Avenue in this part of town, as well as the family-popular OMSI science museum and Tilikum Crossing Bridge. As you move farther east and south, you'll discover beautiful Mt. Tabor Park and up-and-coming Montavilla and Foster-Powell, which is also where you'll find sizable Asian and Latino communities. To the south, the historic and mostly residential neighborhoods of Sellwood and Moreland contain a smattering of notable shops as well as some pretty parks.

Sights

★ Central East Side

NEIGHBORHOOD | This expansive 681-acre tract of mostly industrial and commercial buildings was largely ignored by all but local workers until shops, galleries, and restaurants began opening in some of the neighborhood's handsome, high-ceilinged buildings beginning in the 1990s. These days, it's a legitimately hot neighborhood for shopping and coffee-house-hopping by day, and dining and bar-going at night, and a slew of high-end apartment buildings have added a residential component to the Central East Side. The neighborhood lies just across the Willamette River from Downtown—it extends along the riverfront from the Burnside Bridge south to the Oregon Museum of Science and Industry (OMSI) and Division Street, extending east about a dozen blocks to S.E. 12th Avenue. Businesses of particular note in these parts include urban-chic coffeehouses (Water Avenue, Coava), breweries (Base Camp Brewing, Cascade Brewing Barrel House, Modern Times, Wayfinder Beer), shops and galleries, and restaurants (Kachka, Le Pigeon, Revelry, Afuri). In the past few years, a number of acclaimed craft distilleries and urban wineries have joined the mix. This is a large neighborhood, and some streets are a bit desolate (though still quite safe). If you're coming by car, street parking is becoming tougher with all the new development but still possible to find, especially on quieter side streets. ✉ *Willamette River to S.E. 12th Ave. from Burnside to Division Sts., Central East Side* ⟷ *Reachable via the East Side Streetcar, walking from Downtown, or taking any of several buses across the Hawthorne or Burnside bridges* ⊕ *www. ceic.cc.*

Crystal Springs Rhododendron Garden

GARDEN | FAMILY | For much of the year, this nearly 10-acre retreat near Reed College is frequented mainly by bird-watchers and those who want a restful stroll. But starting in April, thousands of rhododendron bushes and azaleas burst into flower, attracting visitors in larger numbers. The peak blooming season for these woody shrubs is May; by late June the show is over. ✉ *5801 S.E. 28th Ave., Sellwood/Moreland* ☎ *503/771–8386* ⊕ *www.portlandoregon.gov/parks* ✉ *$5 Apr.–Sept., Tues.–Sun.; otherwise free.*

★ Division Street

NEIGHBORHOOD | Back in the early 1970s, Division Street (aka "Southeast Division") was earmarked for condemnation as part of a proposed—and thankfully never built—freeway that would have connected Downtown to Mt. Hood. For many years, this street sat forlornly, just a long stretch of modest buildings and empty lots. These days, Southeast Division—no longer threatened with condemnation—is one of the hottest restaurant rows on the West Coast, and sleek three- and four-story contemporary condos and apartments are popping up like dandelions. If culinary tourism is your thing, head to the 10 blocks of Southeast Division from about 30th to 39th Avenues, where you'll find such darlings of the culinary scene as Pok Pok, Ava Gene's, Bollywood Theater, Olympia Provisions Public House, an outpost of Salt & Straw ice cream, Little T bakery, Lauretta Jean's, and several others. The main draw here is mostly food-and-drink related; there are several great bars, and the excellent Oui!

Wine Bar at SE Wine Collective urban winery. You'll also find a growing number of other noteworthy restaurants and bars extending all the way to 12th Avenue to the west, and 50th Avenue to the east. As well as "Division" and "Southeast Division," you may hear some locals refer to the western end of the neighborhood as "Division/Clinton" referring to Clinton Street, a block south of Division, where you will find lovely early- to mid-20th-century bungalows and houses and a few noteworthy eateries (Broder, La Moule, Magna Kusina, Jaqueline), mostly from 27th to 20th Avenue. ⊠ *S.E. Division St., and parts of S.E. Clinton St., from 12th to 50th Aves., Division/Clinton ✢ Bus 2 crosses the Hawthorne Bridge from Downtown and continues along Division Street; there's also free street parking, although increased development has made it a bit harder to find* ⊕ *www. divisionstreetportland.com.*

Freakybuttrue Peculiarium and Museum
MUSEUM | Portland doesn't get much weirder than this oddball museum packed full of macabre kitsch, science-fiction ephemera, and handmade exhibits on such oddities as zombie brains and alien autopsies. You're encouraged to come in costume (free entry if your outfit impresses the cashier) and snap plenty of selfies. In the shop, peruse gag gifts and tacky souvenirs, and wave farewell to the giant Bigfoot statue on your way out. ⊠ *640 S.E. Stark St., Central East Side* ☎ *503/227–3164* ⊕ *www.peculiarium.com* ⊠ *$5* ☉ *Closed Tues.*

★ Hawthorne District
NEIGHBORHOOD | Stretching from the foot of Mt. Tabor to S.E. 12th Avenue (where you'll find a terrific little food-cart pod), with some blocks far livelier than others, this eclectic commercial thoroughfare was at the forefront of Portland's hippie and LGBTQ scenes in the 1960s and 1970s. As the rest of Portland's East Side has become more urbane and popular among hipsters, young families,

students, and the so-called creative class over the years, Hawthorne has retained an arty, homegrown flavor. An influx of trendy eateries and retailers opening alongside the still-colorful and decidedly low-frills thrift shops and old-school taverns and cafés makes for a hodgepodge of styles and personalities—you could easily spend an afternoon popping in and out of boutiques, and then stay for happy hour at a local nightspot or even later for dinner. Highlights include a small (but still impressive) branch of Powell's Books, House of Vintage emporium, Bagdad Theater, Farmhouse Kitchen Thai, Apizza Scholls, OK Omens wine bar, and the Sapphire Hotel lounge. ⊠ *S.E. Hawthorne Blvd., between S.E. 12th and S.E. 50th Aves., Hawthorne ✢ Bus 14 runs from Downtown along the length of Hawthorne, and there's plenty of free street parking* ⊕ *www.thinkhawthorne.com.*

Laurelhurst Park
CITY PARK | **FAMILY** | Completed in 1914 by Emanuel Mische, who trained with the iconic Olmsted Brothers landscaping design firm, resplendent Laurelhurst Park's hundred-year-old trees and winding, elegant paths are evocative of another time, and may trigger an urge to don a parasol. Listed on the National Register of Historic Places, Laurelhurst offers plentiful trails, playgrounds, tennis courts, soccer fields, horseshoe pits, an off-leash area for dogs, a serene pond with ducks, and many sunny and shady picnic areas. Take a stroll around the large spring-fed pond and keep an eye out for blue heron, the city's official bird. On the south side of this 31-acre park is one of the busiest basketball courts in town. Though the park is always beautiful, it is especially so in fall. The trendy dining and café culture of East Burnside and 28th and Belmont Street are within walking distance. ⊠ *S.E. 39th Ave. and S.E. Stark St., Southeast* ⊕ *www.portlandoregon. gov/parks.*

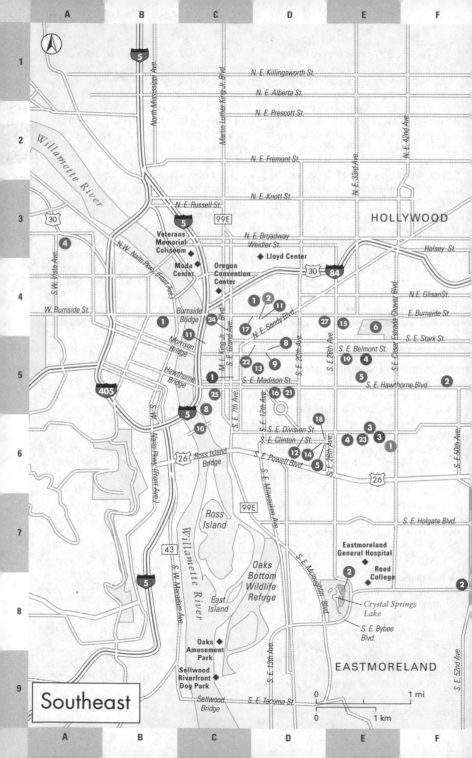

Southeast

TO AIRPORT ↗

Sights ▼

1 Central East Side **D4**
2 Crystal Springs
  Rhododendron
  Garden **E8**
3 Division Street **G6**
4 Freakybuttrue
  Peculiarium
  and Museum **A3**
5 Hawthorne District **E5**
6 Laurelhurst Park **E4**
7 Mt. Tabor Park **G5**
8 Oregon Museum
  of Science
  and Industry.............. **C5**
9 Portland Mercado **H7**
10 Tilikum Crossing
  Bridge...................... **C6**
11 Westward
  Whiskey.................. **C5**

Restaurants ▼

1 Afuri Ramen **B4**
2 Apizza Scholls........... **F5**
3 Ava Gene's................ **E6**
4 Bollywood Theater **E6**
5 Broder..................... **D6**
6 Cheese Bar.............. **G5**
7 Coquine **G5**
8 Delores.................... **D5**
9 Farm Spirit.............. **D5**
10 Ha & VL **H6**
11 Hey Love **D4**
12 Jacqueline............... **D6**
13 Kachka.................... **D5**
14 La Moule................. **D6**
15 Langbaan **E4**
16 Lardo **D5**
17 Le Pigeon **D4**
18 Magna Kusina........... **D6**
19 Nodoguro................. **E5**
20 The Observatory **H4**
21 OK Omens **D5**
22 Pepper Box Cafe........ **D5**
23 Pok Pok **E6**
24 Revelry................... **C4**
25 Stacked
  Sandwich Shop.......... **C5**
26 Tierra del Sol **H7**
27 Tusk **D4**

Quick Bites ▼

1 Coava Coffee
  Roasters **C5**
2 Heart Coffee............. **F8**
3 Lauretta Jean's........... **E6**
4 The Tao of Tea........... **E5**

Hotels ▼

1 Evermore
  Guesthouse.............. **E6**
2 Jupiter NEXT **D4**

N. E. Cully Blvd.

205

N. E. Sandy Blvd.

84

S. E. 60th Ave.

205

S. E. Yamill St.

6
7
7

Mt. Tabor
Park

3 S. E. Division St.

10

S. E. Powell Blvd.

26
9

S. E. Foster Rd.

Lents
Park

S. E. Woodstock Blvd.

205

S. E. 72nd Ave.
S. E. 82nd Ave.

20

KEY

1 Sights
1 Restaurants
1 Quick Bites
1 Hotels

★ **Mt. Tabor Park**

NATIONAL/STATE PARK | FAMILY | A playground on top of a volcano cinder cone? Yup, that's here. The cinders, or glassy rock fragments, unearthed in this 190-acre park's construction were used to surface the respite's roads; the ones leading to the very top are closed to cars, but popular with cyclists. They're also popular with cruisers—each August there's an old-fashioned soapbox derby. Picnic tables and tennis, basketball, and volleyball courts make Mt. Tabor Park a popular spot for outdoor recreation, but plenty of quiet, shaded trails and wide-open grassy lawns with panoramic views of the Downtown skyline appeal to sunbathers, hikers, and nature lovers. The whole park is closed to cars on Wednesday. ■TIP➔ **Just down the hill on the west side of Mt. Tabor, you'll find the lively cafés and restaurants of the hip Hawthorne District.** ✉ S.E. 60th Ave. and S.E. Salmon St., Mt. Tabor ⊕ www.portlandoregon. gov/parks.

★ **Oregon Museum of Science and Industry** (OMSI)

MUSEUM | FAMILY | Hundreds of engaging exhibits draw families to this outstanding interactive science museum, which also contains the Empirical Theater (featuring Portland's biggest screen), and the Northwest's largest planetarium. The many permanent and touring exhibits are loaded with enough hands-on play for kids to fill a whole day exploring robotics, ecology, rockets, animation, and outer space. Moored in the Willamette River as part of the museum is a 240-foot submarine, the USS *Blueback,* which can be toured for an extra charge. OMSI also offers some very cool event programming for adults, including the hugely popular monthly OMSI After Dark nights, where "science nerds" can enjoy food, drink, and science fun, and the twice-monthly OMSI Science Pub nights, where local and national experts lecture on a wide range of topics in the museum's Empirical Theater. ■TIP➔ **OMSI's excellent**

restaurant, Theory, open for lunch, offers great views of the Willamette River and Downtown skyline, and Empirical Café is a great stop for a light bite or drink. ✉ 1945 S.E. Water Ave., Central East Side ☎ 503/797–4000, 800/955–6674 ⊕ www. omsi.edu ✉ Museum $15, planetarium $7.50, Empirical Theater Show $8.50, submarine $7.50, parking $5 ⊗ Closed Mon. early Sept.–early Mar.

★ **Portland Mercado**

MARKET | This colorful and community-driven complex of indoor and outdoor food stalls and markets, flanked by a row of picnic tables, is Portland's own little Latin America with business owners from Mexico, Brazil, Cuba, Venezuela, and elsewhere throughout Central and South America. A great destination for eating and socializing, the colorfully painted Mercado is also a business incubator that helps Latin American entrepreneurs thrive both here and throughout Portland, and it's a thriving anchor of the diverse Foster Powell neighborhood. Be sure to step inside the central interior space to view displays with facts and historic photos about the city's and region's Latin American community. Vendor highlights include Sandino Coffee Roasters, Kaah Neighborhood Market, Tierra del Sol (Oaxacan), Que Bola (Cuban), and Barrio neighborhood bar. ✉ 7238 S.E. Foster Rd., Foster/Powell ☎ 971/200–0581 ⊕ www.portlandmercado.org.

★ **Tilikum Crossing Bridge**

BRIDGE/TUNNEL | Downtown Portland's collection of striking bridges gained a new member in 2015 with the opening of this sleek, cable-stayed bridge a few steps from Oregon Museum of Science and Industry (OMSI). Nicknamed "the Bridge of the People," the Tilikum is unusual in that it's the largest car-free bridge in the country—it's open only to public transit (MAX trains, buses, and streetcars), bikes, and pedestrians. The 1,720-foot-long bridge connects Southeast Portland with the South Waterfront district and

Tilikum Crossing Bridge is the country's largest car-free bridge, meaning it's only open to public transit, bikes, and pedestrians.

rewards those who stroll or cycle across it with impressive skyline views. ⊠ *Tilikum Crossing, Southeast ⊹ Eastbank Esplanade just south of OMSI on the East Side, and S.W. Moody Ave. in South Waterfront.*

Westward Whiskey

WINERY/DISTILLERY | One of the stalwarts of Distillery Row, this highly respected outfit (formerly known as House Spirits) opened in 2004 and now occupies this spacious 14,000-square-foot facility. It's earned international acclaim for its Aviation American Gin (which it has since sold to Davos Brands) and Krogstad Festlig Aquavit. Other favorites include Westward American Single Malt Whiskey, made with locally sourced barley, and Casa Magdalena Rum. In the cozy tasting room, you can also browse a fine selection of barware, books, and other booze-related gifts. Tours are offered every afternoon, but weekends are busy, so best to reserve a spot in advance. There's an additional tasting room at Portland International Airport. ■**TIP→ If**

you plan to check out a few of the spots on Distillery Row, be sure to order a Distillery Row Passport or download the app, which gives credit toward tastings and tours and discounts at a number of restaurants, hotels, and shops around the city. ⊠ *65 S.E. Washington St., Central East Side* ☎ *503/235–3174* ⊕ *www.westwardwhiskey.com.*

 Restaurants

★ Afuri Ramen

$$ | **RAMEN** | When the acclaimed Japanese ramen chain Afuri decided to open an outpost in the United States in 2016, it chose this modern, high-ceilinged dining room in food-obsessed Portland in part because the exacting culinary team appreciated the city's pristine, glacially fed water supply, which plays a significant part in the steaming, savory portions of *yuzu shio* (with chicken broth, yuzu citrus, shimeji mushrooms, seasoned egg, chashu, endive, and nori), one of a half dozen deeply satisfying ramen bowls. The kitchen also turns out flavorful skewers of shishito peppers and chicken thighs, pork dumplings, sushi, and other izakaya-style fare, all of it consistently exceptional. **Known for:** authentic Japanese ramen; meat and veggie skewers; flights of premium sake. $ *Average main: $18* ⊠ *923 S.E. 7th Ave., Central East Side* ☎ *503/468–5001* ⊕ *www.afuri.us.*

Apizza Scholls

$$ | PIZZA | The pies at Apizza Scholls, which have been lauded by Anthony Bourdain, Rachael Ray, and thousands of everyday pizza lovers, deserve the first-class reputation they enjoy. The greatness of the pies rests not in innovation or complexity, but in the simple quality of the ingredients, such as dough made by hand in small batches and baked to crispy-outside, tender-inside perfection and toppings—including basil, pecorino romano, and house-cured bacon—that are fresh and delicious. **Known for:** interesting beer list; the bacon bianca pizza (white, with no sauce); occasionally long waits for a table (reservations are a good idea). $ *Average main: $18* ⊠ *4741 S.E. Hawthorne Blvd., Hawthorne* ☎ *503/233–1286* ⊕ *www.apizzascholls.com* ☉ *No lunch weekdays.*

★ Ava Gene's

$$$$ | MODERN ITALIAN | This highly acclaimed Roman-inspired Italian eatery—with a buzzy dining room with a vaulted ceiling and two long rows of banquette seats—ranks among the top tables in town both in popularity and quality. The menu emphasizes regional, home-style recipes from throughout Italy, but focuses on local produce—you could make an impressive feast of three or four *giardini* (gardens) sides, such as melon with tomatillos, ground cherries, and prosciutto, while the satisfyingly hearty mains might include tagliatelle with chicken ragù or lamb grilled with artichokes and celery root. **Known for:** flatbreads with creative toppings; a top-notch cocktail and wine program; $85 per person family-style "chef's selection"

option. $ *Average main: $32* ⊠ *3377 S.E. Division St., Division/Clinton* ☎ *971/229–0571* ⊕ *www.avagenes.com* ☉ *No lunch weekdays.*

Bollywood Theater

$ | INDIAN | Set beneath a soaring beamed ceiling, and with a welcoming mix of worn wooden seating, kitschy decor, bright fabrics, and intoxicating smells, this lively restaurant along Division Street's hoppin' restaurant row specializes in Indian street food. Order at the counter, and your food—perhaps *vada pav* (spicy potato dumplings with chutney), *gobi* Manchurian (Indo-Chinese fried cauliflower with lemon, curry leaves, and sweet-and-sour sauce), or Goan-style shrimp served with a full complement of chutneys, paratha bread, and dal—will be brought out to you. **Known for:** delicious breads and vegetable side dishes; small Indian gourmet market with spices and curries; mango lassi. $ *Average main: $14* ⊠ *3010 S.E. Division St., Division/Clinton* ☎ *503/477–6699* ⊕ *www.bollywoodtheaterpdx.com.*

★ Broder

$ | SCANDINAVIAN | This adorable neighborhood café—one of the most outstanding brunch spots in town—serves fresh and delicious Scandinavian food with fun-to-pronounce names like *friterade applen* (apple fritter) and *aebleskivers* (Danish pancakes). All the food—the hashes, *lefse* potato crepes, the baked egg scrambles, the Swedish breakfast boards—is delicious, with the Swedish meatballs in sherry cream sauce and salmon fish cakes with caraway vinaigrette being especially tasty among the midday choices. **Known for:** light-filled dining room with rustic-modern furniture; often long waits for a table, especially for breakfast; the largest selection of aquavit in the western United States. $ *Average main: $13* ⊠ *2508 S.E. Clinton St., Division/Clinton* ☎ *503/736–3333* ⊕ *www.broderpdx.com* ☉ *No dinner.*

Cheese Bar

$ | CAFÉ | For years, many of Portland's top restaurateurs have sourced their cheese from nationally renowned cheesemonger Steve Jones, who operates this casual fromagerie near Mt. Tabor Park that functions both as a specialty cheese market and neighborhood bistro. Try the "stinky board" to sample two strong cheeses of the day with crostini. **Known for:** hard-to-find imported and local cheeses (to go or dine-in); an extensive selection of beers, wines, and aperitifs; cheese and charcuterie boards. $ *Average main: $10* ✉ *6031 S.E. Belmont St., Mt. Tabor* ☎ *503/222–6014* ⊕ *www.cheese-bar.com* ⊙ *Closed Mon.*

★ Coquine

$$$ | FRENCH | A sunny neighborhood café serving brunch daily, Coquine blossoms into a romantic, sophisticated French–Pacific Northwest bistro in the evening. Early in the day, sup on sourdough pancakes with huckleberry compote, or black cod–based fisherman's stew with garlic toast, while in the evening, you might encounter pappardelle noodles with pork ragu or roasted whole chicken padron peppers, sungold tomatoes, pole beans, and pickled red onion. **Known for:** four- and seven-course tasting menus (with optional wine pairings); a dim sum–style candy tray offered during the dessert course; cheerful setting near Mt. Tabor. $ *Average main: $27* ✉ *6839 S.E. Belmont St., Mt. Tabor* ☎ *503/384–2483* ⊕ *www.coquinepdx.com* ⊙ *No dinner Mon. and Tues.*

★ Delores

$$ | POLISH | Former *Top Chef* contestant BJ Smith, who established himself as one of Portland's premier barbecue chefs, runs this modern take on Polish food—a tribute to his late mom, for whom the restaurant is named. Many of the artfully plated dishes here showcase Smith's talent for grilling, including smoked kielbasa hash (a brunch favorite) and chicken-fried rabbit with mustard

cream, but you'll also discover ethereal plates of stuffed cabbage rolls and *kopytka* (Polish gnocchi with corn puree and pickled shallots). **Known for:** duck-confit pierogis; Monday family-style ($25 per person) Marczewski Night with polka and traditional Polish food (named in honor of the owner's grandmother); weekend brunch. $ *Average main: $20* ✉ *1401 S.E. Morrison St., Belmont* ☎ *503/231–3609* ⊕ *www.delorespdx.com* ⊙ *Closed Mon. No lunch weekdays.*

★ Farm Spirit

$$$$ | VEGETARIAN | Dinners at this chef-driven vegan restaurant are truly an event—in fact, admission to these several-course repasts, which you can experience at your own table in the dining room or at a lively communal counter (this choice is a bit pricier but includes more courses) overlooking the kitchen, is by advance ticket purchase only. The highly inventive menu changes daily but utilizes about 95% Northwest ingredients and might feature delicata squash with smoked pumpkinseed or fire-roasted plums with oat cream and rosemary. **Known for:** interesting wine, beer, and juice flights; no-tipping policy; nut- and gluten-free menus by advance notice. $ *Average main: $89* ✉ *1403 S.E. Belmont St., Belmont* ☎ *971/255–0329* ⊕ *www.farmspiritpdx.com* ⊙ *Closed Sun.–Tues. No lunch.*

★ Ha & VL

$ | VIETNAMESE | This humble, no-frills banh mi shop amid the many cheap and authentic Asian restaurants on S.E. 82nd stands out not just for its filling sandwiches (these crispy-bread creations come with fillings like spicy Chinese sausage, pork meat loaf, or sardines) but also for the daily featured soup, such as peppery pork-ball noodle soup on Wednesday and Vietnamese turmeric soup, with shrimp cake and sliced pork, on Sunday. There's also a diverse selection of thick milk shakes—top flavors include avocado, mango, and durian. **Known for:** milk shakes in unusual flavors; pork-ball noodle soup (on Wednesday only); barbecue pork loin banh mi sandwiches. $ *Average main: $9* ⊠ *2738 S.E. 82nd Ave., No. 102, Montavilla/82nd Ave.* ☎ *503/772–0103* ⊘ *Closed Tues. No dinner.*

★ Hey Love

$$ | ASIAN FUSION | The food-and-drink component of the stylish Jupiter Next hotel has quickly become one of the East Side's hottest destinations for hobnobbing over drinks and creative bar fare, much of it—salmon poke, Wagyu steak fajitas—framed around Asian and Latin American elements. The space is adorned with hanging and potted greenery and Oriental rugs, which provide a decidedly funky aesthetic. **Known for:** fried chicken chow mein; late-night dining and people-watching; a cast-iron macadamia nut–white chocolate cookie with coconut caramel and sea-salt ice cream. $ *Average main: $19* ⊠ *920 E. Burnside St., Central East Side* ☎ *503/206–6223* ⊕ *www.heylovepdx.com.*

Jacqueline

$$$ | SEAFOOD | This sophisticated but unfussy neighborhood restaurant on a quiet corner of Clinton Street presents a nightly changing menu of superb small and large plates, with an emphasis on seafood. Oysters on the half shell and yellowtail crudo are typically stellar raw-bar offerings, while you might find Dungeness crab toast with saffron hollandaise or sea scallops with a lime leaf-coconut curry elsewhere on the menu. **Known for:** raw oysters ($1 each at happy hour) sourced exclusively from the Pacific Northwest; Monday-night fish fries; family-style supper option ($60 per person). $ *Average main: $27* ⊠ *2039 S.E. Clinton St., Division/Clinton* ☎ *503/327-8637* ⊕ *www.jacquelinepdx. com* ⊘ *Closed Sun. No lunch.*

★ Kachka

$$ | RUSSIAN | This Central East Side establishment decorated to resemble a *dacha* (a Russian country/vacation house) turns out wonderfully creative and often quite light Russian fare, including plenty of shareable small plates, like crispy beef tongue with sweet onion sauce, orange, and pomegranate; panfried sour-cherry *vareniki* (Ukrainian dumplings), and—of course—caviar with blini and all the usual accompaniments. Another crowd-pleaser on the menu is the classic chicken Kiev, prepared the old-fashioned way, oozing with butter. **Known for:** extensive craft vodka list; the cold "zakuski" assorted appetizer experience ($30 per person); hearty Ukrainian dumplings. $ *Average main: $22* ⊠ *960 S.E. 11th Ave., Central East Side* ☎ *503/235–0059* ⊕ *www. kachkapdx.com.*

La Moule

$$ | SEAFOOD | Along quaintly hip Clinton Street, in a fanciful red-roof building, cozy La Moule specializes in the dish for which it's named: Totten Inlet (Washington) mussels with several interesting preparations, such as Korean inspired with ginger and kimchi, or with a cilantro-lime salsa verde. But there are also steak frites, spätzle, and other French-Belgian specialties. **Known for:** braised-oxtail waffles at brunch; an outstanding Belgian beer list; a generous happy hour menu. $ *Average main: $22* ⊠ *2500 S.E. Clinton St., Division/Clinton* ☎ *971/339–2822* ⊕ *www.lamoulepdx. com* ⊘ *No lunch weekdays.*

★ Langbaan

$$$$ | THAI | Guests reach this tiny, wood-paneled, 24-seat gem with an open kitchen by walking through the adjoining PaaDee restaurant and pushing open a faux bookshelf that's actually a door. Of course, you won't even get this far unless you've called ahead to reserve a table; the restaurant serves the most interesting and consistently delicious Southeast Asian food in Portland via a weekly changing 10-course, $95 tasting menu that features unusual dishes like duck breast and tongue skewer with duck yolk jam and fermented fish sauce,

or turmeric broth with Arctic char and clams. **Known for:** some of the most inventive Thai food in the country; a carefully curated wine list; wonderfully creative and flavorful desserts. $ *Average main: $95* ✉ *6 S.E. 28th Ave., East Burnside/28th Ave.* ☎ *971/344–2564* ⊕ *www.langbaanpdx.com* ⊗ *Closed Mon.–Wed. No lunch.*

Lardo

$ | **AMERICAN** | One of several spots around Portland that has become known for advancing the art of sandwich making, Lardo offers a steady roster of about a dozen wonderfully inventive variations, plus one or two weekly specials, along with no-less-impressive sides like maple carrots and escarole Caesar salads. Sandwiches of particular note include the tender Korean-style braised pork shoulder with kimchi, chili mayo, cilantro, and lime, and grilled mortadella with provolone, marinated peppers, and mustard aioli. **Known for:** inviting covered outdoor seating area; excellent craft-beer and cocktail selection; "dirty fries" topped with pork scraps, marinated peppers, and Parmesan. $ *Average main: $12* ✉ *1212 S.E. Hawthorne Blvd., Hawthorne* ☎ *503/234–7786* ⊕ *www.lardosandwiches.com.*

★ Le Pigeon

$$$$ | **FRENCH** | Specializing in adventurous Northwest-influenced French dishes of extraordinary quality, this cozy and unassuming restaurant consistently ranks among the city's most acclaimed dining venues. The menu changes regularly but often features items like beef-cheek Bourguignon, chicken and oxtail with semolina gnocchi, and seared foie gras with chestnuts, raisins, bacon, and cinnamon toast (especially exceptional). James Beard award–winning chef Gabriel Rucker also operates Canard, next door, which serves lighter and less pricey breakfast, lunch, and dinner fare. **Known for:** open kitchen in which diners at the counter can interact with chefs; one of the best

burgers in town; grilled dry-aged pigeon with a seasonally changing preparation. $ *Average main: $34* ✉ *738 E. Burnside St., Central East Side* ☎ *503/546–8796* ⊕ *www.lepigeon.com* ⊗ *No lunch.*

Magna Kusina

$$ | **PHILIPPINE** | This cozy and colorfully decorated corner space, which opened in 2019, has quickly developed a near-fanatical following for flavorful Filipino-fusion food prepared by the restaurant's renowned classically trained chef-owner. Expect creative, artfully prepared renditions of classics like squid-ink crab-fat noodles with peppers and corn, pork-skin cracklings with spiced coconut vinegar, and tender pork adobo. **Known for:** a loud and intimate dining room; hearty main dishes featuring beef, lamb, pork, and other meaty fare; tupig (coconut sticky rice with condensed milk) for dessert. $ *Average main: $19* ✉ *2525 S.E. Clinton St., Division/Clinton* ☎ *503/395–8542* ⊕ *www.magnapdx.com* ⊗ *Closed Sun. and Mon. No lunch.*

★ Nodoguro

$$$$ | **JAPANESE** | A nightly changing selection of exquisitely plated, imaginative Japanese cuisine is served in this small, sophisticated dining room on an otherwise unpretentious stretch of Belmont Street. The 15- to 25-course omakase menus are available exclusively by advance-ticket purchase, and pairings featuring fine sakes and natural wines are available. **Known for:** elaborate 2½-hour feasts; an emphasis on sublime fish and shellfish; knowledgeable and gracious service. $ *Average main: $125* ✉ *2832 S.E. Belmont St., Belmont* ⊕ *www.nodoguropdx.com* ⊗ *Closed Mon. and Tues. No lunch.*

The Observatory

$ | **AMERICAN** | This convivial neighborhood bistro and its adjoining side bar Over and Out have developed a devoted following over the years for friendly service, well-crafted and affordable contemporary American food, and a long, impressive list of local beers and creative cocktails. Start things off with one of the starter platters (smoked fish, Mediterranean, and charcuterie are all options), before graduating to one of the larger plates, such as the lamb burger with local goat cheese, or blackened catfish with remoulade. **Known for:** fantastic happy hour deals; popular weekend brunch; pinball and games in adjoining bar. [$] *Average main: $15* ✉ *8115 S.E. Stark St., Montavilla/82nd Ave.* ☎ *503/445–6284* 🌐 *www.theobservatorypdx.com.*

OK Omens

$$ | WINE BAR | Natural wines from around the world and well-chosen bistro fare are the focus of this charming little neighborhood spot on the edge of historic Ladd's Addition. Shiso-wrapped ahi tartare, Spanish cheeses, and grilled steak with foie gras are representative of the European-inspired but regionally sourced cuisine. **Known for:** spicy spaghetti with Thai chilies and taleggio cheese; the "kinda like a McFlurry" dessert of vanilla ice cream, Butterfingers, and chocolate; an extremely interesting selection of natural wines. [$] *Average main: $18* ✉ *1758 S.E. Hawthorne Blvd., Hawthorne* ☎ *503/231–9939* 🌐 *www.okomens.com* 🕒 *Closed Mon. No lunch.*

Pepper Box Cafe

$ | SOUTHWESTERN | Portlanders flock to this cute and simple breakfast and lunch spot to get their New Mexico food fix with dishes like sopaipillas stuffed with eggs, potatoes, and cheddar and topped with red or green chili, and Albuquerque turkey-avocado-bacon sandwiches on a flour tortilla featured on the menu. The build-your-own chili bowl is a good way to go if you're feeling indecisive. **Known for:** red and green sauces made with New Mexico chilies; smothered breakfast burritos; no alcohol license, but there's good coffee. [$] *Average main: $9* ✉ *932 S.E. Morrison St., Central East Side* ☎ *503/841–5004* 🌐 *www.pepperboxpdx.com* 🕒 *Closed Tues. No dinner.*

★ Pok Pok

$$ | THAI | Andy Ricker, the owner of one of Portland's most talked-about restaurants, regularly travels to Southeast Asia to research street food and home-style recipes to include on the menu of this always-hopping spot. Diners have the option of sitting outside under tents, or in the funky, cavelike interior, while they enjoy enticing dishes like green papaya salad, charcoal-roasted game hen, and Ike's Vietnamese chicken wings, which are deep-fried in caramelized fish sauce and garlic. **Known for:** Ike's Vietnamese chicken wings; charcoal-roasted game hen and other meaty fare; fiery-hot food (although there are plenty of milder dishes—you just have to ask). [$] *Average main: $19* ✉ *3226 S.E. Division St., Division/Clinton* ☎ *503/232–1387* 🌐 *www.pokpokdivision.com.*

Revelry

$$ | KOREAN FUSION | Seattle's renowned Relay Korean restaurant group operates this stylish, industrial-chic restaurant in Portland's white-hot Central East Side. Open late and serving stellar food to a soundtrack of clubby lounge music, Revelry is both a dinner and drinks spot (soju cocktails are a specialty)—noteworthy dishes from the Korean-fusion menu include kimchi pancakes with pork belly, Szechuan Bolognese with lap cheong sausage, and rice bowls with grilled prawns and crushed-pineapple tabbouleh. **Known for:** house-made fudgesicles with banana glaze for dessert; soju cocktails; dinner till midnight on weekends. [$] *Average main: $16* ✉ *210 S.E. Martin Luther King Blvd., Central East Side* ☎ *971/339–3693* 🌐 *www.relayrestaurantgroup.com* 🕒 *No lunch.*

Stacked Sandwich Shop

$ | DELI | A worthy contestant in Portland's ongoing battle for the best sandwich shop honors, this modern industrial space offers not only sensational lunch fare but also well-conceived cocktails. It's hard to decide which of these overstuffed 'wiches is the most amazing, but you can't go wrong with the braised oxtail French dip with cast-iron-charred onions, or the Cubano with pineapple jalapeño relish. **Known for:** generous daily afternoon happy hour from 2 to 5 pm; weekend brunch with fried chicken and waffles; five-cheese truffle mac and cheese. [$] *Average main: $13* ✉ *1643 S.E. 3rd Ave., Central East Side* ☎ *971/279–2731* 🌐 *www.stackedsandwichshop.com* 🕒 *No dinner.*

Tierra del Sol

$ | **MEXICAN** | If you had to choose a star among the several outstanding Latin American food carts at the Portland Mercado, you could make a strong argument for this cheap and friendly purveyor of authentic Oaxacan fare. The owners turn out flavorful renditions of their own long-treasured family recipes, including chicken with *chochoyotes* (masa dumplings) in a complex yellow mole sauce, and *tlayudas* (prodigious corn tortillas) topped with chicharrón, black beans, and Oaxacan cheese. **Known for:** authentic Oaxacan moles; lots of other food and beverage options in the same complex; outdoor (but covered) communal seating. [$] *Average main: $11* ✉ *Portland Mercado, 7238 S.E. Foster Rd., Foster/Powell* ☎ *503/975–4805* 🌐 *www.tierradelsolpdx.com.*

Tusk

$$$ | **MIDDLE EASTERN** | With its clean lines and whitewashed walls, Tusk provides a setting to show off its colorful, beautifully presented modern Middle Eastern fare like flatbread with salmon roe, squash, mustard oil, and yogurt, or grilled sweet potato with hazelnut tahini and dukka. Many of the dishes here are meatless, but you'll also find some pork, lamb, beef, and seafood grills, including a delicious pork schnitzel with carrot-mustard and ancho cress. **Known for:** extensive selection of vegetarian small plates; family-style chef's choice feasts ($60 per person); savory grilled flatbreads with house-made toppings. [$] *Average main: $27* ✉ *2448 E. Burnside St., East Burnside/28th Ave.* ☎ *503/894–8082* 🌐 *www.tuskpdx.com* 🕒 *No lunch weekdays.*

☕ Coffee and Quick Bites

★ Coava Coffee Roasters

$ | **CAFÉ** | The light and open, bamboo wood–filled flagship location of Coava Coffee Roasters offers some of the highest-quality single-origin, pour-over coffees in the city. There's a second branch in Hawthorne, and a separate coffee bar a few blocks away on S.E. Main Street where you can watch the coffee roasting process. **Known for:** honey lattes; coffee roasted to the most exacting standards; sustainable sourcing and production processes. [$] *Average main: $5* ✉ *1300 S.E. Grand Ave., Central East Side* ☎ *503/894–8134* 🌐 *www.coavacoffee.com* 🕒 *No dinner.*

Heart Coffee

$ | **CAFÉ** | Inside this sleek Woodstock café, with additional locations Downtown and on East Burnside, patrons sip fine coffees sourced from Central America, South America, and Africa, and indulge in breakfast and lunch fare, such as savory and sweet porridges, granola, toasts, and salads. Finnish owner Wille Yli-Luoma brings a modern, minimalist aesthetic to this striking space with plenty of tables for working and socializing. **Known for:** well-crafted lattes; decadent pastries; toasts using local Tabor River Bread. [$] *Average main: $8* ✉ *5181 S.E. Woodstock Blvd., Southeast* ☎ *503/208–2710* 🌐 *www.heartroasters.com* 🕒 *No dinner.*

★ Lauretta Jean's

$ | **CAFÉ** | This pie-focused operation began as a stall at Portland's Saturday Farmers Market at PSU and now comprises a couple of charming, homey, brick-and-mortar cafés, one Downtown, but the most atmospheric along Division Street in Southeast. Though it's the delicious pies—with feathery-light crusts and delicious fillings like tart cherry, salted pecan, and chocolate-banana cream—that have made Lauretta Jean's a foodie icon in Portland, these cheerful eateries also serve exceptional brunch fare, including the LJ Classic, a fluffy biscuit topped with an over-easy egg, Jack cheese, bacon, and strawberry jam. **Known for:** salted-caramel apple pie; short but well-curated cocktail list; breakfast sandwich that features the bakery's fluffy biscuits. [$] *Average main: $8* ✉ *3402 S.E. Division St., Division/Clinton* ☎ *503/235–3119* 🌐 *www.laurettajeans.com* ⏲ *No dinner.*

Tao of Tea

$ | **CAFÉ** | With soft music and the sound of running water in the background, the Tao of Tea serves more than 100 loose-leaf teas as well as vegetarian snacks and sweets. The company also operates the serene tearoom inside Old Town's Lan Su Chinese Garden. **Known for:** tranquil ambience; especially good variety of chai and oolong teas; Asian-influenced veggie and noodle bowls. [$] *Average main: $7* ✉ *3430 S.E. Belmont St., Division/Clinton* ☎ *503/736–0119* 🌐 *www.taooftea.com.*

Hotels

Evermore Guesthouse

$ | **B&B/INN** | Just a block from the trendy dining along Southeast Portland's hip Division Street, this beautifully restored, 1909 Arts and Crafts–style mansion contains spacious, light-filled rooms, some with private balconies, claw-foot soaking tubs, and good-size sitting areas; one detached suite has a full kitchen, and a cozy and romantic third-floor room has skylights and pitched ceilings. **Pros:** located in hip, charming neighborhood with many bars and restaurants; reasonably priced with free off-street parking; free laundry and basic breakfast. **Cons:** some rooms face busy Cesar Chavez Boulevard; a 15-minute drive or 30-minute bus ride from Downtown; least expensive rooms are shared bath. [$] *Rooms from: $145* ✉ *3860 S.E. Clinton St., Richmond* ☎ *503/206–6509, 877/600–6509* 🌐 *www.evermoreguesthouse.com* 🛏 *6 rooms* 🍴 *Free breakfast.*

Jupiter NEXT

$$ | **HOTEL** | Across the street from its sister, the original mod-hip Jupiter Hotel (which is a good bet if you need cheap but basic and rather noisy digs), this futuristic-looking mid-rise offers a more upscale—but still moderately priced—lodging experience, complete with several airy outdoor spaces and a sceney lobby bar and restaurant, Hey Love. **Pros:** guest rooms have cool photo collages of Portland landmarks; fun and lively common spaces; excellent restaurant and bar. **Cons:** youthful vibe and quirky design doesn't appeal to everyone; lobby and bar can be loud and busy on weekends; a short drive or bus ride from Downtown. [$] *Rooms from: $155* ✉ *900 E. Burnside St., Central East Side* ☎ *503/230–9200* 🌐 *www.jupiterhotel.com* 🛏 *68 rooms* 🍴 *No meals.*

Nightlife

BARS AND LOUNGES

★ Bible Club

BARS/PUBS | There's a speakeasy-like quality to this hip, vintage-style bar with signs referencing Prohibition and the 18th Amendment. The Bible Club serves up some of the most creative cocktails in the Sellwood and Westmoreland area, as well as a good mix of Oregon beers. Out back there's an expansive seating area with picnic tables and an additional outdoor bar. ✉ *6716 S.E. 16th Ave., Sellwood/Moreland* ☎ *971/279–2198* 🌐 *www.bibleclubpdx.com* ☞ *Closed Mon.–Tues.*

★ Crush

BARS/PUBS | A favorite LGBTQ hangout in the Central East Side, Crush serves up tasty pub grub, strong cocktails, and DJ-fueled dance parties. The front section is mellow and good for conversation, while the back area contains a small but lively dance floor. ✉ *1400 S.E. Morrison St., Belmont* ☎ *503/235–8150* ⊕ *www. crushbar.com.*

★ ENSO Winery

WINE BARS—NIGHTLIFE | Based in a large garagelike space in Southeast Portland's trendy Buckman neighborhood, ENSO is the creation of young and talented wine-maker Ryan Sharp, who sources grapes from Washington, California, and Oregon to produce superb wines that are quickly earning notice in the national wine press. Notable varietals include Petite Sirah, Malbec, Dry Riesling, and the especially popular L'American blend of Zinfandel, Petite Sirah, and Mourvèdre. The high-ceilinged, industrial-chic tasting lounge—with exposed air ducts, a timber-beam ceiling, and a wall of windows (open on warm days)—has become one of the neighborhood's favorite wine bars, serving local Olympia Provisions charcuterie, Woodblock chocolates, Steve's Cheese Bar cheeses, and Little T Baker breads, plus local microbrews and a few wines, mostly from other Portland producers. ✉ *1416 S.E. Stark St., Central East Side* ☎ *503/683–3676* ⊕ *www.ensowinery. com.*

Holocene

DANCE CLUBS | Hosting DJ dance nights that range from indie-pop dance parties to LGBTQ hip-hop nights and poetry slams, the 5,000-square-foot former auto-parts warehouse pulls in diverse crowds. It's sometimes closed early in the week; check the online calendar before you visit. ✉ *1001 S.E. Morrison St., Central East Side* ☎ *503/239–7639* ⊕ *www.holocene.org.*

★ Oui! Wine Bar at SE Wine Collective

WINE BARS—NIGHTLIFE | This hive of bou-tique wine-making has an inviting tasting room–cum–wine bar in which you can sample the vinos of several up-and-com-ing producers. You could carve out a full meal from the extensive menu's tapas, salads, baguette sandwiches, and cheese and meat plates. Although Oregon is chiefly known for Pinot Noir, Pinot Gris, and Chardonnay, the wineries at the collective produce a richly varied assortment of varietals, from racy Sauvi-gnon Blancs to peppery Cabernet Francs. ✉ *2425 S.E. 35th Pl., Division/Clinton* ☎ *503/208–2061* ⊕ *www.sewinecollec-tive.com.*

Scotch Lodge Whisky Bar

BARS/PUBS | This debonair basement space has an elegant marble bar, dark-wood paneling, and a beautiful backlit bar. The specialty here, as the name suggests, is whiskey—in both cocktail and sipping form. And there's superb bar food to boot. ✉ *215 S.E. 9th Ave., base-ment, Central East Side* ☎ *503/208–2039* ⊕ *www.scotchlodge.com.*

BREWPUBS AND MICROBREWERIES

★ Cascade Brewing

BREWPUBS/BEER GARDENS | This laid-back brewpub and pioneer of the Northwest sour-beer movement is a good place for friends and sour-beer lovers to share tart flights of several varieties, including Blackcap Raspberry, Kriek, and potent (10.1% ABV) Sang Noir. You'll find 24 rotating taps, small plates, and sand-wiches to complement the sour beers, and ample outdoor seating. ✉ *939 S.E. Belmont St., Central East Side* ☎ *503/265–8603* ⊕ *www.cascadebrew-ingbarrelhouse.com.*

Gigantic Brewing

BREWPUBS/BEER GARDENS | This well-re-spected craft brewer is in a slightly off-the-beaten-path industrial area that doesn't have a whole lot going on, but this in no way keeps it from pulling in a consistently big crowd most days, and especially on weekend afternoons, when folks sip Gigantic's first-rate beer on the front patio. In addition to conventional Northwest-style IPAs and some terrific German ales, the brewery produces interesting seasonal and barrel-aged varieties. ✉ *5224 S.E. 26th Ave., Southeast* ☎ *503/208–3416* ⊕ *www.giganticbrewing.com.*

LIVE MUSIC
Doug Fir Lounge

MUSIC CLUBS | Part retro diner and part log cabin, the Doug Fir serves food and booze and hosts DJs and live rock shows from both up-and-coming and established bands most nights of the week. It adjoins the trendy Hotel Jupiter. ✉ *830 E. Burnside St., Central East Side* ☎ *503/231–9663* ⊕ *www.dougfirlounge. com.*

★ Revolution Hall

MUSIC CLUBS | Southeast Portland's stately early-1900s former Washington High School building has been converted into a state-of-the-art concert hall, featuring noted pop and world-beat music acts and comedians, from Steve Earle to Tig Notaro, plus film festivals and other intriguing events. There are two bars on-site, including a roof deck with great views of the Downtown skyline. ✉ *1300 S.E. Stark St., Central East Side* ☎ *503/288–3895* ⊕ *www.revolutionhall.com.*

🎭 Performing Arts

FILM
★ Bagdad Theater

FILM | Built in 1927, the stunningly restored, eminently quirky Bagdad Theater shows first-run Hollywood films on a huge screen and serves pizza, burgers, sandwiches, and McMenamins ales. The Bagdad is a local favorite. ✉ *3702 S.E. Hawthorne Blvd., Hawthorne* ☎ *503/249–7474* ⊕ *www.mcmenamins. com/bagdad-theater-pub.*

THEATER
Imago Theatre

THEATER | One of Portland's most outstanding innovative theater companies, the Imago specializes in movement-based work for both young and old. ✉ *17 S.E. 8th Ave., Central East Side* ☎ *503/231–9581* ⊕ *www.imagotheatre. com.*

★ Milagro Theatre Group

THEATER | This well-established nonprofit company in the Central East Side showcases the region's vibrant, and growing, Latino voice through theatrical performances, featuring everything from classic dramas and musicals to experimental works and world premieres. ✉ *525 S.E. Stark St., Central East Side* ☎ *503/236–7253* ⊕ *www.milagro.org.*

🛍 Shopping

CLOTHING
Artifact: Creative Recycle

CLOTHING | You never know what sort of special treasure you might discover while rummaging the aisles of this boho-chic vintage shop with a carefully curated collection of midcentury housewares, 1970s fashion, wicker patio furniture, funky jewelry, and Asian and African bedding and rugs. Artifact is also one of Portland's best places to upcycle your own goods. ✉ *3630 S.E. Division St., Division/Clinton* ☎ *503/230–4831* ⊕ *www.artifactpdx. com.*

Herbivore Clothing

CLOTHING | An animal-rights-minded shop in the Central East Side, Herbivore is a terrific resource if you're seeking clothing and accessories—from cotton-rayon tees and sweaters to braided canvas belts and wallets fashioned out of reclaimed bike and truck tubes—that have been created without the harm or use of animals. There's also a great selection of books on veganism, plus food, health-care products, and gifts. ✉ *1211 S.E. Stark St., Central East Side* ☎ *503/281–8638* ⊕ *www.herbivoreclothing.com.*

Machus

CLOTHING | This small, somewhat under-the-radar, upscale, men's clothier carries one of the best selections of fashion-forward, emerging labels in the city. In addition to Machus's own private-label dress shirts and tees, check out threads by A.P.C., Ksubi, and Purple Brand Denim. You won't find many—or any—pastels or bright prints in here; expect clean classics, with lots of blacks, grays, and whites. ⊠ *542 E. Burnside St., Central East Side* ☎ *503/206–8626* ⊕ *www. machusonline.com.*

★ Una

CLOTHING | The fashion-minded devotees of this chic, upscale women's boutique swear by its staff's discerning eye for international jewelry and clothes. Creations by dozens of vaunted designers are displayed here—hammered sterling silver link collars from Annie Costello Brown, Japanese wool and flax dresses from Vlas Blomme, and Italian leather bags from Massimo Palomba, plus enticing home accessories. ⊠ *922 S.E. Ankeny St., Central East Side* ☎ *503/235–2326* ⊕ *www.unanegozio.com.*

Union Rose

CLOTHING | For distinctive women's fashion and accessories designed and made in Portland, check out this boutique in up-and-coming Montavilla. Though there are scores of dresses for any season, including a very good selection of dresses and skirts in plus sizes, there's also plenty of everyday wear, like hoodies and hats. ⊠ *7909 S.E. Stark St., Montavilla/82nd Ave.* ☎ *503/287–4242* ⊕ *www. unionrosepdx.com.*

FOOD

★ Jacobsen Salt Co.

FOOD/CANDY | Established in 2011 on the Oregon Coast, this artisanal saltworks has become wildly successful and prolific, and you can sample its carefully balanced finishing salts as well as Portland-made Bee Local Honey in this handsome gourmet shop. There's also a wide selection of salty treats—salted caramels, black licorice, and other goodies. ⊠ *602 S.E. Salmon St., Central East Side* ☎ *503/719–4973* ⊕ *www. jacobsensalt.com.*

HOUSEHOLD GOODS AND FURNITURE

Presents of Mind

GIFTS/SOUVENIRS | It happens all the time. You pop into this animated Hawthorne boutique to buy a card or gift for a friend, and you emerge an hour later with knit logo'd socks, a "Gay AF" rainbow coffee mug, a roll of pastel-animal stickers, and a tin of beard balm all for yourself. The owners of this terrific little shop make a strong effort to support local and sustainable makers and designers. ⊠ *3633 S.E. Hawthorne Blvd., Hawthorne* ☎ *503/230–7740* ⊕ *www.presentsofmind.tv.*

Spartan Shop

HOUSEHOLD ITEMS/FURNITURE | As the name suggests, the aesthetic at this trendy lifestyle shop is on the clean and spare side, all the better for browsing the natty selection of muted-tone housewares and accessories. There's a notable selection of bath and apothecary products, plus jewelry, wallets, and other intriguing goods you never knew you needed. ⊠ *1210 S.E. Grand Ave., Central East Side* ☎ *503/360–7922* ⊕ *www.spartan-shop.com.*

★ Urbanite

ANTIQUES/COLLECTIBLES | In this huge warehouse packed with both vintage and contemporary furniture and accessories, you'll find wares from about 40 different designers and sellers. You could easily lose yourself in here for a couple of hours, admiring the antique signs and containers, midcentury lamps, cushy armchairs, industrial tables and drawers, and curious knickknacks. ⊠ *1005 S.E. Grand Ave., Central East Side* ☎ *971/801–2361* ⊕ *www.urbanitepdx.com.*

MUSIC

Music Millennium

MUSIC STORES | The oldest record store in the Pacific Northwest, Music Millennium stocks a huge selection of new and used music in every possible category, including local punk groups. The store also hosts a number of in-store performances, often by top-name artists, which have included Lucinda Williams, Richard Thompson, Sheryl Crow, and Randy Newman. ⊠ *3158 E. Burnside St., Laurelhurst* ☎ *503/231–8926* ⊕ *www.musicmillennium.com.*

TOYS

Cloud Cap Games

TOYS | **FAMILY** | There's more than just run-of-the-mill board games at Cloud Cap. For children and grown-ups alike, the games here challenge the mind and provide hours of entertainment. There's a room with tables to play or try out a game, and game nights some evenings. The knowledgeable owners and staff may sit down and join in the fun and are always happy to answer questions and offer suggestions. ⊠ *1226 S.E. Lexington St., Sellwood/Moreland* ☎ *503/505–9344* ⊕ *www.cloudcapgames.com.*

Chapter 4

OREGON COAST

Updated by
Andrew Collins

● Sights	🍴 Restaurants	🛏 Hotels	💼 Shopping	🍸 Nightlife
★★★★★	★★★★☆	★★★★☆	★★★☆☆	★★★☆☆

WELCOME TO OREGON COAST

TOP REASONS TO GO

★ **Beaches:** Think broad expanses ideal for strolling, creature-teeming tide pools, stunning stretches framed by cliffs and boulders, and the dramatic sands of Oregon Dunes National Recreation Area.

★ **Sip craft beverages:** The coast has developed an impressive bounty of craft breweries, along with a number of first-rate artisanal distilleries, coffeehouses, and cideries.

★ **Rugged hikes:** Breathtaking trails line the coast, many of them leading to lofty mountain summits or rocky ledges that offer great wildlife viewing.

★ **Small-town charms:** You'll find some of the state's most quirky and charming communities along the coast, from hipster-approved Astoria to arty and secluded Port Orford to rustic yet sophisticated Yachats.

★ **Local seafood:** The region has vastly upped its dining game, with talented chefs featuring local crab, razor clams, rockfish, albacore, salmon, and other riches of the Oregon Coast.

1 Astoria. A historic working-class fishing town that abounds with hip cafés, indie boutiques, and restored hotels.

2 Seaside. Family-friendly town with a touristy but bustling boardwalk and old-time amusements.

3 Cannon Beach. Art-fueled and refined with some of Oregon's swankiest coastal accommodations.

4 Manzanita. A cozy seaside hamlet with a laid-back vibe and gorgeous natural scenery.

5 Tillamook. This lush, agrarian valley is home to a famous cheese maker and the stunning Three Capes Scenic Loop.

6 Pacific City. A colorful fleet of dories dots the wide beach of this tiny village that's popular for outdoor recreation.

7 Lincoln City. Visitors can indulge in gaming, shopping, golfing, and beachcombing in this sprawling, family-oriented resort town.

8 Depoe Bay. A coastal town with a teeny-tiny harbor, it's the best place in Oregon for whale-watching.

9 Newport. Home to a stellar aquarium and one of Oregon's largest fishing fleets, expect sophisticated dining and beachfront hotels.

10 Yachats. This less-developed town is a true seaside gem with astounding coastal views and a noteworthy restaurant scene.

11 Florence. With a bustling downtown that hugs the Siuslaw River, this cute village is also the northern gateway to the Oregon dunes.

12 Coos Bay and North Bend. These historic industrial towns offer southern access to Oregon dunes and are close to several beautiful state parks on the ocean.

13 Bandon. A world-class golfing destination that's also known for spectacular boulder-strewn beaches, offshore islands, and lighthouse gazing.

14 Port Orford. Gorgeous beach landscapes and a growing arts scene are the hallmarks of this ruggedly situated and low-key spot.

15 Gold Beach. Entry point for the fabled Rogue River with a nice range of casual seafood eateries and midprice resorts.

16 Brookings. Sterling state parks, lots of redwoods, and plenty of sunshine are accented by a burgeoning restaurant scene.

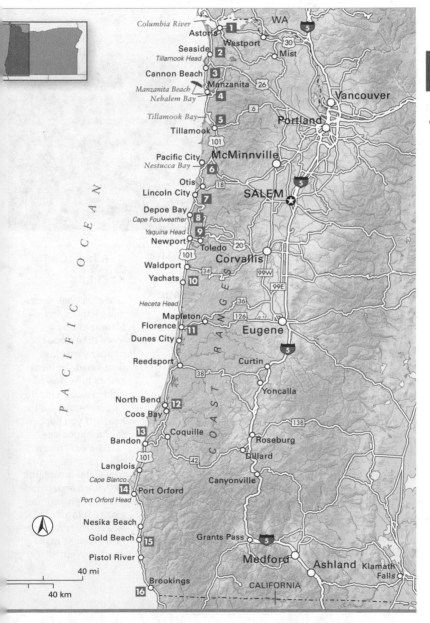

Columbia River
WA
Astoria
Westport
1
30
Seaside
Mist
2
Tillamook Head
Cannon Beach
3
Manzanita
26
Manzanita Beach
4
Nehalem Bay
Vancouver
6
Tillamook Bay
5
Portland
Tillamook
101
Pacific City
McMinnville
6
Nestucca Bay
Otis
18
Lincoln City
7
SALEM
Depoe Bay
8
Cape Foulweather
Yaquina Head
9
Newport
Toledo
20
101
Corvallis
Waldport
34
Yachats
10
99W
99E
Heceta Head
36
Mapleton
126
Florence
11
Eugene
Dunes City
Reedsport
Curtin
38
Yoncalla
North Bend
12
Coos Bay
138
13
Coquille
Bandon
Roseburg
101
42
Dillard
Langlois
Cape Blanco
Canyonville
14
Port Orford
Port Orford Head
Nesika Beach
Gold Beach
15
Grants Pass
Pistol River
40 mi
Medford
Ashland Klamath
Falls
40 km
Brookings
CALIFORNIA
16

PACIFIC OCEAN

COAST RANGES

EXPLORING OREGON'S BEST BEACHES

Oregon's 300 miles of public coastline is the backdrop for thrills, serenity, rejuvenation, and romance. From wide expanses of sand dotted with beach chairs to surf-shaped cliffs, the shoreline is often compared to New Zealand.

Most awe-inspiring are the massive rock formations just offshore in the coast's northern and southern sections. Beaches along the north coast, from Astoria to Pacific City, are perfect for romantic strolls. The central-coast beaches, from Lincoln City to Florence, are long and wide, providing perfect conditions for sunbathers, children, clam diggers, horseback riders, and surfers. The southern coast from Oregon Dunes National Recreation Area to Brookings is less populated, ideal for an escape.

In late July and August the climate is generally kind to sun worshippers. During the shoulder months, keep layers of clothing handy for temperature swings. Winter can be downright blustery.

GLASS FLOATS: FINDERS KEEPERS

Since 1997, between mid-October and Memorial Day, more than 2,000 handcrafted glass floats made by local artists have been hidden along Lincoln City's 7½-mile public beach. If you happen to come upon one, call the local tourism office (800/452–2151) to register it, and find out which artist made it. Although antique glass floats are extremely rare, these new versions make great souvenirs.

THE OREGON COAST'S BEST BEACHES

Cannon Beach. In the shadow of glorious **Haystack Rock,** this family-friendly beach is wide, flat, and perfect for bird-watching, exploring tide pools, building sand castles, and romantic walks in the sea mist. Each June the city holds a **sand-castle contest,** drawing artists and thousands of visitors. The rest of the year the beach is far less populated. The dapper beachfront town has several of the region's swankiest hotels and finest restaurants, as well as spots for surfing, hiking, and beachcombing.

Pacific City. Like Cannon Beach, this town also has a huge (less famous) Haystack Rock that provides the perfect scenic backdrop for horseback riders, beach strollers, and people with shovels chasing sand-covered clams. With safe beach breaks that are ideal for beginners and larger peaks a bit to the south, this is also a great spot for surfers. Winter-storm-watchers love Pacific City, where winds exceeding 75 mph twist Sitka spruce, and tides deposit driftwood and logs on the beach.

Oregon Dunes National Recreation Area. One reason the Pacific Northwest isn't known for its amusement parks is because nature hurls more thrills than any rattling contraption could ever

provide. This certainly is true at this 40-mile stretch of coastal sand dunes, the largest expanse in North America. From Florence to Coos Bay, the dunes draw more than 1.5 million visitors each year. For those who just want to swim, relax, hike, and marvel at the amazing expanse of dunes against the ocean, there are spaces off-limits to motorized vehicles. One of the best places to view the dunes and beach is the gorgeous **Umpqua River Lighthouse.**

Samuel H. Boardman State Scenic Corridor. It doesn't get any wilder than this—or more spectacular. The 12-mile strip of forested, rugged coastline between Gold Beach and Brookings is dotted with smaller sand beaches, some more accessible than others. Here visitors will find the amazing **Arch Rock** and **Natural Bridges** and can hike 27 miles of the **Oregon Coast Trail.** Beach highlights include **Whaleshead Beach, Secret Beach,** and **Thunder Rock Cove,** where you might spy migrating gray whales. From the 345-foot-high **Thomas Creek Bridge,** you can take a moderately difficult hike down to admire the gorgeous, jagged rocks off **China Beach.**

If you aren't from the Pacific Northwest, Oregon's spectacular coastline might still be a secret: it's less visited and less talked about than California's coast, but certainly no less beautiful. In recent decades, however, the state's reputation for scenic drives and splendid hikes, reasonably priced oceanfront hotels and vacation rentals, low-key towns with friendly, creative vibes, and consistently fresh and well-prepared seafood has garnered increased attention. The true draw here is the beaches, where nature lovers delight at their first sight of a migrating whale or a baby harbor seal sitting on a rock.

Oregon's coastline is open to all; not a grain of its more than 300 miles of white-sand beaches is privately owned. The coast's midsize towns and small villages (you won't find any large cities) are linked by U.S. 101, which runs the length of the state. It winds past sea-tortured rocks, brooding headlands, hidden beaches, historic lighthouses, and tiny ports. This is one of the most picturesque driving routes in the country, and it should not be missed. Embracing it is the vast, indigo-blue Pacific Ocean, which presents a range of moods with the seasons. On summer evenings it might be smooth enough to reflect a romantic sunset. In winter the ocean might throw a thrilling tantrum for storm watchers sitting snug and safe in a beachfront cabin.

Active visitors indulge in thrills from racing up a sand dune in a buggy to making par at Bandon Dunes, one of the world's finest links-style golf courses. Bicyclists pedal along misty coastline vistas, cruising past historic lighthouses. Hikers enjoy breezy, open trails along the sea as well as lush, evergreen-studded treks into the adjoining Coast Range. Opportunities abound as well for excursions on jet boats along southern-coast rivers and whale-watching tours along the wildlife-rich central coast. If the weather turns, don't overlook indoor venues like the Oregon Coast Aquarium and Columbia River Maritime Museum.

The region's culinary scene has improved markedly in recent years, with destination-worthy restaurants as well as craft breweries and hip cafés popping up everywhere. Shoppers appreciate the art galleries of Newport and Cannon Beach; for more family-oriented fun, giggle in the souvenir shops of Lincoln City and Seaside while eating fistfuls of caramel corn or chewing saltwater taffy.

MAJOR REGIONS

The **North Coast** is the primary beach playground for residents of Portland, and you'll find a growing number of sophisticated eateries, craft breweries and cocktail bars, colorful art galleries and indie retailers, and smartly restored boutique hotels along this ruggedly beautiful stretch of coastline. What distinguishes the region historically from other areas of the coast are its forts, its graveyard of shipwrecks, historic sites related to Lewis and Clark's early visit, and a town—**Astoria**—that blends the misty temperament and cannery heritage of Monterey, California, with Portland's progressive, hipster personality. To the south, bustling **Seaside** is Oregon's long-time go-to for family-friendly fun, while nearby **Cannon Beach** feels a just a bit fancier than any other town in the area. Farther south are the sleepy and scenic little villages of **Manzanita** and **Pacific City**, as well as **Tillamook,** home to thriving dairy farms and an iconic cheese factory that's a favorite visitor attraction.

The **Central Coast** is Oregon's top destination for families, shoppers, casino goers, kite flyers, deep-sea fishing enthusiasts, and dune-shredding daredevils. Although it's a bit touristy and bisected by a rather tatty commercial stretch of U.S. 101, **Lincoln City** offers a wealth of shops devoted to souvenirs and knickknacks, and visitors can even blow their own glass float at a few local studios. **Depoe**

Bay is popular for whale-watching excursions, and **Newport** is designated the Dungeness crab capital of the world as well as home to bustling bay-front and picturesque ocean beaches, plus plenty of excellent dining and lodging options. As you venture farther south, you'll roll through gorgeous and less-developed **Yachats** and charming **Florence** to reach the iconic mountains of sand that fall within Oregon Dunes National Recreation Area. Even if you're not intent on making tracks in the sand, the dunes provide vast, unforgettable scenery.

Coos Bay-Charleston-North Bend, or Bay Area, is considered to be the gateway to this gorgeous stretch known as the **Southern Coast**. The upper portion is continuation of the Oregon Dunes National Recreation Area, and is the location of its visitor center. In **Bandon** golfers flock to one of the most celebrated clusters of courses in the world at Bandon Dunes. Lovers of lighthouses, sailing, fishing, crabbing, elk viewing, camping, and water sports may wonder why they didn't venture south sooner to explore **Port Orford, Gold Beach,** and **Brookings.**

Planning

When to Go

November through May are generally rainy months (albeit with sporadic stretches of dry and sometimes even sunny days), but once the fair weather comes, coastal Oregon is one of the most gorgeous places on earth. July through September offer wonderful, dry days for beachgoers. Autumn is also a great time to visit, as the warm-enough weather is perfect for crisp beachcombing walks followed by hearty harvest meals paired with ales from the area's growing crop of craft breweries.

Even with the rain, coastal winter and spring do have quite a following. Many hotels are perfectly situated for storm watching, and provide all the trappings for a romantic experience. Think of a toasty (albeit likely gas) fireplace, a smooth Oregon Pinot, and your loved one, settled in to watch the waves dance upon a jagged rocky stage.

Festivals

Astoria Music Festival

FESTIVALS | Fans of opera and classical works flock to this increasingly popular festival, which mounts more than 20 performances, over 16 days in late June and early July. ⊕ www.astoriamusicfestival.org.

Cannon Beach Sandcastle Contest

FESTIVALS | It can be tough to find a room—or parking spot—during this single-day mid-June festival that's been going strong for more than 55 years and showcases the amazingly detailed sand constructions of both professional and amateur teams. ⊕ www.cannonbeach.org.

Cranberry Festival

FESTIVALS | In Bandon each September this three-day festival in celebration of the town's most famous product (well, after seafood) comprises a fair and parade. ⊕ www.bandon.com/cranberry-festival.

Newport Seafood and Wine Festival

FESTIVALS | This renowned foodie gathering takes place the last full weekend in late February and bills itself the premier seafood and wine event of the Oregon Coast. Dozens of wineries are represented at this expansive celebration, which also features myriad crafts and eateries. ⊕ www.seafoodandwine.com.

Getting Here and Around

By far the most practical way to reach and to explore the coast is by car. There's only one small regional airport with limited commercial service, the regional bus lines provide fairly slow and infrequent service from other parts of the state, and there's zero train service. Several two-lane state highways connect the central and northern sections of the coast with the state's two largest cities, Portland and Eugene; the southern portion of the coast is more remote and requires longer drives.

AIR TRAVEL

From Portland, which has Oregon's largest airport, the drive is about 2 hours to Astoria and Cannon Beach, and 2½ hours to Lincoln City and Newport. If you're headed farther south, you have a few other options, including flying into the regional airport in Eugene, which is served by most major airlines and is a 90-minute drive from Florence; flying into the tiny Southwest Oregon Regional Airport in the coast town of North Bend, which is an hour south of Florence and 2½ hours north of Brookings; flying into Rogue Valley International Airport in Medford, which is a 2½-hour drive from Brookings and a 3-hour drive from Bandon; and flying into Del Norte County Airport in Crescent City, California, which is just a 30-minute drive south of Brookings (and has scheduled service only to Oakland).

Southwest Oregon Regional Airport has flights to San Francisco and—from June to early October—Denver on United Express. The airport has Hertz and Enterprise car-rental agencies as well as cab companies serving the area, including Coos Bay and Bandon.

A few shuttle services connect the airports in Portland and Eugene to the coast, but these tend to be far less convenient than renting a car, and not necessarily more economical. Caravan Shuttle runs a daily shuttle service from Portland International Airport to Lincoln City and on down to Waldport (nearly to Yachats). Hub Airport Shuttle provides door-to-door van service from the Eugene airport to the Central Coast, from Florence down to around Bandon.

CONTACTS Caravan Shuttle. ☎ *541/994–9645* ⊕ *www.caravanshuttle.com.* **Hub Airport Shuttle.** ☎ *541/461–7959* ⊕ *www. hubairportshuttle.com.* **Southwest Oregon Regional Airport.** ✉ *1100 Airport La., North Bend* ☎ *541/756–8531* ⊕ *www. cooscountyairportdistrict.com.*

BUS TRAVEL

There is bus travel to the coast from Portland and Eugene, but this is a fairly slow and cumbersome way to explore the area. NW Connector is a nonprofit organization that coordinates travel among five rural transit services in the northwestern corner of the state. From its website, you can plan and book trips from Portland to Astoria, with connecting service between the two along the coast, stopping in Seaside, Cannon Beach, Manzanita, and other communities. You can also purchase three- and seven-day travel passes from drivers on any of the NW Connector buses. Additionally, Point has daily bus service from Portland to Cannon Beach, and then up the coast to Astoria; and daily buses from Klamath Falls to Brookings, via Ashland, Medford, and Crescent City, California; Amtrak handles the company's reservations and ticketing. Pacific Crest Bus Lines connects Florence, Coos Bay, and Reedsport with Eugene and Bend every day.

CONTACTS NW Connector. ⊕ *www. nworegontransit.org.* **Pacific Crest Bus Lines.** ☎ *800/872–7245 ticketing through Amtrak, 800/231–2222 ticketing through Greyhound* ⊕ *www.pacificcrestbuslines. com.* **Point.** ☎ *800/872–7245 ticketing through Amtrak, 541/484–4100 information* ⊕ *www.oregon-point.com.*

CAR TRAVEL

Beautiful U.S. 101 hugs the entire Oregon coastline from Brookings near the California border in the south to Astoria on the Columbia River in the north. The road can be slow in places, especially where it passes through towns and curves over headlands and around coves. In theory, you could drive the entire 345-mile Oregon stretch of U.S 101 in a little under eight hours, but that's without stopping—and, of course, the whole point of driving the coast is stopping regularly to enjoy it. If you want to do a full road trip of the Oregon Coast, give yourself at least three days and two nights; that's enough time to see a few key attractions along the way, enjoy the many scenic viewpoints, and stop to eat and overnight in some small towns along the route.

Several two-lane roads connect key towns on the coast—Astoria, Cannon Beach, Tillamook, Lincoln City, Newport, Waldport (near Yachats), Florence (and nearby Reedsport), and Bandon—with the major towns in the Willamette and Rogue valleys (Portland, Corvallis, Eugene, Roseburg). All these roads climb over the Coast Range, meaning the drives tend to be winding and hilly but quite picturesque. Keep in mind that winter storms in the mountains occasionally create slick conditions and even road closures. Always use numbered, paved state roads when crossing the mountains from the valley to the coast, especially in winter; what might appear to be a scenic alternative or shortcut on a map or GPS device is likely an unmaintained logging or forest road that leads through a secluded part of the mountains, without cell service.

Restaurants

Deciding which restaurant has the best clam chowder or Dungeness crab cakes is just one of the culinary fact-finding expeditions you can embark upon along the Oregon Coast. Chefs here take full advantage of the wealth of sturgeon, salmon, steelhead, and trout that abound in coastal rivers as well as the fresh rockfish, halibut, albacore, and lingcod caught in the Pacific. You'll also find fresh mussels, bay shrimp, oysters, and razor clams. What's changed of late is a notable influx of chef-driven restaurants serving creatively prepared, often globally influenced dishes along with beverage programs that showcase craft spirits, beers, and wines from the Pacific Northwest. The increase in buzz-worthy dining aside, restaurants still tend to be casual and low-key, with a wide range of price points. *Restaurant reviews have been shortened. For full information visit Fodors.com.*

What it Costs in U.S. Dollars			
$	$$	$$$	$$$$
RESTAURANTS			
under $16	$16–$22	$23–$30	over $30
HOTELS			
under $150	$150–$200	$201–$250	over $250

Hotels

Compared with other coastal destinations in the United States, the Oregon Coast offers a pretty good value. You can typically find clean but basic motels and rustic inns, often with beachfront locations, that have nightly rates well below $150, even in high season, although you'll also find a smattering of high-end resorts and boutique inns with summer rates well over $300 nightly. Spring and fall rates often drop by 20% to 30% and the value is even greater in winter. The lodging landscape is dominated by family- or independently owned motels and hotels, a diminishing number of distinctive B&Bs (many have become rentals or private homes in recent years), and a great variety vacation rentals. Airbnb has the greatest selection of rentals along the coast, but you'll also find well-regarded agencies in many communities, and the reputable Oregon-based online agency Vacasa also has dozens of listings.

Properties in much of the North and Central Coast fill up fast in the summer, so book in advance. Many lodgings require a minimum two-night stay on a summer weekend. *Hotel reviews have been shortened. For full information, visit Fodors.com.*

Visitor Information

CONTACTS Oregon Coast Visitors Association. ☎ *541/574–2679, 888/628–2101* ⊕ *www.visittheoregoncoast.com.*

Astoria

96 miles northwest of Portland.

The mighty Columbia River meets the Pacific at Astoria, the oldest city west of the Rockies and a bustling riverfront getaway with a creative spirit and a surprisingly urbane personality for a city of less than 10,000. Astoria cultivates a bit of Portland's hipster vibe, especially when it comes to shopping and nightlife, and its once workaday downtown and cannery wharfs now house trendy restaurants and distinctive lodgings.

It's named for John Jacob Astor, owner of the Pacific Fur Company, whose members arrived in 1811 and established Fort Astoria. In its early days, it was a placid amalgamation of small town and hardworking port city. Its rivers rich with salmon, the city relied on its fishing and canning industries. Settlers built sprawling Victorian houses on the flanks of Coxcomb Hill; many of the homes have since been restored and used as backdrops in movies (*The Goonies,* notably) or been converted into Airbnbs or vacation rentals. Astoria still retains the soul of a fisherman's town, celebrated each February during its FisherPoets Gathering. It's easy to find spectacular views from a number of points in town, both of the river and the richly forested countryside to the south and east, yet it remains a working waterfront, albeit with a superb museum dedicated to the Columbia River. There is little public beach access in the town proper; to reach the Pacific, drive a few miles west to Fort Stevens in the adjacent village of Warrenton.

GETTING HERE AND AROUND

The northernmost town on the Oregon Coast, Astoria is just across the Columbia River from southwestern Washington via U.S. 101 (over the stunning Astoria-Megler Bridge) and a two-hour drive from Portland on U.S. 30. It only takes about 20 extra minutes to get here from Portland via the more scenic route of U.S. 101 south and U.S. 26 east.

ESSENTIALS
VISITOR INFORMATION Travel Astoria.
✉ 111 W. Marine Dr. ☎ 503/325–6311, 800/875–6807 ⊕ www.travelastoria.com.

 Sights

★ **Astoria Column**

MEMORIAL | For the best view of the city, the Coast Range, volcanic Mt. St. Helens, and the Pacific Ocean, scamper up the 164 spiral stairs to the top of the Astoria Column. When you get to the top, you can throw a small wooden plane and watch it glide to earth; each year some 35,000 gliders are tossed. The 125-foot-high structure sits atop Coxcomb Hill, and was patterned after Trajan's Column in Rome. There are little platforms to rest on if you get winded, or, if you don't want to climb, the column's 500 feet of artwork, depicting important Pacific Northwest historical milestones, are well worth a study. ✉ 1 Coxcomb Dr. ☎ 503/325–2963 ⊕ www.astoriacolumn. org ⌲ $5 parking (good for 1 yr).

Astoria Riverfront Trolley

TOUR—SIGHT | **FAMILY** | Also known as "Old 300," this is a beautifully restored 1913 streetcar that travels for 4 miles along Astoria's historic riverfront, stopping at several points between the Astoria River Inn and the foot of 39th Street (although you can easily flag it down at any point along the route by offering a friendly wave). The hour-long ride gives you a close-up look at the waterfront from the Port of Astoria to the East Morring Basin; the Columbia River; and points of interest in between. ☎ 503/325–6311, 800/875–6807 ⊕ www.old300.org ⌲ $1, $2 all-day pass ☉ Limited service Oct.–Apr. (call first).

Clatsop County Historical Society Museums

MUSEUM | In a 1904 Colonial Revival building originally used as the city hall, the Clatsop County Historical Society Museum has two floors of exhibits detailing the history of the early pioneers, Native Americans, and logging and marine industries of Clatsop County, the oldest American settlement west of the Mississippi. Artifacts include finely crafted 19th-century Chinook and Clatsop baskets, otter pelts, a re-created Prohibition-era saloon, and historic logging and fishing tools. The Historical Society also operates two other excellent downtown history museums, the Flavel House (441 8th St.), a graciously restored Queen Anne–style mansion where visitors can imagine what life was like for the wealthy in late-19th-century Astoria; and the Uppertown Firefighters Museum (2968 Marine Dr.), which is filled with old equipment, including hand-pulled and horse-drawn fire engines, and a collection of photos of some of the town's most notable fires make up the exhibits. ✉ 1618 Exchange St. ☎ 503/325–2203 ⊕ www. cumtux.org ⌲ $4 ($6 Flavel House, free Uppertown Firefighters Museum).

★ **Columbia River Maritime Museum**

MUSEUM | **FAMILY** | One of Oregon's best coastal attractions illuminates the

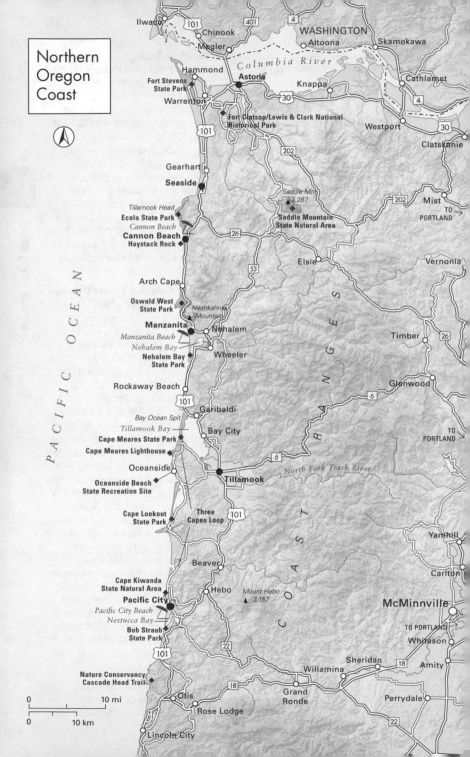

Northern Oregon Coast

Ilwaco Chinook [101] [401] [4] WASHINGTON
Megler Altoona Skamokawa
Columbia River
Hammond Astoria Knappa Cathlamet
Fort Stevens State Park [4]
Warrenton [30] Westport [30]
Fort Clatsop/Lewis & Clark National Historical Park Clatskanie
[101]
[202]
Gearhart Mist TO PORTLAND
Seaside Saddle Mtn [202]
3,287
Saddle Mountain State Natural Area
Tillamook Head [26] Vernonia
Ecola State Park Cannon Beach Elsie
Cannon Beach [53]
Haystack Rock
Arch Cape Timber [26]
Oswald West State Park Neahkahnie Mountain
Manzanita Nehalem
Manzanita Beach Wheeler Glenwood
Nehalem Bay [6]
Nehalem Bay State Park TO PORTLAND
Rockaway Beach [6]
[101]
Garibaldi North Fork Trask River
Bay Ocean Spit
Tillamook Bay Bay City
Cape Meares State Park
Cape Meares Lighthouse
Oceanside Tillamook
Oceanside Beach State Recreation Site
Cape Lookout State Park Three Capes Loop [101]
Yamhill
Beaver Carlton
Cape Kiwanda State Natural Area Hebo
Pacific City Mount Hebo McMinnville
Pacific City Beach 3,157
Nestucca Bay TO PORTLAND
Bob Straub State Park Whiteson
[101] Amity
Sheridan [18]
Nature Conservancy Cascade Head Trail Willamina
[22]
Otis Grand Ronde Perrydale
Rose Lodge
Lincoln City [22]

PACIFIC OCEAN

COAST RANGES

0   10 mi
0   10 km

maritime history of the Pacific Northwest and provides visitors with a sense of the perils of guiding ships into the mouth of the Columbia River. Vivid exhibits recount what it was like to pilot a tugboat and participate in a Coast Guard rescue on the Columbia River Bar. You can tour the actual bridge of a World War II–era U.S. Navy destroyer and the 1951 U.S. Coast Guard lightship *Columbia*. Also on display is a 44-foot Coast Guard motor lifeboat, artifacts from the region's illustrious riverboat heyday, and details about Astoria's seafood-canning history. One especially captivating exhibit displays the personal belongings of some of the ill-fated passengers of the 2,000 ships that have foundered here since the early 19th century. In addition, the theater shows an excellent documentary about the river's heritage as well as rotating 3-D films about sea life. At the east end of the property, the city's former railroad depot now houses the museum's Barbey Maritime Center, which offers classes and workshops on maritime culture and wooden boatbuilding. ⊠ *1792 Marine Dr.* ☎ *503/325–2323* ⊕ *www.crmm.org* ✉ *$14.*

★ **Fort Clatsop at Lewis and Clark National Historical Park**
MEMORIAL | FAMILY | See where the 30-member Lewis and Clark Expedition endured a rain-soaked winter in 1805–06, hunting, gathering food, making salt, and trading with the local Clatsops, Chinooks, and Tillamooks. This memorial is part of the 3,200-acre Lewis and Clark National Historical Park and is a faithful replica of the log fort depicted in Clark's journal. The fort lies within a forested wonderland, with an exhibit hall, gift shop, film, and trails. Park rangers dress in period garb during the summer and perform such early-19th-century tasks as making fire with flint and steel. Hikers enjoy the easy 1½-mile Netul Landing Trail and the more rigorous but still fairly flat 6½-mile Fort to Sea Trail. ⊠ *92343 Fort Clatsop Rd.* ☎ *503/861–2471* ⊕ *www.nps.gov/lewi* ✉ *$7.*

Fort Stevens State Park
MILITARY SITE | FAMILY | This earthen fort at Oregon's northwestern tip was built during the Civil War to guard the Columbia River against attack. None came until World War II, when a Japanese submarine fired upon it. The fort still has cannons and an underground gun battery, of which tours are available in summer (call for details). This 4,300-acre park has year-round camping, with full hookup sites, 11 cabins, and 15 yurts. There are also bike paths, boating, swimming, hiking trails, and a short walk to a gorgeous, wide beach where the corroded skeleton—or the tiny bit that remains of it—of the *Peter Iredale* pokes up through the sand. This century-old English four-master shipwreck is a reminder of the nearly 2,000 vessels claimed by these treacherous waters. ⊠ *100 Peter Iredale Rd., Hammond* ☎ *503/861–3170* ⊕ *www.oregonstateparks.org* ✉ *Day use $5 per vehicle.*

Hanthorn Cannery Museum
MUSEUM | Drive or walk over the rickety-seeming (but actually completely sturdy) bridge onto historic Pier 39, which juts out into the Columbia River on the east side of downtown, to visit this small but interesting museum that occupies the oldest extant cannery building in Astoria. It was once operated by Bumble Bee Seafood, and some 30,000 cans of salmon were processed here annually during the plant's late-19th-century heyday. Exhibits and artifacts, including three vintage gill-net boats, some wonderful old photos, and equipment and cans tell the story of the town's—and facility's—canning history. Also on the pier is Coffee Girl café and Rogue Ales Public House. ⊠ *100 39th St.* ☎ *503/325–2502* ⊕ *www.canneryworker.org* ✉ *Free.*

Oregon Film Museum
MUSEUM | FAMILY | Housed in the old Clatsop County Jail, this small but engaging museum celebrates Oregon's long history of filmmaking and contains

artifacts from and displays about prior productions. The location is apt because it was featured prominently in the famous cult film *The Goonies*, which the town celebrates each June with a one-day Goonies festival. The state's film productions date back to 1908 for *The Fisherman's Bride*. Since then, Oregon has helped give birth to such classics as *The General*, *The Great Race*, *One Flew Over the Cuckoo's Nest*, *Paint Your Wagon*, *Animal House*, and *Twilight*, leading some to call the state Hollywood North. *Kindergarten Cop*, *The Ring II*, *Free Willy I* and *II*, and *Short Circuit* are among those filmed in Astoria. ⊠ *732 Duane St.* ☎ *503/325–2203* ⊕ *www.oregonfilmmuseum.org* ⊒ *$6.*

 ## Restaurants

Astoria Coffeehouse & Bistro

$$ | ECLECTIC | A source of fine coffee drinks and baked goods, this colorful storefront café has both sidewalk seating and a living-room-like interior decorated with old photos. The always-bustling restaurant serves consistently well-prepared food, a mix of American classics and international treats, including a decadent Monte Cristo sandwich at breakfast, and tuna poke with mango and avocado, slow-roasted-beet salad with chèvre and apples, and pad Thai with fresh salmon late in the day. **Known for:** Sunday brunch; excellent drinks, from coffees to cocktails; decadent pastries and baked goods. ⓢ *Average main: $19* ⊠ *243 11th St.* ☎ *503/325–1787* ⊕ *www.astoriacoffeehouse.com.*

Blue Scorcher Bakery Café

$ | CAFÉ | FAMILY | "Joyful work, delicious food, and strong community" is the rallying cry of this family-friendly café known for everything from *huevos scorcheros* (poached eggs with rice, beans, cheese, and salsa) and organic, handcrafted breads to a variety of foods using local, fair trade, and organic ingredients. The offerings change with the seasons, but there are always vegan and gluten-free options, and the inviting dining room's big windows and children's play area overlook downtown and the Columbia River in the distance. **Known for:** delicious desserts; children's play area; funky, light-filled dining room. ⓢ *Average main: $8* ⊠ *1493 Duane St.* ☎ *503/338–7473* ⊕ *www.bluescorcher.com* ⊗ *No dinner.*

Bridgewater Bistro

$$$ | SEAFOOD | In the same complex as the Cannery Pier Hotel, this stylish restaurant has great views of the river and bridge to Washington. Inside, high ceilings are supported by ancient fir timbers, and an extensive menu is strong on creative seafood and meat grills, including roasted spice-encrusted duck breast with orange marmalade glaze, and seared wild local salmon with an arugula-strawberry salad and a star anise–balsamic vinaigrette. **Known for:** Sunday brunch; Columbia River views; fresh, creatively prepared seafood. ⓢ *Average main: $28* ⊠ *20 Basin St., Suite A* ☎ *503/325–6777* ⊕ *www.bridgewaterbistro.com.*

★ Buoy Beer Co

$$ | AMERICAN | One of the most acclaimed craft brewers on the coast, Buoy Beer also serves exceptionally tasty contemporary pub fare in its warm and inviting taproom, set in a converted 1920s grain warehouse on Astoria's riverfront walk—huge windows afford dramatic views of the Columbia. Seafood figures prominently in many dishes here, including rockfish-and-chips and bacon-clam chowder, but you'll also find delicious burgers and meat and cheese boards. **Known for:** hoppy handcrafted IPAs and strong German-style beers; river and sea lion views; panfried oysters with jalapeño jam and goat cheese. ⓢ *Average main: $17* ⊠ *1 8th St.* ☎ *503/325–4540* ⊕ *www.buoybeer.com.*

Carruthers

$$$ | MODERN AMERICAN | The warm lighting, massive fireplace, marble-top bar, and glass-brick transom windows impart

a cosmopolitan vibe to this high-ceilinged downtown bistro that turns out sophisticated, contemporary lunch, dinner, and Sunday brunch fare. Highlights include seared sea scallops with apple-fennel orzo and braised short ribs with andouille and white cheddar grits, but there's also a terrific bar menu of lighter bites—blackened-rockfish tacos, seafood mac and cheese, and the like. **Known for:** great happy hour; well-crafted cocktails; Sunday brunch. $ Average main: $27 ⊠ 1198 Commercial St. ☎ 503/741–3443 ⊙ No dinner Sun.

Coffee Girl

$ | CAFÉ | This cozy café inside a 19th-century cannery building on historic Pier 39 has big windows overlooking the river—you can always take your well-crafted espresso or latte with you for a stroll around the pier. Open until late afternoon each day, Coffee Girl also serves tasty quiches, pastries, soups, bagels with lox, and grilled panini sandwiches. **Known for:** unusual river wharf setting; house-baked granola; top-quality coffee drinks. $ Average main: $6 ⊠ 100 39th St. ☎ 503/325–6900 ⊕ www.thecoffeegirl.com.

Columbian Cafe & Voodoo Room

$ | ECLECTIC | Locals love this funky diner-and-nightclub complex that defies categorization by offering inventive, fresh seafood, spicy vegetarian dishes, and meats cured and smoked on the premises. Located next to the historic Columbian Theater, the café serves simple food, such as crepes with broccoli, cheese, and homemade salsa for lunch. **Known for:** cocktails and very good pizza in the Voodoo Room bar; good people-watching; vintage movies in the adjacent Columbian Theater. $ Average main: $12 ⊠ 1114 Marine Dr. ☎ 503/325–2233 ⊕ www.columbianvoodoo.com/cafe ⊟ No credit cards.

Hotels

★ Cannery Pier Hotel

$$$$ | HOTEL | From every room in this captivating property there's a gorgeous view of the mighty Columbia River flowing toward the Pacific Ocean, and it's almost hypnotic to watch the tugboats shepherding barges to and fro. **Pros:** spectacular river views; complimentary afternoon wine and lox; hotel hot tub and day spa. **Cons:** pricey; a bit of a walk from downtown; some traffic noise from nearby highway bridge. $ Rooms from: $259 ⊠ 10 Basin St. ☎ 503/325–4996, 888/325–4996 ⊕ www.cannerypierhotel.com ⇆ 54 rooms ⊙ Free breakfast.

Clementine's B&B

$ | B&B/INN | This lovingly restored 1888 Italianate Victorian home is just a couple of blocks up the hill from Flavel House Museum and a short walk from several fine restaurants and shops. **Pros:** superb, multicourse breakfast included; handy downtown location; exudes historic charm. **Cons:** the traditional lacy room decor isn't for everyone; rooms are compact; steep steps up to the front door. $ Rooms from: $139 ⊠ 847 Exchange St. ☎ 503/325–2005 ⊕ www.clementines-bb.com ⇆ 5 rooms ⊙ Free breakfast.

Commodore Hotel

$ | HOTEL | An economical but stylish downtown boutique hotel, the Commodore is a favorite with young and artsy souls from Portland and Seattle thanks to its vintage-chic aesthetic, large wall murals and photos, and hip Street 14 Café off the lobby. **Pros:** hip setting; wallet-friendly rates; excellent Street 14 Café on-site. **Cons:** least expensive rooms share a bath; simple decor; on busy downtown street. $ Rooms from: $89 ⊠ 258 14th St. ☎ 503/325–4747 ⊕ www.commodoreastoria.com ⇆ 18 rooms ⊙ No meals.

Hotel Elliott
$$ | **HOTEL** | This atmospheric, five-story hotel stands in the heart of Astoria's historic district and retains the elegance of yesteryear, updated with modern comforts like cozy underfloor heating in the bathrooms and fireplaces and Jacuzzi tubs in the deluxe rooms. **Pros:** captures the city's historic atmosphere beautifully; every effort made to infuse the rooms with upscale amenities; roof deck with stunning views. **Cons:** no on-site dining; some rooms are on the small side; on a busy street downtown. [$] *Rooms from: $179* ✉ *357 12th St.* ☎ *503/325–2222* 🌐 *www.hotelelliott.com* 🛏 *32 rooms* 🍴 *Free breakfast.*

★ Norblad Hotel
$ | **HOTEL** | Formerly a boardinghouse, this attractively renovated, offbeat hotel occupies a stately two-story 1920s building a few steps from Fort George Brewery and offers a mix of small, European-style rooms with shared baths down the hall and a few spacious suites with a private bath. **Pros:** nice common areas and kitchen; short walk from downtown shopping and dining; bargain-priced rooms. **Cons:** fairly basic decor; offbeat, arty vibe isn't for everyone; many rooms share a bath. [$] *Rooms from: $79* ✉ *443 14th St.* ☎ *503/325–6989* 🌐 *www.norbladhotel.com* 🛏 *17 rooms* 🍴 *No meals.*

Nightlife

★ Fort George Brewery
BREWPUBS/BEER GARDENS | The spacious taproom and brewery set in a former 1920s auto showroom has plenty of indoor and outdoor seating where you can sample some of the best craft beers on the coast, including a number of limited-release collaborations with other top regional brewers. There's also tasty pub fare. ✉ *1483 Duane St.* ☎ *503/325–7468* 🌐 *www.fortgeorgebrewery.com.*

Inferno Lounge
BARS/PUBS | Just about every seat in this hip bar situated on a pier that juts into the Columbia River offers stupendous water views. Catch the sunset with a well-crafted cocktail and perhaps a few nibbles—Thai shrimp tacos, pork potstickers—from the tapas menu. This place known for house-infused spirits buzzes until midnight or later. ✉ *77 11th St.* ☎ *503/741–3401.*

★ Reveille Ciderworks
BARS/PUBS | Stop by this friendly downtown taproom with big patio with food trucks to sample superb handcrafted ciders made from a variety of heirloom Northwest apples. These Belgian saison- and English ale-style hard ciders come with a range of complex flavor profiles, from dry and crisp to chai spiced to full-on fruit bombs infused with marionberry or cranberry. ✉ *1343 Duane St., Suite B* ☎ *971/704–2161* 🌐 *www.astoriacider.com.*

Performing Arts

Liberty Theatre
CONCERTS | A massive amber chandelier glows above the 630 seats of this magnificent Italian Renaissance theater that's been a fixture in downtown Astoria since 1925. Painstakingly restored in 2006 and known for its dozen interior murals of Venice, the former vaudeville movie house shows local and nationally prominent dance, classical music, and theater as well as occasional film screenings throughout the year. ✉ *1203 Commercial St.* ☎ *503/325–5922* 🌐 *www.libertyastoria.org.*

Shopping

Astoria Sunday Market
OUTDOOR/FLEA/GREEN MARKETS | Every Sunday between mid-May and mid-October, the town closes three blocks of 12th Street to traffic from 10 to 3 so that as many as 200 vendors can sell goods

they've grown or made. There are booths and tables full of fresh fruits, vegetables, farm products, arts, crafts, and treats of all kinds, plus excellent live music. ✉ *12th and Commercial Sts.* ☎ *503/325–1010* ⊕ *www.astoriasundaymarket.com.*

Doe & Arrow
CLOTHING | This beautifully curated purveyor of urbane women's and men's fashion as well as arty jewelry, hip home accessories, and eco-friendly grooming products occupies a large corner space in downtown's Historic Astor Hotel building. ✉ *380 14th St.* ☎ *503/741–3132* ⊕ *www. doeandarrow.com.*

Josephson's
FOOD/CANDY | Open since 1920, this venerable smokehouse uses alder for all processing and specializes in Pacific Northwest Chinook salmon. The mouthwatering fish that's smoked on the premises includes hot smoked pepper or wine-maple salmon, as well as smoked halibut, sturgeon, tuna, oysters, mussels, rainbow trout, and salmon jerky. ✉ *106 Marine Dr.* ☎ *503/325–2190* ⊕ *www. josephsons.com.*

Seaside

12 miles south of Astoria on U.S. 101.

Established in 1899 as the Oregon Coast's first resort town, Seaside has significantly spruced up its honky-tonk reputation for gaudy arcades and kitschy souvenir shops and now supports a notable selection of mostly midrange hotels, condominiums, and restaurants within walking distance of its traditional paved promenade, aka "the Prom," which stretches 1½ miles along the beachfront. It still has fun games, candy shops, and plenty of carny noise to appeal to kids and teens, but it's also more well-rounded than in the past and offers access to some beautiful natural scenery. Only 90 miles from Portland, Seaside can get crowded, so it's not the place to come

for solitude. Peak times include mid-March to early April during spring break; and late June, when the annual Miss Oregon Pageant is in full swing. Just south of town, waves draw surfers to the Cove, a spot jealously guarded by locals, and the dramatic hike along the Oregon Coast Trail to Tillamook Head connects with Cannon Beach's famous Ecola State Park.

GETTING HERE AND AROUND
Seaside is about a 90-minute drive from Portland via U.S 26 and a 20-minute drive south of Astoria on coastal U.S. 101.

VISITOR INFORMATION
CONTACTS Seaside Visitors Bureau. ✉ *7 N. Roosevelt Ave.* ☎ *503/738–3097, 888/306–2326* ⊕ *www.seasideor.com.*

Sights

Seaside Aquarium
ZOO | **FAMILY** | The first thing you hear at this small but fun 1930s-era aquarium is the clapping and barking of the harbor seals just inside the door (which you can feed). Located on the 1½-mile beachfront Promenade, the aquarium has jellyfish, giant king crab, octopus, moray eels, wolf eels, and other sea life swimming in more than 30 tanks. The discovery center draws curious kids and grown-ups alike for its hands-on touch tanks of starfish, anemones, and urchins, as well as for a close-up exploration of the most minia-ture marine life. No restrooms on-site. ✉ *200 N. Promenade* ☎ *503/738–6211* ⊕ *www.seasideaquarium.com* 🎫 *$8.50.*

Restaurants

Firehouse Grill
$ | **PACIFIC NORTHWEST** | This bustling diner-style café in a former firehouse in downtown Seaside hits the mark with its hearty breakfast fare, including fluffy biscuits with gravy, salmon Benedicts, cinnamon French toast, meat-loaf scram-bles, and a couple of lighter options,

such as house-made granola with fresh fruit. Open only until early afternoon, the restaurant also turns out excellent burgers, panfried oysters, and cod tacos and fish-and-chips at lunch. **Known for:** hearty, creative breakfast fare; cod tacos and fish-and-chips; Sleepy Monk coffee and first-rate Bloody Marys. $ *Average main: $13* ✉ *841 Broadway* ☎ *503/717–5502* ⊕ *www.firehousegrill.org* ⊗ *Closed Tues. and Wed. No dinner.*

★ Osprey Café

$ | **ECLECTIC** | The delicious made-from-scratch breakfast and lunch items at this cheerful café with several outdoor seats reflects the owner's extensive travels around the world, from the Central American arepas with shredded chicken, black beans, and avocado to Indonesian *nasi goreng* to flavorful chilaquiles. There are plenty of classic American dishes, too (the Hangtown fry and Cobb salad are both excellent), and creative cocktails offer a way to liven up your weekend brunch. **Known for:** quiet location near south end of "the Prom"; interesting globally inspired daily specials; weekend brunch. $ *Average main: $12* ✉ *2281 Beach Dr.* ☎ *503/739–7054* ⊗ *Closed Wed. No dinner.*

Hotels

McMenamins Gearhart Hotel

$$ | **HOTEL** | The quirky McMenamins hotel group operates this 34-room boutique inn on the upper floor of the Cape Cod–style Kelly House and in the modern Annex building, in the low-key beach community of Gearhart (a 10-minute drive north of Seaside)—it's next to the esteemed Gearhart Golf Links. **Pros:** short walk from beach; rooms have distinctive and arty flair; excellent 18-hole golf course. **Cons:** ocean view is blocked by condos across the street; 10-minute drive north of Seaside; restaurant on-site is uneven. $ *Rooms from: $155* ✉ *1157 N. Marion Ave., 4 miles north of Seaside, Gearhart* ☎ *503/717–8159, 855/846–7583* ⊕ *www.*

mcmenamins.com/gearhart-hotel ⬏ *34 rooms* ❑❘ *No meals.*

★ Rivertide Suites

$$ | **HOTEL** | **FAMILY** | Although it's not right on the beach, the Rivertide's splendid and spacious accommodations are within walking distance of Seaside's many restaurants, candy shops, and old-time amusements, making it a great choice for families. **Pros:** rates include breakfast and evening manager's reception; lots of different activity-based packages available; near plenty of shopping and boardwalk activities. **Cons:** it's on a river rather than the beach; rooms on lower floors have less of a view; family-friendly vibe isn't ideal for everyone. $ *Rooms from: $169* ✉ *102 N. Holladay Dr.* ☎ *503/717–1100, 877/871–8433* ⊕ *www.rivertidesuites. com* ⬏ *70 suites* ❑❘ *Free breakfast.*

Sandy Cove Inn

$ | **HOTEL** | This small, nicely maintained motel is fun and colorfully decorated, and it's just a couple of blocks away from the quieter and more scenic southern end of Seaside's promenade as well as Seaside Golf Course. **Pros:** relatively quiet, low-key location; distinctive room themes; excellent value. **Cons:** not directly on the beach; about 1 mile south of downtown shops and dining; two-night minimum stay at busy times. $ *Rooms from: $149* ✉ *241 Ave. U* ☎ *503/738–7473* ⊕ *www. sandycoveinn.net* ⬏ *15 rooms* ❑❘ *No meals.*

Nightlife

Seaside Brewing

BREWPUBS/BEER GARDENS | This chatter-filled taproom inside the old city jail is as worthy a stop for well-crafted, European-influenced beers, including a potent Belgian Tripel and sweet but lightly hoppy vanilla cream ale, as for the extensive menu of pub fare. Texas-style brisket and sausages are among the top noshables. ✉ *851 Broadway St.* ☎ *503/717–5451* ⊕ *www.seasidebrewery.com.*

🛍 Shopping

Phillips Candy Kitchen

FOOD/CANDY | **FAMILY** | There are at least a half-dozen candy shops in Seaside's tiny downtown, and shopping for sweets is a favorite pastime here among kids and adults. Phillips has been a favorite since 1897 and presently stocks homemade saltwater taffy, candied fruit slices, caramel popcorn, fudge, stroopwafel, and hand-dipped chocolates in an astonishing array of flavors. ⊠ *217 Broadway* ☎ *503/738–5402* ⊕ *www.phillipscandies. com* 🎫 *Free.*

🏃 Activities

HIKING

★ Saddle Mountain State Natural Area

HIKING/WALKING | One of the most accessible mountain peaks in the Coast Range, 3,290-foot Saddle Mountain is reached via a challenging but beautiful 2½-mile climb, with a 1,640-foot elevation gain—the reward, on clear days, is a view of the ocean to the west and the Cascade peaks—including Mt. Hood—far to the east. Wear sturdy shoes, and be prepared for sections with steep upgrades. There's a zippy change in the altitude as you climb higher, but the wildflowers make it all worthwhile. The trailhead is well signed off U.S. 26, the main highway back to Portland. ⊠ *Saddle Mountain Rd.* ⊕ *Off U.S. 26, 20 miles east of Seaside* ☎ *503/368–5943* ⊕ *www.oregon-stateparks.org.*

Tillamook Head

HIKING/WALKING | A moderately challenging 7½-mile loop from U.S. 101, south of Seaside, brings you through lushly forested Elmer Feldenheimer Forest Reserve and into the northern end of Cannon Beach's Ecola State Park to a nearly 1,000-foot-high viewing point, a great place to see the **Tillamook Rock Light Station,** which stands a mile or so off the coast. The lonely beacon, built in 1881 on a straight-sided rock, towers 41 feet above the ocean and was abandoned in 1957. You can also reach this viewing area by hiking north from Indian Beach in Ecola State Park in Cannon Beach. ⊠ *End of Sunset Blvd.* ⊕ *www. oregonstateparks.org.*

Cannon Beach

9 miles south of Seaside.

Cannon Beach is a mellow but relatively affluent town where locals and part-time residents—many of the latter reside in Portland—come to enjoy shopping, gallery touring, and dining, the sea air, and the chance to explore the spectacular state parks at either end of the area: Ecola to the north and Oswald West to the south. Shops and galleries selling surfing gear, upscale clothing, local art, wine, coffee, and candies line Hemlock Street, Cannon Beach's main thoroughfare. In late June the town hosts the Cannon Beach Sandcastle Contest, for which thousands throng the beach to view imaginative and often startling works in this most transient of art forms. On the downside, this so-called Carmel of the Oregon Coast is more expensive and often more crowded than other towns along U.S. 101.

GETTING HERE AND AROUND

It's a 90-minute drive east from Portland on U.S. 26 to reach Cannon Beach, which is a 10-minute drive south of Seaside. To make a scenic loop, consider returning to Portland by way of Astoria and U.S. 30 (about 2¼ hours) or Tillamook and Highway 6 (about 2½ hours).

ESSENTIALS

VISITOR INFORMATION Cannon Beach Chamber of Commerce. ⊠ *207 N. Spruce St.* ☎ *503/436–2623* ⊕ *www.cannon-beach.org.*

Sights

EVOO Cannon Beach

COLLEGE | Offering fun and interactive culinary experiences as well as a well-stocked gourmet shop, EVOO offers cooking classes as well as demonstration dinners and lunches set around seasonal or specific food themes throughout the year, from artisanal bread making to the art of pasta. The food is always based on what's local and in season, and these meals are always delicious and a great opportunity to learn and meet friends. These experiences are by ticket only and start at $149 per person and include a full meal, with wine pairings. ⊠ *188 S. Hemlock St.* ☎ *503/436–8555, 877/436–3866* ⊕ *www.evoo.biz.*

Beaches

★ Cannon Beach and Ecola State Park

BEACHES | **FAMILY** | Beachcombers love Cannon Beach for its often low foamy waves and the wide stretch of sand that wraps the quaint community, making it ideal for fair-weather play or for hunting down a cup of coffee and strolling in winter. This stretch can get feisty in storms, however, which also makes Cannon Beach a good place to curl up indoors and watch the show. Haystack Rock rises 235 feet over the beach on the south side of downtown, one of nearly 2,000 protected rocks that are part of the Oregon Ocean Island Wildlife Refuge, providing a nesting habitat for birds. Continue south past Tolovana Park—a playground located in the flood plain—to find the quiet side of Cannon Beach with a bevy of tide pools and few other souls. To the north of town, the beach gives way to Ecola State Park, a breathtakingly beautiful series of coves and rocky headlands where William Clark spotted a beached whale in 1806 and visitors still come to view them offshore during the twice-yearly migrations. From here, Sitka spruce and barbecues feature along the sands. There are a few excellent trails that hug the sometimes steep cliffs that rise above sand, including a 6½-mile trail first traced by Lewis and Clark, which runs from this spot past the Tillamook Head lookout and then eventually all the way to Seaside. **Amenities:** parking; toilets. **Best for:** partiers; sunset; walking. ⊠ *Ocean Ave.* ☎ *503/436–2844* ⊕ *www.oregonstateparks.org* ⚐ *Ecola State Park day use $5 per vehicle.*

 Restaurants

Castaways

$$$ | **CARIBBEAN** | At the north end of town, making it a perfect drop-in after a hike at Ecola State Park, this colorfully decorated spot with its own little tiki bar serves big portions of creatively prepared Caribbean and Creole fare, along with a fittingly extensive selection of tropical cocktails (the yellowbird, with fresh-squeezed tangerine and lime juice and Tia Maria, is a favorite). Kick things off with Dungeness crab fritters with mango salsa and Bahamian brown stew, before tucking into a heartier main dish, perhaps Jamaican jerk chicken or New Orleans jambalaya. **Known for:** a pineapple-guava red curry dish with a daily changing protein; easygoing island vibe; Caribbean-inspired cocktails. $ *Average main: $24* ⊠ *316 Fir St.* ☎ *503/436–4444* ⊗ *Closed Tues. No lunch.*

★ Irish Table

$$$ | **IRISH** | Adjacent to the Sleepy Monk café, this cozy restaurant with a timber-beam ceiling and warm lighting serves seasonal food with an Irish twist, such as potato-kale soup, a much-heralded Irish lamb stew, and an always outstanding fresh fish of the day. Start with the curried mussels, and soak up the sauce with slices of piping-hot soda bread, and keep in mind that there's a rich assortment of drinks, including Irish whiskey and a wine list featuring plenty of noted Oregon options. **Known for:** Irish whiskey selection; friendly service;

addictive warm soda bread. $ *Average main: $25* ✉ *1235 S. Hemlock St.* ☎ *503/436–0708* ⊘ *Closed Wed. and Jan. No lunch.*

★ Sleepy Monk

$ | CAFÉ | In a region renowned for artisanal coffee, this small roaster brews some of the best espresso and coffee drinks in the state, and thus attracts java aficionados on caffeine pilgrimages from near and far eager to sample its certified-organic, fair-trade beans. Local, fresh pastries are stacked high and there's also a good selection of herbal and green teas. **Known for:** outstanding coffee; cozy dining room with some outdoor seats; savory and sweet baked goods. $ *Average main: $5* ✉ *1235 S. Hemlock St.* ☎ *503/436–2796* ⊕ *www.sleepymonkcoffee.com* ⊘ *Closed Wed. No dinner.*

Wayfarer Restaurant

$$$$ | PACIFIC NORTHWEST | The dazzling beach and ocean views, especially at sunset, are just part of the story at this casually elegant restaurant at the Surfsand Resort; it's also a reliable if very traditional destination for a leisurely feast of local seafood and steaks, such as panko-breaded Pacific razor clams with rémoulade, seared Chinook salmon with risotto, and the prodigious 22-ounce "tomahawk" rib-eye steak with a Pinot Noir butter. There's a nice list of Oregon wines, and breakfast—featuring delicious crab cake Benedicts and cinnamon roll French toast—is offered daily. **Known for:** great ocean views; classic Northwest seafood and steaks; hearty breakfasts. $ *Average main: $34* ✉ *1190 Pacific Dr.* ☎ *503/436–1108* ⊕ *www.wayfarer-restaurant.com.*

Hotels

Arch Cape Inn & Retreat

$$$ | B&B/INN | Between the lively beach communities of Manzanita and Cannon Beach, this utterly romantic getaway—situated well away from the summer hordes—lies along some of the most gorgeous stretch of coast in the region. **Pros:** elegant, distinctive rooms; peaceful location away from the crowds; most rooms have terrific ocean views. **Cons:** 200 yards from the beach; no kids under 18 permitted; not within walking distance of town. $ *Rooms from: $209* ✉ *31970 E. Ocean La.* ☎ *503/436–2800* ⊕ *www.archcapeinn.com* ⇱ *10 rooms* ❍ *Free breakfast.*

Ecola Creek Lodge

$$ | HOTEL | With a quiet, shady courtyard just off the main road leading into the north side of town, this small, reasonably priced 1940s hotel offers suites and rooms with a mix of configurations, from two-bedroom units with kitchens to cozy standard rooms. **Pros:** simple and tasteful decor; rooms come in wide range of layouts; good value. **Cons:** not on the beach; slight walk from downtown shopping; some rooms are a little small. $ *Rooms from: $160* ✉ *208 E. 5th St.* ☎ *503/436–2776, 800/873–2749* ⊕ *www.ecolacreeklodge.com* ⇱ *22 rooms* ❍ *No meals.*

Ocean Lodge

$$$$ | HOTEL | Designed to capture the feel of a 1940s beach resort, this rustic but upscale lodge is perfect for special occasions and romantic getaways; its rooms—most with oceanfront views—feature wood beams, gas fireplaces, and balconies or decks. **Pros:** beachfront waterfront location; spacious rooms; free passes to local gym and yoga studio. **Cons:** expensive in summer; balconies are shared with neighboring rooms; about a mile from downtown. $ *Rooms from: $289* ✉ *2864 S. Pacific St.* ☎ *503/436–2241, 888/777–4047* ⊕ *www.theoceanlodge.com* ⇱ *45 rooms* ❍ *Free breakfast.*

★ Stephanie Inn

$$$$ | RESORT | One of the coastline's most beautiful views is paired with one of its most splendid hotels, where the focus is firmly on romance, superior service, and luxurious rooms. **Pros:** incredibly plush accommodations; on a gorgeous stretch of beach; fabulous on-site restaurant and spa. **Cons:** among the highest rates of any hotel in the state; not for families with younger children; about a mile from downtown. ⓢ *Rooms from: $469* ✉ *2740 S. Pacific St.* ☎ *503/436–2221, 855/977–2444* ⊕ *www.stephanieinn.com* ⇌ *41 rooms* ⦿ *Free breakfast.*

Tolovana Inn

$ | **HOTEL** | **FAMILY** | Set on the beach at the quieter southern end of town, the large, rambling Tolovana Inn is one of the better-priced options in this tony seaside community, especially considering that most rooms enjoy partial or full views of the Pacific. **Pros:** panoramic beach views; gym, day spa, pool, and other resort amenities; some units have kitchens. **Cons:** a 10-minute drive from downtown; some rooms are relatively small; economy rooms have no water view. ⓢ *Rooms from: $139* ✉ *3400 S. Hemlock St.* ☎ *503/436–2211, 800/333–8890* ⊕ *www.tolovanainn.com* ⇌ *175 rooms* ⦿ *No meals.*

Nightlife

★ Cannon Beach Hardware and Public House

BARS/PUBS | At this oddly endearing gastropub a block from the beach, the view from your table may be of bins filled with assorted lamb knobs or pliers—this is an actual hardware store (with a good supply of gifts, to boot). To drink you'll find a nice list of regional craft brews on tap, plus eclectic cocktails and Northwest wines, and good burgers, sandwiches, seafood apps, and other tavern fare are available. ✉ *1235 S. Hemlock St.* ☎ *503/436–4086* ⊕ *www.cannonbeach-hardware.com.*

Shopping

Cannon Beach Art Galleries

ART GALLERIES | The numerous art galleries that line Cannon Beach's Hemlock Street are an essential part of the town's spirit and beauty. A group of about a dozen galleries featuring beautifully innovative works in ceramic, bronze, photography, painting, and other mediums have collaborated to form the Cannon Beach Gallery Group. You'll find information about exhibits and special events on the website. ✉ *Hemlock St.* ⊕ *www.cbgallerygroup.com.*

Manzanita

15 miles south of Cannon Beach.

Manzanita is a secluded and gorgeously situated seaside community with only around 650 full-time residents—but a fast-growing popularity among weekenders from the Willamette Valley translates to one of the largest selections of vacation rentals along the northern Oregon Coast. The village is on a sandy peninsula, peppered with tufts of grass, on the northwestern side of Nehalem Bay, a noted windsurfing destination. It's a fairly laid-back town, but its growing crop of notable restaurants and boutiques has given it an increasingly fashionable reputation, and nature lovers appreciate its proximity to beautiful Oswald West State Park.

GETTING HERE AND AROUND

Tiny Manzanita is an easy and picturesque 20-minute drive south of Cannon Beach on coastal U.S. 101; from Portland, it takes just less than two hours to get here.

Beaches

Manzanita Beach and Nehalem Bay State Park

BEACHES | FAMILY | The long stretch of white sand that separates the Pacific Ocean from the town of Manzanita is as loved a stretch of coastline as the next, its north side reaching into the shadows of Neahkanie Mountain, right where the mountain puts its foot in the ocean (the mountain itself, which makes for a great hike, lies within Oswald West State Park). The beach is frequented by vacationers, day-trippers, kite flyers, and dogs on its north end, but it extends a breezy 7 miles to the tip of Nehalem Bay State Park, which is accessible on foot over sand or by car along the road (the auto entrance is off Gary Street at Sandpiper Lane). At the south end of the park's parking lot, a dirt horse trail leads all the way to a peninsula's tip, a flat walk behind grassy dunes—you can book horseback excursions from Oregon Beach Rides, which has a stable inside the park. Cross to the right for a secluded patch of windy sand on the ocean, or to the left for a quiet, sunny place in the sun on Nehalem Bay, out of the wind. **Amenities:** toilets. **Best for:** sunset; walking. ✉ *Foot of Laneda Ave.* ☎ *503/368–5154* 🌐 *www.oregonstateparks.org* 🎟 *Nehalem Bay State Park day use $5 per vehicle.*

Restaurants

Bread and Ocean Bakery

$$ | AMERICAN | This small bakery with a simple, cheerful dining room and several more tables on the sunny patio is hugely popular for breakfast and lunch—and dinners some evenings—with the many folks who rent cottages in the friendly beach town. Start the morning with a slice of quiche or breakfast frittata; tuck into a hefty deli sandwich at lunch, and consider the Dungeness crab cakes or slow-cooked pot roast in the evening. **Known for:** picnic lunches (great for the beach or a hike); gourmet groceries, wines, and beers to go or eat in; huge and chewy cinnamon rolls. [$] *Average main: $18* ✉ *154 Laneda Ave.* ☎ *503/368–5823* 🌐 *www.breadandocean.com* 🕒 *Closed Mon. and Tues. No dinner Sun.–Wed.*

★ **Salmonberry Saloon**

$$ | MODERN AMERICAN | With a sweeping wooden deck to watch the magnificent sunsets over Nehalem Bay and Manzanita's sand dunes, this lively saloon in tiny, historic Wheeler could probably get away with serving merely ordinary food. But the owners offer a remarkably ambitious beverage program (especially when it comes to the wine selection) and exceptional seafood-focused tavern fare, such as *brodetto* (Italian fish stew) of local crabs, shrimp, and clams with shaved fennel and toast, and rockfish–melted cheddar sandwiches. **Known for:** dazzling sunset views; nicely curated list of often hard-to-find wines; creative local seafood fare. [$] *Average main: $20* ✉ *380 Marine Dr., Wheeler* ☎ *503/714–1423* 🌐 *www.salmonberrysaloon.com* 🕒 *Closed Tues.*

Yolk

$ | MODERN AMERICAN | The locally sourced, all-day breakfasts at this hip café on Manzanita's main drag include hefty platters of buttery biscuits with fennel sausage–mushroom gravy and lemon-ricotta pancakes with marionberries. For lunch, try the lamb burger with feta and a dill-mint aioli. **Known for:** all-day breakfast; extensive menu; huge portions. [$] *Average main: $14* ✉ *503 Laneda Ave.* ☎ *503/368–9655* 🕒 *Closed Tues. and Wed. No dinner.*

Hotels

Coast Cabins

$$$ | RENTAL | The options at this tranquil little compound within walking distance of the beach and Manzanita's lively shopping-dining strip include six luxury cabins and three loft-style contemporary condos, all of them appointed with carefully chosen, stylish contemporary furnishings. **Pros:** chicly appointed, spacious accommodations; plenty of cushy amenities; there's a nice little gym. **Cons:** not on the beach; not all units have hot tubs; pricey. [$] *Rooms from: $235* ✉ *635 Laneda Ave.* ☎ *503/368–7113* 🌐 *www.coastcabins.com* 🛏 *10 units* 🍴 *No meals.*

★ Inn at Manzanita

$$ | **B&B/INN** | **FAMILY** | Shore pines around this 1987 Scandinavian structure give upper-floor patios a tree-house feel, and it's just half a block from the beach. **Pros:** tranquil setting with a Japanese garden atmosphere; very close to the beach and downtown shops; several rooms good for families. **Cons:** two-night minimum stay on weekends; can book up fast in summer; no water view from some rooms. [$] *Rooms from: $179* ✉ *67 Laneda Ave.* ☎ *503/368–6754* 🌐 *www.innatmanzanita.com* 🛏 *13 rooms* 🍴 *No meals.*

Old Wheeler Hotel

$ | **B&B/INN** | One of the better values along this section of the Oregon Coast, this small and simple 1920s hotel offers eight clean, economical rooms in the center of Wheeler, a tiny historic village on the Nehalem River just a 10-minute drive south of Manzanita. **Pros:** antiques-filled rooms lend a charming atmosphere; some rooms overlook Nehalem Bay; wallet-friendly rates. **Cons:** not many businesses within walking distance; not on the beach; no restaurant on-site. [$] *Rooms from: $129* ✉ *495 U.S. 101, Wheeler* ☎ *503/368–6000* 🌐 *www.oldwheelerhotel.com* 🛏 *8 rooms* 🍴 *Free breakfast.*

Activities

RECREATIONAL AREAS

★ Oswald West State Park

PARK—SPORTS-OUTDOORS | Adventurous travelers will enjoy a sojourn at one of the best-kept secrets on the Pacific coast, at the base of Neahkahnie Mountain. Park in one of the two free lots on U.S. 101 and hike a half-mile trail to dramatic Short Sand Beach, aka "Shorty's," one of the top spots along the Oregon Coast for surfing. It's a spectacular beach with caves and tidal pools. There are several trails from the beach, all offering dazzling scenery; the relatively easy 2½-mile trail to Cape Falcon overlook joins with the Oregon Coast Trail and offers impressive views back toward Shorty's Beach. The arduous 5½-mile trail to the 1,680-foot summit of Neahkahnie Mountain (access the trailhead about 2 miles south of the parking lots marked only by a "Hikers" sign, or get there via Short Sand Beach) provides dazzling views south for many miles toward the surf, sand, and mountains fringing Manzanita and, in the distance, Tillamook. Come in December or March and you might spot pods of gray whales. ✉ *U.S. 101, Arch Cape* ✥ *5 miles north of downtown Manzanita* ☎ *503/368–3575* 🌐 *www.oregonstateparks.org* 🎟 *Free.*

HORSEBACK RIDING

Oregon Beach Rides

HORSEBACK RIDING | **FAMILY** | Saddle up for horseback rides at Nehalem Bay State Park, available Memorial Day through Labor Day weekends. Guides take you on a journey along the beach in Manzanita, and reserved rides can last from one to several hours. There's even a romantic sunset trot. It's appropriate for ages six and up. ✉ *Nehalem Bay State Park, 34600 Gary St., Nehalem* ☎ *971/237–6653* 🌐 *www.oregonbeachrides.com* ✍ *Reservations essential.*

Tillamook

27 miles south of Manzanita.

More than 100 inches of annual rainfall and the confluence of three rivers contribute to the lush green pastures around

Tillamook, probably best known for its thriving dairy industry and cheese factory, and an increasingly noteworthy locavore-driven culinary scene that extends into the nearby villages of Oceanside, Netarts, and Pacific City—for tips on where to explore in the region, visit the Tillamook Coast Visitors Association's North Coast Food Trail website (⊕ www.northcoastfoodtrail.com). The town itself lies several miles inland from the ocean and doesn't offer much in the way of beachy diversions, but it is the best jumping-off point for driving the dramatic Three Capes Loop, which passes over Cape Meares, Cape Lookout, and Cape Kiwanda and offers spectacular views of the ocean and coastline. The small village of Oceanside, just north of Cape Lookout, has several cute restaurants and shops and a lovely beachfront.

GETTING HERE AND AROUND
Tillamook is a 90-minute drive from Portland on U.S. 26 to Highway 6. It's a winding, pretty, 45-minute drive south of Cannon Beach on U.S. 101, and a one-hour drive north of Lincoln City along the same coastal highway.

VISITOR INFORMATION
VISITOR INFORMATION Tillamook Coast Visitors Association. ✉ 4506 3rd St. ☎ 503/842–2672 ⊕ www.tillamookcoast.com.

Sights

★ Cape Lookout State Park
BEACH—SIGHT | Located about 8 miles south of the beach town Netarts, this pristine and diverse park includes a moderately easy (though often muddy) 2-mile trail—marked on the highway as "wildlife viewing area"—that leads through giant spruces, western red cedars, and hemlocks, and ends with views of Cascade Head to the south and Cape Meares to the north. Wildflowers, more than 150 species of birds, and occasional whales throughout the summer months make

this trail a favorite with nature lovers. The section of the park just north of the trail comprises a long, curving stretch of beach with picnic areas and campsites. ✉ Cape Lookout Rd. at Netarts Bay Rd. ☎ 503/842–4981 ⊕ www.oregonstateparks.org ☞ Day-use parking $5.

Cape Meares State Scenic Viewpoint
LIGHTHOUSE | On the northern tip of the Three Capes Loop, this small but spectacular park and vista is the site of the restored **Cape Meares Lighthouse,** built in 1890 and open to the public May through September. It provides a sweeping view from a 200-foot-tall cliff to the caves and sea lion rookery on the rocks below, and this is a great perch for seeing whales during their migrations. A many-trunked Sitka spruce known as the Octopus Tree grows near the lighthouse parking lot. ✉ 3500 Cape Meares Loop, Oceanside ☎ 503/842–3182 ⊕ www.oregonstateparks.org ☞ Free.

★ Tillamook Cheese Creamery
FACTORY | FAMILY | Cheese and ice cream lovers of all ages have long made a stop by the largest cheese-making plant on the West Coast, as much to enjoy free samples and snack on delicious ice cream (try the marionberry, if you're stumped about what to order). In 2018 Tillamook completely revamped and expanded its visitor facilities. You can still learn about cheese making through informative signs and by watching the process from a glassed-in mezzanine, but the gift shop has been expanded into an impressive gourmet market that stocks Tillamook's many varieties of cheddar, produced in part with milk from thousands of local Holstein and brown Swiss cows, as well as chocolates, charcuterie, and all sorts of other mostly Oregon-made snacks and beverages, including wine and craft beer. Additionally, the ice cream café has been reimagined as a huge food hall with soaring windows, plenty of seating, and a full kitchen serving Tillamook cheeseburgers,

pizzas, mac and cheese, and the like. ✉ *4175 U.S. 101 N* ☎ *503/815–1300, 800/542–7290* 🌐 *www.tillamook.com.*

Tillamook Naval Air Station Museum
MUSEUM | FAMILY | In the world's largest wooden structure, a former blimp hangar south of town displays a fine collection of vintage aircraft from World War II, including a vast trove of artifacts and memorabilia, including war uniforms, photos, and remains from the Hindenburg. The 20-story-high building is big enough to hold half a dozen football fields. ✉ *6030 Hangar Rd.* ☎ *503/842–1130* 🌐 *www.tillamookair.com* 🎟 *$10.50* 🕒 *Closed Mon. and Tues.*

Beaches

Oceanside Beach State Recreation Site
BEACHES | FAMILY | This relatively small, sandy cove is a great stop at the midpoint of the cape's loop. It's especially popular with beachcombers in summer for both its shallow, gentle surf and the low-tide bowls and tide pools that make it a great play beach for kids. When the water recedes, it also uncovers a tunnel through the north rock face ensconcing the beach, allowing passage to a second, rocky cove. There are a few fun, casual spots for ice cream and light bites steps from the beach. Parking in summer, however, is tough. The small lot fills quickly, and a walk through the hilly side streets is sometimes required. **Amenities:** none. **Best for:** walking; partiers. ✉ *Pacific Ave. at Rosenberg Loop, Oceanside* ☎ *503/842–3182* 🌐 *www.oregonstateparks.org.*

Restaurants

Hidden Acres Greenhouse & Café
$ | AMERICAN | Set along a stretch of U.S. 101 that courses south of downtown Tillamook, a bit inland and through a lush, agrarian valley, this aptly named oasis of plants, garden gifts, fountains, and art is a delightful spot for a daytime meal that's usually refreshingly far from beach crowds. Count on made-to-order tuna, club, turkey-cranberry, and other sandwiches and wraps (everything can be served on a bed of local greens in place of bread), as well as granola parfait, avocado toast, and Tillamook cheese egg sandwiches at breakfast. **Known for:** charming greenhouse-nursery setting; scones, pies, and other sweets; coffee drinks and smoothies. [$] *Average main: $10* ✉ *6760 S Prairie Rd.* ☎ *503/842–1197* 🕒 *Closed Sun. No dinner.*

Roseanna's Cafe
$$ | SEAFOOD | In a rustic 1915 building on the beach, this café brightened with candlelight and fresh flowers sits opposite Three Arch Rock, a favorite resting spot for sea lions and puffins. The menu includes snapper, halibut, and salmon prepared with several sauce options, baked oysters, and Gorgonzola seafood pasta, and the meal's not complete without marionberry cobbler. **Known for:** marionberry cobbler; baked Washington oysters; lovely water views. [$] *Average main: $22* ✉ *1490 Pacific Ave., Oceanside* ☎ *503/842–7351* 🌐 *www.roseannascafe.com* 🕒 *Closed Tues. and Wed. and most of Dec.*

Shopping

Jacobsen Salt Co
FOOD/CANDY | This little wood-frame contemporary shop on Netarts Bay adjoins the saltworks of this company that's rapidly becoming internationally renowned for pure and artisanally-infused sea salts (with flavors like black garlic, vanilla bean, and ghost chili). You can also purchase the company's honey, salted caramels, peppercorns, and other goodies. ✉ *9820 Whiskey Creek Rd.* ☎ *503/946–9573* 🌐 *www.jacobsensalt.com.*

🏃 Activities

The **Three Capes Loop,** an enchanting 35-mile byway off U.S. 101, winds along the coast between Tillamook and Pacific City, passing three distinctive head-lands—Cape Meares, Cape Lookout, and Cape Kiwanda. Bayocean Road heading west from Tillamook passes what was the thriving resort town of Bayocean, which washed into the sea more than 50 years ago. A road still crosses the levee to Bayocean, and along the beach on the other side you can find the remnants of an old hotel to the north. The pano-ramic views from the north end of the peninsula are worth the walk. A warm and windless road returns hikers on the bay side.

Pacific City

24 miles south of Tillamook.

There's a lot to like about Pacific City, not the least of which is that it's 3 miles off Oregon's busy coastal highway, U.S. 101. That means there's usually no backup at the town's only traffic light—a blinking-red, four-way stop in the center of town. There's just the quiet, happy atmosphere of a town whose 1,000-or-so residents live in the midst of extraor-dinary beauty. It's home to one of the region's most celebrated contemporary resorts, Headlands Coastal Lodge & Spa, along with some wonderful opportunities for recreation. The beach at Pacific City is one of the few places in the state where fishing dories (flat-bottom boats with high, flaring sides) are launched directly into the surf instead of from harbors or docks.

GETTING HERE AND AROUND
Between Tillamook and Lincoln City, the unincorporated village of Pacific City is just off U.S. 101 on the south end of the beautiful Three Capes Loop. It is a two-hour drive from Portland on U.S. 26

to Highway 6, or a 75-minute drive from Salem via Highway 22.

ESSENTIALS
VISITOR INFORMATION Pacific City-Nestucca Valley Chamber of Commerce. ☎ *503/392–4340, 888/549–2632* ⊕ *www. pcnvchamber.org.*

👁 Sights

★ Bob Straub State Park
PARK—SPORTS-OUTDOORS | This 484-acre expanse of coastal wilderness includes a wind-swept walk along the flat white-sand beach that leads to the mouth of the Nestucca River, one of the best fishing rivers on the North Coast. The beach along the Pacific is frequently windy, but it's separated from the stiller, warmer side of the peninsula by high dunes. Multiple trails cross the dunes into a forest that leads to small beaches on the Nestucca. Relax here with a book, and easily find stillness and sunshine. It's possible to skip the Pacific stroll all together, and find trails to the Nestucca straight from the parking lot, but it's hard to resist the views from the top of the dunes. If you choose the ocean side, pitch your beach camp in the dunes, not the flat sand, and you'll find respite from the wind. ⊠ *End of Sunset Dr.* ☎ *503/842–3182* ⊕ *www.oregon-stateparks.org.*

Cape Kiwanda State Natural Area
BEACH—SIGHT | Huge waves pound the jagged sandstone cliffs and caves here, and the much-photographed, 327-foot-high **Haystack Rock** (not to be confused with the 235-foot-tall rock of the same name up in Cannon Beach) juts out of the Pacific Ocean to the south. Surfers ride some of the longest waves on the coast, hang gliders soar above the shore, and beachcombers explore tidal pools and massive sand dunes, and take in unpar-alleled ocean views. ⊠ *Cape Kiwanda Dr.* ☎ *503/842–3182, 800/551–6949* ⊕ *www. oregonstateparks.org.*

Beaches

★ Cape Kiwanda State Natural Area and Pacific City Beach

BEACHES | The town's public beach adjoins Cape Kiwanda State Natural Area, the southernmost section of famously picturesque Three Capes Loop, and extends south to Bob Straub State Park. Adjacent to Cape Kiwanda's massive 240-foot-tall dune, it's a fun place for kids to scamper to its summit just for the thrill of sliding back down again. Hikers also get a thrill from the top, where the view opens on a tiny cove and tide pools below, and the walk down is infinitely easier than the climb. The beach is also popular with tailgaters—it's one of the few places on the Oregon Coast where it's legal to park your vehicle on the sand. Other parking is available off Cape Kiwanda Drive, near the Pelican Pub. For quieter outings, try the Bob Straub. **Amenities:** none. **Best for:** partiers; walking. ✉ *Cape Kiwanda Dr.* ☎ *503/842–3182* 🌐 *www.oregonstateparks.org.*

Restaurants

Grateful Bread Bakery

$ | **AMERICAN** | **FAMILY** | This airy and bright café uses the cod caught by the local dories for its fish sandwiches, and everything served during its popular breakfasts and lunches is made fresh and from scratch, including delicious breads, biscuits, and pastries. Favorite dishes include gingerbread pancakes and *gallo pinto* (a Costa Rican plate of black beans, scrambled eggs, homemade salsa, and corn tortillas) at breakfast, and locally caught albacore tuna melts and bacon-cheddar burgers at lunch. **Known for:** made-from-scratch pastries; filling breakfasts of smoked-salmon scrambles and gingerbread pancakes; local tuna and cod sandwiches. [$] *Average main: $13* ✉ *34805 Brooten Rd.* ☎ *503/965–7337* 🌐 *www.gratefulbreadbakery.com* 🕑 *Closed Tues. and Wed. No dinner.*

★ Meridian Restaurant & Bar

$$$$ | **MODERN AMERICAN** | With its soaring windows, cathedral ceiling, earthy tones, and vibrant timber beams and flooring, this stylish and airy farm-to-table restaurant has become one of the coast's top destinations for a romantic meal—or even just a memorable breakfast or happy hour overlooking the Pacific. The kitchen sources as much as possible from local farms and seafood purveyors with its seasonal menu, which might feature char-grilled, wine-braised octopus with basil-watercress salsa verde, or petrale sole topped with a light citrus beurre blanc, capers, and local pink shrimp. **Known for:** shareable charcuterie, veggie, and cheese plates; huge windows with water and beach views; excellent wine list and craft cocktails. [$] *Average main: $31* ✉ *Headlands Coastal Lodge, 33000 Cape Kiwanda Dr.* ☎ *503/483–3000* 🌐 *www.headlandslodge.com.*

Pelican Pub & Brewery

$$ | **AMERICAN** | **FAMILY** | This craft beer lover's favorite, which overlooks the ocean by Haystack Rock, has garnered considerable kudos for its beers, including the Kiwanda Cream Ale and deep, rich Tsunami Stout, while the pub turns out reliably good comfort fare, such as flatbread pizzas, burgers, and cioppino. Many dishes are infused with homemade beverages, such as pale-malt-crusted salmon and the root beer float. **Known for:** occasional brewers' dinner with international food and house beer pairings; good children's menu; root beer floats. [$] *Average main: $19* ✉ *33180 Cape Kiwanda Dr.* ☎ *503/965–7007* 🌐 *www.pelicanbrewing.com.*

Hotels

★ Headlands Coastal Lodge & Spa

$$$$ | **RESORT** | Newly built in 2018 at the foot of Cape Kiwanda dunes and overlooking the bustling beachfront of Pacific City, this stylish, casually posh boutique resort offers an impressive

selection of wellness pursuits, including yoga classes, surfing lessons, Peloton indoor exercise bikes, and a full slate of soothing spa treatments. **Pros:** first-rate spa and restaurant on-site; fabulous beachfront location; hip, contemporary vibe and aesthetic. **Cons:** quite pricey in summer; busy, sometimes noisy, location; glass-walled bathrooms are cool but don't allow a lot of privacy. [$] *Rooms from: $425* ✉ *33000 Cape Kiwanda Dr.* ☎ *503/483–3000* 🌐 *www.headlandslodge.com* 🛏 *51 rooms* 🍴 *No meals.*

Inn at Cape Kiwanda

$$$ | **HOTEL** | Most of the 35 upscale, fireplace-warmed rooms at this handsome boutique hotel have a view across the street of Pacific City's beach and Haystack Rock in the distance. **Pros:** great views; light and contemporary rooms; terrific restaurants nearby. **Cons:** water views blocked in some rooms by the new hotel across the street; can be a somewhat noisy location in summer; there's a big parking lot between hotel and beach. [$] *Rooms from: $244* ✉ *33105 Cape Kiwanda Dr.* ☎ *888/965–7001, 503/965–7001* 🌐 *www.innatcapekiwanda.com* 🛏 *35 rooms* 🍴 *No meals.*

Lincoln City

16 miles south of Pacific City, 90 miles southwest of Portland.

Lincoln City is an unpretentious, highly social destination whose diversions appeal to families and couples who enjoy hobnobbing and playing on the beach, poking their fingers in tide pools, and trying to harness wind-bucking kites. Once a series of small villages, Lincoln City incorporated into one sprawling municipality without a center in 1965. For its legions of fans, the endless tourist amenities make up for a lack of a small-coastal-town charm. Clustered like barnacles on offshore reefs are fast-food restaurants, gift shops, supermarkets, candy stores, antiques markets, dozens of motels and hotels, a factory-outlet mall, and a busy casino. Lincoln City is the most popular destination city on the Oregon Coast, but its only real geographic claim to fame is the 445-foot-long D River, stretching from its source in Devil's Lake to the Pacific; *Guinness World Records* lists the D as the world's shortest river.

Just south of Lincoln City, quieter and less-developed Gleneden Beach is a small vacation town known primarily for the famed Salishan Resort, which is perched high above placid Siletz Bay.

GETTING HERE AND AROUND

Lincoln City is a 2-hour drive from Portland on Highway 99W and Highway 18, and a 2½-hour drive south of Astoria along coastal U.S. 101.

ESSENTIALS

VISITOR INFORMATION Lincoln City Visitors & Convention Bureau. ✉ *801 S.W. U.S. 101, Suite 401* ☎ *541/996–1274* 🌐 *www.oregoncoast.org.*

Sights

★ Cascade Head Preserve

HIKING/WALKING | At this pristine, slightly off-the-beaten-path property managed by the Nature Conservancy, a dense, green trail winds through a rain forest where 100-inch annual rainfalls nourish 250-year-old Sitka spruces, mosses, and ferns. Emerging from the forest, hikers come upon grassy and treeless Cascade Head, an undulating maritime prairie. There are magnificent views down to the Salmon River and east to the Coast Range. Continuing along the headland, black-tailed deer often graze and turkey vultures soar in the sometimes strong winds. It's a somewhat steep and strenuous but tremendously rewarding hike—allow at least three hours to make the full nearly 7-mile round-trip hike, although you can make it out to the beginning of the headland and back in an hour. ✉ *Savage Rd. at N 3 Rocks Rd., Otis* ✣ *Off U.S. 101*

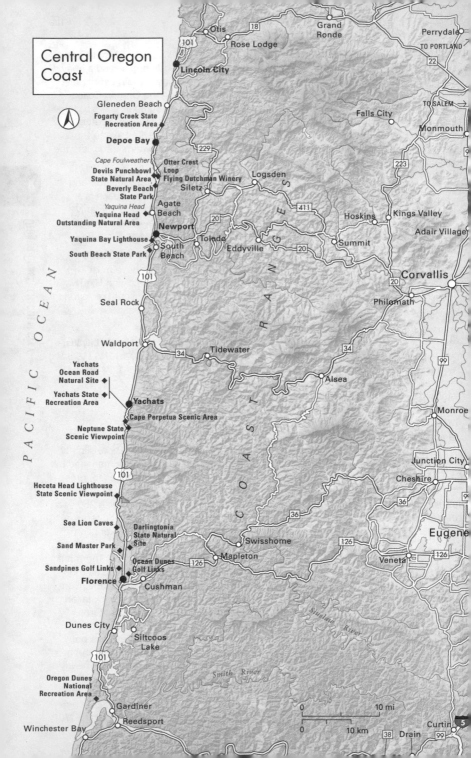

between Lincoln City and Pacific City ⊕ *www.nature.org* ✉ *Free* ◷ *Upper trail closed Jan.–mid-July.*

Restaurants

★ Blackfish Café

$$$ | PACIFIC NORTHWEST | This dapper but unpretentious bistro is known for simple-but-succulent dishes that blend fresh ingredients from local fishermen and gardeners, such as skillet-roasted Chinook salmon basted with fennel-lime butter, Oregon blue-cheese potatoes, and center-cut New York steak au jus with red wine and porcini butter. The Blackfish Ding Dong dessert, with mixed-berry sauce and whipped cream, is the best way to finish a meal. **Known for:** Chinook salmon; Ding Dong dessert; fresh ingredients. Ⓢ *Average main: $28* ✉ *2733 N.W. U.S. 101* ☎ *541/996–1007* ⊕ *www.blackfishcafe.com* ◷ *Closed Mon. and Tues.*

Klementine's Kitchen

$$ | MODERN AMERICAN | Set in an unassuming building along busy U.S. 101 a little north of the Siletz River, this cheerful restaurant with a gas fireplace is a tribute to the owners' Cajun roots, which influence but don't completely define the menu. You'll find authentic versions of Louisiana classics like red beans and rice and crab-and-shrimp gumbo, but other specialties more reflect the bounty of fresh Northwest ingredients—note the blueberry-and-beet salad with chèvre. **Known for:** several dishes featuring Dungeness crab, shrimp, and catfish; warmly welcoming service; butterscotch pudding with a dusting of pink rock salt. Ⓢ *Average main: $17* ✉ *4660 S.E. U.S. 101* ☎ *541/418–5371* ⊕ *www.klementineskitchen.com* ◷ *Closed Mon. and Tues. No lunch.*

Side Door Café

$$$ | PACIFIC NORTHWEST | This dining room, set in an old brick and tile factory with a high ceiling, exposed beams, a fireplace, and many windows, shares its space with Eden Hall performance venue. The menu changes often, but favorites that tend to appear regularly include fire-roasted rack of lamb with vegetable risotto and Northwest bouillabaisse with a lemongrass-saffron-tomato broth. **Known for:** funky and historic industrial setting; seafood-intensive seasonal cuisine; creative quesadillas (bay shrimp; chicken, pear, Gorgonzola) at lunch. Ⓢ *Average main: $24* ✉ *6675 Gleneden Beach Loop Rd., Gleneden Beach* ☎ *541/764–3825* ⊕ *www.sidedoorcafe. com* ◷ *Closed Sun. and Mon.*

Hotels

★ Coho Oceanfront Lodge

$$ | HOTEL | FAMILY | Set on a romantic cliff, the clean and contemporary Coho is a perfect hybrid of family-friendly lodging and a quiet, intimate hideaway for couples—14 of the 65 suites and rooms are relegated to adults, while family-oriented suites have Wii or PS3 game systems, and all have complimentary snack baskets and French press coffeemakers. **Pros:** seating and fire pits overlooking the ocean; family-friendly; DVD and games available in lobby to take to your room. **Cons:** no restaurant; bathrooms can be on the small side; not ideal if seeking a quiet, secluded getaway. Ⓢ *Rooms from: $165* ✉ *1635 N.W. Harbor Ave.* ☎ *541/994–3684, 800/848–7006* ⊕ *www. thecoholodge.com* ⇌ *65 rooms* ⦿| *Free breakfast.*

Historic Anchor Inn

$ | B&B/INN | This quirky bungalow might not be for everyone, but for those who appreciate a warm, spirited inn with a decidedly inventive and whimsical touch, this is a remarkable find. **Pros:** a memorable, truly unique property; central location; on-site pub. **Cons:** not on the beach; very quirky and rustic; on a busy road. Ⓢ *Rooms from: $119* ✉ *4417 S.W. U.S. 101* ☎ *541/996–3810* ⊕ *www.*

historicanchorinn.com 🛏 *19 rooms* 🍴 *Free breakfast.*

Inn at Spanish Head
$$$ | **RESORT** | Driving up to this midcentury condo hotel, you'd think it might be a fairly intimate place, but on further investigation you'll see that the property takes up the entire side of a bluff like a huge staircase. **Pros:** sweeping views of the ocean through floor-to-ceiling windows; good restaurant; easy beach access via elevator. **Cons:** decor varies greatly from room to room; not within walking distance of many restaurants or shops; can get pricey on summer weekends. [$] *Rooms from: $239* ✉ *4009 S.E. U.S. 101* ☎ *541/996–2161, 800/452–8127* 🌐 *www.spanishhead.com* 🛏 *120 units* 🍴 *No meals.*

★ **Salishan Lodge and Golf Resort**
$$$ | **RESORT** | Secluded and refined, this upscale resort designed in the 1960s by renowned architect John Gray is set in a hillside forest preserve near Siletz Bay and offers spacious, art-filled rooms with wood-burning fireplaces, balconies, and large whirlpool tubs. **Pros:** elegantly designed rooms and public spaces; secluded, beautiful natural setting; outstanding spa, golf course, and restaurants. **Cons:** ocean views are few; not within walking distance of town; some rooms receive noise from U.S. 101. [$] *Rooms from: $239* ✉ *7760 N. U.S. 101, Gleneden Beach* ☎ *541/764–3600, 800/452–2300* 🌐 *www.salishan.com* 🛏 *205 rooms* 🍴 *No meals.*

🍸 Nightlife

Black Squid Beer House
BREWPUBS/BEER GARDENS | Bring your dog and grab a seat on the plant-filled brick patio, or grab a seat (and feel free to bring your own food) in the homey taproom. This highly popular bottle shop and drinkery offers a well-chosen selection of ales on tap from both established and cult-favorite microbreweries, plus Northwest wines and cider. There's often live music, too. ✉ *3001 U.S. 101* ☎ *541/614–0733* 🌐 *www.blacksquidbeerhouse.com.*

Chinook Winds Casino Resort
CASINOS | Oregon's only beachfront casino resort has a great variety of slot machines, blackjack, poker, keno, and off-track betting, plus big-name entertainers performing in the showroom. ✉ *1777 N.W. 44th St.* ☎ *541/996–5825* 🌐 *www.chinookwindscasino.com.*

🛍 Shopping

★ **Alder House Glassblowing**
CRAFTS | The imaginative crafts folk at this studio turn molten glass into vases and bowls, which are available for sale. It is the oldest glass-blowing studio in the state. It's closed November–April. ✉ *611 Immonen Rd.* ☎ *541/996–2483* 🌐 *www.alderhouse.com.*

Culinary Center
FOOD/CANDY | The talented chefs here offer everything from small, hands-on classes to full-blown cooking demonstrations for dozens. Frequent themes include baking pizza, making sushi, and even dim sum. ✉ *801 S.W. U.S. 101, Suite 401* ☎ *541/557–1125* 🌐 *www.oregoncoast.org/culinary.*

Lincoln City Glass Center
CERAMICS/GLASSWARE | Blow a glass float or make a glorious glass starfish, heart, or fluted bowl of your own design (prices start at $65 for a glass float). The studio's expert artisans will guide you every step of the way. It's a fun, memorable keepsake of the coast. ✉ *4821 S.W. U.S. 101* ☎ *541/996–2569* 🌐 *www.lincolncityglasscenter.com.*

🏃 Activities

GOLF

Salishan Golf Resort
GOLF | With a layout designed by Peter Jacobsen, this par-71 course

Salishan Golf Resort in Gleneden Beach is a year-round treat for golfers of every level.

is a year-round treat for hackers and aficionados alike. The front nine holes are surrounded by a forest of old-growth timber, while the back nine holes provide old-school, links-style play. There's an expansive pro shop and a great bar and grill, too. High-season greens fees are $99–$119. ⊠ 7760 N. U.S. 101, Gleneden Beach ☎ 541/452–2300 ⊕ www.salishan.com.

Depoe Bay

12 miles south of Lincoln City.

This small but lively town founded in the 1920s bills itself the whale-watching capital of the world. With a narrow channel and deep water, its tiny harbor is also one of the most protected on the coast (and is said to be the nation's smallest navigable harbor). It supports a thriving fleet of commercial and charter fishing boats as well as whale-watching tour outfitters. The Spouting Horn, a natural cleft in the basalt cliffs on the waterfront, blasts seawater skyward during heavy weather. You'll find a small but impressive array of both sophisticated and reasonably priced lodging and dining options in Depoe Bay.

GETTING HERE AND AROUND
Depoe Bay lies right between Newport and Lincoln City along U.S. 101—it's a 20-minute drive to either town.

ESSENTIALS
VISITOR INFORMATION Depoe Bay Chamber of Commerce. ⊠ 223 S.W. U.S. 101, Suite B ☎ 541/765–2889, 877/485–8348 ⊕ www.depoebaychamber.org.

Sights

Fogarty Creek State Recreation Area
NATIONAL/STATE PARK | Bird-watching and viewing the tidal pools are the key draws here, but hiking and picnicking are also popular at this park along U.S. 101. Wooden footbridges wind through the dense forest and tall cliffs rise above the beach. ⊠ U.S. 101 ✛ 3 miles north of Depoe Bay ☎ 541/265–4560 ⊕ www.oregonstateparks.org ⊠ Free.

En Route

Five miles south of Depoe Bay off U.S. 101 (watch for signs), the **Otter Crest Loop**, another scenic byway, winds along the cliff tops. Only parts of the loop are open to motor vehicles, but you can drive to points midway from either end and turn around. The full loop is open to bikes and hiking. British explorer Captain James Cook named the 500-foot-high **Cape Foulweather**, at the south end of the loop, on a blustery March day in 1778—a small visitor center and gift shop at this site affords mesmerizing views and opportunities to spot whales and other marine life. Backward-leaning shore pines lend mute witness to the 100-mph winds that still strafe this exposed spot.

At the viewing point at the **Devil's Punchbowl**, 1 mile south of Cape Foulweather, you can peer down into a collapsed sandstone sea cave carved out by the powerful waters of the Pacific. About 100 feet to the north in the rocky tidal pools of the beach known as **Marine Gardens**, purple sea urchins and orange starfish can be seen at low tide. The Otter Crest Loop rejoins U.S. 101 about 4 miles south of Cape Foulweather near **Yaquina Head**, which has been designated an Outstanding Natural Area. Harbor seals, sea lions, cormorants, murres, puffins, and guillemots frolic in the water and on the rocks below the gleaming, white tower of the **Yaquina Bay Lighthouse**.

Whale, Sealife and Shark Museum

MUSEUM | **FAMILY** | This small but excellent museum on Depoe Bay's tiny harbor is the creation of experienced marine biologist Carrie Newell, who also operates the excellent Whale Research EcoExcursions tour company from the premises. Inside you'll find fascinating exhibits on whales, of course, but also sea lions, sea otters, seals, migratory birds, and the abundance of creatures that inhabit the Oregon Coast's tidal pools. Cut-out murals on the building's exterior depict several "resident" gray whales who spend time in Depoe Bay's waters each summer. The museum also runs a cute little café next door, Whale Bite, that's a fun stop for breakfast or lunch. ✉ *234 S.E. U.S. 101* ☎ *541/912–6734* ⊕ *www.oregonwhales. com* 🎫 *$5.*

The Whale Watching Center

INFO CENTER | **FAMILY** | Here in the most famous whale-watching town in Oregon, this helpful little information center perched on a oceanfront bluff in the heart of town is a valuable resource, whether you're looking for tips on the latest sightings during the peak winter and spring migratory seasons or you simply want to learn about these amazing creatures. The center is staffed with state park naturalists who regularly give talks and can answer your questions, and there's an observation deck that offers fantastic views—you might see gray, humpback, and orcas along with a wide variety of seabirds and other sea mammals. ✉ *119 U.S. 101* ☎ *541/765–3304* ⊕ *www.oregonstateparks.org.*

🍴 Restaurants

★ Restaurant Beck

$$$ | **PACIFIC NORTHWEST** | Immensely gifted chef-owner Justin Wills presents a short but memorable menu of creatively prepared, modern, Pacific Northwest cuisine each night in this romantic, contemporary dining room at the Whale Cove Inn. The menu changes regularly, with chef Wills sourcing largely from local farms, ranches, and fisheries, but you might start with vanilla-cured foie gras or pork belly with caramelized-miso ice cream, followed by Wagyu beef coulotte with parsnip puree, mizuna, chive oil, parsley root, and citrus. **Known for:** panoramic views of Whale Cove; exceptional desserts; one of the best wine lists on the coast. $ Average main: $29 ☒ Whale Cove Inn, 2345 U.S. 101 ☏ 541/765–3220 ⊕ www.restaurantbeck.com ☽ No lunch.

Tidal Raves Seafood Grill

$$$ | **SEAFOOD** | Serving consistently well-prepared modern seafood fare, Tidal Raves uses local and sustainable fish and shellfish in preparations inspired by places far and near. A few steaks and vegetarian dishes round out the lengthy menu, which also includes such local classics as Dungeness crab cakes, panko-crusted razor clams, and rockfish and shrimp green curry with steamed peanut rice, and the dapper bi-level dining room has tall windows overlooking the ocean. **Known for:** local Dungeness crab cakes; ocean views; notable cocktail and wine selection. $ Average main: $25 ☒ 279 U.S. 101 ☏ 541/765–2995 ⊕ www. tidalraves.com.

 ## Hotels

Channel House

$$$ | **B&B/INN** | You can enjoy some of the best whale-watching on the Oregon Coast from your own private balcony and hot tub from many of the spacious rooms in this upscale, contemporary, oceanfront inn that's in the heart of town. **Pros:** you can often see whales right from your room; close to local shops and restaurants; many rooms have decks with hot tubs. **Cons:** no kids under 16; slightly busy location on U.S. 101; steep rates, especially in summer. $ Rooms from: $250 ☒ 35 Ellingson St. ☏ 541/765–2140 ⊕ www.channelhouse.com ↩ 15 rooms ⍢ Free breakfast.

Clarion Surfrider Resort

$ | **HOTEL** | The economical Clarion Surfrider Resort comprises a few two-story clapboard buildings perched on a bluff overlooking the ocean and Fogarty Creek State Park, and amenities include a seafood restaurant and lounge, indoor pool, and exercise room. **Pros:** impressive ocean views; reasonable rates; decent seafood restaurant and bar on-site. **Cons:** rooms have attractive but cookie-cutter chain furniture; not within walking distance of town; smallish bathrooms. $ Rooms from: $139 ☒ 3115 N.W. U.S. 101 ☏ 541/764–2311 ⊕ www.choicehotels.com ↩ 55 rooms ⍢ Free breakfast.

★ Whale Cove Inn

$$$$ | **B&B/INN** | This small and exquisitely decorated high-end inn overlooks the picturesque cove for which it's named and contains just eight spacious suites, each with a balcony that has a large hot tub with a dazzling view of the water. **Pros:** astoundingly good restaurant; stunning building with cushy and spacious suites; terrific ocean views. **Cons:** not a good fit for kids (only those 16 and over are permitted); pricey; not within walking distance of town. $ Rooms from: $520 ☒ 2345 U.S. 101 ☏ 541/765–4300, 800/628–3409 ⊕ www.whalecoveinn. com ↩ 8 suites ⍢ Free breakfast.

 ## Activities

OUTFITTERS

★ Whale Research EcoExcursions

TOUR—SPORTS | **FAMILY** | Knowledgeable marine biologists and naturalists captain the informative and exciting whale-watching excursions offered by this highly respected outfitter that also operates the Whale, Sea Life and Shark Museum from which these 90-minute tours depart. ☒ 234 U.S. 101 ☏ 541/912–6734 ⊕ www. oregonwhales.com ☞ From $45.

Newport

12 miles south of Depoe Bay.

Known as the Dungeness crab capital of the world, Newport offers accessible beaches, a popular aquarium, the coast's premier performing-arts center, and a significant supply of both elegant and affordable accommodations and restaurants. Newport exists on two levels: the highway above, threading its way through the community's main business district, and the old Bayfront along Yaquina Bay below (watch for signs on U.S. 101). With its high-masted fishing fleet, well-worn buildings, seafood markets, art galleries, and touristy shops, Newport's Bayfront is an ideal place for an afternoon stroll. So many male sea lions in Yaquina Bay loiter near crab pots and bark from the waterfront piers that locals call the area the Bachelor Club. Visit the docks to buy fresh seafood or rent a kayak to explore the bay. In 2010 Newport was designated the National Oceanic and Atmospheric Administration's (NOAA) Pacific Marine Operations Center and a $38 million, 5-acre facility (and a port for four ships) opened a year later.

GETTING HERE AND AROUND

Newport is a 2½-hour drive from Portland by way of Interstate 5 south to Albany and U.S. 20 west; the town is a 40-minute drive south along U.S. 101 from Lincoln City, and a 75-minute drive north of Florence.

ESSENTIALS

VISITOR INFORMATION Discover Newport. ☎ 541/265–8801 ⊕ www.discovernewport.com.

TOURS

Marine Discovery Tours
Sea-life cruises, priced from $42 and departing throughout the day, are conducted on a 65-foot excursion boat *Discovery*, with inside seating for 49 people and two viewing levels. The cruise season is March through October. ⊠ 345 S.W. Bay Blvd. ☎ 541/265–6200 ⊕ www.marinediscoverytours.com ☒ From $36.

Sights

Beverly Beach State Park
NATIONAL/STATE PARK | Seven miles north of Newport, this beachfront park extends from Yaquina Head, where you can see the lighthouse, to the headlands of Otter Rock. It's a great place to fly a kite, surf the waves, or hunt for fossils. The campground is well equipped, with a wind-protected picnic area and a yurt meeting hall. ⊠ N.E. Beverly Dr. ✛ Off U.S. 101, 6 miles north of Newport ☎ 541/265–9278 ⊕ www.oregonstateparks.org ☒ Free.

★ Devil's Punchbowl State Natural Area
NATIONAL/STATE PARK | A rocky shoreline separates the day-use area from the surf at this park named for a dramatic rock formation—likely formed by a collapsed sea cave—through which you can observe the violently churning surf. It's a popular setting for whale-watching, and there are excellent tidal pools. ⊠ 1st St., Otter Rock ✛ Off U.S. 101, 8 miles north of Newport ☎ 541/265–4560 ⊕ www.oregonstateparks.org ☒ Free.

Hatfield Marine Science Center
COLLEGE | **FAMILY** | Interactive and interpretive exhibits at Oregon State University appeal to the kid in everyone. More than just showcasing sea life, the center contains exhibits and tide-pool touch tanks, and it holds classes that teach the importance of scientific research in managing and sustaining coastal and marine resources. The staff regularly leads guided tours of the adjoining estuary. ⊠ 2030 S. Marine Science Dr. ☎ 541/867–0100 ⊕ seagrant.oregonstate.edu ☉ Closed Tues. and Wed. in winter.

Oregon Coast Aquarium
ZOO | **FAMILY** | This 4½-acre complex brings visitors face-to-face with the creatures living in offshore and near-shore Pacific marine habitats: frolicking sea otters, colorful puffins, pulsating jellyfish,

and even a several-hundred-pound octopus. There's a hands-on interactive area for children, including tide pools perfect for "petting" sea anemones and urchins. The aquarium houses one of North America's largest seabird aviaries, including glowering turkey vultures. Permanent exhibits include Passages of the Deep, where visitors walk through a 200-foot underwater tunnel with 360-degree views of sharks, wolf eels, halibut, and a truly captivating array of sea life; and Sea-Punk, a nautical take on steampunk with interactive artwork. Large coho salmon and sturgeon can be viewed in a naturalistic setting through a window wall 9 feet high and 20 feet wide. The sherbet-colored nettles are hypnotizing. ✉ *2820 S.E. Ferry Slip Rd.* ☎ *541/867–3474* 🌐 *www.aquarium.org* 🎟 *$24.95.*

South Beach State Park

NATIONAL/STATE PARK | Fishing, crabbing, boating, windsurfing, hiking, and beachcombing are popular activities at this park that begins just across the Yaquina Bay Bridge from Newport and contains a long, lovely stretch of beach. Kayaking tours along Beaver Creek are available for a fee. There's a popular campground, too. ✉ *U.S. 101 S* ☎ *541/867–4715* 🌐 *www.oregonstateparks.org.*

Yaquina Bay Lighthouse

LIGHTHOUSE | **FAMILY** | The state's oldest wooden lighthouse was only in commission for three years (1871–74), because it was determined that it was built in the wrong location. Today the well-restored lighthouse with a candy-apple-red top shines a steady white light from dusk to dawn. Open to the public, it's believed to be Newport's oldest structure, and the only Oregon lighthouse with living quarters attached. ✉ *S.W. Government St. at S.W. 9th St.* ☎ *541/265–5679* 🌐 *www.yaquinalights.org* 🎟 *Free, donations suggested* 🕒 *Closed Mon. and Tues. in winter.*

★ Yaquina Head Lighthouse

LIGHTHOUSE | **FAMILY** | The tallest lighthouse on the Oregon Coast has been blinking its beacon since its head keeper first walked up its 114 steps to light the wicks on the evening of August 20, 1873. Next to the 93-foot tower is an interpretive center. Bring your camera and call ahead to confirm tour times. ✉ *750 N.W. Lighthouse Dr.* ☎ *541/574–3100* 🌐 *www.yaquinalights.org* 🎟 *Free, donations suggested.*

🍴 Restaurants

Canyon Way Restaurant and Bookstore

$$ | **SEAFOOD** | Cod, Dungeness crab cakes, bouillabaisse, and Yaquina Bay oysters—along with homemade pastas—are among the specialties of this weekday-only Newport institution just up the hill from the historic Bayfront and connected to a well-stocked bookstore. The adjacent Club 1216 has live music on Friday nights. **Known for:** dog-friendly patio; deli counter for takeout; excellent bookstore. [$] *Average main: $18* ✉ *1216 S.W. Canyon Way* ☎ *541/265–8319* 🌐 *www.canyonway.com* 🕒 *No dinner Mon.–Thurs. Closed weekends.*

★ Clearwater Restaurant

$$$ | **SEAFOOD** | Part of the fun of dining in this handsome, bi-level restaurant with huge windows overlooking the bay is watching—and listening to—the big posse of sea lions gamboling about on the docks out back, but Clearwater also serves terrifically good seafood. You can't go wrong with any of the shareable starters, including tuna poke bowls and quinoa-crusted avocado fries, but save room for one or two of the signature mains—maybe jumbo sea scallops with roasted-chestnut puree or local Dungeness crab with garlic soba noodles. **Known for:** view of sea lions and Yaquina Bay; coconut curry stew loaded with local seafood; tableside s'mores. [$] *Average main: $25* ✉ *325 S.W. Bay Blvd., Portland* ☎ *541/272–5550* 🌐 *www.clearwaterrestaurant.com.*

Passages of the Deep, at Newport's Oregon Coast Aquarium, is a 200-foot underwater tunnel with 360-degree views of an amazing array of sea life.

Georgie's Beachside Grill

$$ | **SEAFOOD** | **FAMILY** | This stand-alone restaurant serves up some wonderfully innovative dishes and is one of few in town with ocean views—windows line a half-moon of table seating, and tiered booths allow decent views even in the back of the room. From the sea scallops blackened in house-mixed herbs to flame-broiled halibut with pineapple salsa, the food here lives up to the setting. **Known for:** sweeping ocean views; excellent breakfasts; reasonably priced seafood. [$] *Average main: $21* ✉ *Hallmark Resort, 744 S.W. Elizabeth St.* ☎ *503/265–9800* 🌐 *www.georgiesbeachsidegrill.com.*

★ Local Ocean Seafoods

$$ | **SEAFOOD** | At this sustainable fish market and sleek, airy grill with retractable windows that look out across picturesque Yaquina Bay, the operators purchase fish directly from the boats in the fishing fleet right outside. The menu includes such fish lovers' fare as tuna mignon (bacon-wrapped albacore with pan-seared vegetables), panko-buttermilk-crusted oysters, and Fishwives Stew (a tomato broth stew loaded with both shell- and finfish), and nothing is deep-fried—even the fish-and-chips are panfried. **Known for:** market with fresh-caught seafood to go; superb wine list; house-smoked fish and shellfish. [$] *Average main: $22* ✉ *213 S.E. Bay Blvd.* ☎ *514/574–7959* 🌐 *www.localocean.net.*

★ Ove Northwest

$$$ | **PACIFIC NORTHWEST** | The former executive chef of Local Ocean Seafoods opened this stellar Nye Beach restaurant that dazzles with both its ocean views and exquisite modern Pacific Northwest cuisine. The menu changes seasonally but might feature bruschetta with Matiz sardines, pickled fennel, and fromage blanc, and lingcod with Manila clams, Spanish chorizo, and a delicate tomato-saffron cream sauce. **Known for:** sophisticated farm-to-table fare; creative vegetable starters; sunset views over Nye Beach. [$] *Average main: $24* ✉ *749 N.W. 3rd St.*

☎ *541/264–2990* 🌐 *www.ovenorthwest.com* 🕒 *Closed Sun. and Mon.*

Panini Bakery
$ | **CAFÉ** | The owner of this bustling bakery and espresso bar prides himself on hearty and home-roasted meats, hand-cut breads, sourdough pizza, and friendly service. The coffee's organic, the eggs free-range, the orange juice fresh squeezed, and just about everything is made from scratch. **Known for:** made-from-scratch food; outdoor seating; pizzas with interesting toppings. [$] *Average main: $9* ✉ *232 N.W. Coast Hwy.* ☎ *541/272–5322* 🌐 *www.panininye-beach.com* 💳 *No credit cards.*

Tables of Content
$$$$ | **PACIFIC NORTHWEST** | The thoughtful prix-fixe menu at this offbeat restaurant in the outstanding Sylvia Beach Hotel changes nightly, but there's a good chance one of the handful of entrée options will be fresh local seafood, perhaps a moist grilled salmon fillet in a Dijonnaise sauce, served with sautéed vegetables, fresh-baked breads, and rice pilaf; a decadent dessert is also included. Note that dinners, which are at 6 or 7 pm depending on the day, can be long, so young children may get restless. **Known for:** convivial family-style dining; rich desserts; locally sourced seafood. [$] *Average main: $32* ✉ *267 N.W. Cliff St.* ☎ *541/265–5428* 🌐 *sylviabeachhotel.com/restaurant/.*

🛏 Hotels

★ Inn at Nye Beach
$$$ | **HOTEL** | With a prime beachfront location on a bluff in historic Nye Beach, this chic, eco-friendly, boutique hotel has large rooms with a clean, contemporary look and plenty of perks, including DVD players, premium tea and French press coffee, "green" bath amenities, microwaves and refrigerators, and wonderfully comfy beds. **Pros:** ocean views from infinity hot tub; direct beach access; stylish and spacious rooms. **Cons:** the complimentary breakfast is fairly basic; some rooms don't overlook ocean; no restaurant on-site. [$] *Rooms from: $235* ✉ *729 N.W. Coast St.* ☎ *541/265–2477, 800/480–2477* 🌐 *www.innatnyebeach.com* 🛏 *22 rooms* 🍴 *Free breakfast.*

Newport Belle B&B
$$ | **B&B/INN** | This floating B&B is in a fully operational stern-wheeler that's permanently moored at the Newport Marina, where guests have front-row seats to all the boating activity around Yaquina Bay, and it's a short walk from Oregon Coast Aquarium. **Pros:** one-of-a-kind lodging experience; great harbor views; walking distance from Rogue Brewer's pub. **Cons:** not suitable for kids; need a car to get into town; small rooms. [$] *Rooms from: $165* ✉ *Dock H, 2126 S.E. Marine Science Dr.* ☎ *541/867–6290* 🌐 *www.newportbelle.com* 🕒 *Closed Nov.–Mar.* 🛏 *5 rooms* 🍴 *Free breakfast.*

Sylvia Beach Hotel
$$ | **HOTEL** | This quirky 1913-vintage beachfront hotel offers a colorful range of antiques-filled rooms named for famous writers—a pendulum swings over the bed in the Poe room, while the Christie, Twain, Tolkien, Woolf, and Colette rooms feature fireplaces, decks, and great water views. **Pros:** loads of personality; great place to disconnect; very good restaurant. **Cons:** no TV, telephone, or Internet access; idiosyncratic decor isn't to everyone's taste; least-expensive rooms don't have ocean views. [$] *Rooms from: $160* ✉ *267 N.W. Cliff St.* ☎ *541/265–5428, 888/795–8422* 🌐 *sylviabeachhotel.com* 🛏 *20 rooms* 🍴 *Free breakfast.*

🎟 Performing Arts

★ Newport Symphony Orchestra
MUSIC | The only year-round, professional symphony orchestra on the Oregon Coast performs a popular series of concerts in the 328-seat Newport Performing Arts Center fall through spring, and

special events in the summer, including a popular free community concert every July 4. ✉ *777 W. Olive St.* ☎ *541/574–0614* ⊕ *www.newportsymphony.org.*

Yachats

24 miles south of Newport.

The small but utterly enchanting town of Yachats (pronounced "yah- *hots*") lies at the mouth of the Yachats River, and from its rocky shoreline, which includes the highest point directly located on the Oregon Coast (Cape Perpetua), trails lead to beaches and dozens of tidal pools. A relaxed alternative to the more touristy communities to the north, Yachats abounds with coastal pleasures, but without nearly as much traffic: Airbnbs and oceanfront hotels, an impressive bounty of terrific restaurants, quiet beaches, tidal pools, surf-pounded crags, fishing, and crabbing.

GETTING HERE AND AROUND

Yachats lies between Newport and Florence on coastal U.S. 101—it's a 40-minute drive from either town, and a three-hour drive via Interstate 5 and Highway 34 from Portland.

ESSENTIALS

VISITOR INFORMATION Yachats Visitors Center. ✉ *241 U.S. 101* ☎ *800/929–0477, 541/547–3530* ⊕ *www.yachats.org.*

◉ Sights

★ Cape Perpetua Scenic Area

TRAIL | FAMILY | The highest vehicle-accessible lookout on the Oregon Coast, Cape Perpetua towers 800 feet above the rocky shoreline. Named by Captain Cook on St. Perpetua's Day in 1778, the cape is part of a 2,700-acre scenic area popular with hikers, campers, beachcombers, and naturalists. General information, educational movies and exhibits, and trail maps are available at the **Cape Perpetua Visitors Center,** ½ mile south of Devil's

Churn. The easy 1-mile **Giant Spruce Trail** passes through a fern-filled rain forest to an enormous 600-year-old Sitka spruce. Easier still is the marked Auto Tour; it begins just north of the visitor center and winds through Siuslaw National Forest to the ¼-mile **Whispering Spruce Trail.** Views from the rustic rock shelter here extend 50 miles north to south, and some 40 miles out to sea. For a more rigorous trek, hike the **St. Perpetua Trail** to the shelter. Other trails lead from the visitor center down along the shore, including a scenic pathway to **Devil's Churn,** next to which a small snack bar sells sandwiches, sweets, and coffee. ✉ *2400 U.S. 101* ✛ *3 miles south of Yachats* ☎ *541/547–3289* ⊕ *www.fs.usda.gov/siuslaw* ⌑ *Parking fee $5.*

Neptune State Scenic Viewpoint

VIEWPOINT | Visitors have fun searching for whales and other sea life, watching the surf, or hunting for agates at this stretch of shoreline reached via four pulloffs a bit south of Cape Perpetua. The benches set above the beach on the cliff provide a great view of Cumming Creek. At low tide, beachcombers have access to a natural cave and tidal pools. And there's a grassy area that's ideal for picnicking at the northernmost pulloff, by Gwynn Creek. ✉ *U.S. 101* ✛ *4 miles south of Yachats* ☎ *541/547–3416* ⊕ *www.oregonstateparks.org* ⌑ *Free.*

★ Yachats Ocean Road State Natural Site

VIEWPOINT | Drive this 1-mile loop just across the Yachats River from downtown Yachats, and discover one of the most scenic viewpoints on the Oregon Coast. Park along Yachats Ocean Road and scamper out along the broad swath of sand where the Yachats River meets the Pacific Ocean. There's fun to be had playing on the beach, poking around tide pools, and watching blowholes, summer sunsets, and whales spouting. ✉ *Yachats Ocean Rd.* ☎ *541/867–7451* ⊕ *www. oregonstateparks.org.*

Beaches

Yachats State Recreation Area

BEACHES | The public beach in downtown Yachats is more like the surface of the moon than your typical beach. A wooden platform overlooks the coastline, where the waves roll in sideways and splash over the rocks at high tide. As is the case throughout most of the town, the beach itself is paralleled by an upland walking trail and dotted with picnic tables, benches, and interpretive signs. Visit to spot the sea lions that frequent this stretch of coast. Or join the intrepid beachcombers who climb the rocks for a closer look at tide pools populated by sea urchins, hermit crabs, barnacles, snails, and sea stars. **Amenities:** parking; toilets. **Best for:** walking; sunset. ✉ Ocean View Dr. ✛ Off 2nd St. and U.S. 101 ☎ 541/867–7451 ⊕ www.oregonstateparks.org.

Restaurants

★ Beach Street Kitchen

$ | **MODERN AMERICAN** | Duck into this sunny corner café across the street from where the Yachats River empties into the sea for some of the tastiest made-from-scratch breakfast and lunch fare on the central Oregon Coast, along with a full selection of craft beer, wine, and cocktails. From the wild-mushroom frittata and baked French toast with Oregon blueberries in the morning to a killer beef barbacoa sandwich at lunch, the food here is consistently stellar, and the rustic-contemporary dining room, with tables fashioned out of Sitka spruce, is utterly inviting. **Known for:** water views; best espresso drinks in town; carefully sourced ingredients. Ⓢ Average main: $13 ✉ 84 Beach St. ☎ 541/547–4409 ⊕ www.beachstreetkitchen.com ☾ Closed Tues. and Wed. No dinner.

Bread and Roses Baking

$ | **BAKERY** | Artisanal breads are handmade in small batches here, along with pastries, muffins, scones, cookies, cinnamon rolls, and desserts. In the bright, yellow-cottage bakery you can also try the daily soup and sandwiches at lunchtime, or just while away the morning with pastries and good coffee. **Known for:** proximity to Yachats State Recreation Area; delicious pastries and baked goods; organic, fair-trade coffee. Ⓢ Average main: $9 ✉ 238 4th St. ☎ 541/547–4454 ⊕ www.bnrbakery.com ☾ Closed Tues. and Wed. No dinner.

The Drift Inn

$$ | **AMERICAN** | **FAMILY** | This funky, convivial restaurant with affordable, basic overnight accommodations on the upper floor is a reliable bet for all three meals of the day; it's also great for watching live music below a ceiling full of umbrellas, with views of the Yachats River and ocean. Family-friendly and lively, the Drift Inn features fresh razor clams, halibut fish-and-chips, juicy steaks, wood-fired pizzas, and other well-prepared American fare. **Known for:** nice range of Oregon wines and beer; live music nightly; substantial breakfasts. Ⓢ Average main: $20 ✉ 124 U.S. 101 N ☎ 541/547–4477 ⊕ www.the-drift-inn.com.

Luna Sea Fish House

$$ | **SEAFOOD** | **FAMILY** | Sustainable, line-caught wild seafood—including albacore, cod, halibut, and, when in season, Dungeness crab—straight from the owner's boat is the draw at this festive weathered restaurant with colorful indoor and outdoor seating areas. Fish-and-chips of all stripes, including clam and salmon, are served, but the fish tacos and a sinful dish called slumgullion—clam chowder baked with cheese and bay shrimp—are the most popular choices. **Known for:** pet-friendly outdoor patio; slumgullion (a rich clam-and-shrimp chowder baked with cheese); live music many evenings. Ⓢ Average main: $17 ✉ 153 N.W. U.S. 101 ☎ 541/547–4794, 888/547–4794 ⊕ www.lunaseafishhouse.com.

Ona Restaurant

$$$ | **MODERN AMERICAN** | Relatively snazzy for such a laid-back town, this bustling downtown bistro overlooking the confluence of the Yachats River and the Pacific is nonetheless unpretentious and relaxed. The specialty is locally and seasonally sourced Oregon seafood, such as Manila clams steamed with grape tomatoes, dry vermouth, garlic, and butter, or rare seared albacore with togarashi, smoked maitake mushrooms, and tamari green beans—try a glass of wine from the excellent regional wine list. **Known for:** artfully plated contemporary seafood fare; luscious desserts; nice happy hour deals. $ *Average main: $25* ⊠ *131 U.S. 101 N* ☎ *541/547–6627* ⊕ *www.onarestaurant.com* ⊗ *Closed Mon.–Wed. in winter.*

★ Yachats Brewing

$$ | **ECLECTIC** | Inside this lively establishment with pitched-timber ceilings, skylights, and a solarium-style beer garden, you'll find one of the state's most impressive craft breweries and a taproom specializing in house-fermented, -pickled, and -smoked ingredients. It may sound like a slightly odd concept, but the food is creative and absolutely delicious, with dishes like elk-huckleberry sausage sandwiches; a salad of maple-smoked salmon, quail eggs, pickled beets, and seasonal farm veggies; and *khao man gai* (aromatic poached chicken with kimchi and spicy fermented soy sauce) leading the way. **Known for:** unusual craft beers and probiotic drinks; house-fermented foods; burgers and pizzas with interesting seasonal toppings. $ *Average main: $17* ⊠ *348 U.S. 101 N* ☎ *541/547–3884* ⊕ *www.yachatsbrewing.com.*

Hotels

Deane's Oceanfront Lodge

$ | **HOTEL** | This simple single-story, family-run motel is set on a sweeping stretch of beachfront midway between downtown Yachats and Waldport. **Pros:** charming rooms; direct ocean views and beach access; reasonable rates. **Cons:** small rooms; not within walking distance of dining and shopping; books up fast in summer. $ *Rooms from: $89* ⊠ *7365 U.S. 101 N* ☎ *541/547–3321* ⊕ *www.deaneslodge.com* ⇔ *18 rooms* ⊗ *No meals.*

★ Overleaf Lodge

$$$ | **HOTEL** | On a rocky shoreline at the north end of Yachats, this rambling romantic three-story hotel enjoys spectacular sunsets and contains splendidly comfortable and spacious accommodations that have a variety of options, including fireplaces, corner nooks, and whirlpool tubs with ocean views. **Pros:** fantastic oceanfront setting; one of the best full-service spas on the coast; complimentary wine tastings on Friday and Saturday evenings. **Cons:** no restaurant; a bit of a walk from town; rooms with best views can be quite spendy. $ *Rooms from: $239* ⊠ *280 Overleaf Lodge La.* ☎ *541/547–4885, 800/338–0507* ⊕ *www.overleaflodge.com* ⇔ *58 rooms* ⊗ *Free breakfast.*

Florence

25 miles south of Yachats; 64 miles west of Eugene.

The closest beach town to Oregon's second-largest city, Eugene, charming and low-key Florence delights visitors with its restored riverfront Old Town and proximity to one of the most remarkable stretches of Oregon coastline. Some 75 creeks and rivers empty into the Pacific Ocean in and around town, and the Siuslaw River flows right through the historic village center. When the numerous nearby lakes are added to the mix, it makes for one of the richest fishing areas in Oregon. Salmon, rainbow trout, bass, perch, crabs, and clams are among the water's treasures. Fishing boats and pleasure crafts moor in Florence's harbor, forming a pleasant backdrop for the town's restored buildings. Old Town has notable restaurants, antiques stores, fish markets, and other diversions. South of town, the miles of white sand dunes that make up Oregon Dunes National Recreation Area lend themselves to everything from solitary hikes to rides aboard all-terrain vehicles.

GETTING HERE AND AROUND

It's a 75-minute drive west to Florence on Highway 126 from Eugene and a stunningly scenic 40-minute drive south on U.S. 101 from Yachats. It takes about an hour to drive U.S. 101 south to Coos Bay, a stretch that takes in all of Oregon Dunes National Recreation Area.

ESSENTIALS

VISITOR INFORMATION Florence Area Chamber of Commerce. ⊠ *290 U.S. 101* ☎ *541/997–3128* ⊕ *www.florencechamber.com.*

Sights

Darlingtonia State Natural Site
GARDEN | FAMILY | A few miles north of Florence, you'll find this interesting example of the rich plant life found in the marshy terrain near the coast. It's also a surefire child pleaser. A short paved nature trail leads through clumps of insect-catching cobra lilies, so named because they look like spotted cobras ready to strike. This area is most interesting in May, when the lilies are in bloom. ⊠ *U.S. 101, at Mercer Lake Rd.* ☎ *541/997–3851* ⊕ *www.oregonstateparks.org.*

★ Heceta Head Lighthouse State Scenic Viewpoint
VIEWPOINT | A ½-mile trail from the beachside parking lot leads to the oft-photographed Heceta Head Lighthouse built in 1894, whose beacon, visible for more than 21 miles, is the most powerful on the Oregon Coast. More than 7 miles of trails traverse the rocky landscape north and south of the lighthouse, which rises

some 200 feet above the ocean. For a mesmerizing view of the lighthouse and Heceta Head, pull over at the scenic viewpoint just north of Sea Lion Caves. ⊠ *U.S. 101, Yachats* ✛ *11 miles north of Florence* ☎ *541/547–3416* ⊕ *www.oregonstateparks.org* ⊠ *Day use $5, lighthouse tours free.*

★ Oregon Dunes National Recreation Area
NATIONAL/STATE PARK | FAMILY | The Oregon Dunes National Recreation Area is the largest expanse of coastal sand dunes in North America, extending for 40 miles, from Florence to Coos Bay. The area contains some of the best ATV riding in the United States and encompasses some 31,500 acres. More than 1.5 million people visit the dunes each year, many of whom are ATV users. **Honeyman Memorial State Park,** 515 acres within the recreation area, is a base camp for dune-buggy enthusiasts, mountain bikers, hikers, boaters, horseback riders, and dogsledders (the sandy hills are an excellent training ground). There's a campground, too. The dunes are a vast playground for children, particularly the slopes surrounding cool **Cleawox Lake.** If you have time for just a quick scamper in the sand, stop by the Oregon Dunes Overlook off U.S. 101, 11 miles south of Florence and 11 miles north of Reedsport—it's on the west side of the road, just north of Perkins Lake. ⊠ *Visitor Center, 855 U.S. 101, Reedsport* ☎ *541/271–6000* ⊕ *www.fs.usda.gov/siuslaw* ⊠ *Day use $5.*

Sea Lion Caves
CAVE | FAMILY | In 1880 a sea captain named Cox rowed a small skiff into a fissure in a 300-foot-high sea cliff. Inside, he was startled to discover a vaulted chamber in the rock, 125 feet high and 2 acres in size. Hundreds of massive sea lions—the largest bulls weighing 2,000 pounds or more—covered every available surface. Cox's discovery would become one of the Oregon Coast's premier attractions, if something of a tourist trap. An elevator near the cliff-top ticket office

and kitschy gift shop descends to the floor of the cavern, near sea level, where vast numbers of Steller's and California sea lions relax on rocks and swim about (their cute, fuzzy pups can be viewed from behind a wire fence). This is the only known hauling-out area and rookery for wild sea lions on the mainland in the Lower 48, and it's an awesome sight and sound when they're in the cave, typically only in fall and winter (in spring and summer the mammals usually stay on the rocky ledges outside the cave). You'll also see several species of seabirds here, including migratory pigeon guillemots, cormorants, and three varieties of gulls. Gray whales are sometimes visible during their October–December and March–May migrations. ⊠ *91560 U.S. 101* ✛ *10 miles north of Florence* ☎ *541/547–3111* ⊕ *www.sealioncaves.com* ◳ *$14.*

Umpqua Lighthouse State Park

LIGHTHOUSE | Some of the highest sand dunes in the country are found in this 50-acre park between Florence and Coos Bay, near the small town of Reedsport. The first **Umpqua River Lighthouse,** built on the dunes at the mouth of the Umpqua River in 1857, lasted only four years before it toppled over in a storm. It took local residents 33 years to build another one. The "new" lighthouse, built on a bluff overlooking the south side of Winchester Bay and operated by the U.S. Coast Guard, stands at 65 feet and is still going strong, flashing a warning beacon out to sea every five seconds. The **Douglas County Coastal Visitors Center** adjacent to the lighthouse has a museum and can arrange lighthouse tours. ⊠ *Lighthouse Rd., Reedsport* ✛ *Umpqua Hwy., west side of U.S. 101* ☎ *541/271–4118, 541/271–4631 lighthouse tours* ⊕ *www.oregonstateparks.org* ◳ *Tours and museum $8.*

 Restaurants

Bridgewater Fishhouse

$$ | **SEAFOOD** | Freshly caught seafood—20 to 25 choices nightly—is the mainstay of this creaky-floored, Victorian-era restaurant in Florence's Old Town. Whether you opt for patio dining during summer or lounge seating in winter, the eclectic fare of pastas, burgers, salads, and seafood-packed stews is consistently well prepared, and a live jazz band provides some foot-tapping fun many evenings. **Known for:** live music; happy hour deals; lighter fare in Zebra Lounge. Ⓢ *Average main: $19* ⊠ *1297 Bay St.* ☎ *541/997–1133* ⊕ *www.bridgewaterfishhouse.com* ☾ *Closed Tues.*

Harbor Light Restaurant

$$ | **AMERICAN** | **FAMILY** | Located about 20 miles south of Florence in Reedsport, this homey, family-friendly restaurant—think log-cabin-style building decorated with mounted Oregon fish—is a great place to fuel up before playing on the nearby dunes. The food here is straightforward and traditional, from marionberry-stuffed French toast and seafood omelets at breakfast to prosciutto-wrapped prawns and blue-cheese-topped flat-iron steak in the evening, and the use of fresh, often local ingredients results in some of the healthiest and tastiest fare along this stretch of the coast. **Known for:** delicious blackberry, chocolate, and caramel milk shakes; filling breakfasts; proximity to Oregon Dunes National Recreation Area. Ⓢ *Average main: $20* ⊠ *930 U.S. 101, Reedsport* ☎ *541/271–3848* ⊕ *www.harborlightrestaurant.com.*

Homegrown Public House

$$ | **MODERN AMERICAN** | This convivial, intimate gastropub in Old Town Florence—a couple of blocks north of the riverfront—specializes in locally sourced, creatively prepared American fare and offers a well-chosen list of Oregon beers on tap, plus local spirits, iced teas, and kombucha. Stop by for lunch to enjoy the lightly battered albacore fish and hand-cut fries with tartar sauce, or a cheeseburger topped with Rogue blue and served with marinated vegetables and local greens. **Known for:** great selection of Oregon craft beers on tap; seafood curry; popular happy hour. ⓢ *Average main: $17* ✉ *294 Laurel St.* ☎ *541/997–4886* ⊕ *home-grownpublichouse.com/* ⊘ *Closed Mon.*

The Hukilau

$$ | ASIAN FUSION | Well-prepared Pacific Rim–fusion fare and fun tiki-inspired cocktails complete with paper umbrellas, are the draw at this hip, supercasual spot festooned with surfboards, Hawaiian shirts, and tropical artwork. Boldly flavored dishes like Hawaiian-style loco moco, pineapple teriyaki chicken, and Spam musubi may have you feeling like you've been airlifted to Maui, and there's tasty sushi, too. **Known for:** Hawaiian-inspired appetizers; creative sushi; tropical cocktails. ⓢ *Average main: $19* ✉ *185 U.S. 101* ☎ *541/991–1071* ⊕ *www.huki-lauflorence.com* ⊘ *Closed Sun. and Mon.*

River Roasters

$ | CAFÉ | This small, homey café serves cups of drip-on-demand coffee—you select the roast and they grind and brew it on the spot. Beans are roasted on-site, muffins and breads are freshly baked, and a view of the Siuslaw River can be savored from the deck out back. **Known for:** deck with river views; lots of flavored latte options; premium house-roasted coffee. ⓢ *Average main: $4* ✉ *1240 Bay St.* ☎ *541/997–3443* ⊕ *www.coffeeoregon.com.*

★ Waterfront Depot Restaurant and Bar

$$ | SEAFOOD | The detailed chalkboard menu of always intriguing nightly specials says it all: from the fresh, crab-encrusted halibut to classic duck-and-lamb cassoulet to Bill's Flaming Spanish Coffee, this is a place serious about fresh food and fine flavors. Originally located in the old Mapleton train station, moved in pieces and reassembled in Old Town Florence, the atmospheric tavern has a great view

of the Siuslaw River and the Siuslaw River Bridge. **Known for:** patio seating on the river; creative daily specials; excellent wine list. ⓢ *Average main: $21* ✉ *1252 Bay St.* ☎ *541/902–9100* ⊕ *www.thewaterfrontdepot.com* ⊘ *No lunch.*

Hotels

★ Heceta Head Lighthouse B&B

$$$$ | B&B/INN | On a windswept promontory, this unusual late-Victorian property is one of Oregon's most remarkable bed-and-breakfasts; it's located at Heceta Head Lighthouse State Scenic Viewpoint and owned by a gifted chef who prepares an elaborate seven-course breakfast each morning, with seasonal offerings. **Pros:** unique property with a magical setting; exceptionally good food; the promise of potential ghost sightings. **Cons:** remote location; expensive, especially considering some rooms share a bath; tends to book up well in advance. ⓢ *Rooms from: $280* ✉ *92072 U.S. 101* ⊹ *12 miles north of Florence* ☎ *541/547–3696, 866/547–3696* ⊕ *www.hecetalighthouse.com* ⌁ *6 rooms* ��ⓞⵑ *Free breakfast.*

River House Inn

$ | B&B/INN | On the beautiful Siuslaw River, this property has terrific accommodations and is near quaint shops and restaurants in Florence's Old Town. **Pros:** spacious rooms; great views from most rooms; close proximity to dining and shopping. **Cons:** not on the beach; in-town location can be a little busy at times; some rooms receive traffic noise from U.S. 101 bridge. ⓢ *Rooms from: $140* ✉ *1202 Bay St.* ☎ *541/997–3933, 888/824–2454* ⊕ *www.riverhouseflorence.com* ⌁ *40 rooms* ⵑⓞⵑ *Free breakfast.*

Activities

SANDBOARDING
Sand Master Park

LOCAL SPORTS | FAMILY | Everything you need to sandboard the park's private dunes is right here: board rental, wax, eyewear, clothing, and instruction. The staff is exceptionally helpful, and will get beginners off on their sandboarding adventure with enthusiasm. Nevertheless, what must be surfed must first be hiked up, and so on. ⊠ *5351 U.S. 101* ☎ *541/997–6006* ⊕ *www.sandmasterpark.com.*

TOURS

★ Sandland Adventures

TOUR—SPORTS | FAMILY | This outfitter provides everything you need to get the whole family together for the ride of their lives. Start off with a heart-racing dune-buggy ride with a professional that will take you careening up, over, down, and around some of the steepest sand in the Oregon Dunes National Recreation Area. After you're done screaming and smiling, Sandland's park has bumper boats, a go-kart track, a miniature-golf course, and a small railroad. ⊠ *85366 U.S. 101* ☎ *541/997–8087* ⊕ *www.sandland.com.*

Bay Area: Coos Bay and North Bend

45 miles south of Florence on U.S. 101.

The Coos Bay–Charleston–North Bend metropolitan area, collectively known as the Bay Area (population 32,000), is the gateway to rewarding recreational experiences. The small adjoining cities of North Bend and Coos Bay lie on the largest natural harbor between San Francisco Bay and Seattle's Puget Sound. A century ago vast quantities of lumber cut from the Coast Range were milled here and shipped around the world. The area still has a rough-and-ready port-city reputation, but with mill closures and dwindling lumber reserves, they now look increasingly to tourism and other industries for economic growth. In Coos Bay the waterfront is now dominated by an attractive boardwalk with interpretive displays, a casino, and the Coos History Museum.

To see the most picturesque part of the Bay Area, head west from Coos Bay on Newmark Avenue for about 7 miles to **Charleston,** which is home to some beautiful state parks and a bustling marina with casual restaurants and fishing charters. Though it's a Bay Area community, this quiet fishing village at the mouth of Coos Bay is a world unto itself. As it loops into town, the road becomes the Cape Arago Highway and leads to the area's stunning parks.

GETTING HERE AND AROUND

The area lies along a slightly inland stretch of U.S. 101 that's a one-hour drive south of Florence and a 30-minute drive north of Bandon; from the Umpqua Valley and Interstate 5 corridor, Coos Bay is just under two hours' drive west from Roseburg on Highway 42.

Southwest Oregon Regional Airport in North Bend has commercial flights from Denver (summer only) and San Francisco.

ESSENTIALS

VISITOR INFORMATION Oregon's Adventure Coast. ⊠ *50 Central Ave., Coos Bay* ☎ *541/269–0215* ⊕ *www.oregonsadventurecoast.com.*

 Sights

Cape Arago Lighthouse

LIGHTHOUSE | FAMILY | On a rock island just offshore from Charleston near Sunset Bay State Park, this lighthouse has had several iterations; the first lighthouse was built here in 1866, but it was destroyed by storms and erosion. A second, built in 1908, suffered the same fate. The current white tower, built in 1934, is 44 feet tall and towers 100 feet above the ocean. If you're here on a foggy day, listen for its unique foghorn. The lighthouse is connected to the mainland by a bridge. Neither is open to the public, but there's an excellent spot to view

You can experience the Umpqua Sand Dunes via ATV in the 31,500-acre Oregon Dunes National Recreation Area.

this lonely guardian and much of the coastline. From U.S. 101 take Cape Arago Highway to Gregory Point, where it ends at a turnaround, and follow the short trail. ⊠ *Cape Arago Hwy., Charleston* ✛ *Just north of Sunset Bay State Park.*

Cape Arago State Park

NATIONAL/STATE PARK | The distant barking of sea lions echoes in the air at a trio of coves connected by short but steep trails. The park overlooks the **Oregon Islands National Wildlife Refuge,** where offshore rocks, beaches, islands, and reefs provide breeding grounds for seabirds and marine mammals, including seal pups (the trail is closed in spring to protect them). ⊠ *End of Cape Arago Hwy., Coos Bay* ☎ *541/888–3778* ⊕ *www. oregonstateparks.org* ☒ *Free.*

★ Coos History Museum & Maritime Collection

MUSEUM | FAMILY | This contemporary 11,000-square-foot museum with expansive views of the Coos Bay waterfront contains an impressive collection of memorabilia related to the region's

history, from early photos to vintage boats, all displayed in an airy, open exhibit hall with extensive interpretive signage. You'll also find well-designed exhibits on Native American history, agriculture, and industry such as logging, shipwrecks, boatbuilding, natural history, and mining. ⊠ *1210 N. Front St., Coos Bay* ☎ *541/756–6320* ⊕ *www.cooshistory.org* ☒ *$7* ☺ *Closed Mon.*

★ Shore Acres State Park

NATIONAL/STATE PARK | An observation building on a grassy bluff overlooking the Pacific marks the site that held the mansion of lumber baron Louis J. Simpson. The view over the rugged wave-smashed cliffs is splendid, but the real glory of Shore Acres lies a few hundred yards to the south, where an entrance gate leads into what was Simpson's private garden. Beautifully landscaped and meticulously maintained, the gardens incorporate formal English and Japanese designs. From March to mid-October the grounds are ablaze with blossoming daffodils, rhododendrons, azaleas, roses, and dahlias.

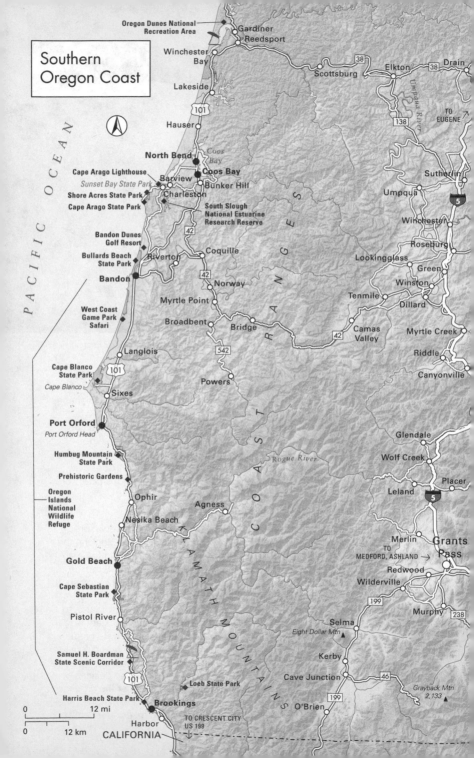

Southern Oregon Coast

PACIFIC OCEAN

Oregon Dunes National Recreation Area
Gardiner
Reedsport
Winchester Bay
Scottsburg
Elkton
Drain
38
38
Lakeside
Umpqua River
TO EUGEN
138
101
Hauser
Sutherlin
Coos Bay
North Bend
Umpqua
Cape Arago Lighthouse
Sunset Bay State Park
Barview
Coos Bay
Bunker Hill
Winchester
Shore Acres State Park
Charleston
Cape Arago State Park
South Slough National Estuarine Research Reserve
Roseburg
Lookingglass
Green
Bandon Dunes Golf Resort
Coquille
Riverton
42
Winston
Bullards Beach State Park
Tenmile
Dillard
Bandon
42
Norway
Myrtle Creek
Myrtle Point
Camas Valley
Riddle
West Coast Game Park Safari
Broadbent
Bridge
42
Canyonville
Langlois
542
Cape Blanco State Park
101
Powers
Cape Blanco
Sixes
Glendale
Port Orford
Wolf Creek
Port Orford Head
Rogue River
Humbug Mountain State Park
Leland
Placer
5
Prehistoric Gardens
Ophir
Agness
Oregon Islands National Wildlife Refuge
Nesika Beach
Merlin
Grants Pass
TO MEDFORD, ASHLAND
Redwood
Gold Beach
Wilderville
Cape Sebastian State Park
199
Murphy
238
Pistol River
Selma
Eight Dollar Mtn
Samuel H. Boardman State Scenic Corridor
Kerby
101
Grayback Mtn 2,133
Loeb State Park
Cave Junction
46
Harris Beach State Park
Brookings
199
O'Brien
Harbor
TO CRESCENT CITY US 199
CALIFORNIA

COAST RANGES

KLAMATH MOUNTAINS

0   12 mi
0   12 km

In December the garden is decked out with a dazzling display of holiday lights. ✉ *89526 Cape Arago Hwy., Coos Bay* ☎ *541/888–2472 gardens, 541/888–3732* 🌐 *www.oregonstateparks.org* 🎟 *$5 parking.*

South Slough National Estuarine Research Reserve

NATURE PRESERVE | **FAMILY** | The 5,900-acre reserve's fragile ecosystem supports everything from algae to bald eagles and black bears. More than 300 species of birds have been sighted at the reserve, which has an interpretive center with interesting nature exhibits, guided walks (summer only), and nature trails that give you a chance to see things up close. ✉ *61907 Seven Devils Rd., Coos Bay* ✥ *4 miles south of Charleston* ☎ *541/888–5558* 🌐 *www.oregon.gov/dsl/ss* 🎟 *Free* ⏲ *Visitor center closed Sun. and Mon.*

🍴 Restaurants

Blue Heron Bistro

$$ | **GERMAN** | The specialty at this bustling downtown bistro is hearty German fare, but you'll also find a number of local seafood items, as well as sandwiches and lighter dishes, from panfried oysters to meatball sandwiches. The skylit, tile-floor dining room has natural wood and mounted animal heads on the walls, and there's a pet-friendly patio outside. **Known for:** great selection of German and local craft beers; pleasant outdoor seating; Sunday brunch. [$] *Average main: $20* ✉ *100 W. Commercial St., Coos Bay* ☎ *541/267–3933* 🌐 *www.blueheronbistro.net.*

Miller's at the Cove

$$ | **SEAFOOD** | Often packed with local fishermen and dock workers as well as tourists en route to and from Sunset Bay and nearby state parks, this lively and fun—if at times raucous—sports bar and tavern makes a great dinner or lunch stop for fresh seafood, and watching a game on TV. Favorites here include the fish-and-chips (available with local snapper or cod), oyster burgers, Dungeness crab melts, meatball subs, clam chowder, and Baja-style fish or crab tacos. **Known for:** laid-back atmosphere; tasty fish tacos; craft beer by the pitcher. [$] *Average main: $16* ✉ *63346 Boat Basin Rd., Charleston* ☎ *541/808–2404* 🌐 *www.millersatthecove.rocks.*

🛏 Hotels

★ Bay Point Landing

$$ | **RESORT** | With striking contemporary architecture and a pristine setting on a section of Coos Bay near Charleston and the ocean, this 100-acre compound is the first luxury glamping venue on the Oregon Coast, though you don't need a tent or sleeping bag to enjoy a stay in its airy cabins and tricked-out Airstream trailers. **Pros:** gorgeous contemporary design; lots of cushy amenities; picturesque bay-side setting. **Cons:** need a car to get to shops and restaurants; some cabins have limited water views; a bit spendy. [$] *Rooms from: $179* ✉ *92443 Cape Arago Hwy., Coos Bay* ☎ *541/351–9160* 🌐 *www.baypointlanding.com* 🔑 *25 units* 🍽 *No meals.*

Coos Bay Manor

$ | **B&B/INN** | **FAMILY** | Built in 1912 on a quiet residential street, this 15-room Colonial Revival manor contains original hardwood floors, detailed woodwork, high ceilings, and antiques and period reproductions. **Pros:** elegantly decorated; family-friendly; central location near restaurants and shops. **Cons:** on a quiet street but still in a busy downtown area; a 15-minute drive from the ocean; traditional, historic vibe isn't everyone's taste. [$] *Rooms from: $145* ✉ *955 S. 5th St., Coos Bay* ☎ *541/269–1224, 800/269–1224* 🌐 *www.coosbaymanor.com* 🔑 *6 rooms* 🍽 *Free breakfast.*

Mill Casino Hotel
$ | **RESORT** | Even if you're not a big fan of gambling, this attractive hotel on the bay and boardwalk in North Bend (a short distance north of downtown Coos Bay) makes a handy and fairly economical base for exploring this stretch of the coast. **Pros:** attractive, contemporary rooms; location close to downtown dining and shopping; nice bay views from many rooms. **Cons:** casino can be noisy and smoky; 25-minute drive from the ocean; rooms in older buildings feel a bit dated. [$] *Rooms from: $125* ✉ *3201 Tremont Ave., North Bend* ☎ *541/756–8800, 800/953–4800* 🌐 *www.themillcasino.com* 🛏 *203 rooms* 🍴 *No meals.*

Bandon

25 miles south of Coos Bay.

Referred to by some who cherish its romantic lure as Bandon-by-the-Sea, Bandon is both a harbor town and a popular beach-vacation town, famous for its cranberry products and its artists' colony, complete with galleries and shops. Two national wildlife refuges, Oregon Islands and Bandon Marsh, are within the town limits, and a drive along Beach Loop Road, just southwest of downtown, affords mesmerizing views of awesome coastal rock formations, especially around Coquille Point and Face Rock State Scenic Viewpoint. The Bandon Dunes links-style golf courses are a worldwide attraction, often ranked among the top courses in the nation.

Tiny Bandon bills itself as Oregon's cranberry capital—10 miles north of town you'll find acres of bogs and irrigated fields where tons of the tart berries are harvested every year. Each September there's the Cranberry Festival, featuring a parade and a fair.

GETTING HERE AND AROUND

Bandon, on U.S. 101, is a half-hour drive south of Coos Bay and North Bend, and a 2-hour drive north up the coast from the California border; allow just under 2 hours to get here from Roseburg in the Umpqua Valley via Highway 42, and 4½ hours from Portland.

ESSENTIALS

VISITOR INFORMATION Bandon Chamber of Commerce. ✉ *300 2nd St.* ☎ *541/347–9616* 🌐 *www.bandon.com.*

Sights

Bandon Historical Society Museum
MUSEUM | In the old city hall building, this museum depicts the area's early history, including Native American artifacts, logging, fishing, cranberry farming, and the disastrous 1936 fire that destroyed the city. The well-stocked gift shop has books, knickknacks, jewelry, myrtlewood, and other little treasures. ✉ *270 Fillmore St.* ☎ *541/347–2164* 🌐 *www.bandonhistoricalmuseum.org* 🎟 *$3* 🕒 *Closed Sun. in winter.*

Bullards Beach State Park
NATIONAL/STATE PARK | At this rugged park along the north bank of the Coquille River (just across from downtown Bandon but reached via a 3½-mile drive up U.S. 101), you can tour the signal room inside the octagonal **Coquille Lighthouse,** built in 1896 and no longer in use; due to safety concerns, visitors can no longer tour the tower, but the signal room is open. From turnoff from U.S. 101, the meandering 2-mile drive to reach it passes through the Bandon Marsh, a prime bird-watching and picnicking area. The 4½-mile stretch of beach beside the lighthouse is a good place to search for jasper, agate, and driftwood—the firm sand is also popular for mountain biking. There's a campground with a wide variety of tent and RV sites as well as pet-friendly yurts. ✉ *52470 U.S. 101* ☎ *541/347–2209* 🌐 *www.oregonstateparks.org* 🎟 *Free.*

Face Rock State Scenic Viewpoint

BEACH—SIGHT | The stone sculptures of Face Rock Wayside, formed only by wind and rain, have names such as Elephant Rock, Table Rock, and Face Rock. To reach them, follow signs from Bandon south along Beach Loop Road; then walk down a stairway to the sand and enjoy the stone sights along this dramatic stretch of beach. ✉ *Beach Loop Rd. at Face Rock Dr.* 🎟 *Free.*

★ Oregon Islands National Wildlife Refuge: Coquille Point Unit

NATURE PRESERVE | FAMILY | Each of the colossal rocks jutting from the ocean between Bandon and Brookings is protected as part of the 19-acre Coquille Point section of this huge refuge that, in total, comprises 1,853 rocks, reefs, islands, and two headland areas spanning 320 miles up and down the Oregon Coast. Thirteen species of seabirds—totalling 1.2 million birds—nest here, and harbor seals, California sea lions, Steller sea lions, and Northern elephant seals also breed within the refuge. Coquille Point, which sits at the edge of Kronenberg County Park close to downtown Bandon, is one of the best places to observe seabirds and harbor seals. The dramatic point atop a steep sea cliff overlooks a series of offshore rocks, and a paved trail that winds over the headland ends in stairways to the beach on both sides, allowing for a loop across the sand when tides permit. Visitors are encouraged to steer clear of harbor seals and avoid touching seal pups. **■ TIP→ A complete list of Oregon Islands Refuge viewpoints and trails is available online, and the refuge headquarters is located up the coast in Newport.** ✉ *11th St. W at Portland Ave. SW* ☎ *541/867–4550* 🌐 *www.fws.gov/refuge/oregon_islands.*

West Coast Game Park Safari

NATURE PRESERVE | FAMILY | The "walk-through safari" on 21 acres has free-roaming wildlife (it's the visitors who are behind fences); more than 450 animals and about 75 species, including lions, tigers, snow leopards, lemurs, bears, chimps, cougars, and camels, make it one of the largest wild-animal petting parks in the United States. The big attractions here are the young animals: bear cubs, tiger cubs, whatever is suitable for actual handling. ✉ *46914 U.S. 101* ☎ *541/347–3106* 🌐 *www.westcoastgameparksafari.com* 🎟 *$20.50* 🕒 *Closed weekdays Jan.–Feb.*

🍴 Restaurants

Alloro Wine Bar

$$$$ | MODERN ITALIAN | Although it bills itself as a wine bar, this casually upscale dining room with local art on the walls is also one of the southern Oregon Coast's most sophisticated little restaurants, with a dinner menu that emphasizes freshly made pastas, often served with local seafood (the wild sea scallops with orange zest–infused spaetzle is a standout). Wines by the glass and bottle are discounted 25% during early evening happy hour. **Known for:** homemade (gluten-free on request) pasta with seafood; extensive Italian and southern Oregon wine list; knowledgeable staff. [$] *Average main: $32* ✉ *375 2nd St. SE* ☎ *541/347–1850* 🌐 *www.allorowinebar.com* 🕒 *Closed Wed. and Sun. No lunch.*

Edgewaters Restaurant

$$ | SEAFOOD | This second-story bar above Edgewaters Restaurant has some of the best west-facing views of the Coquille River and the ocean beyond—you can sometimes see migrating whales. It makes a great happy-hour stop with its tall ceilings, warm fireplace, and many windows, while the main dining downstairs also has great views and serves a great array of fresh seafood, pastas, and creative salads. **Known for:** fish- or prawns-and-chips; impressive river and sunset views; seafood chowder. [$] *Average main: $22* ✉ *480 1st St.* ☎ *541/347–8500* 🌐 *www.edgewaters.net* 🕒 *No lunch Tues.–Thurs. Closed Mon. in winter.*

Lord Bennett's

$$$ | **AMERICAN** | His lordship has a lot going for him: a cliff-top setting, a comfortable and spacious dining area in a dramatic contemporary building, sunsets visible through picture windows overlooking Face Rock Beach, and occasional live music on weekends. The modern American menu features plenty of local seafood; try the nut-crusted halibut, blackened red snapper with potato-horseradish crust, or wild prawns with garlic butter and sherry. **Known for:** Sunday brunch; some of the best steaks in the area; dazzling ocean views. $ *Average main: $29* ✉ *1695 Beach Loop Rd.* ☎ *541/347–3663* ⊕ *www.lordbennetts. com* ✆ *No lunch Mon.–Sat.*

★ Tony's Crab Shack & Seafood Grill

$$ | **SEAFOOD** | Started in 1989 as a bait and tackle shop (which still exists next door), this casual short-order seafooder has become a staple of Bandon's small but picturesque riverfront boardwalk, renowned for its crab cakes, fish tacos, crab and bay shrimp sandwich, and house-smoked salmon. Open only until 6 pm, it's a reliable bet for lunch or a very early dinner. **Known for:** scenic riverfront location; combo crab, steamer clam, and shrimp platters; grilled oysters on the half shell with garlic butter. $ *Average main: $19* ✉ *155 1st St.* ☎ *541/347–2875* ⊕ *www.tonyscrabshack.com.*

 ## Hotels

★ Bandon Dunes Golf Resort

$$$ | **RESORT** | This golfing lodge provides a comfortable place to relax after a day on the world-famous links, with accommodations ranging from single rooms or cottages to four-bedroom condos, many with beautiful views of the famous golf course. **Pros:** if you're a golfer, this adds to an incredible overall experience; if not, you'll have a wonderful stay anyway; lots of on-site dining options. **Cons:** the weather can be wet and wild in the shoulder-season months; not

within walking distance of town; no a/c in rooms. $ *Rooms from: $240* ✉ *57744 Round Lake Dr.* ☎ *541/347–4380, 888/345–6008* ⊕ *www.bandondunesgolf. com* ✆ *186 rooms* ⏸ *Free Breakfast.*

Bandon Inn

$$ | **HOTEL** | This comfy, casual motel offers views of Old Town Bandon and the mouth of Coquille River from every room, each with a small balcony from which to take in the scenery and the town's famous Fourth of July fireworks. **Pros:** steps from downtown dining and shopping; good value; nice views of town and river. **Cons:** walls are a little thin; not directly on the water; busy downtown location. $ *Rooms from: $154* ✉ *355 U.S. 101* ☎ *541/347–4417, 800/526–0209* ⊕ *www.bandoninn.com* ✆ *57 rooms* ⏸ *Free breakfast.*

 ## Shopping

★ Face Rock Creamery

FOOD/CANDY | Launched in 2013, this local creamery has rapidly developed a following for its classic and flavored handmade cheddar as well as its cheese curds and spreadable fromage blanc. At the downtown creamery, you'll also find a wide range of gourmet food items, soups and sandwiches, and ice cream—it's a perfect stop for picnic supplies. The milk comes from a 600-acre dairy farm just 15 miles from Bandon. ✉ *680 2nd St. SE* ☎ *541/347–3223* ⊕ *www.facerockcreamery.com.*

 ## Activities

GOLF

★ Bandon Dunes Golf Resort

GOLF | This windswept, links-style playland for the nation's golfing elite is no stranger to well-heeled athletes flying in to North Bend on private jets to play on the resort's four distinct courses, including the beloved Pacific Dunes layout, many of whose rolling, bunker-laced fairways meander atop high bluffs with breathtaking ocean views. The steep greens fees vary a good bit according to season; they drop sharply during the November–April off-season. The expectation (although not requirement) at Bandon Dunes is that you walk the course with a caddy—adding a refined, traditional touch. Caddy fees are $100 per bag, per round, plus gratuity. ⊠ *57744 Round Lake Dr.* ☎ *541/347–4380, 888/345–6008* ⊕ *www.bandondunesgolf. com* ⊠ *$255–$345* 🍴*. Bandon Dunes Course: 18 holes, 5716 yards, par 72; Bandon Trails Course: 18 holes, 5751 yards, par 71; Old Macdonald Course: 18 holes, 5658 yards, par 71; Pacific Dunes Course: 18 holes, 5775 yards, par 71.*

Port Orford

30 miles south of Bandon.

The westernmost incorporated community in the contiguous United States, Port Orford is surrounded by pristine forests, rivers, lakes, and beaches. Its secluded setting and dramatic natural scenery make it an ideal place to live or visit among artists, hikers, and others who appreciate solitude. The jetty at Port Orford offers little protection from storms, so every night the fishing boats are lifted out and stored on the docks. The town of about 1,150 is a prolific center of commercial fishing (mostly for crab, tuna, snapper, and salmon), diving boats gather sea urchins for Japanese markets—fishing enthusiasts also like to cast a line off the Port Orford dock or the jetty for smelt, sardine, herring, lingcod, and halibut. Dock Beach is a favorite spot for sport divers because of the near-shore, protected reef, and for whale-watchers in fall and early spring.

GETTING HERE AND AROUND
Port Orford is a 30-minute drive south of Bandon and a one-hour drive north of Brookings along U.S. 101.

ESSENTIALS
VISITOR INFORMATION Port Orford Visitors Center. ⊠ *520 Jefferson St.* ☎ *541/332–4106* ⊕ *www.enjoyportorford. com.*

Sights

Battle Rock Park and Port Orford Heads State Park
NATIONAL/STATE PARK | FAMILY | Stroll the mocha-colored sand and admire pristine Battle Rock right in the heart of downtown Port Orford. Named for a battle between white settlers and the Dene Tsut Dah that took place here in 1850, this spot sits just below Port Orford Heads State Park. Atop the bluff that is Port Orford Heads, a trail loops the rocky outcropping between the Pacific and the Port Orford Lifeboat Station, taking in the hillside below, from which crews once mounted daring rescues on the fierce sea. The lifeboat station and adjoining museum is open for free tours Wednesday–Monday, 10–3:30. Their motto? "You have to go out... you don't have to come back." ⊠ *Port Orford Hwy.* ✛ *Follow signs from U.S. 101* ☎ *541/332–6774* ⊕ *www. oregonstateparks.org.*

Cape Blanco State Park
NATIONAL/STATE PARK | FAMILY | Said to be the westernmost point in Oregon and perhaps the windiest—gusts clocked at speeds as high as 184 mph have twisted and battered the Sitka spruces along the 6-mile road from U.S. 101 to the **Cape Blanco Lighthouse.** The lighthouse, atop a 245-foot headland, has been in continuous use since 1870, longer than any other in Oregon. **Hughes House** is all that remains of the Irish settler Patrick Hughes's dairy farm complex built in 1860. The lighthouse and Hughes House are open in summer only. No one knows why the Spaniards sailing past these reddish bluffs in 1603 called them *blanco* (white). One theory is that the name refers to the fossilized shells that glint in the cliff face. Campsites at

the 1,880-acre park are available on a first-come, first-served basis. Four cabins are available for reservation. ⊠ *91814 Cape Blanco Rd., Sixes* ☎ *541/332–2973* ⊕ *www.oregonstateparks.org* ⊠ *Day use and Hughes House tour free; lighthouse tour $2.*

★ Humbug Mountain State Park

NATIONAL/STATE PARK | This secluded, 1,850-acre park, especially popular with campers, usually has warm weather, thanks to the nearby mountains that shelter it from ocean breezes. A 6-mile loop leads to the top of 1,756-foot Humbug Mountain, one of the highest points along the state's coastline. It's a pretty, moderately challenging hike, but the summit is fairly overgrown and doesn't provide especially panoramic views. The campground has tent and RV sites. ⊠ *U.S. 101 ✛ 6 miles south of Port Orford* ☎ *541/332–6774* ⊕ *www.oregon-stateparks.org.*

Prehistoric Gardens

LOCAL INTEREST | **FAMILY** | As you round a bend between Port Orford and Gold Beach, you'll see one of those sights that make grown-ups groan and kids squeal with delight: a huge, open-jawed Tyrannosaurus rex, with a green Brontosaurus peering out from the forest beside it. You can view 23 other life-size dinosaur replicas on the trail that runs through the property. ⊠ *36848 U.S. 101* ☎ *541/332–4463* ⊕ *www.prehistoricgardens.com* ⊠ *$12.*

🍴 Restaurants

Crazy Norwegians Fish and Chips

$ | **SEAFOOD** | **FAMILY** | This quirky and casual hole-in-the-wall in Port Orford excels at what it does: good old-fashioned fish-and-chips. With everything from shrimp to cod to halibut paired with fries, the Crazy Norwegians serve it up with a side of pasta salad or coleslaw. **Known for:** to-go meals to take to the beach or park; the crazy combo platter

(jumbo prawns, cod, and clams); stellar fish-and-chips. **$** *Average main: $13* ⊠ *259 6th St.* ☎ *541/332–8601* ⊕ *the-crazy-norwegians-fish-and-chips.business. site/* ⊗ *Closed Mon.*

★ Redfish

$$$ | **MODERN AMERICAN** | Two walls of windows allow diners at this stylish downtown bistro spectacular ocean panoramas, but the views inside are pretty inviting, too, from the modern artwork provided by sister establishment Hawthorne Gallery to the artfully presented and globally influenced food. Start with the local clams sautéed in butter or the five-spice baked duck eggrolls, before graduating to double-cut pork chops with cranberry-apple chutney or house-made gnocchi with pesto and hazelnuts. **Known for:** crab cakes Benedict at weekend brunch; stunning water views; a noteworthy cocktail, wine, and craft beer program. **$** *Average main: $25* ⊠ *517 Jefferson St.* ☎ *541/366–2200* ⊕ *www. redfishportorford.com* ⊗ *Closed Tues.*

Hotels

Castaway by the Sea

$ | **HOTEL** | **FAMILY** | This old-school motel with a friendly owner offers fantastic views from nearly every room, most of which have enclosed sun porches—the simplest and least expensive accommodations open to an enclosed breezeway that takes in these same views. **Pros:** within walking distance of local restaurants; panoramic ocean views; reasonable rates. **Cons:** decor is a bit dated; not actually on the beach; quirky decor may not please everyone. **$** *Rooms from: $125* ⊠ *545 5th St.* ☎ *541/332–4502* ⊕ *www.castawaybythesea.com* ⊠ *13 rooms* ⊗ *No meals.*

★ WildSpring Guest Habitat

$$$$ | **B&B/INN** | This rustic outpost in the woods above Port Orford blends all the comforts and privacy of a vacation rental with the services of a small resort. **Pros:**

relaxing, secluded, and private; gorgeous rooms; eco-conscious practices. **Cons:** need to drive to the beach and stores; not a good fit if you like bigger hotels; two-night minimum on summer weekends. *$ Rooms from: $259 ⊠ 92978 Cemetery Loop Rd. ☎ 541/332–0977, 866/333–9453 ⊕ www.wildspring.com ➟ 5 cabins ⦿l Free breakfast.*

Gold Beach

28 miles south of Port Orford.

The fabled Rogue River is one of about 150 in the nation to merit federally designated Wild and Scenic status. From spring to late fall, thousands of visitors descend on the town to take one of the daily jet-boat excursions that roar upstream from Wedderburn, an unincorporated hamlet across the bay from Gold Beach, into the Rogue River Wilderness Area. Black bears, otters, beavers, ospreys, egrets, and bald eagles are seen regularly on these trips.

GETTING HERE AND AROUND
It's a 90-minute drive south along U.S. 101 from Coos Bay and North Bend to reach Gold Beach, which is a one-hour drive north of the California border.

ESSENTIALS
VISITOR INFORMATION Gold Beach Visitors Center. ⊠ 94080 Shirley La. ☎ 541/247–7526, 800/525–2334 ⊕ www. visitgoldbeach.com.

Sights

Cape Sebastian State Scenic Corridor
VIEWPOINT | The parking lots at this scenic area are more than 200 feet above sea level. At the south parking vista, you can see up to 43 miles north to Humbug Mountain. Looking south, you can see nearly 50 miles toward Crescent City, California, and the Point Saint George Lighthouse. A deep forest of Sitka spruce covers most of the park. There's

a 1½-mile walking trail. ⊠ U.S. 101 ⊹ 6 miles south of Gold Beach ☎ 541/469– 2021 ⊕ www.oregonstateparks.org.

★ Samuel H. Boardman State Scenic Corridor
PARK—SPORTS-OUTDOORS | This 12-mile corridor through beach forests and alongside rocky promontories and windswept beaches contains some of Oregon's most spectacular stretches of coastline, though seeing some of them up close sometimes requires a little effort. About 27 miles of the Oregon Coast Trail weaves its way through this area, a reach dominated by Sitka spruce trees that stretch up to 300 feet and by rocky coast interspersed with sandy beaches. Starting from the north, walk a short path from the highway turnoff to view Arch Rock. The path travels a meadow that blooms in spring time. Down the road, find **Secret Beach**—hardly a secret— where trails run from two parking lots into three separate beaches below. Visit at low tide to make your way through all three, including through a cave that connects to the third beach close to Thunder Rock. You'll find arguably the most photogenic vista in the park on the short trail to **Natural Bridge,** where several dramatic rock formations form arches over the surf. At **Thunder Rock**, just north of milepost 345 on U.S. 101, walk west for a 1-mile loop that traces inlets and headlands, edging right up to steep drops. Find the highest bridge in Oregon just south—the **Thomas Creek Bridge**—from which a moderately difficult trail extends to wide, sandy **China Beach**. Find some sun on China Beach, or continue south to walk the unusual sculpted sandstone at **Indian Sands**. Easy beach access is at Whaleshead Beach, where shaded picnic tables shelter the view. From farther south at **Lone Ranch**, climb the grassy hillside to the top of **Cape Ferrelo** for a sweeping view of the rugged coastline, also a great spot for whale-watching in fall and summer. ⊠ U.S. 101 between Gold Beach and

Brookings ☎ *541/469–2021* 🌐 *www.oregonstateparks.org* 🎫 *Free.*

🍴 Restaurants

★ Anna's by the Sea

$$$ | MODERN CANADIAN | Dining at Anna's by the Sea is like stepping into one man's artisanal universe: bowed and wood-trimmed ceilings, handmade cheeses, and blackberry honey lemonade, even a hydroponic herb garden, crafted by the owner–head cook. The enchanting, intimate eatery seats only 18, six of those seats stools with a view into the kitchen, and serves what it calls "retro nouvelle Canadian Prairie cuisine," which might include a charcuterie plate of goose prosciutto, smoked local albacore, and beef-tongue pastrami, or Alaskan scallops on a bed of buttered pasta with truffle oil. **Known for:** outstanding selection of Oregon wines and craft spirits; live music; friendly, knowledgeable service. [$] *Average main: $26* ✉ *29672 Stewart St.* ☎ *514/247–2100* 🌐 *www.annasbythesea.com* ⏲ *Closed Sun.–Tues. No lunch.*

Barnacle Bistro

$ | AMERICAN | At this quirky tavern on the main road in downtown Gold Beach, try the lingcod fish-and-chips with ginger-sesame coleslaw and sweet-potato fries, the curry-cider mussels, the shellfish tacos with a Brazilian coconut-peanut sauce, or any of the enormous burgers. It's reliably good pub fare using produce, meat, and seafood sourced locally. **Known for:** beer from nearby Arch Rock Brewery; very reasonable prices; hefty burgers. [$] *Average main: $14* ✉ *29805 Ellensburg Ave.* ☎ *541/247–7799* 🌐 *www.barnaclebistro.com* ⏲ *Closed Sun. and Mon.*

Wild Oaks Grill

$$ | BARBECUE | This bare-bones, counter-service barbecue joint serves up diabolically delicious, house-brined and smoked meaty fare along with sides of fries with decadent toppings (poutine, chili-cheese, and so on). The burgers and sandwiches are delicious, but if you have the appetite for it, consider the sampler of pulled pork, smoked chicken breast, baby back ribs, brisket, and tri-tip with a couple of sides. **Known for:** tri-tip sandwiches; habanero-garlic-Parmesan fries; smoked bacon. [$] *Average main: $16* ✉ *29545 Ellensburg Ave.* ☎ *541/425–5460* 🌐 *www.wildoaksgrill.com.*

🛏 Hotels

Pacific Reef and Resort

$ | HOTEL | FAMILY | This resort offers a little something for everyone: from comfy, clean, economical rooms in the original renovated 1950s hotel to modern two-story condos with expansive ocean views, king-size beds, full kitchens, and outdoor patios. **Pros:** nicely equipped condos with full kitchens; in center of town; glorious water views from the best units. **Cons:** adjoins a rocky beach; on a busy road; could use a little updating. [$] *Rooms from: $89* ✉ *29362 Ellensburg Hwy.* ☎ *541/247–6658* 🌐 *www.pacificreefhotel.com* 🔑 *39 units* 🍽 *Free breakfast.*

★ Tu Tu' Tun Lodge

$$$$ | RESORT | Pronounced "too- *too*-tin," this renowned and rather lavish boutique resort is a slice of heaven on the Rogue River; its rustic-elegant rooms have private decks overlooking the water; some have hot tubs, others have fireplaces, and a few have both. **Pros:** luxurious, beautifully outfitted rooms; exceptional dining; peaceful location overlooking river. **Cons:** no TVs; not well suited for young kids; 15-minute drive from downtown and the ocean. [$] *Rooms from: $295* ✉ *96550 N. Bank Rogue River Rd.* ✥ *7 miles east of Gold Beach* ☎ *541/247–6664, 800/864–6357* 🌐 *www.tututun.com* 🔑 *20 rooms* 🍽 *Free breakfast.*

🏃 Activities

BOATING

★ **Jerry's Rogue Jets**

BOATING | **FAMILY** | These jet boats operate from May through September in the most rugged section of the Wild and Scenic Rogue River, offering 64-, 80-, and 104-mile tours, starting at $50 per person. Whether visitors choose a shorter, six-hour lower Rogue scenic trip or an eight-hour white-water trip, folks have a rollicking good time. Its largest vessels are 40 feet long and can hold 75 passengers. The smaller, white-water boats are 32 feet long and can hold 42 passengers. ✉ 29985 Harbor Way ☎ 541/247–4571, 800/451–3645 ⊕ www.roguejets.com.

Brookings

27 miles south of Gold Beach on U.S. 101.

The coastal gateway to Oregon if you're approaching from California, Brookings is home to a pair of sterling state parks, one overlooking the ocean and another nestled amid the redwoods a bit inland. The only overnight option along the 55-mile stretch between Gold Beach and Crescent City, it's also a handy base, with some reasonably priced hotels and motels, and a growing crop of noteworthy restaurants. A startling 90% of the pot lilies grown in the United States come from a 500-acre area just inland from Brookings. Mild temperatures along this coastal plain provide ideal conditions for flowering plants of all kinds—even a few palm trees, a rare sight in Oregon.

The town is equally famous as a commercial and sportfishing port at the mouth of the turquoise-blue Chetco River. Salmon and steelhead weighing 20 pounds or more swim here.

GETTING HERE AND AROUND

Brookings is the southernmost town on Oregon's coastal 101, just 10 miles north of the California border and a half-hour drive from Crescent City; it's a 2½-hour drive south on U.S. 101 from the Coos Bay and North Bend area. Allow about six hours to get here from Portland via Interstate 5 to Grants Pass and U.S. 199 to Crescent City.

VISITOR INFORMATION

CONTACTS Brookings Harbor Chamber of Commerce. ✉ 703 Chetco Ave. ☎ 541/469–3181 ⊕ www.brookingsharborchamber.com.

👁 Sights

Alfred A. Loeb State Park

NATIONAL/STATE PARK | Some fine hiking trails, one leading to a hidden redwood grove, along with a nice selection of campsites, make up this park a bit inland from Brookings. There's also a grove of myrtlewood trees, which you'll find only in southwest Oregon and northern California. ✉ N. Bank Chetco River Rd. (Hwy. 784) ⊹ 10 miles east of Brookings ☎ 541/469–2021 ⊕ www.oregonstateparks.org ⌂ Reservations not accepted.

★ Harris Beach State Park

NATIONAL/STATE PARK | The views from the parking areas, oceanfront trails, and beaches at this popular tract of craggy rock formations and evergreen forest are some of the prettiest along the southern Oregon Coast. The proximity to downtown Brookings makes this an easy place to head for morning beachcombing or a sunset stroll. You might see gray whales migrate in spring and winter. Just offshore, Bird Island, also called Goat Island, is a National Wildlife Sanctuary and a breeding site for rare birds. The campground here, with tent and RV sites, is very popular. ✉ 1655 Old U.S. 101 ☎ 541/469–2021 ⊕ www.oregonstateparks.org.

Restaurants

★ Oxenfre Public House

$$ | **MODERN AMERICAN** | The kitchen at this upbeat, contemporary gastropub with a welcoming outdoor balcony, from which you can see the ocean in the distance, stands out for its commitment to locally sourced produce and seafood and an ambitious craft-cocktail selection. The eclectic, elevated comfort fare here has an international flair—consider the Baja-style Pacific cod tacos with avocado-mango cruda and Thai chili lime crema, or Korean chicken salad with sesame-soy dressing and charred pineapple. **Known for:** first-rate craft cocktails; excellent happy hour deals; ingredients sourced from local purveyors. $ *Average main: $19* ✉ *631 Chetco Ave.* ☎ *541/813–1985* ⊕ *www.oxenpub.com* ⊘ *No lunch.*

Pacific Sushi & Grill

$$$ | **SUSHI** | You'll find some of the tastiest sushi on the Oregon Coast at this welcoming Japanese restaurant with weathered-timber walls and booths and a friendly adjoining cocktail lounge. Beyond the flavorful and creative jumbo spider and hamachi jalapeño rolls, you'll find a great selection of Japanese dishes, including tonkotsu ramen with chashu pork and crispy fried karaage-style calamari. **Known for:** creative sushi rolls; cucumber-wasabi martinis; late-night menu in the lounge. $ *Average main: $23* ✉ *613 Chetco Ave.* ☎ *541/251–7707* ⊕ *www.pacificsushi.com* ⊘ *Closed Thurs.*

Vista Pub

$ | **AMERICAN** | An affordable, friendly, and attractive family-run tavern in downtown Brookings, Vista Pub is known both for its extensive selection of rotating craft beers and tasty but simple comfort food. Try the hefty bacon-cheddar burgers, beer-cheese soup in a bread bowl, thick-cut fries sprinkled with sea salt, fried locally grown zucchini, and smoked-salmon chowder with bacon. **Known for:** tasty pub fare; excellent craft-beer selection; great burgers.

$ *Average main: $11* ✉ *1009 Chetco Ave.* ☎ *541/813–1638* ⊘ *Closed Mon.*

Hotels

Beachfront Inn

$$$ | **HOTEL** | This spotlessly clean three-story Best Western across the street from the Brookings boat basin has direct beach access and ocean views, making it one of the best-maintained and most appealingly located lodging options along the southern coast. **Pros:** fantastic ocean views; quiet location away from busy U.S. 101; very well kept. **Cons:** rooms don't have much personality; not many restaurants within walking distance; a bit pricey in summer. $ *Rooms from: $219* ✉ *16008 Boat Basin Rd.* ☎ *541/469–7779* ⊕ *www.beachfrontinn.com* ⇆ *102 rooms* ⊚¶ *Free breakfast.*

Nightlife

★ Chetco Brewing Taproom

BREWPUBS/BEER GARDENS | In addition to producing some of the most flavorful, well-crafted beers along the Oregon Coast, Chetco Brewing also has a spacious, inviting taproom with plenty of indoor and outdoor seating, and live music most weekends. ✉ *830 Railroad St.* ☎ *541/661–5347* ⊕ *www.chetcobrew.com.*

Superfly Martini Bar & Grill

BARS/PUBS | The unusual name of this stylish little bar and grill has nothing to do with the Curtis Mayfield '70s funk anthem—rather, owner Ryan Webster named this establishment, which is also an artisanal-vodka distillery, after a fishing fly. Appropriately, the bar serves first-rate cocktails, including a refreshing lemon-basil martini. But the food is tasty, too. ✉ *623 Memory La.* ☎ *541/373–0348* ⊕ *www.superflydistillingcompany.com.*

Chapter 5

5

WILLAMETTE VALLEY AND WINE COUNTRY

Updated by
Margot Bigg

⊙ Sights   🍴 Restaurants   🛏 Hotels   🛍 Shopping   🍸 Nightlife
★★★★☆   ★★★★★   ★★★★☆   ★★★☆☆   ★☆☆☆☆

WELCOME TO WILLAMETTE VALLEY AND WINE COUNTRY

TOP REASONS TO GO

★ **Swirl and sip:** Each region in the Willamette Valley offers some of the finest vintages and dining experiences found anywhere.

★ **Soar through the air:** Newberg's hot-air balloons will give you a bird's-eye view of Yamhill County's wine country.

★ **Run rapids:** Feel the bouncing exhilaration and the cold spray of white-water rafting on the wild, winding McKenzie River outside Eugene.

★ **Walk on the wild side:** Hillsboro's Jackson Bottom Nature Preserve gives walkers a chance to view otters, beavers, herons, and eagles.

★ **Back the Beavers or Ducks:** Nothing gets the blood pumping like an Oregon State Beavers or University of Oregon Ducks football game.

The Willamette Valley is a fertile mix of urban, rural, and wild stretching from Portland at the north to Cottage Grove at the south. It is bordered by the Cascade Range to the east and the Coast Range to the west. The Calapooya Mountains border it to the south and the mighty Columbia River runs along the north. Running north and south, Interstate 5 connects communities throughout the valley. In the mid-1800s the Willamette Valley was the destination of emigrants on the Oregon Trail, and today is home to about two-thirds of the state's population. The Willamette Valley is 150 miles long and up to 60 miles wide, which makes it Oregon's largest wine-growing region.

1 Hillsboro. International dining and excellent parks just outside of Portland.

2 Forest Grove. Douglas firs and sequoias surround the area's numerous wineries and tasting rooms.

3 Newberg. The gateway to Oregon Wine Country.

4 Dundee. A charming town full of wineries and restaurants.

5 Yamhill and Carlton. This area is home to some of the world's finest Pinot Noir vineyards.

6 McMinnville. The largest city in Yamhill County and the commercial hub of Oregon's wine industry, with shops, hotels, and dining galore.

7 Independence. Historic Victorian city in the heart of Oregon's hop country.

8 Salem. Oregon's historic state capital and a gateway to great hiking.

9 Albany. Listed on the National Register of Historic Places and home to some of Oregon's most historic buildings.

10 Corvallis. A small city that's the home of Oregon State University.

11 Eugene. Home to the University of Oregon and a center for athletics, this friendly, bohemian town is a great spot to eat, drink, and spend time outdoors.

12 McKenzie Bridge. Here visitors soak in natural hot springs, hike in dense forest, and run the rapids.

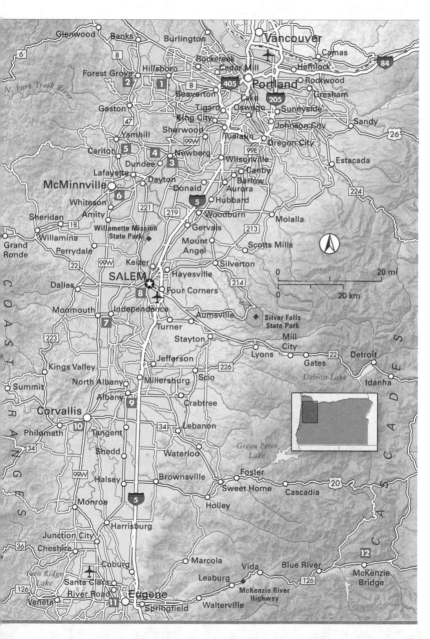

The Willamette (pronounced "wil-*lam*-it") Valley has become a wine lover's Shangri-La, particularly in the northern Yamhill and Washington counties between Interstate 5 and the Oregon Coast, a region that is not only carpeted with vineyards but encompasses small hotels and inns, cozy restaurants, and casual wine bars.

The valley divides two mountain ranges (the Cascade and Coast), and contains more than 500 wineries. The huge wine region is made up of seven subappellations: Chehalem Mountains, Ribbon Ridge, Dundee Hills, Yamhill-Carlton, Eola-Amity Hills, The Van Duzer Corridor, and McMinnville. With its incredibly rich soil perfect for growing Pinot Noir, Pinot Gris, Chardonnay, and Riesling, the valley has received worldwide acclaim for its vintages. The region's farms are famous for producing quality fruits, vegetables, and cheeses that are savored in area restaurants. During spring and summer there are many roadside stands dotting the country lanes, and farmers' markets appear in most of the valley's towns. Also delicious are the locally raised lamb, pork, chicken, and beef. The valley also is a huge exporter of plants and flowers for nurseries, with a large number of farms growing ornamental trees, bulbs, and plants.

The valley definitely has an artsy, expressive, and fun side, with its wine and beer festivals, theater, music, crafts, and culinary events. Many residents and visitors are serious runners and bicyclists, particularly in Eugene, so pay close attention while driving.

There's a long-standing collegiate football rivalry between the Oregon State Beavers in Corvallis and University of Oregon Ducks in Eugene; getting a ticket to the annual "Civil War" game between the two teams is a feat in itself. Across the state, but particularly in the Willamette Valley, Oregonians are passionate fans of one team or the other. If you happen to be visiting the area during the event (usually held in October or November), be prepared for some serious traffic and some closed businesses.

MAJOR REGIONS

Just outside Portland, in the **North Willamette Valley,** the suburban areas of Tigard, **Hillsboro,** and **Forest Grove** have gorgeous wetlands, rivers, and nature preserves. The area has a wealth of golfing, biking, and trails for running and hiking and it's not unusual to spot red-tail hawks, beavers, and ducks on your route. Shopping, fine dining, and proximity to Portland make this a great area in which to begin your exploration of the Willamette Valley and its wine country.

Yamhill County, at the northern end of the Willamette Valley, has a fortunate confluence of perfect soils, a benign climate, and talented winemakers who craft world-class vintages. In recent years several new wineries have been built in Yamhill County's hills, as well as on its flatlands. While vineyards flourished in the northern Willamette Valley in the 19th century, viticulture didn't arrive in Yamhill County until the 1960s and 1970s, with such pioneers as Dick Erath (Erath Vineyards Winery), David and Ginny Adelsheim (Adelsheim Vineyard), and David and Diana Lett (The Eyrie Vineyards). The focus of much of the county's enthusiasm lies in the Red Hills of Dundee, where the farming towns of **Newberg, Dundee, Yamhill-Carlton,** and **McMinnville** have made room for upscale hotels and bed-and-breakfasts, wine bars, and tourists seeking that perfect swirl and sip.

The Yamhill County wineries are only a short drive from Portland, and the roads, especially Route 99W and Route 18, can be crowded on weekends as they link suburban Portland communities to Newport and Lincoln City on the Oregon Coast.

While most of the wineries are concentrated in Washington and Yamhill counties, there are several finds in the **mid–Willamette Valley** that warrant extending a wine enthusiast's journey, with plenty of breweries, flower farms, and state parks along the way. Popular spots to stop include **Salem, Independence, Albany,** and **Corvallis.** The large cluster of factory outlet shops in Woodburn on Interstate 5 will have you thinking about some new Nikes, and Oregon State University will have you wearing orange and black long after Halloween is over. Be aware that many communities in this region are little more than wide spots in the road.

Lane County rests at the southern end of the **South Willamette Valley,** encompassing **Eugene,** Springfield, Drain, **McKenzie**

Bridge, and Cottage Grove. Visitors can enjoy a wide range of outdoor activities such as running, fishing, swimming, white-water rafting, and deep-woods hiking along the McKenzie River, while Eugene offers great food, shopping, and the arts. There are plenty of wineries to enjoy, too, as well as cheering on the Oregon Ducks. To the west lies the Oregon Dunes Recreation Area, and to the east are the beautiful central Oregon communities of Sisters, Bend, and Redmond.

Planning

When to Go

July to October are the best times to wander the country roads in the Willamette Valley, exploring the grounds of its many wineries. Fall is spectacular, with leaves at their colorful peak in late October. Winters are usually mild, but they can be relentlessly overcast and downright rainy. Visitors not disturbed by dampness or chill will find excellent deals on lodging. In the spring rains continue, but the wildflowers begin to bloom, which pays off at the many gardens and nature parks throughout the valley.

FESTIVALS

International Pinot Noir Celebration

FESTIVALS | During the International Pinot Noir Celebration, held the last full weekend in July, wine lovers flock to McMinnville to sample fine regional vintages along with Pinot Noir from around the world. ✉ *Box 1310800, McMinnville* ☎ *800/775–4762* ⊕ *www.ipnc.org.*

Oregon Bach Festival

FESTIVALS | Eugene hosts the world-class Oregon Bach Festival, with two-plus weeks of classical music performances. ✉ *1257 University of Oregon, Eugene* ☎ *541/346–5666, 800/457–1486* ⊕ *oregonbachfestival.com.*

Oregon Country Fair

FESTIVALS | Every July, the weekend after Independence Day, a small patch of fields and forest right outside of Eugene transforms into an enchanting community celebration known as the Oregon Country Fair. This annual event has been going on since the 1960s and maintains much of its flower-child vibe, with all sorts of parades, live music, puppet shows, face painting, and excellent craft shopping. ✉ 24207 Oregon 126, Veneta ☎ 541/343–4298 ⊕ www.oregoncountry-fair.org.

Wooden Shoe Tulip Fest

FESTIVALS | Every April, visitors to Woodburn's Wooden Shoe Tulip Farm can tiptoe (or walk, or take a hayride) through spectacular fields of brightly hued tulips. Other festival features include wine tastings, cutout boards for photos, food booths, and a play area for kids. ✉ 33814 S. Meridian Rd., Woodburn ☎ 503/634–2243 ⊕ www.woodenshoe.com/events/tulip-fest/.

Getting Here and Around

AIR TRAVEL

Portland's airport is an hour's drive east of the northern Willamette Valley. The **Aloha Express Airport Shuttle** provides shuttle service. **Eugene Airport** is more convenient if you're exploring the region's southern end. It's served by Delta, Alaska/Horizon, American, and United/United Express. The flight from Portland to Eugene is 40 minutes. Smaller airports for private aircraft are scattered throughout the valley.

Rental cars are available at the Eugene airport from Budget, Enterprise, and Hertz. Taxis and airport shuttles will transport you to downtown Eugene for about $30. **Omni Shuttle** will provide shuttle service to and from the Eugene airport from anywhere in Oregon.

AIR CONTACTS Aloha Express Airport Shuttle. ☎ 503/356–8848 ⊕ www.aloha-expressshuttle.com. **Hub Airport Shuttle.** ☎ 541/461–7959 ⊕ hubairportshuttle.com.

BUS TRAVEL

Buses operated by Portland's **TriMet** network connect Forest Grove, Hillsboro, and other metro-area suburb communities with Portland and each other; light-rail trains operated by MAX run between Portland and Hillsboro. Many of the **Lane Transit District** buses will make a few stops to the outskirts of Lane County, such as McKenzie Bridge. All buses have bike racks. **Yamhill County Transit Area** provides bus service for Yamhill County, with links to Hillsboro/MAX, Sherwood/TriMet, and Salem/SAMT.

BUS CONTACTS Lane Transit District. (LTD) ☎ 541/687–5555 ⊕ www.ltd.org. **Yamhill County Transit Area.** ☎ 503/474–4900 ⊕ www.ycbus.org.

CAR TRAVEL

Interstate 5 runs north–south the length of the Willamette Valley. Many Willamette Valley attractions sit not too far east or west of Interstate 5. Highway 22 travels west from the Willamette National Forest through Salem to the coast. Highway 99 travels parallel to Interstate 5 through much of the Willamette Valley. Highway 34 leaves Interstate 5 just south of Albany and heads west, past Corvallis and into the Coast Range, where it follows the Alsea River. Highway 126 heads east from Eugene toward the Willamette National Forest; it travels west from town to the coast. U.S. 20 travels west from Corvallis. Most major rental car companies have outposts in Portland and throughout the region.

Restaurants

The buzzwords associated with fine dining in this region are "sustainable," "farm-to-table," and "local." Fresh salmon, Dungeness crab, mussels, shrimp, and oysters are harvested just a couple of hours away on the Oregon Coast. Lamb, pork, and beef are local and plentiful, and seasonal game appears on many menus. Desserts made with local blueberries, huckleberries, raspberries, and marionberries should not be missed. But what really sets the offerings apart are the splendid local wines that receive worldwide acclaim.

Restaurants in the Willamette Valley are low-key and unpretentious. Expensive doesn't necessarily mean better, and locals have a pretty good nose for good value. Reasonably priced Mexican, Indian, Japanese, and Italian do very well. Food carts in the cities are a growing phenomenon. But there's still nothing like a great, sit-down meal at a cozy bistro for some fresh fish or lamb, washed down with a stellar Pinot Noir. *Restaurant reviews have been shortened. For full information visit Fodors.com.*

What it Costs in U.S. Dollars			
$	$$	$$$	$$$$
RESTAURANTS			
under $16	$16–$22	$23–$30	over $30
HOTELS			
under $150	$150–$200	$201–$250	over $250

Hotels

One of the great pleasures of touring the Willamette Valley is the incredible selection of small, ornate bed-and-breakfast hotels sprinkled throughout Oregon's wine country. In the summer and fall they can fill up quickly, as visitors come from around the world to enjoy wine tastings at the hundreds of large and small wineries. Many of these have exquisite restaurants right on the premises, with home-baked goods available

day and night. There are plenty of larger properties located closer to urban areas and shopping centers, including upscale resorts with expansive spas, as well as national chains that are perfect for travelers who just need a place to lay their heads. *Hotel reviews have been shortened. For full information, visit Fodors.com.*

Tours

Oregon Wine Tours and **EcoTours of Oregon** provide informative guided outings across the Willamette Valley wine country.

CONTACTS EcoTours of Oregon. ☎ 503/245–1428 ⊕ www.ecotours-of-oregon.com. **Great Oregon Tours.** ☎ 971/713–1023 ⊕ greatoregontours.com.

Visitor Information

CONTACTS Travel Lane County. ✉ 754 Olive St., Eugene ☎ 541/484–5307, 800/547–5445 ⊕ www.eugenecascadescoast.org. **Washington County Visitors Association.** ✉ 12725 S.W. Millikan Way, Suite 210, Beaverton ☎ 503/644–5555, 800/537–3149 ⊕ www.oregonswashingtoncounty.com. **Willamette Valley Visitors Association.** ☎ 866/548–5018 ⊕ www.oregonwinecountry.org.

Hillsboro

20 miles southwest of Portland.

Hillsboro offers a wealth of eclectic shops, preserves, restaurants, and proximity to the valley's fine wineries. In the past 20 years Hillsboro has experienced rapid growth associated with the Silicon Forest, where high-tech business found ample sprawling room. Several of Intel's industrial campuses are in Hillsboro, as are the facilities of other leading electronics manufacturers. Businesses related

Vineyard and Valley Scenic Tour

Vineyard and Valley Scenic Tour. A 60-mile driving route through the lush Tualatin Valley runs between the city of Sherwood in the southern part of the valley and Helvetia at the northern end. The rural drive showcases much of Washington County's agricultural bounty, including many of the county's wineries and farms (some with stands offering seasonal fresh produce and/or U-pick), along with pioneer and historic sites, wildlife refuges, and scenic viewpoints of the Cascade Mountains. For more information, visit the Washington County Visitors Association's tourist center. ⊠ *Washington County Visitors Association, 12725 S.W. Millikan Way, Suite 210, Beaverton* ☎ *503/644–5555* ⊕ *tualatin-valley.org* ⊙ *Closed weekends.*

to the town's original agricultural roots remain a significant part of Hillsboro's culture and economy. Alpaca ranches, nurseries, berry farms, nut and fruit orchards, and numerous wineries are among the area's most active agricultural businesses.

GETTING HERE AND AROUND

Hillsboro is about a 45-minute drive west from Portland International Airport. The **Aloha Express Airport Shuttle** and the **Beaverton Airporter** provide shuttle service.

From Downtown Portland it's a short 20-minute car ride, or visitors can ride the MAX light rail. The TriMet Bus Service connects to the MAX light rail in Hillsboro, with connections to Beaverton, Aloha, and other commercial areas.

Sights

★ Abbey Creek Winery

WINERY/DISTILLERY | This small winery specializes in small batches of Chardonnay and Pinots, with weekend tastings served to the beats of hip-hop in its cozy North Plains tasting room. Owner-operator Bertony Faustin is the first known black winemaker in the state and has done much to elevate the voices of minorities in the industry, notably through his documentary, *Red, White & Black.* ⊠ *31441 NW Commercial St., North Plains* ☎ *503/389–0619* ⊕ *www. abbeycreekvineyard.com* ⊠ *Tastings $10.*

Hillsboro Farmers' Market

MARKET | Fresh local produce—some from booths, some from the backs of trucks—as well as local arts and crafts are on sale Saturday from May through October. Live music is played throughout the day. The market is just a block from the MAX light rail line. ⊠ *Main St. between 1st and 3rd Aves.* ☎ *503/844–6685* ⊕ *www.hillsboromarkets.org.*

Jackson Bottom Wetlands Preserve

NATURE PRESERVE | Several miles of trails in this 710-acre floodplain and woods are home to thousands of ducks and geese, deer, otters, beavers, herons, and eagles. Walking trails allow birders and other animal watchers to explore the wetlands for a chance to catch a glimpse of indigenous and migrating creatures in their own habitats. The **Education Center** has several hands-on exhibits, as well as a real bald eagle's nest that has been completely preserved (and sanitized) for public display. No dogs or bicycles are allowed. ⊠ *2600 S.W. Hillsboro Hwy.* ☎ *503/681–6206* ⊕ *www.jacksonbottom. org* ⊠ *$2 suggested donation for visitors 10 and over.*

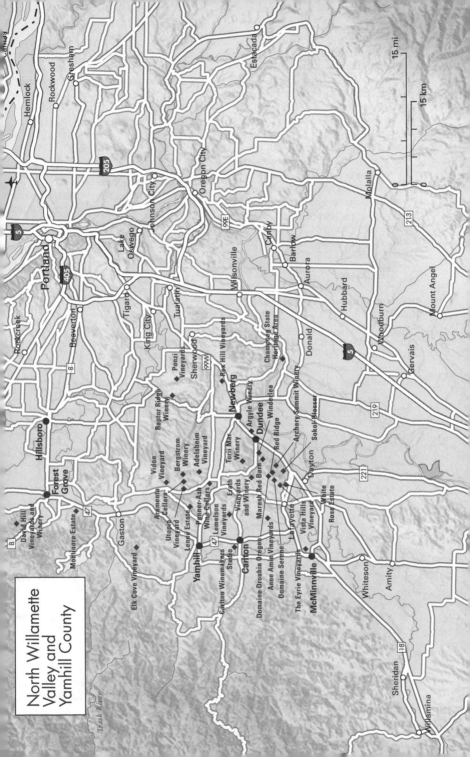

L.L. Stub Stewart State Park

NATIONAL/STATE PARK | FAMILY | This 1,654-acre, full-service park has hiking, biking, and horseback riding trails for day use or overnight camping. There are full hookup sites, tent sites, small cabins, and even a horse camp. Lush rolling hills, forests, and deep canyons are terrific for bird-watching, wildflower walks, and other relaxing pursuits. An 18-hole disc golf course winds its way through a dense forest. In case you don't know, in disc golf players throw a disc at a target and attempt to complete the course with the fewest throws. ✉ *30380 N.W. Hwy. 47, Buxton* ☎ *503/324–0606* 🌐 *www.oregonstateparks.org* 🎫 *$5 for day-use parking.*

Rice Northwest Museum of Rocks and Minerals

MUSEUM | FAMILY | Richard and Helen Rice began collecting beach agates in 1938, and over the years they developed one of the largest private mineral collections in the United States. The most popular item here is the Alma Rose rhodochrosite, a 4-inch red crystal. The museum (in a ranch-style home) also displays petrified wood from all over the world and a gallery of Northwest minerals—including specimens of rare crystallized gold. Tours are offered Saturday at 2 pm. ✉ *26385 N.W. Groveland Dr.* ☎ *503/647–2418* 🌐 *www.ricenorthwestmuseum.org* 🎫 *$12* 🕒 *Closed Tues.*

Tualatin River Wildlife Refuge

NATURE PRESERVE | This sanctuary for indigenous and migrating birds, waterfowl, and mammals is in Sherwood (about 18 miles south of Hillsboro). It is one of only a handful of national urban refuges in the United States and has restored much of the natural landscape common to western Oregon prior to human settlement. The refuge is home to nearly 200 species of birds, 50 species of mammals, 25 species of reptiles and amphibians, and a variety of insects, fish, and plants. It features an interpretive center, a gift shop, photography blinds, and restrooms. This restoration has attracted animals back to the area in great numbers, and with a keen eye, birders and animal watchers can catch a glimpse of these creatures year-round. In May the refuge hosts its Migratory Songbird Festival. ✉ *19255 S.W. Pacific Hwy., Tigard* ☎ *503/625–5944* 🌐 *www.fws.gov/tualatinriver.*

Washington County Museum

MUSEUM | This impressive space on the second floor of the Hillsboro Civic Center houses a range of exhibits focusing on the history and culture of the area. Most of the exhibits include activities for children. ✉ *120 E. Main St.* ☎ *503/645–5353* 🌐 *www.washingtoncountymuseum.org* 🎫 *$5* 🕒 *Closed. Sun.–Wed.*

🍴 Restaurants

Syun Izakaya

$ | JAPANESE | A large assortment of sushi and sashimi, soups, and salads are served in quiet surroundings in the basement of the old Hillsboro Library. Wonderful grilled and fried meats and vegetables are also available, accompanied by a vast sake selection. **Known for:** unique daily specials; a delicious variety of sushi and sashimi; happy hour values. [$] *Average main: $11* ✉ *209 N.E. Lincoln St.* ☎ *503/640–3131* 🌐 *www.syun-izakaya.com* 🕒 *No lunch Sun.*

Virundhu South Indian Cuisine

$ | INDIAN | Though Virundhu does offer a smattering of the North Indian dishes typical to subcontinental restaurants in the States, it mainly focuses on a varied menu of South Indian cuisine, from crepe-like dosas to fragrant biriyanis. If you're not sure what to try, come for the lunch buffet and sample a bit of everything. **Known for:** vegetarian and meat-based South Indian specialties; richly spiced biriyanis; weekday and weekend lunch buffets. [$] *Average main: $12* ✉ *180 E Main St., Suite 105* ☎ *503/941–5976* 🌐 *www.virundhuusa.com* 🕒 *Closed Mon.*

Forest Grove

24 miles west of Portland on Hwy. 8.

This small town is surrounded by stands of Douglas firs and giant sequoia, including the largest giant sequoia in the state. There are nearby wetlands, birding, the Hagg Lake Recreation Area, a new outdoor adventure park, and numerous wineries and tasting rooms. To get to many of the wineries, head south from Forest Grove on Highway 47 and watch for the blue road signs between Forest Grove, Gaston, and Yamhill. To the west of town, you'll find some of the oldest Pinot Noir vines in the valley at David Hill Winery.

GETTING HERE AND AROUND

Forest Grove is about an hour's drive west from Portland International Airport. The **Aloha Express Airport Shuttle** and the **Beaverton Airporter** provide shuttle service.

From Downtown Portland it's a short 35-minute car ride with only a few traffic lights during the entire trip. TriMet Bus Service provides bus service to and from Forest Grove every 15 minutes, connecting to the MAX light rail 6 miles east in Hillsboro, which continues into Portland. Buses travel to Cornelius, Hillsboro, Aloha, and Beaverton.

ESSENTIALS

CONTACTS Forest Grove Chamber of Commerce. ✉ *2417 Pacific Ave.* ☎ *503/357–3006* ⊕ *www.visitforestgrove.com.*

Sights

David Hill Vineyards and Winery

WINERY/DISTILLERY | In 1965 Charles Coury came to Oregon from California and planted some of the Willamette Valley's first Pinot Noir vines on the site of what is now the David Hill Winery. The original farmhouse serves as the tasting room and offers splendid views of the Tualatin Valley. They produce Pinot Noir, some of which comes from the original vines planted by Coury, along with Chardonnay, Gewürztraminer, Merlot, Tempranillo, Pinot Gris, and Riesling. The wines are well made and pleasant, especially the eclectic blend called Farmhouse Red and the estate Riesling. ✉ *46350 N.W. David Hill Rd.* ☎ *503/992–8545* ⊕ *www.davidhillwinery.com* ✉ *Tastings from $10.*

Elk Cove Vineyard

WINERY/DISTILLERY | Founded in 1974 by Pat and Joe Campbell, this established winery covers 600 acres on four separate vineyard sites. The tasting room is set in the beautiful rolling hills at the foot of the coast range overlooking the vines. The focus is on Willamette Valley Pinot Noir, Pinot Gris, and Pinot Blanc. Be sure to also try the limited bottling of their Pinot Noir Rosé if they're pouring it. ✉ *27751 N.W. Olson Rd., Gaston* ☎ *503/985–7760, 877/355–2683* ⊕ *www.elkcove.com* ✉ *Tastings from $15.*

Montinore Estate

WINERY/DISTILLERY | Locals chuckle at visitors who try to show off their French savvy when they pronounce it "Mont-in-or-ay." The estate, originally a ranch, was established by a tycoon who'd made his money in the Montana mines before he retired to Oregon; he decided to call his estate "Montana in Oregon." Montinore (no "ay" at the end) has 232 acres of vineyards, and its wines reflect the high-quality soil and fruit. Highlights include a crisp Gewürztraminer, a light Müller-Thurgau, an off-dry Riesling, several lush Pinot Noirs, and a delightful white blend called Borealis that's a perfect partner for Northwest seafood. ✉ *3663 S.W. Dilley Rd.* ☎ *503/359–5012* ⊕ *www.montinore.com* ✉ *Tastings $15.*

SakéOne

WINERY/DISTILLERY | After the founders realized that the country's best water supply for sake was in the Pacific Northwest, they built their brewery in Forest Grove in 1997. It's one of only six sake brewing facilities in America and

David Hill Vineyards and Winery in Forest Grove produces Pinot Noir, as well as Chardonnay, Gewürztraminer, Merlot, Tempranillo, Pinot Gris, and Riesling.

produces award-winning sake under three labels, in addition to importing from partners in Japan. The tasting room offers three different flights, including one with a food pairing. Be sure to catch one of the tours, offered Friday through Sunday, where your guide will walk you through every phase of the sake-making process, from milling the rice to final filtration and bottling. ⊠ 820 Elm St. ☎ 503/357–7056, 800/550–7253 ⊕ www.sakeone.com 🎫 Tastings from $10.

★ Scoggin Valley Park and Henry Hagg Lake

NATIONAL/STATE PARK | FAMILY | This beautiful area in the Coast Range foothills has a 15-mile-long hiking trail that surrounds the lake. Bird-watching is best in spring. Recreational activities include fishing, boating, waterskiing, picnicking, and hiking, and a 10½-mile, well-marked bicycle lane parallels the park's perimeter road. ⊠ 50250 S.W. Scoggins Valley Rd., Gaston ☎ 503/846–8715 ⊕ www.co.washington.or.us/Support_Services/Facilities/Parks/Hagglake 🎫 Free, parking $7.

Tree to Tree Adventure Park

AMUSEMENT PARK/WATER PARK | FAMILY | At the first public aerial adventure park in the Pacific Northwest—and only the second of its kind in the United States—the aerial adventure course features 19 ziplines and more than 60 treetop elements and obstacles. You can experience the thrills of moving from platform to platform (tree to tree) via wobbly bridges, tightropes, Tarzan swings, and more. The courses range from beginner to extreme, with certified and trained instructors providing guidance to adventurers. "Woody's Ziptastic Voyage" zipline tour features six extreme ziplines (including one that is 1,280 feet long), a bridge, and a 40-foot rappel. Harnesses and helmets are provided, and no open-toed shoes are allowed. Reservations are required. ⊠ 2975 S.W. Nelson Rd., Gaston ☎ 503/357–0109 ⊕ tree2treeadventurepark.com 🎫 Aerial park $55, zip tour $85 ⊙ Closed mid-Nov.–Feb.

Hotels

McMenamins Grand Lodge

$ | HOTEL | On 13 acres of pastoral countryside, this converted Masonic rest home has accommodations that run from bunk-bed rooms to a three-room fireplace suite, with some nice period antiques in all. **Pros:** relaxed, friendly brewpub atmosphere; spa and soaking pool; on-site disc golf course. **Cons:** some rooms have shared bathrooms; not much to do in the area; rooms can be noisy. $ *Rooms from: $60* ✉ *3505 Pacific Ave.* ☎ *503/992–9533, 877/992–9533* ⊕ *www. mcmenamins.com/grandlodge* ⇱ *90 rooms* ❂ *No meals.*

Newberg

24 miles south of Portland on Hwy. 99W.

Newberg sits in the Chehalem Valley, known as one of Oregon's most fertile wine-growing locations, and is called the Gateway to Oregon Wine Country. Many of Newberg's early settlers were Quakers from the Midwest, who founded the school that has become George Fox University. Newberg's most famous resident, likewise a Quaker, was Herbert Hoover, the 31st president of the United States. For about five years during his adolescence, he lived with an aunt and uncle at the Hoover-Minthorn House, now a museum listed on the National Register of Historic Places. Now the town is on the map for the nearby wineries, fine-dining establishments, and a spacious, spectacular resort, the Allison. St. Paul, a historic town with a population of about 325, is about 8 miles south of Newberg, and every July holds a professional rodeo.

GETTING HERE AND AROUND

Newberg is just under an hour's drive from Portland International Airport; **Caravan Airport Transportation** (☎ *541/994–9645* ⊕ *www. caravanairporttransportation.com*) provides shuttle service. The best way to visit Newberg and the Yamhill County vineyards is by car. Situated on Highway 99W, Newberg is 90 minutes from Lincoln City, on the Oregon Coast. Greyhound provides bus service to McMinnville.

Sights

★ Adelsheim Vineyard

WINERY/DISTILLERY | David Adelsheim is the knight in shining armor of the Oregon wine industry—tirelessly promoting Oregon wines abroad, and always willing to share the knowledge he has gained from his long viticultural experience. He and Ginny Adelsheim founded their pioneer winery in 1971. They make their wines from grapes picked on their 230 acres of estate vineyards, as well as from grapes they've purchased. Their Pinot Noir, Pinot Gris, Pinot Blanc, and Chardonnay all conform to the Adelsheim house style of rich, balanced fruit and long, clean finishes. They also make a spicy cool-climate Syrah from grapes grown just outside the beautiful tasting room. ■ **TIP→ Tours are available by appointment.** ✉ *16800 N.E. Calkins La.* ☎ *503/538–3652* ⊕ *www. adelsheim.com* 🍷 *Tastings from $15.*

Aramenta Cellars

WINERY/DISTILLERY | Owners Ed and Darlene Looney have been farming this land for more than 40 years. In 2000, they planted grapevines after keeping cattle on the property. The winery and tasting room are built on the foundation of the old barn, and Ed makes the wine while Darlene runs the tasting room. Of the 27 acres planted in vines, 20 acres are leased to Archrey Summit for its Looney Vineyard Pinot Noir, and the Looneys farm 7 acres for their own wines which have very limited distribution. If you're looking for a break from all the Pinot Noir, try the Tillie Claret—a smooth Bordeaux blend made with grapes from eastern Washington and southern Oregon.

Aramenta offers a great opportunity to interact with farmers who have worked the land for several generations and to taste some great small-production wine. ✉ *17979 N.E. Lewis Rogers La.* ☎ *503/538–7230* ⊕ *www.aramentacellars.com* 🍷 *Tastings $10.*

Bergstrom Winery

WINERY/DISTILLERY | Focusing on classic Oregon Pinot Noir and Chardonnay, this family-owned winery produces elegant and refined wines that represent some of the best the Willamette Valley has to offer. The tasting room is surrounded by the Silice Vineyard, and offers beautiful views of several neighboring vineyards as well. French-trained winemaker Josh Bergstrom sources fruit from his estate vineyards and from several other local sites to produce a wide range of single-vineyard Pinots. Enjoy your tasting on the deck on a warm summer day. ✉ *18215 N.E. Calkins La.* ☎ *503/554–0468* ⊕ *www.bergstromwines.com* 🍷 *Tastings $30* ⏱ *By appointment.*

Bravuro Cellars

WINERY/DISTILLERY | One of the newest additions to the Newberg tasting-room scene, this boutique winery eschews the Pinot Noir prevalent throughout the region in favor of hot-climate varietals— including Zinfandel, Cab, and even a ruby port—all produced in small batches of around 40 to 60 cases. Bravuro's wines are only available at the tasting room or online, and every bottle is individually numbered. ✉ *108. S. College St.* ☎ *503/822–5116* ⊕ *www.bravurocellars. com.*

Champoeg State Heritage Area

NATIONAL/STATE PARK | Pronounced "shampoo-ee," this 615-acre state park on the south bank of the Willamette River is on the site of a Hudson's Bay Company trading post, granary, and warehouse that was built in 1813. This was the seat of the first provisional government in the Northwest. The settlement was abandoned after a catastrophic flood in 1861, then rebuilt and abandoned again after the flood of 1890. The park's wide-open spaces, groves of oak and fir, modern visitor center, museum, and historic buildings provide vivid insight into pioneer life. Tepees and wagons are displayed here, and there are 10 miles of hiking and cycle trails. ✉ *8239 Champoeg Rd. NE, St. Paul* ☎ *503/678–1251* ⊕ *www.oregonstateparks.org* 🍷 *$5 per vehicle.*

Hoover-Minthorn House Museum

HOUSE | In 1885 Dr. Henry Minthorn invited his orphan nephew Herbert "Bertie" Hoover to come west and join the Minthorn family in Newberg. Built in 1881, the restored frame house, the oldest and most significant of Newberg's original structures, still has many of its original furnishings, including the president's boyhood bed and dresser. Hoover maintained his connection to Newberg, and visited several times after his presidency. ✉ *115 S. River St.* ☎ *503/538–6629* ⊕ *hooverminthorn.org* 🍷 *$5* ⏱ *Closed Jan.; Mar.–Nov., Mon. and Tues.; Dec. and Feb., weekdays.*

99W Drive-in

ARTS VENUE | FAMILY | Ted Francis built this drive-in in 1953, and operated it until his death at 98; the business is now run by his grandson. The first film begins at dusk. ✉ *3110 Portland Rd. (Hwy. 99W)* ☎ *503/538–2738* ⊕ *www.99w.com* 🍷 *$9; vehicles with single occupant $14* ⏱ *Closed Mon.–Wed.*

Penner-Ash Wine Cellars

WINERY/DISTILLERY | Lynn Penner-Ash brings years of experience working in Napa and as Rex Hill's winemaker to the winery that she and her husband Ron started in 1998. Although focused primarily on silky Pinot Noir, Penner-Ash also produces very good Syrah, Viognier, and Riesling. From its hilltop perch in the middle of the Dussin vineyard, this state-of-the-art gravity-flow winery and tasting room offers commanding views of the valley below. ✉ *15771 N.E. Ribbon Ridge Rd.* ☎ *503/554–5545* 🌐 *www.pennerash.com* 🎟 *Tastings $25.*

★ Ponzi Vineyards

WINERY/DISTILLERY | One of the founding families of Willamette Valley wine, Dick and Nancy Ponzi planted their original estate vineyard in 1970. While you can still visit the historic estate that looks out over these old vines, your best bet is to drop in at their new visitors facility at the winery just 12 miles south of Hillsboro. Here you'll find red and white flights of the current releases, as well as the occasional older vintage from the library. Enjoy table-side wine service indoors around the fireplace, or out on the covered terrace. Antipasti plates are a nice accompaniment to the wine. Pictures on the walls and displays provide a wonderful visual history of this winery that is still family owned and operated. The Ponzi family also launched the BridgePort Brewing Company in 1984, and runs a wine bar and restaurant in Dundee. ✉ *19500 S.W. Mountain Home Rd., Sherwood* ✣ *7 miles north of Newberg* ☎ *503/628–1227* 🌐 *www.ponziwines.com* 🎟 *Tastings $20.*

Rex Hill Vineyards

WINERY/DISTILLERY | A few hundred feet off the busy highway, surrounded by conifers and overlooked by vineyards, Rex Hill seems to exist in a world of its own. The winery opened in 1982, after owners Paul Hart and Jan Jacobsen converted a former nut-drying facility. It produces first-class Pinot Noir, Pinot Gris, Chardonnay, Sauvignon Blanc, and Riesling from both estate-grown and purchased grapes. The tasting room has a massive fireplace, elegant antiques, and an absorbing collection of modern art. Another highlight is the beautifully landscaped garden, perfect for picnicking. ✉ *30835 N. Hwy. 99W* ☎ *503/538–0666, 800/739–4455* 🌐 *www.rexhill.com* 🎟 *Tastings $15.*

Utopia Vineyard

WINERY/DISTILLERY | Take a trip back in time to when the Oregon wine industry was much smaller and more intimate. Utopia owner and winemaker Daniel Warnhius moved north from California looking for a vineyard site that would produce world-class Pinot Noir, and he found this location with the right combination of location, climate, and soil structure. In the tasting room, you're likely to be served by Daniel himself. In addition to several great Pinot Noirs, they also produce a bright, crisp Chardonnay, and a Pinot Noir Rosé. ✉ *17445 N.E. Ribbon Ridge Rd.* ☎ *503/687–1671* 🌐 *utopiawine.com* 🎟 *Tastings $15* ⏲ *Closed weekdays Dec.–Apr.*

Vidon Vineyard

WINERY/DISTILLERY | This small Newberg-area winery produces seven varieties of Pinot Noir along with small batches of Chardonnay, Pinot Gris, Viognier, Tempranillo, and Syrah. While the wines are enough to merit a visit to Vidon's hilltop tasting room, those with an interest in the science of wine-making will likely get a kick out of chatting with physicist-turned-winemaker Donald Hagge, who has applied his background to come up with some innovative ways to make and store wine. ✉ *17425 N.E. Hillside Dr.* ☎ *503/538–4092* 🌐 *www.vidonvineyard.com* 🎟 *Tastings $20.*

🍴 Restaurants

Jory

$$$$ | **MODERN AMERICAN** | This exquisite hotel dining room is named after one of the soils in the Oregon wine country. Chef Sunny Jin sources the majority of his ingredients locally, many from the on-site garden. **Known for:** Oregon-centric wine list; locally sourced ingredients; open kitchen experience. [$] *Average main: $35* ✉ *The Allison Inn, 2525 Allison La.* ☎ *503/554–2525, 877/294–2525* 🌐 *www.theallison.com.*

Subterra

$$$$ | **AMERICAN** | This casual restaurant offers pizzas, sandwiches, and comfort food at lunch, upping the ante significantly at dinnertime, when it offers three-course prix-fixe menus paired with Pacific Northwest wine. A variety of tapas-style small plates are served throughout the day, too. **Known for:** an extensive list of Oregon wines; three-course dinners paired with local wines; small plates for sharing. [$] *Average main: $32* ✉ *1505 Portland Rd.* ☎ *503/538–6060* 🌐 *subterrarestaurant.com.*

Hotels

The Allison Inn & Spa

$$$$ | **RESORT** | At this luxurious, relaxing base for exploring the region's 200 wineries, each bright, comfortable room includes a gas fireplace, original works of art, a soaking tub, impressive furnishings, bay-window seats, and views of the vineyards from the terrace or balcony. **Pros:** outstanding on-site restaurant; excellent gym and spa facilities; located in the middle of wine country. **Cons:** not many nearby off-property activities other than wine tasting; expensive, particularly by local standards; restaurant can book up early. [$] *Rooms from: $445* ✉ *2525 Allison La.* ☎ *503/554–2525, 877/294–2525* 🌐 *www.theallison.com* 🛏 *85 rooms* 🍴 *No meals.*

Le Puy A Wine Valley Inn

$$$ | **B&B/INN** | This beautiful wine country retreat caters to wine enthusiasts with amenities that include wine bars in each individually decorated room, along with hot tubs and gas fireplaces in some. **Pros:** beautiful surroundings; lots of nice architectural and decorative touches; included breakfast and coffee. **Cons:** a distance from sights other than wineries; strict rules for guests, with no outside food allowed; minimum two-night stays. [$] *Rooms from: $285* ✉ *20300 N.E. Hwy. 240* ☎ *503/554–9528* 🌐 *lepuy-inn.com* 🛏 *8 rooms* 🍴 *Free breakfast.*

Activities

BALLOONING

Hot-air balloon rides are nothing less than a spectacular, breathtaking thrill—particularly over Oregon's beautiful Yamhill County.

★ Vista Balloon Adventures

BALLOONING | Enjoy floating gently above beautiful Oregon wine country as the sun rises behind the vines. Your FAA-licensed pilot will take the balloon up about 1,500 feet and can often steer the craft down to skim the water, then up to view hawks' nests. A champagne brunch is served upon returning to the ground. ✉ *1050 Commerce Pkwy.* ☎ *503/625–7385, 800/622–2309* 🌐 *www.vistaballoon.com* 🎟 *$230 per person.*

Dundee

3 miles southwest of Newberg on Hwy. 99W.

Dundee used to be known for growing the lion's share (more than 90%) of the U.S. hazelnut crop. Today, some of Oregon's top-rated wineries are just outside Dundee, and the area is now best known for wine tourism and wine bars, bed-and-breakfast inns, and restaurants.

GETTING HERE AND AROUND

Dundee is just under an hour's drive from Portland International Airport; **Caravan Airport Transportation** provides shuttle service.

What used to be a pleasant drive through quaint Dundee on Highway 99W now can be a traffic hassle, as it serves as the main artery from Lincoln City on the Oregon Coast to suburban Portland. Others will enjoy wandering along the 25 miles of Highway 18 between Dundee and Grande Ronde, in the Coast Range, which goes through the heart of the Yamhill Valley wine country.

CONTACTS Caravan Airport Transportation. ☎ *541/994–9645* ⊕ */www.caravanshuttle. com.*

Sights

★ Archery Summit Winery
WINERY/DISTILLERY | The winery that Gary and Nancy Andrus, owners of Pine Ridge winery in Napa Valley, founded in the 1990s has become synonymous with premium Oregon Pinot Noir. Because they believed that great wines are made in the vineyard, they adopted such innovative techniques as narrow spacing and vertical trellis systems, which give the fruit a great concentration of flavors. In addition to the standard flight of Pinot Noirs in the tasting room, you can call ahead and reserve a private seated tasting or a tasting paired with small bites or a tour of the winery and, weather permitting, a walk out to the vineyard. You're welcome to bring a picnic, and as at many Oregon wineries, you can bring your dog, too. ⊠ *18599 N.E. Archery Summit Rd., Dayton* ☎ *503/714–2030* ⊕ *www.archerysummit.com* 🍷 *Tastings from $30.*

Argyle Winery
WINERY/DISTILLERY | A beautiful establishment, Argyle has its tasting room in a Victorian farmhouse set amid gorgeous gardens. The winery is tucked into a former hazelnut processing plant—which explains the Nuthouse label on its reserve wines. Since Argyle opened in 1987, it has consistently produced sparkling wines that are crisp on the palate, with an aromatic, lingering finish and bubbles that seem to last forever. And these sparklers cost about a third of their counterparts from California. The winery also produces Chardonnay, dry Riesling, Pinot Gris, and Pinot Noir. ⊠ *691 Hwy. 99W* ☎ *503/538–8520, 888/427–4953* ⊕ *www.argylewinery.com* 🍷 *Tastings from $20.*

The Bistro Bar
WINERY/DISTILLERY | Located right on the main highway between Portland and wine country, The Bistro Bar offers the opportunity to sample wines from both the Ponzi Winery and small local producers without straying far from the beaten path. The tasting menu features current releases of Ponzi wines, as well as a rotating selection of other local wines. If you've had enough wine for a while, you can also get snacks, Italian coffee, or a craft beer to enjoy in the comfortable tasting room. ⊠ *100 S.W. 7th St.* ☎ *503/554–1500* ⊕ *www.dundeebistro. com.*

Dobbes Family Estate
WINERY/DISTILLERY | Joe Dobbes makes a lot of wine, but he's definitely not a bulk winemaker. He provides custom wine-making services to many Oregon wineries that are too small to have their own winery or winemaker. But he also makes several lines of his own wine, ranging from his everyday "Wine By Joe" label to the premium Dobbes Family Estate label featuring great Pinot Noir, Syrah, Sauvignon Blanc, Viognier, and Grenache Blanc. In addition to a few single vineyard Pinot Noir bottlings, Dobbes focuses on blends from multiple vineyards to provide consistent, balanced, and interesting wines. Two different tasting fights are available in the tasting room, and seated tastings and tours can be arranged by appointment. ⊠ *240 S.E. 5th St.* ☎ *503/538–1141* ⊕ *www.dobbesfamilyestate.com* 🍷 *Tastings $20.*

★ Domaine Drouhin Oregon
WINERY/DISTILLERY | When the French winery magnate Robert Drouhin ("the Sebastiani of France") planted a vineyard and built a winery in the Red Hills of Dundee back in 1987, he set local oenophiles abuzz. His daughter Veronique is now the winemaker and produces silky and elegant Pinot Noir and Chardonnay. Ninety acres of the 225-acre estate has been planted on a hillside to take advantage

Continued on page 212

The Willamette Valley is Oregon's premier wine region. With a milder climate than any growing area in California, cool-climate grapes like Pinot Noir and Pinot Gris thrive here, and are being transformed into world-class wines.

There may be fewer and smaller wineries than in Napa, but the experience is often more intimate. The winemaker himself may even pour you wine.

Touring is easy, as most wineries are well marked, and have tasting rooms with regular hours. Whether you're taking a day trip from Portland, or staying for a couple of days, here's how to get the most out of your sipping experience.

By Dave Sandage and John Doerper

Above and right, Willamette Valley

Wine Tasting
in the
Willamette
Valley

OREGON'S WINES: THEN AND NOW

Rex Hill Vineyards

THE EARLY YEARS

The French made wine first—French Canadians, that is. In the 1830s, retired fur trappers from the Hudson's Bay Company started to colonize the Willamette Valley and planted grapes on the south-facing buttes. They were followed by American settlers who made wine.

Although wine-making in the regionlanguished after these early efforts, it never quite vanished. A few wineries hung on, producing wines mainly for Oregonians of European descent.

It wasn't until the 1970s that the state's wine industry finally took off. Only after a group of young California winemakers started making vinifera wines in the Umpqua and Willamette Valleys and gained international acclaim for them, did Oregon's wines really take hold.

WINEMAKING TODAY

Today, Oregon's wine industry is racing ahead. Here the most prolific white and red grapes are Pinot Gris and Pinot Noir, respectively. Other prominent varietals include Riesling, Gewürztraminer, Viognier, Chardonnay, Carbernet Franc, and Syrah.

The wine industry in Oregon is still largely dominated by family and boutique wineries that pay close attention to quality and are often keen to experiment. That makes traveling and tasting at the source an always-interesting experience.

OREGON CERTIFIED SUSTAINABLE WINE

The latest trend in Oregon winemaking is a dedication to responsible grape growing and winemaking. When you see the Oregon Certified Sustainable Wine (OCSW) logo on the back of a wine bottle, it means the winery ensures accountable agricultural and winemaking practices (in conjunction with agencies such as USDA Organic, Demeter Biodynamic, the Food Alliance, Salmon-Safe, and Low Input Viticulture and Enology) through independent third-party certification. For more information on Oregon Certified Sustainable wines and participating wineries, check ⊕ *www.ocsw.org*.

WINE TASTING PRIMER

Ordering and tasting wine—whether at a winery, bar, or restaurant—is easy once you master a few simple steps.

LOOK AND NOTE

Hold your glass by the stem and look at the wine in the glass. Note its color, depth, and clarity.

For whites, is it greenish, yellow, or gold? For reds, is it purplish, ruby, or garnet? Is the wine's color pale or deep? Is the liquid clear or cloudy?

SWIRL AND SNIFF

Swirl the wine gently in the glass to intensify the scents, then sniff over the rim of the glass. What do you smell? Try to identify aromas like:

- **Fruits**—citrus, peaches, berries, figs, melon

- **Minerals**—earth, steely notes, wet stones

- **Flowers**—orange blossoms, honey, perfume

- **Dairy**—butter, cream, cheese, yogurt

- **Spices**—baking spices, pungent, herbal notes

- **Oak**—toast, vanilla, coconut, tobacco

- **Vegetables**—fresh or cooked, herbal notes

- **Animal**—leathery, meaty notes

Are there any unpleasant notes, like mildew or wet dog, that might indicate that the wine is "off?"

SIP AND SAVOR

Prime your palate with a sip, swishing the wine in your mouth. Then spit in a bucket or swallow.

Take another sip and think about the wine's attributes. Sweetness is detected on the tip of the tongue, acidity on the sides of the tongue, and tannins (a mouth-drying sensation) on the gums. Consider the body—does the wine feel light in the mouth, or is there a rich sensation? Are the flavors consistent with the aromas? If you like the wine, try to pinpoint what you like about it, and vice versa if you don't like it.

Take time to savor the wine as you're sipping it—the tasting experience may seem a bit scientific, but the end goal is your enjoyment.

WINE TOURING AND TASTING

Wine tasting at Argyle and Rex Hill

WHEN TO GO

In high season (June through October) and on weekends and holidays during much of the year, wine-country roads can be busy and tasting rooms are often crowded. If you prefer a more intimate tasting experience, plan your visit for a weekday.

To avoid the frustration of a fruitless drive, confirm in advance that wineries of interest will be open when you plan to visit.

Choose a designated driver for the day: Willamette wine-country roads are often narrow and curvy, and you may be sharing the road with bicyclists and wildlife as well as other wine tourists.

IN THE TASTING ROOM

Tasting rooms are designed to introduce newcomers to the pleasures of wine and to the wines made at the winery. At popular wineries you'll sometimes have to pay for your tasting, anything from a nominal $3 fee to $30 and up for a tasting that might include a glass you can take home. This fee is often deducted if you buy wine before leaving.

WHAT'S AN AVA?

AVAs (American Viticultural Areas) are geographic winegrowing regions that vaguely reflect the French concept of terroir, or "sense of place." The vineyards within a given AVA have similar characteristics such as climate, soil types, and/or elevation, which impart shared characteristics to the wines made from grapes grown in that area. AVAs are strictly geographic boundaries distinct from city or county designations. AVAs can also be subdivided into sub-AVAs; each of the AVAs mentioned here is actually part of the larger Willamette Valley AVA.

Each taste consists of an ounce or two. Feel free to pour whatever you don't finish into one of the dump buckets on the bar. If you like, rinse your glass between pours with a little water. Remember, those sips add up, so pace yourself. If you plan to visit several wineries, try just a few wines at each so you won't suffer from palate fatigue, when your mouth can no longer distinguish subtleties. It's also a good idea to bring a picnic lunch, which you can enjoy on the deck of a winery, taking in the surrounding wine country vistas.

FALL FOLIAGE

In autumn, Willamette Valley vineyards are particularly stunning as the leaves change color.

DAY TRIP FROM PORTLAND

With nearly 150 vineyards, the Chehalem Mountain and Ribbon Ridge AVAs offer widely varied soil types and diverse Pinot Noirs. The region is less than an hour away from Portland.

Ponzi Vineyards

CHEHALEM MOUNTAIN AND RIBBON RIDGE AVAS

❶ PONZI VINEYARDS

First planted in 1970, Ponzi has some of Oregon's oldest Pinot Noir vines. In addition to current releases, the tasting room sometimes offers older library wines. **Try:** *Arneis, a crisp Italian white varietal.*

- ✉ 19500 SW Mountain Home Rd., Sherwood
- ☎ 503/628–1227
- 🌐 www.ponziwines.com

❷ REX HILL VINEYARDS

Before grapevines, the Willamette Valley was widely planted with fruits and nuts. Enjoy classic Oregon Pinot Noir in this tasting room built around an old fruit and nut drying facility. **Try:** *dark and spicy Dundee Hills Pinot Noir.*

- ✉ 30835 N. Hwy. 99W, Newberg
- ☎ 800/739–4455
- 🌐 www.rexhill.com

❸ BRAVURO CELLARS

Newberg's new-kid-on-the-block winery features small-batch wines made from hot-climate grapes, including Zinfandels, Cabernets Sauvignons, and even port. **Try:** *crisp and refreshing Pinot Blanc.*

- ✉ 108 S. College St., Newberg
- ☎ 503/822-5116
- 🌐 www.bravuracellars.com

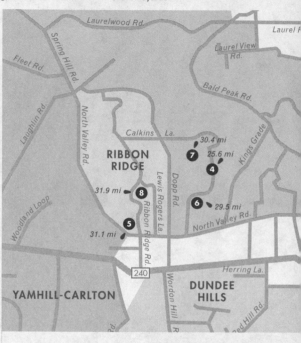

❹ VIDON VINEYARD

Run by a particle physicist-turned-winemaker, this hilltop vineyard features a low-key tasting room plus a covered outdoor seating area for taking in bucolic vineyard views. **Try:** *rich but fruity Pinot Noir Maresh*

- ✉ 17425 NE Hillside Dr., Newberg
- ☎ 503/538-4092
- 🌐 www.vidonvineyard.com

❺ UTOPIA VINEYARD

The tasting room at this small Oregon winery is quite intimate—you'll likely be served by the winemaker himself. **Try:** *light and slightly sweet Rosé.*

- ✉ 17445 N.E. Ribbon Ridge Rd., Newberg
- ☎ 503/298–7841
- 🌐 www.utopiawine.com

Adelsheim Vineyard

REX HILL
VINEYARDS

Rex Hill

Pinot Gris grapes

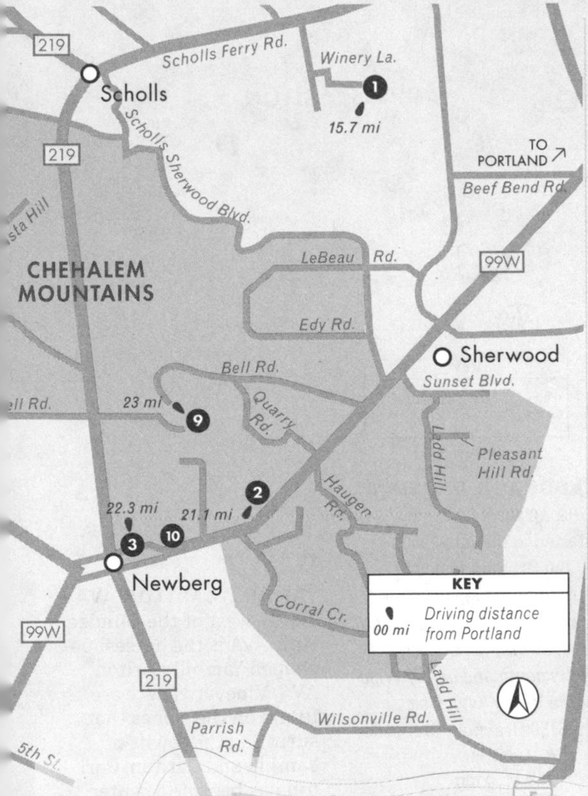
219
Scholls Ferry Rd.
Winery La.
Scholls
15.7 mi
Scholls Sherwood Blvd.
TO PORTLAND
Beef Bend Rd.
CHEHALEM MOUNTAINS
LeBeau Rd.
99W
Edy Rd.
Sherwood
Bell Rd.
Sunset Blvd.
23 mi
Quarry Rd.
Ladd Hill
Pleasant Hill Rd.
Haugen Rd.
22.3 mi
21.1 mi
Newberg
Corral Cr.
KEY
00 mi Driving distance from Portland
99W
219
Parrish Rd.
Wilsonville Rd.
5th St.

❻ ADELSHEIM VINEYARD

One of Oregon's older Pinot Noir producers, Adelsheim has just opened a new tasting room inside its modern winery, with friendly, knowledgeable employees. **Try:** *dark and smoky Elizabeth's Reserve Pinot Noir.*

✉ 16800 N.E. Calkins La., Newberg
☎ 503/538–3652
🌐 www.adelsheim.com

❼ BERGSTROM WINERY

A beautiful tasting room, but the real high point here is the classic Oregon Pinot Noir sourced from several of its estate vineyards as well as other local sites. **Try:** *earthy Bergstrom Pinot Noir.*

✉ 18215 N.E. Calkins La., Newberg
☎ 503/554–0468
🌐 www.bergstromwines.com

❽ ARAMENTA CELLARS

A small, family-run operation that offers tastings in its winery, built on the foundation of an old barn. The on-site vineyard grows primarily Pinot Noir and Chardonnay. **Try:** *smooth and structured Tillie Claret.*

✉ 17979 N.E. Lewis Rogers La., Newberg
☎ 503/538–7230
🌐 www.aramentacellars.com

STOP FOR A BITE

❾ JORY RESTAURANT

Located within the luxurious Allison Inn and Spa, Jory serves creative dishes that highlight the bounty of the Willamette Valley.

✉ 2525 Allison La., Newberg
☎ 503/554–2526
🌐 www.theallison.com

❿ SUBTERRA

Underground cellar restaurant with an impressive regional wine list. Lunch is casual comfort food, while prix-fixe three-course meals dominate at dinner time. Small plates to share are available all day.

✉ 1505 Portland Rd., Newberg
☎ 503/538–6060
🌐 www.subterrarestaurant.com

TWO DAYS IN WINE COUNTRY

Yamhill

DAY 1

DUNDEE HILLS AVA

The Dundee Hills AVA is home to some of Oregon's best known Pinot Noir producers. Start your tour in the town of Dundee, about 30 miles southwest of Portland, then drive up into the red hills and enjoy the valley views from many wineries.

❶ ARGYLE WINERY

If you don't want to drive off the beaten path, this winery is right on Highway 99W in Dundee. They specialize in sparkling wines, but also make very nice still wines. **Try:** *crisp Brut Rosé.*

✉ 691 Hwy. 99 W, Dundee
☎ 503/538–8520
🌐 www.argylewinery.com

❷ THE BISTRO BAR

This cozy wine bar offers a nice selection of local labels, making it a good choice for those who want to sample a large selection side-by-side. **Try:** *bright and fruity Ponzi Pinot Gris.*

✉ 100 S.W. 7th St., Dundee
☎ 503/554–1500
🌐 www.dundeebistro.com

❸ ARCHERY SUMMIT

An Oregon Pinot Noir pioneer, Archery Summit features memorable wines and equally pleasing views. Call in advance to schedule a tour of the winery and aging caves. Try: *dark and rich Premier Cuvée Pinot Noir.*

✉ 18599 NE Archery Summit Rd., Dayton
☎ 503/864–4300
🌐 www.archerysummit.com

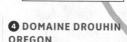

KEY

🝙 *Driving distance from Portland*
00 mi

❹ DOMAINE DROUHIN OREGON

Started in the late 1980s by the Drouhin family of Burgundy fame, this winery makes notable Oregon Pinot Noir, as well as Chardonnay. **Try:** *smooth and earthy Willamette Valley Pinot Noir.*

✉ 6750 Breyman Orchards Rd., Dayton
☎ 503/864–2700
🌐 www.domainedrouhin.com

❺ SOKOL BLOSSER

Producing excellent wines since 1971, Sokol Blosser is worth visiting for the wines alone, but its beautiful tasting areas amongst rolling vineyards certainly don't hurt. **Try:** *Dundee Hills Estate Pinot Noir.*

✉ 5000 Sokol Blosser La., Dayton
☎ 800/582–6668
🌐 www.sokolblosser.com

DAY 2

YAMHILL-CARLTON AVA

To the west of the Dundee Hills AVA is the horseshoe-shaped Yamhill-Carlton AVA. Vineyards here are found on the slopes that surround the towns of Yamhill and Carlton. Carlton has become a center of wine tourism, and you could easily spend a day visiting tasting rooms in town.

❻ PENNER-ASH WINE CELLARS

This state-of-the-art winery and tasting room is atop a hill with an excellent view of the valley below. **Try:** *smooth and dark Shea Vineyard Pinot Noir.*

✉ 15771 N.E. Ribbon Ridge Rd., Newberg
☎ 503/554–5545
🌐 www.pennerash.com

RIBBON RID

240

Blackburn Rd.

YAMHILL-CARLTON

Laughlin Rd.
Woodland Loop
35.2 mi
30.3 mi
Yamhill Rd.
Stag Hollow Rd.
34.8 mi
33.7 mi
Hendricks Rd.
Pine St.
35.8 mi
Malo St.
Oak Spring Farm Rd.
Abbey Rd.
31.2
Mineral Springs Rd.
Hilltop La.
47

Penner-Ash Wine Cellars

Ponzi Wine Bar

Pinot Gris grapes

[Map showing Dundee Hills area with roads including Red Hill Rd., Fairview, Fox Farm Rd., 99W, 5th St., 7th St., 9th St., Albert St., Archery Summit Rd., Orchards Rd., Marion Hill Rd., and locations marked with numbers. TO NEWBERG, PORTLAND. Distances shown: 26.5 mi, 26.4 mi, 29.4 mi, 28.9 mi. Dundee marked.]

STOP FOR A BITE

⓫ THE HORSE RADISH

Located in downtown Carlton, The Horseradish offers a wide selection of local wines as well as cheese from around the world. The sandwiches and small plates make for a great quick lunch.
- ✉ 211 W. Main St., Carlton
- ☏ 503/852–6656
- ⊕ www.thehorseradish.com

⓬ DUNDEE BISTRO

A favorite of winemakers, Dundee Bistro serves seasonal local ingredients paired with Willamette Valley wines. Enjoy outdoor seating, or watch chefs work in the open kitchen inside.
- ✉ 100-A S.W. 7th St., Dundee
- ☏ 503/554–1650
- ⊕ www.dundeebistro.com

⓭ TINA'S

The warm and intimate Tina's features dishes made with seasonal ingredients, organic vegetables, and free-range meats. Stop by for lunch Tuesday–Friday, or nightly dinner.
- ✉ 760 Hwy. 99 W, Dundee
- ☏ 503/538–8880
- ⊕ www.tinasdundee.com

❼ LEMELSON VINEYARDS

Although it specializes in single-vineyard Pinot Noir, Lemelson also makes several crisp white wines. The deck overlooking the vineyards is perfect for picnics. **Try:** *crisp and fruity Riesling.*
- ✉ 12020 N.E. Stag Hollow Rd., Carlton
- ☏ 503/852–6619
- ⊕ www.lemelsonvineyards.com

❽ KEN WRIGHT CELLARS TASTING ROOM

Well-known winemaker Ken Wright is known for producing big reds. The tasting room is in the historic Carlton train station. **Try:** *bold and spicy Del Rio Claret.*
- ✉ 120 N. Pine St., Carlton
- ☏ 503/852–7070
- ⊕ kenwrightcellars.com

❾ CARLTON WINEMAKERS STUDIO

A wide range of small-batch wine producers are showcased at this winery cooperative, with a rotating selection of offerings, including plenty of Pinot. **Try:** *Studio Benchmark Pinot Noirs*
- ✉ 801 N. Scott St., Carlton
- ☏ 503/852–6100
- ⊕ www.winemakersstudio.com

❿ LENNÉ ESTATE

Lenné specializes in highly regarded Pinot Noir, although it's often pouring a couple of non-Pinot wines from other wineries as well. The tasting room in a small stone building overlooks the vineyards. **Try:** *complex and earthy Estate Pinot Noir.*
- ✉ 18760 Laughlin Rd., Yamhill
- ☏ 503/956–2256
- ⊕ www.lenneestate.com

of the natural coolness of the earth and to establish a gravity-flow winery. No appointment is needed to taste the Oregon wines, but if you can plan ahead for the tour (reservations required), you can taste Oregon and Burgundy side by side. ⊠ *6750 N.E. Breyman Orchards Rd., Dayton* ☎ *503/864–2700* ⊕ *www. domainedrouhin.com* ⊠ *Tastings $25* ⊘ *Closed mid-Oct.–May, Mon. and Tues.*

Erath Vineyards Winery

WINERY/DISTILLERY | When Dick Erath opened one of Oregon's pioneer wineries more than a quarter century ago, he focused on producing distinctive Pinot Noir from grapes he'd been growing in the Red Hills since 1972—as well as full-flavored Pinot Gris, Pinot Blanc, Chardonnay, Riesling, and late-harvest Gewürztraminer. The wines are excellent and reasonably priced. In 2006 the winery was sold to Washington State's giant conglomerate Ste. Michelle Wine Estate. The tasting room is in the middle of the vineyards, high in the hills, with views in nearly every direction; the hazelnut trees that covered the slopes not so long ago have been replaced with vines. The tasting-room terrace, which overlooks the winery and the hills, is a choice spot for picnicking. Crabtree Park, next to the winery, is a good place to stretch your legs after a tasting. ⊠ *9409 N.E. Worden Hill Rd.* ☎ *503/538–3318, 800/539–9463* ⊕ *www.erath.com* ⊠ *Tastings $30.*

Red Ridge

FARM/RANCH | A good place to clean your palate after all that wine tasting is Red Ridge, home to the first commercial olive mill in the Pacific Northwest. Stop by the gift shop to taste some of the farm's signature oils or head out back to see an old-fashioned (and not-in-use) olive press imported from Spain. ⊠ *5510 N.E. Breyman Orchards Rd., Dayton* ☎ *503/864–8502* ⊕ *redridgefarms.com.*

★ Sokol Blosser

WINERY/DISTILLERY | One of Yamhill County's oldest wineries (it was established in 1971) makes consistently excellent wines and sells them at reasonable prices. Set on a gently sloping south-facing hillside and surrounded by vineyards, lush lawns, and shade trees, it's a splendid place to learn about wine with tableside tastings held across a number of indoor and outdoor spaces. Winery tours and summer Sunday vineyard hikes can be booked in advance. ⊠ *5000 Sokol Blosser La., Dayton* ✛ *3 miles west of Dundee off Hwy. 99W* ☎ *503/864–2282, 800/582–6668* ⊕ *www.sokolblosser.com* ⊠ *Tastings $15, tours $40.*

Torii Mor Winery

WINERY/DISTILLERY | Established in 1993, Torii Mor makes small quantities of handcrafted Pinot Noir, Pinot Gris, and Chardonnay and is set amid Japanese gardens with breathtaking views of the Willamette Valley. The gardens were designed by Takuma Tono, the same architect who designed the renowned Portland Japanese Garden. The owners, who love all things Japanese, named their winery after the distinctive Japanese gate of Shinto religious significance; they added a Scandinavian mor, signifying "earth," to create an east-west combo: "earth gate." Jacques Tardy, a native of Nuits Saint Georges, in Burgundy, France, is the current head winemaker. Under his guidance Torii Mor wines have become more Burgundian in style. ⊠ *18323 N.E. Fairview Dr.* ☎ *503/538–2279* ⊕ *www.toriimorwinery. com* ⊠ *Tastings $35.*

Winderlea

WINERY/DISTILLERY | The tasting room looks over the acclaimed former Goldschmidt vineyard, first planted in 1974, and the view can be enjoyed on the outside deck on a warm summer day. Winemaker Robert Brittan crafts lush Pinot Noir and Chardonnay from several nearby vineyards in both single-vineyard offerings and blends from multiple vineyards. Proceeds from the tasting fee are donated to ¡Salud!, a nonprofit providing health-care services to Oregon's vineyard workers and their families. ⊠ *8905 N.E. Worden Hill Rd.* ☎ *503/554–5900* ⊕ *www.winderlea. com* 🍷 *Tastings $25.*

🍴 Restaurants

Dundee Bistro

$$$ | **CONTEMPORARY** | Owned by the Ponzi wine family, this bistro showcases Italian-style fare dominated by locally grown and raised produce, while the on-site Fratelli Ponzi Fine Food & Wine Bar serves Ponzi wines from Oregon and Italy. Vaulted ceilings provide an open feeling inside, warmed by abundant fresh flowers and the works of local Oregon artists. **Known for:** part of the Ponzi wine family; wines from Oregon and Italy; Italian fare with options for special diets. $ *Average main: $25* ⊠ *100-A S.W. 7th St.* ☎ *503/554–1650* ⊕ *www.dundeebistro.com.*

Red Hills Market

$ | **PACIFIC NORTHWEST** | **FAMILY** | Serving great sandwiches, salads, and pizza, this is the perfect stop for a quick lunch in the middle of a day of wine tasting, or a casual no-frills dinner at the end of the day. In addition to wine, there are cocktails and a great selection of local and imported craft beers. **Known for:** great stop during wine tasting; takeout options; kids' menu. $ *Average main: $12* ⊠ *155 S.W. 7th St.* ☎ *971/832–8414* ⊕ *www. redhillsmarket.com.*

★ Tina's

$$$$ | **FRENCH** | Opened back in 1991, this Dundee institution has long been known for luring Portlanders away from their own restaurant scene, offering country-French fare cooked lovingly with locally grown produce. Service is as intimate and laid-back as the interiors; a double fireplace divides the dining room, with heavy glass brick shrouded by bushes on the highway side, so you're not bothered by the traffic on Highway 99. **Known for:** attracting Portland foodies; delicious homemade soups; hearty French-country cuisine. $ *Average main: $35* ⊠ *760 Hwy. 99W* ☎ *503/538–8880* ⊕ *www.tinasdundee.com.*

Hotels

The Dundee

$$ | **HOTEL** | Right on the main road in Dundee, this boutique property offers spacious, light-filled rooms with living areas and tall ceilings; there's even a "Squad Room" with six bunk beds for traveling groups. **Pros:** contemporary, stylish surroundings; close to many wineries; spacious rooms remodeled in 2019. **Cons:** located on the main highway through town rather than the country; check-in time is later than usual; breakfast is not included. $ *Rooms from: $199* ⊠ *1410 N. Hwy. 99W* ☎ *503/538–7666* ⊕ *www.innatredhills.com* 🛏 *22 rooms* ⊙ *No meals.*

The Vintages Trailer Resort

$ | **RESORT** | **FAMILY** | Just off the road that runs from Dundee to McMinnville, this quirky retro resort boasts 34 lovingly refurbished vintage trailers, most dating from the 1940s–60s. **Pros:** authentic vintage trailers with quirky, retro-chic decor; each comes with its own gas grill; some trailers are dog-friendly. **Cons:** $29 cleaning fee added at check-in; near the highway and can get traffic noise; bathrooms are compact. $ *Rooms from: $145* ⊠ *16205 SE Kreder Rd., Dayton* ☎ *971/267–2130* ⊕ *www.the-vintages.com* 🛏 *34 trailers* ⊙ *No meals.*

Yamhill-Carlton

14 miles west of Dundee.

Just outside the small towns of Carlton and Yamhill are neatly combed benchlands and hillsides, an American Viticultural Area (AVA) established in 2004, and home to some of the finest Pinot Noir vineyards in the world. Carlton has exploded with many small tasting rooms in the past few years, and you could easily spend an entire day tasting wine within three or four blocks. The area is a gorgeous quilt of nurseries, grain fields, and orchards. Come here for the wine tasting, but don't expect to find too much else to do.

GETTING HERE AND AROUND

Having your own car is the best way to explore this rural region of Yamhill County, located a little more than an hour's drive from Portland International Airport. The towns of Yamhill and Carlton are about an hour's drive from Downtown Portland, traveling through Tigard, to Newberg and west on Highway 240.

CONTACTS Yamhill County Transit Area.
☎ *503/474–4900* ⊕ *www.ycbus.org.*

Sights

Carlton Winemakers Studio

WINERY/DISTILLERY | Oregon's first cooperative winery was specifically designed to house multiple small premium wine producers. This gravity-flow winery has up-to-date wine-making equipment as well as multiple cellars for storing the different makers' wines. You can taste and purchase bottles from the different member wineries. The emphasis is on Pinot Noir, but more than a dozen other types of wines are poured, from Cabernet Franc to Gewürztraminer to Mourvèdre on a rotating basis. The selection of wines available to taste changes every few days. ⊠ *801 N. Scott St., Carlton* ☎ *503/852–6100* ⊕ *www.winemakersstudio.com* 🍷 *Tastings from $25.*

Ken Wright Cellars Tasting Room

WINERY/DISTILLERY | Carlton's former train depot is now the tasting room for Ken Wright Cellars and his warm-climate label, Tyrus Evan. The winery specializes in single-vineyard Pinot Noirs, each subtly different from the next depending on the soil types and grape clones. The wines are poured side by side, giving you an opportunity to go back and forth to compare them. The Tyrus Evan wines are quite different from the Ken Wright Pinots: they are warm-climate varieties like Cabernet Franc, Malbec, Syrah, and red Bordeaux blends, from grapes Wright buys from vineyards in eastern Washington and southern Oregon. You can also pick up cheeses and other picnic supplies, as well as wine country gifts and souvenirs. ⊠ *120 N. Pine St., Carlton* ☎ *503/852–7070* ⊕ *www.kenwrightcellars.com* 🍷 *Tastings from $20.*

Lemelson Vineyards

WINERY/DISTILLERY | This winery was designed from the ground up to be a no-compromises Pinot Noir production facility with an eye to Willamette Valley aesthetics, and the highlight is a diverse range of single-vineyard Pinot Noirs. But don't neglect the bright Pinot Gris and Riesling, perfect with seafood or spicy fare. The spacious high-ceiling tasting room is a great place to relax and take in the view through the floor-to-ceiling windows, or bring a picnic and enjoy the deck on a warm summer day. ⊠ *12020 N.E. Stag Hollow Rd., Carlton* ☎ *503/852–6619* ⊕ *www.lemelsonvineyards.com* 🍷 *Tastings from $25.*

Lenné Estate

WINERY/DISTILLERY | The small stone building that houses the tasting room is surrounded by the estate vineyard and looks like something right out of Burgundy. Steve Lutz was looking for the perfect site to grow Pinot Noir and bought the property in 2000. In addition to offering his own rich and elegant estate Pinot Noirs for tasting, he often pours other varietals from other wineries. ⊠ *18760 N.E. Laughlin Rd., Yamhill* ☎ *503/956–2256* ⊕ *www.lenneestate.com* ☜ *$15.*

 Restaurants

The Horse Radish

$ | **DELI** | The perfect stop in the middle of a day of wine tasting offers a wide selection of artisanal cheese and meats, as well as a great lunch menu. Pick up some sandwiches and a soup or salad to go, and you'll be all set for a picnic at your favorite winery. **Known for:** live music on Friday and Saturday nights; tasting room featuring Marshall Davis wines; kids' menu. $ *Average main: $8* ⊠ *211 W. Main St., Carlton* ☎ *503/852–6656* ⊕ *www.thehorseradish.com.*

 Hotels

Abbey Road Farm Silo Suites B&B

$$$ | **B&B/INN** | Situated on a small farm and winery overlooking a lush expanse of farmland, this unusual bed-and-breakfast is housed in a trio of old silos that have been converted into a small inn. **Pros:** gorgeous views; delicious gourmet breakfast; casual but chic on-site tasting room. **Cons:** lumpy beds; not much within the immediate area; resident roosters may awaken light sleepers. $ *Rooms from: $250* ⊠ *10501 NE Abbey Rd., Carlton* ☎ *503/687–3100* ⊕ *abbeyroadfarm. com* ☜ *5 rooms* ⦿ *Free breakfast.*

McMinnville

11 miles south of Yamhill on Hwy. 99W.

The Yamhill County seat, McMinnville lies in the center of Oregon's thriving wine industry. There is a larger concentration of wineries in Yamhill County than in any other area of the state. Among the varieties are Chardonnay, Pinot Noir, and Pinot Gris. Most of the wineries in the area offer tours and tastings.

McMinnville's downtown area has a few shops worth a look; many of the historic district buildings, erected 1890–1915, are still standing, and are remarkably well maintained.

GETTING HERE AND AROUND

McMinnville is a little more than an hour's drive from Downtown Portland; **Caravan Airport Transportation** provides shuttle service to Portland International Airport. McMinnville is just 70 minutes from Lincoln City on the Oregon Coast, and 27 miles west of Salem.

ESSENTIALS

VISITOR INFORMATION Visit McMinnville. ⊠ *328 N.E. Davis St., Suite 1* ☎ *503/857–0182* ⊕ *visitmcminnville.com.*

 Sights

Evergreen Aviation & Space Museum and Wings & Waves Waterpark

MUSEUM | **FAMILY** | Howard Hughes's *Spruce Goose,* the largest plane ever built and constructed entirely of wood, is on permanent display, but if you can take your eyes off the giant you will also see more than 45 historic planes and replicas from the early years of flight and World War II, as well as the postwar and modern eras. Across the parking lot from the aviation museum is the space museum with artifacts that include a German V-2 rocket and a Titan missile, complete with silo and launch control room. The adjacent Wings and Waves Waterpark (separate admission) has 10 waterslides, including one that starts at a Boeing 747-100 that sits on *top* of the building. The IMAX theater is open daily and features several different films each day. There are a museum store and two cafés, as well as ongoing educational programs and special events. ⊠ *500 N.E. Michael King Smith Way* ☎ *503/434–4185* ⊕ *www. evergreenmuseum.org* ☜ *$27, includes IMAX movie; $29 water park.*

The Eyrie Vineyards

WINERY/DISTILLERY | When David Lett planted the first Pinot Noir vines in the Willamette Valley in 1965, he was setting in motion a series of events that caused Willamette Valley Pinot Noir to be recognized as among the best in the world. Affectionately known as Papa Pinot, Lett, along with several other pioneering winemakers, nurtured the Oregon wine industry to what it is today. Today, David's son Jason Lett is now the winemaker and vineyard manager, and continues to make Pinot Noir, Pinot Gris, and Chardonnay that reflect the gentle touch that has always characterized Eyrie wines. In recent years, many small wineries have sprung up in the neighborhood around this historic winery. ✉ *935 N.E. 10th Ave.* ☎ *503/472–6315, 888/440–4970* 🌐 *www.eyrievineyards.com* 🎫 *Tastings $40* 🕓 *Closed Tues. and Wed.*

★ Maysara Winery

WINERY/DISTILLERY | Set on 497 acres, this sprawling winery specializes in biodynamic farming and wine production, a sustainable alternative to commercial agriculture based on the works of Rudolf Steiner (best known as the force behind Waldorf education). Instead of commercial fertilizers and chemical pesticides, the focus here is on a holistic approach to farming—turkeys roam the fields, fending off insects, and manure and compost are used to enrich the soil. The result is some fantastic Pinots and wines without any worry of chemical residues. Owner Moe Momtazi's belief in sustainability carries into the tasting room, a cavernous space built of stone from the farm and upcycled wood; even the bar stools are made from old wine barrels. ✉ *15765 S.W. Muddy Valley Rd.* ☎ *503/843–1234* 🌐 *maysara.com.*

🍴 Restaurants

Joel Palmer House

$$$$ | **CONTEMPORARY** | Wild mushrooms and truffles are the stars at this 1857 home, named after an Oregon pioneer, that is now on the National Register of Historic Places; there are three small dining rooms, each seating about 15 people. The standard dinner is a seasonal three-course prix-fixe menu, but if you really, really like mushrooms, have your entire table order chef Christopher's Mushroom Madness Menu, a six-course extravaganza. **Known for:** mushrooms, mushrooms, mushrooms; three-course prix-fixe menu; chef Christopher's Mushroom Madness Menu. [$] *Average main: $50* ✉ *600 Ferry St., Dayton* ☎ *503/864–2995* 🌐 *www.joelpalmerhouse.com* 🕓 *Closed Sun. and Mon. No lunch.*

★ Nick's Italian Cafe

$$$ | **ITALIAN** | Famed for serving Oregon's wine country enthusiasts, this fine-dining venue is a destination for a special evening or lunch. Modestly furnished but with a voluminous wine cellar, Nick's serves spirited and simple food, reflecting the owner's northern Italian heritage. **Known for:** five-course prix fixe with wine pairings; expansive wine cellar; extensive dessert menu. [$] *Average main: $26* ✉ *521 N.E. 3rd St.* ☎ *503/434–4471* 🌐 *nicksitaliancafe.com.*

☕ Coffee and Quick Bites

Serendipity Ice Cream

$ | **CAFÉ** | **FAMILY** | Historic Cook's Hotel, built in 1886, is the setting for a true, old-fashioned ice-cream-parlor experience. Try a sundae, and take home cookies made from scratch. **Known for:** locally made ice cream (dairy- and sugar-free varieties); open all year; the shop provides workplace experience and job training for adults with developmental disabilities. [$] *Average main: $4* ✉ *502*

N.E. 3rd St. ☎ *503/474–9189* 🌐 *serendipityicecream.com* ⏲ *Closed Mon.*

Hotels

★ Atticus Hotel

$$$$ | **HOTEL** | Smack in the middle of downtown McMinnville, this chic boutique hotel offers elegant, high-ceilinged rooms that feature an eclectic mix of local art and amenities and vaguely Edwardian soft furnishings. **Pros:** elegant digs in downtown McMinnville; on-site dining and room service from Red Hills Kitchen; unlimited free espresso at the front desk. **Cons:** no self-parking (except on the street); fee for room service; rooms get some ambient noise. [$] *Rooms from: $315* ✉ *375 N.E. Ford St.* ☎ *503/472–1975* 🌐 *atticushotel.com* 🛏 *36 rooms* 🍴 *No meals.*

Youngberg Hill

$$$$ | **B&B/INN** | Situated on a hilltop overlooking the ridiculously bucolic outskirts of McMinnville, this family-run winery and B&B features nine elegant rooms, all with gas or electric fireplaces and some with whirlpool hot tubs; a couple of the top-floor units even have private balconies. **Pros:** incredible wine country views; included two-course breakfasts; some rooms have Jacuzzis. **Cons:** no on-site restaurant (except for breakfast); some rooms lack views; removed from town. [$] *Rooms from: $309* ✉ *10660 S.W. Youngberg Hill Rd.* ☎ *503/472–2727* 🌐 *youngberghill.com* 🛏 *9 rooms* 🍴 *Free breakfast.*

Salem

24 miles from McMinnville, south on Hwy. 99W and east on Hwy. 22, 45 miles south of Portland on I–5.

The state capital has a rich pioneer history, but before that it was the home of the Calapooia Indians, who called it Chemeketa, which means "place of rest." Salem is said to have been renamed by missionaries. Although trappers and farmers preceded them in the Willamette Valley, the Methodist missionaries had come in 1834 to minister to Native Americans, and they are credited with the founding of Salem. In 1842 they established the first academic institution west of the Rockies, which is now known as Willamette University. Salem became the capital when Oregon achieved statehood in 1859 (Oregon City was the capital of the Oregon Territory). Salem serves as the seat to Marion County as well as the home of the state fairgrounds. Government ranks as a major industry here, while the city's setting in the heart of the fertile Willamette Valley stimulates rich agricultural and food-processing industries. More than a dozen wineries are in or near Salem. The main attractions in Salem are west of Interstate 5 in and around the Capitol Mall.

GETTING HERE AND AROUND

Salem is located on Interstate 5 with easy access to Portland, Albany, and Eugene. **Hut Portland Airport Shuttle** provides transportation to Portland International Airport, which is one hour and 15 minutes away. Salem's McNary Field no longer has commercial airline service, but serves general aviation aircraft.

Bus transportation throughout Salem is provided by **Cherriots.** Amtrak operates regularly, and its train station is located at 500 13th Street SE.

ESSENTIALS

CONTACTS Cherriots. 🌐 *www.cherriots.org.* **Hut Portland Airport Shuttle.** ☎ *503/364–4444* 🌐 *hutshuttle.cim.*

VISITOR INFORMATION Salem Convention & Visitors Center. ✉ *181 High St. NE* ☎ *503/581–4325, 800/874–7012* 🌐 *www.travelsalem.com.*

Mid-Willamette
Valley and
South Willamette
Valley

Mount
Angel
213 Scotts
Mills
Bethel Heights
Vineyard
Witness Tree
Vineyard
Silverton
Keizer
Hayesville
Oregon
Garden
Salem
214
22
99W
Four Corners
Dallas
Silver Falls
State Park
Independence
Aumsville
Monmouth
Turner
Enchanted
Forest
Stayton
Lyons
Gates
22
Detroit
Jefferson
Mill
City
Scio
226
Detroit
Lake
North Albany
Millersburg
Albany
Crabtree
Oregon State
University
Corvallis
Tangent
34
Lebanon
Shedd
Waterloo
Green Peter
Lake
Halsey
Brownsville
Foster
20
99W
Sweet Home
Cascadia
20
Monroe
Holley
Harrisburg
Junction City
McKenzie
Bridge
Cheshire
Marcola
Vida
Blue River
126
Coburg
McKenzie Pass
Leaburg
Cougar Dam
Santa Clara
126
McKenzie River
Highway
Terwilliger Hot Springs
Cougar
Reservoir
River Road
Walterville
Eugene
Springfield
Cascades
Raptor Center
Mt. Pisgah
Arboretum
Sweet Cheeks
Winery
Creswell
5
King Estate
Winery
Lowell
58
Lookout Point
Lake
Cottage Grove
0   15 mi
0   15 km
58

◉ Sights

Bethel Heights Vineyard

WINERY/DISTILLERY | Founded in 1977, Bethel Heights was one of the first vineyards planted in the Eola Hills region of the Willamette Valley. It produces Pinot Noir, Chardonnay, Pinot Blanc, and Pinot Gris. The tasting room has one of the most glorious panoramic views of any winery in the state; its terrace and picnic area overlook the surrounding vineyards, the valley below, and Mt. Jefferson in the distance. ⊠ *6060 Bethel Heights Rd. NW* ☎ *503/581–2262* ⊕ *www.bethelheights. com* 🍽 *Tastings $20*.

Bush's Pasture Park and Bush House

HOUSE | These 105 acres of rolling lawn and formal English gardens include the remarkably well-preserved Bush House, an 1878 Italianate mansion at the park's far-western boundary. It has 10 marble fireplaces and virtually all of its original furnishings, and can be visited only on informative tours. Bush Barn Art Center, behind the house, exhibits the work of Northwest artists and has a sales gallery. ⊠ *600 Mission St. SE* ☎ *503/363–4714* ⊕ *bushhousemuseum.org* 🍽 *House $6*.

Elsinore Theatre

ARTS VENUE | This flamboyant Tudor Gothic vaudeville house opened on May 28, 1926, with Edgar Bergen in attendance. Clark Gable (who lived in nearby Silverton) and Gregory Peck performed on stage. The theater was designed to look like a castle, with a false-stone front, chandeliers, ironwork, and stained-glass windows. It's now a lively performing arts center with a busy schedule of bookings, and there are concerts on its Wurlitzer pipe organ. ⊠ *170 High St. SE* ☎ *503/375–3574* ⊕ *www.elsinoretheatre.com*.

Enchanted Forest

AMUSEMENT PARK/WATER PARK | **FAMILY** | South of Salem, the Enchanted Forest is the closest thing Oregon has to a major theme park. The park has several attractions in forestlike surroundings, including a Big Timber Log Ride. On it, you ride logs through flumes that pass through a lumber mill and the woods. The ride—the biggest log ride in the Northwest—has a 25-foot roller-coaster dip and a 40-foot drop at the end. Other attractions include the Ice Mountain Bobsled roller coaster, the Haunted House, English Village, Storybook Lane, the Fantasy Fountains Water Light Show, Fort Fearless, and the Western town of Tofteville. ⊠ *8462 Enchanted Way SE, Turner* ✛ *7 miles south of Salem at Exit 248 off I–5* ☎ *503/363–3060, 503/371–4242* ⊕ *www. enchantedforest.com* 🍽 *$13.50, $12 children, rides cost extra* ⊙ *Closed Apr. and Labor Day–end of Sept., weekdays, and Nov.–Mar.*

Gilbert House Children's Museum

MUSEUM | **FAMILY** | This is a different kind of kids' museum; an amazing place to let the imagination run wild. Celebrating the life and the inventions of A.C. Gilbert, a Salem native who became a toy manufacturer and inventor, the historic houses included many themed interactive rooms along with a huge outdoor play structure. In addition to the children's activities, many beloved toys created by A.C. Gilbert are on display, including Erector sets and American Flyer trains. The wide range of indoor and outdoor interactive exhibits will appeal to children (and adults) of all ages. ⊠ *116 Marion St. NE* ☎ *503/371–3631* ⊕ *www.acgilbert. org* 🍽 *$8* ⊙ *Closed Mon. except during school holidays.*

★ Mount Angel Abbey

RELIGIOUS SITE | This Benedictine monastery on a 300-foot-high butte was founded in 1882 and is the site of one of two Modernist buildings in the United States designed by Finnish architect Alvar Aalto. A masterpiece of serene and thoughtful design, Aalto's library opened its doors in 1970, and has become a place of pilgrimage for students and aficionados of modern architecture. You also can sample beers produced by the abbey's in-house

The Sprague Fountain, also known as the Capitol Fountain, can be found in Salem's Capitol Mall in front of the capitol building.

brewery (the aptly named Benedictine Brewery) at its taproom just up the road (closed Monday and Tuesday). ⊠ *1 Abbey Dr., St. Benedict ✛ 18 miles from Salem; east on Hwy. 213 and north on Hwy. 214* ☎ *503/845–3030* ⊕ *www.mountangelabbey.org* ▧ *Free.*

Oregon Capitol

GOVERNMENT BUILDING | A brightly gilded bronze statue of the *Oregon Pioneer* stands atop the 140-foot-high Capitol dome, looking north across the Capitol Mall. Built in 1939 with blocks of gray Vermont marble, Oregon's Capitol has an elegant yet austere neoclassical feel. East and west wings were added in 1978. Relief sculptures and deft historical murals soften the interior. Guided tours of the rotunda, the House and Senate chambers, and the governor's office leave from the information center under the dome at 10:30 am, 11:30 am, 1:30 pm, and 2:30 pm. ⊠ *900 Court St. NE* ☎ *503/986–1388* ⊕ *www.oregonlegislature.gov* ▧ *Free* ☉ *Closed weekends and public holidays.*

Oregon Garden

GARDEN | Just outside the town of Silverton, a 25-minute drive from Salem, the Oregon Garden showcases the botanical diversity of the Willamette Valley and Pacific Northwest. Open 365 days a year, the 80-acre garden features themed plots ranging from a conifer forest to medicinal plants. There's also a whimsical children's garden complete with a model train, and another garden featuring the agricultural bounty of the area. A free narrated hop-on hop-off tram tour operates from April through October and stops at six points across the garden. ⊠ *879 W. Main St., Silverton* ☎ *503/874–8100, 877/674–2733* ⊕ *www.oregongarden.org* ▧ *$8–$14 depending on season* ☉ *Closed Nov.–Mar., Mon.–Thurs.*

Oregon State Hospital Museum of Mental Health

MUSEUM | This former insane asylum served as the primary set for the legendary 1975 blockbuster *One Flew Over the Cuckoo's Nest*, starring Jack Nicholson. In the late- 19th-century facility, volunteers operate this nonprofit museum, which explores the somber history of psychiatry through artifacts such as straitjackets sewn by patients and now-regrettable treatment devices. A popular permanent exhibit is dedicated to the Academy Award–winning film. ⊠ 2600 Center St. NE ☎ 971/599–1674 ⊕ oshmuseum.org ✉ $7 ۞ Closed Mon.

Silver Falls State Park

NATIONAL/STATE PARK | Hidden amid old-growth Douglas firs in the foothills of the Cascades, this is the largest state park in Oregon (8,700 acres). South Falls, roaring over the lip of a mossy basalt bowl into a deep pool 177 feet below, is the main attraction here, but 13 other waterfalls—half of them more than 100 feet high—are accessible to hikers. The best time to visit is in the fall, when vine maples blaze with brilliant color, or early spring, when the forest floor is carpeted with trilliums and yellow violets. There are picnic facilities and a day lodge; in winter you can cross-country ski. Camping facilities include tent and trailer sites, cabins, and a horse camp. ⊠ 20024 Silver Falls Hwy. SE, Sublimity ☎ 503/873–8681, 800/551–6949 ⊕ www.oregonstateparks.org ✉ $5 per vehicle.

Willamette Heritage Center

MUSEUM VILLAGE | FAMILY | Take a trip back in time to experience the story of Oregon's early pioneers and the industrial revolution. The **Thomas Kay Woolen Mill Museum** complex (circa 1889), complete with working waterwheels and millstream, looks as if the workers have just stepped away for a lunch break. Teasel gigging, napper flock bins, and the patented Furber double-acting napper are but a few of the machines and processes on display. The **Jason Lee House,** the **John D. Boon Home,** and the **Methodist Parsonage** are also part of the village. There is nothing grandiose about these early pioneer homes, the oldest frame structures in the Northwest, but they reveal a great deal about domestic life in the wilds of

Oregon in the 1840s. ⊠ 1313 Mill St. SE ☎ 503/585–7012 ⊕ www.willametteheritage.org ✉ $8 ۞ Closed Sun.

Willamette Mission State Park

NATIONAL/STATE PARK | Along pastoral lowlands by the Willamette River, this serene park holds the largest black cottonwood tree in the United States. A thick-barked behemoth by a small pond, the 275-year-old tree has upraised arms that bring to mind J.R.R. Tolkien's fictional Ents. Site of Reverend Jason Lee's 1834 pioneer mission, the park also offers quiet strolling and picnicking in an old orchard and along the river. The Wheatland Ferry, at the north end of the park, began carrying covered wagons across the Willamette in 1844 and is still in operation today. ⊠ Wheatland Rd. ✛ 8 miles north of Salem, I–5 Exit 263 ☎ 503/393–1172, 800/551–6949 ⊕ www.oregonstateparks.org ✉ $5 per vehicle.

Willamette University

COLLEGE | Behind the Capitol, across State Street but half a world away, are the brick buildings and grounds of Willamette University, the oldest college in the West. Founded in 1842, Willamette has long been a breeding ground for aspiring politicians. **Hatfield Library,** built in 1986 on the banks of Mill Stream, is a handsome brick-and-glass building with a striking campanile; tall, prim **Waller Hall,** built in 1867, is one of the oldest buildings in the Pacific Northwest. ⊠ 900 State St. ☎ 503/370–6300 ⊕ www.willamette.edu ۞ Closed weekends.

Witness Tree Vineyard

WINERY/DISTILLERY | Named for the ancient oak that towers over the vineyard (it was used as a surveyor's landmark in the 1850s), this winery produces premium Pinot Noir made entirely from grapes grown on its 100-acre estate nestled in the Eola Hills northwest of Salem. The vineyard also produces limited quantities of estate Chardonnay, Viognier, Pinot Blanc, Dolcetto, and a sweet dessert wine called Sweet Signé. Tours are available by appointment. ✉ *7111 Spring Valley Rd. NW* ☎ *503/585–7874* ⊕ *www. witnesstreevineyard.com* ☲ *Tastings from $10* ⊘ *Closed Mon.–Wed. Mar.– mid-Dec. and mid-Dec.–Feb.*

 Restaurants

★ DaVinci

$$$ | ITALIAN | Salem politicos flock to this two-story downtown gathering spot for Italian-inspired dishes cooked in a wood-burning oven. No shortcuts are taken in the preparation, so don't come if you're in a rush. **Known for:** pasta made in-house; good wines by the glass; live music. Ⓢ *Average main: $24* ✉ *180 High St. SE* ☎ *503/399–1413* ⊕ *www.davinci-sofsalem.com* ⊘ *Closed Sun. No lunch.*

Hotels

Grand Hotel in Salem

$$ | HOTEL | Salem is short on choices, but this hotel offers large rooms, with comfortable and luxurious furnishings; it's a good base for guests attending shows and meetings at Salem Conference Center or touring the region. **Pros:** spacious rooms; centrally located; free hot breakfast. **Cons:** some street noise; lacks character; check-in times are late. Ⓢ *Rooms from: $189* ✉ *201 Liberty St. SE* ☎ *503/540–7800, 877/540–7800* ⊕ *www.grandhotelsalem.com* ⇆ *193 rooms* ❘⊙❘ *Free breakfast.*

Oregon Garden Resort

$$ | RESORT | Bright, spacious, classically decorated rooms, each with a fireplace and a private landscaped patio or balcony, neighbor the Oregon Garden (admission is included in the rates). **Pros:** gorgeous grounds; rooms have fireplaces and patios or balconies; spa and plenty of other amenities. **Cons:** a distance from other activities; room decor is simple and old-fashioned; pool is outdoors and seasonal. Ⓢ *Rooms from: $159* ✉ *895 W. Main St., Silverton* ☎ *503/874–2500* ⊕ *www.oregongardenresort.com* ⇆ *103 rooms* ❘⊙❘ *Free breakfast.*

Shopping

Reed Opera House

SHOPPING CENTERS/MALLS | These days the 1869 opera house in downtown Salem contains an eclectic collection of locally owned stores, shops, restaurants, bars, and bakeries, everything from art galleries to tattoo parlors. Its Trinity Ballroom hosts special events and celebrations. ✉ *189 Liberty St. NE* ☎ *503/391–4481* ⊕ *www.reedoperahouse.com.*

Woodburn Premium Outlets

SHOPPING CENTERS/MALLS | Located 18 miles north of Salem just off Interstate 5 are more than 100 brand-name outlet stores, including Nike, Adidas, Calvin Klein, Bose, Coach, Ann Taylor, Levi's, Pendleton, and Columbia Sportswear. There's also a small playground and a couple of places to eat. ✉ *1001 Arney Rd., Woodburn* ☎ *503/981–1900, 888/664–7467* ⊕ *www.premiumoutlets. com/outlet/woodburn.*

Independence

13 miles southwest of Salem on Hwy. 22 W and Hwy. 51 S.

Founded by Oregon Trail pioneers (who named the city after their hometown in Missouri), Independence thrived largely as a trading port owing to its location right on the Willamette River and its proximity to Oregon's hop country. Much of the city was built in the 1880s and its National Register of Historic Places–listed Independence Historic District features around 250 buildings spread over about 30 blocks.

GETTING HERE AND AROUND

Independence is located right on the Willamette River, between 99W and Interstate 5 and directly east of the college town of Monmouth. It's about 15 minutes from Salem, while the Portland International Airport is about 90 minutes away without traffic.

ESSENTIALS

VISITOR INFORMATION Independence Downtown Association. ✉ *278 S Main St., Independence* 🌐 *www.downtownindependence.com.*

Sights

Independence Heritage Museum

MUSEUM | Housed in the old First Baptist Church building, built in 1888, this history museum does a striking job at telling the story of Independence and its surrounding regions through the eyes of various communities that have contributed to its history, not just white settlers. Kids love the skeleton of "Betsy the Cow," used in local classrooms to teach anatomy since her bones were first discovered by a group of schoolboys in the 1960s. Pick up a historic district map for a self-guided tour. ✉ *112 S. 3rd St., Independence* ☎ *503/838–1811* 🌐 *www.ci.independence.or.us/museum.*

Redgate Vineyard

WINERY/DISTILLERY | Though the Independence area is more known for hops than vineyards, Red Gate produces a wide variety of wines, from Pinots to Syrah, Tempranillo, and even port-style dessert wines. The small, publike tasting room has some of the most reasonably priced flights in the area. ✉ *8175 Buena Vista Rd., Independence* ☎ *503/428–7115* 🌐 *redgatevineyard.com* 🎟 *Tastings $10* ⏲ *Closed Mon.–Thurs.*

Rogue Farms Tasting Room

WINERY/DISTILLERY | If you want to try out some of Rogue Ales' most popular brews, you can't get much fresher than right on the grounds of the celebrated Oregon brewery's massive hop farm. A selection of 12 beers are on tap at any given time (along with pretzels and sandwiches); there's also a gift shop with merch and beer for sale, plus a series of educational panels that tell the story of hop production in the area. ✉ *3590 Wigrich Rd., Independence* ☎ *503/838–9813* 🌐 *www.rogue.com/locations/rogue-farms-chatoe-tasting-room.*

Restaurants

Jubilee Champagne and Dessert Bar

$ | **WINE BAR** | Though champagne, prosecco, and mimosas are the star attraction at this bright, feminine dessert bar, it also offers espresso drinks, tea, and beer. Beautifully presented desserts, from glittery red velvet cake to pastel-hued cupcakes, and macarons, round out the menu, and there are a few savory snacks, including a popular dill-pickle soup, for those wanting something more substantial. **Known for:** sparkling wine, champagne, and espresso drinks; a huge selection of fresh cakes and pastries; dill pickle soup. [$] *Average main: $8* ✉ *296 S. Main St., Independence* ☎ *837–0888* ⏲ *Closed Mon.*

Mangiare Italian Restaurant

$$ | **ITALIAN** | Italian-food lovers frequently make the drive from neighboring towns to dine on Mangiare's celebrated pasta dishes and traditional desserts (it also does pizzas, salads, and even meatball sandwiches). The wine list isn't too shabby, either, with an even balance of Willamette Valley and Italian options. **Known for:** generous portions of pasta; traditional Italian desserts; charming outdoor patio area. [$] *Average main: $19* ✉ *114 S. Main St., Independence* ☎ *503/838–0566* 🌐 *www.mangiareitalianrestaurantor.com* ⏲ *No lunch Sun.*

Hotels

The Independence

$$ | **HOTEL** | Overlooking the Willamette River, this business-boutique hotel draws decor inspiration from its local geography, with oceanic blues and wavelike patterns paired with locally sourced furnishings (even the mattresses were

made in the region). **Pros:** beautiful riverfront location right in town; cyclist-friendly facilities, with workshops and in-room bike storage; lovely restaurant with indoor and outdoor seating. **Cons:** bathrooms have automatic light switches and abrasively bright lights; rooms lack safes; no room service. [$] *Rooms from: $189* ✉ *201 Osprey La., Independence* ☎ *503/837–0200* 🌐 *theindependenthotel.com* 🛏 *75 rooms* 🍴 *No meals.*

Albany

20 miles from Salem, south on I–5 and west on U.S. 20.

Known as the grass-seed capital of the world, Albany has some of the most historic buildings in Oregon. Some 700 buildings, scattered over a 100-block area in three districts, include every major architectural style developed in the United States since 1850. The area is listed on the National Register of Historic Places. Eight covered bridges can also be seen on a half-hour drive from Albany. Oregon has the largest collection of covered bridges in the western United States, and the Willamette Valley has more than 34 of the wooden structures.

GETTING HERE AND AROUND

Albany is located on Interstate 5 with easy access to Portland, Salem, and Eugene. Portland International Airport is one hour, 40 minutes away, and the Eugene airport is one hour away to the south. Several shuttle services are available from both airports.

Albany Transit System provides two routes for intercity travel. The Linn-Benton loop system provides for transportation between Albany and Corvallis. Albany is served by Amtrak.

ESSENTIALS

VISITOR INFORMATION Independence Downtown Association. ✉ *278 S Main St., Independence* 🌐 *www.downtownindependence.com.*

Sights

Albany Historic Carousel and Museum
CAROUSEL | FAMILY | It's not often that you get to watch a carousel being built, but that's exactly what's happening here. Craftsmen and volunteers from the Albany area have come together to contribute thousands of hours to carving and painting a huge array of whimsical carousel creatures ranging from traditional horses to giant frogs and dragons. ✉ *250 S.W. Broadalbin St.* ☎ *541/791–3340* 🌐 *albanycarousel.com* 🎟 *Free, carousel rides $2.*

Albany Regional Museum
MUSEUM | This 1887 Italianate building in the heart of historic downtown Albany previously housed a department store and was located several blocks away, but the entire building was moved to its current location in 1912. Exhibits change every few months and include subjects ranging from the Willamette Valley hops industry to early aviation. The Rod and Marty Tripp Reference Room has many historical documents and provides ample room to spread books out and do research projects. ✉ *136 Lyons St. SW* ☎ *541/967–7122* 🌐 *www.armuseum.com* 🎟 *$2 Suggested donation* 🕒 *Closed Sun. and Mon.*

Restaurants

Novak's Hungarian
$ | HUNGARIAN | Since 1984, the Novak family has been a delightful fixture in Albany's dining scene. Whether you're ordering Hungarian hash and eggs in the morning or chicken paprika served over homemade Hungarian pearl noodles for dinner, you can't go wrong in this establishment. **Known for:** good, hearty Hungarian fare; locally sourced ingredients;

familial atmosphere. $ *Average main: $14* ⊠ *208 2nd St. SW* ☎ *541/967–9488* ⊕ *www.novakshungarian.com.*

★ **Sybaris**

$$ | **ECLECTIC** | A rotating menu at this fine bistro in Albany's historic downtown changes monthly and features flavorful cuisine at reasonable prices. The restaurant strives to ensure that most of the ingredients, including the lamb, eggs, and vegetables, are raised within 10 miles. **Known for:** reasonable prices; menu changes monthly; locally sourced products. $ *Average main: $20* ⊠ *442 1st Ave. W* ☎ *541/928–8157* ⊕ *www. sybarisbistro.com* ⊙ *Closed Sun. and Mon. No lunch.*

Corvallis

10 miles southwest of Albany on U.S. 20.

Corvallis is a small city that's best known as the home of Oregon State University and its Beavers athletic teams. Driving the area's economy are a growing engineering and high-tech industry, a burgeoning wine industry, and more traditional local agricultural crops, such as grass and legume seeds. The town and its environs offer plenty of outdoor activities as well as scenic attractions, from covered bridges to wineries and gardens.

GETTING HERE AND AROUND

Corvallis Transit System (CTS) operates eight bus routes throughout the city. **Hut Shuttle** provides transportation between Corvallis and the Portland airport, located one hour, 53 minutes away. **OmniShuttle** provides transportation between Corvallis and the Eugene airport, 50 minutes away. Corvallis Municipal Airport is a public airport 4 miles south of the city.

ESSENTIALS

VISITOR INFORMATION Corvallis Tourism. ⊠ *420 N.W. 2nd St.* ☎ *541/757–1544, 800/334–8118* ⊕ *www.visitcorvallis.com.*

 Sights

Oregon State University

COLLEGE | It's a thrill to be on campus on game day, when students are a sea of orange and black cheering on their beloved Beavers. This 400-acre campus, west of the city center, was established as a land-grant institution in 1868. OSU has more than 26,000 students, many of them studying the university's nationally recognized programs in conservation biology, agricultural sciences, nuclear engineering, forestry, fisheries and wildlife management, community health, pharmacy, and zoology. ⊠ *15th and Jefferson Sts.* ☎ *541/737–1000* ⊕ *oregon-state.edu.*

Osborn Aquatic Center

AMUSEMENT PARK/WATER PARK | **FAMILY** | This is not your ordinary lap pool. There's an outdoor water park, "Otter Beach," featuring waterslides, a water channel, water cannons, and floor geysers. The indoor pools are open all year. ⊠ *1940 N.W. Highland Dr.* ☎ *541/766–7946* ⊕ *www.corvallisoregon.gov* ⊠ *$6.*

★ **Siuslaw National Forest**

FOREST | The forest, starting just 2 miles from Corvallis and extending to the coast, includes the Oregon Dunes National Recreation Area and the Cape Perpetua Interpretive Center. Within the park is the highest point in the Coast Range, Mary's Peak (4,097 feet), offering panoramic views of the Cascades, the Willamette Valley, and the rest of the Coast Range. On a clear day you can see as far as the Pacific Ocean. There are several picnicking areas, more than 10 miles of hiking trails, and a small campground, as well as stands of noble fir and alpine meadows. You can access Mary's Peak from Highway 34 between Corvallis and Newport and the central coast. Several other major highways (Highways 26, 6, 18, 26, and 126) also run through the forest between the Willamette Valley and the coast, providing access to recreation areas. ✉ *Forest office, 3200 S.W. Jefferson Way* ☎ *541/750–7000* 🌐 *www.fs.fed.us/r6/siuslaw* 🎫 *$5 per vehicle at some recreation sites.*

🍴 Restaurants

Del Alma

$$$ | LATIN AMERICAN | This multilevel waterfront eatery gives every table a nice view of the river and puts a modern spin on tapas, bringing unexpected flavors and textures to classic Latin food. The menu also features larger dishes, with a strong emphasis on seafood and beef. **Known for:** tapas; Latin-inspired cocktails; great river views. [$] *Average main: $27* ✉ *136 S.W. Washington Ave.* ☎ *541/753–2222* 🌐 *delalmarestaurant.com* 🕒 *Closed Sun. No lunch.*

★ Gathering Together Farm

$$$ | MODERN AMERICAN | Fresh vegetables, pizzas, local lamb, pork, and halibut are frequent highlights on a menu that features simple, fresh, and primarily organic ingredients impeccably prepared. Local wines and tempting desserts make the evening perfect. **Known for:** coppa (cured pork from the shoulder of the pig); organic produce from collective of local farms; local wines. [$] *Average main: $25* ✉ *25159 Grange Hall Rd., Philomath* ☎ *541/929–4270* 🌐 *www.gatheringtogetherfarm.com* 🕒 *Closed Mon., no dinner Sun.–Tues.*

🛏 Hotels

★ Boulder Falls Inn

$ | HOTEL | One of the chicest places to stay in the area, this business-boutique hotel features sleek rooms and suites filled with locally produced furniture, many of which look out on a huge koi pond surrounded by an authentic Japanese garden. **Pros:** sleek rooms; excellent dining; on-site Japanese garden. **Cons:** location somewhat removed from area attractions; chain hotel ambience; thin walls between rooms. [$] *Rooms from: $149* ✉ *505 Mullins Dr., Lebanon* ☎ *541/405–7025* 🌐 *boulderfallsinn.com* 🛏 *84 rooms* 🍽 *Free breakfast.*

Eugene

63 miles south of Corvallis on I–5.

Eugene was founded in 1846, when Eugene Skinner staked the first federal land-grant claim for pioneers. Eugene is consistently given high marks for its "livability." As the home of the University of Oregon, a large student and former-student population lends Eugene a youthful vitality and countercultural edge. Full of parks and oriented to the outdoors, Eugene is a place where bike paths are used, pedestrians *always* have the right-of-way, and joggers are so plentiful that the city is known as the Running Capital of the World. Shopping and commercial streets surround the Eugene Hilton and the Hult Center for the Performing Arts, the two most prominent downtown buildings. During football season you can count on the U of O Ducks being the primary topic of most conversations.

GETTING HERE AND AROUND

Eugene's airport has rental cars, cabs, and shuttles that make the 15-minute trip to Eugene's city center. By train, Amtrak stops in the heart of downtown. Getting around Lane County's communities is easy with **Lane Transit District** public transportation. Eugene is very bicycle-friendly.

ESSENTIALS

VISITOR INFORMATION Travel Lane County. ✉ *754 Olive St.* ☎ *541/484–5307, 800/547–5445* 🌐 *www.eugenecascadescoast.org.*

👁 Sights

Alton Baker Park

CITY PARK | This parcel of open land on the banks of the Willamette River is named after the late publisher of Eugene's newspaper, the *Register-Guard,* and is the site of many community events. Live music is performed in summer at the Cuthbert Amphitheater. There's fine hiking and biking on a footpath that runs along the river for the length of the park, and an 18-hole disc golf course. Also worth seeing is the Whilamut Natural Area, an open space with 13 "talking stones," each with an inscription. ⊠ *200 Day Island Rd.* ☎ *541/682–4906* ⊕ *www. altonbakerpark.com.*

Cascades Raptor Center

NATURE PRESERVE | FAMILY | This birds-of-prey nature center and hospital hosts more than 30 species of birds. A visit is a great outing for kids, who can learn what owls eat, why and where birds migrate, and all sorts of other raptor facts. Some of the full-time residents include turkey vultures, bald eagles, owls, hawks, falcons, and kites. ⊠ *32275 Fox Hollow Rd.* ☎ *541/485–1320* ⊕ *www.eraptors. org* ⊠ *$9* ⊘ *Closed Mon.*

Civic Winery

WINERY/DISTILLERY | This intimate wine shop focuses on small-batch producers, with a solid list of some of Oregon's finest biodynamic growers. Civic also makes a few wines of its own, all fermented naturally, without added yeast, in terra-cotta amphorae using locally sourced biodynamic and organic grapes. ⊠ *50 E 11th Ave.* ☎ *541/636–2990* ⊕ *www.civicwinery.com* ⊘ *Closed Mon. and Tues.*

Eugene Saturday Market

MARKET | Held every Saturday from April through the middle of November, the Saturday Market is a great place to browse for handicrafts, try out local food carts, or simply kick back and people-watch while listening to live music at the Market Stage. ⊠ *126 E. 8th Ave.* ☎ *541/686–8885* ⊕ *www.eugenesaturdaymarket.org.*

Eugene Science Center

MUSEUM | FAMILY | Formerly the Willamette Science and Technology Center (WISTEC), and still known to locals by its former name, Eugene's imaginative, hands-on museum assembles rotating exhibits designed for curious young minds. The adjacent **planetarium,** one of the largest in the Pacific Northwest, presents star shows and entertainment events. ⊠ *2300 Leo Harris Pkwy.* ☎ *541/682–7888* ⊕ *www.sciencefactory. org* ⊠ *$5 for exhibit hall or planetarium show, $8 for both* ⊘ *Closed Mon. and during Oregon Ducks home football games; planetarium timings vary.*

Hayward Field

SPORTS VENUE | University of Oregon's historic Hayward Field was demolished and rebuilt from scratch to host the 2021 IAAF World Athletics Championships, and the results have been fantastic. Featuring gargantuan indoor and outdoor practice areas along with extensive world-class facilities for runners and spectators alike, from an antigravity treadmill room to a theater created specifically for optimal viewing of track-and-field events. ⊠ *1580 E 15th Ave.*

★ Jordan Schnitzer Museum of Art

MUSEUM | Works from the 20th and 21st centuries are a specialty in these handsome galleries on the University of Oregon campus. They feature works by many leading Pacific Northwest artists, and European, Korean, Chinese, and Japanese works are also on view, as are 300 works commissioned by the Works Progress Administration in the 1930s and '40s. You can also view an ever-changing collection of important works from private collections by internationally recognized artists through the museum's Masterworks On Loan program. ⊠ *1430 Johnson La.* ☎ *541/346–3027* ⊕ *jsma. uoregon.edu* ⊠ *$5* ⊘ *Closed Mon. and Tues.*

King Estate Winery

WINERY/DISTILLERY | One of Oregon's largest producers is known for its crisp Pinot Gris and silky Pinot Noir and boasts the world's largest organic vineyard. The visitor center offers wine tasting and

Fresh produce can be found at numerous farmers' markets throughout the state including the Eugene Saturday Market, held April through November.

production tours, and the restaurant highlights local meats and organic produce grown in the estate gardens. ✉ 80854 Territorial Rd. ☎ 541/942-9874 ⊕ www.kingestate.com 🍷 Tastings $15.

Lane County Farmers' Market

MARKET | Across the street from the Eugene Saturday Market, the Lane County market offers produce grown or made in Oregon. Hours and days vary throughout the year. ✉ Corner of 8th Ave. and Oak St. ☎ 541/431-4923 ⊕ www.lanecountyfarmersmarket.org/markets ◷ Closed Jan.

Mount Pisgah Arboretum

GARDEN | FAMILY | This beautiful nature preserve near southeast Eugene includes extensive all-weather trails, educational programs for all ages, and facilities for special events. Its visitor center holds workshops and features native amphibian and reptile terraria; microscopes for exploring tiny seeds, bugs, feathers, and snakeskins; "touch me" exhibits; reference books; and a working viewable beehive. ✉ 34901 Frank Parrish Rd.

☎ 541/747-3817 ⊕ www.mountpisgaharboretum.org 🅿 Parking $4.

Ninkasi Brewing Company

WINERY/DISTILLERY | Named after the Sumerian goddess of fermentation, Ninkasi has grown from a little start-up in 2006 to a major supplier of craft beer. Its flagship beer, Total Domination IPA, is signature Northwest, with bold flavor and lots of hops. Visit the tasting room and enjoy a tasting flight or a pint, either indoors or on the patio. The beer menu changes often and includes a few hard-to-find limited-production beers. If you'd like a little food to go with your beer, you'll usually find one of Eugene's many food carts right there on the patio. Free brewery tours are offered daily. ✉ 272 Van Buren St. ☎ 541/344-2739 ⊕ www.ninkasibrewing.com.

Skinner Butte Park

NATIONAL/STATE PARK | FAMILY | Rising from the south bank of the Willamette River, this forested enclave provides the best views of any of the city's parks; it also has the greatest historic cachet, since it was here that Eugene Skinner staked the claim that put Eugene on the map. Children can scale a replica of Skinner Butte, uncover fossils, and cool off under a rain circle. Skinner Butte Loop leads to the top of Skinner Butte, traversing sometimes difficult terrain through a mixed-conifer forest. ✉ *248 Cheshire Ave.* ☎ *541/682–4800* 🎫 *Free.*

Sweet Cheeks Winery

WINERY/DISTILLERY | This estate vineyard lies on a prime sloping hillside in the heart of the Willamette Valley appellation. It also supplies grapes to several award-winning wineries. Bring a picnic and enjoy the amazing view from the lawn outside the tasting room, or take advantage of the food available for purchase. Friday-night tastings are embellished with cheese pairings and live music. They also have a second tasting room in the Fifth Street Public Market. ✉ *27007 Briggs Hill Rd.* ☎ *541/349–9463, 877/309–9463* 🌐 *www.sweetcheekswinery.com.*

University of Oregon

COLLEGE | The true heart of Eugene lies southeast of the city center at its university. Several fine old buildings can be seen on the 250-acre campus; **Deady Hall,** built in 1876, is the oldest. More than 400 varieties of trees grace the bucolic grounds, along with outdoor sculptures that include *The Pioneer* and *The Pioneer Mother.* The two bronze figures by Alexander Phimster Proctor were dedicated to the men and women who settled the Oregon Territory and less than a generation later founded the university. ✉ *1585 E. 13th Ave.* ☎ *541/346–1000* 🌐 *www.uoregon.edu.*

University of Oregon Museum of Natural and Cultural History

MUSEUM | Relics on display are devoted to Pacific Northwest anthropology and the natural sciences. Highlights include the fossil collection of Thomas Condon, Oregon's first geologist, and a pair of 9,000-year-old sandals made of sagebrush. ✉ *1680 E. 15th Ave.* ☎ *541/346–3024* 🌐 *mnch.uoregon.edu* 🎫 *$6* 🕒 *Closed Mon.*

★ **WildCraft Cider Works**

WINERY/DISTILLERY | With a long list of house-crafted ciders, many seasonal, this casual spot is a great place to try out WildCraft's locally celebrated wild-ferment ciders, many of which highlight the diversity of the Willamette Valley's apple bounty. Local favorites include the botanical Wild Rose cider (made with locally harvested rose petals) and "perries," unpasteurized pear ciders stored in wax-sealed bottles. WildCraft also has its own event space with regular live music. Peckish guests can order meals and snacks from Krob Krua, an independently operated Thai restaurant that rents out a section of the cidery. ✉ *232 Lincoln St.* ✣ *The main parking area is off Lawrence St., 1 block west of Lincoln* ☎ *541/735–3506* 🌐 *wildcraftciderworks.com* 🕒 *Closed Sun. and Mon.*

🍴 Restaurants

Café 440

$$ | MODERN AMERICAN | Putting a modern twist on classic comfort food, this airy, industrial-chic space features pub food and comfort fare made from locally grown ingredients and a great local beer list. Along with updated classics like mac and cheese, burgers, and fish-and-chips, you'll find innovative versions of ahi poke and salmon cakes. **Known for:** upscale takes on comfort food; homemade desserts; supporting local charities. [$] *Average main: $22* ✉ *440 Coburg Rd.* ☎ *541/505–8493* 🌐 *www.cafe440.com.*

Grit Kitchen and Wine

$$$ | PACIFIC NORTHWEST | Local, seasonal ingredients are the star attraction at this Whiteaker neighborhood mainstay, with a changing menu featuring complex and unexpected flavors and a wide range of textures. Eat inside and take advantage of the open kitchen to watch the chefs at

work, or enjoy a pleasant outdoor dining experience on either of the two decks. **Known for:** the monthly changing four-course feast; locally sourced ingredients; handmade noodles. $ *Average main: $27* ⊠ *1080 W. 3rd St.* ☏ *541/343–0501* ⊕ *gritkitchen.com* ☉ *No lunch.*

Marché

$$$ | **FRENCH** | Located in the bustling Fifth Street Market, this renowned Eugene restaurant works with more than a dozen local farmers to bring fresh, local, organic food to the table. Specialties include salmon, halibut, sturgeon, and beef tenderloin, braised pork shoulder, and outstanding local oysters paired with an extensive wine list featuring lots of Oregon wines. **Known for:** fresh beignets on Sunday; locally sourced ingredients; solid wine list with plenty of local options. $ *Average main: $30* ⊠ *296 E. 5th Ave.* ☏ *541/342–3612* ⊕ *www.marcherestaurant.com.*

★ Morning Glory Cafe

$ | **VEGETARIAN** | Eugene's oldest vegetarian restaurant serves up huge, hearty breakfasts and delicious espresso drinks all day along with a great lunchtime menu of soups, salads, and sandwiches. The interiors are decked with local art pieces and there's a small seating area outside for sunny-day dining. **Known for:** breakfast served all day; house-made baked goods; hearty lunch menu with generous portions. $ *Average main: $9* ⊠ *450 Willamette St.* ☏ *541/687–0709* ⊕ *morninggloryeugene.squarespace.com.*

★ Ristorante Italiano

$$$$ | **ITALIAN** | The chef uses fresh local produce from the restaurant's own farm, but this bistro-style café across from the University of Oregon is best known for its authentic Italian cuisine, with a heavy emphasis on fresh local seafood. The menu changes according to the season, but staples include delicious salads and soups, ravioli, grilled chicken, pizza, and sandwiches plus a variety of specials. **Known for:** Italian fare, with lots of seafood; farm-sourced produce; lovely outdoor seating area. $ *Average main: $33* ⊠ *Excelsior Inn, 754 E. 13th Ave.* ☏ *541/342–6963, 800/321–6963* ☉ *No lunch Sat.*

Hotels

Campbell House

$ | **B&B/INN** | Built in 1892 and later restored with fastidious care, this luxurious bed-and-breakfast features elegant rooms spread across a main house and a carriage house that are surrounded by an acre of landscaped grounds. **Pros:** classic architecture and decor; evening wine receptions; well-kept grounds. **Cons:** rooms lack some of the amenities of nearby hotels; rooms get train noise; uncomfortable mattresses. $ *Rooms from: $109* ⊠ *252 Pearl St.* ☏ *541/343–1119, 800/264–2519* ⊕ *www.campbellhouse.com* ⇄ *21 rooms* ⦶ *Free breakfast.*

C'est la Vie Inn

$$ | **B&B/INN** | Listed on the National Register of Historic Places, this 1891 Queen Anne Victorian bed-and-breakfast provides old-world comfort and modern-day amenities in its luxurious and romantic guest rooms. **Pros:** intimate ambience; beautiful grounds; helpful staff. **Cons:** few rooms; breakfast is average; not as central as some alternatives. $ *Rooms from: $175* ⊠ *1006 Taylor St.* ☏ *541/302–3014* ⊕ *cestlavieinn.com* ⇄ *4 rooms* ⦶ *Free breakfast.*

EVEN Hotel Eugene

$ | **HOTEL** | With an excellent gym, an indoor pool, and extensive in-room exercise equipment, this sleek business hotel is ideal for visiting athletes (and anyone who values a good workout); its location near the jogging trails at Alton Baker Park is an added bonus. **Pros:** in-room fitness equipment and modern gym; free and ample on-site parking; 24-hour gift shop selling healthy snacks and fresh-squeezed OJ. **Cons:** lacks local charm of smaller properties; room thermostat; thin walls. [$] *Rooms from: $104* ✉ *2133 Centennial Plaza* ☎ *541/342–3836* 🌐 *www.ihg.com/evenhotels* 🛏 *100 rooms* 🍴 *No meals.*

Excelsior Inn

$ | **B&B/INN** | Quiet sophistication, attention to architectural detail, and rooms furnished in a refreshingly understated manner, each with a marble-and-tile bath and some with fireplaces, suggest a European inn. **Pros:** romantic accommodations; excellent service and restaurant; close to the University of Oregon campus. **Cons:** some rooms are tiny; limited parking; front desk has limited hours. [$] *Rooms from: $135* ✉ *754 E. 13th Ave.* ☎ *541/342–6963, 800/321–6963* 🌐 *www.excelsiorinn.com* 🛏 *14 rooms* 🍴 *Free breakfast.*

★ **Graduate Eugene**

$$$$ | **HOTEL** | The University of Oregon is celebrated with stylish fervor at Graduate Eugene, from the gargantuan wooden duck mascot that greets guests in the lobby to room decor featuring reproductions of local frat and field ephemera; they even have lamps designed to resemble waffle irons (the inspiration for homegrown-brand Nike's first soles). **Pros:** right next to Autzen Stadium in downtown Eugene; tasteful University of Oregon–inspired decor throughout; extensive conference facilities, including rooftop. **Cons:** rooms near ice machines get noise; a trek from the university; no room service. [$] *Rooms from: $277* ✉ *66 E 6th Ave.* ☎ *541/342–2000* 🌐 *graduatehotels.com/eugene* 🛏 *295 rooms* 🍴 *No meals.*

Inn at the 5th

$$$$ | **HOTEL** | This upscale boutique hotel, set among the shops and restaurants of the trendy Fifth Street Public Market, features subtly elegant rooms and suites. **Pros:** most rooms have fireplaces; great location surrounded by boutiques and restaurants; great amenities, including fitness center. **Cons:** no self-parking; expensive by local standards; some rooms get train noise. [$] *Rooms from: $259* ✉ *205 E. 6th Ave.* ☎ *541/743–4099* 🌐 *www.innat5th.com* 🛏 *69 rooms* 🍴 *No meals.*

Performing Arts

Hult Center for the Performing Arts

ARTS VENUE | This is the locus of Eugene's cultural life. Renowned for the quality of its acoustics, the center has two theaters that are home to Eugene's symphony and opera. ✉ *1 Eugene Center* ☎ *541/682–5087 administration, 541/682–5000 tickets* 🌐 *www.hultcenter.org.*

★ **Oregon Bach Festival**

FESTIVALS | Conductor Helmuth Rilling leads the internationally known Oregon Bach Festival every summer. Concerts, chamber music, and social events—held mainly in Eugene at the Hult Center and the University of Oregon School of Music but also in Corvallis and Florence—are part of this three-week event. ✉ *1 Eugene Center* ☎ *541/346–5666* 🌐 *oregonbachfestival.com.*

Shopping

Fifth Street Public Market

SHOPPING CENTERS/MALLS | Tourists coming to the Willamette Valley, especially to Eugene, can't escape without experiencing the Fifth Street Public Market in downtown Eugene. There are plenty of boutiques and crafts shops, a large gourmet food hall with a bakery, and restaurants serving sushi, pizza, and seafood. ✉ *296 E. 5th Ave.* ☎ *541/484–0383* 🌐 *www.5stmarket.com.*

Marley's Monsters EcoShop

HOUSEHOLD ITEMS/FURNITURE | What started as a homegrown Etsy business focusing on eco-friendly, machine-washable, reusable items has quickly mushroomed into a major operation. Here you'll find everything from rolls of cloth "unpaper towels" to reusable sponges in simple whites or fun, colorful patterns; they even do custom orders. ⊠ *234 W. 6th Ave.* ☎ *541/505–9417.*

Activities

BIKING AND JOGGING

The **River Bank Bike Path,** originating in Alton Baker Park on the Willamette's north bank, is a level and leisurely introduction to Eugene's topography. It's one of 120 miles of trails in the area. **Prefontaine Trail,** used by area runners, travels through level fields and forests for 1½ miles.

RECREATIONAL AREAS

Dexter State Recreation Site

BOATING | FAMILY | A 20-minute drive southeast of Eugene on the western shores of Dexter Reservoir, this recreation site offers disc golf, picnic areas, boat launches, and plenty of hiking. ⊹ *Hwy. 58, between mileposts 11 and 12.*

McKenzie Bridge

58 miles east of Eugene on Hwy. 126.

On the beautiful McKenzie River, lakes, waterfalls, and covered bridges surround the town of McKenzie Bridge and wilderness trails in the Cascades. Fishing, skiing, backpacking, and rafting are among the most popular activities in the area.

GETTING HERE AND AROUND

McKenzie Bridge is about an hour from Eugene, on Highway 126. It is just 38 miles from Hoodoo Ski Area, but its proximity can be deceiving if the snow is heavy. Bend also is close at 64 miles to the east.

Sights

Cougar Dam and Reservoir

DAM | Four miles outside of McKenzie Bridge is the highest embankment dam ever built by the Army Corps of Engineers—452 feet above the streambed. The resulting reservoir, on the South Fork McKenzie River, covers 1,280 acres. The dam generates 25 megawatts of power, and includes a fish collection and sorting facility, and a temperature control tower to keep the downstream water at a suitable temperature for spawning. The public recreation areas are in the Willamette National Forest. You can visit the dam year-round, but some campgrounds are open only from April to September. ⊠ *Willamette National Forest, Forest Rd. 19* ☎ *541/822–3381* ☜ *Free.*

McKenzie River Highway

SCENIC DRIVE | Highway 126, as it heads east from Eugene, is known as the McKenzie River Highway. Following the curves of the river, it passes grazing lands, fruit and nut orchards, and the small riverside hamlets of the McKenzie Valley. From the highway you can glimpse the bouncing, bubbling, blue-green McKenzie River, one of Oregon's top fishing, boating, and white-water rafting spots, against a backdrop of densely forested mountains, splashing waterfalls, and jet-black lava beds. The small town of McKenzie Bridge marks the end of the McKenzie River Highway and the beginning of the 26-mile McKenzie River National Recreation Trail, which heads north through the Willamette National Forest along portions of the Old Santiam Wagon Road. ⊠ *McKenzie Bridge.*

Terwilliger Hot Springs (Cougar Hot Springs)

HOT SPRINGS | Bring a towel and enjoy the soaking pools in this natural hot-springs area. Located an hour east of Eugene off of Highway 126, the pools are a short hike from the parking area, and include a changing area. Soaking aficionados will find Terwilliger to be rustic, which many regard as an advantage, though the popularity of this beautiful spot can be a drawback. The pools are in a forest of old-growth firs and cedars, and just downstream is a beautiful lagoon complete with waterfall that is also suitable for swimming. Clothing is optional. ✉ *Off Forest Rd. 19, Blue River* ☎ *541/822–3381* 💲 *$7.*

★ Willamette National Forest

FOREST | Stretching 110 miles along the western slopes of the Cascade Range, this forest boasts boundless recreation opportunities, including waterfall exploration, camping, hiking, boating, ATV riding, and winter sports. It extends from the Mt. Jefferson area east of Salem to the Calapooya Mountains northeast of Roseburg, encompassing 1,675,407 acres. ✉ *3106 Pierce Pkwy., Suite D, Springfield* ☎ *541/225–6300* ⊕ *www.fs.usda.gov/willamette.*

Restaurants

Obsidian Grill Restaurant

$ | **AMERICAN** | On an expansive patio at the back of the McKenzie General, this restaurant offers a great menu of sandwiches, wraps, burgers, and wings, but it's the ambience that really sets it apart. Wooden tables and chairs are clustered around fire pits, with a covered area that has European-style heat lamps for cooler weather and plenty of twinkling fairy lights. **Known for:** dog-friendly patio; solid vegan and gluten-free options; great beer selection. 💲 *Average main: $12* ✉ *91837 Taylor Rd., Blue River* ☎ *541/822–3221* ⊕ *www.mckenziegeneral.com.*

Takoda's Restaurant

$ | **AMERICAN** | **FAMILY** | A popular roadside café serves burgers, sandwiches, great soups, salads, pizza, and daily specials. The burger selection includes not only beef, but seafood, chicken, turkey, and veggie options. **Known for:** great burger options; video game room for kids;

lovely outdoor seating area. 💲 *Average main: $11* ✉ *91806 Mill Creek Rd., Milepost 47.5 McKenzie Hwy., Blue River* ☎ *541/822–1153* ⊕ *www.takodasrainbow.com.*

Hotels

★ Eagle Rock Lodge

$ | **B&B/INN** | These wood-paneled rooms filled with quilts and gorgeous custom furniture are surprisingly luxurious and provide a romantic, relaxing riverside retreat in the woods. **Pros:** great location on the McKenzie River; comfortable atmosphere; delicious free breakfast. **Cons:** a distance from nonoutdoor activities; only one ADA room; limited property features. 💲 *Rooms from: $130* ✉ *49198 McKenzie Hwy., Vida* ☎ *541/822–3630, 888/773–4333* ⊕ *www.eaglerocklodge.com* 🍴 *8 rooms* ¶ *Free breakfast.*

Loloma Lodge

$$ | **RESORT** | **FAMILY** | This sprawling riverside retreat offers spacious, vintage cabins that pair colorful decor with Oregon forest touches (think stone fireplaces and lots of wood and wicker). **Pros:** convenient self check-in; beautiful, quiet location; all cabins have full-sized kitchens. **Cons:** no daily housekeeping; limited amenities, with no front desk; Wi-Fi can be spotty. 💲 *Rooms from: $200* ✉ *56687 McKenzie Hwy.* ☎ *541/813–6018* ⊕ *www.lolomalodge.com* 🍴 *5 cabins, 1 lodge* ¶ *No meals.*

Shopping

McKenzie General Store

CONVENIENCE/GENERAL STORES | With an impressive selection of gourmet and organic grocery items, plus its own on-site restaurant with regular music events, this is not your average small-town general store. ✉ *91837 Taylor Rd., Blue River* ☎ *541/822–3221* ⊕ *www.mckenziegeneral.com.*

Organic Redneck

FOOD/CANDY | On the way to McKenzie Bridge from Eugene, this farm stand offers seasonal, certified organic produce grown right on the family's farm. Blueberries are the specialty here, and they've got dried versions available for those who visit out of season. ⊠ *44382 Mckenzie Hwy., Leaburg* ☎ *541/896–3928* ⊕ *www. ogredneck.com.*

 Activities

GOLF

Tokatee Golf Club

GOLF | Ranked one of the best golf courses in Oregon by *Golf Digest*, this 18-hole beauty is tucked away near the McKenzie River with views of the Three Sisters Mountains, native ponds, and streams. *Tokatee* is a Chinook word meaning "a place of restful beauty." The course offers a practice range, carts, lessons, rentals, a coffee shop and snack bar, and Wi-Fi. ⊠ *54947 McKenzie Hwy.* ☎ *541/822–3220, 800/452–6376* ⊕ *www.tokatee. com* 🗐 *18 holes $55; 9 holes $35* 🏌 *9 or 18 holes, 6806 yards, par 72.*

WHITE-WATER RAFTING

High Country Expeditions

WHITE-WATER RAFTING | FAMILY | Raft the white waters of the McKenzie River on a guided full- or half-day tour. You'll bounce through rapids, admire old-growth forest, and watch osprey and blue herons fishing. The outfit provides life jackets, splash gear, wet suits, booties (if requested), boating equipment, paddling instructions, river safety talk, a three-course riverside meal, and shuttle service back to your vehicle. Full-day trips are $92, half-day trips $62. ⊠ *Belknap Hot Springs Resort, 59296 N. Belknap Springs Rd.* ☎ *541/822–8288, 888/461–7238* ⊕ *www. highcountryexpeditions.com.*

Chapter 6

COLUMBIA RIVER GORGE AND MT. HOOD

Updated by
Andrew Collins

👁 Sights	🍴 Restaurants	🛏 Hotels	💼 Shopping	🍸 Nightlife
★★★★★	★★★★☆	★★★☆☆	★★★☆☆	★★★☆☆

WELCOME TO COLUMBIA RIVER GORGE AND MT. HOOD

TOP REASONS TO GO

★ **Orchards and vineyards:** Dozens of farm stands selling apples, pears, peaches, cherries, and berries, as well as a growing crop of seriously acclaimed wineries, thrive here.

★ **Outdoor rec mecca:** From kiteboarding in the Columbia River to mountain biking the slopes of Mt. Hood to hiking among the roaring waterfalls of the Gorge, this is a region tailor-made for adventure junkies.

★ **Historico-luxe:** Grand dames like Timberline Lodge and the Columbia Gorge Hotel exude history and architectural distinction.

★ **Road-tripping:** From Portland you can make a full 250-mile scenic loop through the Gorge out to Maryhill, Washington, returning to Hood River and then circling Mt. Hood to the south.

★ **Hop havens:** The Gorge-Hood region has a fast-growing proliferation of craft-beer taprooms, from Stevenson's quirky Walking Man Brewing to Pfriem, Ferment, and several others in Hood River.

1 Historic Columbia River Highway. The country's oldest scenic highway is a great way to see the Gorge.

2 Cascade Locks. Early-20th-century dams turned the raging Columbia River into a comparatively docile waterway.

3 Stevenson, Washington. This is a quiet base for outdoor adventures and Oregon cliff views.

4 Hood River. The hub of the Gorge area has restaurants, lodgings, taprooms, wineries, and amazing mountain views.

5 White Salmon, Washington. This scenic spot is handy for wine touring, hiking, and other adventures on the eastern Gorge.

6 The Dalles. Old West meets workaday city in north-central Oregon's economic hub.

7 Goldendale, Washington. The Gorge's eastern edge has the Maryhill Museum, Maryhill Winery, and Goldendale Observatory State Park.

8 Mt. Hood. Mt. Hood is a mecca for mountaineers, sightseers, and year-round skiers. You'll find the alpine resort village of Government Camp, as well as Welches and Zigzag villages.

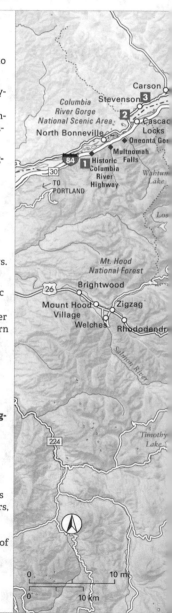

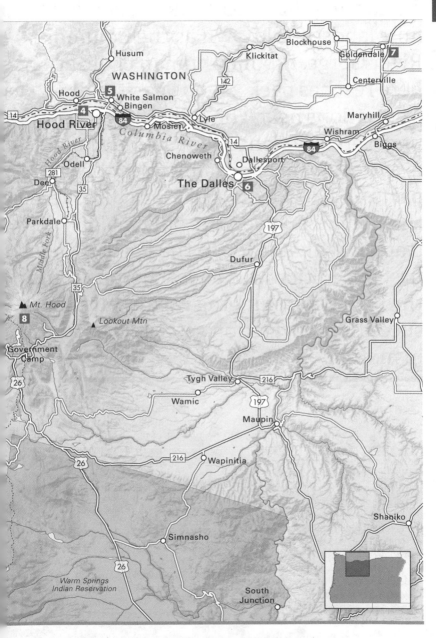

Volcanoes, lava flows, ice-age floodwaters, and glaciers were nature's tools of choice for carving this breathtaking, nearly 100-mile landscape known as the Columbia River Gorge. Proof of human civilization here reaches back 31,000 years, and excavations near The Dalles have uncovered evidence that salmon fishing is a 10,000-year-old tradition in these parts. In 1805 Lewis and Clark discovered the Columbia River, the only major waterway that leads to the Pacific. Their first expedition was a treacherous route through wild, plunging rapids, but their successful navigation set a new exodus in motion.

Today the river has been tamed by a comprehensive system of hydroelectric dams and locks, and the towns in these parts are laid-back though increasingly sophisticated recreation hubs whose residents harbor a fierce pride in their shared natural resources. Sightseers, hikers, bikers, windsurfers, kiteboarders, and skiers have long found contentment in this robust region, officially labeled a National Scenic Area in 1986 and on par with some of the country's top national parks when it comes to eye-popping natural scenery. Rapidly, the region is drawing those in search of farm-to-table cuisine, craft breweries, artisanal bakeries and coffeehouses, and seriously stellar—if still a bit underrated—wineries. Highlights of the area include Multnomah Falls, Bonneville Dam, the rich orchard and vineyard lands of Hood River and White Salmon (and the agrarian hamlets nearby), and Maryhill Museum of Art.

To the south of Hood River are all the alpine attractions of the 11,249-foot-high Mt. Hood. With more than 2.5 million people living just up the road in greater Portland, you'd think this mountain playground would be overrun, but it's still easy to find solitude in the 1,067,000-acre national forest surrounding the peak. Some of the world's best skiers take advantage of the powder on Hood, and they stick around in summer for North America's longest ski season at Palmer Snowfield, above Timberline Lodge.

MAJOR REGIONS

When glacial floods carved out most of the **Columbia River Gorge** at the end of the last ice age, they left behind massive, looming cliffs where the river bisects the Cascade mountain range. The size of the canyon and the wildly varying elevations make this small stretch of Oregon as ecologically diverse as anyplace in the state. In a few days along the Gorge you can mountain bike through dry canyons near **The Dalles,** hike through temperate rain forests in the Columbia Gorge along the **Historic Columbia River Highway,** or drive across the Bridge of Gods, which connects **Cascade Locks** with it's twin city, **Stevenson, Washington.** At night you'll be rewarded with historic lodging and good food in one of a half-dozen mellow river towns and one very bustling one, **Hood River. White Salmon, Washington,** is a great base for exploring the Washington side of the Gorge, and farther east, you'll find some notable attractions in Maryhill and **Goldendale.**

Towering at 11,249 feet above sea level, **Mt. Hood** offers the longest ski season in North America, with three major ski resorts that also offer great mountain biking, hiking, and climbing opportunities in the summer. The small resort village of **Government Camp** is located on Mt. Hood, while **Welches and Zigzag** are part of a group of small hamlets known as the Villages of Mt. Hood.

Planning

When to Go

Winter weather in the Mt. Hood area is much more severe than in Portland and the Willamette Valley, and occasionally rough conditions permeate the Gorge, too. Interstate 84 rarely closes because of snow and ice. If you're planning a winter visit, be sure to carry plenty of warm clothes. High winds and single-digit temps are par for the course around 6,000 feet—the elevation of Timberline Lodge on Mt. Hood—in January. Note that chains are sometimes required for traveling over mountain passes.

Temperatures in the Gorge are mild year-round, rarely dipping below 30°F in winter and hovering in the high 70s in midsummer. As throughout Oregon, however, elevation is often a more significant factor than season, and an hour-long drive to Mt. Hood's Timberline Lodge can reduce those midsummer temps by 20–30 degrees. Don't forget that the higher reaches of Mt. Hood retain snow year-round.

In early fall, look for maple, tamarack, and aspen trees around the Gorge, bursting with brilliant red and gold color. No matter the season, the basalt cliffs, the acres of lush forest, and that glorious expanse of water make the Gorge one of the West's great scenic wonders.

Getting Here and Around

The Columbia Gorge, which is easily accessed from Portland, is most easily explored by car. The same is generally true for the Mt. Hood area, but in season, the area ski resorts do have shuttle services from Portland and the airport. Even light exploring of the region, however, requires an automobile—take heart that the driving in these parts is scenic and relatively free of traffic (exceptions being the Historic Columbia River Highway, which can get backed up on weekends). Just keep in mind that winter storms can result in road closures around Mt. Hood and, occasionally, even in the Gorge. It's just a 20-minute drive east of Portland to reach the beginning of the Columbia Gorge, in Troutdale. From Portland it's a one-hour drive to Hood River, a 90-minute drive to Mt. Hood, and a two-hour drive to Goldendale, Washington *(the farthest-away point covered in this chapter)*. If you're trying to visit the region without a car, there are some limited bus options, and you could even take Amtrak to White Salmon–Bingen and then cab it to Hood River, but it'll be tricky to explore the countryside. For tips and details on leaving the car behind, visit ⊕ *www. columbiagorgecarfree.com.*

CAR TRAVEL

Interstate 84 is the main east–west route into the Columbia River Gorge, although you can also reach the area on the Washington side via slower but quite scenic Highway 14, which skirts the north side of the river. U.S. 26, which leads east from Portland, is the main route to Mt. Hood.

The scenic Historic Columbia River Highway (U.S. 30) from Troutdale to just east of Oneonta Gorge (which is, itself, closed indefinitely due to wildfire damage) passes Crown Point State Park and Multnomah Falls. Interstate 84/U.S. 30 continues on to The Dalles. Highway 35 heads south from Hood River to the Mt. Hood area, intersecting with U.S. 26 near Government Camp. From Portland the Columbia Gorge–Mt. Hood Scenic Loop is the easiest way to fully explore the Gorge and the mountain. Take Interstate 84 east to Troutdale and then follow U.S. 26 east to Mt. Hood, Highway 35 north to Hood River, and Interstate 84 back to Portland. Or make the loop in reverse.

Restaurants

A prominent locavore mentality pervades western Oregon generally, and low elevations around the Gorge mean long growing seasons for dozens of local producers. Fresh foods grown, caught, and harvested in the Northwest dominate menus in the increasingly sophisticated restaurants in the Gorge, especially in the charming town of Hood River, but even in smaller White Salmon and up around Mt. Hood. Columbia River salmon is big; fruit orchards proliferate around Hood River; delicious huckleberries flourish in Mount Hood National Forest; and the Gorge nurtures a bounty of excellent vineyards. Additionally, even the smallest towns around the region have their own lively and consistently excellent brewpubs with tasty comfort fare and tap after tap of craft ales. In keeping with the region's green and laid-back vibe, outdoor dining is highly popular. *Restaurant reviews have been shortened. For full information visit Fodors.com.*

What it Costs in U.S. Dollars			
$	$$	$$$	$$$$
RESTAURANTS			
under $16	$16–$22	$23–$30	over $30
HOTELS			
under $150	$150–$200	$201–$250	over $250

Hotels

The region is close enough that you could spend a day or two exploring the Gorge and Mt. Hood, using Portland hotels as your base. The best way to fully appreciate the Gorge, however, is to spend a night or two—look to Hood River and The Dalles for the largest selections of lodging options, although you'll also find some noteworthy resorts, motels, and B&Bs in some of the towns between Portland and The Dalles (on both sides of the river). There are a couple of run-of-the-mill motels in Goldendale, but otherwise, you won't find any accommodations in the region east of The Dalles.

The slopes of Mt. Hood are dotted with smart ski resorts, and towns like Government Camp and Welches have a mix of rustic and contemporary vacation rentals. The closer you are to Mt. Hood in any season, the earlier you'll want to reserve. With ski country working ever harder to attract summer patrons, Mt. Hood resorts like Timberline Lodge and Mt. Hood Skibowl offer some worthwhile seasonal specials. *Hotel reviews have been shortened. For full information visit Fodors.com.*

Tours

EverGreen Escapes
GUIDED TOURS | The energetic crew at this highly respected tour operator provides both regularly scheduled and customizable tours of the Gorge (with themes that range from wine to hiking) and Mt. Hood, where options include hiking and snowshoeing. ☎ *503/252–1931* ⊕ *www. evergreenescapes.com* ✉ *From $149.*

Martin's Gorge Tours
GUIDED TOURS | Wine tours, waterfall hikes, and spring wildflower tours are among the popular trips offered by this Portland-based guide. ☎ *503/349–1323* ⊕ *www.martinsgorgetours.com* ✉ *From $70.*

Visitor Information

CONTACTS Columbia Gorge Tourism Alliance. ☎ *509/427–8911* ⊕ *www. visitcolumbiarivergorge.com.* **Hood-Gorge. com.** ⊕ *www.hood-gorge.com.* **Mt. Hood Territory.** ☎ *800/424–3002, 503/655–8490* ⊕ *www.mthoodterritory.com.*

Historic Columbia River Highway

U.S. 30, paralleling I–84 for 22 miles between Troutdale and Interstate Exit 35.

The oldest scenic highway in the United States is a construction marvel that integrates asphalt path with cliff, river,

and forest landscapes. Paralleling the interstate, U.S. 30 climbs to forested riverside bluffs, passes half a dozen waterfalls, and provides access to hiking trails leading to still more falls and scenic overlooks. Completed in 1922, the serpentine highway was the first paved road in the Gorge built expressly for automotive sightseers. Technically, the Historic Columbia River Highway extends some 74 miles to The Dalles, but much of that is along modern Interstate 84—the 22-mile western segment is the real draw. Along this stretch as well as some additional spans closer to Hood River, you'll find pull-outs with parking for dozens of popular day hikes, including Angel's Rest, Bridal Veil Falls, Dry Creek Falls, Latourell Falls, Wahkeena Falls, Horsetail Falls, Mitchell Point, and Starvation Creek. Sadly, the Eagle Creek Fire of 2017—begun accidentally by a careless teenager illegally using fireworks on a trail—burned about 50,000 acres of the Gorge, and a number of once popular trails (including those around Eagle Creek and Oneonta Gorge) are closed indefinitely as the forest restores itself. For an up-to-date list of trail closures and other useful information on hiking and helping to protect this beloved wilderness, visit the excellent website of **Friends of the Columbia Gorge** (⊕ *www.gorgefriends. org*).

GETTING HERE AND AROUND
U.S. 30 heads east out of downtown Troutdale, a suburb about 15 miles east of Portland, but you can also access the route from Interstate 84 along the way, via Exit 22 near Corbett, Exit 28 near Bridal Veil Falls, Exit 31 at Multnomah Falls, and Exit 35, where it rejoins the interstate.

ESSENTIALS
VISITOR INFORMATION Multnomah Falls Visitor Center. ✉ *53000 E. Historic Columbia River Hwy., Bridal Veil* ✛ *Exit 31 off I–84* ☎ *503/695–2376* ⊕ *www. multnomahfallslodge.com.* **West Columbia**

Columbia
River Gorge

WASHINGTON

TO
FALL CREEK
FALLS

Fall Creek Falls

Carson

Stevenson

Cascade Locks

Columbia Gorge Interpretive Center Museum

North Bonneville

Bonneville Dam and Fish Hatchery

Beacon Rock State Park

Washougal

Camas

Kanser Rock State Trail

Troutdale

GREATER PORTLAND

Vista House at Crown Point

Historic Columbia River Hwy.

Historic Columbia River Hwy.

Ainsworth State Park

Oneonta Gorge

Multnomah Falls

Bridge of the Gods

Pacific Coast Trail

Columbia River Gorge National Scenic Area

Wahtum Lake

Lost Lake

Lost Lake Resort

Pacific Coast Trail

Husum

141

White Salmon

Bingen

Syncline Winery

Hood

Aniche Cellars

Marchesi Vineyards

Hood River

Gorge White House

Glassometry Studio

Hood River Lavender Farm

Odell

Dee

Mt. Hood Railroad

Parkdale

Mt. Hood
see detail map

Mt. Hood National Forest

Brightwood

Mount Hood Village

Rhododendron

Government Camp

Salmon River

Pacific Coast Trail

Timothy Lake

Sandy

Boring

Estacada

Klickitat

142

Mayer State Park

Lyle

Mosier

Chenoweth

Fort Dalles Museum

The Dalles

The Dalles Dam

Columbia Gorge Discovery Center

Wasco County Historical Museum

Dallesport

14

Wishram

Celilo

84

Centerville

Goldendale

Goldendale Observatory State Park

Blockhouse

Maryhill

Maryhill Museum of Art

Rufus

Cliffs

Biggs

TO → PENDLETON

Moro

Grass Valley

Dufur

197

Columbia Gorge–Mt. Hood Scenic Highway

Tygh Valley

Wamic

Maupin

216

Wapinitia

197

TO BEND
26

Warm Springs Indian Res.

224

26

Columbia River

Hood River

White Salmon River

Wohkum Lake

Middle Fork

Mt. Hood

TO FALL CREEK FALLS

10 mi

10 km

0

0

14

30

281

35

35

26

26

224

84

Gorge Chamber of Commerce. ⊠ *107 E. Historic Columbia River Hwy., Troutdale* ☎ *503/669–7473* ⊕ *www.westcolumbiagorgechamber.com.*

Sights

★ Multnomah Falls

TRAIL | FAMILY | A 620-foot-high double-decker torrent, the second-highest year-round waterfall in the nation, Multnomah is by far the most spectacular of the Gorge cataracts east of Troutdale. You can access the falls and Multnomah Lodge via a parking lot at Exit 31 off Interstate 84, or via the Historic Columbia River Highway; from the parking area, a paved path winds to a bridge over the lower falls. A much steeper, though paved, 1.1-mile trail climbs to a viewing point overlooking the upper falls, and from here, unpaved but well-groomed trails join with others, allowing for as much as a full day of hiking in the mountains above the Gorge, if you're up for some serious but scenic trekking. Even the paved ramble to the top will get your blood pumping, but worth it to avoid the crowds that swarm the lower falls area in every season. ⊠ *53000 E. Historic Columbia River Hwy., Bridal Veil* ✛ *15 miles east of Troutdale* ☎ *503/695–2376* ⊕ *traveloregon.com.*

★ Rooster Rock State Park

NATIONAL/STATE PARK | FAMILY | The most famous beach lining the Columbia River is right below Crown Point. Three miles of sandy beaches, panoramic cascades, and a large swimming area make this a popular spot for lazing on the sand, picnicking, and hanging out with friends. Naturists appreciate that one of Oregon's two designated nude beaches is at the east end of Rooster Rock, and that it's completely secluded and clearly marked—the area has a bit of a party vibe and is hugely popular with the LGBTQ community, but all are welcome. The other section of the park, where nudity is not permitted, is also beautiful

and draws a good number of families. Rooster Rock is 9 miles east of Troutdale, accessible only via the interstate. ⊠ *I–84, Exit 25, Corbett* ☎ *503/695–2261* ⊕ *www.oregonstateparks.org* 🖃 *$5 parking.*

★ Vista House at Crown Point

BUILDING | A two-tier octagonal structure perched on the edge of this 730-foot-high cliff offers unparalleled 30-mile views up and down the Columbia River Gorge. The building dates to 1917, its rotunda and lower level filled with displays about the Gorge and the highway. Vista House's architect Edgar Lazarus was the brother of Emma Lazarus, author of the poem displayed at the base of the Statue of Liberty. ⊠ *40700 E. Historic Columbia River Hwy., Corbett* ✛ *10 miles east of Troutdale* ☎ *503/344–1368* ⊕ *www.vistahouse.com.*

 Restaurants

Multnomah Falls Lodge

$$ | AMERICAN | Vaulted ceilings, stone fireplaces, and exquisite views of Multnomah Falls are complemented by friendly service and reliably good American fare at this landmark restaurant, which is listed on the National Register of Historic Places. Consider the smoked salmon starter with apple-huckleberry compote, cod fish-and-chips, or the elk burger with aged Tillamook cheddar and garlic-sesame mayo. **Known for:** amazing waterfall views; Sunday champagne brunch; scenic patio. 🖇 *Average main: $22* ⊠ *53000 Historic Columbia River Hwy., Bridal Veil* ✛ *Exit 31 off I–84, 15 miles east of Troutdale* ☎ *503/695–2376* ⊕ *www.multnomahfallslodge.com.*

★ Sugarpine Drive-In

$ | MODERN AMERICAN | This modern take on a classic drive-in is a fantastic first stop when setting out from Portland for a drive along the Historic Columbia River Highway—it adjoins a leafy park in Troutdale overlooking the Sandy River.

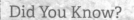

Did You Know?

The Columbia River Highway travels over graceful stone bridges built by Italian immigrant masons and winds through quiet forest glades. More than a dozen waterfalls pour over fern- and lichen-covered cliffs in a 10-mile stretch, including Multnomah Falls (pictured), the second-highest year-round waterfall in the nation.

Favorites from the creative menu of locally sourced fare include pulled-pork barbecue sandwiches, seasonal harvest veggie salads, and the Larch Mountain sundae with vanilla and chocolate soft serve, blondie brownie, blueberry-lavender sauce, and pine-nut honeycomb crunch. **Known for:** creative soft-serve sundaes; craft beer and artisanal ciders; creative locavore-driven food. [$] *Average main: $13* ✉ *1208 E. Historic Columbia River Hwy., Troutdale* ☎ *503/665–6558* 🌐 *www.sugarpinedrivein.com* 🕒 *Closed Tues. and Wed.*

Hotels

★ McMenamins Edgefield

$ | RESORT | Set in 74 acres of gardens, murals, orchards, and vineyards, this Georgian Revival manor—once home to the county poor farm—is now an offbeat resort that offers intriguing amenities and large but basic rooms filled with vintage furnishings; some rooms are hostel-style or have shared baths. **Pros:** plenty of eating and drinking choices; on-site movie theater and live-music concerts; great spa. **Cons:** this busy place can get pretty crowded; no TVs, phones, or air-conditioning in the rooms; most rooms share baths. [$] *Rooms from: $145* ✉ *2126 S.W. Halsey St., Troutdale* ☎ *503/669–8610, 800/669–8610* 🌐 *www.mcmenamins.com/edgefield* 🛏 *114 rooms* 🍴 *No meals.*

Cascade Locks

13 miles east of Multnomah Falls on Historic Columbia River Hwy. and I–84; 30 miles east of Troutdale on I–84.

In pioneer days, boats needing to pass the bedeviling rapids near the town of Whiskey Flats had to portage around them. The locks that gave the town its new name were completed in 1896, allowing waterborne passage for the first time. In 1938 they were submerged beneath the new Lake Bonneville when the Bonneville Lock and Dam became one of the most massive Corps of Engineers projects to come out of the New Deal. The town of Cascade Locks hung onto its name, though. A historic stern-wheeler still leads excursions up and down the river from the town's port district, and the region's Native American tribes still practice traditional dip-net fishing near the current locks.

GETTING HERE AND AROUND

Cascade Locks is 45 miles east of Portland and 20 miles west of Hood River on Interstate 84. The town is also home to Bridge of the Gods ($2 toll), which featured prominently in the 2014 movie *Wild* and is the only auto bridge that spans the Columbia River (it connects with Stevenson, Washington) between Portland and Hood River.

Sights

Bonneville Dam

DAM | FAMILY | President Franklin D. Roosevelt dedicated the first federal dam to span the Columbia in 1937. Its generators (visible from a balcony on a self-guided tour or up close during free guided tours offered daily in summer and on weekends the rest of the year) have a capacity of more than a million kilowatts, enough to supply power to more than 200,000 single-family homes. There's an extensive visitor center on Bradford Island, complete with underwater windows where gaggles of kids watch migrating salmon and steelhead as they struggle up fish ladders. The best viewing times are between April and October. In recent years the dwindling runs of wild Columbia salmon have made the dam a subject of much environmental controversy. ✉ *I–84, Exit 40* ✥ *Follow signs 1 mile to visitor center* ☎ *541/374–8820* 🌐 *www.nwp.usace.army.mil.*

Bonneville Fish Hatchery

FISH HATCHERY | FAMILY | Built in 1909 and operated by the Oregon Department of Fish & Wildlife, the largest state-operated fish hatchery is next door to Bonneville Dam. Visitors can view the fishponds in which Chinook, coho, and steelhead spawn—October and November are the most prolific times. Other ponds hold rainbow trout (which visitors can feed) and mammoth Columbia River sturgeon, some exceeding 10 feet in length. ✉ *70543 N.E. Herman Loop* ✣ *Off exit 40 of I–84* ☎ *541/374–8393* 🌐 *www.myodfw.com.*

Cascade Locks Marine Park and Portland Spirit Cruises

LIGHTHOUSE | This riverfront park is the home port of the 500-passenger stern-wheeler *Columbia Gorge*, which churns upriver, then back again, on one- and two-hour excursions through some of the Columbia River Gorge's most impressive scenery, mid-May to early October; brunch and dinner cruises are also available. The ship's captain discusses the Gorge's fascinating 40-million-year geology and pioneering spirits and legends, such as Lewis and Clark, who once triumphed over this very same river. The park itself, which includes a pedestrian bridge to leafy and tranquil Thunder Island, is a lovely spot for picnicking. ✉ *Marine Park, S.W. Portage Rd.* ☎ *503/224–3900* 🌐 *www.portlandspirit.com* 🎟 *Cruises from $28* ✍ *Reservations essential.*

🍴 Restaurants

Brigham Fish Market

$$ | SEAFOOD | This casual seafood market is a great stop for fish and shellfish to go—maybe to enjoy on a hike or a picnic at Rooster Rock—but there's casual seating to dine in. Fish-and-chips are available with several different proteins (halibut, cod, clam, and—most cherished of all—Columbia River salmon), and there are three kinds of chowder, as well as ceviche and a great selection of po'boy sandwiches. **Known for:** fish-and-chips with Columbia River salmon; three kinds of seafood chowder; great takeout spot when exploring the Historic Columbia River Hwy. [$] *Average main: $17* ✉ *681 Wa Na Pa St.* ☎ *541/374–9340* 🌐 *www.brighamfish.com* ⏲ *Closed Wed. No dinner.*

★ **Thunder Island Brewing**

$ | AMERICAN | Hikers, boaters, and others exploring the Gorge gather at this laid-back, funky brewpub that in 2019 moved into striking new contemporary building overlooking the Columbia River, the Bridge of the Gods, and the little island for which the brewery is named. Order a glass of hoppy Pacific Crest Trail Pale Ale or malty Scotch Porter, and enjoy it with one of the light dishes from the pub menu. **Known for:** great beer from on-site brewery; cheese platters and hummus plates; stellar river views from outdoor dining area. [$] *Average main: $10* ✉ *601 Wa Na Pa St.* ☎ *971/231–4599* 🌐 *www.thunderislandbrewing.com.*

🛏 Hotels

Best Western Plus Columbia River Inn

$ | HOTEL | The draw here is an enviable setting with great views of the Columbia River and Bridge of the Gods—many rooms, which are done in soft tans and grays and hung with framed black-and-white photos of the Gorge, overlook the river, as does a deck in back and the breakfast room. **Pros:** excellent river views; handy location midway between Portland and Hood River; spotless, modern rooms. **Cons:** cookie-cutter furnishings; some rooms face away from the river; no restaurant. [$] *Rooms from: $140* ✉ *735 Wa Na Pa St.* ☎ *541/374–8777, 800/780–7234* 🌐 *www.bwcolumbiariverinn.com* 🛏 *62 rooms* 🍴 *Free breakfast.*

Activities

HIKING
Pacific Crest Trail
HIKING/WALKING | Cascade Locks bustles with grubby thru-hikers refueling along the 2,650-mile Canada-to-Mexico Pacific Crest Trail, which was immortalized in the 2014 movie *Wild* starring Reese Witherspoon. Check out a scenic and strenuous portion of it, heading south from the trailhead at Herman Creek Horse Camp, just east of town. The route heads up into the Cascades, showing off monster views of the Gorge. Backpackers out for a longer trek will find idyllic campsites at Wahtum Lake, 14 miles south. You can also access the trail from the free parking area at Toll House Park, by the Bridge of the Gods. ☒ *Off N.W. Forest La.* ✛ *1 mile east of downtown* ☎ *541/308–1700* ⊕ *www.pcta.org.*

Stevenson, Washington

Across the river from Cascade Locks via the Bridge of the Gods and 1 mile east on Hwy. 14.

With the Bridge of the Gods toll bridge spanning the Columbia River above the Bonneville Dam, Stevenson acts as a sort of "twin city" to Cascade Locks on the Oregon side. Tribal legends and the geologic record tell of the original Bridge of the Gods, a substantial landslide that occurred here sometime between AD 1000 and 1760, briefly linking the two sides of the Gorge before the river swept away the debris. The landslide's steel namesake now leads to tiny Stevenson, where a quiet Main Street is lined with a few casual eateries and shops. Washington's Highway 14 runs through the middle of town, and since the cliffs on the Oregon side are more dramatic, driving this two-lane highway actually offers better views. About 5 miles east and slightly north, the village of Carson also has a handful of notable businesses

and is a good access point to hiking north of the Gorge in Gifford Pinchot National Forest.

GETTING HERE AND AROUND
From the Oregon side of the Gorge, cross the Columbia River at the Bridge of the Gods ($2 toll).

ESSENTIALS
VISITOR INFORMATION Skamania County Chamber of Commerce. ☒ *167 N.W. 2nd St., Stevenson* ☎ *509/427–8911, 800/989–9178* ⊕ *www.skamania.org.*

⊙ Sights

★ Beacon Rock State Park
NATIONAL/STATE PARK | For several hundred years this 848-foot rock was a landmark for river travelers, including Native Americans, who recognized this point as the last rapids of the Columbia River. Lewis and Clark are thought to have been the first white men to see the volcanic remnant. Even most casual hikers can make the steep but safe trek up to the top of the rock—allow about 45–60 minutes round-trip. More serious hikers should head to the trailhead for Hamilton Mountain, which is reached via a beautiful, though arduous, 8-mile ramble over a roaring waterfall, through dense temperate rain forest, and finally up to the 2,400-foot summit with breathtaking views up and down the Gorge. ☒ *34841 Hwy. 14, Skamania* ✛ *7 miles west of Bridge of the Gods* ☎ *509/427–8265* ⊕ *www.parks.wa.gov* ⊠ *$10 parking.*

Bridge of the Gods
BRIDGE/TUNNEL | For a magnificent vista 135 feet above the Columbia, as well as a short and quick (despite its 15 mph speed limit) route between Oregon and Washington, $2 will pay your way over the grandly named bridge that Reese Witherspoon memorably strolled across in the 2014 movie *Wild*. Hikers cross the bridge from Oregon to reach the Washington segment of the **Pacific Crest Trail**, which picks up just west of the bridge.

✉ *Off Hwy. 14, Stevenson* 🌐 *portofcascadelocks.org/bridge-of-the-gods/.*

Columbia Gorge Interpretive Center Museum

MUSEUM | FAMILY | A petroglyph whose eyes seem to look straight at you, "She Who Watches" or "Tsagaglalal" is the logo for this museum. Sitting among the dramatic basaltic cliffs on the north bank of the Columbia River Gorge, the museum explores the life of the Gorge: its history, culture, architecture, legends, and much more. Younger guests enjoy the reenactment of the Gorge's formation in the DeGroote Theater, and the 37-foot-high fish wheel, a device like a mill wheel equipped with baskets for catching fish, from the 19th century. Historians appreciate studying the water route of the Lewis and Clark Expedition. There's also an eye-opening exhibit that examines current environmental impacts on the area. ✉ *990 S.W. Rock Creek Dr., Stevenson* ☎ *509/427–8211, 800/991–2338* 🌐 *www.columbiagorge.org* 🎟 *$10.*

🍴 Restaurants

Big River Grill

$$ | AMERICAN | A tradition with hikers, bikers, fishermen, and scenic drivers out exploring the Gorge, especially for weekend breakfast but also at lunch and dinnertime, this colorful roadhouse in the center of town is festooned with license plates, vintage signs, and kitschy artwork. Grab a seat at the counter or in one of the high-back wooden booths, and tuck into grilled wild salmon sandwich, home-style fried chicken with eggs, home-style meat loaf with buttermilk-garlic mashed potatoes, and other hearty, reasonably priced fare. **Known for:** grilled wild salmon sandwiches; weekend breakfast; hiker and biker crowd. [$] *Average main: $20* ✉ *192 S.W. 2nd St., Stevenson* ☎ *509/427–4888* 🌐 *www.thebigrivergrill.com.*

Cascade Room at Skamania Lodge

$$$$ | PACIFIC NORTHWEST | At Skamania Lodge's signature restaurant, with its stunning views of sky, river, and cliff scapes, the chef draws on local seafood and regionally sourced meats. Try dishes like a Dungeness crab tower with avocado, beet coulis, and basil oil; and bacon-cured Carlton Farms pork chops. **Known for:** stunning Gorge views; lavish Sunday brunch; hefty steaks and grills. [$] *Average main: $33* ✉ *Skamania Lodge, 1131 S.W. Skamania Lodge Way, Stevenson* ☎ *509/427–7700* 🌐 *www.skamania.com.*

Red Bluff Tap House

$ | AMERICAN | With exposed-brick walls, varnished wood tables, and a sleek long bar, this downtown gastropub excels both with its extensive craft-beer and drinks selection and its modern take on comfort food. Snack on shareable starters like deep-fried brussels sprouts with pork belly and apple-cider reduction and smoked salmon flatbread, while popular mains include ale-battered seasonal fish-and-chips and bacon-jam Gouda burgers. **Known for:** ample selection of craft beers and Columbia Gorge wines; fish-and-chips; tasty, shareable appetizers. [$] *Average main: $15* ✉ *256 2nd St., Stevenson* ☎ *509/427–4979* 🌐 *www.redblufftaphouse.com.*

🛏 Hotels

Carson Ridge Luxury Cabins

$$$$ | B&B/INN | For a romantic, cushy getaway in the piney woods near Gifford Pinchot National Forest, book one of these luxurious rustic-chic cabins outfitted with hot tubs and separate walk-in showers, iPod docks, DVD players, fireplaces, sitting areas, and private porches. **Pros:** serene woodland setting; fireplaces and two-person hot tubs in each cabin; across the street from Backwoods Brewing. **Cons:** in a small, slightly remote village; steep rates; not designed for kids. [$] *Rooms from: $299* ✉ *1261 Wind River Hwy.* ✣ *10-min drive northeast of*

Stevenson ☎ 509/427–7777 🌐 www.carsonridgecabins.com 🛏 10 cabins 🍴 Free breakfast.

★ Skamania Lodge

$$$ | RESORT | FAMILY | This warm, woodsy lodge on an expansive, verdant swath of forest and meadows impresses with a multitude of windows overlooking the surrounding mountains and Gorge, an outstanding array of recreational facilities, and handsome, Pacific Northwest–chic accommodations, many with fireplaces and all with views. **Pros:** secluded and totally relaxing; loads of fun outdoorsy activities; first-rate spa and dining facilities. **Cons:** expensive in high season; can get crowded; set back from the river. [$] *Rooms from: $209 ✉ 1131 S.W. Skamania Lodge Way, Stevenson ☎ 509/427–7700, 800/221–7117 🌐 www.skamania.com 🛏 254 rooms 🍴 No meals.*

Nightlife

Backwoods Brewing

BREWPUBS/BEER GARDENS | A favorite destination for well-crafted ales and reliably good pub fare before or after hiking at nearby Falls Creek Falls or venturing deeper into Gifford Pinchot National Forest, Backwoods is in the heart of the small town of Carson, a short drive northeast of Stevenson. Top brews include the crispy and piney Logyard IPA, and a seasonal Imperial Maple Porter that warms the soul on rainy winter days. ✉ *1162 Wind River Hwy., Carson ☎ 509/427–3412 🌐 www.backwoodsbrewingcompany.com.*

Walking Man Brewing

BARS/PUBS | The sunshiny patio and cozy interior are great spots for creative pizzas and sampling the dozen-or-so craft ales. After a couple of pints of the strong Homo Erectus IPA and Walking Stick Stout, you may go a little ape. Live music on summer weekends skews twangy and upbeat. ✉ *240 S.W. 1st St., Stevenson ☎ 509/427–5520 🌐 www.walkingmanbeer.com.*

Activities

HIKING

Falls Creek Falls

HIKING/WALKING | You'll find one of the most spectacular waterfall hikes in the Northwest in the Wind River section of 1½-million-acre Gifford Pinchot National Forest. The large, free parking area (with restrooms) is at the end of graded, unpaved forest road off paved Wind River Road, about 20 miles north of Stevenson. The trail meanders through dense forest and crosses a couple of sturdy suspension bridges en route to the more spectacular Lower Falls (a relatively easy 3½-mile round-trip). If you're up for more of an adventure, continue to the Upper Falls overlook, which adds about 3 more miles and makes it a loop hike—parts of this section are quite steep. ✉ *End of NF 057, Carson ✥ 16 miles north of Carson via Wind River Rd. and NF 3062 ☎ 509/395–3400 🌐 www.fs.usda.gov/main/giffordpinchot.*

Hood River

20 miles east of Cascade Locks and 60 miles east of Portland on I–84.

This picturesque riverside community of about 7,700 residents affords visitors spectacular views of the Columbia River and the snowcapped peaks of Mt. Hood and—on the Washington side—Mt. Adams. The bustling downtown of more than 40 buildings dating from the 1890s to the 1930s and more recently developed Columbia River waterfront make this charming town the Gorge's hub for dining, lodging, and shopping and a hugely popular weekend destination among Portlanders. You'll find plenty of urbane farm-to-table restaurants, up-and-coming craft breweries and wine-tasting rooms, and nicely curated boutiques and art galleries. The surrounding countryside abounds with orchards and vineyards, enticing fans of U-pick farmsteads and tasting rooms. Wineries in Hood River and also across the river from roughly White Salmon to Maryhill grow a much broader range of grapes than Oregon's famous Willamette Valley, and wine touring has become one of the area's top draws.

And then there are Hood River's recreational pursuits. For years, the incessant easterly winds blowing through town were nothing more than a slight nuisance. Then somebody bolted a sail to a surfboard, waded into the fat part of the Gorge, and a new recreational craze was born. A fortuitous combination of factors—mainly the reliable gale-force winds blowing against the current—has made Hood River the self-proclaimed windsurfing capital of the world. Especially in summer, the town swarms with colorful "boardheads" from as far away as Europe and Australia.

GETTING HERE AND AROUND

Reach Hood River from Portland via Interstate 84, or from Mt. Hood by heading 40 miles north on Highway 35.

ESSENTIALS

VISITOR INFORMATION Hood River County Chamber of Commerce. ⊠ 720 E. Port Marina Dr. ☎ 541/386–2000, 800/366–3530 ⊕ www.visithoodriver.com.

TOURS

MountNbarreL

BICYCLE TOURS | This outfitter's knowledgeable guides offer 6.5- and 8-mile wine country bike tours in two different areas of Hood River, each one stopping for tastings at wineries as well as a U-pick fruit farm. E-bike tours are also available. ⊠ Hood River ☎ 541/490–8687 ⊕ www.mountnbarrel.com ⌂ From $169.

Sol Rides Electric Bike Tours

BICYCLE TOURS | Explore the area on state-of-the-art e-bikes on the four guided excursions offered by Sol Rides. There

are two options for touring the Columbia Gorge, one trip through Hood River Valley, and a winery tour of Lyle, Washington, just across the Columbia River. ⊠ 101 Oak St. ☎ 503/939–4961 ⊕ www.solrides.com ⌂ From $99.

 # Sights

Columbia Center for the Arts

ARTS VENUE | FAMILY | Hood River's premier venue for both visual and performing arts is a great place to start your explorations of the town's growing creative scene. The center's excellent gallery presents rotating exhibits throughout the year and also offers a range of classes. And it's worth checking the CCA's calendar to see what's upcoming in the venue's theater, which offers plays, musicals, and children's theater. ⊠ 215 Cascade Ave. ☎ 541/387–8877 ⊕ www.columbiaarts.org.

★ Fruit Loop

SCENIC DRIVE | Either by car or bicycle, tour the quiet country highways of Hood River Valley, which abounds with about 30 fruit stands, a handful of U-pick berry farms, about 10 wineries, and 3 cideries. You'll see apples, pears, cherries, and peaches fertilized by volcanic soil, pure glacier water, and a conducive harvesting climate. Along the 35 miles of farms are a host of outlets for delicious baked goods, wines, flowers, and nuts. While on the loop, consider stopping in the small town of **Parkdale** to lunch, taste beer at Solera Brewery, and snap a photo of Mt. Hood's north face. ⊠ Hood River ✛ Begins just east of downtown on Hwy. 35 ⊕ www.hoodriverfruitloop.com.

★ Gorge White House

FARM/RANCH | You'll find pretty much everything the Hood River Valley is famous for growing and producing at this picturesque, century-old farm anchored by a Dutch Colonial farmhouse and surrounded by acres of U-pick flowers, apple and peach trees, and blackberry and blueberry bushes. After strolling through the farm fields, stop inside the main house to sample wines—the tasting room carries one of the largest selections of Columbia River wines in the region. Out back, there's a farm store, another tasting room serving local craft beer and cider, and a garden patio with seating and a food-truck-style café serving delicious strawberry salads, burgers, pear-cheddar pizzas, and other light fare. ⊠ 2265 Hwy. 35 ☎ 541/386–2828 ⊕ www.thegorge-whitehouse.com.

★ Historic Columbia River Highway State Trail–Mark O. Hatfield Trailheads

TRAIL | This peaceful and picturesque 4½-mile section of the old Historic Columbia River Highway begins just east of downtown Hood River at the Mark O. Hatfield West Trailhead and Visitor Center. Known as the Twin Tunnels segment, this paved trail that's closed to vehicular traffic is great for biking, jogging, or strolling. It first twists and turns upwardly through a dense ponderosa-pine forest before passing through the tunnels and descending past jagged volcanic-rock formations and semi-arid terrain into the small town of Mosier. This portion of the trail is one of a few segments of the old highway that's been converted to paved trail—there are currently about 13 miles in all, with additional sections west of Hood River with access at Starvation Creek and Veinto state parks, and well west of here in Cascade Locks, with access from the parking lot at the Bridge of the Gods. ⊠ End of Old Columbia River Rd. ✛ 2 miles east of downtown Hood River ☎ 541/387–4010 ⊕ www.oregonstateparks.org ☞ $5 parking.

Hood River Waterfront Park

CITY PARK | FAMILY | The recreational anchor of Hood River's contemporary waterfront district has been opened in phases, starting in 2010, and includes a sheltered sandy cove with a children's play area, picnic tables, a swimming beach, a launch ramp for windsurfing and stand-up paddleboarding, and access to a walking trail that connects with Waucoma Basin Marina to the west (a great spot to watch the sunset over the Gorge) and Nichols Boat Basin to the east. Events take place here and elsewhere along the park all throughout the year, and a number of hip new eateries and bars are steps away. ⊠ 650 Portway Ave. ☎ 541/387–5201 ⊕ www.hoodriverwater-front.org.

Lavender Valley

FARM/RANCH | FAMILY | During the warmer months, and especially during the late June–August full-bloom season, saunter the beautiful lavender fields of this farm near Parkdale. The small shop sells honeys, soaps, teas, and dozens of other products infused with lavender grown on-site. ⊠ 5965 Boneboro Rd., Parkdale ☎ 541/386–1906 ⊕ www.lavendervalley.com ⊙ Closed Oct.–Apr.

★ Lost Lake Resort

BODY OF WATER | One of the most-photographed spots in the region, this lake's waters reflect towering Mt. Hood and the thick forests that line its shore. Open May through mid-October, the blissfully quiet 240-acre wilderness resort in Mt. Hood National Forest offers cabins and campsites for overnight stays, but it's also a popular destination for day-use recreation, offering miles of hiking trails, as well as fishing for rainbow trout, kayaking, rowboating, stand-up paddling, swimming, canoeing, and other nonmotorized boating. There's also a camp store and a grill offering burgers, ice cream, and other light fare. ⊠ 9000 Lost Lake Rd. ✛ 25 miles southwest of Hood River via Hwy. 35 and Hwy. 281 ☎ 541/386–6366 ⊕ www.lostlakeresort.org ☞ Day use parking $9.

★ Marchesi Vineyards

WINERY/DISTILLERY | Somewhat unusual for the Pacific Northwest, this boutique winery with a small, airy tasting room and a verdant garden patio specializes in Italian varietals—Moscato, Ramato,

Dolcetto, Sangiovese, Barbera, Nebbiolo, and a few others. Owner Franco Marchesi hails from Italy's Piemonte region, and he's earned serious kudos for his finesse as a winemaker. ⊠ *3955 Belmont Dr.* ☎ *541/386–1800* ⊕ *www.marchesivineyards.com.*

Mt. Hood Railroad

SCENIC DRIVE | FAMILY | Scenic passenger excursions along a small rail line established in 1906 offer a picturesque and relaxing way to survey Mt. Hood and the Hood River Valley. Chug alongside the Hood River through vast fruit orchards before climbing up steep forested canyons, glimpsing Mt. Hood along the way. There are several trip options, from $35: a four-hour excursion (serves light concessions), dinner, brunch, and several themed trips, like murder mysteries and Old West robberies, and a family-favorite holiday-inspired Train to Christmas Town runs throughout much of November and December. The friendly service enhances the great scenery. ⊠ *110 Railroad Ave.* ☎ *541/386–3556, 800/872–4661* ⊕ *www.mthoodrr.com* ☽ *Closed Jan.–Apr.*

Mt. Hood Winery

WINERY/DISTILLERY | In addition to producing increasingly acclaimed wine—with particularly impressive Pinot Gris, dry Riesling, Zinfandel (which is seldom bottled in these parts), Pinot Noir, Barbera, and Tempranillo—this winery adjacent to the long-running Fruit Company (fruit and gift baskets) has a beautiful, contemporary tasting room with gorgeous Mt. Hood views from inside and the expansive patio. ⊠ *2882 Van Horn Dr.* ☎ *541/386–8333* ⊕ *www.mthoodwinery.com* ☽ *Closed Dec.–Feb.*

Stave & Stone Winery

WINERY/DISTILLERY | With one of the most dramatic settings of any Hood River winery, this lodge-style tasting room is a wonderful locale for sampling Stave & Stone's expressive vinos. The dry, strawberry-inflected Dorothy Pinot Noir Rosé and zesty Pinot Gris have each garnered plenty of awards, but the reds are terrific, too. If you can't make it to the vineyard, there's a cute tasting room in downtown Hood River, too. ⊠ *3827 Fletcher Dr.* ☎ *541/946–3750* ⊕ *www.staveandstone.com.*

Viento Wines

WINERY/DISTILLERY | Focused more on whites than most of the winemakers in the Gorge region, Viento has a stunning tasting room with vaulted ceilings, soaring windows, and a large patio overlooking the on-site vineyard of Riesling grapes. This is a lovely space for tasting and chatting with fellow oenophiles. Notable wines here include a crisp Grüner Veltliner, a food-friendly Brut Rosé, and one of the better Oregon Pinot Noirs you'll find in the Hood River region. ⊠ *301 Country Club Rd.* ☎ *541/386–3026* ⊕ *www.vientowines.com.*

Western Antique Aeroplane and Automobile Museum

MUSEUM | FAMILY | Housed at Hood River's tiny airport (general aviation only), the museum's impressive, meticulously restored, propeller-driven planes are all still in flying condition. The antique steam cars, Model Ts, and sleek Depression-era sedans are road-worthy, too. Periodic car shows and an annual fly-in draw thousands of history buffs and spectators. ⊠ *1600 Air Museum Rd.* ☎ *541/308–1600* ⊕ *www.waaamuseum.org* ☒ *$16.*

🍴 Restaurants

Broder Øst

$ | SCANDINAVIAN | Portland's wildly popular modern Scandinavian restaurant Broder has a branch just off the lobby of downtown's historic Hood River Hotel. Breakfast and lunch are the main event, although dinner is served during the busy summer months, and you may have to wait, especially on weekend mornings, for the chance to sample such delicacies as *abeleskivers* (Danish pancakes) with lingonberry jam and lemon curd or the open-faced gravlax (salmon) sandwich

Vineyards in the Hood River Valley

with mustard sauce. **Known for:** Danish favorites like pancakes with lingonberry sauce; covered sidewalk tables overlooking bustling Oak Street; fresh house-baked pastries (weekends only). [$] *Average main: $14* ✉ *Hood River Hotel, 102 Oak St.* ☎ *541/436–3444* 🌐 *www.brodereast.com* 🕓 *No dinner Mon. and Tues. or Sept.–May.*

Celilo Restaurant

$$$ | **PACIFIC NORTHWEST** | Refined and relaxing, this high-ceilinged restaurant in a contemporary downtown building is popular both for dinner and enjoying a glass of local wine in the bar. Notable examples of the kitchen's deftly crafted Pacific Northwest fare, which emphasizes seasonal ingredients, include pan-seared scallops over goat cheese spaetzle and tender pork schnitzel with house-made choucroute garnie (a traditional Alsatian dish of sauerkraut and sausages). **Known for:** one of the best local wine lists in the Gorge; attractive sidewalk seating; lively and inviting bar. [$] *Average main: $28* ✉ *16 Oak St.* ☎ *541/386–5710* 🌐 *www.celilorestaurant.com* 🕓 *No lunch Mon.–Thurs. or Nov.–Apr.*

Doppio Coffee + Lounge

$ | **CAFÉ** | Sunshine fills the small dining room and outdoor seating area of this high-ceilinged, contemporary downtown coffee bar that serves fine espresso drinks as well as local wines and craft beers. It's great for light snacking—there's a nice selection of baked goods and fine chocolates—but there are also substantial grilled panini sandwiches, salads, and soups. **Known for:** rich Ghiradelli hot chocolate; great selection of Columbia Gorge wines by the glass; delicious breakfast sandwiches. [$] *Average main: $8* ✉ *310 Oak St.* ☎ *541/386–3000* 🌐 *www.doppiohoodriver.com* 🕓 *No dinner.*

★ Kin

$$ | **MODERN EUROPEAN** | This intimate and charming downtown bistro offers a short but enticing menu of beautifully prepared modern European dishes, such as grilled bread topped with raclette cheese and

smoked paprika, and duck confit with sauerkraut, potato, and bacon. Save room for the pot de crème. **Known for:** friendly service; small but well-chosen wine selection; intimate, romantic space. [$] *Average main: $20* ✉ *110 5th St.* ☎ *541/387–0111* 🌐 *www.kineatery.com* 🕒 *Closed Mon. and Tues. No lunch.*

★ Pfriem Family Brewers

$ | **PACIFIC NORTHWEST** | Inside a striking contemporary building on the Columbia River, Pfriem (pronounced "freem") is all about the marriage of Belgium's brewing traditions and Oregon's distinctive, often hoppy, styles. But the on-site restaurant serves stellar pub fare, too, including mussels and fries, lentil burgers with grilled-leek aioli, and house-made bratwurst—it's a legit dining option even if you're not a big fan of craft beer. **Known for:** well-crafted Belgian-influenced beers; plenty of veggie options; dog-friendly patio with fire pit. [$] *Average main: $15* ✉ *707 Portway Ave.* ☎ *541/321–0490* 🌐 *www.pfriembeer.com.*

★ Solstice Wood Fire Pizza Café

$$ | **PIZZA** | This snazzy, high-ceilinged space along the Hood River waterfront is wildly popular for its wood-fire-grilled pizzas with unusual toppings—such as the Cherry Girl, layered with local cherries, spicy chorizo, goat cheese, mozzarella, and marinara sauce. There are several tasty salads, apps, and non-pizza entrées, too, as well as tantalizing wood-fired s'mores for dessert. **Known for:** creative pizzas; wood-fired mac 'n' cheese; wood-fired s'mores. [$] *Average main: $18* ✉ *501 Portway Ave.* ☎ *541/436–0800* 🌐 *www.solsticewoodfirecafe.com* 🕒 *Closed Tues.*

Hotels

Best Western Plus Hood River Inn

$$ | **HOTEL** | This low-slung, rambling hotel beside the Hood River Bridge offers some of the best river views of any hotel in the Gorge, and many units have private balconies or patios on the water; the deluxe accommodations have full kitchens, fireplaces, and Jacuzzi tubs. **Pros:** riverfront location with great views; good restaurant and lounge; spacious rooms. **Cons:** a little pricey in summer; downtown shopping and dining not within walking distance; room decor is a bit cookie-cutter. [$] *Rooms from: $170* ✉ *1108 E. Marina Way* ☎ *541/386–2200, 800/828–7873* 🌐 *www.hoodriverinn.com* 🛏 *194 rooms* 🍴 *Free breakfast.*

★ Columbia Cliff Villas Hotel

$$ | **HOTEL** | **FAMILY** | This elegant condo-style compound on a sheer cliff overlooking the Columbia River contains some of the plushest accommodations in the region—units have one to three bedrooms, fireplaces, terraces or patios, stone-and-tile bathrooms, and fine linens. **Pros:** private apartment-style accommodations; great river views; sophisticated decor and top-flight amenities. **Cons:** no restaurant or fitness center on-site; need a car to get into town; some rooms experience highway noise. [$] *Rooms from: $199* ✉ *3880 Westcliff Dr.* ☎ *541/490–8081, 866/912–8366* 🌐 *www.columbiacliffvillas.com* 🛏 *37 suites* 🍴 *No meals.*

Columbia Gorge Hotel & Spa

$$$ | **HOTEL** | Charming though somewhat dated-looking period-style rooms at this grande dame of Gorge hotels are fitted out with plenty of wood, brass, and antiques and overlook the Gorge, impeccably landscaped formal gardens, or a 208-foot-high waterfall. **Pros:** historic structure built by Columbia Gorge Highway visionary Simon Benson; unbeatable Gorge views; full-service spa. **Cons:** smallish rooms with rather dated decor; rooms facing away from river pick up noise from nearby Interstate 84; often books up with weddings on summer and fall weekends. [$] *Rooms from: $219* ✉ *4000 Westcliff Dr.* ☎ *541/386–5566, 800/345–1921* 🌐 *www.columbiagorgehotel.com* 🛏 *40 rooms* 🍴 *No meals.*

Hood River Hotel

$ | **HOTEL** | In the heart of the lively and hip business district, steps from great restaurants and shops, this handsomely restored 1911 boutique hotel has a grand, Old West facade, behind which are simple rooms with tasteful period-style antiques and a few larger suites that have kitchenettes and large sitting rooms. **Pros:** excellent downtown location; good-value rafting and ski packages; antiques-heavy interiors have feel of a European inn. **Cons:** smallish rooms; no king-size beds; rooms in back have great river views but tend to receive some freeway noise. [$] *Rooms from: $99* ✉ *102 Oak St.* ☎ *541/386–1900* 🌐 *www.hoodriverhotel.com* 🛏 *41 rooms* 🍴 *Free breakfast.*

★ **Sakura Ridge**

$$$ | **B&B/INN** | Located on a 72-acre farm on the south side of town, the five warm but sleekly furnished rooms at this contemporary lodge-style B&B offer magical panoramas of Mt. Hood, and the inn's gorgeous gardens, amid a welcome absence of clutter. **Pros:** spectacular mountain views; rustic yet urbane decor; lush gardens and orchards on the grounds. **Cons:** secluded location is a 15-minute drive from downtown; closed in winter. [$] *Rooms from: $225* ✉ *5601 York Hill Rd.* ☎ *541/386–2636, 877/472–5872* 🌐 *www.sakuraridge.com* 🕒 *Closed Nov.–Mar.* 🛏 *5 rooms* 🍴 *Free breakfast.*

Nightlife

★ **Camp 1805**

BARS/PUBS | Yet another delicious reason to spend time around Hood River's sleek new waterfront district, this artisanal producer of rum, vodka, and bracing white whiskey offers an interesting menu of creative cocktails, from new-school mai tais to soothing drinks made with CBD-infused mint oil or elderflower-lavender bitters. There's a noteworthy food menu, too, with pulled-pork nachos and smoked tri-tip sandwiches leading the charge. ✉ *501 Portway Ave., Suite 102* ☎ *541/386–1805* 🌐 *www.camp1805.com.*

Double Mountain Brewery & Taproom

BREWPUBS/BEER GARDENS | Notable for its European-style beers, including the rich Black Irish Stout and the refreshing Kölsch, Double Mountain also produces seasonal cherry-infused Kriek ales and a hoppy India Red Ale. The bustling, homey downtown taproom is also a great source for pizzas, salads, and sandwiches. There's a second location in Portland. ✉ *8 4th St.* ☎ *541/387–0042* 🌐 *www.doublemountainbrewery.com.*

★ **Ferment Brewing Company**

BREWPUBS/BEER GARDENS | One of the latest venues to further Hood River's reputation as something of a mini Brewvana, Ferment uses traditional farmhouse techniques to craft complex beers as well as kombucha, from Bavarian-inspired smoked dunkelweisse to Japanese-style sensa kombucha. The gorgeous, airy tasting room has huge windows overlooking the waterfront, and the kitchen turns out tasty gastropub fare. ✉ *403 Portway Ave.* ☎ *541/436–3499* 🌐 *www.fermentbrewing.com.*

Full Sail Tasting Room and Pub

BARS/PUBS | A glass-walled microbrewery with a windswept deck overlooking the Columbia, Full Sail was a pioneer brewpub in Oregon, helping to put Hood River on the map as a major beer hub. Free, on-site brewery tours are given during the afternoons. ✉ *506 Columbia St.* ☎ *541/386–2247* 🌐 *www.fullsailbrewing.com.*

Activities

KAYAKING

Gorge Paddling Center

KAYAKING | Whether you want to practice your Eskimo roll in the safety of a pool, run the Klickitat River in an inflatable kayak, or try out a stand-up paddleboard on the Columbia, the Gorge's premier kayak guides can arrange the trip or rent you the equipment you need. ⊠ *101 N. 1st St.* ☎ *541/806–4190* ⊕ *www.gorgekayaker. com.*

WINDSURFING
Big Winds

WINDSURFING | The retail hub for Hood River's windsurfing and kiteboarding culture also rents gear and provides windsurfing lessons for beginners. Lessons and clinics begin at $89 for windsurfing, and $49 for stand-up paddling. ⊠ *207 Front St.* ☎ *541/386–6086, 888/509–4210* ⊕ *www. bigwinds.com.*

White Salmon, Washington

5 miles north of Hood River on Hwy. 14.

Tiny White Salmon, which sits on a bluff with commanding views of the Columbia River as well as the town of Hood River, is handy for exploring the Washington side of the eastern end of the Gorge. A few noteworthy restaurants and shops in the village center cater to hikers, kayakers, and wine- and beer-tasting aficionados checking out this quieter but similarly scenic counterpart to Hood River. Just down the hill in the tiny adjacent village of Bingen, you'll find increasingly more tourism-related businesses. Several first-rate wineries offer tastings in the nearby rural communities of Underwood (just west) and Lyle (just east) along Highway 14. There's also excellent hiking and white-water rafting in the vicinity, and if you drive north of town about 20 miles on Highway 141, you'll reach secluded Trout Lake, the access point for hiking and recreation in and around 12,281-foot Mt. Adams, a soaring "twin" of Mt. Hood that's similarly visible from many points in the Gorge.

GETTING HERE AND AROUND

You reach White Salmon by driving across the Hood River Bridge (toll $2), turning east onto Highway 14, and then north in the small village of Bingen onto Highway 141—it's a 10-minute drive from Hood River. Amtrak's *Empire Builder* also stops once a day in each direction in Bingen–White Salmon, en route from Portland to Spokane.

ESSENTIALS

CONTACTS Mt. Adams Chamber of Commerce. ⊠ *1 Heritage Plaza, White Salmon* ⊹ *Off Hwy. 14, just west of Hood River Bridge* ☎ *509/493–3630* ⊕ *www.mtad-amschamber.com.*

 Sights

Aniche Cellars

WINERY/DISTILLERY | Just a short drive west of White Salmon, this friendly boutique winery has one of the prettiest tasting-room settings in the area—it's high on Underwood Mountain, with outdoor seating that affords spectacular views looking east toward Hood River and deep into the Gorge. The cleverly named wines here—Puck, an Albarino, and Three Witches, a Rhône-style blend of Cinsault, Carignan, and Counoise—are paired with little amuse-bouche-style nibbles, typically chocolate, prosciutto, or fruit. ⊠ *71 Little Buck Creek Rd., Underwood* ☎ *360/624–6531* ⊕ *www.anichecellars. com* ⊘ *Closed Mon. and Tues.*

Catherine Creek Recreation Area

NATIONAL/STATE PARK | Administered by the U.S. Forest Service, this ruggedly beautiful patch of wilderness in generally sunny and dry Lyle, less than 2 miles east of Coyote Wall, comprises a well-signed network of trails through what had been a sprawling ranch. This is one of the top spots in the region for wildflower viewing in the spring, but there's plenty to see and do here year-round. A paved multiuse trail curves down along a bluff overlooking the river, while longer trails meander up into the foothills. ✉ *Old Hwy. 8, Lyle* ✛ *1½ miles east of junction with Hwy. 14* ☎ *541/308–1700* ⊕ *www.fs.usda.gov/ recarea/crgnsa/recarea.*

COR Cellars
WINERY/DISTILLERY | Appreciated for its sleek, glass-walled tasting room and landscaped courtyard as well as for producing complex, eclectic wines, COR is one of several excellent Lyle wineries. The Cabernet Franc is one of the best in the state, but don't overlook the distinctive Merlot-Malbec and co-fermented Pinot Gris and Gewürztraminer blends. ✉ *151 Old Hwy. 8, Lyle* ☎ *509/365–2744* ⊕ *www.corcellars.com* ☾ *Closed Tues. and Wed.*

★ Coyote Wall–Labyrinth Loop
TRAIL | The Coyote Wall trail, accessed about 5 miles east of town off Highway 14, affords hikers unobstructed views of the Columbia River and the surrounding mountains, including Mt. Hood. The trail leads from a disused section of roadway up a gradual slope, through tall grass and wildflower meadows, from sea level up the side of a sheer cliff that rises to about 1,900 feet elevation. You can descend the way you came up or by looping back down through an intriguing valley of basalt rock formations (known as the Labyrinth)—the full round-trip is about 8 miles, but you could hike part of the way up the trail and back, taking in the impressive vistas, in less than an hour. ✉ *Old Hwy. 8 at Courtney Rd., White Salmon.*

★ Savage Grace Wines
WINERY/DISTILLERY | Celebrated Woodinville winemaker Michael Savage opened this intimate tasting room at the vineyard on which he grows the grapes in several of his most acclaimed bottles, including a vibrant Riesling, a lean and elegant Pinot Noir, and an earthy Grüner Veltliner. Enjoy the sweeping Gorge and Mt. Hood views while you sip. ✉ *442 Kramer Rd., Underwood* ☎ *206/920–4206* ⊕ *www.*

savagegracewines.com ☾ *Closed Mon.–Thurs.*

★ Syncline Wines
WINERY/DISTILLERY | The focus at this intimate winery with lovely seating set among beautiful gardens is predominantly on elegant, full-bodied Rhône-style wines. The friendly, knowledgeable tasting room has garnered plenty of awards for its aromatic Cuvée Elena Grenache-Syrah-Mourvèdre blend, as well as a first-rate stand-alone Syrah, and several racy, dry whites—Picpoul, Grenache Blanc, Grüner Veltliner—that seem tailor-made for the Gorge's warm summer nights. Note that several other outstanding small wineries—Domaine Pouillon and Tetrahedron among them—are in the same rural town, 10 miles east of White Salmon. ✉ *111 Balch Rd., Lyle* ☎ *509/365–4361* ⊕ *www.synclinewine. com* ☾ *Closed Mon.–Wed.*

🍴 Restaurants

Feast Market & Delicatessen
$ | PACIFIC NORTHWEST | Although this handsome space with Edison lights and a tile-back bar fits the bill when you're seeking wines and food (coffee, cheeses, sandwiches, prepared foods, cookies) to go, it's also an inviting dine-in restaurant with a spacious back patio offering glorious views of Mt. Hood. The kitchen sources regionally to create many of the enticing dishes, including roasted bone marrow with chimichurri and sea-salt grilled bread, and pan-seared Columbia salmon with red quinoa, leeks, and a pomegranate vinaigrette. **Known for:** gourmet groceries and sandwiches to go; superb beer and wine list; patio views of Mt. Hood. 💲 *Average main: $15* ✉ *151 E. Jewett Blvd., White Salmon* ☎ *509/637–6886* ⊕ *www.feastmarket.org* ☾ *Closed Sun. No dinner Mon. and Tues.*

Henni's Kitchen & Bar

$$ | **PACIFIC NORTHWEST** | This warm and inviting neighborhood bistro serves well-priced, creatively prepared international fare with a decided Northwest focus—think broccolini with sumac and mint raita, salmon cakes with kimchi and remoulade, and Goat-style organic-chicken yellow curry. The bar serves terrific, innovative cocktails, and food prices during the weekday evening (5–6 pm) happy hour represent one of the best deals around. **Known for:** excellent cocktails; inventive food; fun, lively ambience. [$] *Average main: $21* ✉ *120 E. Jewett Blvd., White Salmon* ☎ *509/493–1555* 🌐 *www.henniskitchenandbar.com* 🕓 *No lunch.*

★ White Salmon Baking Co

$ | **BAKERY** | The formidable redbrick, wood-fired oven toward the back of this artisanal bakery's airy dining room hints at the delicious treats on offer here, from local-mushroom scrambles over rustic toast in the morning to line-caught-albacore melts and house-made falafel-and-beet-kraut sandwiches at lunch. There's also a vast selection of savory breads, chewy cookies, and a nice selection of espresso drinks, beers, and wines. **Known for:** made-to-order tartines, frittatas, and toasts; wood-fired savory breads and sweets; Monday pizza nights. [$] *Average main: $9* ✉ *80 N.E. Estes Ave., White Salmon* ☎ *509/281–3140* 🌐 *www.whitesalmonbaking.com* 🕓 *Closed Tues. No dinner.*

Hotels

Lyle Hotel

$ | **HOTEL** | Built in the early 20th century a block from still very active train tracks (rooms are equipped with ear plugs), this friendly and slightly quirky 10-room boutique hotel is a well-situated and affordable base for exploring the many exceptional wineries between Lyle and Maryhill. **Pros:** short drive from several excellent wineries; terrific bar and restaurant on-site; reasonably priced. **Cons:** noise from passing trains; need a car to get around; rooms have shared bathrooms. [$] *Rooms from: $110* ✉ *100 7th St., Lyle* ☎ *509/365–5953* 🌐 *www.thelylehotel.com* 🛏 *10 rooms* 🍴 *No meals.*

★ Society Hotel Bingen

$$ | **HOTEL** | This stylish but unpretentious Scandinavian-inspired compound—a converted 1937 schoolhouse and a ring of sleek cabins set around a spa and bathhouse—is a perfect base for hiking, wine touring, and chilling out on the Washington side of the Columbia Gorge. **Pros:** stunning contemporary design; soothing bathhouse with hot tubs and sauna; kitchenettes in cabins. **Cons:** some rooms share bath; not within walking distance of many restaurants; bathhouse can get crowded on weekends. [$] *Rooms from: $155* ✉ *210 N. Cedar St., Bingen* ☎ *509/774–4437* 🌐 *www.thesocietyhotel.com* 🛏 *30 rooms* 🍴 *No meals.*

Nightlife

Everybody's Brewing

BREWPUBS/BEER GARDENS | Head to this stylish downtown brewpub with a back patio overlooking Mt. Hood for seriously impressive beers, with the potent Cryo IPA and roasty and rich Cash Oatmeal Stout leading the way. There's live music many evenings, and tasty pub fare, too. ✉ *177 E. Jewett Blvd., White Salmon* ☎ *509/637–2774* 🌐 *www.everybodysbrewing.com.*

Activities

WHITE-WATER RAFTING

Wet Planet Whitewater

KAYAKING | This outfitter just outside White Salmon offers half- and full-day white-water rafting trips on the White Salmon, Wind, Klickitat, Farmlands, Hood, and Tieton rivers, which rank among some of the top waterways for this activity in the region. The Wind and

Hood rivers contain stretches of hairy Class IV–Class V rapids (previous experience is required), but the other trips are suitable for beginners. The company also offers kayaking instruction and trips. ☒ *860 Hwy. 141, Husum* ☎ *509/493–8989, 877/390–9445* ⊕ *www.wetplanetwhitewater.com.*

The Dalles

20 miles east of Hood River on I–84.

The seat of Wasco County and the economic hub of the region, The Dalles lies on a crescent bend of the Columbia River where it narrows and once spilled over a series of rapids, creating a flagstone effect. French voyagers christened it *dalle,* or "flagstone." The town gained fame early in the region's history as the town where the Oregon Trail branched, with some pioneers departing to travel over Mt. Hood on Barlow Road and the others continuing down the Columbia River. This may account for the small-town, Old West feeling that still permeates the area. In this workaday town, you'll find some excellent museums as well as a mix of independent and chain restaurants and hotels. As you're strolling around, watch for the eight historic downtown murals that depict important events in Oregon's past.

GETTING HERE AND AROUND

From Hood River, it's a 22-mile drive east on Interstate 84 to reach The Dalles. Alternatively, you can take the slightly slower and more scenic Highway 14, on the Washington side of the Columbia, from White Salmon to U.S. 197, which leads you into town via The Dalles Bridge.

ESSENTIALS

VISITOR INFORMATION Dalles Area Chamber of Commerce. ☒ *404 W. 2nd St.* ☎ *541/296–2231, 800/255–3385* ⊕ *www.thedalleschamber.com.*

👁 Sights

★ Analemma Winery

WINERY/DISTILLERY | It's worth the trip to the rugged Mosier Hills, midway between The Dalles and Hood River, to enjoy some sips at this serene winery and tasting room that's developed a cult following for its exceptional wines. Using grapes grown at upwards of 1,800 feet in elevation, Analemma produces superb Pinot Noir, Gewürztraminer, and Mosier Hills Tinto, a sleek Grenache-Tempranillo-Syrah blend. ☒ *1120 State Rd., Mosier* ☎ *541/478–2873* ⊕ *www.analemmawines.com* ⊘ *Closed Mon.–Thurs. and Oct.–Mar.*

Columbia Gorge Discovery Center & Museum

MUSEUM | **FAMILY** | Exhibits and artwork at this expansive, contemporary museum just off Interstate 84 as you approach The Dalles from the west highlight the geological history of the Columbia Gorge, back 40 million years when volcanoes, landslides, and floods carved out the area. History exhibits focus on 10,000 years of Native American life and exploration of the region by white settlers, from Lewis and Clark to the early-20th-century engineers who developed the Historic Columbia River Highway. ☒ *5000 Discovery Dr.* ☎ *541/296–8600* ⊕ *www.gorgediscovery.org* 🎫 *$9.*

The Dalles Lock and Dam

DAM | At this hydroelectric dam 50 miles east of the Bonneville Dam, you can tour a visitor center, which is located on the Oregon side of the river at Seufert Park, with surprisingly even-handed exhibits presenting differing perspectives on the Columbia River dams, with input from farmers, utility companies, environmentalists, and indigenous tribes. There's also a surreal live feed of salmon and sturgeon scaling the fish ladder. Call ahead for the guided tours, which include the powerhouse and fish ladder, offered most weekends. Photo ID required. ☒ *3545*

Bret Clodfelter Way ✣ *2 miles east of The Dalles, off I-84, Exit 87* ☎ *541/296–9778* 🌐 *www.nwp.usace.army.mil/The-Dalles* 🎫 *Free* 🕒 *Closed Oct.–Apr. and Mon.–Thurs. in May and Sept.*

Fort Dalles Museum

MUSEUM | The 1856-vintage Fort Dalles Surgeon's Quarters ranks among the state's oldest history museums. The first visitors came through the doors in 1905. On display in authentic hand-hewn log buildings, originally part of a military base, are the personal effects of some of the region's settlers and a collection of early automobiles. The entrance fee gains you admission to the Swedish log-style **Anderson Homestead** museum across the street, which also displays pioneer artifacts. ✉ *500 W. 15th St.* ☎ *541/296–4547* 🌐 *www.fortdallesmuseum.org* 🎫 *$8* 🕒 *Closed except by appointment Nov.–Feb.*

★ National Neon Sign Museum

MUSEUM | **FAMILY** | Dozens of dazzling, in many cases strikingly ornate, neon signs that have been designed from the late-19th through the mid-20th centuries are displayed in this handsomely restored 20,000-square-foot former Elks Club building in the center of downtown. The museum's owner, David Benko, often personally leads visitors through the two floors of exhibits. In addition to often instantly recognizable vintage neon signs for Shell Oil, Buster Brown Shoes, and Coca-Cola, you'll see countless signs from diners, shops, and other independently owned businesses. There's also quite a cache of photos, documents, and other historical materials that trace the development of neon signage and how its use influenced American culture and commercial design through the midcentury. ✉ *200 E. 3rd St.* ☎ *541/370–2242* 🌐 *www.nationalneonsignmuseum.org* 🎫 *$10* 🕒 *Closed Sun.*

★ Rowena Crest Viewpoint and Tom McCall Nature Preserve

NATURE PRESERVE | Views from atop Rowena Crest bluff are a knockout, especially during the March and April wildflower season, and there are a couple of fairly short and wonderfully scenic hikes that lead from the bluff parking lot through a pristine nature preserve operated by the Nature Conservancy. The 3½-mile (round-trip) trek up to McCall Point is especially scenic—it affords great views of Mt. Hood. ✉ *U.S. 30* ✣ *15 miles west of The Dalles* 🌐 *www.nature.org.*

Sunshine Mill Winery

WINERY/DISTILLERY | You won't find many wineries situated in more unusual buildings than Quenett, which operates out of an early-1900s flour mill with huge grain elevators that soar over the southern end of The Dalles's downtown. Inside this dramatic old structure that nearly fell to the wrecking ball before winemakers James and Molli Martin bought it, you'll find the tasting room for Quenett, which produces first-rate Grenache, Viognier, Barbera, and red and white blends. You can also order cheese boards and other snacks, and sample wines from the company's other line, Copa Di Vino, an inexpensive brand of single-serving table wines sold throughout the country. ✉ *901 E. 2nd St.* ☎ *541/298–8900* 🌐 *www.sunshinemill.com.*

🍴 Restaurants

Baldwin Saloon

$ | **AMERICAN** | The walls of this historic downtown watering hole and restaurant are an engagingly authentic mix of landscape art and Early American oil-painting erotica. The extensive, traditional menu runs the gamut from pastas to fish-and-chips to burgers—portions are substantial. **Known for:** convivial old-time vibe; dinner accompanied by the saloon's 1894 piano; good pub fare in big portions. [$] *Average main: $14* ✉ *205 Court St.* ☎ *541/296–5666* 🕒 *Closed Sun.*

Mosier Company

$ | **AMERICAN** | This contemporary roadhouse with vaulted ceilings, big windows, and a sprawling patio is an ideal go-to after hiking at Rowena Crest or wine touring at one of several nearby vineyards—it's in tiny Mosier, between The Dalles and Hood River. Count on well-crafted tavern fare using top-quality local ingredients, including prodigious burgers and fried-chicken sandwiches and poutine slathered in mushroom gravy and melted cheese curds. **Known for:** crispy-tender fried chicken sandwiches; first-rate cocktail, wine, and beer program; inviting and expansive outdoor patio seating. [$] *Average main: $13* ✉ *904 2nd Ave., Mosier* ☎ *541/705–0302* 🌐 *www.mosiercompany.com* 🕒 *Closed Tues. and Wed.*

Petite Provence

$ | **CAFÉ** | This popular downtown bistro-bakery-dessertery, which also has branches in Portland, serves delicious eggs, crepes, and croissants for breakfast; hot and cold sandwiches and salads for lunch, and fresh-baked pastries and breads (you can take a loaf home). The sparkling display case tempts with a good selection of napoleons, éclairs, tarts, and mousses. **Known for:** delicious French pastries; nice selection of wines; lavish breakfast fare. [$] *Average main: $11* ✉ *408 E. 2nd St.* ☎ *541/506–0037* 🌐 *www.provencepdx.com* 🕒 *No dinner.*

Hotels

Balch Hotel

$ | **HOTEL** | Just a 20-minute drive south of The Dalles, this charming and distinctive redbrick 1907 inn offers a wealth of restorative activities, including spa treatments, art therapy sessions, yoga classes in the garden, and delicious breakfasts (included in the rates) and dinners in the easygoing bistro. **Pros:** good location en route to Bend; some rooms have Mt. Hood views; peaceful setting with spa. **Cons:** least expensive rooms share a bath; 15 miles from The Dalles; no TVs in rooms. [$] *Rooms from: $110* ✉ *40 Heimrich St.* ☎ *541/467–2277* 🌐 *www.balchhotel.com* 🛏 *20 rooms* 🍴 *Free breakfast.*

★ Celilo Inn

$ | **HOTEL** | A prototypical retro motor lodge gone high design, with exterior-entry rooms and a '50s light-up motel sign that disguise a slick, boutique feel, commands a hilltop overlooking the Columbia River and Dalles Dam. Flat-screen TVs, pillow-top mattresses, and smart decorating come standard, and the outdoor pool and patio are mighty inviting during The Dalles' dry summers. **Pros:** cool design; terrific wine-touring packages; most rooms have great views. **Cons:** not all rooms have views; those on the far end feel far away from the front desk; need a car to get downtown. [$] *Rooms from: $139* ✉ *3550 E. 2nd St.* ☎ *541/769–0001* 🌐 *www.celiloinn.com* 🛏 *46 rooms* 🍴 *No meals.*

Fairfield Inn & Suites

$$ | **HOTEL** | Although it's part of Marriott's midrange brand, this four-story hotel a couple of blocks from Interstate 84 does have some of the brightest and most up-to-date rooms in the eastern end of the Gorge, with spacious work areas, comfy bedding, mini-refrigerators, microwaves, and marble-accented bathrooms. **Pros:** upscale decor; nice indoor pool; good exercise room. **Cons:** bland setting; bit of a long walk from downtown; looks like any other member of the chain. [$] *Rooms from: $189* ✉ *2014 W. 7th St.* ☎ *541/769–0753, 800/306–1665* 🌐 *www.marriott.com* 🛏 *80 rooms* 🍴 *Free breakfast.*

Goldendale, Washington

34 miles northeast of The Dalles via Hwy. 14 and U.S. 97.

Although the actual town of Goldendale lies about 12 miles north of the Columbia River, this easygoing community with a few prosaic eateries and two basic chain motels is a useful base for exploring the Gorge's eastern reaches, in particular Maryhill Museum of Art and small but excellent Goldendale Observatory State Park. Views on the drive to Goldendale and in town itself are some of the most dramatic in the drier, eastern reaches of the Gorge—you'll see soaring white wind turbines lining the grassy bluffs and cliffs on both sides of the river, and along U.S. 97 as it leads into Goldendale, you can see the snowcapped summit of 12,281-foot Mt. Adams.

GETTING HERE AND AROUND

Although it's quickest to drive east along Interstate 84 and then north on U.S. 97 to reach Goldendale and the attractions around Maryhill, it takes only a few extra minutes and is far more scenic to cross the Columbia via The Dalles Bridge into Washington and drive east on Highway 14 to U.S. 97.

ESSENTIALS

CONTACTS Greater Goldendale Chamber of Commerce. ⊠ *903 E. Broadway St., Goldendale* ☎ *509/773–3400* ⊕ *www.goldendalechamber.org.*

Sights

Goldendale Observatory State Park

OBSERVATORY | FAMILY | This 5-acre park on a 2,100-foot-elevation bluff just north of Goldendale's compact downtown contains one of the nation's largest public telescopes, and the town's remote location, far from the lights of any cities, is ideal. Fascinating astronomy programs and sky-watching events are held during the day and evening, year-round. ⊠ *1602 Observatory Dr., Goldendale* ☎ *509/773–3141* ⊕ *www.goldendaleobservatory. com* ✉ *$10 parking* ⊗ *Closed Apr.–Sept., Mon. and Tues.; Oct.–Mar., most weekdays (call).*

★ Maryhill Museum of Art

BUILDING | A wonderfully eclectic mix of artworks, including the largest assemblage of Rodin works outside France; posters, glasswork, and ephemera related to the modern-dance pioneer Loïe Fuller; an impressive cache of Native American artifacts; furniture and art that belonged to another Hill companion, Queen Marie of Romania; an art nouveau glass collection; and a large collection of mostly Victorian-era European and American landscape paintings: they're all housed within the walls of a grandiose mansion built rather improbably in the middle of nowhere by Sam Hill, the man who spearheaded the development of a scenic highway through the Columbia Gorge. The main Beaux Arts building dates to 1914, and a daring, beautifully executed, LEED-certified modern wing extends from the back, with a terraced slope overlooking the Columbia River—it contains the museum café, a lovely spot for lunch. The extensive, harmoniously landscaped grounds include a sculpture garden and pathways along the Gorge rim. ⊠ *35 Maryhill Museum of Art Dr., Goldendale* ✛ *Off Hwy. 14, 3 miles west of junction with U.S. 97* ☎ *509/773–3733* ⊕ *www.maryhillmuseum.org* ✉ *$12* ⊗ *Closed mid-Nov.–mid-Mar.*

★ Maryhill Winery

WINERY/DISTILLERY | Just down the road from Maryhill Museum, this large winery enjoys the same phenomenal views up and down the Gorge. The largest tasting room in the Gorge has a good-size gift shop as well as a market selling cheese, charcuterie, and other gourmet goodies. Maryhill produces dozens of wines at a variety of prices—the reserves, including stellar Cabernet Franc, Cabernet Sauvignon, Malbec, and Chardonnay, tend to earn most acclaim. In summer, the outdoor amphitheater on the grounds hosts a series of pop concerts. Maryhill runs three additional tasting rooms and bistros elsewhere around the state in Spokane, Vancouver, and Woodinville. ⊠ *9774 Hwy. 14, Goldendale* ☎ *509/773–1976* ⊕ *www. maryhillwinery.com.*

Stonehenge Memorial

MEMORIAL | Built by Maryhill Museum founder Sam Hill, this remarkable full-scale replica of England's legendary Neolithic stone creation was constructed in 1918 as the nation's first memorial to servicemen who perished in World War I. The memorial is a five-minute drive east of the museum, on a promontory with dramatic vistas overlooking the Columbia River. ⊠ *Stonehenge Dr., Goldendale* ⊹ *Off Hwy. 14, just east of U.S. 97* ☎ *509/773–3733* ⊕ *www.maryhillmuseum.org* ⊠ *Free.*

Mt. Hood

The Multnomah tribe call Mt. Hood "Wy'East," named, according to popular legend, for a jealous lover who once sparred over a woman with his rival, Klickitat. When their fighting caught the Great Spirit's attention, Wy'East and Klickitat were transformed into two angry, smoke-bellowing mountains—one became Washington's Mt. Adams, the other became Mt. Hood. Wy'East has mellowed out a bit since then, but the mountain is still technically an active volcano, and it's had very minor, lava-free eruptive events as recently as the mid-1800s.

Today Mt. Hood is known for the challenge it poses to climbers, its deep winter snows, and a dozen glaciers and snowfields that make skiing possible nearly year-round. A few small resort villages are arranged in a semicircle around the north side of the mountain, offering après-ski bars and rental cabins that host

hordes of fun-loving Portlanders each weekend. In every direction from the postcard-perfect peak, the million-acre Mount Hood National Forest spreads out like a big green blanket. Mule deer, black bears, elk, and the occasional cougar share the space with humans who come to hike, camp, and fish in the Pacific Northwest's quintessential wild ecosystem.

Around the Mountain

About 60 miles east of Portland on U.S. 26, and 42 miles south of Hood River via Hwy. 35 and U.S. 26.

Towering majestically at 11,249 feet above sea level, Mt. Hood is what remains of the original north wall and rim of a volatile crater. Although the peak no longer spews ash or fire, active vents regularly release steam high on the mountain, which was named in 1792 for the naval officer who helmed the first European sailing expedition up the Columbia River. Mt. Hood offers the longest ski season in North America, with three major ski areas, as well as extensive areas for cross-country skiing and snowboarding. Many of the ski runs turn into mountain-bike trails in summer. The mountain is also popular with climbers and hikers. In fact, some hikes follow parts of the Oregon Trail, and signs of the pioneers' passing are still evident.

GETTING HERE AND AROUND

From Portland U.S. 26 heads east into the heart of Mount Hood National Forest, while Highway 35 runs south from Hood River, skirting the mountain's east face. The roads meet 60 miles east of Portland, near Government Camp, forming an oblong loop with Interstate 84 and the Historic Columbia River Highway. It's about a 75-minute drive from Downtown Portland to Government Camp via U.S. 26. **Sea to Summit**—call for timetables and pickup and drop-off sites—offers shuttle service from Portland International

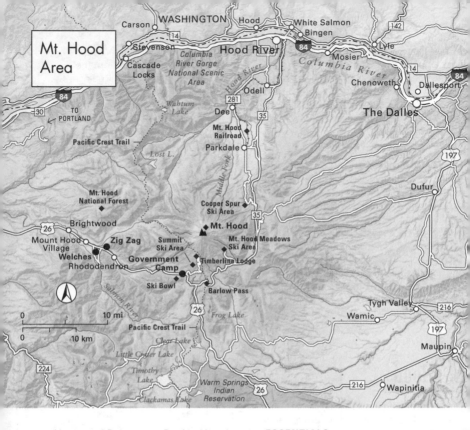

Mt. Hood Area

WASHINGTON

Airport and Downtown Portland hotels to Mt. Hood resorts; the fare is $59 each way, with discounted lift-ticket and ski-rental packages available. Additionally, the **Mt. Hood Express** bus line operates daily and links the villages along the corridor—including Welches, Government Camp, and Timberline Lodge—to the Portland suburb of Sandy, which you can reach via TriMet commuter bus. This option is slower (it takes 2½ to 3 hours each way from the airport or Downtown to Timberline Lodge, for example) than a direct shuttle but costs just $2 ($5 for all-day ticket), plus $2.50 for TriMet bus fare to Sandy.

CONTACTS Mt. Hood Express. ☎ 503/668–3466 ⊕ www.mthoodexpress.com. **Sea to Summit.** ☎ 503/286–9333 ⊕ www. seatosummit.net.

ESSENTIALS
VISITOR INFORMATION Mount Hood National Forest Headquarters. ✉ 16400 Champion Way, Sandy ☎ 503/668–1700 ⊕ www.fs.usda.gov/mthood. **Mt. Hood Area Chamber of Commerce.** ☎ 503/622–3017 ⊕ www.mthoodchamber.com.

TOURS
Mt. Hood Outfitters
ADVENTURE TOURS | The only business on Mt. Hood that rents snowmobiles and offers snowmobile tours is also a well-respected tour company for snowshoe tours and sleigh rides in winter, and mountain hikes, biking trips, and boat excursions on area rivers—the shop is also a good place to buy gear and ask for advice on outdoorsy activities in the area. ✉ 88220 Government Camp Loop Rd., Government Camp ☎ 503/715–2175

🌐 *www.mthoodoutfitters.com* 🎟 *From $119; snowmobile tours from $225.*

Sights

★ Mount Hood National Forest

HIKING/WALKING | The highest spot in Oregon and the fourth-highest peak in the Cascades, "the Mountain" is a focal point of the 1.1-million-acre forest and all-season playground. Beginning 20 miles southeast of Portland, it extends south from the Columbia River Gorge for more than 60 miles and includes more than 315,000 acres of designated wilderness. These woods are perfect for hikers, horseback riders, mountain climbers, and cyclists. Within the forest are dozens of campgrounds as well as lakes stocked with brown, rainbow, cutthroat, brook, and steelhead trout. The Sandy, Salmon, Clackamas, and other rivers are known for their fishing, rafting, canoeing, and swimming. Both forest and mountain are crossed by an extensive trail system for hikers, cyclists, and horseback riders. The **Pacific Crest Trail,** which begins in British Columbia and ends in Mexico, crosses at the 4,155-foot-high Barlow Pass. As with most other mountain destinations within Oregon, weather can be temperamental, and snow and ice may affect driving conditions as early as mid-September and as late as June. Bring tire chains and warm clothes as a precaution.

Since this forest is close to the Portland metro area, campgrounds and trails are potentially crowded over the summer months, especially on weekends. If you're planning to camp, get info and permits from the Mount Hood National Forest Headquarters. Campgrounds are managed by the U.S. Forest Service and a few private concessionaires, and standouts include a string of neighboring campgrounds on the south side of Mt. Hood: Trillium Lake, Still Creek, Timothy Lake, Little Crater Lake, Clackamas Lake, Summit Lake, Clear Lake, and Frog Lake. Each varies in what it offers and in price. The mountain overflows with day-use areas. From mid-November through April, all designated Winter Recreation Areas require a Sno-Park permit, available from the U.S. Forest Service and many local resorts and sporting goods stores. ✉ *Headquarters, 16400 Champion Way, Sandy* ☎ *503/668–1700* 🌐 *www.fs.usda.gov/mthood* 🎟 *$5 parking.*

Restaurants

Cascade Dining Room

$$$$ | **PACIFIC NORTHWEST** | Vaulted wooden beams and a wood-plank floor, handcrafted furniture, handwoven drapes, and a lion-sized stone fireplace set the scene in Timberline Lodge's esteemed restaurant, from which views of neighboring mountains are enjoyed, except when snow drifts cover the windows. The atmosphere is traditional and historic, and the menu emphasizes local and organic ingredients in dishes like alpine spaetzle with applewood-smoked bacon, green cabbage, apples, aged Gouda, and your choice of several protein options (salmon, flat-iron steak, etc.). **Known for:** less expensive menu in atmospheric Ram's Head Bar; grand views from many tables; historic setting. [$] *Average main: $42* ✉ *27500 E. Timberline Rd., Timberline Lodge* ☎ *503/272–3104* 🌐 *www.timberlinelodge.com.*

Hotels

★ Timberline Lodge

$$ | **RESORT** | **FAMILY** | Guest rooms are simple, rustic, and charming (a handful of them lack private baths), but don't expect a cushy experience—the reason for staying here is the location and setting. **Pros:** a thrill to stay on the mountain itself; great proximity to all snow activity; amazing architecture. **Cons:** rooms are small and the least expensive ones have shared bathrooms; views from rooms are often completely blocked by snow in winter; lots of tourists milling. [$] *Rooms*

A snowboarder catches some air on Mt. Hood.

from: $175 ⊠ 27500 E. Timberline Rd., Timberline Lodge ☎ 503/272–3311, 800/547–1406 ⊕ www.timberlinelodge. com ⤳ 70 rooms ⧉ No meals.

Activities

DOWNHILL SKIING

Cooper Spur Mountain Resort

SKIING/SNOWBOARDING | FAMILY | On the northern slope of Mt. Hood, Cooper Spur caters to families and has one double chair and a tow rope. The longest run is ⅔ mile, with a 350-foot vertical drop, but you'll also find a tubing run as well as groomed cross-country and snowshoeing trails. Facilities and services include rentals, instruction, repairs, and a ski shop, day lodge, snack bar, restaurant, and a handful of log cabin–style overnight accommodations. ⊠ 10755 Cooper Spur Rd., Mount Hood ✛ Follow signs from Hwy. 35 for 2½ miles to ski area ☎ 541/352–6692 ⊕ www.cooperspur. com.

Timberline Lodge & Ski Area

SKIING/SNOWBOARDING | The longest ski season in North America unfolds at this full-service ski area, where the U.S. ski team conducts summer training. Thanks to the omnipresent Palmer Snowfield, it's the closest thing to a year-round ski area in the Lower 48 (it's typically closed for just a few weeks in September). Timberline is famous for its Palmer chairlift, which takes skiers and snowboarders to the high glacier for summer skiing. There are five high-speed quad chairs, one triple chair, and one double. The top elevation is 8,500 feet, with a 3,700-foot vertical drop, and the longest run is 3 miles. Facilities include a day lodge with fast food and a ski shop; lessons and equipment rental and repair are available. Parking requires a Sno-Park permit. The Palmer and Magic Mile lifts are popular with both skiers and sightseers. ⊠ 27500 E. Timberline Rd., Timberline Lodge ☎ 503/272–3311 ⊕ www.timberlinelodge. com.

HIKING

Tamanawas Falls

HIKING/WALKING | This relatively easy (it's 3½ miles round-trip), family-friendly hike on the lower eastern slopes of Mt. Hood is popular from late spring through midautumn, although it's on the hottest days of summer that folks flock here to cool off and splash around in Cold Spring Creek and the roaring Tamanawas Falls. These dramatic cascades tumble from a 150-foot-tall lava cliff and make quite an impression on Instagram feeds. ✉ *Hwy. 35, Mount Hood* ✣ *Just north of Sherwood Campground* ☞ *$5 parking.*

Government Camp

54 miles east of Portland on I–84 and U.S. 26, and 42 miles south of Hood River via Hwy. 35 and U.S. 26.

This alpine resort village with a laid-back vibe has several hotels and restaurants popular with visitors exploring Mt. Hood's ski areas.

GETTING HERE AND AROUND

Government Camp is on U.S. 26, about 55 miles east of Portland, and just down the hill from Timberline Lodge.

🍴 Restaurants

Charlie's Mountain View

$ | **AMERICAN** | Old and new ski swag plasters the walls, lift chairs function as furniture, and photos of famous (and locally famous) skiers and other memorabilia abound in this raucous local institution for après-ski fun and listening to live music on weekend nights. Open-flame-grilled steaks, beer-bratwurst sandwiches, and hamburgers are worthy here, as are generous portions of biscuits and gravy for breakfast (weekends only). **Known for:** live music on weekends; large burgers with lots of toppings; rowdy and fun vibe. [$] *Average main: $14* ✉ *88462 E. Government Camp Loop* ☎ *503/272–3333* 🌐 *www.charliesmountainview.com.*

Glacier Public House

$$ | **MODERN AMERICAN** | Formerly run by different owners and known as Glacier Haus Bistro, this lively spot in the center of Government Camp reopened in late 2019 as a cool gastropub offering tasty, elevated comfort fare. It's a great go-to before or after a day of skiing or summer outdoor fun, and there's a great list of local wines and craft beers. **Known for:** well-crafted comfort food; family-friendly atmosphere; good selection of craft beer. [$] *Average main: $19* ✉ *88817 E. Government Camp Loop Rd.* ☎ *503/272–3471* 🌐 *www.glacierpublichouse.com* 🕑 *Closed Mon. and Tues.*

Mt. Hood Brewing

$$ | **AMERICAN** | Producing finely crafted beers—Multorporter Smoked Porter, Ice Axe IPA, Highland Meadow Blond Ale—since the early '90s, this casual brewpub with stone walls, a fireplace, and both booth and table seating buzzes in the early evening for après-ski dining and drinking. It's popular for its creative comfort food, including poutine with fontina cheese and peppercorn demi-glace, cast-iron-skillet-baked fondue, Alsatian pizza topped with smoked ham and crème fraîche, barbecue pulled-pork-and-porter sandwiches. **Known for:** root-beer—and beer—ice-cream floats; giant salted pretzel with beer-cheese dip; hearty chilis and chowders. [$] *Average main: $20* ✉ *87304 E. Government Camp Loop* ☎ *503/272–3172* 🌐 *www.mthood-brewing.com.*

🛏 Hotels

Best Western Mt. Hood Inn

$$ | **HOTEL** | Clean, well maintained, and inexpensive, all rooms have microwaves and refrigerators, and some have kitchenettes and whirlpool tubs. **Pros:** handy location for skiing and hiking; clean and modern rooms; great value. **Cons:** cookie-cutter decor and design; not ski-in, ski-out (but very close); parking can be limited when hotel is full. [$] *Rooms from:*

$160 ✉ 87450 E. Government Camp Loop ☎ 503/272–3205 🌐 www.bestwesternoregon.com 🛏 57 rooms 🍴 Free breakfast.

★ Collins Lake Resort

$$$ | RESORT | FAMILY | This contemporary 28-acre compound of poshly furnished chalets and "Grand Lodge" town homes with fireplaces and dozens of other amenities is scattered around an alpine lake and offers the cushiest accommodations in the Mt. Hood area. **Pros:** within walking distance of Government Camp restaurants and bars; spacious layouts are ideal for groups and families; fireplaces and private decks in all units. **Cons:** two- or three-night minimum during busy times; can be expensive for just one or two occupants; decor varies from unit to unit. *[$] Rooms from: $239 ✉ 88149 E. Creek Ridge Rd. ☎ 503/928–3498, 800/234–6288 🌐 www.collinslakeresort.com 🛏 66 condos 🍴 No meals.*

Shopping

Govy General Store

CONVENIENCE/GENERAL STORES | Good thing this is a really nice grocery store, because it's the only one for miles around. Govy General stocks all the staples, plus a nice selection of gourmet treats like cheeses and chocolates. **■ TIP→ Buy your Sno-Park permit here in winter.** *✉ 30521 E. Meldrum St. ☎ 541/272–3107 🌐 www.govygeneralstore.com.*

Activities

DOWNHILL SKIING

★ Mt. Hood Meadows Ski Resort

SKIING/SNOWBOARDING | The mountain's largest resort has more than 2,150 skiable acres, 85 runs, five double chairs, six high-speed quads, a top elevation of 9,000 feet, a vertical drop of 2,777 feet, and a longest run of 3 miles. If you're seeking varied, scenic terrain with plenty of trails for all skiing abilities, this is your best choice among the region's ski areas. Facilities include a day lodge, nine restaurants, two lounges, a ski-and-snowboard school, a children's learning center with daycare, and two ski shops with equipment rentals. *✉ Hwy. 35 ⊕ 10 miles east of Government Camp ☎ 503/337–2222 🌐 www.skihood.com.*

Mt. Hood Skibowl

SKIING/SNOWBOARDING | FAMILY | The ski area closest to Portland is also known as "America's largest night ski area," with 36 runs lighted each evening. It has 960 skiable acres serviced by four double chairs and five surface tows, a top elevation of 5,100 feet, a vertical drop of 1,500 feet, and a longest run of 3 miles. You can take advantage of two day lodges, a midmountain warming hut, four restaurants, and two lounges. Sleigh rides are conducted, weather permitting, and a hugely popular tubing and adventure park has several tubing hills, plus "cosmic tubing," which features music, 600,000 LED lights, and a laser show. In summer the resort morphs into the Adventure Park at Skibowl, with mountain biking, ziplines, bungee jumping, a five-story free-fall Tarzan Swing, disc golf, and kid-friendly tubing and alpine slides. *✉ 87000 E. U.S. 26 ☎ 503/272–3206 🌐 www.skibowl.com.*

Welches and Zigzag

12 miles west of Government Camp and 40 miles east of Portland.

One of a string of small communities known as the Villages of Mt. Hood, Welches' claim to fame is that it was the site of Oregon's first golf course, built near the base of Mt. Hood in 1928 and still going strong (as part of the Mt. Hood Oregon Resort). Vacationers hover around both towns for proximity to Mt. Hood along with easy access to basic services like gas, groceries, and dining. Others come to pull a few trout out of the scenic Zigzag River or to access trails and streams in the adjacent Salmon–Huckleberry Wilderness.

GETTING HERE AND AROUND

Most of Welches is just off U.S. 26, sometimes called the Mt. Hood Corridor, about 45 miles east of Portland.

Sights

North American Bigfoot Center

MUSEUM | **FAMILY** | In the town of Boring along the main route from Portland to Mt. Hood (about 20 miles before you reach Welches), this museum devoted to all things Bigfoot opened in 2019 by one of the world's foremost researchers on the topic and has quickly become a favorite stop, especially with kids. Inside you'll find a 7½-foot-tall replica of a rather stern-looking Sasquatch (his name is Murphy), along with framed and cast footprints, indigenous masks, photos, books, and other artifacts that help visitors to decide for themselves about the likelihood that this creature actually exists. ✉ *31297 S.E. U.S. 26, Boring* ☎ *503/912–3054* 🌐 *www.northamerican-bigfootcenter.com* 🎟 *$8* 🕒 *Closed Tues. and Wed.*

Restaurants

Altitude

$$$ | **MODERN AMERICAN** | Mt. Hood Oregon Resort's flagship restaurant aims for a sleek, modernist look in its glitzy—for this rustic region at least—dining room with recessed lighting and contemporary art. **Known for:** popular lounge with lighter menu; nice views of resort's greenery; extensive wine list. [$] *Average main: $26* ✉ *Mt. Hood Oregon Resort, 68010 E. Fairway Ave., Welches* ☎ *503/622–2214* 🌐 *www.mthood-resort.com* 🕒 *No lunch.*

Koya Kitchen

$ | **JAPANESE** | One of the few options for Asian cuisine near Mt. Hood, this affordable Japanese spot is nestled beneath a grove of towering pines and offers simple yet artfully designed dining areas inside and out. Make a feast of a few of the good-sized sushi rolls (which include veggie options) or tuck into a steaming bowl of Oregon mushroom ramen with tofu, chicken, or pork, or ponzu-avocado fried rice with a sunny fried egg on top. **Known for:** nice selection of sushi; pine-shaded beer garden; ramen and noodle bowls. [$] *Average main: $13* ✉ *67886 E. U.S. 26, Welches* ☎ *503/564–9345* 🕒 *Closed Mon. and Tues.*

★ Rendezvous Grill

$$ | **MODERN AMERICAN** | "Serious food in a not-so-serious place" is the slogan of this casual roadhouse with surprisingly sophisticated food—it's been a locals' favorite since it opened back in the mid-'90s. For a joint many miles from the coast, the 'Vous sure does a nice job with seafood, turning out appetizing plates of sautéed shrimp, Willapa Bay oysters, Dungeness crab, and chargrilled wild salmon. **Known for:** creatively prepared comfort fare; cocktails with house-infused spirits; attractive patio seating. [$] *Average main: $21* ✉ *67149 E. U.S. 26, Welches* ☎ *503/622–6837* 🌐 *www.thevousgrill.com* 🕒 *Closed Mon. in winter.*

Hotels

The Cabins Creekside at Welches

$ | **RENTAL** | Affordability, accessibility to recreational activities, and wonderful hosts make these cabins with knotty-pine vaulted ceilings, log furnishings, and full-size kitchens a great lodging choice in the Mt. Hood area. **Pros:** friendly owners who can dispense fly-fishing advice; quiet, off-highway location; close to hiking and skiing. **Cons:** no dining within walking distance; no cabin-side parking; simple but clean, functional furnishings. [$] *Rooms from: $129* ✉ *25086 E. Welches Rd., Welches* ☎ *503/622–4275* 🌐 *www.mthoodcabins.com* 🛏 *10 cabins* 🍴 *No meals.*

Mt. Hood Oregon Resort

$$ | RESORT | In the evergreen-forest foothills of Mt. Hood, this expansive golf and spa resort is popular year-round both with outdoorsy sorts and couples seeking romantic alpine hideaways. **Pros:** every sport available; plenty of choices in room size; closer to Portland than most Mt. Hood area lodgings. **Cons:** can get crowded; less appealing if you're not a golfer; a 20-minute drive from ski areas. [$] *Rooms from: $199* ✉ *68010 E. Fairway Ave., Welches* ☎ *503/622–3101* 🌐 *www.mthood-resort.com* 🛏 *157 rooms* 🍴 *No meals.*

Mt. Hood Vacation Rentals

$$ | RENTAL | Doggedly determined to ensure a great time for the two- and four-pawed vacationer alike, this company welcomes the family pet into the majority of its homes, cabins, and condos, yet the properties are still on the upscale side: you'll find fireplaces or wood-burning stoves, hot tubs, river views, and full kitchens. **Pros:** knowledgeable, hospitable staff; family- and pet-friendly; many secluded sites. **Cons:** bring your own shampoo; two- to five-night minimum stays; there's an additional guest services fee. [$] *Rooms from: $180* ✉ *67898 E. Hwy. 26, Welches* ☎ *888/424–9168* 🌐 *www.mthoodrentals.com* 🛏 *32 units* 🍴 *No meals.*

Activities

FISHING

The Fly Fishing Shop

FISHING | This heritage shop full of self-proclaimed "fish-aholics" has been peddling flies and guiding trips for three decades. Drop in to ask about the huge variety of customizable float trips, clinics, and by-the-hour walking trips for seasonal steelhead and salmon ($60 an hour). Great nearby rivers include the glacial-fed Sandy and its tributary the Zigzag, which hides some native cutthroat. ✉ *67296 E. U.S. 26, Welches* ☎ *503/622–4607, 800/266–3971* 🌐 *www.flyfishusa.com.*

GOLF

Mt. Hood Oregon Resort

GOLF | The three 9-hole tracks at this esteemed resort include the Pine Cone Nine, Oregon's oldest golf course, built on a rented hayfield in 1928—you can mix any combination of the three courses to complete a full 18-hole round. There's also a lighted 18-hole putting course that's popular with families and adults working on their short game. Resort guests receive a 10% discount. ✉ *68010 E. Fairway Ave., Welches* ☎ *503/622–3151* 🌐 *www.mthood-resort.com* 🎫 *$67–$83 for 18 holes* ⛳ *Pine Cone: 9 holes, 3299 yards, par 36. Foxglove: 9 holes, 3106 yards, par 36. Thistle: 9 holes, 2956 yards, par 34.*

RECREATIONAL AREAS

Salmon–Huckleberry Wilderness

PARK—SPORTS-OUTDOORS | Named for the two main food groups of both black bears and frequent Mt. Hood restaurant diners, this sizeable wilderness area just south of Welches occupies the eroded foothills of the "Old Cascades," ancient mountains made mellow by time, water, and wind. Not surprisingly, trailside huckleberry picking is big here in late August and September. Inquire at the Zigzag Ranger Station for regulations and recommended trails, and to buy National Forest parking passes ($5). ✉ *Mt. Hood National Forest Zigzag Ranger Station, 70220 E. U.S. 26, Zigzag* ☎ *503/622–3191* 🌐 *www.fs.usda.gov/recarea/mthood.*

Chapter 7

CENTRAL OREGON

7

Updated by
Jon Shadel

👁 Sights	🍴 Restaurants	🛏 Hotels	🛍 Shopping	🍸 Nightlife
★★★★★	★★★☆☆	★★★★☆	★★★☆☆	★★☆☆☆

WELCOME TO CENTRAL OREGON

TOP REASONS TO GO

★ **Escape into the wild:** Pack your hiking boots, carabiners, snowboard, and camera to explore snowy mountains, rock formations, rivers, lakes, forests, ancient lava flows, and desert badlands.

★ **Get a taste of Bend:** See the refined side of the high desert in Bend's walkable city center, which is packed with upscale restaurants and bars, taprooms, boutiques, and food carts.

★ **Kick back at Sunriver:** This riverfront resort has bike paths, hiking trails, horse stables, hot tubs, four golf courses, and several restaurants.

★ **Tour the brewery scene:** With nearly three dozen breweries—and more on the horizon—you can discover nearly any type of beer that fits your tastes.

★ **Discover the Old West:** Historic ranching towns such as Sisters keep frontier heritage alive with annual festivals.

Central Oregon provides a natural meeting place between the urban west side and the rural east side. It's set below the Columbia River basin and drained by the Deschutes River, which flows from south to north. Skiers and snowboarders flock to winter sports areas on the western edge; anglers head to the Deschutes, the Metolius, and the Cascade Lakes; and climbers, campers, rockhounds, and wanderers explore the arid landscapes on the east side. Bend, the largest town for more than 120 miles in any direction, sits roughly in the center of this region.

1 **Bend.** This quickly gentrifying resort city has a new wave of culinary ambition to fuel outdoor adventurers.

2 **Sisters.** Famous for its namesake rodeo and quilt festival, this kitschy little town looks like an Old West theme park.

3 **Redmond.** The hub for air travel in central Oregon is also the gateway to Smith Rock State Park.

4 **Prineville.** Ranchlands and the Ochoco National Forest border the region's oldest community.

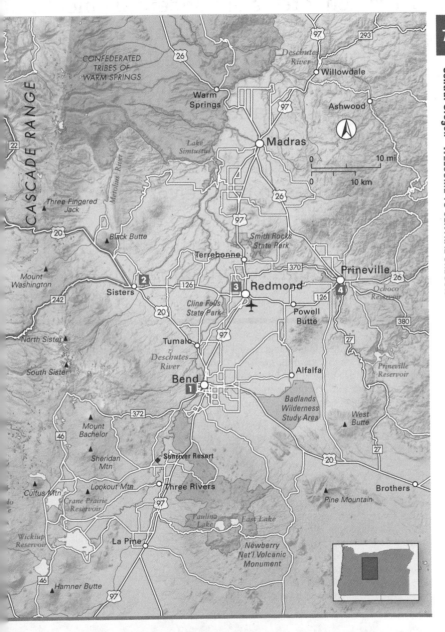

As you zip along highways through the straw-colored high deserts and past evergreen forests of ponderosa pines, you may feel like a star in a commercial for some four-wheel-drive vehicle. Yes, central Oregon's sunny landscapes capture the romance of the open road: snowfields so white they sharpen the edges of the mountains; canyons so deep and sudden as to induce vertigo; water that ripples in mountain lakes so clear that boaters can see to the bottom, or rushes through turbulent rapids favored by rafters.

A region born of volcanic tumult is now a powerful lure for the adventurous, the solitude seeking, and even the urbane— Bend has grown into a sophisticated city nearing 100,000 residents, a haven for hikers, athletes, and barflies.

From Bend it's easy to launch to the outdoor attractions that surround it. To the northwest, Camp Sherman is a fisher's destination for rainbow trout or kokanee. The Smith Rocks formation to the north draws climbers and boulderers, and, to the south, Lava Lands and the Lava River Caves fascinate budding geologists more than 6,000 years after they were chiseled out of the earth. Hikers and equestrians trot across the untamed Oregon Badlands Wilderness to the east. Lake Billy Chinook to the north is a startling oasis, where summer visitors drift in houseboats beneath the high walls of the Deschutes River canyon. The Deschutes River itself carries rafters of all descriptions, from young families to solo drifters.

And after a pulse-raising day exploring the rugged setting, you can settle into one of the many rustic but luxurious resorts that compete with each other for upscale amenities. They dot the landscape from the dry terrain around Warm Springs to the high road to Mt. Bachelor.

MAJOR REGIONS

Sunshine, crisp pines, pure air, rushing waters, world-class skiing and snowboarding at Mt. Bachelor, destination golf resorts, a touch of the frontier West at **Sisters,** an air of sophistication in **Bend**— the forested side of **west central Oregon** serves up many recreational flavors. The area draws young couples, seniors, families, athletes, and adventurers, all of whom have no problem filling a week (or more) with memorable activities, from rafting and biking to beer tasting and fine dining.

East of the Cascades, **east central Oregon** changes to desert. The land is austere, covered mostly in sage and juniper, with a few hardy rivers and great extrusions of lava, which flowed or was blasted across the prehistoric landscape. In recent years resorts have emerged to draw Portlanders, especially in winter when the Willamette Valley gets rainy. They venture here to bask in the sun and to soak up the feeling of the frontier, reinforced by ranches and resilient towns like **Redmond** and **Prineville.**

Planning

When to Go

Central Oregon is a popular destination year-round. Skiers and snowboarders come from mid-December through March, when the powder is deepest and driest. During this time, guests flock to the hotels and resorts along Century Drive, which leads from Bend to Mt. Bachelor. In summer, when temperatures reach the upper 80s, travelers are more likely to spread throughout the region. But temperatures fall as the elevation rises, so take a jacket if you're heading out for an evening at the high lakes or Newberry Crater.

You'll pay a premium at the mountain resorts during ski season, and Sunriver and other family and golf resorts are busiest in summer. It's best to make reservations as far in advance as possible; six months in advance is not too early.

Getting Here and Around

AIR TRAVEL

Visitors fly into Redmond Municipal Airport–Roberts Field (RDM), about 17 miles north of downtown Bend. Rental cars are available for pickup at the airport from several national agencies. The Redmond Airport Shuttle provides transportation throughout the region (reservations requested); a ride from the airport to addresses within Bend costs about $40. Taxis are available at curbside, or can be summoned from the call board inside the airport; rideshare services Uber and Lyft both service RDM. Portland's airport is 160 miles northwest of Bend, and daily flights connect the two cities.

AIR CONTACTS Redmond Airport Shuttle. ☎ 541/382–1687, 888/427–4888 ⊕ www. redmondairportshuttle.net. **Redmond Municipal Airport–Roberts Field.** (RDM) ✉ 2522 S.E. Jesse Butler Circle, Redmond ☎ 541/548–0646 ⊕ www.flyrdm. com.

BUS TRAVEL

The Central Oregon Breeze, a regional carrier, runs one bus a day each way between Portland and Bend, with stops in Redmond and Madras. Cascades East Transit is Bend's intercity bus service, and connects Redmond, La Pine, Madras, Prineville, Bend, and Sisters. Trips from the airport require reservations. Greyhound also serves the area with direct routes from Bend to Eugene and Salem, with connections onward to Portland.

BUS CONTACTS Cascades East Transit. ✉ 334 Hawthorn Ave., Bend ☎ 541/385–8680, 866/385–8680 ⊕ www.cascadeseasttransit.com. **Central Oregon Breeze.** ✉ 2045 N.E. Hwy. 20, Bend ☎ 541/389–7469, 800/847–0157 ⊕ www.cobreeze. com. **Greyhound Bend.** ✉ 334 N.E. Hawthorne Ave., Bend ☎ 541/923–1732 ⊕ www.greyhound.com.

CAR TRAVEL

U.S. 20 heads west from Idaho and east from the coastal town of Newport into central Oregon. U.S. 26 goes southeast from Portland to Prineville, where it heads northeast into the Ochoco National Forest. U.S. 97 heads north from California and south from Washington to Bend. Highway 126 travels east from Eugene to Prineville; it connects with U.S. 20 heading south (to Bend) at Sisters. Major roads throughout central Oregon are well maintained and open throughout the winter season, although it's always advisable to have tire chains in the car. Some roads are closed by snow during winter, including Highway 242. Check the Oregon Department of Transportation's TripCheck (⊕ *www.tripcheck. com*) or call ODOT (☎ *800/977–6368*).

Festivals

★ Bend Film Festival

FESTIVALS | This local film festival, among the most popular in the state, takes place in October. ✉ *Bend* ☎ *541/388–3378* ⊕ *www.bendfilm.org*.

Bend Summer and Fall Festival

FESTIVALS | Downtown Bend is blocked off with food, crafts, art booths, and music in July and October. ✉ *Bend* ☎ *541/508– 4280* ⊕ *www.bendsummerfestival.com; www.bendfallfestival.com*.

Oregon Winterfest

FESTIVALS | February brings music, food, brews, wine, ice carving, and other winter sports to Bend's Old Mill District. ✉ *Bend* ☎ *541/323–0964* ⊕ *www.oregon- winterfest.com*.

Pole, Pedal, Paddle

FESTIVALS | Bend's popular ski, bike, run, and kayak or canoe race is held in May. ✉ *Bend* ☎ *541/388–0002* ⊕ *www. pppbend.com*.

Sisters Folk Festival

FESTIVALS | A celebration of American music is held in September. ✉ *Sisters* ☎ *541/549–4979* ⊕ *www.sistersfolkfes- tival.org*.

Sisters Outdoor Quilt Show

FESTIVALS | The second Saturday in July, Sisters transforms into a western town covered with colorful quilts hanging from building exteriors. ✉ *Sisters* ☎ *541/549– 0989* ⊕ *www.sistersoutdoorquiltshow. org*.

Sisters Rodeo

FESTIVALS | Multiple rodeo and community events, held annually for more than 75 years, take place over a weekend in June. ✉ *67637 U.S. 20, south of Sisters, Sisters* ☎ *541/549–0121, 800/827–7522* ⊕ *www.sistersrodeo.com*.

Restaurants

The center of culinary ambition is in downtown Bend, where the restaurant scene has exploded since about 2010. Decent restaurants also serve diners in Sisters, Redmond, Prineville, and the major resorts. Styles vary, but many hew to the Northwest preference for fresh foods grown, caught, and harvested in the region.

Central Oregon also has many down-home places and brewpubs, and family-run Mexican restaurants have emerged to win faithful followings in Prineville, Redmond, Madras, and Bend. *Restaurant reviews have been shortened. For full information visit Fodors.com.*

What it Costs in U.S. Dollars			
$	$$	$$$	$$$$
RESTAURANTS			
under $16	$16–$22	$23–$30	over $30
HOTELS			
under $150	$150– $200	$201– $250	over $250

Hotels

Central Oregon has lodging for every taste, from upscale resort lodges to an in-town brewpub village, eclectic bed-and-breakfasts, rustic western inns, and a range of independent and chain hotels and motels. If you're drawn to the rivers, stay in a pastoral fishing cabin along the Metolius near Camp Sherman. If you came for the powder, you'll want a ski-snowboard condo closer to the mountain. For soaking up the atmosphere, you might favor one of downtown Bend's luxurious hotels, or Old St. Francis, the Catholic school–turned-brewpub village. *Hotel reviews have been shortened. For full information, visit Fodors.com.*

Tours

Cog Wild Bicycle Tours
BICYCLE TOURS | Half-, one-, and multiday mountain bike tours are offered for people of all skill levels and interests. ⊠ *LOGE Bend, 19221 S.W. Century Dr., Suite 135, Bend* ☎ *541/385–7002* ⊕ *www.cogwild.com* ⌨ *From $60.*

Sun Country Tours
ADVENTURE TOURS | A longtime provider of raft and tube trips on central Oregon rivers offers rafting excursions that range from two hours to full days May through September. ⊠ *531 S.W. 13th St., Bend* ☎ *541/382–1709* ⊕ *www.suncountrytours.com* ⌨ *From $59.*

★ Wanderlust Tours
ADVENTURE TOURS | Popular and family-friendly half-day or evening excursions are offered around Bend, Sisters, and Sunriver. Options include kayaking, canoeing, snowshoeing, and caving. ⊠ *61535 S. Hwy. 97, Suite 13, Bend* ☎ *541/389–8359* ⊕ *www.wanderlusttours.com* ⌨ *From $80.*

Visitor Information

CONTACTS Central Oregon Visitors Association. ⊠ *57100 Beaver Dr., Bldg. 6, Suite 130, Sunriver* ☎ *541/389–8799, 800/800–8334* ⊕ *www.visitcentraloregon.com.*

Bend

160 miles southeast of Portland.

No longer a sleepy timber town, Bend is booming as one of the top recreational playgrounds on the West Coast thanks to its proximity to skiing, rivers, and seemingly endless trails. Invigorated start-up and culinary scenes add fresh energy to the urban core, while active families fleeing California's high cost of living are, in turn, pushing up the cost of real estate here. Even as Oregon's biggest city east of the Cascades grows more cosmopolitan, it remains a monoculture—demographically, it's overwhelmingly white and at times, it seems everybody is an athlete, a tech bro, or a brewer. But thankfully, everyone strives to make a good first impression. Bend's heart is a handsome area of about four square blocks, centered on Wall and Bond Streets. Here you'll find boutique stores, galleries, independent coffee shops, brewpubs, creative restaurants, and historic landmarks such as the Tower Theatre, built in 1940. A few traditional barbershops and taverns are also spread around, keeping it real.

Neighboring Mt. Bachelor, though hardly a giant among the Cascades at 9,065 feet, is blessed by an advantage over its taller siblings—by virtue of its location, it's the first to get snowfall, and the last to see it go. Inland air collides with the Pacific's damp influence, creating skiing conditions immortalized in songs by local rock bands and raves from the ski press.

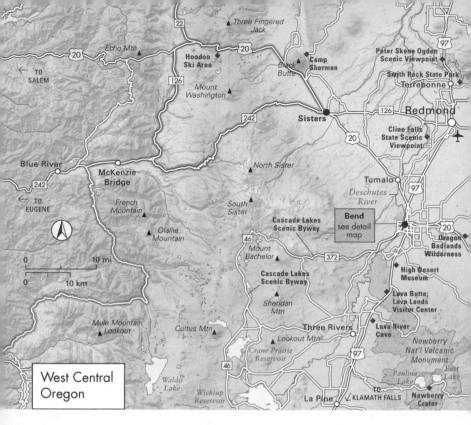

West Central Oregon

GETTING HERE AND AROUND

Portlanders arrive via car on U.S. 20 or U.S. 26, and folks from the mid–Willamette Valley cross the mountains on Highway 126. Redmond Municipal Airport, 17 miles to the north, is an efficient hub for air travelers, who can rent a car or take a shuttle or cab into town. Greyhound also serves the area with direct routes to Eugene and Salem. The Central Oregon Breeze, a privately operated regional carrier, runs daily between Portland and Bend, with stops in Redmond and Madras. Bend is served by a citywide bus system called Cascades East Transit, which also connects to Redmond, La Pine, Sisters, Prineville, and Madras. To take a Cascades East bus between cities in central Oregon, reservations are not required but recommended. *For more on bus travel to and from Bend, see Getting Here and Around in the Central Oregon Planner.*

If you're trying to head out of or into Bend on a major highway during the morning or 5 pm rush, especially on U.S. 97, you may hit congestion. Parking in downtown Bend is free for the first two hours (three hours at the centrally located parking garage), or park for free in the residential neighborhoods just west of downtown. In addition to the car-rental counters at the airport, Avis, Budget, Enterprise, and Hertz also have rental locations in Bend.

ESSENTIALS

VISITOR INFORMATION Bend Chamber of Commerce. ✉ 777 N.W. Wall St., Suite 200 ☎ 541/382–3221 ⊕ www.bendchamber.

org. **Visit Bend/Bend Visitor Center.** ⊠ *750 N.W. Lava Rd., Suite 160* ☎ *541/382–8048, 877/245–8484* ⊕ *www.visitbend.com.*

Sights

★ Cascade Lakes Scenic Byway
SCENIC DRIVE | For 66 miles, this nationally designated Scenic Byway meanders past a series of high mountain lakes and is good for fishing, hiking, and camping in the summer months. (Much of the road beyond Mt. Bachelor is closed by snow during the colder months.) ⊠ *Bend* ✛ *Take Century Dr./Hwy. 372 out of Bend and follow it around Mt. Bachelor. To complete as a loop, take U.S. 97 to return* ⊕ *www.tripcheck.com.*

Deschutes Brewery
WINERY/DISTILLERY | Central Oregon's first and most famous brewery produces and bottles its beer in this facility separate from the popular brewpub. Join one of the four daily tours ($5) and learn from the beer-obsessed staff; be sure to make reservations online or by phone, since groups fill quickly. The tour ends in the tasting room and gift shop, where participants get to try samples of the fresh beer. ⊠ *901 S.W. Simpson Ave.* ☎ *541/385–8606* ⊕ *www.deschutes-brewery.com.*

Deschutes Historical Museum
MUSEUM | **FAMILY** | The Deschutes County Historical Society operates this museum, which was originally built as a school-house in 1914. Exhibits depict historical life in the area, including a pioneer schoolroom, Native American artifacts, and relics from the logging, ranching, homesteading, and railroading eras. ⊠ *129 N.W. Idaho Ave.* ☎ *541/389–1813* ⊕ *www.deschuteshistory.org* ⊠ *$5.*

Deschutes National Forest
FOREST | This 1½-million-acre forest has 20 peaks higher than 7,000 feet, including three of Oregon's five highest mountains, more than 150 lakes, and 500 miles of streams. If you want to park your car at

a trailhead, some of the sites require a Northwest Forest Pass; day-use passes are also needed May through September at many locations for boating and picnicking. Campgrounds are operated by a camp host. ⊠ *63095 Deschutes Market Rd.* ☎ *541/383–5300* ⊕ *www.fs.usda.gov/centraloregon* ⊠ *Park pass $5.*

Drake Park and Mirror Pond
CITY PARK | At its western edge, down-town Bend slopes down to these 13 acres of manicured greensward and trees lining the edge of the Deschutes, attracting flocks of Canada geese as well as strollers from downtown. Various events, such as music festivals, occur in the park during the summer months. Note the 11-foot-high wheel log skidder, harkening back to Bend's logging industry in the early 20th century, when four draft horses pulled the wheel to move heavy logs. ⊠ *Bend* ✛ *Bounded on the west by N.W. Brooks St. and Drake Park; N.W. Lava Rd. on the east; N.W. Franklin Ave. to the south; and N.W. Greenwood Ave. to the north* ⊕ *www.downtownbend.org.*

★ High Desert Museum
MUSEUM | **FAMILY** | The West is actually quite wild, and this combo muse-um-zoo proves it. Kids will love the up-close-and-personal encounters with Gila monsters, snakes, porcupines, birds of prey, Vivi the bobcat, and Snowshoe the lynx. Characters in costume take part in the Living History series, where you can chat with stagecoach drivers, boomtown widows, pioneers, home-steaders, and sawmill operators. Peruse the 110,000 square feet of indoor and outdoor exhibits, such as Spirit of the West and a historic family ranch, to expe-rience how the past can truly come alive. ⊠ *59800 S. Hwy. 97* ✛ *7 miles south of downtown Bend* ☎ *541/382–4754* ⊕ *www.highdesertmuseum.org* ⊠ *$17 Apr.–Oct., $14 Nov.–Mar.*

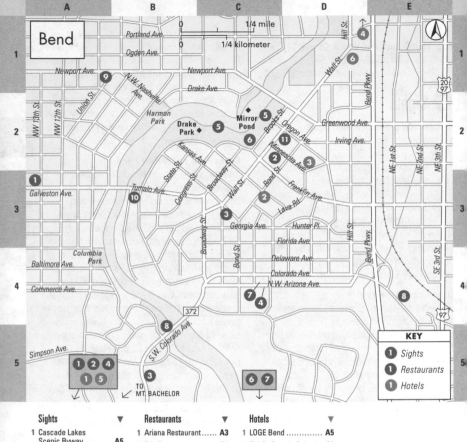

Bend

Sights ▼

1 Cascade Lakes
  Scenic Byway........... **A5**
2 Deschutes Brewery.... **A5**
3 Deschutes Historical
  Museum **C3**
4 Deschutes National
  Forest **A5**
5 Drake Park
  and Mirror Pond **C2**
6 High Desert Museum.... **C5**
7 Newberry National
  Volcanic Monument
  and Lava Lands **C5**
8 Vector Volcano
  Classic Arcade.......... **B5**

Restaurants ▼

1 Ariana Restaurant...... **A3**
2 Bos Taurus **C2**
3 Deschutes Brewery
  & Public House **B5**
4 Foxtail Bakeshop
  & Kitchen **C4**
5 Pine Tavern............... **C2**
6 Pizza Mondo.............. **C2**
7 The Podski................ **C4**
8 Sparrow Bakery **E4**
9 Spork...................... **A1**
10 10 Barrel Brewing
  West Side................ **B3**
11 Zydeco Kitchen
  & Cocktails **D2**

Hotels ▼

1 LOGE Bend **A5**
2 Old St. Francis School... **C3**
3 The Oxford Hotel........ **D2**
4 Riverhouse
  on the Deschutes....... **D1**
5 Sunriver Resort **A5**
6 Wall Street Suites **D1**

KEY
1 Sights
1 Restaurants
1 Hotels

Newberry National Volcanic Monument and Lava Lands
VOLCANO | **FAMILY** | The last time hot lava flowed from Newberry Volcano was about 13 centuries ago. The north end of the monument has several large basalt flows, as well as the 500-foot **Lava Butte** cinder cone—a coal-black and scorched-red, symmetrical mound thrust from the depths 7,000 years ago. The cone is now home to the **Lava Lands Visitor Center,** which features interpretive exhibits that explain the volcanic and early human history of the area. **Lava River Cave,** a 1-mile-long lava tube, takes about 90 minutes to explore on your own with a lantern (available for rent, $5). On the south end of the monument, an unpaved road leads to beautiful views from **Paulina Peak.** Along the shores of **Paulina Lake** and **East Lake,** you can hike, fish, camp, or stay at the rustic resorts. You can also hike a trail to **Paulina Falls,** an 80-foot double waterfall. The monument offers 100 miles of summer trails, and may be accessible during winter months, depending on snowmelt, for snowmobiling, snowshoeing, and skiing. ✉ *58201 S. Hwy. 97* ☎ *541/593–2421* 🌐 *www.fs.usda.gov/centraloregon* 🎟 *$5 per vehicle* 🕒 *Lava River Cave closes Oct. 1 to protect bat population.*

Vector Volcano Classic Arcade
LOCAL INTEREST | **FAMILY** | One of the few spots in central Oregon where you should head indoors to stare at screens, this arcade doubles as a gallery for playing retro arcade games and pinball machines, all while sipping craft beer or kombucha. Thankfully, you won't need to slide any spare change into the 40-plus games from the 1980s and '90s; instead, you pay for an hour or full-day of nostalgia-tripping. ✉ *111 N.W. Oregon Ave.* 🌐 *www.vectorvolcanoarcade.com* 🎟 *Unlimited play for $5–$15* 🕒 *Closed Mon.*

🍴 Restaurants

Ariana Restaurant
$$$$ | **AMERICAN** | For the good part of a decade, the 12 tables inside this Craftsman bungalow were the top real estate in the city for celebrating special occasions. Bend's dining scene has evolved considerably since 2004, but Ariana continues to draw national acclaim—landing twice on OpenTable's list of Top 100 Restaurants in America—for its French-, Italian-, and Spanish-inspired dishes. **Known for:** an Oregon take on European classics; intimate dinner-party atmosphere; extensive list of Pacific Northwest wines. [$] *Average main: $35* ✉ *1304 N.W. Galveston Ave.* ☎ *541/330–5539* 🌐 *www.arianarestaurantbend.com* 🕒 *Closed Mon. No lunch.*

★ **Bos Taurus**
$$$$ | **STEAKHOUSE** | After 10 Barrel Brewing Co. sold to Anheuser-Busch, the brewery's founding team veered into more upscale territory with the 2018 opening of Bos Taurus. The always-packed modern steak house seems like a central Oregonian's hungry vision of a big-city restaurant—aspiring to be a sort of gallery for some of the finest cuts of meat in town. **Known for:** sourcing top-rated steak from around the world; California- and Washington-centric wine list; attentive service. [$] *Average main: $50* ✉ *163 N.W. Minnesota Ave.* ☎ *541/241–2735* 🌐 *www.bostaurussteak.com* 🕒 *No lunch.*

Deschutes Brewery & Public House
$ | **AMERICAN** | Established in 1988, Bend's original brewpub remains a happening spot to get a taste of the city's beer scene. The menu includes a diverse lineup of craft brews, including rotating seasonals, and pub food, such as hearty burgers on homemade brioche rolls. **Known for:** central Oregon–inspired brews; sometimes long waits for a table; elk burgers. [$] *Average main: $15* ✉ *1044*

Newberry National Volcanic Monument's Paulina Falls has an 80-foot double waterfall.

N.W. Bond St. ☎ *541/382–9242* 🌐 *www.deschutesbrewery.com.*

★ Foxtail Bakeshop & Kitchen

$ | **CAFÉ** | More artful than hearty, brunch is the sleeper hit at this twee bakeshop, where the kitchen struggles to keep up with the weekend demand. A mural of buzzing bees, fluttering bats and butterflies, and a big fox lends a storybook setting to the café's compact dining room, while a spacious patio is prime real estate on warm mornings. **Known for:** slim menu of savory brunch entrées; sourcing ingredients from nearby farms; long waits during the midmorning rush. [$] *Average main: $14* ✉ *555 N.W. Arizona St., Suite 60* ☎ *541/213–2275* 🌐 *www.foxtailbakeshop.com* 🕒 *Closed Mon. No dinner.*

Pine Tavern

$$ | **AMERICAN** | A pair of ponderosa pine trees actually grow through the back dining room in this downtown landmark, which two venturesome women opened in the height of the Great Depression. As the longest-operating restaurant in the city, it keeps old-timers coming back for what hasn't changed: the focus on traditional American cooking and the warm scones with honey butter. **Known for:** an idyllic patio overlooking Mirror Pond; comfort food classics like meat loaf and three-cheese mac; happy hour specials. [$] *Average main: $20* ✉ *967 N.W. Brooks St.* ☎ *541/382–5581* 🌐 *www.pinetavern.com.*

Pizza Mondo

$$ | **PIZZA** | **FAMILY** | The Maui Wowie and Run Little Piggy are just a few topping combinations at this New York–style pizza restaurant downtown, a fan favorite among families and hungry hikers. Visit the cozy digs for the lunch special—pizza slice, salad, and soda—or order an "after mountain special" (two slices and a beer) in the late afternoon. **Known for:** hand-tossed thin-crust pizza; stellar vegan and "gluten sensitive" pies; limited seating. [$] *Average main: $20* ✉ *811 N.W. Wall St.* ☎ *541/330–9093* 🌐 *www.pizzamondo-bend.com.*

Central Oregon Brewery Boom

With nearly three dozen breweries and counting, central Oregon rivals the Portland metro area for brewpubs per capita, but it only hit the map as a beer travel destination in recent years.

Since the first microbrewery opened its doors in 1988 (Deschutes Brewery in downtown Bend), the industry has continued to grow and expand. Each brewery and brewpub approaches the craft beer experience in an original manner, often supported by locals and a combination of live music, good food, unique marketing, experimental brews, and standbys that keep pint glasses and growlers filled.

Residents may buoy the industry, but breweries in turn support the community. Local artists design labels, many beer proceeds go to neighborhood causes, and brews are continually concocted with local events and culture in mind.

Bend Ale Trail

Pick up a Bend Ale Trail brochure, or download the app, to guide you through nearly 20 of Bend's breweries. Stop at each brewery, have a taste or a pint, and receive a stamp in your passport. Once you've visited 10 locations, drop by the Bend Visitor Center to receive the prize: a durable silicone pint glass.

★ The Podski

$ | **ECLECTIC** | This tightly packed cluster of street-food vendors feels less like a typical food-cart pod and more like a year-round party—even the trash cans are decorated with a disco ball. Choose from a half-dozen carts serving dishes like pierogies, charcuterie, vegan toast, and stuffed Korean-style pancakes. **Known for:** Bend's most creative food carts; on-site taproom pouring craft beer; indoor seating. [$] *Average main: $12* ✉ *536 N.W. Arizona Ave.* 🌐 *www.thepodski.com* 🕑 *No breakfast.*

Sparrow Bakery

$ | **BAKERY** | Groggy locals start lining up every morning for this bakery's signature treat: the Ocean Roll, a croissant-like pastry that's wrapped like a cinnamon roll and filed with cardamom and vanilla. Pastry chefs also hand-make the caramel used in the house espresso drinks. **Known for:** hand-folded croissants and Ocean Rolls; stacked breakfast and lunch sandwiches; French-style bread. [$] *Average main: $10* ✉ *50 S.E. Scott St.* ☎ *541/330–6321* 🌐 *www.thesparrowbakery.net* 🕑 *No dinner.*

Spork

$ | **INTERNATIONAL** | Interpretations of street food staples from around the world come out of the kitchen at this beloved counter-serve spot, which draws a health-conscious crowd. Originally opened as a mobile kitchen housed in a 1962 Airstream, the restaurant keeps the good vibes alive with its colorful, hippie-industrial decor. **Known for:** eclectic, wide-ranging menu; globally inspired house cocktails; popular for takeout. [$] *Average main: $12* ✉ *937 N.W. Newport Ave.* ☎ *541/390–0946* 🌐 *www.sporkbend.com.*

★ 10 Barrel Brewing West Side

$ | **AMERICAN** | One of Bend's favorite brewpubs, 10 Barrel's founders faced threats of boycotts from many fans when they sold the operation to conglomerate Anheuser-Busch in 2014. Thankfully, the tap list at their original outpost remains one of the most creative and varied in this very suds-obsessed city and the beer still pairs best with the signature pizzas. **Known for:** innovative brews; patio with fire pits; noisy dining room. $ *Average main: $12* ✉ *1135 N.W. Galveston Ave.* ☎ *541/678–5228* ⊕ *www.10barrel.com.*

Zydeco Kitchen & Cocktails

$$$ | AMERICAN | The blended menu of Northwest specialties and Cajun influences has made this elegant but welcoming restaurant (named after a style of Creole music) a popular lunch and dinner spot for more than a decade. On the menu, fillet medallions, chicken, and pasta sit alongside jambalaya and redfish dishes. **Known for:** gluten-free menu; expert bartenders; seasonal specials. $ *Average main: $23* ✉ *919 N.W. Bond St.* ☎ *541/312–2899* ⊕ *www.zydecokitchen. com* ☉ *No lunch weekends.*

Hotels

LOGE Bend

$$$ | HOTEL | No hotel in Bend caters more to outdoor adventurers than LOGE, an old-school motel stylishly renovated in 2018 with recreation-focused amenities that take advantage of the property's proximity to the Deschutes National Forest. **Pros:** close to the Mt. Bachelor ski area; on-site gear rental center; year-round hot tub. **Cons:** motel-style layout; bare-bones café menu; a bit far from the city center. $ *Rooms from: $210* ✉ *19221 S.W. Century Dr.* ☎ *541/382–4080* ⊕ *www.logecamps.com* ☞ *79 rooms* ❢⊙❢ *No meals.*

Old St. Francis School

$$$ | RESORT | Part of the eclectic McMenamins chain of pubs, movie theaters, and hotels, this fun outpost in a restored 1936 Catholic schoolhouse has classrooms turned into lodging quarters, restaurant and bars, a brewery, a stage, a mosaic-tile soaking pool, and a movie theater with couches and food service. **Pros:** a bohemian-styled destination village; smack in downtown Bend; a semi-secret bar known as the

Broom Closet. **Cons:** many rooms feel quite small; few modern appliances; rooms near on-site pubs can get noisy. $ *Rooms from: $215* ✉ *700 N.W. Bond St.* ☎ *541/382–5174, 877/661–4228* ⊕ *www.mcmenamins.com* ☞ *60 rooms* ❢⊙❢ *No meals.*

★ The Oxford Hotel

$$$$ | HOTEL | Unrivaled for its downtown views and close proximity to the city's top restaurants, this jazz-inspired boutique sets the rhythm for urban lodging in Bend, with in-room vinyl record players and loaner acoustic guitars. **Pros:** generous and environmentally sustainable amenities; luxurious spa and fitness room; loaner bikes in summer months. **Cons:** parking limited to valet or adjacent pay-per-day garage; location is less convenient for outdoor adventures; basement restaurant underwhelms. $ *Rooms from: $425* ✉ *10 N.W. Minnesota Ave.* ☎ *541/382–8436* ⊕ *www.oxfordhotel-bend.com* ☞ *59 rooms* ❢⊙❢ *No meals.*

Riverhouse on the Deschutes

$$ | HOTEL | FAMILY | Extensively renovated in 2016, this lodge-inspired hotel and convention center overlooks the Deschutes River and appeals to family travelers with its indoor and outdoor pools, hot tubs, and on-site dining. **Pros:** spacious standard rooms and suites; convenient facilities for family and business travelers; dining and shopping nearby. **Cons:** rooms lack character; not ideal for those looking to walk downtown; room-service menu disappoints. $ *Rooms from: $199* ✉ *3075 N. Business Hwy. 97* ☎ *541/389–3111* ☞ *221 rooms* ❢⊙❢ *No meals.*

Sunriver Resort

$$$$ | RESORT | FAMILY | Central Oregon's premier family playground and luxurious destination resort encapsulates so many things that are distinctive about central Oregon, from the mountain views and winding river to the biking, rafting, golfing, skiing, and family or romantic getaways. **Pros:** many activities for kids and adults; much pampering in elegant lodge

facilities; close to The Village at Sunriver. **Cons:** decor looks a tad dated; vibe is very family-centric; gets quite crowded on summer weekends. [$] *Rooms from: $259* ✉ *17600 Center Dr., Sunriver* ✣ *15 miles south of Bend on Hwy. 97* ☎ *800/801–8765* 🌐 *www.sunriver-resort.com* 🛏 *245 rooms, 284 houses* 🍴 *No meals.*

Wall Street Suites

$$$ | **HOTEL** | Built in the 1950s as a motel and reopened in 2013 after getting a complete makeover, these spacious suites and rooms are both woodsy and stylishly contemporary, with stunning pine, hardwood, and granite surfaces. **Pros:** room to spread out; pet-friendly; walkable to downtown. **Cons:** basic rooms with few amenities; no lobby common area; still looks like a motel. [$] *Rooms from: $230* ✉ *1430 Wall St.* ☎ *541/706–9006* 🌐 *www.wallstreet-suitesbend.com* 🛏 *17 rooms* 🍴 *No meals.*

Nightlife

The Ale Apothecary

BREWPUBS/BEER GARDENS | The ancient process of wild fermentation gives an unusual sense of terroir to the oak-barrel-aged sours at The Ale Apothecary, setting this small-batch operation apart from most other IPA-driven beer ventures in the region. The tasting room feels more like a winery's than a brewery's—and it keeps similar hours, too, so check ahead to ensure they're open. ✉ *30 S.W. Century Dr., Suite 140* ☎ *541/797–6265* 🌐 *www.thealeapothecary.com.*

Boss Rambler Beer Club

BREWPUBS/BEER GARDENS | Bright pastels and whitewashed shiplap walls make this west-side Bend tasting room look more like an ice cream shop. Indeed, a beachy vibe permeates Boss Rambler's ever-changing tap list—highlighting the house brewer's preference for brewery collaborations and beers intended for sipping on the typically sunny street-side patio. ✉ *1009 N.W. Galveston Ave.* 🌐 *www.bossrambler.com.*

Crux Fermentation Project

BREWPUBS/BEER GARDENS | Housed in a converted auto repair shop, this experimental brewery has no flagship beer. Instead, the brewmaster, a Deschutes Brewery alum, produces an ever-changing variety of pale ales and other craft brews, all of which are on tap in the lively tasting room. On-site food carts and a sprawling patio make this a popular hangout in summer months. ✉ *50 S.W. Division St.* ☎ *541/385–3333* 🌐 *www.cruxfermentation.com.*

900 Wall Restaurant and Bar

WINE BARS—NIGHTLIFE | In a historic corner brick building on a downtown Bend crossroads, this sophisticated restaurant and bar serves hundreds of bottles and about 50 different wines by the glass, earning it the Wine Spectator Award of Excellence. ✉ *900 N.W. Wall St.* ☎ *541/323–6295* 🌐 *www.900wall.com.*

★ Velvet Lounge

BARS/PUBS | In a city where nightlife seems to end when the Tower Theatre locks up, the nearby Velvet Lounge has earned loyal fans. Join the flannel-clad crowd for a happy-hour brew or an after-show cocktail in the narrow, bi-level bar, which is filled with hanging houseplants and, frequently, the sounds of acoustic-guitar-picking locals. ✉ *805 N.W. Wall St.* ☎ *541/728–0303* 🌐 *www.velvetbend.com.*

Shopping

In addition to Bend's compact downtown, the Old Mill District draws shoppers from throughout the region. Chain stores and franchise restaurants have filled in along the approaches to town, especially along U.S. 20 and U.S. 97.

★ Box Factory

SHOPPING CENTERS/MALLS | A converted mill building from the early 1900s houses more than two dozen of Bend's most eclectic shops, restaurants, and studios. Browse leather goods at Danner and the latest opening at the Bend Art Center, or embark on a round-the-block tasting tour of Immersion Brewery, AVID Cider, River Pig Saloon, and Riff, a café dedicated to cold-brewed coffee. ✉ *550 S.W. Industrial Way.*

Dudley's Bookshop Cafe

BOOKS/STATIONERY | Bookshelves stacked with new and used titles surround café tables and couches in this two-floor, dual-purpose space that hosts all kinds of activities, from tango classes to philosophical debates. Order an espresso drink at the bar and then browse the city's widest selection of central Oregon trail guides. ✉ *135 N.W. Minnesota Ave.* ☎ *541/749–2010* ⊕ *www.dudleysbookshopcafe.com.*

Goody's

FOOD/CANDY | If the aroma of fresh waffle cones causes a pause on your downtown stroll, you've probably hit one of central Oregon's favorite soda fountain and candy shops. Try the Oreo cookie ice cream, a local favorite, or the homemade chocolate. If you purchase a stuffed toy animal that calls the store home, expect for it to smell sweet for weeks to come. ✉ *957 N.W. Wall St.* ☎ *541/389–5185* ⊕ *www.goodyschocolates.com.*

Hot Box Betty

CLOTHING | This fun, casual shop helps set women's style trends in central Oregon, with its ethically sourced selection of utilitarian apparel and handbags from Pacific Northwest and international brands. ✉ *903 N.W. Wall St.* ☎ *541/383–0050* ⊕ *www.hotboxbetty.com.*

Old Mill District

SHOPPING CENTERS/MALLS | Bend was once the site of one of the world's largest sawmill operations, with a sprawling industrial complex along the banks of the Deschutes. In recent years the abandoned shells of the old factory buildings have been transformed into an attractive shopping center, a project honored with national environmental awards. National chain retailers mingle with restaurants, boutiques, a 16-screen multiplex and IMAX movie theater, and the Les Schwab Amphitheater that attracts nationally renowned artists, local bands, and summer festivals. ✉ *450 S.W. Powerhouse Dr.* ☎ *541/312–0131* ⊕ *www.oldmilldistrict.com.*

Oregon Body & Bath

SPA/BEAUTY | If adventures in the high desert's arid climate have left your skin feeling dry and dehydrated, head to this body and bath boutique in downtown Bend for locally made soaps, lotions, bath bombs, and body butters. The store also stocks home goods, such as fragrant candles and scents. ✉ *1019 N.W. Wall St.* ☎ *541/383–5890* ⊕ *www. oregonbodyandbath.com.*

Pine Mountain Sports

CLOTHING | Part of Bend's fleet of outdoors stores, this shop sells high-quality clothing, energy bars, and the locally famous Hydro Flask water bottles. Recreation equipment such as mountain bikes, backcountry skis, and snowshoes are also available for rent or purchase. ✉ *255 S.W. Century Dr.* ☎ *541/385–8080* ⊕ *www.pinemountainsports.com.*

🏃 Activities

BIKING

U.S. 97 north to the Crooked River Gorge and Smith Rock and the route along the Cascade Lakes Highway out of Bend provide bikers with memorable scenery and a good workout. Sunriver has more than 30 miles of paved bike paths.

Hutch's Bicycles

BICYCLING | Rent road, mountain, and kids' bikes at this shop as well as a location at 725 N.W. Columbia Street. ✉ *820*

Accommodations at Sunriver Resort Accommodations range from vacation-house rentals to guest rooms and condos.

N.E. 3rd St. ☎ *541/382–6248 3rd St. shop, 541/382–9253 Columbia St. shop* ⊕ *www.hutchsbicycles.com.*

BOATING AND RAFTING

A popular summer activity is floating the Deschutes River at your own pace.

Bend Whitewater Park

BOATING | The first white-water park in Oregon, at McKay Park in the Old Mill District, is the result of an extensive renovation to a 1915 dam, which previously made this section of the Deschutes River impassable. Three separate channels below the dam cater to rafters, kayakers, tubers, and even surfers. ⊠ *166 S.W. Shevlin Hixon Rd.* ☎ *541/389–7275* ⊕ *www.bendparksandrec.org.*

Riverbend Park

BOATING | In Bend, rent an inner tube at Riverbend Park from a kiosk operated from Memorial Day to Labor Day by **Tumalo Creek Kayak & Canoe** and float an hour and a half downriver to Drake Park, where you can catch a shuttle back for a minimal cash fee. ⊠ *799 S.W. Columbia St.* ☎ *541/389–7275* ⊕ *www.bendpark-sandrec.org.*

Tumalo Creek Kayak & Canoe

BOATING | Rent a kayak or stand-up paddleboard and enter the river from the store's backyard, but be prepared to paddle upriver before a leisurely float downstream. Tumalo also operates out of a seasonal shop in Sunriver and a rental kiosk in Riverbend Park. ⊠ *805 S.W. Industrial Way, Suite 6* ☎ *541/317–9407* ⊕ *tumalocreek.com.*

SKIING

Many Nordic trails—more than 165 miles of them—wind through the Deschutes National Forest.

Mt. Bachelor

SKIING/SNOWBOARDING | **FAMILY** | This alpine resort area has 60% of downhill runs that are rated advanced or expert, with the rest geared for beginner and intermediate skiers and snowboarders. One of 10 lifts takes skiers all the way to the mountain's 9,065-foot summit. One run has a vertical drop of 3,265 feet for thrill seekers, and the longest of the 88 runs is 4 miles. Facilities and services include equipment rental and repair, a ski school, retail shop, and day care; you can enjoy seven restaurants, three bars, and six lodges. Other activities include cross-country skiing, a tubing park, sled-dog rides, snowshoeing, and in summer, hiking, biking, disc golfing, and chairlift rides. The 35 miles of trails at the **Mt. Bachelor Nordic Center** are suitable for all abilities.

During the off-season, the lift to the **Pine Marten Lodge** provides sightseeing, stunning views, and fine sunset dining. Visitors can play disc golf on a downhill course that starts near the lodge. At the base of the mountain, take dry-land dog-sled rides with four-time Iditarod musher Rachael Scdoris. ⊠ *13000 S.W. Century Dr.* ☎ *541/382–1709, 541/382–7888* ⊕ *www.mtbachelor.com* ⌨ *Lift tickets $56–$99 per day; kids five and under free.*

Sisters

21 miles northwest of Bend.

If Sisters looks as if you've stumbled onto the set of a western film, that's entirely by design. The town strictly enforces an 1800s-style architecture, which can make its walkable center feel like an Old West theme park. Rustic cabins border ranches on the edge of town, and you won't find a stoplight on any street. Frontier store-fronts give way to touristy gift shops, the century-old hotel now houses a restaurant and bar, and a bakery occupies the former general store. Although its population is just a little more than 2,000, Sisters increasingly attracts visitors as well as urban runaways who appreciate its tranquillity and kitsch. If you're driving over from the Willamette Valley, note how the weather seems to change to sunshine when you cross the Cascades

at the Santiam Pass and begin descending toward the town.

Black Butte, a perfectly conical cinder cone, rises to the northwest. The Metolius River/Camp Sherman area to the west is a special find for fly-fishermen and abounds with springtime wildflowers.

GETTING HERE AND AROUND

Travelers from Portland and the west come to Sisters over the Santiam Pass on Highway 126. This is also the route for visitors who fly into Redmond Municipal Airport, rent a car, and drive 20 miles west. Those coming from Bend drive 21 miles northwest on U.S. 20. Cascades East, a regional bus carrier, runs routes between Sisters and the Redmond airport by reservation.

ESSENTIALS

VISITOR INFORMATION Sisters Chamber of Commerce. ⊠ *291 E. Main Ave.* ☎ *541/549–0251* ⊕ *www.sisterscountry. com.*

 ## Sights

Camp Sherman

RESORT—SIGHT | Surrounded by groves of whispering yellow-bellied ponderosa pines, larch, fir, and cedars and miles of streamside forest trails, this small, peaceful resort community of about 250 full-time residents (plus a few stray cats and dogs) is part of a designated conservation area. The area's beauty and natural resources are the big draw: the spring-fed Metolius River prominently glides through the community. In the early 1900s Sherman County wheat farmers escaped the dry summer heat by migrating here to fish and rest in the cool river environment, making Camp Sherman one of the first destination resorts in central Oregon. As legend has it, to help guide fellow farmers to the spot, devotees nailed a shoebox top with the name "camp sherman" to a tree at a fork in the road. Several original buildings still stand from the early days, including some cabins, a schoolhouse, and a tiny railroad chapel. Find the source of local information at the **Camp Sherman Store & Fly Shop**, built in 1918, adjacent to the post office. ⊠ *25451 S.W. Forest Service Rd. 1419* ⊹ *10 miles northwest of Sisters on U.S. 20, 5 miles north on Hwy. 14* ☎ *541/595–6711* ⊕ *www.campsherman-store.com.*

🍴 Restaurants

The Cottonwood Café

$ | **AMERICAN** | **FAMILY** | Occupying a cute cottage hemmed by a white-picket fence, Sisters' signature brunch spot serves breakfast all day. The menu features such recognizable dishes as scrambles, hash, and eggs Benedict—all elevated by the chef's attention to sourcing ingredients from regional growers and bakers. **Known for:** homey brunch atmosphere; pup-friendly backyard patio with fire pit; standard lunch menu of salads and sandwiches. Ⓢ *Average main: $12* ⊠ *403 E. Hood Ave.* ☎ *541/549–2699* ⊕ *www.cottonwoodinsisters.com* ⊘ *Closed Wed. fall and winter.*

The Open Door

$$ | **WINE BAR** | This wine bar and Mediterranean-inflected restaurant exudes an artsy, small-town eccentricity, with the dining room's mix of mismatched tables and chairs opening into a gallery displaying work from regional craftspeople. The rather tacky art and trinkets all look swell after a few glasses of vino from the well-curated bottle collection. **Known for:** boards with charcuterie from Sisters Meat and Smokehouse; live music on most Monday nights; a leafy patio. Ⓢ *Average main: $16* ⊠ *303 W. Hood Ave.* ☎ *541/549–6076* ⊕ *www.theclearwatergallery.com* ⊘ *Closed Sun.*

Sisters Meat and Smokehouse

$ | **DELI** | A retired fire chief works his smoky magic at this modern butchery and smokehouse, where you can sample the house meats—from pastrami to bologna to cheddar bratwurst—on thick deli-style sandwiches, served with baked beans. For a snack, try the beef jerky, pepperoni sticks, and squeaky cheese curds. **Known for:** smoked and cured meats; counter-serve lunch hot spot; craft beer on tap. Ⓢ *Average main: $12* ⊠ *110 S. Spruce St.* ☎ *541/719–1186* ⊕ *www.sistersmeat.com* ⊘ *No dinner.*

Sno Cap Drive In

$ | **AMERICAN** | Since the golden age of the automobile, this iconic drive-in has served sizzling hamburgers, crispy fries, and handmade milk shakes and ice cream. Stop in for a good helping of roadside Americana, though expect lines in the summer, when travelers driving across the mountain stop here for lunch. **Known for:** historic drive-in; made-to-order burgers; tiny dining area with checkered floors. Ⓢ *Average main: $8* ⊠ *380 W. Cascade Ave.* ☎ *541/549–6151.*

☕ Coffee and Quick Bites

Sisters Bakery

$ | **BAKERY** | In a rustic western-looking former general store built in 1925, Sisters Bakery smells precisely how you want it to—the scent of fresh-baked pastries, doughnuts, and specialty breads wafts out the door from 6 am to 5 pm. **Known for:** traditional baked treats; simple doughnuts; cash and check only. Ⓢ *Average main: $4* ⊠ *251 E. Cascade St.* ☎ *541/549–0361* ⊕ *www.sistersbakery. com* ▭ *No credit cards.*

Sisters Coffee Co.

$ | **CAFÉ** | When it comes to a correctly prepared latte, there's only one gunner in town—Sisters Coffee Co. operates out of a lofty log cabin, where the only specialty baristas in miles pull shots of the single-origin espresso and prepare perfect pour-overs. It's also the top spot for an early morning bite or to camp out with a laptop on the mezzanine. **Known for:** house-sourced and-roasted beans;

classic breakfast muffins; a bakery case filled with pastries and scones. $ *Average main: $8* ✉ *273 W. Hood Ave.* ☎ *541/549–0527* ⊕ *www.sisterscoffee. com.*

 Hotels

★ FivePine Lodge
$$$ | RESORT | FAMILY | This upscale western-style resort resembles an alpine village with a cluster of cabins surrounding the main lodge, where every room is rustically decorated with custom-built furnishings. **Pros:** peaceful atmosphere on the fringes of Sisters; on-site brewery and cinema; popular athletic club and spa. **Cons:** limited breakfast options; some cabins are too close to neighbors; main lodge is near U.S. 20, where traffic gets heavy. $ *Rooms from: $219* ✉ *1021 Desperado Trail* ☎ *541/549–5900* ⊕ *www. fivepinelodge.com* ⊷ *8 suites, 36 cabins* ⏹ *Free breakfast.*

Metolius River Resort
$$$$ | RENTAL | Each of the cabins set amid the pines and aspen at this peaceful resort has splendid views of the sparkling Metolius River, decks furnished with Adirondack chairs, a full kitchen, and a fireplace. **Pros:** peaceful forest setting; feels truly off-grid; wake up to the sound of the river. **Cons:** no additional people (even visitors) allowed; no cell-phone service; bring supplies on winter weekdays when Camp Sherman closes down. $ *Rooms from: $300* ✉ *25551 S.W. Forest Service Rd. 1419, Camp Sherman* ⨁ *Off U.S. 20, northeast 10 miles from Sisters, turn north on Camp Sherman Rd., stay to left at fork (1419), and then turn right at only stop sign* ☎ *800/818– 7688* ⊕ *www.metoliusriverresort.com* ⊷ *11 cabins* ⏹ *No meals.*

★ Suttle Lodge
$$$$ | RESORT | If the famed director Wes Anderson built a wilderness lodge, it'd probably look something like this whimsically updated lakeside retreat in the Deschutes National Forest, where the vintage summer-camp vibes come with the finest craft cocktails you'll find between here and Portland. **Pros:** the only Sisters-area resort with its own lake; lobby bar and on-site restaurant; year-round accessibility to outdoor sports. **Cons:** no air-conditioning; unreliable Wi-Fi and cell reception; Boathouse restaurant only operates in summer. $ *Rooms from: $265* ✉ *13300 U.S. 20* ⨁ *13 miles northwest of Sisters* ☎ *541/638–7001* ⊕ *www.thesuttlelodge.com* ⊷ *11 rooms, 14 cabins* ⏹ *No meals.*

 Nightlife

Sisters Saloon & Ranch Grill
BARS/PUBS | Pass through the swinging saloon doors into this Old West watering hole, originally built more than a century ago as the Hotel Sisters. Head to the bar, which is decorated with a mural of can-can dancers, weathered saddles hanging on the wall, and a mounted stuffed buffalo head. The menu remains rooted in ranch favorites but gets updated with vegetarian-friendly offerings. ✉ *190 E. Cascade Ave.* ☎ *541/549–7427* ⊕ *www. sisterssaloon.net.*

Three Creeks Brewing Co.
BREWPUBS/BEER GARDENS | Currently Sisters' only brewery, Three Creeks offers a selection of beers at its brewing facility and brewpub that play on Northwest culture and the outdoor lifestyle. The brewery system is visible from the pub, which serves a range of burgers, pizzas, salads, and other bar mainstays. Order a frothing pint of the popular Knotty Blonde, or try one of their seasonal brews. ✉ *721 Desperado Ct.* ☎ *541/549–1963* ⊕ *www. threecreeksbrewing.com.*

 Shopping

Hop in the Spa
SPA/BEAUTY | More of a fun novelty than luxe experience, America's first beer spa takes advantage of the medicinal,

nonintoxicating qualities of hops and other beer ingredients. Call ahead to schedule a microbrew soak and massage, or one of the other beer-centric spa packages. ⊠ *371 W. Cascade Ave.* ☎ *541/588–6818* ⊕ *www.hopinthespa.com.*

Paulina Springs Books

BOOKS/STATIONERY | Select a book from the discounted staff recommendation table, or from categories such as history, outdoor recreation, field guides, regional, science, and fiction. Sisters' leading independent bookstore also sells toys and games, and has a substantial young readers section. ⊠ *252 W. Hood Ave.* ☎ *541/549–0866* ⊕ *www.paulinaspringsbooks.com.*

Stitchin' Post

CRAFTS | Owned by a mother-and-daughter team, the famous knitting, sewing, and quilting store opened its doors in 1975. The spacious store not only inspires the senses with colorful fabric, patterns, and yarns, but also conducts classes throughout the year. The **Sisters Outdoor Quilt Show**, annually held the second Saturday of July, is the largest in the world and intertwines its origins with the store's early years. ⊠ *311 W. Cascade St.* ☎ *541/549–6061* ⊕ *www.stitchinpost.com.*

 Activities

FISHING

Fly-fishing the Metolius River attracts anglers who seek a challenge.

Camp Sherman Store & Fly Shop

FISHING | This local institution—the center of life in the tiny riverside community—sells gear and provides information about where and how best to fish. ⊠ *25451 Forest Service Rd. 1419, Camp Sherman* ☎ *541/595–6711* ⊕ *www.campshermanstore.com.*

Fly & Field Outfitters

FISHING | This large Bend-based supplier of gear also sets anglers up with expert guides. ⊠ *35 S.W. Century Dr., Bend* ☎ *866/800–2812* ⊕ *www.flyandfield.com.*

RECREATIONAL AREAS

Metolius Recreation Area

PARK—SPORTS-OUTDOORS | On the eastern slope of the Cascades and within the 1.6-million-acre Deschutes National Forest, this bounty of recreational wilderness is drier and sunnier than the western side of the mountains, giving way to bountiful natural history, outdoor activities, and wildlife. There are spectacular views of jagged, 10,000-foot snowcapped Cascade peaks, looming high above the basin of an expansive evergreen valley clothed in pine.

Five miles south of **Camp Sherman** (2 miles to headwaters), the dark and perfectly shaped cinder cone of **Black Butte** rises 6,400 feet. At its base the **Metolius River** springs forth. Witness the birth of this "instant" river by walking a short paved path embedded in ponderosa forest, eventually reaching a viewpoint with the dramatic snow-covered peak of **Mt. Jefferson** on the horizon. At this point, water gurgles to the ground's surface and pours into a wide trickling creek cascading over moss-covered rocks. Within feet it funnels outward, expanding its northerly flow; becomes a full-size river; and meanders east alongside grassy banks and a dense pine forest to join the Deschutes River downstream. Within the 4,600-acre area of the Metolius and along the river, there are ample resources for camping, hiking, biking, and floating. Enjoy fly-fishing for rainbow, brown, and bull trout in perhaps the best spot within the Cascades. ⊠ *Camp Sherman* ✛ *Off U.S. 20, 9 miles northwest of Sisters* ⊕ *www.metoliusriver.com.*

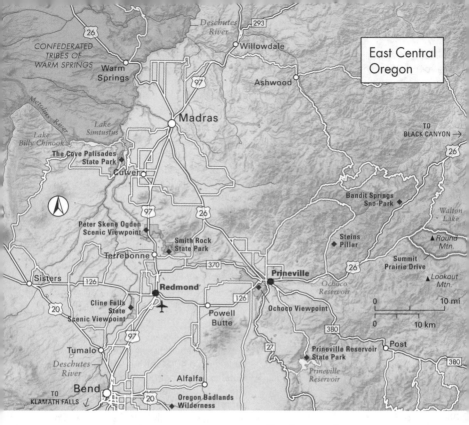

SKIING
Hoodoo Ski Area

SKIING/SNOWBOARDING | On a 5,703-foot summit, this winter sports area has more than 800 acres of skiable terrain. With 34 runs and five lifts, skiers of all levels will find suitable thrills. Upper and lower Nordic trails are surrounded by silence, and an inner tube run and night skiing round out the range of activities. At a 60,000-square-foot lodge at the mountain's base, you can take in the view, grab a bite, shop, or rest your weary feet. The ski area has kids' activities and child-care services available. Lift tickets range from $12 to $61, depending on the type and day. ⊠ *U.S. 20 ⊹ 20 miles northwest of Sisters* ☎ *541/822-3799* ⊕ *www.hoodoo. com.*

Redmond

20 miles east of Sisters, 17 miles northeast of Bend.

If you find yourself in Redmond, chances are you're on your way somewhere else. The town nearest Eagle Crest Resort and Smith Rock, Redmond is where windswept ranches meet runways, as it serves as the regional hub for air travel. It's experienced notable growth in the past decade, largely owing to its proximity to cross-country skiing, fishing, hiking, mountain biking, and rockhounding. Still, this is no gentrified resort town à la Bend, as a stroll through the compact and historic downtown will attest. A few blocks of vintage buildings remain and Centennial Park serves as an attractive civic center, but north–south traffic mostly hustles through the city core, with the majority of the 30,000 residents in suburban neighborhoods sprawling out to the west. A bevy of taquerias and a couple of breweries make Redmond a convenient pit stop or rather quiet base camp for outdoor adventurers.

GETTING HERE AND AROUND

A couple of highways—U.S. 97 and Highway 126—cross in Redmond. U.S. 97 carries travelers north and south to Washington and California, and Highway 126 runs between Sisters in the west to Prineville in the east. Taxis and the Redmond Airport Shuttle ferry travelers to the Redmond Municipal Airport. Two bus lines, the Central Oregon Breeze and Cascades East Transit, serve Redmond. The Central Oregon Breeze links Bend, Redmond, Madras, and Portland, and Cascades East runs buses to and from Redmond and Madras, Prineville, and Bend. Passengers should call to ensure a ride.

ESSENTIALS

VISITOR INFORMATION Redmond Chamber of Commerce and Convention Visitor's Bureau. ⊠ 446 S.W. 7th St. ☎ 541/923–5191 ⊕ www.visitredmondoregon.com.

Sights

Cline Falls State Scenic Viewpoint

VIEWPOINT | Picnicking and fishing are popular at this 9-acre rest area commanding scenic views on the Deschutes River. ⊠ Hwy. 126 ✛ 4 miles west of Redmond ☎ 800/551–6949 ⊕ www.oregonstateparks.org.

★ The Cove Palisades State Park

NATIONAL/STATE PARK | Many people who drive through this part of north-central Oregon are more intent on their distant destinations than on the arid landscape they're passing through. But venture down the two-lane roads to this mini Grand Canyon of red-rock cliffs and gorges 14 miles west of small-town Madras. On a clear day a column of snowcapped Cascades peaks lines the horizon during

the drive from town. Lake Billy Chinook, a glittering oasis amid the rocks, snakes through the park. It's formed by the Deschutes, Metolius, and Crooked rivers.

The park is accessible year-round, but high season is summertime, when families camp on the lakeshore and houseboats drift unhurriedly from cliff to cleft. The lake is renowned for its wildlife, from the lake's bull trout to turkey vultures that fill the sky with their cries. Nature lovers also flock to the park in February for the annual eagle watch. The Crooked River Day Use Area is the most immediately accessible part of the park, a great place to cast a line into the water, launch a boat, or raid your picnic basket. Nearby is the Cove Palisades Marina, where you can rent fishing and houseboats, clean fish, and buy sandwiches and boat supplies, including kids' water toys.

In addition to nearly 10 miles of hiking trails, The Cove Palisades has a driving loop around its craggy rim. Near the Ship Rock formation, you may see petroglyphs carved into a boulder by indigenous people centuries ago.

A full-service campgrounds has full hookups, electrical sites with water, and tent sites, boat slips, and cabins. ⊠ 7300 Jordan Rd., Culver ✛ Off U.S. 97, 27 miles north of Redmond ☎ 541/546–3412, 800/551–6949, 541/546–3412 ⊕ www.oregonstateparks.org ☒ Day use $5 per vehicle.

The Museum at Warm Springs

MUSEUM | If you're driving on U.S. 26 from Portland, stop by the Confederated Tribes of Warm Springs Reservation to check out this museum. It's worth a stop to see the collection of Native American artifacts and exhibits on the culture and history of the Confederated Tribes. ⊠ 2189 U.S. 26, Warm Springs ☎ 541/553–3331 ⊕ www.museumatwarmsprings.org ⊘ Closed Sun. and Mon.

Cove Palisades State Park in north-central Oregon is like a mini Grand Canyon of red-rock cliffs and gorges.

Peter Skene Ogden State Scenic Viewpoint
VIEWPOINT | Even the most seasoned traveler may develop vertigo peering from the cliff top into a deep river canyon. It is a view that gives insight into why Oregon's high desert looks the way it does, with sheer drops and austere landscapes. You'll want to take pictures, but hang on to your camera. ⊠ *U.S. 97 N* ⊹ *9 miles north of Redmond* ☎ *800/551–6949* ⊕ *www.oregonstateparks.org.*

★ Smith Rock State Park
NATIONAL/STATE PARK | Eight miles north of Redmond, this park is world famous for rock climbing, with hundreds of routes of all levels of difficulty. A network of hiking trails serves both climbers and families dropping in for the scenery. In addition to the stunning rock formations, the Crooked River, which helped shape these features, loops through the park. You might spot golden eagles, prairie falcons, mule deer, river otters, and beavers. Due to the environmental sensitivity of the region, the animal leash law is strongly enforced. It can get quite hot in

midsummer, so most prefer to climb in the spring and fall. ⊠ *9241 N.E. Crooked River Dr., Terrebonne* ⊹ *Off U.S. 97* ☎ *541/548–7501, 800/551–6949* ⊕ *www. oregonstateparks.org* ⊠ *Day use $5 per vehicle.*

🍴 Restaurants

General Duffy's Waterhole
$ | **ECLECTIC** | **FAMILY** | A glimmer of Portland's street-food scene in Redmond, this no-frills food-cart pod is a neighborhood hangout with a half-dozen vendors clustered around a bar with 20 taps dedicated to West Coast beer and cider. **Known for:** low-key lunch and dinner; plenty of indoor and outdoor seating; filling growlers with to-go beer. **$** *Average main: $12* ⊠ *404 S.W. Forest Ave.* ☎ *541/527–4345* ⊕ *www.generalduffys. com* ⊗ *No breakfast.*

Seventh Street Brew House
$ | **AMERICAN** | **FAMILY** | A hometown hero since the 1990s, Cascade Lakes Brewing operates this no-frills tap house, which

ranks among the most popular spots for dinner in Redmond, where Seventh Street doesn't have much competition. Dig into typical pub fare—sandwiches, burgers, tacos, and so on—and try a flight of the hoppy ales. **Known for:** reliable dinner in a town with limited options; sunny, dog-friendly patio; rotating seasonal beers. ⑤ *Average main: $12* ⊠ *855 S.W. 7th St.* ☎ *541/923–1795* ⊕ *www. cascadelakes.com* ⊘ *No breakfast.*

Terrebonne Depot

$$ | AMERICAN | Former food-cart proprietors operate this traditional American restaurant and full bar in an old train depot, where you can chow down on burgers and nachos after braving the Misery Ridge Trail at nearby Smith Rock State Park. **Known for:** restaurant nearest the iconic Smith Rock; hearty meals for hikers and climbers; sizeable happy-hour dishes for a late lunch. ⑤ *Average main: $18* ⊠ *400 N.W. Smith Rock Way, Terrebonne* ☎ *541/527–4339* ⊕ *www.terrebonnedepotrestaurant.com* ⊘ *Closed Tues.*

Hotels

Eagle Crest Resort

$$$ | RESORT | FAMILY | Three golf courses are the big draw at this 1,700-acre destination resort, set on high-desert grounds covered with juniper and sagebrush; accommodations include rental houses as well as rooms and suites in the main lodge. **Pros:** a full-service resort with a spa and restaurants; near Smith Rock State Park; kid- and pet-friendly. **Cons:** clean but not luxurious; noisy, unreliable air-conditioning in some units; gets crowded with families. ⑤ *Rooms from: $226* ⊠ *1522 Cline Falls Hwy.* ⊹ *5 miles west of Redmond* ☎ *541/923–2453, 888/306–9643* ⊕ *www.eagle-crest.com* ⇨ *100 rooms, 70 town houses* ⑩ *No meals.*

ⓨ Nightlife

Wild Ride Brew

BREWPUBS/BEER GARDENS | Occupying a block on the edge of downtown, Wild Ride's tasting room and outdoor patio bustle late into the evening thanks to a quartet of food carts serving meals until the bartenders stop pouring. As its name suggests, the brewery takes a cue from the locals' adventurous lifestyles and names its flagship beers for various "wild rides"—from motorcycles to skiing to rock climbing. ⊠ *332 S.W. 5th St.* ☎ *541/516–8544* ⊕ *www.wildridebrew. com.*

Activities

ROCK CLIMBING

Smith Rock Climbing Guides

CLIMBING/MOUNTAINEERING | Professionals with emergency medical training take visitors to the Smith Rock formation for climbs of all levels of difficulty; they also supply equipment. Guided climbs—you meet at Smith Rock—can run a half day or full day, and are priced according to the number of people. ⊠ *Smith Rock State Park, Terrebonne* ☎ *541/788–6225* ⊕ *www.smithrockclimbingguides.com.*

Prineville

18 miles east of Redmond.

Prineville is the oldest town in central Oregon, and the only incorporated city in Crook County. Tire entrepreneur Les Schwab founded his regional empire here, and this community of around 10,000 remains a key hub for the company. In more recent years, Facebook and Apple have chosen Prineville as the location for data centers. Surrounded by verdant ranch lands and the purplish hills of the Ochoco National Forest, Prineville will likely interest you chiefly as a jumping-off point for some of the region's more secluded outdoor adventures.

Oregon's Ghost Towns

Oregon's many ghost towns captivate the imaginations of road-trippers and photographers with the mysteries of who might've called these frontier communities home. Shaniko, about 75 minutes north of Redmond on U.S. 97, is a picture-perfect example of one of these towns, with a decaying hotel, jail, and schoolhouse among the still-standing structures. Considered the "Wool Capital of the World" at the turn of the century, the town peaked at nearly 500 residents; today Shaniko looks like the abandoned set of a Wild West film.

Other ghost towns in Eastern Oregon include Galena, an 1860s gold mining town near Prairie City; Hardman, an 1870s agricultural hub south of Heppner; and Sumpter, a defunct 1860s gold mining town in the Elkhorn Mountain Range that has become a bit of a destination.

The area attracts thousands of anglers, boaters, sightseers, and rockhounds to its nearby streams, reservoirs, and mountains. Rimrocks nearly encircle Prineville, and geology fans dig for free agates, limb casts, jasper, and thunder eggs. Downtown Prineville consists of a handful of small buildings along a quiet strip of U.S. 26, dominated by the Crook County Courthouse, built in 1909. Shopping and dining opportunities are mostly on the basic side.

GETTING HERE AND AROUND

Travelers approaching Prineville from the west on Highway 126 descend like a marble circling a funnel, dropping into a tidy grid of a town from a high desert plain. It's an unfailingly dramatic way to enter the seat of Crook County, dominated by the courthouse on N.E. Third Street, aka U.S. 26, the main drag. Prineville is 19 miles east of Redmond Municipal Airport. If you're coming to Prineville from the airport, it's easiest to rent a car and drive. Nevertheless, two bus lines, **Central Oregon Breeze** and **Cascades East Transit,** run routes.

ESSENTIALS

VISITOR INFORMATION Ochoco National Forest Office. ⊠ *3160 N.E. 3rd St.* ☎ *541/416–6500* ⊕ *www.fs.usda.gov/*

centraloregon. **Prineville-Crook County Chamber of Commerce & Visitor Center.** ⊠ *185 N.E. 10th St.* ☎ *541/447–6304* ⊕ *www.prinevillechamber.com.*

Sights

A. R. Bowman Memorial Museum

MUSEUM | A tough little stone building (it was once a bank, and banks out here needed to be solid) is the site of the museum of the Crook County Historical Society. The 1910 edifice is on the National Register of Historic Places, with the inside vault and teller cages seemingly untouched. Prominent in the museum are old guns, relics from the lumber mills, and Native American artifacts that define early Prineville. An expansion houses a research library and life-size representations of an Old West street. ⊠ *246 N. Main St.* ☎ *541/447–3715* ⊕ *www.bowmanmuseum.org* ⊠ *Free* ⊗ *Closed Jan.*

Ochoco National Forest

FOREST | Twenty-five miles east of the flat, juniper-dotted countryside around Prineville, the landscape changes to forested ridges covered with tall ponderosa pines and Douglas firs. Sheltered by the diminutive Ochoco Mountains and with only about a foot of rain each year, the national forest, established in 1906 by President Theodore Roosevelt, manages to lay a blanket of green across the dry, high desert of central Oregon. This arid landscape—marked by deep canyons, towering volcanic plugs, and sharp ridges—goes largely unnoticed except for the annual influx of hunters during the fall. The Ochoco, part of the old Blue Mountain Forest Reserve, is a great place for camping, hiking, biking, and fishing in relative solitude. In its three wilderness areas—Mill Creek, Bridge Creek, and Black Canyon—it's possible to see elk, wild horses, eagles, and even cougars. ✉ *Office, 3160 N.E. 3rd St. (U.S. 26)* ☎ *541/416–6500* 🌐 *www.fs.usda.gov/ochoco.*

Ochoco Viewpoint

VIEWPOINT | This scenic overlook commands a sweeping view of the city, including the prominent Crook County Courthouse built in 1909, and the hills, ridges, and buttes beyond. ✉ *U.S. 126* ✣ *½ mile west of Prineville.*

Oregon Badlands Wilderness

NATIONAL/STATE PARK | This 29,000-acre swath of Oregon's high desert was designated a national wilderness in 2009, following the longtime advocacy of Oregonians enamored by its harshly beautiful landscape riven by ancient lava flows and home to sage grouse, pronghorn antelope, and elk. Motorized vehicles are prohibited, but visitors can ride horses on designated trails and low-impact hikers are welcome. Bring a camera to capture the jagged rock formations, birds, and wildflowers. ✉ *BLM Office, 3050 N.E. 3rd St. (U.S. 26)* ☎ *541/416–6700* 🌐 *www.blm.gov.*

Prineville Reservoir State Park

NATIONAL/STATE PARK | Mountain streams flow out of the Ochoco Mountains and join together to create the Crooked River, which is dammed near Prineville. Bowman Dam on the river forms this park, where recreational activities include boating, swimming, fishing, hiking, and camping. Some anglers return here year after year, although temperatures can get uncomfortably hot and water levels relatively low by late summer. The reservoir is known for its bass, trout, and crappie, with fly-fishing available on the Crooked River below Bowman Dam. ✉ *19020 S.E. Parkland Dr.* ☎ *541/447–4363, 800/452–5687* 🌐 *www.oregonstateparks.org* 🎟 *Campsites $21–$31.*

Summit Prairie Drive

SCENIC DRIVE | The scenic drive winds past Lookout Mountain, Round Mountain, Walton Lake, and Big Summit Prairie. The prairie abounds with trout-filled creeks and has one of the finest stands of ponderosa pines in the state; wild horses, coyote, deer, and sometimes even elk roam the area. The prairie can be glorious between late May and June, when wildflowers with evocative names like mule ears, paintbrush, checkermallow, and Peck's mariposa lily burst into bloom. ✉ *Prineville* ✣ *From Prineville, head 16 miles east on U.S. 26, go right on County Rd. 123, turn east and travel 8½ miles to Forest Rd. 42, turn southeast and travel 9½ miles to Forest Rd. 4210* ☎ *541/416–6500.*

🍴 Restaurants

Ochoco Brewing Company

$ | **AMERICAN** | **FAMILY** | Burgers are as big a draw as the craft beer at Prineville's prime hangout, which borrows its name from the first brewery known to operate in Oregon in the 1870s. The ⅓-pound grass-fed beef patties come from a ranch just outside town. **Known for:** carb-heavy brewpub favorites; various IPA styles; a few vegetarian options. [$] *Average main: $12* ✉ *380 N. Main St.* ☎ *541/233–0883* 🌐 *www.ochocobrewing.com.*

Tastee Treet

$ | **DINER** | **FAMILY** | The stuff of childhood memories, this old-school establishment is locally renowned for its traditional burgers, hand-cut French fries, and milk shakes. Saunter up to the horse-shoe-shaped counter to sit on swiveling stools and chat with locals and out-of-towners, some of whom never miss a chance to drop by while passing through. **Known for:** 1950s-era burger joint; greasy deep-fried appetizers; iconic neon ice-cream cone sign. $ *Average main: $9* ⊠ *493 N.E. 3rd St.* ☎ *541/447–4165* ⊕ *www.tasteetreetprineville.com.*

 Hotels

★ Brasada Ranch

$$$$ | RESORT | This top-rated but lesser-known luxury resort places an emphasis on feeling good, with a series of 2019 renovations expanding the fitness center and adding an adults-only pool and a new studio space dedicated to wellness classes. **Pros:** on-site restaurants and spa; range of on-site facilities and activities; serene views of mountain horizons. **Cons:** beautiful but somewhat isolated setting; Ranch House suites do not permit kids; not all units have hot tubs. $ *Rooms from: $289* ⊠ *16986 S.W. Brasada Ranch Rd., Powell Butte* ☎ *855/561–7953* ⊕ *www.brasada.com* ⌁ *8 suites, 119 cabins* ❍❘ *No meals.*

 Activities

FISHING

It's helpful to check the Oregon Department of Fish and Wildlife's (⊕ *ww.dfw. state.or.us*) recreation report before you head out.

Ochoco Reservoir

FISHING | This lake is annually stocked with fingerling trout, and you might also find a rainbow, bass, or brown bullhead tugging on your line. ⊠ *U.S. 26* ⊹ *6 miles east of Prineville* ☎ *541/447–1209* ⊕ *www.ccprd.org* ⌑ *Campsites $20.*

HIKING

Pick up maps at the Ochoco National Forest office for trails through the nearly 5,400-acre Bridge Creek Wilderness and the demanding Black Canyon Trail (11½ miles one way with a hazardous river crossing in spring) in the Black Canyon Wilderness. The 1½-mile Ponderosa Loop Trail follows an old logging road through ponderosa pines growing on hills. In early summer wildflowers take over the open meadows. The trailhead begins at Bandit Springs Rest Area, 29 miles east of Prineville on U.S. 26. A 2-mile, one-way trail winds through old-growth forest and mountain meadows to Steins Pillar, a giant lava column with panoramic views; be prepared for a workout on the trail's poorly maintained second half, and allow at least three hours for the hike. To get to the trailhead, drive east 9 miles from Prineville on U.S. 26, head north (to the left) for 6½ miles on Mill Creek Road (also signed as Forest Service Road 33), and head east (to the right) on Forest Service Road 500.

SKIING

Bandit Springs Sno-Park

SKIING/SNOWBOARDING | A network of cross-country trails starts here at a rest area. Designed for all levels of skiers, the trails traverse areas near the Ochoco Divide and have snow globe–like views of the wilderness area dotted with ponderosa pines. ⊠ *U.S. 26* ⊹ *29 miles east of Prineville.*

Prineville Department of Motor Vehicles

SKIING/SNOWBOARDING | The office can provide the required Sno-Park permits. ⊠ *Ochoco Plaza, 1595 E. 3rd St., Suite A-3* ☎ *541/447–7855* ⊕ *www.oregondmv. com.*

Chapter 8

CRATER LAKE
NATIONAL PARK

8

Updated by
Andrew Collins

 Sights
★★★★★

 Restaurants
★★★☆☆

 Hotels
★★★★☆

 Shopping
★★☆☆☆

 Nightlife
★★☆☆☆

WELCOME TO CRATER LAKE NATIONAL PARK

TOP REASONS TO GO

★ **The lake:** Cruise inside the caldera basin and gaze into the extraordinary sapphire-blue water of the country's deepest lake, stopping for a ramble around Wizard Island.

★ **Native land:** Enjoy the rare luxury of interacting with totally unspoiled terrain.

★ **The night sky:** Billions of stars glisten in the pitch-black darkness of an unpolluted sky.

★ **Splendid hikes:** Accessible trails spool off the main roads and wind past colorful bursts of wildflowers and cascading waterfalls.

★ **Lake-rim lodging:** Spend the night perched on the lake rim at the rustic yet stately Crater Lake Lodge.

Crater Lake National Park covers 183,224 acres, and only a relatively small portion of it encompasses the lake for which it's named. In southern Oregon less than 75 miles from the California border, the park is surrounded by several Cascade Range forests, including the Winema and Rogue River national forests. The town of Klamath Falls, 50 miles south of the park, has the most convenient Amtrak stop; Ashland and Medford, to the southwest, are 73 miles and 85 miles, respectively, from the park's southern (Annie Spring) entrance. Roseburg is 85 miles northwest of the park's northern entrance, which is open only during the warmer months.

1 Crater Lake. The park's focal point, this scenic destination is known for its deep-blue hue.

2 Wizard Island. Visitors can take boat rides to this protruding landmass rising from the western section of Crater Lake; it's a great place for hiking and picnicking.

3 Mazama Village. About 5 miles south of Rim Drive, the village is your best bet for stocking up on snacks, beverages, and fuel.

4 Cleetwood Cove Trail. The only designated trail to hike down the caldera and reach the lake's edge is on the rim's north side off Rim Drive; boat tours leave from the dock at trail's end.

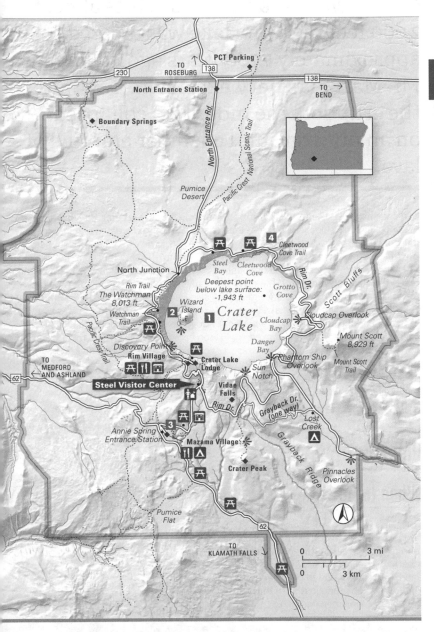

TO
ROSEBURG

230

138

PCT Parking

TO
BEND

138

North Entrance Station

◆ Boundary Springs

North Entrance Rd.

Pacific Crest National Scenic Trail

Pumice
Desert

🏕 🏕 4   Cleetwood
Cove Trail

Steel
Bay   Cleetwood
Cove

Rim Dr.

North Junction

Deepest point
below lake surface:
-1,943 ft

Grotto
Cove

Scott Bluffs

Rim Trail
The Watchman
8,013 ft

Wizard
Island

Crater
Lake

Cloudcap
Bay

Cloudcap Overlook

Watchman
Trail

2

1

Mount Scott
8,929 ft

Pacific Crest Trail

Discovery Point

🏕

Danger
Bay

Mount Scott
Trail

TO
MEDFORD
AND ASHLAND

62

Rim Village

🏕 🍴 📷

🏕   Crater Lake
Lodge

Phantom Ship
Overlook

Sun
Notch

Steel Visitor Center

🚻

Vidae
Falls

Rim Dr.

Grayback Dr.
(one way)

Lost
Creek

Annie Spring
Entrance Station

3

🏕

Mazama Village

🏕 🛖

Grayback Ridge

🏕 🛖 🍴 ⛺

Crater Peak

Pinnacles
Overlook

🏕

Pumice
Flat

62

0   3 mi

TO
KLAMATH FALLS

0   3 km

🏕

The pure, crystalline blue of Crater Lake astounds visitors at first sight. More than 5 miles wide and ringed by cliffs almost 2,000 feet high, the lake was created approximately 7,700 years ago, following Mt. Mazama's fiery explosion. Days after the eruption, the mountain collapsed on an underground chamber emptied of lava.

Rain and snowmelt filled the caldera, creating a sapphire-blue lake so clear that sunlight penetrates to a depth of 400 feet (the lake's depth is 1,943 feet). Crater Lake is both the clearest and deepest lake in the United States—and the ninth deepest in the world. For most visitors, the star attractions of Crater Lake are the lake itself and the breathtakingly situated Crater Lake Lodge. Although it takes some effort to reach it, Wizard Island is another outstanding draw. Other park highlights include the natural, unspoiled beauty of the forest and the geological marvels you can access along the Rim Drive.

Planning

When to Go

The park's high season is July and August. September and early October tend to draw smaller crowds. By mid-October until well into June, nearly the entire park closes due to heavy snowfall. The road is kept open just from the South Entrance to the rim in winter, except during severe weather. Early summer snowmelt often creates watery breeding areas for large groups of mosquitoes. Bring lots of insect repellent in June and July, and expect mosquito swarms in the early morning and at sunset. They can also be a problem later in the summer in campgrounds and on the Cleetwood Cove Trail, so pack repellent if you plan on camping or hiking. You might even consider a hat with mosquito netting.

Planning Your Time

CRATER LAKE IN ONE DAY
Begin at the **Steel Visitor Center,** a short drive from Annie Spring, the only park entrance open year-round. The center's interpretive displays and a short video describe the forces that created the lake and what makes it unique. From here begin circling the crater's rim by heading northeast on **Rim Drive,** allowing an hour to stop at overlooks—be sure to check out the Phantom Ship rock formation in the lake—before you reach the trailhead of **Cleetwood Cove Trail,** the only safe and legal way to access the lake. If you're game for a good workout, hike down the trail to reach the dock at trail's end

AVERAGE HIGH/LOW TEMPERATURES					
JAN.	FEB.	MAR.	APR.	MAY	JUNE
34/18	35/18	37/19	42/23	50/28	58/34
JULY	AUG.	SEPT.	OCT.	NOV.	DEC.
68/41	69/41	63/37	52/31	40/23	34/19

and hop aboard a **tour boat** for a two-hour ranger-guided excursion. If you'd prefer to hike on your own, instead take the late-morning shuttle boat to **Wizard Island** for a picnic lunch and a trek to the island's summit.

Back on Rim Drive, continue around the lake, stopping at the **Watchman Trail** for a short but steep hike to this peak above the rim, which affords a splendid view of the lake and a broad vista of the surrounding southern Cascades. Wind up your visit at **Crater Lake Lodge.** Allow time to wander the lobby of this 1915 structure that perches right on the rim. Dinner at the lodge's restaurant, overlooking the lake, caps the day—reservations are strongly advised, although you can enjoy drinks, appetizers, and desserts in the Great Hall or out on the back terrace without having booked ahead.

Getting Here and Around

Rogue Valley International–Medford Airport (MFR) is the nearest commercial airport. About 75 miles southwest of the park, it's served by Alaska, Allegiant, American, Delta, and United Airlines and has rental cars. Amtrak trains stop in downtown Klamath Falls, 50 miles south of the park, and car rentals are available in town.

Crater Lake National Park's South Entrance, open year-round, is off Highway 62 in southern Oregon. If driving here from California, follow Interstate 5 north to Medford and head east on Highway 62, or take U.S. 97 north past Klamath Falls, exiting northwest on Highway 62. From Portland, Oregon, allow from 5½

to 6 hours to reach the park's South Entrance, by taking Interstate 5 to Medford. In summer, when the North Entrance is open, the drive from Portland takes just 4½ hours via Interstate 5, Highway 58 (through Oakridge), U.S. 97, and Highway 138. If coming from Portland in summer, staying at an Oakridge, Chemult, or Diamond Lake lodging the night before your arrival will get you fairly close to the park the following morning.

Most of the park is accessible only from late June or early July through mid-October. The rest of the year, snow blocks park roadways and entrances except Highway 62 and the access road to Rim Village from Mazama Village. Rim Drive is typically closed because of snow from mid-October to mid-July, and you could encounter icy conditions at any time of year, particularly in the early morning.

Park Essentials

ACCESSIBILITY

All the overlooks along Rim Drive are accessible to those with impaired mobility, as are Crater Lake Lodge, the facilities at Rim Village, and Steel Visitor Center. A half dozen accessible campsites are available at Mazama Campground.

PARK FEES AND PERMITS

Admission to the park is $30 per vehicle in summer, $20 in winter, good for seven days. For all overnight trips, backcountry campers and hikers must obtain a free wilderness permit at Canfield Ranger Station, which is at the park headquarters adjacent to Steel Visitor Center and open daily 9–5 from mid-April through early November, and 10–4 the rest of the year.

PARK HOURS

Crater Lake National Park is open 24 hours a day year-round; however, snow closes most park roadways from October to June. Lodging and most dining facilities are open usually from late May to mid-October (Rim Village Café the one year-round dining option). The park is in the Pacific time zone.

CELL PHONE RECEPTION

Cell phone reception in the park is unreliable, although generally it works around Crater Lake Lodge, which—along with Mazama Village—also has public phones.

Educational Offerings

RANGER PROGRAMS

★ Boat Tours

ISLAND | FAMILY | The most popular way to tour Crater Lake itself is on a two-hour ranger-led excursion aboard a 37-passenger launch. The first narrated tour leaves the dock at 9:30 am; the last departs at 3:45 pm. Several of the 10 daily boats stop at Wizard Island, where you can get off and reboard three or six hours later. Some of these trips act as shuttles, with no ranger narration. They're perfect if you just want to get to Wizard Island to hike. The shuttles leave at 8:30 and 11:30 and return to Cleetwood Cove at 12:15, 3:05, and 4:35. To get to the dock you must hike down Cleetwood Cove Trail, a strenuous 1.1-mile walk that descends 700 feet in elevation along the way; only those in excellent physical shape should attempt the hike. Bring adequate water with you. Purchase boat-tour tickets at Crater Lake Lodge, Annie Creek Restaurant and gift shop, the top of the trail, and through reservations. Restrooms are available at the top and bottom of the trail. ⊠ Crater Lake National Park ⊕ Access Cleetwood Cove Trail off Rim Dr., 11 miles north of Rim Village ☎ 866/292–6720 ⊕ www.travelcraterlake. com ▤ $28–$55.

Junior Ranger Program

TOUR—SIGHT | FAMILY | Kids ages 6–12 learn about Crater Lake while earning a Junior Ranger patch in daily sessions during summer months at the Rim Visitor Center, and year-round they can earn a badge by completing the Junior Ranger Activity Book, which can be picked up at either visitor center. ☎ 541/594–3100 ⊕ www.nps.gov/crla/learn/kidsyouth.

TOURS

Main Street Adventure Tours

GUIDED TOURS | This Ashland-based outfitter's guided tours in southern Oregon include seven-hour ones to Crater Lake. During these tours, available year-round, participants are driven around part of the lake and, seasonally, given the chance to take a boat tour. Along the way to the park there are stops at the Cole M. Rivers Fish Hatchery, two waterfalls, and Lake of the Woods. ⊠ Ashland ☎ 541/625–9845 ⊕ www.ashland-tours. com ▤ From $139.

Restaurants

There are just a few casual eateries and convenience stores within the park, all near the main (southern) entrance. For fantastic upscale dining on the caldera's rim, head to the Crater Lake Lodge. Outside the park, Klamath Falls has a smattering of good restaurants, and both Medford and Ashland abound with first-rate eateries serving farm-to-table cuisine and local Rogue Valley wines. *Restaurant reviews have been shortened. For full information visit Fodors.com.*

What It Costs in U.S. Dollars			
$	$$	$$$	$$$$
RESTAURANTS			
under $16	$16–$22	$23–$30	over $30
HOTELS			
under $150	$150–$200	$201–$250	over $250

Hotels

Crater Lake's summer season is relatively brief, and Crater Lake Lodge, the park's main accommodation, is generally booked up a year in advance. If you are unable to get a reservation, check availability as your trip approaches—cancellations do happen on occasion. The other in-park option, the Cabins at Mazama Village, also books up early in summer. Outside the park there are a couple of options in nearby Prospect as well as Fort Klamath and Union Creek, and you'll find numerous lodgings a bit farther afield in Klamath Falls, Medford, Ashland, and Roseburg. Additionally, if visiting the park via the North Entrance in summer, you might consider staying in one of the handful of lodgings in Diamond Lake, Oakridge, and Chemult. Even Bend is an option, as it's just a two-hour drive from North Entrance, which is only slightly longer than the drive from Ashland to the main entrance. *Hotel reviews have been shortened. For full information, visit Fodors.com.*

Visitor Information

PARK CONTACT INFORMATION Crater Lake National Park. ☎ 541/594–3000 ⊕ www.nps.gov/crla.

PARK LITERATURE AND INFORMATION Crater Lake Natural History Association. ☎ 541/594–3111 ⊕ www.craterlakeoregon.org.

VISITOR CENTERS
Rim Visitor Center

INFO CENTER | In summer you can obtain park information at the center, introduce your kids to a number of Junior Ranger activities, or stop into the nearby Sinnott Memorial Overlook, which has a small museum and a 900-foot view down to the lake's surface as well as ranger talks several times per day. In winter, snow-shoe walks are offered on weekends and holidays. A short walk away, the Rim Village Gift Store and cafeteria are the only services open in winter. ⊠ *Rim Dr. ✛ 7 miles north of Annie Spring entrance station* ☎ *541/594–3000* ⊕ *www.nps.gov/crla.*

Steel Visitor Center

INFO CENTER | Open year-round, the center, part of the park's headquarters, has restrooms, a small post office, and a shop that sells books, maps, and postcards. There are fewer exhibits than at comparable national park visitor centers, but you can view an engaging 22-minute film, *Crater Lake: Into the Deep,* which describes the lake's formation and geology and examines the area's cultural history. ⊠ *Rim Dr. ✛ 4 miles north of Annie Spring entrance station* ☎ *541/594–3000* ⊕ *www.nps.gov/crla.*

Sights
SCENIC DRIVES
★ Rim Drive

SCENIC DRIVE | Take this 33-mile scenic loop for views of the lake and its cliffs from every conceivable angle. The drive takes two hours not counting frequent stops at overlooks and short hikes that can easily stretch this to a half day. Rim Drive is typically closed due to heavy snowfall from mid-October to mid-June, and icy conditions can be encountered any month of the year, particularly in early morning. ⊠ *Crater Lake National Park ✛ Drive begins at Rim Village, 7 miles from (Annie Spring) South Entrance; from North Entrance, follow North Entrance Rd. south for 10 miles* ⊕ *www.nps.gov/crla.*

Wildlife in Crater Lake

Wildlife in the Crater Lake area flourishes in the water and throughout the surrounding forest.

Salmon and Trout

Two primary types of fish swim beneath the surface of Crater Lake: kokanee salmon and rainbow trout. Kokanees average about 8 inches in length, but they can grow to nearly 18 inches. Rainbow trout are larger than the kokanee but are less abundant in Crater Lake. Trout—including bull, Eastern brook, rainbow, and German brown—swim in the park's many streams and rivers.

Elk, Deer, and More

Remote canyons shelter the park's elk and deer populations, which can sometimes be seen at dusk and dawn feeding at forest's edge. Black bears and pine martens—cousins of the short-tailed weasel—also call Crater Lake home. Birds such as hairy woodpeckers, California gulls, red-tailed hawks, and great horned owls are more commonly seen in summer in forests below the lake.

HISTORIC SITES

★ Crater Lake Lodge

HOTEL—SIGHT | Built in 1915, this regal log-and-stone structure was designed in the classic style of western national park lodges, and the original lodgepole-pine pillars, beams, and stone fireplaces are still intact. The lobby, fondly referred to as the Great Hall, serves as a warm, welcoming gathering place where you can play games, socialize with a cocktail, or gaze out of the many windows to view spectacular sunrises and sunsets by a crackling fire. Exhibits off the lobby contain historic photographs and memorabilia from throughout the park's history. ⊠ *Rim Village* ⊕ *www.travelcraterlake. com.*

SCENIC STOPS

Cloudcap Overlook

VIEWPOINT | The highest road-access overlook on the Crater Lake rim, Cloudcap has a westward view across the lake to Wizard Island and an eastward view of Mt. Scott, the volcanic cone that is the park's highest point. ⊠ *Crater Lake National Park* ✛ *2 miles off Rim Dr., 13 miles northeast of Steel Visitor Center.*

Discovery Point

VIEWPOINT | This overlook marks the spot at which prospectors first spied the lake in 1853. Wizard Island is just northeast, close to shore. ⊠ *West Rim Dr.* ✛ *1½ miles north of Rim Village.*

Mazama Village

INFO CENTER | In summer, a campground, cabin-style motel, restaurant, gift shop, amphitheater, and gas station are open here. No gasoline is available in the park from mid-October to mid-May. Snowfall determines when the village and its facilities open and close for the season. Hours vary; call ahead. ⊠ *Mazama Village Rd.* ✛ *Off Hwy. 62, near Annie Spring entrance station* ☎ *541/594–2255, 866/292–6720* ⊕ *www.travelcraterlake. com.*

Phantom Ship Overlook

VIEWPOINT | From this point you can get a close look at Phantom Ship, a rock formation that resembles a schooner with furled masts and looks ghostly in fog. ⊠ *East Rim Dr.* ✛ *7 miles northeast of Steel Visitor Center.*

★ Pinnacles Overlook

VIEWPOINT | Ascending from the banks of Sand and Wheeler creeks, unearthly

Wizard Island in Craker Lake is accessible only by boat.

spires of eroded ash resemble the peaks of fairy-tale castles. Once upon a time, the road continued east to a former entrance. A path now replaces the old road and follows the rim of Sand Creek (affording more views of pinnacles) to where the entrance sign still stands. ⊠ *Pinnacles Rd.* ✚ *12 miles east of Steel Visitor Center.*

Sun Notch

VIEWPOINT | It's a relatively easy ½-mile loop hike through wildflowers and dry meadow to this overlook, which has views of Crater Lake and Phantom Ship. Mind the cliff edges. ⊠ *East Rim Dr.* ✚ *About 4½ miles east of Steel Visitor Center.*

★ Wizard Island

ISLAND | The volcanic eruption that led to the creation of Crater Lake resulted in the formation of this magical island a quarter mile from the lake's western shore. The views at its summit—reached on a somewhat strenuous 2-mile hike—are stupendous.

Getting to the island requires a strenuous 1-mile hike down (and later back up) the steep Cleetwood Cove Trail to the cove's dock. There, board either the shuttle boat to Wizard Island or a Crater Lake narrated tour boat that includes a stop on the island. If you opt for the latter, you can explore Wizard Island a bit and reboard a later boat to resume the lake tour.

The hike to Wizard Summit, 763 feet above the lake's surface, begins at the island's boat dock and steeply ascends over rock-strewn terrain; a path at the top circles the 90-foot-deep crater's rim. More moderate is the 1¾-mile hike on a rocky trail along the shore of Wizard Island, so called because William Steel, an early Crater Lake booster, thought its shape resembled a wizard's hat. ⊠ *Crater Lake National Park* ✚ *Access Cleetwood Cove Trail off Rim Dr., 11 miles north of Rim Village* ☎ *541/594–2255, 866/292–6720* ⊕ *www.travelcraterlake.com* ⊠ *Shuttle boat $28, tour boat $55.*

Activities

HIKING

Annie Creek Canyon Trail

HIKING/WALKING | This somewhat challenging 1½-mile hike loops through a deep stream-cut canyon, providing views of the narrow cleft scarred by volcanic activity. This is a good area to look for flowers and deer. *Moderate.* ⊠ *Mazama Campground, Mazama Village Rd.* ⊹ *Trailhead: behind amphitheater between D and E campground loops.*

Boundary Springs Trail

HIKING/WALKING | If you feel like sleuthing, take this moderate 5-mile round-trip hike to the headwaters of the Rogue River. The trail isn't well marked, so a detailed trail guide is necessary. You'll see streams, forests, and wildflowers along the way before discovering Boundary Springs pouring out of the side of a low ridge. *Moderate.* ⊠ *Crater Lake National Park* ⊹ *Trailhead: pullout on Hwy. 230, near milepost 19, about 5 miles west of Hwy. 138.*

★ Castle Crest Wildflower Trail

HIKING/WALKING | This picturesque 1-mile round-trip trek passes through a spring-fed meadow and is one of the park's flatter hikes. Wildflowers burst into full bloom here in July. You can also access Castle Crest via a similarly easy half-mile loop trail from East Rim Drive. *Easy.* ⊠ *Crater Lake National Park* ⊹ *Trailhead: either East Rim Dr. or across road from Steel Visitor Center parking lot.*

Cleetwood Cove Trail

HIKING/WALKING | This strenuous 2¼-mile round-trip hike descends 700 feet down nearly vertical cliffs along the lake to the boat dock. Be in very good shape before you tackle this well-maintained trail—it's the hike back up that catches some visitors unprepared. Bring along plenty of water. *Difficult.* ⊠ *Crater Lake National Park* ⊹ *Trailhead: on Rim Dr., 11 miles north of Rim Village.*

Godfrey Glen Trail

HIKING/WALKING | This 1-mile loop trail is an easy stroll through an old-growth forest with canyon views. Its dirt path is accessible to wheelchairs with assistance. *Easy.* ⊠ *Crater Lake National Park* ⊹ *Trailhead: Mission Valley Rd., 2½ miles south of Steel Visitor Center.*

★ Mt. Scott Trail

HIKING/WALKING | This strenuous 4½-mile round-trip trail takes you to the park's highest point—the top of Mt. Scott, the oldest volcanic cone of Mt. Mazama, at 8,929 feet. The average hiker needs 90 minutes to make the steep uphill trek—and about 60 minutes to get down. The trail starts at an elevation of about 7,679 feet, so the climb is not extreme, but the trail is steep in spots. The views of the lake and the broad Klamath Basin are spectacular. *Difficult.* ⊠ *Crater Lake National Park* ⊹ *Trailhead: 14 miles east of Steel Visitor Center on Rim Dr., across from road to Cloudcap Overlook.*

Pacific Crest Trail

HIKING/WALKING | You can hike a portion of the Pacific Crest Trail, which extends from Mexico to Canada and winds through the park for 33 miles. For this prime backcountry experience, catch the trail off Highway 138 about a mile east of the North Entrance, where it heads south and then toward the west rim of the lake and circles it for about 6 miles, then descends down Dutton Creek to the Mazama Village area. You'll need a detailed map for this hike; check online or with the PCT association. *Difficult.* ⊠ *Crater Lake National Park* ⊹ *Trailhead: at Pacific Crest Trail parking lot, off Hwy. 138, 1 mile east of North Entrance* ⊕ *www.pcta.org.*

★ Watchman Peak Trail

HIKING/WALKING | This is one of the park's best and most easily accessed hikes. Though it's just more than 1½ miles round-trip, the trail climbs more than 400 feet—not counting the steps up to the actual lookout, which has great views of

Wizard Island and the lake. *Moderate.* ✉ *Crater Lake National Park ⊕ Trailhead: at Watchman Overlook, Rim Dr., about 4 miles northwest of Rim Village.*

Restaurants

IN THE PARK
Annie Creek Restaurant

$ | **AMERICAN** | **FAMILY** | This family-friendly dining spot in Mazama Village serves hearty if unmemorable comfort fare, and service can be hit or miss. Blue cheese–bacon burgers, Cobb salads, sandwiches, meat loaf, and a tofu stir-fry are all on the menu, and American standards are served at breakfast. **Known for:** pine-shaded outdoor seating area; convenient to lake and the park's southern hiking trails; several varieties of burgers. $ *Average main: $13 ✉ Mazama Village Rd. and Ave. C ⊕ Near Annie Spring entrance station* ☎ *541/594–2255 ⊕ www.travelcraterlake. com ⊙ Closed late Sept.–late May.*

★ Crater Lake Lodge Dining Room

$$$ | **PACIFIC NORTHWEST** | The only upscale restaurant option inside the park (dinner reservations are essential), the dining room is magnificent, with a large stone fireplace and views of Crater Lake's clear-blue waters. Breakfast and lunch are enjoyable here, but the dinner is the main attraction, with tempting dishes that emphasize local produce and Pacific Northwest seafood—think wild mushroom–and–caramelized onion flatbread and pan-seared wild salmon with seasonal veggies. **Known for:** nice selection of Oregon wines; Oregon berry cobbler; views of the lake. $ *Average main: $28 ✉ Crater Lake Lodge, 1 Lodge Loop Rd.* ☎ *541/594–2255 ⊕ www.craterlakelodges.com ⊙ Closed mid-Oct.–mid-May.*

PICNIC AREAS
Godfrey Glen Trail

RESTAURANT—SIGHT | In a small canyon abuzz with songbirds, squirrels, and chipmunks, this picnic area has a south-facing, protected location. The half dozen picnic tables here are in a small meadow; there are also a few fire grills and a pit toilet. ✉ *Crater Lake National Park ⊕ 2½ miles south of Steel Visitor Center.*

Rim Drive

RESTAURANT—SIGHT | About a half dozen picnic-area turnouts encircle the lake; all have good views, but they can get very windy. Most have pit toilets, and a few have fire grills, but none have running water. ✉ *Rim Dr.*

★ Rim Village

RESTAURANT—SIGHT | This is the only park picnic area with running water. The tables are set behind the visitor center, and most have a view of the lake below. There are flush toilets inside the visitor center. ✉ *Rim Dr., Rim Village ⊕ By Crater Lake Lodge.*

★ Wizard Island

RESTAURANT—SIGHT | The park's best picnic venue is on Wizard Island; pack a lunch and book yourself on one of the early-morning boat tour departures, reserving space on an afternoon return. There are no formal picnic areas and just pit toilets, but you'll discover plenty of sunny and shaded spots where you can enjoy a quiet meal and appreciate the astounding scene that surrounds you. The island is accessible by boat only. ✉ *Crater Lake ⊕ Boat dock at end of Cleetwood Cove Trail, off Rim Dr., 11 miles north of Rim Village ⊕ www.travelcraterlake.com.*

🛏 Hotels

IN THE PARK
The Cabins at Mazama Village

$$ | **HOTEL** | In a wooded area 7 miles south of the lake, this complex is made up of several A-frame buildings and has modest rooms with two queen beds and a private bath. **Pros:** clean and well-kept facility; very close to the lake and plenty of hiking trails; most affordable of the park lodgings. **Cons:** lots of traffic into adjacent campground; no a/c, TVs, or phones in rooms; not actually on

Best Campgrounds in Crater Lake

Tent campers and RV enthusiasts alike enjoy the heavily wooded and well-equipped setting of Mazama Campground. Lost Creek is much smaller, with minimal amenities and a more "rustic" Crater Lake experience. Pack bug repellent and patience if camping in the snowmelt season.

Lost Creek Campground. The 16 small, remote tent sites here are usually available on a daily basis; in summer arrive early to secure a spot (it's open early July–mid-October). The cost is $5 nightly. ✉ *3 miles south of Rim Rd. on Pinnacles Spur Rd. at Grayback Dr.* ☎ *541/594–3100.*

Mazama Campground. This campground is set well below the lake caldera in the pine and fir forest of the Cascades not far from the main access road (Highway 62). Drinking water, showers, and laundry facilities help ensure that you don't have to rough it too much. About half the 214 spaces are pull-throughs, some with electricity and a few with hookups. The best tent spots are on some of the outer loops above Annie Creek Canyon. Tent sites cost $21, RV ones $31–$36. ✉ *Mazama Village, near Annie Spring entrance station* ☎ *541/594–2255, 866/292–6720* 🌐 *www.craterlakelodges.com.*

Crater Lake (but a short drive away). [$] *Rooms from: $165* ✉ *Mazama Village* ✣ *Near Annie Spring entrance station* ☎ *541/594–2255, 866/292–6720* 🌐 *www.travelcraterlake.com* ⏲ *Closed mid-Oct.–late May* 🛏 *40 rooms* 🍴 *No meals.*

★ Crater Lake Lodge

$$$ | **HOTEL** | The period feel of this 1915 lodge on the caldera's rim is reflected in its lodgepole-pine columns, gleaming wood floors, and stone fireplaces in the common areas, and the simple guest rooms. **Pros:** ideal location for watching sunrise and sunset reflected on the lake; exudes rustic charm; excellent restaurant. **Cons:** books up far in advance; rooms are small and have tubs only, no shower; no air-conditioning, phone, or TV in rooms. [$] *Rooms from: $201* ✉ *1 Lodge Loop Rd.* ✣ *Rim Village, east of Rim Visitor Center* ☎ *541/594–2255, 866/292–6720* 🌐 *www.travelcraterlake.com* ⏲ *Closed mid-Oct.–mid-May* 🛏 *71 rooms* 🍴 *No meals.*

Chapter 9

SOUTHERN OREGON

Updated by
Andrew Collins

👁 Sights	🍴 Restaurants	🛏 Hotels	🛍 Shopping	🍸 Nightlife
★★★★★	★★★★☆	★★★★☆	★★☆☆☆	★★★☆☆

WELCOME TO SOUTHERN OREGON

TOP REASONS TO GO

★ **Discover Oregon's other wine regions:** The once underrated Umpqua and Rogue River wine regions offer a fast-growing bounty of critically acclaimed tasting rooms.

★ **Go underground:** Explore deep into mysterious underground chambers and marble caves at Oregon Caves National Monument.

★ **Shakespeare Festival:** The acclaimed Oregon Shakespeare Festival draws drama lovers to Ashland nine months a year for both classic and contemporary theater.

★ **Enjoy quaint towns:** Southern Oregon's own throwback to the Old West, Jacksonville abounds with well-preserved buildings, while Ashland has one of the state's prettiest downtowns.

★ **Get wet and wild:** Each fall millions of waterfowl descend upon Klamath Basin National Wildlife Refuge Complex. The Rogue River is Oregon's white-water-rafting capital, and the entire region is laced with stunning hiking trails.

1 Roseburg. Located on the pristine Umpqua River, there's fishing, waterfall hikes, several excellent wineries, and a Wildlife Safari nearby.

2 Grants Pass. The lively downtown has a growing number of restaurants and boutiques, and it's the launching point for great white-water rafting.

3 Medford. The region's largest city and transportation hub boasts reasonably priced lodgings and a burgeoning craft-beer, wine, and distilling scene.

4 Jacksonville. Founded during the 1851 gold rush, this historic downtown has lively boutiques and eateries, and several excellent wineries nearby.

5 Ashland. The Oregon Shakespeare Festival and an abundance of historic buildings have made this into a hub of arts, dining, and luxury inns.

6 Klamath Falls. This slightly off-the-beaten-path town is a great base for visiting the Klamath Basin and Crater Lake.

7 Cave Junction. Along the scenic highway from Grants Pass to Crescent City, California, this modest village is home to the Oregon Caves National Monument.

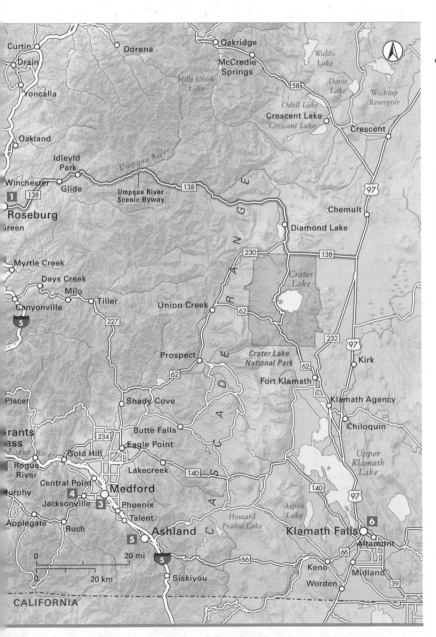

Southern Oregon begins where the verdant lowlands of the Willamette Valley give way to a complex collision of mountains, rivers, and ravines. The intricate geography of the "Land of Umpqua," as the area around Roseburg is somewhat romantically known, signals that this is territory distinct from neighboring regions to the north, east, and west.

Wild rivers—the Rogue and the Umpqua are legendary for fishing and boating—and twisting mountain roads traverse this landscape that saw Oregon's most violent Indian wars and became the territory of a self-reliant breed. "Don't-Tread-on-Me" southern Oregonians see themselves as markedly different from fellow citizens of the Pacific Wonderland. In fact, several early-20th-century attempts to secede from Oregon (in cahoots with northern California) and proclaim a "state of Jefferson" survive in local folklore and culture. That being said, Ashland and parts of the surrounding area have steadily become more progressive and urbane in recent decades, as wineries, breweries, art galleries, and farm-to-table restaurants continue to proliferate. The mix of folks from all different political, social, and stylistic bents is a big part of what makes southern Oregon so interesting—and appealing.

Some locals describe this sun-kissed, sometimes surprisingly hot landscape as Mediterranean; others refer to it as Oregon's banana belt. It's a climate built for slow-paced pursuits and a leisurely outlook on life, not to mention agriculture—the region's orchards, farms, and increasingly acclaimed vineyards have lately helped give southern Oregon cachet among food and wine aficionados. The restaurant scene has grown partly thanks to a pair of big cultural draws, Ashland's Oregon Shakespeare Festival and Jacksonville's open-air, picnic-friendly Britt Festivals concert series.

Roseburg, Medford, and Klamath Falls are all popular bases for visiting iconic Crater Lake National Park (see Chapter 8), which lies at the region's eastern edge, about two hours away by car. Formed nearly 8,000 years ago by the cataclysmic eruption of Mt. Mazama, this stunningly clear-blue lake is North America's deepest.

MAJOR REGIONS

The northernmost part of southern Oregon, beginning about 40 miles south of Eugene and the Willamette Valley, the rural and sparsely populated **Umpqua Valley** is the gateway to this part of the state's sunny and relatively dry climate. As you drive down Interstate 5 you'll descend through twisting valleys and climb up over scenic highlands. In summer you can follow the dramatic Rogue-Umpqua River Scenic Byway (Highway 138) east over the Cascades to access Crater Lake from the north—it's the prettiest route to the lake.

Known increasingly for its up-and-coming wineries, including superb Abacela, the Umpqua Valley is home to bustling **Roseburg** and its family-friendly Wildlife Safari park, and the Rogue-Umpqua River Scenic Byway, a particularly scenic route that leads to the northern (summer only) entrance of Crater Lake before doubling back to the southwest toward Medford.

Encompassing the broad, curving, southeasterly swath of towns from Grants Pass through Medford down to Ashland, the mild and sun-kissed **Rogue Valley** is southern Oregon's main population center, and also where you'll find the bulk of the region's lodging, dining, shopping, and recreation.

Interstate 5 cuts through the valley en route to northern California, but venture away from the main thoroughfare and you'll discover the many superb wineries that have lately begun earning the same kind of attention that the state's more famous Willamette Wine Country has been receiving for decades. Foodies are also drawn to the region's abundance of local producers, from nationally acclaimed cheese makers and chocolatiers to farms growing pears, blackberries, and cherries. With warmer temperatures, this area is conducive to growing a wide range of grape varieties—from reds like Syrah, Tempranillo, and Cabernet Sauvignon to increasingly well-known old-world whites like Viognier, Sauvignon Blanc, and Pinot Gris. At the north end of the valley, the bustling river-rafting hub of **Grants Pass** has several excellent restaurants and marks the northern gateway to the Rogue and adjacent Applegate Valley wine regions. Farther south are charmingly historic **Jacksonville,** home to the

annual three-week Britt Music Festival, and the small city (population 82,000) of **Medford**, whose downtown has been enjoying a resurgence of late. The artsy college town of **Ashland** is one of Oregon's top restaurant destinations and home to the world-renowned Oregon Shakespeare Festival.

Flanked by about a 2-million-acre Rogue–Siskiyou National Forest, the Rogue Valley is a hub of outdoor recreation, from Oregon Caves National Monument in the sleepy town of **Cave Junction** to fishing and white-water rafting along its clear rivers and mountain biking, hiking, and even skiing in the higher elevations. **Klamath Falls** lies technically a bit east of the Rogue Valley but shares the region's abundance of unspoiled wilderness and opportunities for getting in touch with nature.

Planning

When to Go

Southern Oregon's population centers, which all lie chiefly in the valleys, tend to be warmer and quite a bit sunnier than Eugene and Portland to the north, receiving almost no snow in winter and only 2 to 3 inches of rain per month. In summer, temperatures regularly climb into the 90s, but the low humidity makes for a generally comfortable climate. This makes most of the region quite pleasant to visit year-round, with spring and fall generally offering the best balance of sunny and mild weather.

The exceptions, during the colder months, are southern Oregon's mountainous areas to the east and west, which are covered with snow from fall through spring. Some of the roads leading from the Umpqua and Rogue valleys up to Crater Lake are closed because of snow from mid-October through June, making summer the prime time to visit.

Festivals

Britt Music & Art Festival

FESTIVALS | The Northwest's oldest performing arts showcase features three midsummer weekends of concerts by some 90 international artists, offering everything from classical to bluegrass to pop. ⊠ *Britt Festival Pavilion, 350 1st St., Jacksonville* ☎ *541/773–6077, 800/882–7488* ⊕ *www.brittfest.org.*

★ Oregon Shakespeare Festival

FESTIVALS | Ashland's biggest attraction is this festival of Shakespeare and other plays, which runs mid-February through early November. Book tickets and lodging well in advance. ⊠ *15 S. Pioneer St., Ashland* ☎ *800/219–8161* ⊕ *www.osfashland.org.*

Winter Wings Festival

FESTIVALS | Each February, nature enthusiasts flock to the Klamath Basin for the Winter Wings Festival, the nation's oldest birding festival. ⊠ *Klamath Falls* ☎ *877/541–2473* ⊕ *www.winterwingsfest.org.*

Getting Here and Around

AIR TRAVEL

Medford's Rogue Valley International Airport (MFR) is the state's third-largest facility, with direct flights to Denver, Las Vegas, Los Angeles, Phoenix, Portland, Salt Lake City, San Francisco, and Seattle, and service by Allegiant, Alaska, American, Delta, and United. Most national car-rental branches are at the airport. A few taxi and shuttle companies provide transportation from the airport to other towns in the area, as do Lyft and Uber; these are used mostly by locals, as a car is the only practical way to explore this relatively rural part of Oregon. The one exception is Ashland, where many attractions, restaurants, and accommodations are within walking distance. Cascade Airport Shuttle offers door-to-door service from the airport to Ashland for about $30 to $35. Among taxi companies, Valley Cab serves the Rogue Valley region, with fares costing $2.75 base per trip, plus $3 per mile thereafter.

Roseburg is a 75-mile drive from Oregon's second-largest airport, in Eugene (EUG). Ashland is about 300 miles south of the state's largest airport, in Portland, and 350 miles north of San Francisco. Although it's often cheaper to fly into these larger airports than it is to Medford, what you lose in gas costs, time, and inconvenience will likely outweigh any savings.

CONTACTS **Cascade Airport Shuttle.** ☎ *541/488–1998, 888/760–7433* ⊕ *www.cascadeshuttle.com.* **Rogue Valley International Airport.** ☎ *541/772–8068* ⊕ *www.jacksoncountyor.org/airport.* **Valley Cab.** ☎ *541/772–1818* ⊕ *www.myvalleycab.com.*

CAR TRAVEL

Unquestionably, your best way to explore the region is by car, although key attractions, hotels, and restaurants in a few downtowns—such as Ashland, Grants Pass, and Jacksonville—are within walking distance of one another. Interstate 5 runs north–south the length of the Umpqua and Rogue river valleys, linking Roseburg, Grants Pass, Medford, and Ashland. Many regional attractions lie not too far east or west of Interstate 5. Jacksonville is a short drive due west from Medford. Highway 138 (aka the Rogue-Umpqua Scenic Byway) winds scenically along the Umpqua River east of Roseburg to the less-visited northern end of Crater Lake National Park. Highway 140 leads from Medford east to Klamath Falls, which you can also reach from Ashland via Highway 66 and Bend via U.S. 97.

Restaurants

Southern Oregon's dining scene varies greatly from region to region, with the more tourism-driven communities of Ashland, Jacksonville, and Grants Pass leading the way in terms of sophisticated farm-to-table restaurants, hip coffeehouses, and noteworthy bakeries and wine bars. Other larger towns in the valleys, including Roseburg and Medford, have grown in culinary as well as craft-brewing stature of late, while Klamath Falls and Cave Junction have few dining options of note. In the top culinary communities you'll find chefs emphasizing Oregon-produced foods; regional wines, including many from the Rogue and Umqua valleys, also find their way onto many menus. *Restaurant reviews have been shortened. For full information visit Fodors.com.*

What it Costs in U.S. Dollars			
$	$$	$$$	$$$$
RESTAURANTS			
under $16	$16–$22	$23–$30	over $30
HOTELS			
under $150	$150–$200	$201–$250	over $250

Hotels

Ashland has the region's greatest variety of distinctive lodgings, from the usual midpriced chain properties to plush B&Bs set in restored Arts and Crafts and Victorian mansions. Nearby Jacksonville also has a few fine, upscale inns. Beyond that, in nearly every town in southern Oregon you'll find an interesting country inn or small hotel, and in any of the key communities along Interstate 5—including Roseburg, Grants Pass, and Medford—a wide variety of chain motels and hotels. Rooms in this part of the state book up earliest in summer, especially on weekends. If you're coming to Ashland or Jacksonville, try to book at least a week or two ahead. Elsewhere, you can usually find a room in a suitable chain property on less than a day's notice. *Hotel reviews have been shortened. For full information visit Fodors.com.*

Tours

Hellgate Jetboat Excursions
BOAT TOURS | FAMILY | You'll see some of Oregon's most magnificent scenery on these excursions, which depart from the Riverside Inn in Grants Pass. The 36-mile round-trip runs through Hellgate Canyon and takes two hours. There is also a 5½-hour, 75-mile round-trip from Grants Pass to Grave Creek, with a stop for a meal on an open-air deck (cost of meal not included). Trips are available May through September, conditions permitting. ☎ 541/479–7204 ⊕ www.hellgate.com ✉ From $33.

Premier Wine Tours
SPECIAL-INTEREST | Getting to know some of the region's more than 130 wineries can be a challenge to visitors, especially when you factor in having to drive from tasting room to tasting room. This outfitter with knowledgeable guides leads five-hour tours leaving daily from Ashland, Medford, and Jacksonville—the day includes a tour of a winery, picnic lunch, and tasting at a few of the area's top producers. ☎ 541/261–6389 ⊕ www.southernoregonwinetour.com ✉ From $79.

Visitor Information

CONTACTS Travel Southern Oregon. ☎ 541/708–1994 ⊕ www.southernoregon.org.

Roseburg

73 miles south of Eugene on I–5.

Fishermen the world over hold the name Roseburg sacred. The timber town on the Umpqua River attracts anglers in search of a dozen popular fish species, including bass, brown and brook trout, and Chinook, coho, and sockeye salmon. The native steelhead, which makes its run to the sea in the summer, is king of them all.

The north and south branches of the Umpqua River meet up just north of Roseburg. You can drive alongside the North Umpqua via the Rogue-Umpqua Scenic Byway, which provides access to trails, hot springs, waterfalls, and the Winchester fish ladder. White-water rafting is also popular here, although not to the degree that it is farther south in the Rogue Valley.

About 80 miles west of the northern gateway to Crater Lake National Park and in the Hundred Valleys of the Umpqua, Roseburg and the surrounding countryside are home to about 25 wineries, many of them well regarded and most within easy reach of Interstate 5.

GETTING HERE AND AROUND

Roseburg is the first large town you'll reach driving south from Eugene on Interstate 5. It's also a main access point into southern Oregon via Highway 138 if you're approaching from the east, either by way of Crater Lake or U.S. 97, which leads down from Bend. And from the North Bend–Coos Bay region of the Oregon Coast, windy but picturesque Highway 42 leads to just south of Roseburg. It's a 75-mile drive north to Eugene's airport, and a 95-mile drive south to Rogue Valley Airport in Medford.

ESSENTIALS

VISITOR INFORMATION Roseburg Area Visitor Center. ⊠ *410 S.E. Spruce St.* ☎ *541/672–2648* ⊕ *www.roseburgchamber.com.*

◉ Sights

★ Abacela Vineyards and Winery

WINERY/DISTILLERY | The name derives from an archaic Spanish word meaning "to plant grapevines," and that's exactly what this winery's husband-wife team started doing in the late '90s. Abacela has steadily established itself as one of the best Oregon wineries outside the Willamette Valley. Hot-blooded Spanish Tempranillo is Abacela's pride and joy, though inky Malbec and a subtly floral Albariño also highlight a repertoire heavy on Mediterranean varietals, which you can sample in a handsome, eco-friendly tasting room where you can also order light appetizers to snack on. ⊠ *12500 Lookingglass Rd.* ☎ *541/679–6642* ⊕ *www.abacela.com.*

Douglas County Museum

MUSEUM | One of the best county museums in the state surveys 10,000 years of human activity in the region. The fossil collection is worth a stop, as is the state's second-largest photo collection, numbering more than 24,000 images, some dating to the 1840s. ⊠ *123 Museum Dr.* ☎ *541/957–7007* ⊕ *www.umpquavalleymuseums.org* 🎟 *$8* ⊘ *Closed Sun. and Mon.*

Henry Estate Winery

WINERY/DISTILLERY | One of the earliest wineries to develop into a serious success in southern Oregon, this picturesque estate sits alongside the Umpqua River about 15 miles northwest of Roseburg and turns out exceptional Pinot Noir and Alsace-style Pinot Gris, along with some European wines less often seen in the United States, such as Müller-Thurgau and Veraison. The winery hosts a number of events, including a

Cajun blues festival each June. ✉ *687 Hubbard Creek Rd., Umpqua* ☎ *541/459–5120* 🌐 *www.henryestate.com.*

Rogue-Umpqua River Scenic Byway

SCENIC DRIVE | Roseburg is the starting point for this dramatic route that climbs east through dense stands of old-growth Douglas fir and hemlock trees and into the Cascade Range for about 80 miles en route to the northern entrance to Crater Lake National Park (this section, which runs alongside the North Umpqua Wild and Scenic River, is also known as Highway 138). Just after Diamond Lake, the route turns southwest via Highways 230, 62, and 234 along a stunning stretch of the Rogue River, before ending northeast of Medford in the small town of Eagle Point. If you're planning to drive this entire 172-mile route, give yourself at least six hours (and as many as nine) to stop here and there to enjoy the scenery, and perhaps even hike some portions of the North Umpqua Trail. Signposted trailheads along the drive lead to some magnificent waterfalls—Deadline Falls and Fern Creek Falls are a couple of favorites. Note that this route differs from the Umpqua River Scenic Byway, which you can also access near Roseburg. This stretch of Highway 138 starts about 15 miles north of Roseburg in Oakland and twists and turns for 66 miles over the Coast Range—through famous fishing holes and rugged timber towns—before ending at U.S. 101 (aka the Oregon Coast Highway) in Reedsport, on the central coast. ✉ *Hwy. 138* ✣ *It runs east starting at the junction with Hwy. 99* 🌐 *www.blm.gov/or/districts/roseburg/recreation/ScenicByway.*

★ Wildlife Safari

ZOO | **FAMILY** | Come face-to-face with some 500 free-roaming animals at the 600-acre drive-through wildlife park. Inhabitants include alligators, bobcats, cougars, gibbons, lions, giraffes, grizzly bears, Tibetan yaks, Siberian tigers, and more than 100 additional species. There's also a petting zoo, a miniature train, up-close animal feedings and encounters, and engaging wildlife talks. The admission price includes two same-day drive-throughs. This nonprofit zoological park is a respected research facility with full accreditation from the American Zoo and Aquarium Association, with a mission to conserve and protect endangered species through education and breeding programs. Through its cheetah breeding program, for example, more than 215 of these animals have been born here. ✉ *1790 Safari Rd., Winston* ☎ *541/679–6761* 🌐 *www.wildlifesafari.net* 🎟 *$22.*

🍴 Restaurants

Brix

$$ | **AMERICAN** | This handsome downtown American bistro with exposed-brick walls, curving leather banquettes, and high ceilings serves reasonably priced breakfast and lunch fare daily, and somewhat more upscale dinners. Highlights include mango-mahi nachos, and Sicilian-style, rare-seared ahi tuna steak with olive tapenade; several more affordable sandwiches, burgers, and salads are available, too. **Known for:** mix of affordable and upscale dishes; impressive wine and cocktail list; pumpkin-cranberry ricotta pancakes at breakfast. [$] *Average main: $18* ✉ *527 S.E. Jackson St.* ☎ *541/440–4901* 🌐 *www.facebook.com/brixgrill/* 🕒 *No dinner Sun. and Mon.*

The Parrot House

$$$ | **AMERICAN** | This ornate Victorian house filled with antiques, chandeliers, and framed mirrors and artwork provides a grand setting for everything from a romantic dinner by the fireplace to a relaxed brunch or lunch with friends on the heated patio—you'll find both formal and casual spaces. The farm-to-table menu is similarly varied, with burgers, pizzas, pastas to more elaborately sauced steaks and seafood grills, and there's live music many evenings. **Known for:** setting inside a gracious Victorian house; lavish

Sunday brunch (with buffet and à la carte option); barrel-aged bourbons in the classy Reform Bar. $ *Average main: $28* ⊠ *1851 S.E. Stephens St.* ☎ *541/580–0600* ⊕ *www.parrotthouseroseburg.com.*

★ True Kitchen + Bar

$$$ | MODERN AMERICAN | A dapper, upmarket downtown bistro with a friendly, easy-going vibe, True excels both in its gastropub menu that often draws on seasonal ingredients and arguably the region's best beverage program, which features a terrific selection of Umpqua Valley wines and Oregon craft beers. The cuisine borrows a bit from different parts of the world; with short-rib bao buns, shrimp and grits, and adobo-lime chicken among the favorites, and several juicy burgers to choose from as well. **Known for:** generous food deals during the daily (bar-seating only) happy hour; impressive craft cocktail list; creatively topped burgers. $ *Average main: $25* ⊠ *629 S.E. Main St.* ☎ *541/900–1000* ⊕ *www. truekitchenandbar.com* ⊘ *Closed Sun. No lunch.*

Hotels

Hampton Inn & Suites Roseburg

$$ | HOTEL | Although its straight out of the Hampton Inn cookie-cutter mold, this clean and modern property offers the comfiest rooms of any property in town, and it's a quick drive from downtown. **Pros:** nice indoor pool and gym; conveniently located just off the interstate; rooms have microwaves and refrigerators. **Cons:** looks and feels like any other Hampton Inn; no pets allowed; not an especially inspired setting. $ *Rooms from: $162* ⊠ *1620 N.W. Mulholland Dr.* ☎ *541/492–1212* ⊕ *www.hamptoninn3.hilton.com* ⤳ *84 rooms* ⦿ *Free breakfast.*

★ The Steamboat Inn

$$$ | B&B/INN | The world's top fly-fishermen converge at this secluded forest inn, high in the Cascades above the North Umpqua River; others come simply to relax in the reading nooks or on the decks of the riverside guest cabins nestled below soaring fir trees. **Pros:** good option if en route to Crater Lake; access to some of the best fishing in the West; an excellent restaurant (open to the general public; call for hours). **Cons:** far from any towns or cities; often books up well in advance in summer; no TV or Wi-Fi. $ *Rooms from: $215* ⊠ *42705 N. Umpqua Hwy., Idleyld Park* ✥ *38 miles east of Roseburg on Hwy. 138, near Steamboat Creek* ☎ *541/498–2230* ⊕ *www.thesteamboatinn.com* ⤳ *20 units* ⦿ *No meals.*

Nightlife

Backside Brewing

BREWPUBS/BEER GARDENS | Situated just north of downtown, this lively, rambling brewpub turns out well-crafted pilsners, red ales, and hazy IPAs. There are pool tables and sports on TV in the spacious taproom and a grassy lawn with picnic tables outside. They serve pretty tasty pizza, too. ⊠ *1640 N.E. Odell Ave.* ☎ *541/671–2552.*

Activities

FISHING

You'll find some of the best river fishing in Oregon along the Umpqua, with smallmouth bass, shad, steelhead, salmon (coho, Chinook, and sockeye), and sturgeon—the biggest reaching 10 feet in length—among the most prized catches. In addition to the Steamboat Inn, several outfitters in the region provide full guide services, which typically include all gear, boats, and expert leaders. There's good fishing in this region year-round, with sturgeon and steelhead at their best during the colder months, Chinook and coho salmon thriving in the fall, and most other species prolific in spring and summer.

Kayaking Rainey Falls on the Rogue River

Big K Guest Ranch

FISHING | Set along a 10-mile span of the upper Umpqua River near Elkton (about 35 miles north of Roseburg), Big K is a 2,500-acre guest ranch. Accommodations are geared primarily to groups and corporate retreats, but the ranch offers individual half- and full-day fishing trips starting at $350 for one or two anglers, and two-day/three-night fishing and lodging packages (meals included) for around $940 per person. Adventures include fly-fishing for smallmouth bass and summer steelhead, as well as spin-casting and drift-boat fishing. ⊠ *20029 Hwy. 138 W, Elkton* ☎ *541/584–2295* ⊕ *www. big-k.com.*

Oregon Angler

FISHING | One of the state's most respected and knowledgeable guides, Todd Hannah, specializes in jet-boat and drift-boat fishing excursions along the famed "Umpqua Loop," an 18-mile span of river that's long been lauded for exceptional fishing. Full-day trips start around $200 per person. ⊠ *Elkton* ☎ *541/459–7922* ⊕ *www.theoregonangler.com.*

RAFTING

There's thrilling Class III and higher white-water rafting along the North Umpqua River, with several outfitters providing trips ranging from a few hours to a few days throughout the year.

North Umpqua Outfitters

WHITE-WATER RAFTING | Since 1987, this trusted provider has offered half-, full-, and two-day rafting and kayaking trips, starting at $105 per person, along the frothy North Umpqua. ⊠ *Idleyld Park* ☎ *888/454–9696* ⊕ *www.umpquarivers. com.*

Grants Pass

70 miles south of Roseburg on I–5.

"It's the Climate!" So says a confident 1950s vintage neon sign presiding over Josephine County's downtown. Grants Pass bills itself as Oregon's white-water

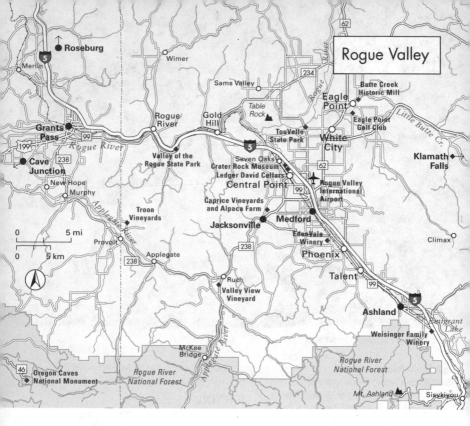

capital: the Rogue River, preserved by Congress in 1968 as a National Wild and Scenic River, runs right through town. Downtown Grants Pass is a National Historic District, an attractive little enclave of 19th-century brick storefronts housing a mix of folksy businesses harking back to the 1950s and newer, trendier cafés and boutiques. It's all that white water, however, that compels most visitors—and not a few moviemakers (*The River Wild* and *Rooster Cogburn* were both filmed here). If the river alone doesn't serve up enough natural drama, the sheer rock walls of nearby Hellgate Canyon rise 250 feet.

GETTING HERE AND AROUND

Grants Pass is easily reached via Interstate 5, and it's also where Highway 238 curves in a southeasterly direction through the Applegate Valley wine region en route to Jacksonville and Medford (a very pretty alternative route to driving south on Interstate 5), and where U.S. 199 cuts southwest toward Oregon Caves National Monument and, eventually, the northernmost section of California's coast (and Redwood National Park). Many visitors to the southern Oregon coastline backtrack inland up U.S. 199 to create a scenic loop drive, ultimately intersecting with Interstate 5 at Grants Pass. Medford's airport is a 30-mile drive south.

ESSENTIALS

VISITOR INFORMATION Experience Grants Pass. ⊠ *198 S.W. 6th St.* ☎ *541/476–7574* ⊕ *www.travelgrantspass.com.*

Sights

Del Rio Vineyards & Winery

WINERY/DISTILLERY | In the small town of Gold Hill, about 15 miles east of Grants Pass, one of the Rogue Valley's most established vineyards stands out as much for its elegant wines as for its setting—the tasting room is set inside one of the region's oldest structures, the former Rock Point Hotel, which dates to 1865. In this grand building or out on the breezy patio, you can sample Del Rio's finest bottles, including an age-worthy Claret Bordeaux-style blend, a heady Rhône-style Syrah, and the most appealing rosés in the valley. Del Rio manages about 300 acres of grapes and sends its fruit to more than 20 wineries on the West Coast. ⊠ 52 N. River Rd., Gold Hill ☎ 541/855–2062 ⊕ www.delriovineyards.com.

The Oregon Vortex and House of Mystery

MUSEUM | In southern Oregon, between Grants Pass and Medford, there's a place that seems to defy all the laws of physics—where a ball rolls uphill and a person's height appears to change as they move. Optical illusion or some strange paranormal activity? That question has made the Oregon Vortex and House of Mystery a popular diversion since the 1930s. ⊠ 4303 Sardine Creek Left Fork Rd., Gold Hill ✛ 27 miles northeast of Grants Pass on I-5 S ☎ 541/855–1543 ⊕ www.oregonvortex.com ⊡ $13.75 ⊗ Closed Nov.–Feb.

★ Troon Vineyards

WINERY/DISTILLERY | Few winemakers in southern Oregon have generated more buzz than Troon, whose swank tasting room and winery is patterned after a French country villa. Troon produces relatively small yields of exceptional wines more typical of Sonoma than Oregon (Malbec and Zinfandel are the heavy hitters), but they also offer less typical U.S. bottles, such as Vermentino orange wines and Tannat. The winery is 14 miles southeast of downtown Grants Pass, in the northern edge of the Applegate Valley; there's a second Troon tasting room in Carlton, in the Willamette Valley. ⊠ 1475 Kubli Rd. ☎ 541/846–9900 ⊕ www.troonvineyard.com.

Wildlife Images Rehabilitation Center

ZOO | FAMILY | Begun in 1981 as a nonprofit care center for orphaned, injured, and otherwise in-need wildlife, this 24-acre facility on the Rogue River also educates the public by offering tours of the property and opportunities to view the animals, which include bobcats, bears, eagles, owls, otters, and dozens of other species native to the region. ⊠ 11845 Lower River Rd. ☎ 541/476–0222 ⊕ www.wildlifeimages.org ⊡ $14 ⊗ Closed Mon.–Thurs.

★ Wooldridge Creek Winery

WINERY/DISTILLERY | A trip to this peaceful hillside winery in the Applegate Valley offers the chance to view a herd of adorable dairy goats who provide the milk that Wooldridge uses to produce its organic fresh and aged cheeses. Enjoy a platter of cheeses along with house-made charcuterie while you relax on the patio, sipping the winery's exceptional estate wines, including Malbec, Pinot Noir, Tempranillo, and Chardonnay. If you're in downtown Grants Pass, you can enjoy these same treats at Wooldridge's terrific little tasting room, VinFarm, which also serves a full menu of lunch, dinner, and Sunday brunch items. ⊠ 818 Slagle Creek Rd. ☎ 541/846–6364 ⊕ www.wcwinery.com.

Restaurants

Gtano's

$$ | LATIN AMERICAN | Although set in a nondescript downtown shopping center, this cozy and welcoming restaurant is cheerful inside, and the kitchen turns out superb Nuevo Latino cuisine. Specialties include the starter of Puerto Rico "nachos," with Jack cheese, black beans, chicken, grilled pineapples,

and mango salsa; and hearty main dishes, such as Peruvian-style grilled pork ribs with aji amarillo sauce, and Bolivian-style steak strips with a smoky roasted-tomato sauce. **Known for:** fresh-fruit margaritas; guacamole prepared table-side; a variety of Mexican burritos, tacos, and enchiladas. $ Average main: $18 ⊠ 218 S.W. G St. ☎ 541/507–1255 ☉ Closed Sun. and Mon.

★ Ma Mosa's

$ | **AMERICAN** | Sustainability is the name of the game at this lively breakfast and lunch café in downtown Grants Pass, with a cozy dining room of colorfully painted tables and mismatched chairs, and a large adjacent patio with picnic tables and lush landscaping. The kitchen sources from local farms and purveyors to create beer-battered fried chicken and waffles, kale Caesar salads, and line-caught-fish tacos with seasonal slaw and house-made salsa. **Known for:** refreshing mimosa and other cocktails at brunch; pet-friendly patio; coconut rice porridge topped with seasonal fruit and granola. $ Average main: $11 ⊠ 118 N.W. E St. ☎ 541/479–0236 ⊕ www.mamosas.com ☉ Closed Mon. and Tues. No dinner.

★ Twisted Cork Wine Bar

$$ | **WINE BAR** | With a mission to showcase southern Oregon's fast-growing reputation for acclaimed vino, this dapper, art-filled space lends a bit of urbane sophistication to downtown Grants Pass. In addition to pouring varietals from throughout the Umpqua and Rogue valleys, Twisted Cork carries wines from more than 115 wineries throughout the Northwest, along with a few from California, and it offers a menu of small plates ideal for sharing—fruit-and-cheese plates, cured meats—as well as creative and quite affordable larger plates, including pomegranate-cinnamon flank steak, ginger-glazed salmon, and wild-mushroom flatbread with butternut-mint hummus. **Known for:** local ports and dessert wines; shareable platters of cheese and

charcuterie; a good mix of affordable and fancier menu options. $ Average main: $19 ⊠ 210 S.W. 6th St. ☎ 541/295–3094 ⊕ www.thetwistedcorkgrantspass.com ☉ Closed Sun. and Mon.

 ## Hotels

Lodge at Riverside

$$$ | **HOTEL** | At this contemporary lodge at the southern end of downtown, the pool and many rooms overlook the Rogue River, and all but a few rooms, furnished with stylish country house–inspired armoires, plush beds, and oil paintings, have private balconies or patios; suites have river-rock fireplaces and Jacuzzi tubs. **Pros:** central location overlooking the river; spacious rooms, many with balconies; very good breakfasts. **Cons:** no restaurant on-site; some rooms contend with a bit of traffic noise; rates can get steep in summer. $ Rooms from: $205 ⊠ 955 S.E. 7th St. ☎ 541/955–0600, 877/955–0600 ⊕ www.thelodgeatriverside.com ↻ 33 rooms ⧉ Free breakfast.

★ Weasku Inn

$$$ | **B&B/INN** | Pacific Northwest–inspired art, handmade furnishings, and fine fabrics fill this rambling timber-frame home overlooking the Rogue River, 11 handsomely outfitted cabins, and an A-frame bungalow that comprise the most luxurious accommodations between Ashland and Eugene. **Pros:** set directly on the Rogue River; impeccably decorated; evening wine reception and full hot breakfast included. **Cons:** 10-minute drive east of downtown; you may hear some road noise if you're in the main lodge; no restaurant on-site. $ Rooms from: $210 ⊠ 5560 Rogue River Hwy., Wolf Creek ☎ 541/471–8000, 800/493–2758 ⊕ www.weaskuinn.com ↻ 17 rooms ⧉ Free breakfast.

Wolf Creek Inn & Tavern

$ | **B&B/INN** | Following a multiyear closure and renovation, one of the Pacific

Northwest's most historic inns is once again open for overnight stays in the homey, old-fashioned rooms and meals in the convivial tavern. **Pros:** exudes historic charm; paranormal ghost-hunting tours are available; enchanting restaurant, known especially for its Sunday brunch. **Cons:** in a small town 20 miles north of Grants Pass; you can sometimes hear Interstate 5 traffic in the distance; restaurant is closed some nights for dinner. [$] *Rooms from: $90* ✉ *100 Front St.* ☎ *541/866–2474* 🌐 *www.wolfcreekinn.com* 🛏 *9 rooms* 🍴 *No meals.*

Nightlife

Bohemian Bar & Bistro
BARS/PUBS | A chatter-filled, brick-walled modern tavern in the historic district of downtown Grants Pass, Bohemian is a great option for well-prepared cocktails, and it's also a great choice for a late dinner, dessert, or even happy hour snacking in the afternoon. ✉ *233 S.W. G St.* ☎ *541/471–7158* 🌐 *www.bohemianbarandbistro.com.*

Shopping

The Glass Forge
ART GALLERIES | **FAMILY** | Check out the extensive array of colorful, contemporary glass art, from lamps to vases to paperweights, at this spacious gallery that also offers tours and demonstrations. ✉ *501 S.W. G St.* ☎ *541/955–0815* 🌐 *www.glassforge.com.*

Activities

RAFTING

More than a dozen outfitters guide white-water rafting trips along the Rogue River in and around Grants Pass. In fact, this stretch of Class III rapids ranks among the best in the West. The rafting season lasts from about July through August and often into September, and the stretch of river running south from Grants Pass, with some 80 frothy rapids, is exciting but not treacherous, making it ideal for novices, families, and others looking simply to give this enthralling activity a try.

Morrisons Rogue Wilderness Adventures
WHITE-WATER RAFTING | If you're up for an adventure that combines rafting with overnight accommodations, consider booking one of these exciting excursions that run along a 34-mile stretch of the Rogue River. They last for four days and three nights, with options for both lodge and camping stays along the way. Half- and full-day trips are also available. ✉ *325 Galice Rd., Merlin* ☎ *800/336–1647, 541/476–3825* 🌐 *www.rogueriverraft.com* 🎟 *From $69.*

Orange Torpedo Trips
WHITE-WATER RAFTING | One of the most reliable operators on the Rogue River offers half-day to several-day trips, as well as relaxed dinner-and-wine and morning float trips along a calmer stretch of river. Klamath and North Umpqua river trips are also available. ✉ *210 Merlin Rd., Merlin* ☎ *541/479–5061, 800/635–2925* 🌐 *www.orangetorpedo.com* 🎟 *From $69.*

RECREATIONAL AREAS

Rogue River–Siskiyou National Forest, Grants Pass
PARK—SPORTS-OUTDOORS | In the Klamath Mountains and the Coast Range of southwestern Oregon, the 2-million-acre forest contains the 35-mile-long Wild and Scenic section of the Rogue River, which races through the Wild Rogue Wilderness Area, and the Illinois and Chetco Wild and Scenic rivers, which run through the 180,000-acre Kalmiopsis Wilderness Area. Activities include white-water rafting, camping, and hiking, but many hiking areas require trail-park passes. You can get advice on exploring the rivers and forest, and buy passes both online and at the Grants Pass Wild Rivers Ranger District office. ✉ *2164 N.E. Spalding Ave.* ☎ *541/471–6500* 🌐 *www.fs.usda.gov/rogue-siskiyou.*

Valley of the Rogue State Park

PARK—SPORTS-OUTDOORS | A 1¼-mile hiking trail follows the bank of the Rogue, the river made famous by novelist and fisherman Zane Grey; it joins with a picturesque 4-mile stretch of the multiuse Rogue River Greenway Trail, which will eventually span 30 miles and connect Grants Pass with Gold Hill and Central Point. There's a campground along 3 miles of shoreline with full RV hookups as well as yurts (some of them pet-friendly). Day visitors appreciate the picnic tables, walking trails, playgrounds, and restrooms. ⊠ *3792 N. River Rd., Gold Hill* ✢ *12 miles east of Grants Pass* ☎ *541/582–1118, 800/551–6949* ⊕ *www. oregonstateparks.org.*

Medford

30 miles southeast of Grants Pass on I–5.

Medford is the professional, retail, trade, and service hub for eight counties in southern Oregon and northern California. As such, it offers more professional and cultural venues than might be expected for a city of its size (with a population of about 82,000). The historic downtown has shown signs of gentrification and rejuvenation in recent years, with a rapidly growing craft-brewing and distilling scene having taken hold, and in the outskirts you'll find several major shopping centers and the famed fruit and gourmet-food mail-order company Harry & David.

Lodging tends to be cheaper in Medford than in nearby Ashland or Jacksonville, although cookie-cutter chain properties dominate the hotel landscape. The city is also 75 miles southwest of Crater Lake and 80 miles northeast of the Oregon Caves, making it an affordable and convenient base for visiting either.

GETTING HERE AND AROUND

Medford is in the heart of the Rogue Valley on Interstate 5, and is home to the state's third-largest airport, Rogue Valley International. A car is your best way to get around the city and surrounding area.

ESSENTIALS

VISITOR INFORMATION Travel Medford. ⊠ *101 E. 8th St.* ☎ *541/776–4021, 800/469–6307* ⊕ *www.travelmedford. org.*

 Sights

Crater Rock Museum

MUSEUM | Jackson County's natural history and collections of the Roxy Ann Gem and Mineral Society are on display at this impressive 12,000-square-foot museum in Central Point (6 miles northwest of Medford). Fossils, petrified wood, scrimshaw, fluorescent rocks, thunder eggs, and precious minerals from throughout Oregon and elsewhere in the West are included, plus works of glass by renowned artist Dale Chihuly. ⊠ *2002 Scenic Ave., Central Point* ☎ *541/664–6081* ⊕ *www.craterrock.com* ⊠ *$7* ☉ *Closed Sun. and Mon.*

Dancin Vineyard

WINERY/DISTILLERY | This gorgeous wine estate with a handsome tasting room and patio is technically in Medford, but it's actually closer to historic downtown Jacksonville and a great stop if you're exploring either area. Dancin turns out an interesting mix of wines, from a jammy Zinfandel to a bright, bramble-accented Barbera that's a perfect match with any of the artisanal pizzas served from the tasting room kitchen. ⊠ *4477 S. Stage Rd.* ☎ *541/245–1133* ⊕ *www.dancin.com* ☉ *Closed Mon. and Tues. (also Wed. in winter).*

EdenVale Winery and Orchards

WINERY/DISTILLERY | Four miles southwest of downtown Medford amid a bucolic patch of fruit orchards, this winery and tasting room adjoins a stately

19th-century white-clapboard farmhouse surrounded by flower beds and vegetable gardens. Inside the tasting room you can sample and buy EdenVale's noted reds, a late-harvest dessert Viognier, a white port, and a first-rate cider produced with estate-grown pears. ⊠ *2310 Voorhies Rd.* ☎ *541/512–2955* ⊕ *www.edenvaleyorchards.com.*

Kriselle Cellars

WINERY/DISTILLERY | About 12 miles north of Medford on the way to Crater Lake and near the area's two famous Table Rock hikes, Kriselle offers tastings in an airy, contemporary wood-frame bar with spectacular vineyard and Cascades Range views and spacious patio. The winery produces one of the best Sauvignon Blancs in Oregon, along with a superb Cabernet Franc. ⊠ *12956 Modoc Rd., Eagle Point* ☎ *541/830–8466* ⊕ *www.krisellecellars.com.*

★ Ledger David Cellars

WINERY/DISTILLERY | Sandwiched handily between Rogue Creamery and Lillie Belle Chocolates in the small downtown of Central Point, this boutique winery produces an interesting portfolio of wines that earn top praise at competitions and from major critics. Standouts include a bright, balanced Chenin Blanc and a berry-forward, medium-body Sangiovese. Enjoy your tasting on the patio if it's a nice day. ⊠ *245 N. Front St., Central Point* ☎ *541/664–2218* ⊕ *www.ledgerdavid. com.*

Rogue River–Siskiyou National Forest, Medford

NATIONAL/STATE PARK | Covering 1.7 million acres, this immense tract of wilderness woodland has fishing, swimming, hiking, and skiing. Motorized vehicles and equipment—even bicycles—are prohibited in the 113,849-acre Sky Lakes Wilderness, south of Crater Lake National Park. Its highest point is the 9,495-foot Mt. McLoughlin. Access to most of the forest is free, but there are fees at some trailheads. ⊠ *Forest Office, 3040 Biddle*

Rogue River Views

Nature lovers who want to see the Rogue River at its loveliest can take a side trip to the Avenue of the Boulders, Mill Creek Falls, and Barr Creek Falls, off Highway 62, near Prospect, which is about 45 miles northeast of Medford—it's a scenic one-hour drive, and it's on the way to Crater Lake. Here the wild waters of the upper Rogue foam past volcanic boulders and the dense greenery of the Rogue River National Forest.

Rd. ☎ *541/618–2200* ⊕ *www.fs.usda. gov/rogue-siskiyou.*

Rogue Valley Family Fun Center

LOCAL INTEREST | **FAMILY** | You'll find an impressive array of kids' games and recreation at this complex just off Exit 33 of Interstate 5. Miniature golf, batting cages, a golf driving range, bumper boats, and go-karts are among the offerings, and there's also a video arcade and game room. ⊠ *1A Peninger Rd., Central Point* ☎ *541/664–4263* ⊕ *www.rvfamilyfuncenter.com.*

★ Table Rock

LOCAL INTEREST | This pair of monolithic rock formations rise some 700 to 800 feet above the valley floor. Operated by a partnership between the Bureau of Land Management and the Nature Conservancy, the Table Rock formations and surrounding 4,864 acres of wilderness afford panoramic valley views from their summits, and glorious wildflower viewing and migratory bird-watching in spring. This is one of the best venues in the Rogue Valley for hiking; you can reach Lower Table Rock on a moderately challenging trail, and Upper Table Rock via a shorter, less-steep route. ⊠ *Off Table Rock Rd., Central Point* ✦ *About 10 miles north of*

Medford and just a couple of miles north of TouVelle State Park ☎ *541/618–2200* 🌐 *www.blm.gov.*

Restaurants

Elements Tapas Bar

$$$ | **TAPAS** | A stylish setting and a taste of impressively authentic Spanish fare—these are the draws of this handsome tapas restaurant in downtown Medford's turn-of-the-20th-century "Goldy" building. Pass around plates of mussels in romesco sauce, apricot-braised-pork empanadas, chorizo-studded Andalucian paella, and lamb-sausage flatbread, while sampling selections from the lengthy beer and cocktail menus. **Known for:** late-night dining; several types of paella (that serves three to four); extensive, international beer, wine, and cocktail selection. *Average main: $25* ✉ *101 E. Main St.* ☎ *541/779–0135* 🌐 *www.elementsmedford.com* ⏲ *No lunch.*

Jaspers Café

$ | **BURGER** | This cute roadhouse-style building a few miles northwest of downtown Medford has made a name for itself serving absurdly large, decadently topped, and deliciously crafted burgers. Polish off the chuck wagon wild-boar burger with maple-glazed bacon, country gravy, cheddar, a hash-brown patty, and a fried egg, and you probably won't be experiencing any hunger pains for the rest of the day; veggie and game (from lamb to antelope to kangaroo) burgers are offered, too. **Known for:** old-fashioned shakes and malts in about 20 flavors; tasty sides—sweet potatoes, pork pot stickers; excellent craft beer and wine selection. *Average main: $9* ✉ *2739 N. Pacific Hwy.* ☎ *541/776–5307* 🌐 *www.jasperscafe.com.*

Hotels

Inn on the Commons

$ | **HOTEL** | This smartly revamped and reasonably priced hotel with a pool and excellent restaurant is within walking distance of downtown Medford's restaurants and shops as well as leafy Hawthorne Park and the Rogue River (which some rooms have views of). **Pros:** prettier and more distinctive decor than most of Medford's chain properties; a branch of Ashland's notable Larks restaurant is on-site; free passes to the health club across the street. **Cons:** some rooms have street and freeway traffic noise; busy downtown location; although nicely updated, it's much older than several new chain properties in town. *Rooms from: $107* ✉ *200 N. Riverside Ave.* ☎ *541/779–5811, 866/779–5811* 🌐 *www.innatthecommons.com/* *118 rooms* *Free breakfast.*

Resort at Eagle Point

$$ | **HOTEL** | The setting adjacent to one of the state's top golf courses is a major draw for this small boutique hotel with a dozen contemporary chalet-style suites featuring fireplaces and either balconies or patios. **Pros:** adjacent to and overlooking a beautiful golf course; peaceful setting; location handy for visiting Rogue Valley and Crater Lake. **Cons:** remote setting about a 20-minute drive from Medford; setting is less exciting for nongolfers; no elevator for upper-level rooms. *Rooms from: $150* ✉ *Eagle Point Golf Club, 100 Eagle Point Dr., Eagle Point* ☎ *541/879–3700* 🌐 *www.resortateaglepoint.com* *12 rooms* *Free breakfast.*

Rodeway Inn–Medford

$ | **HOTEL** | If you're on a budget and seeking a simple and immaculately clean base camp, check into this friendly, family-run '50s vintage motor court on the city's south side. **Pros:** vintage charm; convenient to sights in Medford as well Jacksonville and Ashland; super low rates. **Cons:** few amenities and luxuries;

rather dated (though that's part of the charm); bland setting on busy commercial strip. $ *Rooms from: $74* ✉ *901 S. Riverside Ave.* ☎ *541/776–9194* ⊕ *www. choicehotels.com* ⌁ *40 rooms* ⦶ *Free breakfast.*

Nightlife

Common Block Brewing
BREWPUBS/BEER GARDENS | This convivial downtown spot with a huge patio is a great microbrewery pick whether you're a serious beer aficionado or you're just seeking a laid-back spot to quaff a pint or two of Tangerine Squeeze IPA or Wild Turkey Bourbon barrel–aged Stout and enjoy good pizza and elevated pub food. ✉ *315 E. 5th St.* ☎ *541/326–2277* ⊕ *www. commonblockbrewing.com.*

Immortal Spirits & Distillery Company
BARS/PUBS | Part of the boom of craft beverage makers that's redefining downtown Medford, this inviting tasting room with tables fashioned out of barrels and rotating art exhibits offers a full bar and restaurant with creative (and big) burgers and sandwiches and creative cocktails. But you can also just stop in to sample Immortal's first-rate single-barrel whiskey, Genever-style gin, blackberry brandy, and other heady elixirs. ✉ *141 S. Central Ave.* ☎ *541/816–4344* ⊕ *www. immortalspirits.com.*

★ Jefferson Spirits
BARS/PUBS | This hip nightspot has helped to spur downtown Medford's ongoing renaissance by creating a swanky environment for hobnobbing and enjoying creative craft cocktails, like the blue linen, with gin, cucumber, lemon, and local blueberries. Barrel-aged cocktails are a specialty, and you'll also find local and international wines, mostly Oregon beers, and tasty pub fare. There's a similarly inviting branch in downtown Ashland. ✉ *404 E. Main St.* ☎ *541/622–8190* ⊕ *www.jeffersonspirits.com.*

★ The Urban Cork
WINE BARS—NIGHTLIFE | You can sit at a table or on a black leather sofa lining the brick wall as you enjoy one of the extensive selection of southern Oregon wines—more than 120 choices. Try one of the many flight options or order 2-ounce pours of whatever you'd care to try. There's tasting food to pair with your sips as well, including cheese and charcuterie plates, salads, and a flourless chocolate cake. ✉ *330 N. Fir St.* ☎ *541/500–8778* ⊕ *www.theurbancork. com.*

 Performing Arts

Craterian Theater at the Collier Center for the Performing Arts
ARTS CENTERS | This beautifully restored 750-seat 1920s performing arts center with state-of-the-art acoustics is steps from downtown restaurants and microbreweries and hosts a wide range of concerts and shows, including some big-name talents and national touring companies. ✉ *23 S. Central Ave.* ☎ *541/779–3000* ⊕ *www.craterian.org.*

Shopping

Harry & David
FOOD/CANDY | Famous for holiday gift baskets, Harry & David is based in Medford and offers hour-long tours of its huge facility on weekdays at 9:15, 10:30, 12:30, and 1:45. The tours cost $5 per person, but the fee is refunded if you spend $40 in the mammoth Harry & David store, great for snagging picnic supplies to carry with you on any winery tour. Reservations are recommended, as space is limited. ✉ *1314 Center Dr.* ☎ *541/864–2278, 877/322–8000* ⊕ *www. harryanddavid.com.*

★ Lillie Belle Farms
FOOD/CANDY | Next door to Rogue Creamery, this artisanal chocolatier handcrafts outstanding chocolates using local, often organic ingredients. A favorite

treat is the Smokey Blue Cheese ganache made with Rogue River blue, but don't overlook the dark-choco-late–marionberry bonbons (made with organic marionberries grown on-site) or the delectable hazelnut chews. ⊠ *211 N. Front St., Central Point* ☏ *541/664–2815* ⊕ *www.lilliebellefarms.com.*

★ Rogue Creamery

FOOD/CANDY | Just a few miles up the road from Medford in the little town of Central Point, you'll find one of the planet's most respected cheese makers (in 2019, Rogue became the first U.S. cheese maker ever to take the top prize at the prestigious World Cheese Awards). Begun in 1935 by Italian immigrants and now run by David Gremmels, this factory store sells all of the company's stellar cheeses, from Smokey Blue to a lavender-infused cheddar, and you can often watch the production through a window. Delicious grilled-cheese sandwiches and local wines and beers are also available— enjoy them at one of the sidewalk tables outside. ■**TIP**➜ **Ardent fans of this place might want to check out Rogue Creamery Dairy Farm, outside Grants Pass, and about 30 miles away from Central Point. Tours of the milking operations and the farm are available, and you can buy cheese and other gourmet goods there as well.** ⊠ *311 N. Front St., Central Point* ☏ *541/665–1155* ⊕ *www.roguecreamery.com.*

 Activities

GOLF

Eagle Point Golf Club

GOLF | One of the most challenging and best-designed in southern Oregon, this course is 10 miles northeast of Medford and was designed by legendary architect Robert Trent Jones Jr. and adjoins an upscale boutique resort. ⊠ *100 Eagle Point Dr., Central Point* ☏ *541/826–8225* ⊕ *www.resortateaglepoint.com* ☑ *$55* ⚑ *18 holes, 6576 yards, par 72.*

HIKING

Table Rock is one of the best venues for hiking in the Rogue Valley. You reach Lower Table Rock by way of a moderately challenging 5½-mile round-trip trail, and Upper Table Rock via a shorter (about 3 miles round-trip) and less-steep route. The trailheads to these formations are a couple of miles apart—just follow the road signs from Table Rock Road, north of TouVelle State Park (reached from Exit 33 of Interstate 5).

Jacksonville

5 miles west of Medford on Hwy. 238.

This perfectly preserved town found-ed in the frenzy of the 1851 gold rush has served as the backdrop for several western flicks. It's easy to see why. Jacksonville is one of only a small number of towns corralled into the National Register of Historic Places lock, stock, and barrel. These days, a bounty of lively shops, eat-eries, and inns set in downtown's historic buildings and the world-renowned Britt Festivals (held from late July to mid-August) of classical, jazz, and pop music are the draw, rather than gold. Trails winding up from the town's center lead to the festival amphitheater, mid-19th-century gardens, exotic madrona groves, and an intriguing pioneer cemetery. The sur-rounding countryside contains a number of noteworthy wineries, making Jacksonville one of the prime base camps in the Rogue Valley for winery touring.

GETTING HERE AND AROUND

Most visitors to Jacksonville come by way of Medford, 5 miles east, on Highway 238—it's a scenic drive over hilly farmland and past vineyards. Alternatively, you can reach the town coming the other way on Highway 238, driving southeast from Grants Pass. This similarly beautiful drive through the Applegate Valley takes about 45 minutes.

ESSENTIALS

VISITOR INFORMATION Jacksonville Visitor Information Center. ✉ *185 N. Oregon St.* ☎ *541/899–8118* 🌐 *www.jacksonville-oregon.com.*

Sights

★ Jacksonville Cemetery

CEMETERY | FAMILY | A trip up the winding road—or, better yet, a hike via the old cart track marked Catholic access—leads to the resting place of the clans (the Britts, the Beekmans, and the Orths) that built Jacksonville. You'll also get a fascinating, if sometimes unattractive, view of the social dynamics of the Old West: older graves (the cemetery is still in use) are strictly segregated, Irish Catholics from Jews from Protestants. A somber granite plinth marks the pauper's field, where those who found themselves on the losing end of gold-rush economics entered eternity anonymously. The cemetery closes at sundown, and guided daytime and sunset strolls are offered about once a month in summer. ✉ *Cemetery Rd. at N. Oregon St.* ☎ *541/826–9939* 🌐 *www.friendsjvillecemetery.org.*

Quady North Tasting Room

WINERY/DISTILLERY | You can try the complex, mostly Rhône-inspired wines—such as Viognier and Syrah, and Grenache—of this respected Rogue Valley producer that uses grapes from a few different area vineyards. The cute, cozy, brick tasting room is one of the only ones within walking distance of downtown Jacksonville inns and restaurants. ✉ *255 E. California St.* ☎ *541/702–2123* 🌐 *www.quadynorth.com* 🕒 *Closed Tues.*

Rellik Winery and Alpaca Farm

FARM/RANCH | FAMILY | Among the many vineyards throughout the Rogue Valley, Rellik stands out both for producing well-balanced wines (including a quite tasty oak-aged Cabernet Sauvignon) and for having a herd of curious, friendly alpacas, which makes this a fun stop for the entire family. You can admire and even pet the alpacas, and sip wine while snacking on cheese and charcuterie on the tasting room or on the shaded patio. The vineyard is just over a mile up the road from historic Jacksonville. ✉ *970 Old Stage Rd., Central Point* ☎ *541/499–0449* 🌐 *www.rellikwinery.com.*

Restaurants

Back Porch Bar & Grill

$$ | SOUTHERN | For an excellent, mid-priced alternative to Jacksonville's more upscale eateries, head to this roadhouse-style clapboard building six blocks northeast of the town's historic main drag. Authentic central Texas–style barbecue is served here: chargrilled red-hot sausage, slow-cooked pork ribs, and ½-pound burgers, plus a few steak and pasta dishes. **Known for:** tangy slow-cooked barbecue; down-home, Wild West decor; good selection of local wines. [$] *Average main: $19* ✉ *605 N. 5th St.* ☎ *541/899–8821* 🌐 *www.backporchjacksonville.com.*

C Street Bistro

$$ | MODERN EUROPEAN | Casual and warmly decorated with shelves of cookbooks, pickled veggies, jams, and wine bottles, and with a few choice outdoor tables that you should definitely consider on a softly breezy summer day, this welcoming bistro is a perfect lunch or dinner stop after a tasting or two at a nearby winery. The kitchen specializes in creative takes on comfort fare, including house-made pastas, brioche-bun burgers with fingerling potatoes, and Alsatian-style pizzas with garlic bechamel sauce, smoked ham, and Swiss cheese. **Known for:** terrific wine list; the market-fresh red meat and fish of the day specials; organic-crust pizzas. [$] *Average main: $20* ✉ *230 E. C St.* ☎ *541/261–7638* 🌐 *www.cstbistro.com* 🕒 *Closed Sun. and Mon. No dinner Wed.*

★ Gogi's

$$$ | **MODERN AMERICAN** | This low-key favorite among foodies and locals lies just down the hill from Britt Gardens and serves sophisticated contemporary cuisine and a discerning selection of local and international wines. The menu changes regularly, but might feature squash-and-ricotta ravioli with pancetta, shallot confit, and Marsala brown butter sauce; or white-wine-and-tomato-braised lamb shank with Parmesan polenta, grilled broccolini, and fresh horseradish gremolata. **Known for:** terrific wine list; artfully presented, innovative dishes; excellent cheese and charcuterie boards. [$] *Average main: $28* ✉ *235 W. Main St.* ☎ *541/899–8699* 🌐 *www.gogisrestaurant.com* 🕒 *Closed Sun.–Tues. No lunch.*

Hotels

Jacksonville Inn

$$ | **B&B/INN** | The spotless pioneer period antiques and the wealth of well-chosen amenities (fireplaces, saunas, whirlpool tubs, double steam showers) at this eight-room 1861-vintage inn—with four additional luxury cottages—evoke the Wild West with an urbane, sophisticated aesthetic. **Pros:** in heart of downtown historic district; one of the town's most historically significant buildings; very good restaurant on-site. **Cons:** rather old-fashioned decor for some tastes; on busy street; often books up well ahead on summer weekends. [$] *Rooms from: $165* ✉ *175 E. California St.* ☎ *541/899–1900, 800/321–9344* 🌐 *www.jacksonvilleinn.com* 🛏 *12 rooms* 🍴 *Free breakfast.*

★ Magnolia Inn

$$ | **B&B/INN** | The nine warmly appointed, reasonably priced rooms in the Mediterranean-inspired 1920s inn steps from many of Jacksonville's best restaurants and boutiques have plush bedding, well-designed bathrooms, and tasteful but not overly frilly furnishings. **Pros:** walking distance from shops and dining; beautifully landscaped grounds; pet-friendly rooms. **Cons:** tends to book up far ahead on summer weekends; on a slightly busy street; excellent continental breakfast but no hot entrées. [$] *Rooms from: $154* ✉ *245 N. 5th St.* ☎ *541/899–0255, 866/899–0255* 🌐 *www.magnolia-inn.com* 🛏 *9 rooms* 🍴 *Free breakfast.*

Shopping

Jacksonville's historic downtown has several engaging galleries, boutiques, and gift shops. It's best just to stroll along California Street and its cross streets to get a sense of the retail scene.

The English Lavender Farm

SPECIALTY STORES | **FAMILY** | Part of the fun of browsing the lavender-infused essential oils, honeys, salted caramels, soaps, sachets, and other products here is visiting the pastoral Applegate Valley farm, which is about 20 miles southwest of Jacksonville. Although it's only open a few days a week in June and July, the farmstead has two big festivals each summer, and they sell their products throughout much of the rest of the year at farmers' markets in Jacksonville, Medford, and Grants Pass. ✉ *8040 Thompson Creek Rd., Applegate* ☎ *541/846–0375* 🌐 *www.englishlavenderfarm.com.*

The Miners Bazaar

GIFTS/SOUVENIRS | **FAMILY** | An oddly endearing little gallery and gift shop that's set in a pretty, little, crooked, white house built during the town's mining heyday, the bazaar sells handmade jewelry, crafts, fiber arts, and other goods, and also offers its customers supplies and art kits to create their own DIY creations. It's great fun for kids and adults, and there's also a café serving locally sourced food as well as coffee and tea drinks, and local beer and wine. ✉ *235 E. California St.* ☎ *541/702–2380* 🌐 *www.theminersbazaar.com.*

Ashland

20 miles southeast of Jacksonville and 14 miles southeast of Medford on I–5.

Known for its hilly streets dotted with restored Victorian and Craftsman houses, sophisticated restaurants and cafés, and surrounding natural scenery that's ideal for hiking, biking, rafting, and winery-hopping most of the year (and skiing in winter), Ashland's greatest claim to fame is the prestigious Oregon Shakespeare Festival, which attracts thousands of theater lovers every year, from late February to early November (prime season is June through September). The influx of visitors means that Ashland is more geared toward the arts, more eccentric, and more expensive than its size (about 21,000 people) might suggest. The mix of well-heeled theater tourists, bohemian students from Southern Oregon University, and dramatic show folk imbues the town with an urbane sensibility.

GETTING HERE AND AROUND

The southernmost community in the Rogue Valley, Ashland is also the first town you'll reach via Interstate 5 if driving north from California. You can also get here from Klamath Falls by driving west on winding, scenic Highway 66. Cascade Airport Shuttle offers door-to-door service from the airport to Ashland for about $30 to $35, and Uber and Lyft serve the area as well. A car isn't necessary to explore downtown and to get among many of the inns and restaurants, but it is helpful if you're planning to venture farther afield or visit more than one town, which most visitors do.

ESSENTIALS

VISITOR INFORMATION Ashland Chamber of Commerce and Visitors Information Center. ✉ *110 E. Main St.* ☎ *541/482–3486* ⊕ *www.ashlandchamber.com.*

Sights

Belle Fiore Winery

WINERY/DISTILLERY | As you pull up before this over-the-top, opulent, Mediterranean-inspired chateau nestled in the mountains a few miles east of downtown Ashland, it's easy to guess that it's a favorite destination for weddings. But the winery's elegant Pavilion Tasting Room is also a memorable spot to sip Belle Fiore's excellent Cabernet Franc, Riesling, and more than a dozen other finely crafted wines. There's an art gallery, too, and there's light dining on the upper level, with its gracious terrace. ✉ *100 Belle Fiore La.* ☎ *541/552–4900* ⊕ *www.bellefiorewine.com.*

★ Irvine & Roberts Winery

WINERY/DISTILLERY | This relatively young rising star among southern Oregon wineries specializes in two varietals the region generally isn't known for: Pinot Noir and Chardonnay. The vineyard's cooler, higher-elevation setting is perfect for these grapes usually associated with the Willamette Valley, and you can sample them, along with a refreshing, dry rosé of Pinot Noir—with one of their impressive cheese-and-charcuterie boards, perhaps—amid the cushy seating in the airy, modern tasting room and sweeping patio, with its grand mountain views. ✉ *1614 Emigrant Creek Rd.* ☎ *541/482–9383* ⊕ *www.irvinerobertsvineyards.com* ☾ *Closed Mon. and Tues.*

★ Lithia Park

CITY PARK | FAMILY | The Allen Elizabethan Theatre overlooks this park, a wooded 93-acre jewel founded in 1916 that serves as Ashland's physical and psychological anchor. The park is named for the town's mineral springs, which supply water fountains by the band shell and on the town plaza—be warned that the slightly bubbly water has a strong and rather disagreeable taste. From morning through evening, picnickers, joggers, dog walkers, and visitors congregate amid this park's most popular areas, which include dozens of paved and unpaved trails, two duck ponds, a rose garden, a Japanese garden, and ice-skating rink, and a reservoir with a beach and swimming. A great way to get a sense of Lithia Park's vastness, and just how much wilderness there is in the northern section, is to make the 3-mile loop drive around its border. On weekends from mid-March through October, the park hosts a lively artisans' market, and free concerts take place Thursday evenings in summer. Each June the Oregon Shakespeare Festival opens its outdoor season by hosting the Feast of Will in the park, with music, dancing, bagpipes, and food. Tickets ($16) are available through the festival box office (☎ 541/482–4331 ⊕ www.osfashland.org). ⊠ N. Main St. at Winburn Way ⊕ www.ashland.or.us.

★ Oregon Shakespeare Festival

FESTIVAL | From mid-February to early November, more than 100,000 Bard-loving fans descend on Ashland for some of the finest Shakespearean productions you're likely to see outside of London—plus works by both classic (Ibsen, O'Neill) and contemporary playwrights, including occasional world premieres. Eleven plays are staged in repertory in the 1,200-seat Allen Elizabethan Theatre, an atmospheric re-creation of the Fortune Theatre in London; the 600-seat Angus Bowmer Theatre, a state-of-the-art facility typically used for five different productions in a single season; and the 350-seat Thomas Theatre, which often hosts productions of new or experimental work. The festival, which dates to 1935, generally operates close to capacity, so it's important to book ahead. ⊠ 15 S. Pioneer St. ☎ 541/482–4331, 800/219–8161 ⊕ www.osfashland.org.

Schneider Museum of Art

MUSEUM | On the beautifully landscaped campus of Southern Oregon University, this museum includes a light-filled gallery devoted to special exhibits by Oregon, West Coast, and international artists. The permanent collection has grown considerably over the years, and includes pre-Columbian ceramics and works by such notables as Alexander Calder, George Inness, and David Alfaro Siqueiros. Hallways and galleries throughout the rest of the 66,000-square-foot complex display many works by students and faculty. ■TIP➜ Steps from the museum, the university's Hannon Library is a gorgeous building with a dramatic four-story atrium, plenty of comfy seating, and quite a few notable artworks as well. ⊠ 1250 Siskiyou Blvd. ☎ 541/552–6245 ⊕ www.sma.sou. edu ⊗ Closed Sun.

ScienceWorks Hands-On Museum

MUSEUM | FAMILY | Geared toward kids but with some genuinely fascinating interactive exhibits that will please curious adults, too, this 26,000-square-foot science museum is close to the Southern Oregon University campus. In the main hall, you can explore touch-friendly exhibits on nanotechnology and sports science, and Discovery Island has curious games and puzzles geared to tots under age five. There's outdoor fun amid the plantings and pathways in the xeriscape Black Bear Garden, as well as a weather station, solar-power nursery, and kid-appropriate climbing wall. ⊠ 1500 E. Main St. ☎ 541/482–6767 ⊕ www.scienceworksmuseum.org ⊠ $10 ⊗ Closed Mon. and Tues.

Weisinger Family Winery

WINERY/DISTILLERY | Just a short drive east of downtown, this long-established winemaker occupies a leafy hilltop with broad views of the surrounding mountains. Specialties include a fine Malbec, a well-respected Viognier, both conventional (crisp, minerally) and late-harvest (for dessert) Gewürztraminer, and a nicely balanced Tempranillo. The winery also rents out a stylish one-bedroom cottage with a kitchen and hot tub for overnight stays. ⊠ 3150 Siskiyou Blvd. ☎ 541/488–5989 ⊕ www.weisingers.com.

Ashland's 93-acre Lithia Park is named for the town's mineral springs, which supply water fountains by the band shell and on the town plaza.

🍴 Restaurants

Amuse

$$$$ | **PACIFIC NORTHWEST** | The Northwest-driven French cuisine here, which is infused with seasonal, organic meat and produce, changes regularly but might feature charcoal-grilled prawns, duck-leg confit, or braised pork shoulder. Try to save room for one of the local-fruit desserts, such as wild huckleberry tart with a pecan crust or Gravenstein apple crisp. **Known for:** intimate, romantic setting; reasonable $20 corkage fee to bring your own wine; delectable desserts and cheese-course options. [$] *Average main: $31* ✉ *15 N. 1st St.* ☎ *541/488–9000* 🌐 *www.amuserestaurant.com* 🕒 *Closed Mon. and Tues. No lunch.*

Hearsay

$$ | **MODERN AMERICAN** | The lush, tranquil garden patios of this sophisticated bar and bistro attached to the Oregon Cabaret Theatre and a short stroll from the Shakespeare Festival are so appealing it's easy to forget the charming interior, with its art deco–inspired paintings and live piano lounge. This restaurant inside a 1911 former church turns out eclectic, creative dishes like beer-cured salmon tartare and burgers topped with wild mushrooms, Rogue Oregonzola cheese, and truffle aioli, and the desserts are fabulous, too. **Known for:** romantic garden seating; creative craft cocktails; great happy hour deals (lounge only). [$] *Average main: $22* ✉ *40 S. 1st St.* ☎ *541/625–0505* 🌐 *www.hearsayashland.com* 🕒 *Closed Tues. No lunch.*

★ Hither Coffee & Goods

$$ | **MODERN AMERICAN** | Set in a minimalist downtown space with bare floors, a vaulted painted-white timber ceiling, and bounteous floral arrangements, Hither serves as an inviting coffeehouse and café by day, featuring heavenly pastries and artfully composed egg dishes and tartines. Later in the day, stop in for a light dinner of grilled duck breast with aioli and frites, or house-made pasta with 'nduja, bitter greens, and lemon bread crumbs, along with a glass or two from

the well-curated natural wine list. **Known for:** clean, uncluttered aesthetic; delicious sweets and baked goods; craft beverages, from Sightglass Coffee to local wines and beers. $ *Average main: $19* ⊠ *376 E. Main St.* ☎ *541/625–4090* ⊕ *www. hithermarket.com* ⊗ *No dinner Sun.*

Larks

$$$ | MODERN AMERICAN | In a swanky yet soothing dining room off the lobby of the historic Ashland Springs Hotel, Larks pairs the freshest ingredients from local farms with great wines, artisanal chocolate desserts, and drinks, and features modern interpretations of classic comfort food, such as Southern fried chicken with bacon pan gravy. Dessert offerings include old-fashioned chocolate sundaes, s'mores, and a seasonal cheesecake selection. **Known for:** pretheater dining; outstanding Sunday brunch; fine cocktails in the adjoining 1920s bar. $ *Average main: $28* ⊠ *Ashland Springs Hotel, 212 E. Main St.* ☎ *541/488–5558* ⊕ *www. larksrestaurant.com.*

★ MÄS

$$$$ | PACIFIC NORTHWEST | Book ahead several days—or even weeks for Friday and Saturday—for the chance to dine at this intimate prix-fixe restaurant that features the modern, farm-to-table culinary masterpieces of young and extraordinary chef-owner Josh Dorcak. Feasts generally of 6 to 10 courses are available, with the seats at the cozy and lively chef's counter the most desirable—wine and sake pairings are available. **Known for:** exquisitely plated tasting menus; dining at the chef's counter; a hyperlocal approach to Northwest cuisine. $ *Average main: $75* ⊠ *141 Will Dodge Way* ⊕ *Next to Yogurt Hut, off Lithia Way* ☎ *541/581–0090* ⊕ *www.masashland. com* ⊗ *Closed Mon.–Wed.*

Morning Glory

$ | AMERICAN | Expect a wait for a table, especially on weekend or summer mornings, when dining at this wildly popular, eclectically furnished, blue Craftsman-style bungalow across the street from Southern Oregon University. The extraordinarily good food emphasizes breakfast fare—omelets filled with crab, artichokes, Parmesan, and smoked-garlic cream and lemon-poppy waffles with seasonal berries—but the lamb burgers, pressed Cuban sandwiches, and other lunch items are tasty, too. **Known for:** large portions; long lines, especially for a table on the pretty patio; crab omelets and crab melts. $ *Average main: $14* ⊠ *1149 Siskiyou Blvd.* ☎ *541/488–8636* ⊗ *No dinner.*

★ New Sammy's Cowboy Bistro

$$$$ | PACIFIC NORTHWEST | Ardent foodies have been known to make reservations weeks in advance, especially for weekends, to dine in this stucco Southwest-style roadhouse a few miles northwest of Ashland. Surrounded by orchards and gardens, the menu finds its way into the exquisite—and mostly farm-to-table—Northwestern fare with typical dishes from the seasonal menu ranging from green-garlic flan with spiced Washington spot prawns, cherry tomatoes, avocado, and epazote to pan-roasted king salmon with garden gazpacho, three basils, and tapenade. **Known for:** artful desserts; funky yet romantic setting; nicely curated beer and wine list. $ *Average main: $32* ⊠ *2210 S. Pacific Hwy.* ☎ *541/535–2779* ⊕ *newsammys.com* ⊗ *Closed Sun.–Tues.*

Peerless Restaurant & Bar

$$$ | MODERN AMERICAN | This hip neighborhood bistro and wine bar adjoins the stylish little Peerless Hotel and anchors the up-and-coming Railroad District, on the north side of downtown, just a few blocks from Main Street and the Shakespeare theaters. Regulars appreciate the well-crafted cocktails and thoughtful wine list as much as the consistently tasty locally sourced American food, such as fig-and-horseradish salad with apples and blue cheese and grilled lamb T-bone with apricot-glazed carrots and avocado-yogurt sauce. **Known for:** delicious

desserts with suggested drink pairings; first-rate cocktails; beautiful outdoor garden dining area. $ *Average main: $28* ✉ *265 4th St.* ☎ *541/488–6067* ⊕ *www. peerlesshotel.com* ⊘ *Closed Sun. and Mon. No lunch.*

Sammich

$ | **DELI** | In this unassuming deli tucked into a small shopping center across the street from Southern Oregon University, you'll find some of the biggest and tastiest sandwiches in the state—they've been featured on TV's *Diners, Drive-Ins and Dives,* and there's also a branch in Portland. Owner Melissa McMillan bases her menu on the Italian-style sandwiches of Chicago, where she's from, and unless you're absolutely starving, it's not a bad idea to order a half or share a whole with a friend. **Known for:** truly prodigious sandwiches; the Pastrami Zombie with Swiss, slaw, and Russian dressing on rye; grilled cheese with tomato soup. $ *Average main: $11* ✉ *424 Bridge St.* ☎ *541/708– 6055* ⊕ *www.sammichrestaurants.com* ⊘ *No dinner.*

☕ Coffee and Quick Bites

Noble Coffee Roasting

$ | **CAFÉ** | The fair-trade, organic beans used in the espresso drinks at Noble Coffee Roasting, in the hip Railroad District, are among the best in town. The spacious, high-ceilinged dining room is a comfy and attractive place to socialize or get work done while you sip and munch. **Known for:** cold-brew, ice-dripped, and other cool espresso drinks; tasty pastries; house-made Tonic sparkling beverage with coffee fruit, lemon, and agave. $ *Average main: $5* ✉ *281 4th St.* ☎ *541/488–3288* ⊕ *www.noblecof- feeroasting.com.*

🛏 Hotels

The Oregon Shakespeare Festival has stimulated one of the most extensive networks of B&Bs in the Northwest—more than 30 in all. High season for Ashland-area bed-and-breakfasts is June–October.

Ashland B&B Network

The network provides referrals and has an online booking system for about a dozen of the town's top inns. ⊕ *www. stayashland.com.*

★ Ashland Creek Inn

$$$$ | **B&B/INN** | Every plush suite in this converted late-19th-century mill has a geographic theme—the Normandy is outfitted with rustic country French prints and furniture, while Moroccan, Danish, and New Mexican motifs are among the designs in other units—and each sitting room–bedroom combo has its own entrance, a full kitchen or kitchenette, and a deck amid stunning gardens and just inches from burbling Ashland Creek. **Pros:** exceptionally good breakfasts; short walk to downtown shopping, Lithia Park, and theaters; enormous suites. **Cons:** among the priciest inns in town; limited common areas; two-night minimum stay most of the year. $ *Rooms from: $320* ✉ *70 Water St.* ☎ *541/482–3315* ⊕ *www. ashlandcreekinn.com* ⇌ *10 suites* ⦿ *Free breakfast.*

★ Ashland Hills Hotel & Suite

$$ | **HOTEL** | Hoteliers Doug and Becky Neuman (who also run the excellent Ashland Springs Hotel and Lithia Springs Resort) transformed this long-shuttered '70s-era resort into a stylish yet affordable retro-cool compound, retaining the property's fabulous globe lights, soaring lobby windows, and beam ceilings while adding many period-style furnishings. **Pros:** great rates considering all the amenities; terrific restaurant on-site; attractive grounds, including patio and sundeck. **Cons:** just off the interstate a 10-minute drive from downtown; some rooms face parking lot; fitness rooms are small and dark. $ *Rooms from: $162* ✉ *2525 Ashland St.* ☎ *541/482–8310, 855/482–8310* ⊕ *www.ashlandhillshotel. com* ⇌ *173 rooms* ⦿ *Free breakfast.*

Ashland Springs Hotel

$$ | **HOTEL** | Ashland's stately 1925 landmark hotel towers seven stories over the center of downtown, with 70 rooms done with a preponderance of gentle fall colors and unconventional decor—think French-inspired botanical-print quilts and lampshades with leaf designs. **Pros:** rich with history; upper floors have dazzling mountain views; the excellent Larks restaurant is on-site. **Cons:** central location translates to some street noise and bustle; many rooms are quite small; no gym (but discount at a local fitness center nearby). $ *Rooms from: $175* ✉ *212 E. Main St.* ☏ *541/488–1700, 888/795–4545* ⊕ *www.ashlandspringshotel.com* ⇌ *70 rooms* ⦿ *Free breakfast.*

The Palm

$$ | **HOTEL** | This cheerfully restored, eco-friendly, midcentury modern complex has a hip, quirky vibe and offers the convenience of a downtown location with relatively moderate prices. **Pros:** retro-chic vibe; pretty gardens and a pool with cool deck chairs and cabanas; convenient location near Southern Oregon University and not far from theaters. **Cons:** on a busy street; the economical rooms are quite small; cabana rentals can be spendy on summer weekends. $ *Rooms from: $157* ✉ *1065 Siskiyou Blvd.* ☏ *541/482–2636, 800/691–2360* ⊕ *www.palmcottages.com* ⇌ *16 rooms* ⦿ *No meals.*

The Winchester Inn

$$$$ | **B&B/INN** | **FAMILY** | Rooms and suites in this upscale Victorian have character and restful charm—some have fireplaces, refrigerators, and wet bars, and private exterior entrances, and most are well suited to having one or two children in the room. **Pros:** the adjacent Alchemy wine bar and restaurant serve outstanding international fare; one of the more child-friendly B&Bs in town; surrounded by lush gardens. **Cons:** among the more expensive lodgings in town; downtown location can feel a bit busy in summer; some rooms are reached via steep flights of stairs. $ *Rooms from: $295* ✉ *35 S. 2nd St.* ☏ *541/488–1113* ⊕ *www.winchesterinn.com* ⇌ *24 rooms* ⦿ *Free breakfast.*

Nightlife

With its presence of college students, theater types, and increasing numbers of tourists (many of them fans of local wine), Ashland has developed quite a festive nightlife scene. Much of the activity takes place at bars inside some of downtown's more reputable restaurants in the center of town.

Caldera Brewery & Restaurant

BREWPUBS/BEER GARDENS | At this renowned brewery just off Interstate 5 you can sample the signature Hopportunity Knocks IPA, Old Growth Imperial Stout, and an extensive selection of tasty apps, burgers, and pub fare. ✉ *590 Clover La.* ☏ *541/482–4677* ⊕ *www.calderabrewing.com.*

Ostras! Tapas + Bottle Shop

TAPAS BARS | There's definitely an impressive and extensive enough selection of beautifully plated Spanish tapas—half-shell oysters with cava mignonette, braised pork cheeks—to make this a sophisticated, high-ceilinged bar a dinner option (there's even paella). But, it's also one of the coolest little bars in southern Oregon, offering up a stellar list of Spanish and local wines as well as fine after-dinner drinks. ✉ *47 N. Main St.* ☏ *541/708–0528* ⊕ *ostrasashland.com.*

Performing Arts

Oregon Cabaret Theatre

THEATER | Shakespeare isn't the only game in this town, although the presence of OSF no doubt contributes to the wealth of talented performers in Ashland. You can see some of the region's top talents in five or six musicals throughout the year at this handsome cabaret theater set inside a converted 1911 church, and the on-site restaurant serves tasty dinner and brunch fare to enjoy before each show. ⊠ *241 Hargadine St.* ☎ *541/488–2902.*

 ## Shopping

Bloomsbury Books

BOOKS/STATIONERY | If you're looking for a book copy of the work you're seeing at Oregon Shakespeare Festival, this cheerful, literary-minded indie bookshop in the center of town is sure to have it. Readings and book discussions are also offered regularly. ⊠ *290 E. Main St.* ☎ *541/488–0029* ⊕ *www.bloomsburyashland.com.*

Gathering Glass Studio

CERAMICS/GLASSWARE | The striking, contemporary works of glassblower Keith Gabor are displayed in this spacious gallery and hot shop where you can also watch demonstrations and even take a class. ⊠ *322 N. Pioneer St.* ☎ *541/488–4738* ⊕ *www.gatheringglass.com.*

Activities

MULTISPORT OUTFITTERS
Momentum River Expeditions

WHITE-WATER RAFTING | Known primarily for its multiday white-water rafting as well as fishing, hiking, trail running, and climbing trips, Momentum also offers excellent half- and full-day rafting adventures on the Rogue, Upper Klamath, and Scott rivers. ⊠ *3195 E. Main St.* ☎ *541/488–2525* ⊕ *www.momentumriverexpeditions.com* ☞ *From $70.*

RAFTING
★ **Noah's River Adventures**

WHITE-WATER RAFTING | This long-running outfitter provides white-water rafting and wilderness fishing trips throughout the region—the company can lead single- or multiple-day adventures along the mighty Rogue River, the Upper Klamath, and—just across the border—in northern California, on the Salmon and Scott rivers. ⊠ *53 N. Main St.* ☎ *541/488–2811, 800/858–2811* ⊕ *www.noahsrafting.com* ☞ *From $95.*

SKIING
Mt. Ashland Ski Area

SKIING/SNOWBOARDING | This winter-sports playground in the Siskiyou Mountains receives about 265 inches of snow annually and is halfway between San Francisco and Portland. The owners have invested heavily on upgrades in recent years, adding an impressive new chalet-style day lodge with rentals and a bar and restaurant. There are 23 trails, nearly all of them intermediate and advanced, in addition to chute skiing in a glacial cirque called the bowl. Two triple and two double chairlifts accommodate a vertical drop of 1,150 feet; the longest of the runs is 1 mile. A couple of days a week, usually Thursday and Friday, there's also lighted twilight skiing until 9 pm. Anytime of year the drive up the twisting road to the ski area is incredibly scenic, affording views of 14,162-foot Mt. Shasta, some 90 miles south in California. Free shuttle bus service from downtown Ashland is offered on weekends from mid-January through March. ⊠ *Mt. Ashland Access Rd.* ⊹ *Off Exit 6 from I–5, 18 miles south of downtown* ☎ *541/482–2897* ⊕ *www.mtashland.com* ☜ *Lift ticket $52.*

Klamath Falls

65 miles east of Ashland via Hwy. 66, 75 miles east of Medford via Hwy. 140.

Apart from being a handy base for visiting several different wildlife refuges as well as Crater Lake, the actual town of Klamath Falls is somewhat prosaic and is somewhat overlooked by visitors traveling the Interstate 5 corridor, but it does have a few small but engaging museums. With a population of about 21,400 people, the city stands at an elevation of 4,100 feet, on the southern shore of Upper Klamath Lake—one of 82 bodies of water in the area. The highest elevation in Klamath County is the peak of Mt. Scott, at 8,926 feet.

GETTING HERE AND AROUND

Klamath Falls lies along U.S. 97, one of the Northwest's main north–south routes—it's a prime stop between Bend, 140 miles north, and Weed, California, about 70 miles south. You can also get here from the Rogue Valley, either by way of Highway 66 from Ashland or Highway 140 from Medford, which is home to the nearest airport (about a 90-minute drive).

ESSENTIALS

VISITOR INFORMATION Discover Klamath. ⊠ *205 Riverside Dr.* ☎ *541/882–1501, 800/445–6728* ⊕ *www.discoverklamath. com.*

 ## Sights

Favell Museum

MUSEUM | Created by the late and devoted art collector Gene Favell, this superb and underrated art museum overlooking the Link River features arrowheads, textiles, baskets, and more than 100,000 other indigenous artifacts from throughout the western United States and Canada as well as Mexico and Peru. There's also an impressive collection of contemporary western art that includes an oil painting by Charles Russell as well as bronze sculptures, wood carvings, dioramas, and an astonishing collection of miniature firearms. ⊠ *125 W. Main St.* ☎ *541/882–9996* ⊕ *www.favellmuseum. org* ☱ *$10* ⊗ *Closed Sun. and Mon.*

Klamath County Museum

MUSEUM | The anthropology, history, geology, and wildlife of the Klamath Basin are explained at this extensive museum set inside the city's historic armory building, with special attention given to the hardships faced by early white settlers. Also part of the museum's domain are the Baldwin Hotel Museum, which is also downtown, and the Fort Klamath

Museum and 8-acre frontier-era military garrison that you reach by driving 35 miles north on Highway 62. ⊠ *1451 Main St.* ☎ *541/883–4208* ⊕ *www.klamath-countymuseum.squarespace.com* ☱ *$5* ⊗ *Closed Sun. and Mon.*

★ Lower Klamath National Wildlife Refuge

NATURE PRESERVE | As many as 500 bald eagles make Klamath Basin their rest stop, amounting to the largest wintering concentration of these birds in the contiguous United States. Located along the Pacific Flyway bird migration route, the nearly 40,000 acres of freshwater wetlands in this complex of six different refuges serve as a stopover for nearly 1 million waterfowl in the fall. Any time of year is bird-watching season; more than 400 species of birds—including about 30 types of raptors—have been spotted in the Klamath Basin, along with many mammals, reptiles, and amphibians. For a leisurely excursion by car, follow the tour routes in the Lower Klamath and Tule Lake refuges—the latter has a superb bookstore and visitor center and is also a short drive from Lava Beds National Monument. ⊠ *Tule Lake Refuge Visitor Center, 4009 Hill Rd., Tulelake* ⊹ *27 miles south of Klamath Falls via Hwy. 39* ☎ *530/667–2231* ⊕ *www.fws.gov/refuge/ Lower_Klamath* ☱ *Free.*

 ## Restaurants

Basin Martini Bar

$$ | AMERICAN | Although the name of this elegant storefront spot in the heart of the downtown historic district suggests an option for evening cocktails, the bar is just as well regarded for its reliably tasty dinner fare—New York strip steaks, burgers topped with Crater Lake blue cheese, and bacon-wrapped scallops are among the highlights. There's seating in a handful of comfy booths or at stools along the modern bar, where you can order one of the creative drinks—consider the lemon-basil martini. **Known for:** well-prepared craft cocktails; decadent mac and cheese; urbane, deco-inspired dining room. [$] *Average main: $19* ✉ *632 Main St.* ☎ *541/884–6264* 🕒 *Closed Sun. No lunch.*

Gathering Grounds Cafe

$ | CAFÉ | Although this bustling coffeehouse with comfortable seating and exposed-brick walls is a hot spot for espresso drinks made from house-roasted coffee beans, it's also a great option for grabbing healthful, flavorful picnic items. Fresh-fruit parfaits and croissant and English muffin sandwiches are popular for breakfast, while lunch favorites include asparagus-prosciutto panini, sausage-lentil soup, and salads. **Known for:** panini sandwiches at breakfast and lunch; best coffee in town, roasted in-house; comfy armchairs. [$] *Average main: $9* ✉ *116 S. 11th St.* ☎ *541/887–8403* 🕒 *Closed Sun. No dinner.*

Hotels

Running Y Ranch Resort

$$$ | RESORT | FAMILY | Golfers rave about the Arnold Palmer–designed course at this 3,600-acre resort in a juniper-and-ponderosa–shaded canyon overlooking Upper Klamath Lake. **Pros:** indoor pool; 8 miles of paved trails; spacious, modern rooms. **Cons:** may be too far off the beaten path for some; pricey in summer; sometimes fills up with meetings and conventions. [$] *Rooms from: $205* ✉ *5500 Running Y Rd.* ✣ *8 miles north of Klamath Falls* ☎ *541/850–5500* 🌐 *www.runningy.com* 🛏 *82 rooms* 🍴 *No meals.*

Activities

MULTISPORT OUTFITTERS

The Ledge Outdoor Store

CAMPING—SPORTS-OUTDOORS | For advice, gear, clothing, books, and maps for hiking, birding, mountaineering, canoeing, camping, and fishing throughout the area, visit this extensively stocked shop in downtown Klamath Falls, which carries all kinds of equipment, and also offers guided fly-fishing trips. There's also a climbing gym. ✉ *369 S. 6th St.* ☎ *541/882–5586.*

RECREATIONAL AREAS

GOLF

Running Y Ranch Golf Course

GOLF | The outstanding Arnold Palmer–designed 18-hole course at Running Y Ranch delights golfers of all abilities. Ponderosa pines line the relatively short, undulating course, which is heavy on doglegs and has a number of holes in which water comes into play. There's also an 18-hole putting course that's ideal for honing your short game and fun for families. ✉ *5115 Running Y Rd.* ☎ *541/850–5580* 🌐 *www.runningy.com* 🎫 *$95 (discount for hotel guests)* ⛳ *18 holes, 5976 yards, par 72.*

Spence Mountain

BICYCLING | In 2018, JWTR timber company opened the first portion of a fantastic new trail system on a nearly 7,500-acre tract of pristine conifer forest about 12 miles northwest of town, near the western shore of Upper Klamath Lake. There are currently 35 well-groomed trails open for mountain biking, running, and hiking (as well as cross-country skiing and snowshoeing in winter), with the nearly 10-mile Spence Mountain Loop the property's showpiece. The trail rises steadily to a 5,800-foot peak that offers spectacular views of Upper Klamath Lake and the surrounding mountains. ✉ *Trailhead, Hwy. 140* ✣ *Just north of Howard Bay Park* 🌐 *www.klamathtrails.org/spence-mountain-project.*

Cave Junction

30 miles southwest of Grants Pass via U.S. 199, 60 miles west of Jacksonville via Hwy. 238 and U.S. 199.

One of southern Oregon's least populated and most pristine areas, Cave Junction and the surrounding Illinois Valley attract outdoors enthusiasts of all kinds for hiking, backpacking, camping, fishing, and hunting. Expect rugged terrain and the chance to view some of the tallest Douglas fir trees in the state. Other than those passing through en route from Grants Pass to the northern California coast via U.S. 199, most visitors come here to visit Oregon Caves National Monument, one of the world's few marble caves (formed by erosion from acidic rainwater). Sleepy Cave Junction makes an engaging little base camp, its main drag lined with a handful of quirky shops, gas stations, and very casual restaurants.

GETTING HERE AND AROUND

Cave Junction lies along U.S. 199, the main road leading from Grants Pass. You can also get here by heading west from Jacksonville on Highway 238 to U.S. 199. From Cave Junction, head east on Highway 46 to reach Oregon Caves National Monument. Cave Junction is about a 75-minute drive southwest of Medford's regional airport. Alternatively, the small airport (served by Contour Airlines, with service from Oakland) in Crescent City, California, is the same distance.

ESSENTIALS

VISITOR INFORMATION Illinois Valley Chamber of Commerce. ⊠ *201 Caves Hwy. (Hwy. 46)* ☎ *541/592–3326* ⊕ *www. ivchamberofcommerce.com.*

Sights

★ **Oregon Caves National Monument**
CAVE | Marble caves, large calcite formations, and huge underground rooms shape this rare adventure in geology. Guided cave tours take place late March through early November. The 90-minute half-mile tour is moderately strenuous, with low passageways, twisting turns, and more than 500 stairs; children must be at least 42 inches tall to participate. Cave tours aren't given in winter. Aboveground, the surrounding valley holds an old-growth forest with some of the state's largest trees, and offers some excellent and generally uncrowded hiking. Note that the park lodge, the Oregon Caves Chateau, is closed for a major renovation through 2020. ⚠ **GPS coordinates for the caves often direct drivers onto a mostly unpaved forest service road meant for four-wheel-drive vehicles. Instead, follow well-signed Highway 46 off U.S. 199 at Cave Junction, which is also narrow and twisting in parts; RVs or trailers more than 32 feet long are not advised.** ⊠ *19000 Caves Hwy. (Hwy. 46)* ⊹ *20 miles east of U.S. 199, 140 miles southwest of Crater Lake* ☎ *541/592–2100* ⊕ *www.nps.gov/ orca* ⊡ *Park free, tours $10.*

Hotels

Out 'n' About
$$ | B&B/INN | FAMILY | You sleep among the leaves in the tree houses of this extraordinary resort—the highest is 37 feet from the ground, one has an antique claw-foot bath, and another has separate kids' quarters connected to the main room by a swinging bridge. **Pros:** kids love the Swiss Family Robinson atmosphere; lots of fun activities are offered, from ziplining to horseback riding; amazingly quiet and peaceful. **Cons:** accommodations are extremely rustic; some units don't have private bathrooms; two-night minimum during week and three-night minimum weekends during spring to fall. $ *Rooms from: $160* ⊠ *300 Page Creek Rd.* ☎ *541/592–2208* ⊕ *www.treehouses. com* ⇱ *15 tree houses, 1 cabin* ○ *Free breakfast.*

Chapter 10

EASTERN OREGON

Updated by
Margot Bigg

● Sights	🍴 Restaurants	🛏 Hotels	● Shopping	🍸 Nightlife
★★★★★	★★★☆☆	★★★★☆	★★★☆☆	★☆☆☆☆

WELCOME TO EASTERN OREGON

TOP REASONS TO GO

★ **Wallowa wonder:** The usually snowcapped peaks of the Wallowa Range ornament one of the West's most overlooked alpine playgrounds, with Wallowa Lake resting at its base and Hells Canyon beckoning nearby.

★ **Historic Baker City:** See architecture from Oregon's mining-era heyday in Baker City's authentically restored downtown, where a short walking tour takes you past more than 100 historic buildings, many of which now contain indie boutiques and cafés.

★ **Snow day:** The family-friendly Anthony Lakes Ski Area offers skiing, snowboarding, and miles of Nordic trails.

★ **Rodeo:** Pendleton's famous rodeo attracts 50,000 people every September, but the cowboy mystique sticks around all year.

★ **Otherworldly scenery:** The buff-colored, crumpled-looking Painted Hills seem to change hues throughout the day.

At its eastern end, Oregon begins in a high, sage-scented desert plateau that covers nearly two-thirds of the state's 96,000 square miles. To the north, the border with Washington follows the Colombia River, then stretches eastward across the Colombia River Plateau to meet the Snake River, itself forming much of the state's eastern border with Idaho. East-central Oregon is carved out by the forks and tributaries of the John Day River, the country's third-largest undammed waterway. Its north–south course to the Columbia marks an invisible line extending southward, separating eastern Oregon from central Oregon's high plateaus and Cascade foothills. To the south, the Nevada border is an invisible line slicing through a high, desolate region sometimes known as the Oregon outback— it's one of the most sparsely settled areas in the lower 48 states.

1 Pendleton. At the foot of the Blue Mountains, this Wild West town is the heart of Oregon's ranching and agricultural communities.

2 La Grande. At the center of the Grand Ronde Valley, the home of Eastern Oregon University is a great stop en route to the Wallowa Mountains.

3 Joseph. In this former frontier town, old-school ranchers and cowboys mingle with a swelling population of artisans, foodies, and creative spirits.

4 Hells Canyon. North America's deepest river-carved gorge has great outdoor recreation options.

5 Halfway. Closest town to Hells Canyon and the scenic Wallowa Mountain Loop.

6 Baker City. Another former frontier town, this city has maintained its mining-era integrity—the restored Geiser Grand Hotel is a must-visit.

7 John Day. Plentiful outdoor recreation opportunities and proximity to the John Day Fossil Beds, make this former gold rush town a great base.

8 John Day Fossil Beds National Monument. Divided into three units—Sheep Rock, Painted Hills, and Clarno—the geological formations that make up this national monument cover hundreds of square miles.

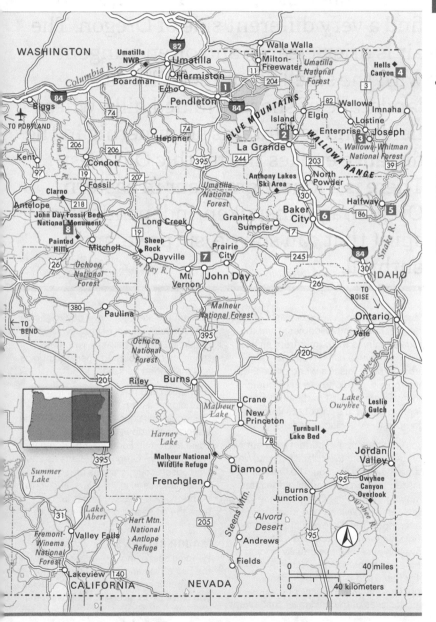

Travel east from The Dalles, Bend, or any of the foothill communities blossoming in the shade of the Cascades, and you'll find a very different side of Oregon. The air is drier, clearer, and often pungent with the smell of juniper. The vast landscape of sharply folded hills, wheat fields, and mountains shimmering in the distance evokes the mythic Old West. There is a lonely grandeur in eastern Oregon, a plainspoken, independent spirit that can startle, surprise, and enthrall.

Much of eastern Oregon consists of national forest and wilderness, and the population runs the gamut from spur-janglin' cowboys to conservationists and urban expats. This is a world of ranches and rodeos, pickup trucks and country and western music. For the outdoor-adventure crowd, it's one of the West's last comparatively undiscovered playgrounds.

Some of the most important moments in Oregon's history took place in the towns of northeastern Oregon. The Oregon Trail passed through this corner of the state, winding through the Grande Ronde Valley between the Wallowa and Blue mountain ranges. The discovery of gold in the region in the 1860s sparked a second invasion of settlers, eventually leading to the displacement of the Native American Nez Perce and Paiute tribes. Pendleton, La Grande, and Baker City were all beneficiaries of the gold fever that swept through the area. Yet signs of even earlier times have survived, especially visible in the John Day Fossil Beds, with fragments of saber-toothed tigers, giant pigs, and three-toed horses.

Recreation and tourism are gaining a foothold in eastern Oregon today, but the region still sees only a fraction of the visitors that drop in on Mt. Hood or the coast each year. For off-the-beaten-path types, eastern Oregon's mountains and high desert country are as breathtaking as any landscape in the West, and you'd be pretty hard-pressed to get farther from the noise and distractions of city life.

MAJOR REGIONS
Heading east along the interstate through the beige flats and monoculture croplands between Hermiston and **Pendleton**, you could be forgiven for supposing that

the most interesting part of Oregon was behind you. But just off the beaten path in the **East Gorge** country are seasonal wetlands chock-full of avian wildlife, road-side relics of the Old West, and dusty frontier towns undergoing commercial rebirths. Parks like Hat Rock State Park offer boaters and anglers access to the vast Columbia River Gorge, one of the country's most impressive waterways. A few dozen miles away in Pendleton, one of the world's largest and oldest rodeos anchors a town with an unexpectedly hip dining and shopping scene. Look south and east to where the river plateau gives way to the forested foothills of the Blue Mountains.

No part of eastern Oregon repudiates the region's reputation for flat and barren landscapes quite like lush and mountainous **northeast Oregon.** The Wallowa Mountains are among the most underrated outdoor recreation hot spots in the Rockies, with 565 square miles of backpacker-friendly wilderness, abundant wildlife, and proximity to **Hells Canyon,** North America's deepest gorge. If you're planning to explore Hells Can-yon, **Halfway** is a good base. The nearby Blue Mountains are no slouches either, home to some of the state's best alpine and Nordic skiing. Towns like **Baker City, Joseph,** and **La Grande** have transitioned more thoroughly than much of the region from pastoral and extractive economies to hospitality and recreation, making them eastern Oregon's de facto capitals of art, food, and culture. Each city has a vibrant downtown with a growing number of sophisticated galleries and boutiques, and you'll find locals swapping fish stories and trail tales in one of the area's excellent brewpubs.

About 80 miles west of Baker City, **John Jay** is known for its plentiful outdoor recreational opportunities, is also a great base if you plan to visit **John Day Fossil Beds National Monument.**

Planning

When to Go

Though skiers and snowboarders appreciate the Blues and the Wallowas in winter, summer is eastern Oregon's primary travel season. It comes late in the state's northeast corner, where snow can remain on the mountains until July, and May flurries aren't uncommon at lower elevations. July and August are the best months for wildflowers in the high northeast, and they're also the only months when many remote-but-scenic Forest Service roads are guaranteed to be open.

Summer temps in northeast Oregon generally level out in the 80s around July and August. In midwinter 20-degree days are the norm. Bear in mind: elevation varies greatly in eastern Oregon, and this can render seasonal averages pretty meaningless. It's not uncommon to gain or lose several thousand feet during the course of an hour's drive, and for much of the year this can mean the difference between flip-flops and snow boots.

Getting Here and Around

AIR TRAVEL
Eastern Oregon Regional Airport at Pend-leton is not serviced by any major airline, but San Francisco–based airline, Boutique Air, runs flights between Pendleton and Portland and has a codeshare partnership with United. There's a Hertz car-rental agency on-site. Across the Washington border, Tri-Cities Airport is just 35 miles from Hermiston and 70 miles from Pend-leton and has service on Allegiant, Delta, Alaska/Horizon, and United Express from several major cities in the West. If visiting Baker City or other communities in the eastern edge of the region, your best bet is flying into Boise, which is about a two-hour drive from Baker City. To reach the

John Day region, it's easiest to fly into Bend, which is 2½ to 3 hours away.

CONTACTS Eastern Oregon Regional Airport at Pendleton. ☎ 541/276–7754 ⊕ www. pendletonairport.com. **Tri-Cities Airport.** ☎ 509/547–6352 ⊕ www.flytricities.com.

BUS TRAVEL

The major Greyhound route travels along Interstate 84, passing through Pendleton, Baker City, and Ontario, but buses are an extremely impractical way to get around the vast distances of this part of the state.

CONTACTS Greyhound. ☎ 800/231–2222 ⊕ www.greyhound.com.

CAR TRAVEL

Virtually all visitors to eastern Oregon get around by car. Interstate 84 runs east along the Columbia River and dips down to Pendleton, La Grande, Baker City, and Ontario. U.S. 26 heads east from Prineville through the Ochoco National Forest, passing the three units of the John Day Fossil Beds. U.S. 20 travels southeast from Bend in central Oregon to Burns. U.S. 20 and U.S. 26 both head west into Oregon from Idaho.

In all these areas, equip yourself with chains for winter driving, and remember that many roads are closed by snow and can remain inaccessible for months. Check the **Oregon Department of Transportation's TripCheck** (⊕ www.tripcheck.com) or call **ODOT** (☎ 800/977–6368). Four-wheel drive is beneficial on a lot of eastern Oregon's designated Scenic Byways. Plan ahead for gas, since service stations can be few and far between. They often close early in small towns, and because drivers in Oregon can't legally pump their own gas, you'll be out of luck until morning.

Restaurants

Chef-driven restaurants serving anything beyond traditional pub fare and hearty steaks are rare on the eastern Oregon range, but it's not hard to find a tasty, authentic meal if you know where to look. Restaurants around the Wallowas, in particular, have a burgeoning locavore-organic ethos: locally grown produce abounds, farmers' markets are a big draw, and the rural country even has its own Slow Food chapter. A few noteworthy brewpubs have also cropped up around Pendleton, the Wallowas, and Baker City.

Elsewhere in the high desert, an entrenched ranching culture means big eating: farm-boy breakfasts and steak house after spur-jangling steak house. Generations of *braceros* (Hispanic laborers) have left their mark on the region's culinary scene as well, and excellent taquerias can be found in even the dustiest ranch towns. Pack a lunch if you're touring more remote areas, where traveler services are few and far between. *Restaurant reviews have been shortened. For full information visit Fodors.com.*

What it Costs in U.S. Dollars			
$	$$	$$$	$$$$
RESTAURANTS			
under $16	$16–$22	$23–$30	over $30
HOTELS			
under $150	$150–$200	$201–$250	over $250

Hotels

Chain hotels are easy to find in the Gorge and in bigger towns like Baker City and Pendleton, but elsewhere, small motels and bed-and-breakfasts are more typical. Although much of the region's lodging hasn't seen a major renovation since the Eisenhower administration, refurbished boutique inns are slowly starting to pop up in some of the area's bigger towns.

Triple-digit rates are an anomaly in eastern Oregon, and you'd have to work pretty hard to spend more than $150 on a night's lodging. Parts of eastern Oregon shut down in the off-season, so don't count on winter lodging without calling first. *Hotel reviews have been shortened. For full information, visit Fodors.com.*

Tours

Hells Canyon Adventures
ADVENTURE TOURS | From May through October, Hells Canyon Adventures leads full- and half-day jet-boat tours of the country's deepest gorge. ☎ *800/422–358, 541/785–3352* ⊕ *www.hellscanyonadventures.com* ✉ *From $70.*

TREO Bike Tours
BICYCLE TOURS | Local guides offer multiday, all-inclusive bicycle tours and customize routes based on the interest of groups. ☎ *541/676–5840* ⊕ *www.treobiketours.com* ✉ *From $560.*

Visitor Information

CONTACTS Eastern Oregon Visitors Association. ☎ *800/332–1843* ⊕ *www.visiteasternoregon.com.*

Pendleton

200 miles east of Portland, 130 miles east of The Dalles.

At the foot of the Blue Mountains amid waving wheat fields and cattle ranches, Pendleton is a quintessential western town with a rip-roaring history. It was originally acquired in a swap for a couple of horses, and the town's history of wild behavior was evident from the first city ordinance, which outlawed public drunkenness, fights, and shooting off one's guns within the city limits. But Pendleton is also the land of the Umatilla Tribe—the herds of wild horses that once thundered across this rolling landscape were at the center of the area's early Native American culture (today the tribe operates the Wildhorse Resort & Casino). Later Pendleton became an important pioneer junction and home to a sizable Chinese community. The current cityscape still carries the vestiges of yesteryear, with many of its century-old homes still standing, from simple farmhouses to stately Queen Anne Victorians.

Given its raucous past teeming with cattle rustlers, saloons, and bordellos, the largest city in eastern Oregon (population 17,000) looks unusually sedate. But all that changes in September when the **Pendleton Round-Up** draws thousands.

GETTING HERE
Nearly all visitors arrive by car on Interstate 84. Pendleton does have the region's only airport, the Eastern Oregon Regional Airport, but it is not currently serviced by any major airlines.

VISITOR INFORMATION
CONTACTS Travel Pendleton. ✉ *501 S. Main St.* ☎ *541/246–7411, 541/276–7411* ⊕ *www.travelpendleton.com.*

Sights

★ Pendleton Round-Up
SPORTS—SIGHT | FAMILY | More than 50,000 people roll into town during the second full week in September for one of the oldest and most prominent rodeos in the United States. With its famous slogan of "Let 'er Buck," the Round-Up features eight days of parades, races, beauty contests, and children's rodeos, culminating in four days of rodeo events. Vendors line the length of Court Avenue and Main Street, selling beadwork and curios, while country bands twang in the background. ✉ *1205 S.W. Court Ave.*

☎ *541/276–2553, 800/457–6336* ⊕ *www. pendletonroundup.com.*

★ **Pendleton Underground Tours**

TOUR—SIGHT | This 90-minute tour transports you below ground and back through Pendleton's history of gambling, girls, and gold. The Underground Tours depict town life from more than a century ago (when 32 saloons and 18 brothels were operating in full swing) to the 1953 closure of the Cozy Rooms, the best-known bordello in town. The Underground Tour eventually resurfaces, climbing the "31 Steps to Heaven" to those Cozy Rooms where madam Stella Darby reigned. The secret gambling lairs, opium dens, and bathhouses that lie directly below the pavement will give you a whole new perspective of the streets of Pendleton. Reservations are required. ⊠ *31 S.W. Emigrant Ave.* ☎ *541/276–0730* ⊕ *www. pendletonundergroundtours.org* ⛬ *$15* ⊘ *Closed Sun. and Tues.* ☞ *No children under six.*

Pendleton Woolen Mills

FACTORY | Pendleton's most significant source of name recognition in the country comes from this mill, home of the trademark wool plaid shirts and colorful woolen Indian blankets. This location is the company's blanket mill; there's also a weaving mill in the Columbia Gorge town of Washougal, Washington, near Portland and about three hours west of Pendleton. If you want to know more about the production process, the company gives 20-minute tours on weekdays at 9 am, 11 am, 1:30 pm, and 3 pm. The mill's retail store stocks blankets, towels, and clothing with good bargains on factory seconds in the back room. ⊠ *1307 S.E. Court Pl.* ☎ *541/276–6911* ⊕ *www.pendleton-usa.com.*

Round-Up Hall of Fame Museum

MUSEUM | **FAMILY** | The museum's collection spans the rodeo's history since 1910, with photographs—including glamorous glossies of prior Rodeo Queens and the Happy Canyon Princesses (all Native American)—as well as saddles, guns, and costumes. A taxidermied championship bronco named War Paint is the museum's cool, if slightly creepy, prize artifact. ⊠ *1114 S.W. Court Ave.* ⊹ *Across from Round-Up grounds* ☎ *541/278–0815* ⊕ *www.pendletonhalloffame.com* ⛬ *$5* ⊘ *Closed Sun.*

★ **Tamástslikt Cultural Institute**

MUSEUM | **FAMILY** | Located at the Wildhorse Resort and Casino, this impressive 45,000-square-foot interpretive center depicts history from the perspective of the Cayuse, Umatilla, and Walla Walla tribes (*Tamástslikt* means "interpret" in the Walla Walla native language). An art gallery showcases the work of local and regional tribal artists, and on Saturday in summer you can visit the adjacent Living Culture Village, Naami Nishaycht, and watch a variety of talks and demonstrations on everything from tepee building to traditional community games. There's also a museum gift shop, a theater showing a short film about the tribe's heritage, and a café. ⊠ *47106 Wildhorse Blvd.* ☎ *541/429–7700* ⊕ *www.tamastslikt.org* ⛬ *$10.*

Umatilla National Forest

FOREST | Three rugged, secluded wilderness areas attract backpackers to this 1.4-million-acre forest: the Wenaha-Tucannon, the North Fork Umatilla, and the North Fork John Day. *Umatilla* is derived from a word in the indigenous Shahaptian language meaning "water rippling over sand," and the forest has its share of fishable rivers and streams as well. Home to the Blue Mountain Scenic Byway and 40 campgrounds, the diverse forestland is found both east and south of Pendleton, and extends south almost as far as John Day, where it borders the Malheur National Forest. To the east it is bordered by the Wallowa-Whitman National Forest. Major thoroughfares through the forest include Interstate 84, U.S. 395, and Highways 204 and 244. ⊠ *Supervisor's Office, 72510 Coyote*

Rd. ☎ 541/278–3716 ⊕ www.fs.usda. gov/umatilla ▨ Northwest Forest Pass required at some trailheads, $5/day or $30 annual.

 Restaurants

Great Pacific Wine & Coffee Co

$ | CAFÉ | Set in a stately 1880s former Masonic lodge in downtown Pendleton, what began as a coffeehouse and wine bar has expanded over the years into a full restaurant serving reasonably priced salads, sandwiches, soups, pizzas, and appetizers. The food tends toward traditional American café fare, with focaccia topped with kalamata olives and chèvre, smoked-salmon Caesar salads, and barbecued-pork pizzas among the favorites. **Known for:** extensive selection of beer and wine; Naples-style pizza; live music on most weekends. $ Average main: $10 ⊠ 403 S. Main St. ☎ 541/276–1350 ⊕ www.greatpacific.biz ⊘ Closed Sun.

Hamley Steakhouse

$$$ | STEAKHOUSE | A large downtown complex of western-style brick and log cabin buildings holds a steak house, café, and saloon, and captures Pendleton's cowboy heritage with its ornate interior. The swanky steak house is open for dinner only, the saloon serves a lighter bar menu (and produces its own whiskey), and the café serves breakfast and lunch. **Known for:** meat-heavy menu of steaks and burgers; Old West setting with 19th-century mahogany bar and period memorabilia; twice-daily happy hours. $ Average main: $28 ⊠ 8 S.E. Court St. ☎ 541/278–1100 ⊕ www.hamleysteakhouse.com.

The Prodigal Son

$ | AMERICAN | A cavernous and historic former car dealership houses this hip brewpub, which also has a kitchen serving tasty pub food, such as Tillamook cheeseburgers and beer-battered fish-and-chips. Since it opened in 2010, it's become known for its nicely crafted

beers, including the heady Max Power IPA, faintly tart Huckleberry Wheat beer, and robust Bruce/Lee Porter. **Known for:** laid-back, saloon-inspired atmosphere; rotating tap list of seasonal beers; solid menu of pub food. $ Average main: $14 ⊠ 230 S.E. Court Ave. ☎ 541/276–6090 ⊕ www.prodigalsonbrewery.com ⊘ Closed Mon.

Rainbow Cafe

$ | AMERICAN | A downtown institution since 1883, this historic saloon hasn't changed much in more than a hundred years. Locals donning cowboy hats and leather boots still belly up to the bar seven days a week for no-frills breakfast, lunch, and dinner. **Known for:** truly authentic Old West ambience; colorful and talkative regulars. $ Average main: $10 ⊠ 209 S. Main St. ☎ 541/276–4120 ▭ No credit cards.

Hotels

★ The Pendleton House Historic Inn

$ | B&B/INN | This gorgeous, 6,000-square-foot pink stucco home in Pendleton's North Hill neighborhood dates to 1917 and abounds with handsome decorative details, including Chinese silk wallpaper and custom woodwork; it's a grand reminder that the Old West had its share of wealth and worldly sophistication. **Pros:** glorious home with lavishly decorated rooms; small pets allowed; quiet location just across the river from downtown. **Cons:** one room has a shared bathroom; not staffed around the clock; most rooms lack TVs. $ Rooms from: $135 ⊠ 311 N. Main St. ☎ 541/276–8581 ⊕ www.pendletonhousebnb.com ⤶ 6 rooms ⦿| Free breakfast.

Wildhorse Resort & Casino

$ | RESORT | Situated on a sweeping mesa 6 miles southeast of downtown Pendleton, this contemporary hotel at Wildhorse Resort (operated by the Umatilla tribe) offers plenty of perks even if you're not a gamer. **Pros:** great views and stylish decor in tower hotel; lots of amenities and dining options on-site; scenic location outside town. **Cons:** casino can be noisy and reeks of cigarette smoke; a 15-minute drive from downtown restaurants; rooms in courtyard building feel a bit dated, and some still allow smoking. [$] *Rooms from: $115* ✉ *46510 Wildhorse Blvd.* ☎ *800/654–9453* 🌐 *www.wildhorseresort.com* 🛏 *300 rooms* 🍴 *No meals.*

Working Girls Hotel
$ | **B&B/INN** | From boardinghouse to bordello to affordable and historic inn, this refurbished 1890s edifice owned and operated by Pendleton Underground Tours advertises its "Old West Comfort" with a large vertical sign hanging from the side of the building. **Pros:** centrally located in downtown Pendleton; fun decor; common kitchen for guest use. **Cons:** bathrooms are down the hall; no children or pets allowed; no lobby or front office. [$] *Rooms from: $75* ✉ *17 S.W. Emigrant Ave.* ☎ *541/276–0730* 🌐 *www.pendletonundergroundtours.org* 🛏 *5 rooms* 🍴 *Free breakfast.*

Shopping

Hamley & Co. Western Store & Custom Saddlery
SHOES/LUGGAGE/LEATHER GOODS | On-site craftspeople at this western superstore fashion hand-tooled saddles considered among the best in the world. You'll also find authentic cowboy/cowgirl gear and quality leather products, plus gifts and art. The store is next to Hamley's massive—and gorgeous—steak house, saloon, and café. ✉ *30 S.E. Court Ave.* ☎ *541/278–1100* 🌐 *www.hamleywesternstore.com.*

Montana Peaks Hat Co
CLOTHING | If the custom-sized felt hats in this shop and workspace look familiar, it's for good reason—the owners of Montana Peaks have outfitted celebrities and major Hollywood stars. They'll happily size anyone's head for a hat with their rare 19th-century equipment. ✉ *24 S.W. Court Ave.* ☎ *541/215–1400* 🌐 *www.montanapeaks.net.*

Activities

FISHING

Blue Mountain Anglers and Fly Shop
FISHING | Oregon's largest full-service fly shop east of the Cascades also has a fishing school and information about angling in the area; the focus here is on fishing in the Umatilla River for steelhead trout and salmon. ✉ *1847 Westgate Pl.* ☎ *541/966–8770* 🌐 *www.bluemountainanglers.com.*

Shopping

Hamley & Co. Western Store & Custom Saddlery
SHOES/LUGGAGE/LEATHER GOODS | On-site craftspeople at this western superstore fashion hand-tooled saddles considered among the best in the world. You'll also find authentic cowboy/cowgirl gear and quality leather products, plus gifts and art. The store is next to Hamley's massive—and gorgeous—steak house, saloon, and café. ✉ *30 S.E. Court Ave.* ☎ *541/278–1100* 🌐 *www.hamleywesternstore.com.*

Montana Peaks Hat Co
CLOTHING | If the custom-sized felt hats in this shop and workspace look familiar, it's for good reason—the owners of Montana Peaks have outfitted celebrities and major Hollywood stars. They'll happily size anyone's head for a hat with their rare 19th-century equipment. ✉ *24 S.W. Court Ave.* ☎ *541/215–1400* 🌐 *www.montanapeaks.net.*

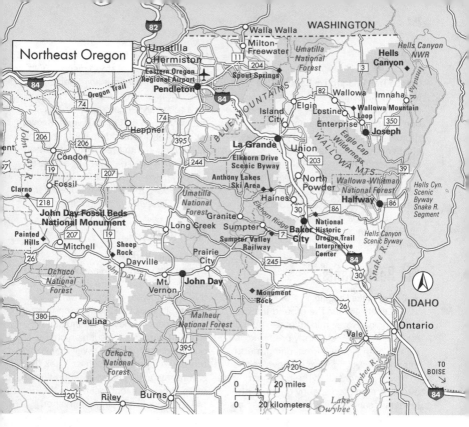

La Grande

52 miles southeast of Pendleton.

Home to Eastern Oregon University, a small state college, La Grande is a quiet little city of 13,000, which sits at the center of the Grand Ronde Valley. It's a convenient stop if you're heading to the Wallowa Mountains, and La Grande's historic frontier character charms visitors. The city started life in the late 1800s as a farming community. It grew slowly while most towns along the Blue Mountains were booming or busting in the violent throes of gold-fueled stampedes. When the railroad companies were deciding where to lay their tracks through the valley, a clever local farmer donated 150 acres to ensure that the Iron Horse would run through La Grande. With steam power fueling a new boom, the town quickly outgrew its neighbors and took the title of county seat from fading Union City. Today the city is home to a handful of attractions and restaurants, and makes a good base for hiking and other outdoor adventures in the mountains.

GETTING HERE

La Grande sits at the intersection of Interstate 84 and Highway 82, the primary route through the Wallowa Valley to Joseph and Enterprise. It's a 4-hour drive from Portland and 2½ hours from Boise, Idaho.

VISITOR INFORMATION

CONTACTS Visit Union County. ✉ *207 Depot St.* ☎ *541/963–8588, 800/848–9969* ⊕ *www.unioncountychamber.org.*

Sights

Oregon Trail Interpretive Park at Blue Mountain Crossing

LOCAL INTEREST | Trace the steps of Oregon Trail pioneers at this nature park in the Blue Mountains, where pine trees still bear the scars made by passing covered wagons more than 150 years ago. Signs along the various unpaved hiking trails highlight the history of the journey west. ✉ *La Grande* ☎ *541/523-6391* 🌐 *www.fs.usda.gov/wallowa-whitman* 🎟 *$5 per vehicle* ⏲ *Closed mid-Sept.–early May.*

Restaurants

★ Dining at the Landing

$$$$ | **EUROPEAN** | On the ground floor of The Landing Hotel, this intimate, upscale restaurant serves elegantly prepared dishes, with a regularly changing menu offering everything from sockeye salmon to Italian rib-eye steak. The breakfast offerings aren't too shabby either, with breakfast sandwiches, hot daily specials, and high-end tea and coffee. **Known for:** extensive daily specials; headed by a celebrated Oregon chef; great cocktail and wine list. [$] *Average main: $32* ✉ *1501 Adams Ave.* ☎ *541/786–0123* 🌐 *www.merlynscatering.net.*

Joe and Sugar's

$ | **CAFÉ** | If you want to remain an anonymous tourist, don't visit Joe and Sugar's. You can't avoid being chatted up by the funny, friendly, and helpful owner of this sweet-smelling café and coffee shop that's popular for breakfast, lunch, and light snacks. **Known for:** home-style omelets; self-serve coffee bar; chatty locals. [$] *Average main: $8* ✉ *1119 Adams Ave.* ☎ *541/975–5282* ⏲ *Closed Mon. and Tues.*

Ten Depot Street

$$$ | **AMERICAN** | In a stylish historic brick building, Ten Depot Street serves an eclectic menu of classic American favorites, everything from burgers to hearty steak and seafood dishes. With dark wood throughout accented by plum tablecloths and teal plates and napkins, it's a relatively elegant spot for this dressed-down part of the world. **Known for:** meat and seafood-heavy fine dining; adjoining bar with great wine list; attentive service in an elegant atmosphere. [$] *Average main: $23* ✉ *10 Depot St.* ☎ *541/963–8766* 🌐 *www.tendepotstreet.com* ⏲ *Closed Sun. No lunch.*

Hotels

The Landing Hotel

$ | **B&B/INN** | Housed in a historic building dating to the turn of the 20th century, this cozy downtown inn features five beautifully appointed rooms, complete with elegant homey decor including wooden furniture, pincushion chairs, and original paintings on the walls, plus contemporary upgrades such as sleek tiled bathrooms and window air-conditioning units. **Pros:** excellent location in the heart of La Grande; charmingly furnished rooms; convenient self-check-in. **Cons:** no front desk or 24-hour staff; glass bathroom doors compromise privacy; train noise may awaken light sleepers. [$] *Rooms from: $140* ✉ *1501 Adams Ave.* ☎ *541/663–1501* 🌐 *lagrandelandinghotel.com* 🛏 *5 rooms* 🍴 *No meals.*

★ Minam River Lodge

$$$ | **RESORT** | In a remote corner of the Eagle Cap Wilderness that's only accessible by plane or an 8.5-mile hike or horseback ride, this rustic-meets-chic resort offers woodstove-heated cabins, cozy lodge rooms, and gourmet meals served family style against the backdrop of the crystalline Minam River. **Pros:** gorgeous location in a pristine forest; delicious, gourmet meals; hot tub and sauna. **Cons:** rooms aren't well lit; no Wi-Fi or phone service; meals are very expensive. [$] *Rooms from: $245* ✉ *Eagle Cap Wilderness, Wallowa-Whitman National Forest* ✥ *Accessible on foot from the*

Moss Springs Trailhead, 8.5 miles away ☎ *541/508–1373* ⊕ *minam-lodge.com* 🕙 *Closed mid-Oct.–Memorial Day weekend* 🛏 *16 rooms* 🍴 *No meals.*

Joseph

70 miles southeast of La Grande.

The area around Wallowa Lake was the traditional home of the Nez Perce Indians—the town of Joseph is named for Chief Joseph, their famous leader. The peaks of the Wallowa Mountains, typically snow covered until July, tower 5,000 feet above the regional tourist hubs of the town. Joseph itself isn't much more than a nice Main Street speckled with shops, galleries, brewpubs, and cafés. Follow Main Street a mile out of town, though, to reach the gorgeous Wallowa Lake, where you'll find a whole separate hospitality village of rental cabins, outfitters, go-karts, and ice-cream stands. The busy area on the south end of the lake is also the site of two of the most popular access points for the mountains, the Wallowa Lake trailhead and the Wallowa Lake Tramway.

GETTING HERE
Highway 82 ends at Joseph, which is reachable primarily by car. A free shuttle bus to area attractions and hotels stops at the Joseph Visitor's Center.

VISITOR INFORMATION
CONTACTS Joseph Chamber of Commerce. ✉ *Visitor's Center, Main St. and Joseph Ave.* ☎ *541/432–1015* ⊕ *www.josephoregon.com.*

 Sights

★ Eagle Cap Wilderness
FOREST | At more than 360,000 acres, this is the largest wilderness area in Oregon, encompassing most of the Wallowa range with 535 miles of trails for hardcore backpackers and horseback riders. Most of the popular trailheads are along

Eagle Cap's northern edge, accessible from Enterprise or Joseph, but you also can find several trailheads 20 to 30 miles southeast of La Grande along Route 203. Some areas of the wilderness are accessible year-round, while the high-elevation areas are accessible only for a few months in summer. To park at many trailheads you must purchase a Northwest Forest Pass for $5 per day, or $30 per year. To hike into the wilderness, you also need to get a free permit that will alert rangers of your plans. ✉ *Wallowa Mountains Ranger Office, 201 E. 2nd St.* ☎ *541/426–5546* ⊕ *www.fs.usda.gov/detail/wallowa-whitman.*

★ Valley Bronze of Oregon
MUSEUM | This impressive gallery displays sculptures by the many artists who cast their work at the nearby foundry, plus quite a few international pieces. The foundry itself is a half mile away; tours are available on weekdays at 11 am. Your tour guide will lead you there after the group has gathered at the gallery. ✉ *18 S. Main St.* ☎ *541/432–7445* ⊕ *www.valleybronzegallery.com* 🎟 *Gallery free, tours $15* 🕙 *Gallery closed Mon.–Wed.*

Wallowa County Farmers' Market
MARKET | More than just a cluster of produce tents, Joseph's Saturday farmers' markets are the social hub of the community. Grab groceries or treats from rows of veggie vendors, specialty-food producers, and sustainable-cattle ranchers, then hang around for live outdoor music and bronze-sculpture street art. ✉ *N. Main St. and E. Poplar St.* ⊕ *www.wallowacountyfarmersmarket.com.*

Wallowa County Museum
MUSEUM | Joseph's history museum has a small but poignant collection of artifacts and photographs chronicling the flight of the Nez Perce, a series of battles against the U.S. Army that took place in the late 1870s. Built as a bank in 1888, the building was robbed in 1896, an event commemorated by a number of the museum's artifacts, including a massive

Teepees overlooking Joseph Canyon

old safe and some yellowing newspaper accounts. ✉ 110 S. Main St. ☎ 541/432–6095 ⊕ www.co.wallowa.or.us/community_services/museum ✇ $4 ⊙ Closed late-Sept.–Memorial Day.

★ Wallowa Lake State Park

NATIONAL/STATE PARK | FAMILY | On the south shore of beautiful Wallowa Lake, just a 10-minute drive south of downtown Joseph, this alpine park with a highly popular campground is surrounded on three sides by 9,000-foot-tall snow-capped mountains. Popular activities include fishing and powerboating on the lake, plus hiking wilderness trails, horseback riding, and canoeing. Nearby are a marina, bumper boats, miniature golf, and the tramway to the top of Mt. Howard. ✉ 72214 Marina La. ✛ Off Hwy. 351 ☎ 541/432–4185, 800/551–6949 ⊕ www.oregonstateparks.org ✇ Day use $5 per vehicle.

Wallowa Lake Tramway

TRANSPORTATION SITE (AIRPORT/BUS/FERRY/TRAIN) | The steepest tram in North America rises 3,700 feet in 15 minutes, rushing you up to the top of 8,150-foot Mt. Howard. Vistas of mountain peaks, forest, and Wallowa Lake far below will dazzle you, both on the way up and at the summit. Early and late in the season, 2½ miles of cross-country skiing trails await at the top, and the interpretive trails are open for hiking during the snowless months of midsummer, as are mountain-bike trails. A casual lunch is available at the Summit Grill and Alpine Patio, but keep in mind that it's more about the view than the sometimes uneven food and service. ✉ 59919 Wallowa Lake Hwy. ☎ 541/432–5331 ⊕ www.wallowalakeramway.com ✇ $35 ⊙ Closed Oct.–Apr. and weekdays in May.

★ Wallowa Mountain Loop

SCENIC DRIVE | This is a relatively easy way to take in the natural splendor of the Eagle Cap Wilderness and reach Baker City without backtracking to La Grande. The three-hour trip from Joseph to Baker City, designated the Hells Canyon Scenic Byway, winds through the national forest and part of Hells Canyon Recreation

Area, passing over forested mountains, creeks, and rivers. Before you travel the loop, check with the Forest Service about road conditions; the route can be impassable when snowed over. From Joseph, take Highway 350 east for 8 miles, turn south onto Forest Service Road 39, and continue until it meets Highway 86, which winds past the town of Halfway and then continues to Baker City. ✉ *Joseph* ✥ *Begins at Hwy. 82 and Hwy. 350* ☎ *541/426–5546* 🌐 *www.fs.usda.gov/wallowa-whitman.*

★ Wallowa Mountains

MOUNTAIN—SIGHT | Forming a rugged U-shaped fortress between Hells Canyon on the Idaho border and the Blue Mountains, the Wallowas are sometimes called the American Alps or Little Switzerland. The granite peaks in this range are between 5,000 and 9,000 feet in height. Dotted with crystalline alpine lakes and meadows, rushing rivers, and thickly forested valleys that fall between the mountain ridges, the Wallowas have a grandeur that can take your breath away. Bighorn sheep, elk, deer, and mountain goats populate the area. Nearly all the trails in the Wallowa Mountains are at least partially contained within the Eagle Cap Wilderness. The offices and visitor center for the mountains are in Joesph at the Wallowa Mountains ranger office of Wallowa-Whitman National Forest, but you can access different parts of the range from different towns in the region, including Enterprise, La Grande, and Baker City. ✉ *Wallowa Mountains Ranger Office, 201 E. 2nd St.* ☎ *541/426–5546* 🌐 *www.fs.usda.gov/detail/wallowa-whitman.*

Wallowology Discovery Center

MUSEUM | **FAMILY** | This interactive museum is aimed at teaching young visitors about the ecosystems of Northeastern Oregon through a mix of museum-style exhibits and special events. Highlights include a Discovery Room full of animal skulls and minerals, an exhibit dedicated to birds of prey, and an exhibit on the geology of the Wallowa Mountains. **■ TIP→ Check the Wallowology website for details on lectures and other special events.** ✉ *508 N. Main St.* ☎ *541/263–1663* 🌐 *www.wallowology.org* 🎟 *Free* 🕓 *Closed Mon. and Oct.–Memorial Day.*

🍴 Restaurants

Old Town Cafe

$ | **CAFÉ** | Both the keen early riser ready for the day's adventure and the groggy late sleeper up for a lazy afternoon will find bottomless cups of coffee and hearty breakfast standbys at this stalwart café smack in the middle of Joseph's main strip. **Known for:** French toast made with homemade bread; sunny breakfast classics; breakfast served till closing. [$] *Average main: $9* ✉ *8 S. Main St.* ☎ *541/432–9898* 🌐 *www.oldtowncafejoseph.com* 🕓 *No dinner.*

Red Horse Coffee Traders

$ | **CAFÉ** | In this modest yellow clapboard cottage in downtown Joseph, you can sample some of the finest coffee in eastern Oregon. The owners roast carefully sourced, organic, fair-trade beans and serve a selection of sandwiches, breakfast burritos, and baked goods. **Known for:** the best cup of coffee for miles; simple breakfast and lunch fare to go; homemade baked goods. [$] *Average main: $9* ✉ *306 N. Main St.* ☎ *541/432–3784* 🌐 *www.redhorsecoffeetraders.com* 🕓 *Closed Mon.–Wed.*

🛏 Hotels

★ Bronze Antler B&B

$$ | **B&B/INN** | This cozy 1920s Craftsman bungalow on the south end of downtown Joseph is along Main Street, a short walk from local shops and restaurants; it's surrounded by perennial gardens laced with pathways and containing a bocce court and picnic area. **Pros:** beautiful grounds with great mountain views; friendly and helpful innkeepers; free breakfast and

Did You Know?

The Eagle Cap Wilderness area is one of Oregon's premier backpacking destinations, with more than 500 miles of trails. It is home to more than 50 alpine lakes, including the highest lake in Oregon, Legore Lake.

Baker City is a great place for outdoor enthusiasts.

highways as well, including scenic Highway 7 through the Blue Mountains to John Day.

VISITOR INFORMATION

CONTACTS **Baker County Chamber of Commerce and Visitors Center.** ⊠ *490 Campbell St.* ☎ *541/523–5855, 800/523–1235* ⊕ *www.visitbaker.com.*

Sights

Adler House Museum

MUSEUM | The Baker Heritage Museum also operates the nearby Adler House Museum, an 1889 Italianate house that was once home to an eccentric publishing magnate and philanthropist. ⊠ *2305 Main St.* ☞ *$7.*

Baker Heritage Museum

MUSEUM | Located in a stately brick building that once housed the community's swimming pool, Baker's history center has one of the most impressive rock collections in the West. Assembled over a lifetime by a local amateur geologist, the Cavin-Warfel Collection includes

thunder eggs, glowing phosphorescent rocks, and a 950-pound hunk of quartz. Other exhibits highlight pioneering, ranching, gold mining, and antique furniture. ⊠ *2480 Grove St.* ☎ *541/523–9308* ⊕ *www.bakerheritagemuseum.com* ☞ *$6.*

Eastern Oregon Museum

MUSEUM | In the tiny town of Haines, several miles north of Baker City, this humble museum almost resembles an antiques store or flea market at first glance, and has 10,000 household, farming, mining, and pioneer artifacts. Kids enjoy the one-room schoolhouse, as well as the 100-plus antique dolls and teddy bears. On the grounds is the old Union Pacific depot, built in the 1880s and given to the museum when the railroad discontinued stops at Haines in 1962. ⊠ *610 3rd St., Haines* ☎ *541/856–3233* ☞ *$2 per person, $5 per family* ⊘ *Closed Mon.–Wed.*

Elkhorn Drive Scenic Byway

SCENIC DRIVE | This scenic 106-mile loop winds from Baker City through the

Elkhorn Range of the Blue Mountains. Only white-bark pine can survive on the range's sharp ridges and peaks, which top 8,000 feet; spruce, larch, Douglas fir, and ponderosa pine thrive on the lower slopes. The route is well marked; start in Baker City on Highway 7, head west to Sumpter, turn onto County Road 24 toward Granite, turn north on Forest Road 73 and take that over Granite Pass and eventually by Anthony Lakes ski area to Haines, and then return to Baker City along U.S. 30. ✉ *Baker City.*

★ National Historic Oregon Trail Interpretive Center

INFO CENTER | Head 5 miles east of Baker City to this sprawling facility, containing 12,000 square feet of galleries, for a superb exploration of pioneer life in the mid-1800s. From 1841 to 1861 about 300,000 people made the 2,000-mile journey from western Missouri to the Columbia River and the Oregon Coast, looking for agricultural land in the West. A simulated section of the Oregon Trail will give you a feel for camp life and the settlers' impact on Native Americans; an indoor theater presents movies and plays. A 4-mile round-trip trail winds from the center to the actual ruts left by the wagons. ✉ *22267 Hwy. 86* ☎ *541/523–1843* 🌐 *www.blm.gov/or/oregontrail* 🎫 *$8 Apr.–Oct., $5 Nov.–Mar.*

Sumpter Valley Railway

TRANSPORTATION SITE (AIRPORT/BUS/FERRY/TRAIN) | Though the original track was scrapped in 1947, an all-volunteer workforce has rebuilt more than 7 miles of track on the railroad's original right-of-way. Today the train operates along a 5-mile route in Sumpter. The historic trains leave from the McEwen and Sumpter stations; call ahead for departure information. A few additional fall foliage runs and Christmas trains are offered in October and December respectively. ✉ *211 Austin St., Sumpter* ✣ *22 miles west of Bakery City via Hwy. 7* ☎ *541/894–2268, 866/894–2268* 🌐 *www.sumptervalleyrailroad.org* 🎫 *$24.*

Wallowa-Whitman National Forest

FOREST | The 2.3-million-acre forest, found both east and west of Baker City, ranges in elevation from 875 feet in the Hells Canyon Wilderness to 9,845 feet in the Eagle Cap Wilderness. There are two other wilderness areas: Monument Rock and North Fork John Day. ✉ *1550 Dewey Ave.* ☎ *541/523–6391* 🌐 *www.fs.usda.gov/wallowa-whitman* 🎫 *Northwest Forest Pass required at some trailheads, $5/day or $30 annual.*

🍴 Restaurants

★ Barley Brown's Brewpub

$$ | **AMERICAN** | A frequent winner at American beer festivals, Barley Brown's is just as famous in the area for its food, which is prepared with locally sourced ingredients (the hand-cut fries are Baker County potatoes) and hormone-free beef for burgers and other tasty grub. The "Shredders Wheat" American Wheat Ale has beaten out international contenders for a gold at the World Beer Cup. **Known for:** crowds in high season; award-winning craft beer; locally sourced ingredients. [$] *Average main: $16* ✉ *2190 Main St.* ☎ *541/523–4266* 🌐 *www.barleybrownsbeer.com.*

Charley's Deli & Ice Cream

$ | **DINER** | No historic Main Street would be complete without its soda fountain, and Charley's Ice Cream Parlor fits the bill, serving all manner of treats, frozen and otherwise. You can also get hearty soups, sandwiches, and salads, and cheese and meats cut to order. **Known for:** pie shakes; homemade soups and sandwiches; delicious ice cream in a variety of flavors. [$] *Average main: $4* ✉ *2101 Main St.* ☎ *541/524–9307.*

Hotels

★ Geiser Grand Hotel

$ | **HOTEL** | Built in 1889, the stately Geiser Grand sits like the dowager duchess of Main Street, her cupola clock tower cutting a sharp figure against a wide Baker City sky—the Italianate Renaissance Revival beauty was once known as the finest hotel between Portland and Salt Lake City, though today it's showing its age. **Pros:** great downtown location; fascinating history; two on-site restaurants. **Cons:** rooms are decidedly old-fashioned and not to everyone's taste; worn interiors; many rooms lack views. [$] *Rooms from: $109* ✉ *1996 Main St.* ☎ *541/523–1889, 888/434–7374* 🌐 *www.geisergrand.com* 🛏 *30 rooms* 🍴 *No meals.*

Shopping

MAD Habit Boutique

CLOTHING | Whimsical crafts and decorative goods are sold at this large downtown boutique on historic Main Street, along with jewelry and women's clothing. Be sure to say hello to the friendly shop cats, Earl and Pearl, whose images appear on the shop's own line of greeting cards. ✉ *1798 Main St.* ☎ *541/829–3157.*

No. 1911

ANTIQUES/COLLECTIBLES | This hip but unpretentious lifestyle and home-accessories shop stocks an eclectic assortment of goods, from upcycled handbags to one-of-a-kind antiques. You'll also find soaps, balms, and lotions along with candles and women's apparel. ✉ *1911 Main St.* ☎ *541/523–4321.*

Activities

Anthony Lakes Ski Area

SKIING/SNOWBOARDING | **FAMILY** | Find some of the state's best powder at this hill in the Wallowa-Whitman National Forest, along with a vertical drop of 900 feet and a top elevation of 8,000 feet. There are 21 trails, one triple chairlift, and a cross-country network spanning over 18 miles. Snowboards are permitted. ✉ *47500 Anthony Lake Hwy., North Powder* ✥ *35 miles northwest of Baker City* ☎ *541/856–3277* 🌐 *www.anthonylakes.com* 🎟 *Lift tickets $40.*

John Day

80 miles west of Baker City; 150 miles east of Bend.

More than $26 million in gold was mined in the John Day area. The town was founded shortly after gold was discovered there in 1862. Yet John Day is better known to contemporaries for the plentiful outdoor recreation it offers and for the nearby John Day Fossil Beds. The town is also a central location for trips to the Malheur National Wildlife Refuge and the towns of Burns, Frenchglen, and Diamond to the south.

As you drive west through the dry, shimmering heat of the John Day Valley on U.S. 26, it may be hard to imagine this area as a humid subtropical forest filled with lumbering 50-ton brontosauruses and 50-foot-long crocodiles. But so it was, and the eroded hills and sharp, barren-looking ridges contain the richest concentration of prehistoric plant and animal fossils in the world.

GETTING HERE

The town is a scenic, 90-minute drive from Baker City on Highways 7 and 26. To the west, it's about a three-hour drive to Bend via U.S. 26.

VISITOR INFORMATION

CONTACTS Grant County Chamber of Commerce. ✉ *301 W. Main St.* ☎ *541/575–0547* 🌐 *www.gcoregonlive.com.*

Sights

Grant County Historical Museum
MUSEUM | Two miles south of John Day, Canyon City is a small town that feels as if it hasn't changed much since the Old West days. Memorabilia from the gold rush is on display at the town's small museum, along with Native American artifacts and antique musical instruments. Drop in at the neighboring pioneer jail, which the locals pilfered years ago from a nearby crumbling ghost town. ✉ *101 S. Canyon City Blvd., Canyon City* ☎ *541/575–0362, 541/575–0509 off-season* 🌐 *grantcountyhistoricalmuseum.org* 🎟 *$4* 🕒 *Closed Sun. and Mon. and Oct.–Apr.*

★ Kam Wah Chung State Heritage Site
MUSEUM | This ramshackle building operated by the state park system was a trading post on The Dalles Military Road in 1866 and 1867, then later served as a general store, a Chinese labor exchange for the area's mines, a doctor's shop, and an opium den. Listed on the National Register of Historic Places, the museum is an extraordinary testament to the early Chinese community in Oregon. ■ **TIP→ Tours are on the hour with groups limited to eight people; if you miss it, you can always catch a 5- or 30-minute video at the interpretive center across the street.** ✉ *125 N.W. Canton St.* ☎ *541/575–2800, 800/551–6949* 🌐 *www.oregonstateparks.org* 🎟 *Free* 🕒 *Closed Nov.–Apr.*

Restaurants

Outpost Pizza, Pub & Grill
$ | **AMERICAN** | **FAMILY** | The Outpost occupies one of the sleekest spaces in town: a large building with a log-cabin exterior, a vast entry lobby, and a bright, spacious, high-ceilinged dining room. The kitchen serves creative pizzas and has a lengthy menu of standard entrées including burgers, steak, seafood, salads, and quesadillas. **Known for:** typical steakhouse menu; large pizzas; heavy breakfasts served from early in the morning. [$] *Average main: $12* ✉ *201 W. Main St.* ☎ *541/575–0250* 🌐 *www.outpostpizzapubgrill.com.*

Squeeze-In Restaurant & Deck
$ | **AMERICAN** | This casual Main Street eatery serves three meals a day and has a sunny deck overlooking Canyon Creek as well as a bustling, casual dining room. Regulars pile in at breakfast for buttermilk pancakes and biscuits with sausage gravy, while hearty American fare, including burgers, rib-eye steaks, salmon pasta bowls, and smothered pork ribs, is served later in the day. **Known for:** all-day breakfast; dog-friendly outdoor deck; hearty American fare. [$] *Average main: $13* ✉ *423 W. Main St.* ☎ *541/575–1045.*

Hotels

★ The Retreat, Links & Spa at Silvies Valley Ranch
$$$$ | **RESORT** | Spread out over 220 square miles, most of which serves as a working cattle and goat ranch, this luxury retreat caters primarily to golfers, though there's plenty for non-golfers, too, with a luxury spa, Clydesdale-powered wagon rides, and gourmet dining for all three meals. **Pros:** on a par 2 golf course that can be played in two different ways; elegant spa with full menu plus gym and indoor pool; incredible meals, with huge wine list and lots of options for special diets. **Cons:** no phone service; walkie-talkies instead of phones can be difficult to use; meal timings are limited. [$] *Rooms from: $369* ✉ *10000 Rendezvous La.* ☎ *800/745–8437* 🌐 *silvies.us* 🛏 *28 rooms* 🍴 *No meals.*

John Day Fossil Beds National Monument covers hundreds of square miles and preserves a diverse record of plant and animal life that spans more than 40 million years.

John Day Fossil Beds National Monument

40 miles west of John Day, 150 miles south of Pendleton.

The geological formations that compose this peculiar monument cover hundreds of square miles and preserve a diverse record of plant and animal life spanning more than 40 million years of the Age of Mammals. The national monument itself is divided into three units: Sheep Rock, Painted Hills, and Clarno—each of which looks vastly different and tells a different part of the story of Oregon's history. Each unit has picnic areas, restrooms, visitor information, and hiking trails. The main visitor center is in the Sheep Rock Unit, 40 miles northwest of John Day; Painted Hills and Clarno are about 70 and 115 miles northwest of John Day, respectively. If you only have time for one unit of the park, make it Painted Hills, where the namesake psychedelic mounds most vividly expose the region's unique geology.

GETTING HERE
Reach the Sheep Rock Unit of the John Day Fossil Beds Monument driving 38 miles west of John Day on U.S. 26, then 2 miles north on Highway 19. The Painted Hills unit is an additional 35 miles west on U.S. 26. To reach the Clarno unit, follow Highway 19 north from the Sheep Rock Unit, 60 miles northwest to Fossil. From Fossil, drive west on Highway 218 for 20 miles to the entrance. Be prepared to stop for frequent roadside interpretive exhibits between the three units. From other towns in central and eastern Oregon, it's a two-hour drive to the Sheep Rock Unit from The Dalles and Redmond, and a two-hour drive from Bend to the Painted Hills unit.

VISITOR INFORMATION
The Thomas Condon Paleontology Center at Sheep Rock serves as the area's primary visitor center.

Sights

Clarno

NATURE SITE | The 48-million-year-old fossil beds in this small section have yielded the oldest remains in the John Day Fossil Beds National Monument. The drive to the beds traverses forests of ponderosa pines and sparsely populated valleys along the John Day River before traveling through a landscape filled with spires and outcroppings that attest to the region's volcanic past. A short trail that runs between the two parking lots contains fossilized evidence of an ancient subtropical forest. Another trail climbs ½ mile from the second parking lot to the base of the Palisades, a series of abrupt, irregular cliffs created by ancient volcanic mud flows. ✉ *Hwy. 218* ✣ *18 miles west of Fossil* ☎ *541/987–2333* 🌐 *www.nps.gov/joda.*

The Painted Hills

NATURE SITE | The fossils at the Painted Hills, a unit of the John Day Fossil Beds National Monument, date back about 33 million years, and reveal a climate that has become noticeably drier than that of Sheep Rock's era. The eroded buff-colored hills reveal striking red and green striations created by minerals in the clay. Come at dusk or just after it rains, when the colors are most vivid. If traveling in spring, the desert wildflowers are most intense between late April and early May. Take the steep, ¾-mile **Carroll Rim Trail** for a commanding view of the hills or sneak a peek from the parking lot at the trailhead, about 2 miles beyond the picnic area. A few Forest Service roads lead north toward the Spring Basin Wilderness and the town of Antelope, but these can only be managed safely by high-clearance vehicles and when dry. ✉ *37375 Bear Creek Rd., Mitchell* ✣ *Off U.S. 26, 9 miles west of Mitchell* ☎ *541/987–2333* 🌐 *www.nps.gov/joda/planyourvisit/ptd-hills-unit.htm.*

Thomas Condon Paleontology Center

INFO CENTER | The center serves as the area's primary visitor center, with a museum dedicated to the fossil beds, fossils on display, in-depth informational panels, handouts, and an orientation movie. Two miles north of the visitor center on Highway 19 is the impressive **Blue Basin**, a badlands canyon with sinuous blue-green spires. Winding through this basin is the ½-mile **Island in Time Trail,** where trailside exhibits explain the area's 28-million-year-old fossils. The 3-mile Blue Basin Overlook Trail loops around the rim of the canyon, yielding some splendid views. Blue Basin is a hike with a high effort-to-reward ratio, and in summer rangers lead interpretive jaunts Friday to Sunday at 10 am. ✉ *32651 Hwy. 19, Kimberly* ☎ *541/987–2333* 🌐 *www.nps.gov/joda.*

Hotels

★ Hotel Condon

$ | **HOTEL** | A popular option for visitors exploring the Clarno (35 miles south) and Painted Hills (60 miles south) sections of John Day Fossil Beds National Monument, this three-story 1920 redbrick hotel anchors the small town of Condon. **Pros:** charming old small-town hotel; friendly staff; large rooms with comfy furnishings. **Cons:** few dining options in the area; remote location; limited on-site amenities. [$] *Rooms from: $149* ✉ *202 S. Main St., Condon* ☎ *541/384–4624, 800/201–6706* 🌐 *www.hotelcondon.com* 🛏 *20 rooms* 🍴 *Free breakfast.*

Index

Photo Credits

Front Cover: Robert Potts [Description: Cape Arago Lighthouse near Charleston, Oregon]. **Back cover, from left to right:** Josemaria Toscano/Shutterstock, Mkopka/Dreamstime, Michal Hlewk/Dreamstime. **Spine:** Dancestrokes/Shutterstock. **Interior, from left to right:** 4nadia/iStockphoto (1). Ahorica/iStockphoto (2). San Juan Safaris (5). **Chapter 1: Experience Oregon:** AndrewSoundarajan/iStockphoto (6-7). zschnepf/Shutterstock (8). Torsten Kjellstrand/Travel Portland (9). Stephen Moehle/Shutterstock (9). Manuela Durson/Shutterstock (10). tusharkoley/Shutterstock (10). Wollertz/Shutterstock (10). Taylor Higgins (11). Carolyn Wells-Kramer (11). T. Charles Erickson/Oregon Shakespeare Festival (12). Joshua Rainey Photography/Shutterstock (12). SERRA (12). Jamie Hooper/Dreamstime (12). Wanderlust Tours (13). James R. Hearn/Shutterstock (13). Peng Ge/Dreamstime (13). Satoshi ETO/Travel Oregon (13). Explore Lincoln City (14). BLM Oregon/Washington (14). Laura Ragsdale Photo/Shutterstock (14). Jeanne Provost/Shutterstock (15). Jon Lovette/Alamy (16). davidkrug/Shutterstock (16). www.travelportland.com (16). Timothy Horn (16). C.Echeveste/Shutterstock (17). JPL Designs/Shutterstock (17). Jamie Francis/Travel-Portland.com (17). JPL Designs/Shutterstock (17). Marnie Patchett/Dreamstime (18). Gregor Halenda (18). Courtesy of Enchanted Forest (18). Ken Goldman Photography/Oregon Parks and Recreation Dept (19). Courtesy of Evergreen Aviation & Space Museum (19). Andréa Johnson Photography (20). King Estate Winery (20). Andrea Johnson Photography (20). Serge Chapuis (20). Andrea Johnson Photography (21). Stuart Westmorland/agefotostock (31). Thomas Kitchin/agefotostock (33). San Juan Safaris (34). **Chapter 3: Portland:** Torsten Kjellstrand (47). zrfphoto (60). Strekoza2/Dreamstime (74). Joshuaraineyphotography/Dreamstime.com (76). Joshuaraineyphotography/Dreamstime (80). Joshuaraineyphotography/Dreamstime (96). Appalachianviews/Dreamstime (115). **Chapter 4: Oregon Coast:** Glebtarro/Dreamstime (127). Tom Wald/iStockphoto (130). John Norris/Flickr (131). Scott Catron/wikipedia.org (131). Greg Vaughn (159). Oregon Coast Aquarium (164). Greg Vaughn (173). **Chapter 5: Willamette Valley and Wine Country:** Dennis Frates / Alamy (185). GREG VAUGHN (196). GREG VAUGHN (202-203). Jason Tomczak (202). REX HILL, Newberg, OR (204). REX HILL, Newberg, OR (206). Jason Tomczak (206). Doreen L. Wynja (207). Polara Studio (208). Kent Derek (209). REX HILL, Newberg, OR (209). Norman Eder/iStockphoto (209). Polara Studio (211). Andrea Johnson Photography (211). Dundee Bistro (211). Jpldesigns/Dreamstime (220). Oregonlass/Dreamstime (228). **Chapter 6: Columbia River Gorge and Mt. Hood:** William Blacke/iStockphoto (235). zschnepf/Shutterstock (244). Greg Vaughn (253). Melissa & Bryan Ripka/Flickr (266). **Chapter 7: Central Oregon:** Livingstonatlarge/Dreamstime (271). Svetlana55/Dreamstime (282). Sunriver Resort (287). davemantel/iStockphoto (294). **Chapter 8: Crater Lake National Park:** William A. McConnell (299). Photographer and videographer from Ukraine/iStockphoto (307). **Chapter 9: Southern Oregon:** Greg Vaughn (311). nwrafting/flickr (321). Viviansviews/Dreamstime (335). **Chapter 10: Eastern Oregon:** Fokket/flickr (343). IDAK/Shutterstock (356). Danny Warren/iStockphoto (358-359). Cacophony/wikimedia (363). AmySelleck/flickr (367). **About Our Writers:** All photos are courtesy of the writers except for the following: Andrew Collins, courtesy of Fernando Nocedal.

*Every effort has been made to trace the copyright holders, and we apologize in advance for any accidental errors. We would be happy to apply the corrections in the following edition of this publication.

Notes

Notes

Notes

Notes

Notes

Notes

Fodor's OREGON

Publisher: Stephen Horowitz, *General Manager*

Editorial: Douglas Stallings, *Editorial Director*; Jill Fergus, Jacinta O'Halloran, Amanda Sadlowski, *Senior Editors*; Kayla Becker, Alexis Kelly, Rachael Roth, *Editors*

Design: Tina Malaney, *Director of Design and Production*; Jessica Gonzalez, *Graphic Designer;* Mariana Tabares, *Design & Production Intern*

Production: Jennifer DePrima, *Editorial Production Manager*; Carrie Parker, *Senior Production Editor*; Elyse Rozelle, *Production Editor;* Jackson Pranica, *Editorial Production Assistant*

Maps: Rebecca Baer, *Senior Map Editor*; Mark Stroud (Moon Street Cartography), David Lindroth, *Cartographers*

Photography: Viviane Teles, *Senior Photo Editor;* Namrata Aggarwal, Ashok Kumar, Carl Yu, *Photo Editors;* Rebecca Rimmer, *Photo Intern*

Business and Operations: Chuck Hoover, *Chief Marketing Officer*; Robert Ames, *Group General Manager*; Devin Duckworth, *Director of Print Publishing*; Victor Bernal, *Business Analyst*

Public Relations and Marketing: Joe Ewaskiw, *Senior Director Communications & Public Relations*; Esther Su, *Senior Marketing Manager*

Fodors.com: Jeremy Tarr, *Editorial Director*; Rachael Levitt, *Managing Editor;* Teddy Minford, *Editor*

Technology: Jon Atkinson, *Director of Technology;* Rudresh Teotia, *Lead Developer*; Jacob Ashpis, *Content Operations Manager*

Writers: Margot Bigg, Andrew Collins, Jon Shadel

Editor: Alexis Kelly

Production Editor: Elyse Rozelle

8th Edition

ISBN 978–1–64097–266–7

ISSN 1523–8776

About Our Writers

Margot Bigg is a freelance travel writer and editor based in Portland, Oregon. She's lived and worked all over the world, most recently in India, where she worked at *Time Out Magazine* and contributed to four editions of Fodor's Essential India. She's contributed to publications around the world, from *Rolling Stone India* to *Travel + Leisure.* Margot updated the Willamette Valley and Eastern Oregon chapters for this edition.

Former Fodor's staff editor **Andrew Collins** is based in Mexico City, but resides part-time in Portland, where he's the editor of *The Pearl* magazine (which focuses on the city's trendy Pearl District). A long-time contributor to more than 200 Fodor's guidebooks, including Pacific Northwest, Santa Fe, New England, Inside Mexico City, and National Parks of the West, he's also written for dozens of mainstream and LGBTQ publications—*Travel + Leisure, New Mexico Magazine, AAA Living, The Advocate,* and *Canadian Traveller* among them. Additionally, Collins teaches travel writing and food writing for New York City's Gotham Writers Workshop. He updated Portland, Oregon Coast, Columbia River Gorge and Mt. Hood, Crater Lake National Park, and Southern Oregon chapters this edition. You can find more of his work at ⊕ *AndrewsTraveling.com.*

Jon Shadel is a Portland-based writer, editor, and multimedia journalist, whose work appears in *The Washington Post, VICE,* Condé Nast's *them., The Atlantic CityLab,* and many other outlets. Prior to embarking on a career as a roving freelancer, they worked as the top editor at MEDIAmerica, a publisher of Pacific Northwest magazines and travel guides. They updated the Central Oregon, Experience Oregon, and Travel Smart chapters in this book. Learn more about their work covering culture, travel, and technology at ⊕ *www.jdshadel.com.*

mines of Cornucopia. The mines are long gone now, but this small (population just under 300), straightforward town on the southern flanks of the Wallowas has an appealing main street and a quiet rural flavor. Most visitors to Halfway are prepping for Hells Canyon or passing through along the scenic Wallowa Mountain Loop.

GETTING HERE

Halfway is reachable by car on Highway 86, part of the Hells Canyon National Scenic Byway. Interstate 84 at Baker City is 55 miles east. The summer-only Wallowa Mountain Loop road leads to Joseph, a scenic three-hour drive through the mountains.

Hotels

Inn at Clear Creek Farm

$ | **B&B/INN** | Amid 170 acres of orchards, ponds, woods, and fields on the southeastern flank of the Wallowa Mountains, this 1912 Craftsman-style farmhouse is a comfortable rural retreat on a working ranch. **Pros:** glorious views; peaceful and secluded; many recreational activities available. **Cons:** not exactly on the beaten path; only six rooms; only breakfast available. [$] *Rooms from: $95* ✉ *48212 Clear Creek Rd.* ✣ *Off Fish Lake Rd., 3½ miles north of Halfway* ☎ *541/742-2238* 🌐 *www.clearcreekinn.com* 🛏 *6 rooms* 🍴 *Free breakfast.*

Pine Valley Lodge

$ | **B&B/INN** | From the outside, this lodge on Main Street is constructed like many others built in eastern Oregon during the timber boom of the late 1920s, using wood from the original mines' construction. **Pros:** well-maintained rooms; recreation options close by; breakfast with baked goods is included. **Cons:** in a tiny remote town with few services and amenities; not many options for dinner; rooms have dated decor. [$] *Rooms from: $110* ✉ *163 N. Main St.* ☎ *541/742-2027* 🌐 *www.pvlodge.com* 🛏 *13 rooms, 1 cottage* 🍴 *Free breakfast.*

Shopping

Halfway Whimsical

CRAFTS | This artists' co-op is chock-full of landscape photography, textile art, and handcrafted jewelry. Some of the gallery's more "whimsical" items are clever remixes of household materials—think lamps made of toasters and jewelry made from cutlery. ✉ *231 Gover La.* ☎ *541/742-6040.*

Baker City

44 miles south of La Grande, 305 miles southeast of Portland, 114 miles south of Joseph.

During the 1860s gold rush, Baker City was the hub of the action. Many smaller towns dried up after the gold rush, but Baker City transformed itself into the seat of the regional logging and ranching industries that are still around today. Remnants of its turn-of-the-20th-century opulence, when it was the largest city between Salt Lake and Portland, are still visible in the many restored Victorian houses and downtown storefronts, many of which now hold distinctive boutiques, design shops, and cafés.

Baker City may not have that much gold left in its surrounding hills—but what hills they are. The Wallowas and Eagle Cap, the Elkhorn Ridge of the Blue Mountains, the Umatilla National Forest, the Wallowa-Whitman, Hells Canyon, Monument Rock—the panorama almost completes a full circle. Outdoors enthusiasts flock here for the climbing, fishing, hunting, waterskiing, canoeing, hiking, cycling, and skiing. It seems Baker City's gold rush has been supplanted by the "green rush."

GETTING HERE

Baker City is easily accessed by Interstate 84, a five-hour drive east of Portland and a two-hour drive west of Boise, Idaho. The city is the hub for several smaller check with rangers at the Wallowa Mountains Ranger Office in Joseph for road conditions and trip-planning advice. Even in perfect conditions, these forest roads can be slow going; allow two to three hours, for instance, to drive the 50-mile Wallowa Mountain Loop. Most float trips originate from the Hells Canyon Creek site below the Hells Canyon Dam.

VISITOR INFORMATION
CONTACTS Hells Canyon Chamber of Commerce. ☏ *541/540–4222* ⊕ *www. hellscanyonchamber.com.*

 Sights

Hells Canyon
CANYON | Most travelers take a scenic peek from the overlook on the 45-mile **Wallowa Mountain Loop**, which follows Forest Service Road 39 (part of the Hells Canyon Scenic Byway) from just east of Halfway on Route 86 to just east of Joseph on Route 350. At the junction of Forest Service Road 39 and Forest Service Road 3965, take the 6-mile round-trip spur to the 5,400-foot-high rim at Hells Canyon Overlook. This is the easiest way to get a glimpse of the canyon, but be aware that Forest Service Road 39 is open only during summer and early fall. During the late fall, winter, and spring the best way to experience Hells Canyon is to follow a slightly more out-of-the-way route along the **Snake River Segment** of the Wallowa Mountain Loop. Following Snake River Road north from Oxbow, the 60-mile round-trip route winds along the edge of Hells Canyon Reservoir on the Idaho side, crossing the Snake River at Hells Canyon Dam on the Oregon-Idaho border. ■**TIP→ Be sure you have a full tank before starting out, since there are no gas stations anywhere along the route.** ✉ *Halfway.*

Hells Canyon National Recreation Area
NATURE PRESERVE | This is the site of one of the largest elk herds in the United States, plus 422 other species, including bald eagles, bighorn sheep, mule deer, white-tailed deer, black bears, bobcats, cougars, beavers, otters, and rattlesnakes. The peregrine falcon has also been reintroduced here. Part of the area was designated as Hells Canyon Wilderness, in parts of Oregon and Idaho, with the establishment of the Hells Canyon National Recreation Area in 1975. Additional acres were added as part of the Oregon Wilderness Act of 1984, and the recreation area currently extends across more than 652,000 wild and rugged acres. Nine hundred miles of trails wind through the wilderness area, closed to all mechanized travel. If you want to visit the wilderness it must be on foot, mountain bike, or horseback. Three of its rivers (the Snake, Imnaha, and Rapid) have been designated as Wild and Scenic. Environmental groups have proposed the creation of Hells Canyon National Park to better manage the area's critical habitat. You can access the canyon from several points—see the website for an overview map. ✉ *Wallowa Mountains Office, 201 E. 2nd St., Joseph* ☏ *541/426–5546* ⊕ *www.fs.usda.gov/wallowa-whitman.*

🏃 Activities

FISHING AND BOATING
Hells Canyon Adventures
BOATING | Book a fishing trip or jet-boat excursion on the Snake River through Hells Canyon with this well-respected company that offers half- and full-day trips. ✉ *Oxbow* ☏ *541/785–3352, 800/422–3568* ⊕ *www.hellscanyonadventures.com* ✆ *From $100.*

Halfway

63 miles southeast of Joseph, 40 miles south of Hells Canyon Dam, 55 miles east of Baker City.

Halfway, the closest town to Hells Canyon, got its name because it was midway between the town of Pine and the gold afternoon snacks. **Cons:** on the slightly busy main road through town; rooms have busy decor; only four rooms. $ *Rooms from: $156* ✉ *309 S. Main St.* ☏ *541/432–0230* ⊕ *www.bronzeantler. com* ⌂ *4 rooms* ♦ *Free breakfast.*

Wallowa Lake Lodge
$ | **HOTEL** | This friendly 1920s lodge offers simple yet appealing rooms (the grandest have balconies facing the lake) plus knotty-pine cabins, some with fireplaces and lake views, and all with kitchens. **Pros:** affordable rates; a visual and historical treat; staff goes out of its way to accommodate. **Cons:** no TV, phones, or Internet; closed in winter; rooms are quite rustic and simple. $ *Rooms from: $145* ✉ *60060 Wallowa Lake Hwy., Wallowa Lake* ☏ *541/432–9821* ⊕ *www.wallowalakelodge.com* ⊘ *Closed late-Sept.–late May* ⌂ *22 rooms, 8 cabins* ♦ *No meals.*

Shopping

★ Arrowhead Chocolates
FOOD/CANDY | Take a break from browsing at Joseph's several galleries and boutiques to indulge in first-rate caramels and truffles at this popular downtown shop. You'll also find rich, hot mochas that blend chocolate with Portland's Stumptown coffee. The sweets come in novel flavors, including caramels topped with alder-smoked sea salt and lavender-honey chocolate truffles. ✉ *4 S. Main St.* ☏ *541/432–2871* ⊕ *www.arrowheadchocolates.com.*

ToZion
CERAMICS/GLASSWARE | Check out the well-curated collection of fair-trade clothing, soaps, skin-care products, Buddha statuary, jewelry, pottery, and artwork at this colorful two-story boutique carrying both local and international goods. ✉ *200 N. Main St.* ☏ *541/432–0745.*

Activities

HORSEBACK RIDING
Wallowa Lake Pack Station
HORSEBACK RIDING | **FAMILY** | Book a short or full-day guided summer pack trip from the south end of Wallowa Lake into the Eagle Cap Wilderness. ✉ *59761 Wallowa Lake Hwy.* ☏ *541/432–7433* ⊕ *www. eaglecapwildernesspackstation.com.*

RAFTING AND BOATING
Wallowa Lake Marina
BOATING | From Memorial Day to Labor Day, you can rent paddleboats, motorboats, rowboats, and canoes by the hour or by the day. ✉ *Marina La.* ✛ *South end of Wallowa Lake, off Hwy. 351* ☏ *541/432–9115* ⊕ *www.wallowalakemarina.com.*

Winding Waters River Expeditions
BOATING | Experienced river guides at this Joseph-based company lead white-water rafting and kayaking trips, as well as fly-fishing outings, on the Snake River and the nearby Grande Ronde and Salmon rivers. ✉ *Joseph* ☏ *888/906–3816, 541/886–5078* ⊕ *www.windingwatersrafting.com.*

Hells Canyon

30 miles northeast of Joseph, 80 miles east of Baker City.

This remote place along the Snake River is the deepest river-carved gorge in North America (7,900 feet), with many rare and endangered animal species. There are three different routes from which to view and experience the canyon, though only one is accessible year-round.

GETTING HERE
Many seasonal National Forest Service roads access Hells Canyon from Imnaha east of Joseph and the Wallowa Mountain Loop. Four-wheel drive can be necessary on certain roads, but Forest Service Road 39 is paved the entire way;